2d Edition

# Information
# Resource
# Management

Betty R. Ricks, CRM

Associate Professor of Management
Old Dominion University
Norfolk, Virginia

Kay F. Gow

Consultant,
Records Management and Automated Office Systems
Norfolk, Virginia

A Records
Systems Approach

G51    *Published by*

**SOUTH-WESTERN
PUBLISHING CO.**

CINCINNATI    WEST CHICAGO, IL
CARROLLTON, TX    LIVERMORE, CA

ISBN: 0-538-07511-2

Library of Congress Catalog Card Number: 87-61231


Cover photograph: © Clayton J. Price


1 2 3 4 5 6 7 D 3 2 1 0 9 8 7
Printed in the United States of America

# CONTENTS

# PART TWO
## Organizing the System

# PART THREE
## Staffing the System

# PART FOUR
## Controlling the System

## 19 MICRORECORDS CONTROL     522

## 20 RECORDS SAFETY AND SECURITY     556

## APPENDIX A • ARCHIVES MANAGEMENT     591

# ACKNOWLEDGMENTS

For permission to reproduce the photographs on the pages indicated, acknowledgment is made to the following:

**Chapter 3**     p. 49 — Reprinted by permission: Tribune Media Services

            p. 71 (Fig. 3-6) — Floor Model — Michael Business Machines Corporation

            Desk-top Model — HEAVY DUTY DESK-TOP SHREDDER FROM SECURITY ENGINEERED MACHINERY (SEM)

**Chapter 4**     p. 94 (Fig. 4-5) — Photo Courtesy of ARMA QUARTERLY

            p. 102 — By permission of Johnny Hart and News America Syndicate

**Chapter 5**     p. 119 — By permission of Ford Button

            p. 141 — SALLY FORTH by Greg Howard © by and permission of News America Syndicate

**Chapter 6**     p. 161 (Fig. 6-3) — Permission by Supreme Equipment & Systems Corp.

            p. 162 (Fig. 6-4) — Photography courtesy of GAYLORD BROS., INC.

            p. 162 (Fig. 6-5) — Manufactured by Business Efficiency Aids, Inc., Skokie, IL

            p. 164 (Fig. 6-7) — Wright Line Inc.

            p. 164 (Fig. 6-8) — RING KING VISIBLES, INC.

            p. 165 (Fig. 6-11) — Photo Courtesy of FELLOWES MANUFACTURING

            p. 165 (Fig. 6-12) — Photo Courtesy of KEUFFEL & ESSER COMPANY

            p. 166 (Fig. 6-13) — Photography courtesy of GAYLORD BROS., INC.

            p. 167 (Fig. 6-14) — Permission by Supreme Equipment & Systems Corp.

            p. 168 (Fig. 6-16) — DELCO ASSOCIATES, INC. "ROTARY DELCO-FILE"

            p. 169 (Fig. 6-17) — Kardex Systems, Inc.

            p. 170 (Fig. 6-18) — Multiple User Stations are a feature of the Datafile Automated Records Management System

            p. 171 (Fig. 6-19) — Computer Assisted Retrieval System — Com Squared Systems, Inc.

|              | p. 173 (Fig. 6-20) | Courtesy of TAB Products Co. |
|              | p. 176 (Fig. 6-23) | Courtesy of TAB Products Co. |
| **Chapter 7** | p. 192 (Fig. 7-4) | Photo Courtesy of Bell and Howell |
|              | p. 193 (Fig. 7-5) | Photo Courtesy of Bell and Howell |
|              | p. 193 (Fig. 7-6) | Photo Courtesy of Bell and Howell |
|              | p. 194 (Fig. 7-7) | Photo Courtesy of NCR CORPORATION |
|              | p. 200 (Fig. 7-10) | Floor Model — Photo Courtesy of CANON U.S.A. Hand-held Model — Photo Courtesy of Bell and Howell |
| **Chapter 9** | p. 244 (Fig. 9-4) | Hamilton Sorter Company, Inc. Vertical Sorting System, Fairfield, Ohio |
|              | p. 263 (Fig. 9-13) | Photo Courtesy of EASTMAN KODAK CO. |
|              | p. 264 (Fig. 9-14) | Kardex Systems, Inc. |
| **Chapter 10** | p. 289 (Fig. 10-4) | Photo Courtesy of Sperry Corporation |
|              | p. 295 (Fig. 10-8) | Courtesy of Ricoh Corporation |
|              | p. 297 (Fig. 10-9) | Courtesy of AT&T |
| **Chapter 15** | p. 424 | Reprinted by permission: Tribune Media Services |
| **Chapter 16** | p. 450 (Fig. 16-6) | Infortext Systems Inc.; Schaumburg, Illinois |
| **Chapter 20** | p. 567 (Fig. 20-2) | Meilink Safe Company, Whitehouse, Ohio |
|              | p. 570 (Fig. 20-3) | Photo by Beverly McVay |
|              | p. 577 (Fig. 20-4) | PERPETUAL STORAGE, INC. — SALT LAKE CITY, UTAH |
|              | p. 584 (Fig. 20-6) | Push-button — Photo Courtesy of SIMPLEX SECURITY SYSTEMS, INC. Card — Photo, Courtesy of Rusco Electronic Systems, Glendale, CA |

# PREFACE

Information is a vital organizational resource. Organizations depend on accurate, readily available information to assist in management decision making, to provide litigation support, to improve organizational efficiency, to document compliance with legislative and regulatory requirements, and to provide a historical reference. As this dependency on information has become more widely recognized, organizations have begun to focus on the management of this resource. Information recorded on any medium becomes a record. INFORMATION RESOURCE MANAGEMENT *A Records Systems Approach* addresses the need for a systematic approach to managing the information resource (record) throughout its life cycle — from creation to final disposition — and presents a functional management approach to the implementation and operation of a records management system.

INFORMATION RESOURCE MANAGEMENT is written for instructors, students, and records professionals. Instructors of college courses in records management will find information to expand their expertise and to assist students preparing for careers in records management. Records professionals will find this book a ready reference to be used in expanding or updating their knowledge on all aspects of a records management system.

The twenty chapter text consists of an introductory chapter (which presents the records management system) and four parts. "Part I ● Planning the System" addresses the planning function and its importance in attaining organizational goals. This part describes the development and use of a records retention program, procedures for planning records facilities, selection of a classification system, selection of equipment and supplies, and the determination of the feasibility of microrecords applications.

"Part II ● Organizing the System" introduces the organizing subsystem which coordinates the records management system to ensure its efficient operation. This part addresses the preparation and maintenance of the records management manual, examines storage and retrieval systems, describes the implementation and operation of an integrated information system, and examines the special records problems of banks, governmental agencies, insurance organizations, medical facilities, libraries, and multinational organizations.

"Part III ● Staffing the System" describes the role of the records manager within the organization, examines the records manager's human resources development responsibilities, and provides information on career paths in records management.

"Part IV ● Controlling the System" addresses the control function as it specifically relates to correspondence, copies, directives, forms, reports, microrecords, and the physical and content security of the records.

INFORMATION RESOURCE MANAGEMENT also includes profiles of the records management programs of ten organizations. A glossary and appendixes on archives management, the history of records management, and alphabetic filing rules are also provided. Each chapter includes competencies, cases that introduce chapter concepts, a terminology review, a competency review, applications, and concluding cases. A comprehensive case for each part of the text is also provided.

The accompanying instructor's manual suggests additional resources and provides chapter outlines, teaching suggestions for each chapter, solutions to end-of-chapter questions, applications, and comprehensive cases, a text bank, pretests and posttests of alphabetic filing rules, and 50 transparency masters.

The information resource includes all of the systems and procedures, personnel and organizational structure, equipment, supplies, and facilities necessary to create, collect, store, retrieve, distribute, use, maintain, and control information. INFORMATION RESOURCE MANAGEMENT presents a systematic approach to planning, organizing, staffing, directing, and controlling for the efficient use of this vital organizational resource.

A book is seldom the work of one or two people. The authors wish to express their gratitude to the many records professionals and information managers who contributed information about current practices in this field, or reviewed portions of the text. These professionals include:

Beverly Amoroso — Kirkwood Community College, Cedar Rapids, IA
Dave Ashby — Manuals Dynamics
Don M. Avedon — Executive Director, International Information
                   Management Congress (IMC)
Bill Benedon — Lockheed Corp.
Daniel A. Brathal — 3M
DiAnn Conyers — Laramie County Clerk's Office, Cheyenne, WY
E. T. Durand — Information Resource Management Corporation

J. M. Flanagan — RCA
Frances E. Fuller — The Coastal Corporation
Lillian R. Greathouse — Eastern Illinois University
Geneva Hagedorn — University of Houston
Earl E. Halvas
James E. Hepp — 3M
Mary Lou Hodge — Records Management Consultant
Allen N. Keegan — Cities Service Oil & Gas Corporation
Mark Langemo — University of North Dakota
Clarice Marx — Northern States Power Company
Carol O'Reilly Messer — Tulsa Junior College
Robert B. Mitchell — University of Arkansas at Little Rock
Nancy P. Mulder — Grand Rapids Junior College
Peggy Reno
Walter W. Riese — Northwestern Mutual Life Insurance Company
Beverly Ann Roberts — Maryland National Bank
William L. Rofes
Charles Schiell — Mountain Bell Telephone Company
Preston W. Shimer — Rockwell International
Jean Shull — St. Louis Community College at Meramec
Janet C. Whitehead — Laramie County Clerk's Office, Cheyenne,
        WY
Christine Zanotti — Association of Records Managers and Adminis-
        trators, Inc.

Our special thanks go to the following individuals and organizations who worked closely with us in the preparation of the profiles included in this book:

Henrietta S. Barbour — Hardee's Food Systems, Inc.
Bill Burd — Hardee's Food Systems, Inc.
DiAnn Conyers — Laramie County Clerk's Office, Cheyenne, WY
Mavis Eppes — Vinson & Elkins
William Gainey — United Telephone of Florida
Dennis F. Morgan — Florida Power & Light Company
Denis G. Perks — Alcan Aluminum Ltd.
Walter W. Riese — Northwestern Mutual Life Insurance Company
Stuart Shilling — Citicorp
Linda M. Shurites — University of Maryland Medical System
Elizabeth A. Sontum — University of Maryland Medical System
Jean E. Tucker — The Library of Congress

Comments and suggestions from teachers using this text are
welcomed at any time by the authors.

Betty R. Ricks
Kay F. Gow

# 1

# THE RECORDS MANAGEMENT SYSTEM

## Competencies

After completing this chapter, you should be able to

1. specify major reasons for establishing an effective, efficient, economical system of records management.
2. identify the system components of a records management system and describe the relationships among the components.
3. describe the life cycle of a record and state the methods for reaching each stage.
4. classify examples of records as active, inactive; long-term, temporary; record, nonrecord; and provide a rationale for your decision.
5. distinguish between records management and filing activities.
6. describe the functional approach to system management.

# Introductory Case

Jerry McGrath graduated from a well-known university last year with a degree in marketing management. During his four years as a college student, he worked part-time as an assistant manager of Sports World, a large sporting goods chain. When Jerry received his degree, he was asked to stay on at Sports World as manager of their largest volume store.

After several months as manager, Jerry began to be frustrated by the lack of information available to him as well as the untimely manner in which the information was provided. Jerry felt that he often had to make tough decisions based on incomplete or incorrect information. He discussed this problem with the regional vice president, who suggested that Jerry examine the current records management system for deficiencies.

1. What contribution does the records management system make to the availability of information within the organization?
2. What are the elements of a records management system?

Information is becoming increasingly critical to the continuing success of organizations. Information is, therefore, a vital organizational resource. As organizations have begun to recognize this vital resource and their dependency on it, they have also begun to realize that a system for managing this resource is essential. Information recorded on any medium becomes a record. A system must be developed for planning, organizing, and controlling records, and for staffing; this system is the records management system.

**Records management** is the systematic control of records from creation to final disposition. This systematic approach to the control of all phases of records life is essential if an organization is to reduce paperwork proliferation, have efficient access to requested information, dispose of obsolete records, provide documentation of compliance to state and federal courts and agencies, and maintain a historical organizational record.

*Definition of records management*

Figure 1–1
Forms of Records

**Records** (recorded information) refers to all books, papers, photographs, maps, or other documentary materials, regardless of physical form or characteristics, made or received for legal and operational purposes in connection with the transaction of business. Records contain information about and evidence of organizational functions, policies, decisions, procedures, operations, and other activities. The term **documentary materials** includes all forms of

*Definition of records*

*Forms of records*

correspondence, letters, memos, directives, and reports; forms, generated both internally and externally; drawings; specifications; maps; photographs; and creative materials. A record may take various forms—paper, microfilm, computer tape, word processing disk, microfiche, video disk, or such unique forms as sacks of seed corn or the original manuscript of *Gone With the Wind*. Northrup King Grain Company in Minneapolis, Minnesota, stores grain seeds so that if a blight destroys one particular strain of corn, there will be a "record" (seed stock) to use to start over again. Whatever the form, any recorded information constitutes a record.

## NEED FOR RECORDS MANAGEMENT SYSTEM

*"Last year my company lost a million-dollar account because the information I needed to complete the proposal was not available when I needed it."*

*"Our organization went to court on a contractual matter and lost the case because we did not have complete documentation."*

*"The paperwork volume in our office has doubled in the past year—quadrupled in the past five years. We cannot afford this acceleration of costs."*

*"We cannot find important records and our overall efficiency is impaired."*

*"Our records are regularly audited by state and federal agencies. Over the years we have spent thousands of hours and millions of dollars in procedural justification to these agencies."*

*"Our company celebrates its 100th anniversary in June. I have been asked to prepare the company history, but all of our early records are gone."*

*Corporate memory*

Records are the corporate memory of the organization. Consider the inaccuracy of individual recollections of events. Ask any number of persons to observe a scene and report their individual observations. The results of this experiment are consistent—each person's memory of the event is different. An organization must not depend on elusive memory and conflicting recollections. Further, organizations depend on recorded past accomplishments to provide a foundation for future development. Accurate records are necessary to provide this background information for planning for the future while taking advantage of the past.

*Organizational resource/asset*

Records are, therefore, both an organizational resource and an organizational asset. As a resource, records provide information; as an asset, they provide documentation.

## Management Decision Making

*"Last year my company lost a million-dollar account because the information I needed to complete the proposal was not available when I needed it."*

In order to make appropriate decisions, managers must have appropriate information. Decisions are only as good as the information on which they are based. Most of the information necessary for decision making is found in records.

*Decision-making tool*

The decision-making process includes defining the problem, developing alternatives, evaluating the alternatives, choosing and implementing the best solution, and evaluating (validating) that decision. To make professional decisions, managers should have background information (documentation provided by records), bases for evaluating the alternatives (forecasting, past experiences, consequences experienced by other organizations — provided by records), and means for validating the decisions (feedback and control mechanisms provided by records).

Records also provide the information required for routine or programmed decisions. These types of decisions are made based on established organizational policies, procedures, and rules, all of which are a part of the organizational records system.

## Litigation Support

*"Our organization went to court on a contractual matter and lost the case because we did not have complete documentation."*

The importance of documentation to the continuing life and success of organizations has become critical as more and more consumers, individuals, and organizations turn to the court systems as a forum for their concerns and as an avenue of recourse. In a 1984 decision in Carlucci vs. Piper Aircraft Corporation, the absence of an effective program of records management cost Piper Aircraft $10 million.

Virtually all organizations are vulnerable to discrimination and privacy violation suits. Organizations rely on records for documentation to provide evidence that these practices do not occur and, further, that the organization has established policies and procedures to prevent such actions.

When an organization initiates legal action against another, records must provide the necessary documentation to win the case in court. Clear documentation of an organization's intent and subsequent actions is a safeguard for protection from litigation consequences and an imperative for their records system.

*Provide evidence/ documentation*

## Paperwork Volume/Cost Reduction

*"The paperwork volume in our office has doubled in the past year — quadrupled in the past five years. We cannot afford this acceleration of costs."*

Many executives are concerned with the increasing volume of records and the increasing costs associated with creating, using, and maintaining these records. Illustrations of the massive volume of records that have accumulated and will continue to accumulate are common.

- There are 318 billion paper documents on file.
- There are five file cabinets for each worker.
- The amount of information handled by office workers has doubled during the past 19 years and is expected to double again by 1991.
- Copies, laid end to end, would stretch 22 million miles, the equivalent of about 47 trips to the moon.

*Most references are to recent records*

While the projected volume increase is 62 million file drawers each year, reference is never made to 80 percent of the stored records, and 95 percent of the references made are to records created within the past three years.

Concern over increasing paperwork is understandable when one considers that 130 billion of the 350 billion copies made in American offices this year are not needed — wasted, unnecessary, or for personal use. The cost of processing these copies is about $2.6 billion, not counting the time spent standing by the copier. Although recognition is given to the problem of records proliferation, the recognition is primarily due to inconvenience created by the mass of records and to the spiraling costs of maintaining the records. It is only when space becomes a premium, records become difficult to locate, misfiles are prevalent, and the cost exceeds the benefits that organizations seriously consider implementing a records management system.

*Records control requires systematic approach*

Recognition should be given to the need for a systematic approach to the entire records concept — from generation to disposition — in an effort to control the increased volume and the increased costs of creating and maintaining necessary records.

## Organizational Efficiency

*"We cannot find important records and our efficiency is impaired."*

Frustration and reduced efficiency occur when the individual responsible for making a decision is unable to locate the information necessary to efficiently develop and evaluate alternatives. Statistics show that employees spend an average of 50 minutes per day looking for misplaced files. Not only is this searching costly in terms of the records clerk's time, but a loss of productive time to the person requiring the information also occurs.

*Costly misfiles*

Organizational efficiency can be seriously impaired if needed information is not readily available. A systematic approach to records management provides the vehicle for information availability to enhance the efficiency of the employees and, ultimately, the organization.

## Legislative/Regulatory Requirements

*"Our records are regularly audited by state and federal agencies. Over the years we have spent thousands of hours and millions of dollars in procedural justification to these agencies."*

Many organizations are involved with state and federal government programs and must operate using established policies and procedures. The records of such organizations are subject to state and/or federal records retention and disposition criteria as well as the established corporate criteria. Organizations engaged in pharmaceutical, insurance, banking, public utilities, and investment activities are subject to stringent regulatory constraints. These organizations must be able to substantiate their positions through complete and accessible records. At Goodyear Tire and Rubber Company, the company's computer cranked out 345,000 pages of paper weighing 3,200 pounds in one week, to meet *one* government regulation.

*Regulatory constraints*

Organizations engaged in interstate commerce, such as trucking firms, telephone companies, and banks, are accountable to regulatory agencies. All of these organizations must be able to document their compliance and to provide that documentation upon request.

## Historical Reference

*"Our company celebrates its 100th anniversary in June. I have been asked to prepare the company history, but all of our early records are gone."*

It is often said that "the past is prologue" — prologue being defined as a preliminary act or course of action foreshadowing greater events, or an introduction to events that follow. Records document this past and provide information for future events.

*Preserve*
*organizational*
*history*

They preserve history for future generations. When recorded information is lost or destroyed, much of it is never regained. Those portions of the information regained are often a result of recollection and may contain considerable distortion from the original record.

Records provide a reference base not only in a historical sense but also in a current sense. Technical reference files consist of specialized information for use as a technical reference library. Materials housed in a technical reference library include copies of books, periodicals, special reports and studies, catalogs, and data sheets. Project histories may be maintained as a historical reference base for researchers. Therefore, organizations must maintain this historical base both as evidence of their past achievements and as their prologue to the future.

■

## A LOOK AT THE CASE

As Jerry begins to examine the current records management system, he reviews the basic reasons (needs) for a system of controlling records from their creation to their final disposition. He lists the following primary reasons:

- Management decision making
- Litigation support
- Paperwork volume/cost reduction
- Organizational efficiency
- Legislative/regulatory requirements
- Historical reference

Jerry believes that all of the reasons noted are important, and he plans to investigate the current records management system's ability to meet these needs. He also believes that an established system is necessary to provide appropriate information and has made a note to discuss what a system is, what elements comprise a system, and to describe a records management system when he meets with the vice president.

1. What is the system concept?
2. What are the components of a records management system?

■

## THE SYSTEM CONCEPT

A **system** is a group of interrelated parts acting together to accomplish a goal. The goal of the records management system is the ability to provide the right information to the right person at the right time at the lowest possible cost. Reaching this goal is more easily accomplished by applying the system approach to records management.

*Records management goal*

All systems are composed of three basic elements—input into the system, process of the input, and generation of the output of the system. The input, process, and output components of the records management system contribute to the achievement of the established goal of the system. (See Figure 1–2.)

*System components*

Figure 1–2
Records Management System

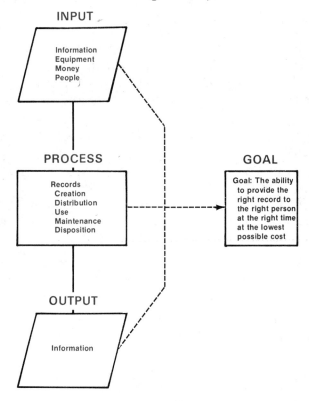

## Input Component

The input of a records management system includes those factors that provide the necessary ingredients for the system to process and reach its goal. The input factors include information, equipment, money, and people. Each factor is essential to the system, and the factors are interdependent.

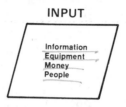

INPUT

Information
Equipment
Money
People

Information as an input may take any of the forms of recorded material. As discussed earlier, recorded material takes many forms and is generated by many sources.

Equipment as an input to the system includes all of the hardware used in processing records. Organizations may choose traditional equipment such as four- or five-drawer cabinets or shelf units, or they may select automated equipment with computer-assisted retrieval, as discussed in Chapter 6.

The money input into the system provides the resources for expenditures necessary in planning, implementing, operating, and controlling the total system of records administration.

People as an input into the system include the administrative support personnel necessary to provide the "right record to the right person at the right time at the lowest possible cost." The "people input" also includes administrative and managerial personnel who generate records which serve as an input in the form of information into the system.

The four inputs into the records management system—information, equipment, money, and people—provide the bases for the processing of records within the system.

## Process Component

The processing portion of the total system includes the functions of records management—records creation, distribution, use, maintenance, and disposition.

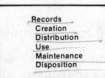

PROCESS

Records
Creation
Distribution
Use
Maintenance
Disposition

Information is processed through each of the functions. The five functional phases of the process element of the system represent the **life cycle** of a record—the evolution of a record from its birth (creation) to its death (disposition). (See Figure 1–3.) Some sources refer to the life cycle of a record as "creation to cremation."

*Creation to disposition*

Figure 1–3
Life Cycle of a Record

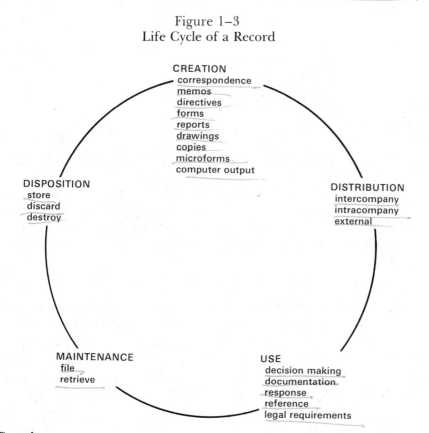

CREATION
correspondence
memos
directives
forms
reports
drawings
copies
microforms
computer output

DISTRIBUTION
intercompany
intracompany
external

USE
decision making
documentation
response
reference
legal requirements

MAINTENANCE
file
retrieve

DISPOSITION
store
discard
destroy

## Creation

Records originate internally through dictation, handwritten drafts, or by using word or data processors and externally from mail, computer output, telecommunication systems, or word or data processors. When a letter is written, an invoice typed, a report prepared, an engineering drawing made, or a new formula recorded, a record has been created and information has been processed. Records are created at all levels of the organization—from clerk to chief executive officer.

## Distribution

If the process stopped at the creation phase, information would not be available to persons requiring the data in the performance of their jobs. Following the creation phase, therefore, is the distribution phase, during which the information can be distributed to the appropriate persons. Distribution may be intercompany, intracompany, or external to the organization. Information may be distributed by electronic mail, the U.S. Postal Service, special courier, interoffice mail systems, or direct access to computer databases.

### Use

Records have many uses. They provide information for decision making, for documentation, for response to inquiries, for reference, or for supporting legal requirements. In this phase of the life cycle, information is put to its intended use.

### Maintenance

Maintenance refers to filing and retrieving records. A **file** is a collection of records arranged according to a predetermined system; filing is the preparation and placement of materials into their places within the system. Although records management is often confused with filing, the filing activities comprise only one portion of the total records management system. **Retrieval** refers to finding and retrieving a requested file or information contained within the file.

### Disposition

When records are no longer frequently referenced, these records are stored or disposed of. The decision to store or dispose of records is based on a predetermined organizational plan (schedule) for retaining or disposing of records. This schedule, which takes legal and other business needs into consideration, is known as the records retention schedule and is discussed in detail in Chapter 3.

*Store.* The storage of records is based largely on whether the records are classified as active or inactive, long term or temporary, a record or a nonrecord. Records may be classified as active or inactive depending on how often they are used. A record is considered to be an **active record** if it is referenced (used) on a regular basis. For example, the personnel records of current employees are considered to be active records. Other examples of active records include invoices for the current fiscal period, correspondence, or creative works in progress. All of these would be referenced on a regular basis. **Inactive records** include long-term records, semi-active records, and inactive records. A record is classified as a **semi-active record** if it is referenced once a month and inactive if referenced fewer than ten times annually. This reference rate clas-

*Active/inactive records*

sifies long-term, semiactive, and inactive records in the broad category of inactive records. Examples of inactive records include personnel files of terminated employees, paid invoices for previous periods, and canceled checks.

Records may also be classified as long term or temporary according to whether the records have continuing value to the organization. **Long-term records** have continuing value and are held indefinitely or for a specified period identified in the retention schedule. For many years, records that had continuing value were classified as *permanent* records when, in fact, the records were not intended to be kept permanently. Records managers now recognize that few, if any, records are to be kept permanently — one day after forever. When asked about permanent retention of a record, one records manager inquired if 500 years would be adequate. The trend is to establish a record life in finite terms (20 years, for example) or to use the concept "life of the organization." The term "permanent" refers to the ability of the record to last for long periods of time rather than referring to retaining a record forever.

*Long-term/ temporary records*

Records designated long-term may include documentation of organizational history, policies and procedures, and individual papers having historical significance. Also included in the category of long-term records are vital records. **Vital records** are those records that are essential to the operation of the organization, the continuation and/or resumption of operations following a disaster, the recreation of legal and financial status of the organization, or to the fulfillment of its obligations to stockholders and employees in the event of a disaster. Examples of vital records include accounts receivable, inventory lists, contracts, and creative works in progress. Based on their reference rates, long-term records may also be either active or inactive.

**Temporary records** are all records not classified as long term. Being labeled "temporary" does not reduce their importance; it only suggests that the records do not have continuing or lasting value to the organization. Temporary records are sometimes referred to as transitory records, indicating their temporary value to the organization. Temporary, or transitory, records may include responses to letters, routine requests, memos for specific short-term activities, project control cards, or forms that are routine in nature and do not have continuing reference value.

A record may also be classified as a **record copy** or a **nonrecord copy**. For incoming records, the original copy is the record copy. For outgoing records, one copy is designated as the official

*Record/ nonrecord copy*

record copy which serves the documentation needs of the organization. Nonrecord refers to copies of documents maintained in more than one location, materials not identified in the retention schedule, documents not required to be retained, or materials available from public sources.

*Records span categories*

Records are not limited to one category. They are, however, active or inactive, long term or temporary, and the record or nonrecord copy. Not only do records span categories, but they may also change status over time. For example, most records move from active status to inactive status as the reference rates decrease. In general, it is unlikely that a record will change from long term to temporary status and vice versa, or from record to nonrecord status and vice versa. Table 1–1 illustrates how the same record may have more than one classification. General correspondence, for example, may be active or inactive depending on its reference rate; depending on its value to the organization, it may be either long term or temporary. The official organizational copy of a piece of general correspondence is the record copy. Extra copies retained in various locations within the organization are nonrecord copies. When unneeded records are allowed to accumulate, the cost of maintenance and storage rises accordingly.

Table 1–1
Records Classification

| Example | Active | Inactive | Long Term | Temporary | Record | Nonrecord |
|---|---|---|---|---|---|---|
| Current orders | × | | × | | × | |
| Last week's *Business Week* magazine | × | | | × | | × |
| General correspondence | × | × | × | × | × | × |
| Personnel records for 1982–83 | | × | | | × | |
| Creative work in progress | × | | × | | × | |

***Discard/destroy.*** The predetermined organizational plan (schedule) for records storage and disposition provides the organization with a timetable for records disposal. When a record reaches the disposition phase of its life cycle, the record may be either discarded or destroyed. The choice of disposition form depends largely on the type of document and its contents.

*Disposition of records*

Every record may not proceed through each of the stages in the life cycle. For example, a memo may be created and distributed. A notation may be made by the user and the memo discarded, bypassing the maintenance or storage phases. A FYI (for your information) report may go from creation to distribution to maintenance, omitting the use phase.

*Every record does not proceed through each stage of the life cycle*

The process portion of the records management system represents the life cycle of a record. During the process phase, input (information, equipment, money, and people) is processed through the system and provides the output of the total records management system.

## Output Component

The output of the records management system is information — information that has been processed through the system and is available in recorded form to the right person at the right time and at the lowest possible cost.

**OUTPUT**

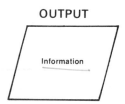

Information

The records management system, then, is composed of three elements — input, process, and output — acting together to accomplish the records management goal.

**GOAL**

Goal: The ability to provide the right record to the right person at the right time at the lowest possible cost

The terms records manager and records management are used throughout this text; however, other terms such as information manager and information resource management are also used in the industry to denote the position and the function. These terms are often used interchangeably and should be regarded in that manner.

■

## A LOOK AT THE CASE

Several days after his meeting with the regional vice president, Jerry received a phone call from Sports World's vice president for information services, Arlene Schlitzteig. The annual manager's meeting is scheduled in two months, and Arlene would like Jerry to conduct one of the sessions dealing with information resource management. She also asked Jerry to include a segment on the functional approach to system management.

1. What is the functional approach to system management?
2. How is the functional approach applied to a records management system?

■

## FUNCTIONAL APPROACH TO SYSTEM MANAGEMENT

The functional approach to the management of a system involves planning, organizing, staffing, directing, and controlling. Each function plays an essential role in the efficient and effective operation of a system. Although the functions are discrete, they have direct relationships to each other and are operationally interdependent.

### Planning

**Planning** is determining what the organization wishes to achieve and deciding on the means for achieving the desired outcomes.

*Determining goals and objectives*

Setting goals, determining specific objectives, and making a plan to achieve the goals and objectives of the organization and its subunits are major components of the planning function.

Planning for a records management system includes setting goals for the organization (What are the goals of the organization with regard to its records management system?) and setting objectives for each of the subunits of the organization (What are the objectives of each of the subunits and how will these objectives contribute to achieving the overall records management goals of the organization?). Plans are made that include planning for the system, the facilities, and the equipment and supplies necessary for implementation.

## Organizing

**Organizing** is the process of putting plans into action. The organizing function involves allocating the available resources and providing the structure for implementation of the plans. An organization allocates available resources (money, equipment, people) to the records management system based on the established priorities of the organization and its perception of the contribution of records management to achieving the goals of the organization.

*Implementing plans*

Structure refers to establishing formal relationships in order to make the best use of resources. Formal organizational structure is usually shown on the organizational chart which defines authority levels and reporting relationships.

The process of organizing the records management system includes developing a records management manual, establishing a retrieval system, integrating information technologies, and developing special records applications. These activities provide the vehicle for "putting the plans into action."

## Staffing

**Staffing** is human resource planning. An organization must determine present and future personnel needs and make plans to meet these needs. Staffing includes determining the quantity and type of personnel needed in order for the organization to reach its goals, recruiting and placing new personnel, training and developing employees, and appraising employee performance.

*Planning for personnel selection and development*

Staffing the records management system includes anticipating the needs of the organization for the present and for the future in terms of the number of persons needed and the types of skills necessary to operate the current system and any anticipated changes in the future system. Technological advances resulting in equipment updating and system changes may require personnel with a different type of qualifications than are currently employed. In this case, it may be necessary to offer additional training to current personnel or to employ new workers.

## Directing

**Directing** is the leading and motivating function. The purpose of the directing function is to provide a climate that stimulates employees to work toward achieving organizational goals and unit objectives. The records manager plays a primary role in motivating the employees who work in the records management unit. The

*Leading and motivating employees*

records manager and the records management supervisors set the tone for the employees and lead and influence their workers in a way that provides the motivation to achieve the goals and objectives of the records management system.

## Controlling

*Comparing results and goals*

**Controlling** is the function that compares achieved results with planned goals. The control function is the process of ordering, evaluating, and providing feedback to the records management system in order to determine whether the plans have been successfully implemented and have achieved the desired results.

Specifically, the records manager examines and obtains feedback regarding the control exercised in correspondence creation and maintenance, directives creation and maintenance, copy creation and maintenance, forms and reports creation and maintenance, micrographics creation and maintenance, and the physical safety and security of stored records.

The functional approach to records management is an interrelational and interdependent approach. The planning function provides the basis for the other functions; each of the other functions depends on the accuracy and thoroughness of the organizational plans. Organizing (putting plans into action) must be complemented by the staffing and directing functions in order to achieve the desired results. Finally, controlling provides information regarding whether the planned objectives and implementation have been accomplished. If the objectives have not been accomplished, plans must be reviewed, revisions made, and the cycle begins again.

*Ongoing and cyclical*

If the desired results have been achieved, goals are again determined for the future, plans are made to accomplish these goals, plans are put into action, staffing requirements are reviewed, a motivational climate is created, and a comparison is made of the plans and the results achieved. The functional approach is cyclical and ongoing.

The records manager, using the functional approach to managing the records management system, follows the same cyclical pattern. Organizational goals are established, objectives that contribute to achieving organizational goals are determined for the records management unit, plans are made to accomplish the stated objectives, and the plans are implemented. Staffing needs of the records management unit are reviewed in light of the plans, and the records manager and staff create a climate that will encourage goal accomplishment. Finally, feedback is obtained and a comparison made of the plans and the results achieved.

## A LOOK AT THE CASE

Jerry McGrath has long recognized the importance of a functional approach to managing any system. In his presentation he has decided to emphasize the functions of planning, organizing, staffing, directing, and controlling as they apply to information availability through the records management systems for Sports World.

## TERMINOLOGY REVIEW

*Active record.* A record that is referenced (used) on a regular basis.

*Controlling.* The management function that compares achieved results with planned goals.

*Directing.* The management function of leading and motivating by providing a climate that stimulates employees to work toward achieving organizational goals and unit objectives.

*Documentary materials.* All forms of correspondence (letters, memos, directives, and reports); forms; drawings; specifications; maps; photographs; and creative materials.

*File.* A collection of records arranged according to a predetermined system.

*Inactive record.* A record that is referenced fewer than ten times annually.

*Life cycle.* Creation, distribution, use, maintenance, and disposition of a record.

*Long-term record.* A record that has continuing value to the organization.

*Nonrecord copy.* A copy of a record maintained in addition to the record copy, such as materials not identified in the retention schedule; documents not required to be retained; materials available from public sources.

*Organizing.* The management function of putting plans into action through allocating available resources and providing a structure for the implementation of the plans.

*Planning.* The management function of determining what the organization wishes to achieve and deciding the means for achieving the desired outcomes.

*Record copy.* A record that serves the documentation needs of the organization.

*Records.* Recorded information (books, papers, photographs, maps, or other documentary materials) regardless of form or characteristics, made or received for legal or operational purposes in connection with the transaction of business.

*Records management.* The systematic control of records from creation to final disposition.

*Retrieval.* Finding a requested file or information contained within the file.

*Semiactive record.* Records that are referenced once a month.

*Staffing.* Planning for the human resource needs of an organization, including determining types and number of personnel required, recruiting, selecting, training, promoting, appraising, and terminating employees.

*System.* A group of interrelated parts acting together to accomplish a goal.

*Temporary record.* A record that does not have continuing or lasting value to the organization; sometimes called a transitory record.

*Vital record.* A record that is essential to the operation of the organization, the continuation and/or resumption of operations following a disaster, the recreation of legal or financial status of the organization, or to the fulfillment of its obligations to stockholders and employees in the event of a disaster.

## COMPETENCY REVIEW

1. Explain five major reasons for establishing a systems approach to records management.
2. Describe the components of a records management system and the relationships among the components.
3. Describe the life cycle of a record and state the methods for accomplishing each stage.

4.  Classify the following types of records as active, inactive; long term, temporary; record, nonrecord. Provide a rationale for your decisions.
    a.  directives
    b.  advertising brochures received
    c.  Christmas party announcement
    d.  current purchase orders
    e.  accounts receivable, 1985
5.  How does filing differ from records management?
6.  Define the functions within the functional approach to system management and describe their relationship.

## APPLICATIONS

1.  Because records serve as the corporate memory, information must be accurate and complete. Unrecorded information is often unreliable, lost, or distorted as it is relayed from one person to another. The following activity emphasizes this problem.
    a.  Five participants will be selected from the class.
    b.  One participant will be given a copy of an office scene and allowed five minutes to study the scene.
    c.  Three of the remaining four participants will leave the room.
    d.  The person who has studied the office scene will be instructed to describe the scene to the remaining participant. The person describing the scene should have the option of using any technique or combination of techniques to describe the scene, such as use of chalkboard or summarizing and repeating. The person to whom the scene is described may ask questions, ask to have information repeated, and so forth.
    e.  The process is continued with each of the remaining participants in grapevine style; as the next participant is brought back into the room, the most recent participant describes the office scene.
    f.  Student observers (the rest of the class) will identify
        (1)  items omitted from the scene (never mentioned by the first participant)
        (2)  items mentioned by the first participant but later dropped
        (3)  items that were modified to change their meaning or position within the scene
        (4)  items that were added by the participants
        (5)  opinion statements by one participant that became facts. For example, "Two people were at the door; they may have been leaving" becomes "There were two people leaving the office."
    g.  Discuss what you have learned about the importance of recording information.
2.  Identify the many types of records that are in your dorm room or bedroom.

CONCLUDING CASES

## ■ A. Delilah Recording Studios

Delilah Recording Studios has been one of the leaders in vocal jazz recordings for over a decade. Recently, however, a new recording company has begun to make a name in the business, and Delilah is beginning to "feel the heat."

As the records manager for Delilah Recording Studios, Sally Myers is aware of the pressure everyone is under. Sally is passing the vice president's office when she overhears the following conversation:

*Jack S. (vice president)* "We must have more current and correct information about our market position. At this point, we receive sales reports at the end of the month only, and they are sometimes late."

*Monica L. (marketing manager)* "And I have no idea what new talent the agents have signed until well after the fact. It makes the marketing job much more difficult. We just don't seem to have any coordination of effort—or at least knowledge of what's going on in the other parts of the company."

*Jack S.* "I am going to call a staff meeting for early next week to discuss this situation. If both of us see that problems exist, others probably have some problems they would like to 'put on the table' too. We need a system around here."

*Monica L.* "We also need to look at the entire approach to making information available. I think we should include Sally Myers in this meeting next week. Maybe she can help us to understand the records management function better. That system needs to be working for us, not against us!"

Sally hurries along to her office. She wants to be prepared when Jack or Monica calls her, so she begins to make notes.

1.  What information should Sally provide to justify an improved records management system?
2.  How can Sally explain to the group what a system is and how a systems approach can contribute to information availability?
3.  Why is it important for Delilah Recording Studios to adopt a functional approach to its records management system?

## B. Jensen Enterprises

Gene Jenkins is a recent graduate of a large university and is now in the management training program of Jensen Enterprises. Jensen Enterprises has been in the nursery and garden equipment business for over 100 years. The business is now run by the founder's grandson Ron. Ron tends to manage the business in the traditional way of his grandfather Carl. Grandfather Carl kept records, but they were not maintained in any systematic manner.

Gene believes that improvement is necessary in order for the records to provide the "right information to the right person at the right time and at the lowest possible cost." When Gene approached Ron regarding his suggestion that the system of keeping records be reviewed, Ron's first response was "Why do we need the records?"

Prepare a memo to Ron Jensen, president of Jensen Enterprises, explaining the value of records to the organization.

## READINGS AND REFERENCES

Austin, Robert B. "10,000,000 Reasons for Records Management," *Records Management Quarterly,* Vol. 19, No. 3 (July, 1985), p. 3.

Benedon, William. "Computer Records Management," presented at 30th Annual Conference of the Association of Records Managers and Administrators, Inc., New York, September 9–12, 1985.

Blount, Gail. "Two Steps Not to Be Overlooked When Organizing Your Records Management Program," *Records Management Quarterly,* Vol. 18, No. 4 (October, 1984), p. 17.

Morgan, Dennis F., and Maryanne Nawoczenski. "Memory Loss: Combatting Corporate Senility," *Records Management Quarterly*, Vol. 19, No. 3 (July, 1985), p. 6.

Penn, Ira A. "Understanding the Life Cycle Concept of Records Management," *Records Management Quarterly,* Vol. 17, No. 3 (October, 1983), p. 5.

Rumer, Thomas A. "Corporate History and the Records Manager," *Records Management Quarterly,* Vol. 18, No. 4 (July, 1984), p. 12.

Winter, Ralph E. "Many Businesses Blame Governmental Policies for Productivity Lag," *The Wall Street Journal,* October 28, 1980, p. 1.

## THE TERM PROJECT

The term project relates many of the records management concepts discussed in INFORMATION RESOURCE MANAGEMENT to what is being done in local organizations. Through visitations with selected local organizations, you will develop in-depth profiles of records management programs. Your instructor will provide some working parameters for the term project, such as

1. establishing a due date for the project, with interim target dates, if necessary.

2. requiring all students to submit for approval the name of an organization to be profiled. Some businesses may be too small or too new to have a fully developed records management program, and you would not benefit from selecting such a business. The approval process also prevents more than one student from profiling the same organization.

3. establishing a minimum and a maximum length for the profile. Length will be defined in terms of double-spaced, typewritten pages. Additional pages may be allowed for photographs or sketches.

Important points that should be included in the profile are:

- Philosophy of the organization regarding its records management program.
- Placement of the records manager and staff within the organization. Show this with an organizational chart.
- Classification system(s) in use and rationale for selection.
- Description of filing and retrieval system(s) in place (manual, mechanical, or automated).
- Description of types of equipment in place; any plans for changes or additional equipment. (May use photographs from the organization or from vendor brochures to illustrate.)
- Description of the organization's records retention program.
- Types of microrecords used and specific applications; location of microforms processing.
- Description and drawing of layout of facility(ies) for active and inactive records.
- Description of vital records program and security provided for these records.
- Development of records management manual(s).
- Extent of office automation and its effect on the records management system.
- Control programs in use (correspondence, forms, reports, directives, copies, and microrecords).
- Presentation of the content of the profile, correct use of grammar and punctuation, and eye-appealing quality of the profile.

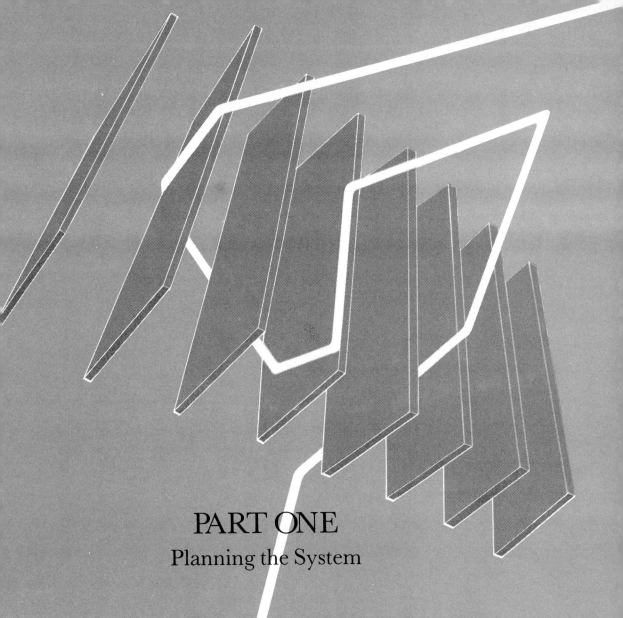

# PART ONE
## Planning the System

# 2
# THE PLANNING FUNCTION

## Competencies

After completing this chapter, you should be able to

1. explain the relationship among organizational goals, objectives, and plans.
2. define the components of a feasibility study.
3. compare and contrast effective oral and written presentations.
4. explain methods for obtaining management support for programs.
5. explain methods for obtaining user support for programs.

# Introductory Case

In 1985, Sampson Industries paid over $1 million dollars in lawsuits resulting from non-compliance with several federal statutes. Immediately after the suits were settled, Sampson's Board of Directors demanded that a total program of records management be implemented.

In keeping with the Board's mandate, Sampson Industries has made a commitment to a strong records management program. Their annual plan includes a goal of "providing each user with requested records in a timely manner at the least possible cost in order to promote efficient and effective decision making." To achieve the overall goal organization wide, specific objectives to be achieved during the coming year include

- developing an organization-wide records management program,
- maximizing personnel and space utilization,
- controlling communication costs, and
- providing high-quality communications at all levels.

Within this framework, each department has its own objectives which contribute to attaining the goals and objectives of the organization. One department submitted the following records management objectives.

- Provide users with records within 15 minutes following a request.
- Reduce the number of records now held by 20 percent.
- Reduce the space required for departmental records by 25 percent.
- Decrease misfiles to a maximum of 2 percent.
- Re-evaluate the mix of records media in use (paper, microfilm, magnetic, optical media).

The vice president for planning, Rebecca Cozart, has been charged with the responsibility of implementing a systems approach to records management consistent with the goals of Sampson Industries. Ms. Cozart has appointed a task force headed by Simon Hertzberg, a recognized expert in the field of records management. The charge to the task force is to make a recommendation regarding the best approach for Sampson in order to comply with applicable laws and to improve its internal system of records management.

1. How do the organizational and departmental objectives affect Simon's task?
2. What plans should Simon and his group make?

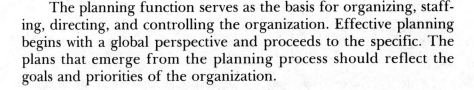

The planning function serves as the basis for organizing, staffing, directing, and controlling the organization. Effective planning begins with a global perspective and proceeds to the specific. The plans that emerge from the planning process should reflect the goals and priorities of the organization.

## ESTABLISH GOALS

Planning involves determining where the organization wants to go and how it will get there.

*"If you don't know where you are going, any road will get you there."*
*—Hildebrandt's Plotting Principle*

Planning is a subsystem of the overall records management system and should be viewed as part of the process portion of that system. As with any system, the planning subsystem includes input, process, and output. (See Figure 2–1.)

*Planning subsystem*

Figure 2–1
Relationship Between Records Management System
and Planning Subsystem

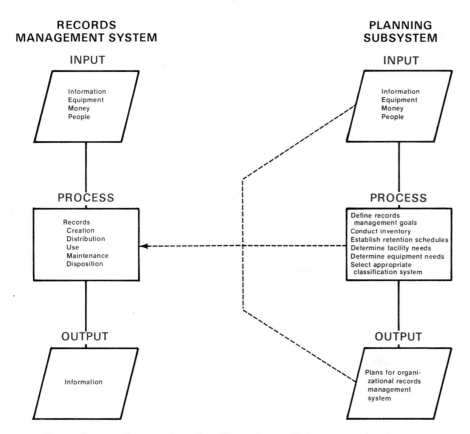

RECORDS
MANAGEMENT SYSTEM

INPUT

Information
Equipment
Money
People

PROCESS

Records
  Creation
  Distribution
  Use
  Maintenance
  Disposition

OUTPUT

Information

PLANNING
SUBSYSTEM

INPUT

Information
Equipment
Money
People

PROCESS

Define records
  management goals
Conduct inventory
Establish retention schedules
Determine facility needs
Determine equipment needs
Select appropriate
  classification system

OUTPUT

Plans for organi-
zational records
management
system

In order to determine the direction of the organization, overall organizational goals are established—both short and long term. The organization must know where it is going (goals) and how it is going to get there (plans).

## Define Goals and Objectives

The goals of an organization are established at the highest levels of management; **goals** reflect the philosophy and aspirations of management for the organization. Goals are usually stated in general

*Goals are stated in general terms*

terms. For example, one organizational goal might be to reduce the cost of administrative services. In keeping with this organizational goal, goals in records management might be to increase the capabilities and reduce the cost of providing information to managers. After the goal(s) have been defined, specific objectives relating to *Objectives are* the goals are developed. An **objective** is a statement of how one *stated in specific* step in reaching a goal is to be completed and measured. A specific *terms* objective for the organizational goal of a reduction in costs might be to reorganize the administrative services to streamline its operation to produce an eight percent savings during the next two years. A specific objective of the records management goal of reducing the cost of providing information to managers might be to determine a more cost-efficient method of maintaining and storing records.

*Plans are* Plans are then written to accomplish the objectives and, conse-
*based on* quently, to attain the goals. Given the records management goals
*goals/objectives* and one of the objectives as defined above, a plan for achieving the objective would be devised. The plan would include ways to accomplish the objective, a timetable for the planned action, and a cost projection. Plans serve as the foundation for all organizational achievements.

## Obtain Management Support

*Obtain* A firm commitment from top management is essential to achieving
*commitment* cooperation and promoting coordination from those involved in the implementation of plans for a records management program. Support and commitment should be obtained at the beginning of the planning process and must be continued throughout the planning and implementation stages. Support and commitment can be achieved by maintaining open communication with management

through both informal communication and interval reporting. Communication allows management to be knowledgeable about the progress of the plans and to provide input to the records management unit.

## DETERMINE THE PRESENT SITUATION

Before plans can be finalized for a records management program, the records manager should assess the current situation and its compatibility with the goals of the organization. There are a number of tools available to aid planners in the assessment process. One planning tool is a feasibility study.

### Plan a Feasibility Study

A **feasibility study** is an examination of the practicality of implementing new or modified procedures, methods, or technologies. Feasibility studies range from simple, informal observations to complex, formal analyses. The complexity and formality of the study are directly related to the number of people affected by the proposed change, the potential extent of the change, and the cost of implementation. An example of a simple feasibility study is an examination of how a file room might be rearranged to allow for more convenient access by users. If, however, the feasibility study is an examination of an entire organization's records system, and the outcome of the proposed changes affects many employees and involves spending large sums of money, the feasibility study is complex. Studies, of course, may fall at any point within these two extremes.

*Studies may be simple to complex*

Whether a feasibility study is simple or complex or formal or informal, careful planning is a must. The person designated to be responsible for the study may be selected from an organization's staff, or a consultant may be employed to conduct the study. In either case, decisions must be made regarding the scope of the study, time frame of the study, information needed, and the methods used to conduct the study.

*Designate person responsible*

#### Scope of the Study

Who will be included in the study? Will the study include one department, several departments, or the whole organization? The **scope of the study** defines the boundaries of the study in terms of who will be included. In certain instances, it is desirable to limit the

*Department(s) or organization-wide*

study to a small group and to implement the changes on a pilot basis in that small group. The scope decision is based on the interdependence of each of the departments and the need for consistent procedures for managing the records program throughout the organization.

## Time Frame

How long will the study last? A predetermined time frame forces the project manager to plan in order to meet the target dates. The time frame is usually projected in a schedule. (See Figure 2–2.) The arrows shown on the schedule indicate continuous time frames; the X notations indicate a specific date such as April 1, July 1, and so forth.

Figure 2–2
Feasibility Study Schedule

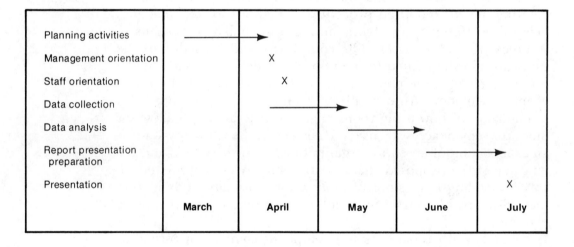

| | March | April | May | June | July |
|---|---|---|---|---|---|
| Planning activities | → | | | | |
| Management orientation | | X | | | |
| Staff orientation | | X | | | |
| Data collection | | → | | | |
| Data analysis | | | → | | |
| Report presentation preparation | | | | → | |
| Presentation | | | | | X |

## Information Needed

What kinds of data are needed in order to make a judgment on the proposed changes in the records management system? The proposed changes may be in automating records retrieval, in procedures, in types of equipment or supplies, or in adding, redistributing, or terminating personnel. All categories of data essential to determination of objectives should be collected. The person or group conducting the feasibility study should collect only essential data. Often, too much information is collected, which makes summarizing the data and extracting needed information more difficult.

*Collect only essential data*

**Study Methods**

How will the information be obtained? A number of methods exist for gathering data for records management feasibility studies. Among the more commonly used methods are records inventory, activity sampling, questionnaires, time/activity charts, and interviews.

A **records inventory** is a complete listing of the locations and contents of an organization's records. The records inventory is covered in detail in Chapter 3. A random sampling of records activities may be obtained for a short period of time (generally two to three weeks) in which records activities are tracked on a randomly selected basis. A **records time/activity chart** provides information regarding the volume of records, types of records activities within each department or file station, and time spent in records activities. Individual time/activity charts may be used to identify the specific activities of records clerks and the amount of time that is spent on various types of records. (See Figure 2–3.) Interviews may be conducted with key personnel to obtain information for the study. Any combination of these methods may be used; gathering information need not be limited to one method.

*Questionnaires, records inventory, random sampling, time/activity charts, interviews*

Figure 2–3
Records Activity Chart

**RECORDS ACTIVITY CHART**

Division*_____ Department_____ Chart maintained by_____

Directions: Beginning on _____ and continuing for ten working days, maintain this chart for all record activity in your department. Place "tick marks" ( ~~HH~~ ) each time you file, refile, or charge out a record. Follow the same procedure for identifying the record as correspondence, forms, or other types of records.

| Date | File | Refile | Charge-out | Correspondence | Forms | Other |
|------|------|--------|------------|----------------|-------|-------|
|      |      |        |            |                |       |       |
|      |      |        |            |                |       |       |
|      |      |        |            |                |       |       |

*Only for large divisions where there are several departments using the same file station. In this case, please use separate Activity Charts for each department within the division.

■

## A LOOK AT THE CASE

Having examined the goal of Sampson Industries to "provide
each user with requested records in a timely manner at the
least possible cost in order to promote efficient and effective
decision making," Simon Hertzberg has decided to conduct a
feasibility study to determine if a centralized system is the most
appropriate system for Sampson Industries to use in its records
management program. He will need to determine (1) the scope
of the study, (2) the time frame of the study, (3) the information needed, and (4) the method to be used.

Because the Board of Directors of Sampson Industries has
mandated that each division shall have a program of records
management, the task force will want the organization as a
whole to participate in the study (scope). The entire study will
probably take two to three months with an additional month
for analyzing the data and preparing the report (time frame).
Mr. Hertzberg's group may gather the information in the most
expedient way, while employing a method(s) that would be
most productive to meet the needs (goals) of the total organization (method). The task force would probably wish to have a
records inventory and to use a survey questionnaire.

Before the decision of "how" can be made, the determination must be made regarding "what." The question "What information is needed in order to decide whether a centralized,
decentralized, or combination system is more appropriate?"
must be asked. Much of the desired information can be obtained from the records inventory. Information, such as volume of records maintained and their locations, classification of
records, current filing procedures, records flow, and current
costs for personnel, space, and equipment, is available from the
records inventory. The questionnaire will gather attitudinal
and subjective information. In addition, a records time/activity
chart should be maintained at each file station. This will
provide information such as volume of new files, volume of refiles, volume of requested records, and method of requesting
records.

■

## Conduct the Feasibility Study

Total management support of the study must be evident to persons
charged with the responsibility of conducting the study and to participants. Methods used to obtain and broadcast this support will be

discussed later in this chapter. At this point, it is only necessary to know that commitment of top management, made known by both oral and written communication to all affected personnel, is essential to the success of a study.

The task force must prepare the forms to be used in the study. *Prepare forms* Even personal interviews should have a definite format of prepared questions so that each person interviewed will be asked to respond to the same set of questions asked in the same way. When it is time to tabulate responses, this standardized procedure will prove to be a great asset. Figure 2–4 is a list of some of the questions an interviewer might use to determine attitudes and subjective information from managers.

Orientation meetings are held for information purposes—to *Plan* introduce the persons conducting the study; to explain why the *orientation* study is necessary; to reinforce the commitment of management to the goal of an improved records management program; to explain in detail the procedures to be followed; to allow doubters to ask questions and receive responses; and to gain cooperation.

Orientation should be planned for two groups of people. If numbers are large, divide the groups into smaller orientation groups. The number of people in each orientation group should not exceed 40 or 50. Management is the first group to participate in orientation sessions. Subsequent sessions would involve the administrative support personnel, major budget unit directors, and others who have direct responsibility for records management.

Following the orientation sessions, collection of data begins. *Collect data* Data may be collected through the use of records inventories, questionnaires, records activity sampling, and records time/activity charts. An investigator should make appointments for interviews and give each manager a copy of a questionnaire prior to the interview. If specific information is to be required, this should be communicated to interviewees at the time appointments are made. For *Prepare for* example, if the question "How many times a week do you request *interview* information from your correspondence files?" is asked and the response is expected to be an exact number, persons to be interviewed should have an opportunity to prepare their responses. However, if questions are general in nature or aimed at obtaining attitudinal information, this procedure is not necessary.

Arrangements must be made to distribute records time/activity *Distribute* charts, which are to be maintained at each file station, and to *time/activity* provide directions for their use. Records time/activity charts *charts* provide information regarding the volume and types of records ac-

Figure 2–4
Records Management Interview Instrument

**Name of Person Interviewed** _____ **Title** _____

**Department** _____ **Office Location (No.)** _____ **Telephone No.** _____

1. Is there at least one person responsibile for managing the records in this department? Yes _____ No _____

2. If so, what are the responsibilities of that person(s)?

3. Do you have a retention and disposition schedule? Yes _____ No _____
Is the schedule regularly used? Yes _____ No _____

4. Is your storage area adequate for current needs? Yes _____ No _____
Is your storage area adequate for projected five-year needs (including paper, microforms, optical data disks, magnetic media)? Yes _____ No _____

5. Do government regulations affect your departmental records? Yes _____ No _____
If so, what specific regulations?

6. Do you have a records management manual? Yes _____ No _____
Is the manual regularly used? Yes _____ No _____

7. Do you have a directives management program? Yes _____ No _____
Is the program regularly used? Yes _____ No _____

8. Do you have a correspondence management program? Yes _____ No _____
Is the program regularly used? Yes _____ No _____

9. Do you have a forms management program? Yes _____ No _____
Is the program regularly used? Yes _____ No _____

10. Do you have a reports management program? Yes _____ No _____
Is the program regularly used? Yes _____ No _____

11. Do you have a copy management program? Yes _____ No _____
Is the program regularly used? Yes _____ No _____

12. Explain your perception of records management.

13. What problems do you encounter in your daily records use?

14. What kinds of records security are exercised?

15. Diagram the flow of records in your office. (Use the back of this page.)

tivity within each department or file station. Contact is first made with the person having overall responsibility for records within each unit, followed by a personal explanation (preferably on a one-to-one basis) with each records supervisor and records clerk. Time frames are explained, procedures to be followed are reinforced, and opportunity is given for questions. In addition, arrangements are made to collect the data. Will the records supervisor send the records activity sheets to the investigator, or will the records activity sheets be collected by the investigator? In what order should the sheets be collated? Should they be stapled or loose? Are any of the records confidential or specified as limited access records requiring special precautions? All of these considerations should be discussed in detail with the persons responsible for maintaining the records activity charts.

## DETERMINE AIDS AND BARRIERS TO GOALS

Information derived from a feasibility study can provide investigators with data regarding aids and obstacles to goal attainment. Identification of these factors makes implementation of plans more efficient and goal achievement more likely.

### Analyze the Feasibility Study Data

Once the data are received, in whatever format (records inventory, questionnaire, random sample, records activity charts), a data summary is made. Summaries allow easier, more efficient analyses of data. Summaries may be made in many forms — from a simple tallying where the tabulations are merely tick marks (卌) to computer prepared summaries that provide means, medians, percentages, frequency distributions, and statistical summaries.

*Summarize data*

    From the basic information provided by the data summaries, various analyses may be made. Given a summary of the records action by department (as provided by time/activity charts), an analysis may be made of the levels of records activity within each department. Does one department have a greater volume of processed records than other departments? Are the records that are processed original files, refiles, or charge-outs? Are most of the processed records correspondence, forms, or other types of records? Or, provided a summary of the locations and space required for inactive records, along with the costs of housing records in prime space, an analysis may be made of the cost efficiency of the records storage.

*Make analyses*

## Perform a Cost Benefit Analysis

A primary component of a feasibility study is a **cost benefit analysis**, which is a comparison of the benefits of a new procedure, system, or technology with its costs. The analysis is a comparison of costs of current systems with the costs of proposed changes. Costs of personnel, equipment, space, and system conversion should be taken into consideration. Attention should be given to long-term continuing operational costs as well as immediate expenditures. The cost benefit analysis should be clearly presented in a manner that assists readers in making comparisons. All comparisons should be parallel; if data is presented to compare the costs of a new system with a current one, then all information should be compatible. Comparisons should be made of costs over the long term, not just start-up costs of the new system as compared to maintenance costs of the existing system.

*Make comparisons*

Costs should be analyzed, but the benefits accruing from the new system should be evaluated also. One way to evaluate is to list the benefits of the changes and compare them to any potential problems that may result from the changes. But consideration must also be given to future costs and ramifications that may occur as a result of making no change in the system. Basically, the cost benefit analysis will address the following questions:

- What are the costs of the changes?
- What costs may be eliminated by the new system?
- What are the benefits to be derived from the changes?
- What are the problems that may result from the changes?
- What are the long-term costs associated with maintaining the current system?
- What are the benefits of maintaining the current system?
- What are the problems associated with maintaining the current system?
- What are the opportunity costs — what opportunities may be lost by not developing the new system and what opportunities may be lost by channeling the resources into the new system rather than in other activities?

*Be objective*

Analysis of the current and proposed systems should be made and presented objectively. A cost benefit analysis is no place for personal biases.

■

## A LOOK AT THE CASE

Simon Hertzberg's task force will have to develop the instruments to be used in the interviews and records activity analyses unless instruments are available which are acceptable in current or modified form. Orientation meetings must be planned and scheduled for managers and other personnel responsible for records within Sampson Industries. Data is then collected by using the records inventory/survey, interviews, and records activity charts. This information will be analyzed, and recommendations will be made to the vice president for planning, Ms. Rebecca Cozart.

How may the recommendations be presented in order to obtain management support?

■

## DEVELOP A PLAN FOR REACHING GOALS

A plan includes recommendations to management for reaching the established goal(s). Recommendations are presented in writing and included in the final report to management.

### Make Recommendations

Recommendations are made to management based on information obtained from the study and results of the cost benefit analysis. Each recommendation should be accompanied by a rationale. For example:

*Recommendation:* Consolidate purchase order files of the purchasing and finance departments.

*Rationale:* The departments of purchasing and finance currently maintain duplicate files. Duplication could be eliminated by consolidating files of the two departments.

*Recommendation:* Route the purchasing department copy of purchase orders to the finance department for processing.

*Rationale:* Current procedure is for copies of purchase orders to be retained in the purchasing department and a copy forwarded to the finance department for processing. A more efficient procedure would be to retain the copy in the purchasing department until the order has been completed. At this time, the copy would be attached to the invoice/delivery receipt and routed to the finance department for processing payment.

## Assure Management Approval

The most carefully planned and conducted study may never get off the ground unless the presentation to management is just as carefully planned and conducted. Many excellent studies have found their way to the "round file" or have been ignored because of the lack of quality in a presentation to management. Presentations may be oral or written, and a follow-up may be used in either format.

### Oral Presentations

*Planning the presentation*

When planning the method of presentation, strong consideration should be given to using an oral presentation accompanied by a written report. The plan for an oral presentation includes making decisions regarding the order of presentation, type of visuals to be used, when visual reinforcement will be used, who will be responsible for making the oral presentation, the time to be allocated, how and when to allow for questions, and so forth.

Oral presentations are intended to sell a viewpoint, product, or service. In preparing an oral presentation, consideration should be given to the following items as part of the sales technique.

- State the present situation and get agreement
- State the problems resulting from the present situation
- Outline the benefits attainable if the problems were solved
- Identify the problem causes (get agreement that these are the causes)
- Show alternative solutions investigated
- Recommend a specific alternative, showing why it is the best solution
- Restate the benefits to be gained (using the best alternative)
- Show your specific plan of action
- Get a commitment

Visuals should be prepared professionally to enhance, not detract from, the information to be presented. Professionally prepared visuals are not necessarily expensive. However, professionally prepared visuals do employ all of the principles of effective visual preparation. Visuals which display concepts clearly, are attractively arranged, and are easily readable convey the desired effect on the audience and are considered to be professionally prepared. Good visuals serve the purpose of gaining and holding attention, reinforcing what the speaker says, and providing emphasis to important aspects of the oral presentation.

The person selected to make an oral presentation should also employ the principles of good public speaking. Certainly, the presenter must be technically competent, comfortable with the subject matter, articulate, and well prepared. Visual materials should be used during practice sessions. Anyone who has experienced the frustration and embarrassment of having visuals in incorrect order or slides upside down knows the importance of practicing the entire presentation. When the presentation can be made smoothly and within a predetermined time frame, practice has been sufficient. The important point is—don't ruin a good study by making a poor presentation.

*Making the presentation*

## Written Presentations

The oral presentation should be followed by the presentation of a written report to management. Generally, withholding distribution of the written report until all questions resulting from the oral presentation have been addressed is preferable. If handouts are to be distributed in conjunction with an oral presentation, the distribution should be carefully timed. When handouts are distributed prior to oral presentations, time should be allowed for participants to read the handouts. Prior distribution prevents the tendency of the participants to be distracted by receiving the handouts throughout the presentation.

Preparation of a written report to management is a time-consuming project and should never be left until the last moment. During the writing of the first draft of the report, careful consideration should be given to the order in which the information will be presented. A decision must also be made regarding the necessity of preparing more than one report. One type of report for top-level management and another for middle management is often desirable.

*Preparing the written report*

When this approach is selected, the report to top-level management should be concise. Executives are interested primarily in final recommendations, costs involved, and positive/negative benefits that would accrue from any changes. A report to top-level management, therefore, should reflect these interests.

A concise **executive summary** of the report should be limited to two or three pages and be attached to the top of the complete report. Busy executives then have the option of reading only the summary report or reading the entire report at their convenience.

*Executive summary*

The report (or section of the report) that is specifically tailored for middle-level management is more detailed, comprehensive in scope, and includes information necessary to operations personnel. Middle-level managers are interested in all of the collected information, the ramifications (particularly to their operations), and the methods to be used in implementing the changes. The report to middle-level managers should reflect these concerns and interests. Detailed information on implementation is particularly important to managers at the operations level.

As with an oral presentation, a written presentation must be developed in a logical sequence, be grammatically and technically correct, and be attractively packaged. A report of this caliber is more likely to produce a positive initial response than a report that is sloppily prepared and presented. Often an association is made between the way the information is prepared and presented and the quality of information contained in the report.

### Follow-Up

*Suggest tentative date for further review/decision*

At the conclusion of the oral and written presentations, a tentative date may be suggested for further review or to reach a decision on the proposal. This suggestion must be handled tactfully. Top management, especially, may regard the suggestion as an encroachment on their authority. However, few managers resent a carefully worded request to meet at their convenience within the next several weeks in order to review, clarify, or finalize plans for implementation.

# PROMOTE THE PLAN

*Sell the program*

What plans can be made to promote the records management program? Plan to "sell" the program with the same preparation and enthusiasm that you would use to sell any other product. Define your market; plan your strategy to interest that market; implement your plans. Plans should be developed for two major markets — management and users.

## Management Support/Commitment

Management is primarily interested in the organization-wide benefits a records management program will provide. Top levels of management often do not recognize the need for a comprehensive program of records management. Basic education regarding the scope of records management is needed, because too many managers equate records management with cabinets and boxes for housing paper records. Before the educational process can begin, assess the personalities, politics, and policies currently in action, the reasons they were established, and who was involved in the process. In other words, know your market.

*Educate managers about the need for planning for records*

Managers must be aware of existing or potential problems in order to perceive a need for change. For some managers, this knowledge comes late and is costly. One organization became aware of the importance of records protection only after all of their records were destroyed by fire.

Gaining management support may not start with the "grand design." Sometimes an elaborate plan scares off potential supporters. You may have to start with a single phase of a multiphase plan; for example, begin by instituting a program of records retention and disposition. Again, know your market and be prepared to present a well-designed plan for change.

*Know your market*

Management support must be publicized. This support may be evidenced in many ways. For example, if a study is to be conducted in any area of records management, a letter from management to all participants will convey the support of management. In addition, the first item on the agenda at the orientation meetings should be a brief introduction of the project by a member of top management. This introduction should emphasize the importance of the study and the commitment of top management for its successful conclusion. Get the support, then broadcast it!

*Publicize managers' support*

## User Support

User support is achieved in two major ways: positive top-down attitudes and user involvement in the processes. People's attitudes often reflect the attitudes of their superiors; thus, positive attitudes of top management tend to create positive user attitudes. The other tool used to gain user support—user involvement in the processes—has long been accepted as a successful supervisory technique. Early user involvement; routine updates; accepting, even soliciting, suggestions; encouraging participation; and making potential benefits known to the users are effective in gaining support.

*Educate users to accept changes in records management procedures*

Support for any program must be obtained from the people who will ultimately be responsible for the system's implementation and maintenance. In almost all instances, management and users share this responsibility.

## A LOOK AT THE CASE

The task force, headed by Simon Hertzberg, now turns its attention to the preparation of the oral presentation to Ms. Rebecca Cozart and other managers. Because it is important to present the information in a professional manner, Simon and his group will be particularly careful in their preparation for the presentation. Equal care will be given to the preparation and presentation of the written report. The feasibility study, which has been carefully planned, conducted, and prepared, will not be diminished by improper presentation.

## TERMINOLOGY REVIEW

*Cost benefit analysis.* A comparison of the benefits of a new procedure, system, or technology with its costs.

*Executive summary.* A two- to three-page concise summary of a report made especially for top management.

*Feasibility study.* An examination of the practicality of implementing new or modified procedures, methods, or technologies.

*Goals.* General statements of the philosophy and aspirations of management for the organization.

*Objective.* A statement of how one step in reaching a goal is to be completed and measured.

*Records inventory.* A complete listing of the locations and contents of an organization's records.

*Records time/activity chart.* Provides information regarding the volume, types of records activity within each department or file station, and time spent in records activities.

*Scope of study.* Defines the boundaries of the study in terms of who will be included.

## COMPETENCY REVIEW

1. Describe the relationship among organizational goals, objectives, and plans.
2. The four components of feasibility studies—planning the study, conducting the study, analyzing the data, and making recommendations—all have elements of their own. Define and discuss.

3. Oral and written presentations are important to obtaining management approval.
   a. Discuss commonalities in effective oral and written presentations.
   b. Discuss elements unique to each type of presentation.
4. How can management program support be obtained?
5. How can user program support be obtained?

## APPLICATIONS

1. To make goal setting and objectives definition more realistic, define your personal and/or professional goals and specific objectives for the next twelve-month period. Then write a plan for achieving one of the goals.
   a. My goal(s) for the next twelve months is (are)
   b. My specific objectives are
   c. My plan for reaching my goal of
2. Prepare a checklist of actions that should be taken in preparing and presenting a formal presentation to management.

## CONCLUDING CASES

### A. Summit Manufacturers

Marjorie Hon is the divisional purchasing manager for Summit Manufacturers, a large manufacturing company located in the midwest. Each of four plants is responsible for its own purchasing. However, a new policy has been adopted requiring all contracts in excess of $10,000 to be approved by Miss Hon's office.

The suggestion has been made to decide upon and implement a uniform system of records management. Currently each plant uses its own unique system. There have been some problems recently, however, in coordinating requests. One branch uses a geographic classification; another uses an alphabetic system by vendor name; a third uses a numeric system; the fourth plant uses whatever system the current records clerk happens to know.

Marjorie Hon received a proposal from Raul Perez, a management consultant, to study the system. Since Miss Hon reports to the vice president for production, the proposal must be cleared with him. The vice president suggests that two of the other vice presidents should be present for the proposal presentation. Marjorie discussed this with Raul Perez who said that he would assume the responsibility for preparing the oral and written presentations.

The meeting is scheduled for Tuesday at 10:30 a.m. At 10:45 Raul arrives out of breath. "I've just been copying the handouts. They are on the back table. Please pick them up." What follows is a real fiasco. Slides that Raul is using are blurred and difficult to read. The bulb burns out on the projector. Raul is nervous; he reads the entire report. He apologizes for his lack of familiarity with the content.

When the oral presentation is finally over, Marjorie Hon thanks the VPs for coming and announces that the written report will be distributed next week.

1.  Why did Miss Hon announce that the written report would be distributed next week?
2.  What planning elements were missing in this case?
3.  What mistakes did Marjorie Hon make?
4.  How did the quality of the oral report affect the possibility of gaining management support?
5.  What actions would you suggest at this point in the project?

## B. Western Gear

Jefferson Turner, a retired senior partner of Easterlin Systems Management Consultants and an active member of SCORE (Service Corps of Retired Executives), has received a request from the Small Business Administration to provide assistance to Traci Long, owner of Western Gear.

Western Gear was opened in January, 1980, and has financial difficulties. Among other problems, Traci is inexperienced in planning. Her projections for future sales are always far too optimistic (as much as 36 percent above actual revenue), and her projections of expenses are always too low (as much as 32 percent below actual expenditures).

When Jeff contacted Traci, he asked her to have some information available to him when they met; a meeting was scheduled for two weeks later. Jeff asked Traci to have the documentation that she used in making her projections and to provide the goals and objectives for Western Gear (both short-term and long-range).

At the meeting, it was obvious that Traci had little documentation for the activities of Western Gear since 1980. If you were Jefferson Turner, what advice would you give Traci regarding the importance of accurate records in her planning activities?

## READINGS AND REFERENCES

Blount, Gail L. "If Records Management Is Such a Neat Idea — Why Is It So Tough to Sell?" *Records Management Quarterly*, Vol. 19, No. 4 (October, 1985), p. 12.

General Services Administration, National Archives and Records Service, Office of Records and Information Management. *Methods and Procedures for Conducting Word Processing Feasibility Studies* (Advance Edition). Washington, D.C.: U.S. Government Printing Office, September, 1979.

Pennix, Gail B., and Jan Schouw. "When All Else Fails — Smile." *Records Management Quarterly*, Vol. 19, No. 4 (October, 1985), p. 40.

# 3
# RECORDS RETENTION PROGRAM

## Competencies

After completing this chapter, you should be able to

1. define a records retention program and explain its goals.
2. explain the function of a records inventory in the records management program.
3. outline the steps in planning a records inventory.
4. discuss the considerations in selecting personnel to conduct the records inventory.
5. explain the advantages and disadvantages of the two most common methods of conducting the records inventory.
6. define a record series and give examples of those found in most organizations.
7. list and explain the procedures for conducting the records inventory.
8. outline the steps in preparing the status report at the conclusion of the records inventory.
9. define records appraisal and the types of values which a record series might have to the organization.
10. differentiate between organizational, governmental, and archival requirements for records retention.
11. outline the steps in implementing a records retention program.
12. explain the importance of timely records transfer to the effectiveness of a records retention program and list the steps to be completed in a records transfer.
13. define methods of records destruction.
14. list criteria which affect an organization's selection of a destruction method.

# Introductory Case

Spencer Construction Corp. has experienced rapid growth in services provided and in the number of personnel employed in the past two years. Last month, Susan Spencer, president of Spencer's, hired Gordon Marshall as the records manager to help Spencer's out of their paperwork jungle.

Gordon's first assignment was to prepare and present a plan for the organization and implementation of a records retention program to Susan Spencer and her staff.

1. What is a records retention program?
2. How should a retention program be developed?

**SHOE**

The *Shoe* cartoon illustrates the reason that a retention program is a crucial element of a records management program. If every important record was placed in the "Urgent" file and remained there indefinitely, files would become cumbersome and costly to maintain; they would lose their value as a means of organizing information for efficient retrieval. A records retention program provides a timetable and consistent procedures for maintaining the organization's records, moving the records to inactive storage when appropriate, and destroying records when they are no longer valuable to the organization. The development of a records retention program requires establishing goals and objectives, conducting a records inventory, completing a records appraisal, establishing a retention schedule, and implementing scheduled transfer and disposal of records.

*Procedures for maintaining records*

## GOALS

A records retention program is developed and implemented under the direction of the records manager. During this process, the records manager must work closely with the organization's top executives, division heads, and department heads in identifying and appraising the records of each office.

The first task in developing a records retention program is to determine the goals and objectives of the organization's retention program. A records retention program has three main goals: (1) cost reduction, (2) retrieval efficiency, and (3) retention consistency. Each of these goals is important to the success of the total records management program.

## Cost Reduction

*Methods of achieving cost reduction*

An established retention program reduces the cost of records maintenance in three ways. First, the destruction of unneeded records and the transfer of semiactive and inactive records to low-cost storage areas improve the utilization of expensive office space. Second, the equipment required for the storage of semiactive and inactive records (usually metal shelving and transfer boxes) is less costly than storage cabinets or shelves for office use. A third cost reduction is realized when the retention of duplicate records by various departments is eliminated. Only one copy, the record copy, needs to be retained during semiactive and inactive periods.

## Retrieval Efficiency

*Rapid retrieval*

The proliferation of information and sound management practices prohibit organizations from considering the indefinite retention of all documents and micromedia. In addition to storage costs, another (perhaps more important) need — retrieval efficiency — is sacrificed in an uncontrolled accumulation of records. In order to be used, records must be found. Time spent in searching through old documents is costly to the organization. An established retention program requires that semiactive and inactive records be transferred from the active files at scheduled intervals. At these same intervals, records which are no longer of value to the organization are destroyed. This eliminates clutter and allows more rapid retrieval of those records with high accession rates. Proper transfer procedures allow semiactive and inactive records to be readily retrieved. These procedures are described in the section on records transfer.

## Retention Consistency

*Consistent retention procedures*

Retention procedures which are consistent throughout the organization provide control over division or department heads who might be either "pack rats" who keep everything or "nonsavers" who dispose of records too quickly. Top executives must be able to depend on the availability of similar types of records for each division or department during the periods that these records have value to the organization.

The records manager may establish additional goals to meet the organization's needs. The records manager may also wish to determine specific objectives for the records retention program. These objectives may include the volume of records to be transferred or destroyed annually, the maximum allowable amount of in-office storage space, or the establishment of more central files areas.

■

## A LOOK AT THE CASE

Gordon Marshall realizes how impractical it is to plan a records retention program without detailed information on the types, volume, and current locations of the organization's records. Consequently, Gordon approaches top management with a plan for conducting a records inventory.

1. What information can be gathered in a records inventory?
2. How should a records inventory be conducted?
3. How should the results of the inventory be reported?

■

## RECORDS INVENTORY

Before a retention program can be developed, an organization must conduct a records inventory. The records inventory provides answers to the following questions: (1) What kinds of records do we have? (2) Where are the records located? (3) How many records are there? (4) Are the records active, inactive, or nonessential? This information provides the database for the development of a retention program and for many other decisions in the development of an effective records management program. For example, the answers to these four questions provide a database for determining what facilities, equipment, supplies, and staff are required to handle the organization's records; what training the staff needs; what controls should be placed on the creation and duplication of records; and what measures must be taken to protect the organization's vital records.

*List of records contents and locations*

### Planning the Inventory

A records inventory should not be undertaken without careful planning because the data provided affects most aspects of the records management program. The records manager is responsible for determining how to conduct this project. Steps in planning this project should include obtaining the authorization of top management, selecting the personnel to conduct the inventory, determining the method to be used, selecting or developing the appropriate forms, and planning the schedule for the inventory.

## Project Director

One of the first tasks in planning the records inventory is selecting a project director. The project director must have a thorough knowledge of inventory techniques and of the importance of the records inventory as a basis for a sound records management program. Should someone on the staff be appointed to serve as the project director or should the organization hire an outside consultant for this position? Each choice has advantages and disadvantages.

*Internal director.* If the organization employs a records manager, this person should be given first consideration as the project director. The records manager has an understanding of the goals and operating methods of the organization. In addition, the records manager is motivated to provide the most sound basis possible for the records management program to be planned and implemented following the records inventory.

*Knowledge of organization*

The records manager may not be familiar with inventory procedures. If so, a records consultant may be hired to train the records manager in techniques of taking a records inventory. This additional training time may cause some delay in beginning the inventory but should enhance the usefulness of the results.

*External director.* When an organization hires an outside consultant or group of consultants, it is hiring an expert who has experience in doing a particular task or group of related tasks. The consultant knows the most up-to-date techniques and how these techniques have been applied in other organizations. A consultant also comes to the job with no bias toward any particular department or procedure within the organization.

*Knowledge of techniques*

A disadvantage to hiring consultants is the brief length of time the consultants are in the organization. Because of their limited knowledge of the organization's operating procedures, consultants may overlook some problem areas. As a result, the final report may be based on generalizations and may not include all the details necessary for the staff to implement the recommended procedures.

Careful selection of a consultant helps to ensure proper assistance for the organization. Ask for references and contact these references to determine their satisfaction or dissatisfaction with the consultant or consultants being considered for the position.

The consultant should be asked to present a written proposal to the organization. This proposal should include a detailed list of activities to be completed, a schedule for completing the activities, and a cost estimate.

## Authorization and Responsibility

Completion of a records inventory involves every department within the organization. Cooperation of staff members within each department is essential in obtaining an accurate and complete records inventory. Because taking an inventory causes some interruption of normal work flow and increases the responsibilities of key departmental personnel, these individuals must know that top management recognizes the importance of this task and expects their cooperation. Photos or slides showing unorganized and overflowing storage areas may be instrumental in gaining the approval of top management for the records inventory project.

*Commitment of top management*

Once top management is committed to taking a records inventory, the staff should be informed of the importance this task has in establishing a records management program that will assist smooth operations in all departments. This commitment should be conveyed to the staff in writing. The same communication should, if possible, name the project director and request support for that person in completing the task as expeditiously as possible.

## Methods

The records inventory may be conducted by questionnaire or by a physical survey.

*Questionnaire.* Many organizations find the most expeditious way to complete a records inventory is to develop a survey form to collect the necessary data about volume and type of records in each department. These forms can be distributed to all departments simultaneously. Departmental personnel complete the forms and return them to the project director as requested.

*Survey form*

Two problems frequently develop when this method is employed. First, departmental personnel may not be experienced in records inventory procedures. Instructions may be interpreted differently; if this occurs, the collected data will have little or no consistency. Meeting with the key departmental personnel prior to distributing the inventory forms — to explain their use and to answer questions — may eliminate or minimize this problem.

Second, the departmental personnel who are assigned to complete the questionnaire may view it as one more job to be done. Completing the questionnaire may not seem the essential task that it is. Departmental personnel may procrastinate in completing the inventory form and then do it in a haphazard manner. In addition, resentment may develop toward any effort to implement records controls within the organization. The commitment of the organization's key managers may be enough to alleviate these concerns. An enthusiastic project director who simplifies the task as much as possible also decreases the probability of having to deal with poorly prepared responses from resentful personnel.

*Physical survey.* A physical survey of all the active and inactive records of each department within an organization is time-consuming; however, this method is the most accurate one for determining the current volume, types, dates, and locations of an organization's records. One person can usually survey 1,000 cubic feet of records (approximately 700 letter-size drawers) per week.

*Inspect records*

Training those who actually conduct the physical survey of the records provides consistency in the collected data and speeds the actual completion of the survey. In a small organization, training may not be necessary, as the project director may be the only person involved in the survey. Specific steps in completing the physical survey are discussed in the section on conducting the inventory.

### Forms

Information required on the inventory form may vary somewhat from organization to organization. An inventory form is completed for each record series within each department. A **record series** is a

*Group of related records*

group of records filed together in a unified arrangement which results from, or relates to, the same function or activity. Examples of frequently used record series are paid vouchers, departmental correspondence, and personnel records.

The inventory form should also indicate the locations, dates, types, and volume of the records; whether the record is a record copy or a nonrecord copy; and the name of the person who surveyed the records and the date on which they were surveyed. This information provides an audit trail. A sample inventory form is shown in Figure 3–1. The lower half of this form is completed after the records inventory and is discussed in the section on establishing retention periods.

### Schedule

Before the records inventory is begun, a detailed schedule should be prepared, presented to key managers for approval, and published throughout the organization. (Some records managers prefer to notify each department near the time of the survey to

Figure 3–1
Records Inventory and Retention Sheet

| RECORDS INVENTORY AND RETENTION SHEET | | | |
|---|---|---|---|
| Department  Human Resources | Records Series Title  Annual Performance Appraisals | | Date 1/10/-- |

### INVENTORY

☒ Record Copy    ☐ Computer Tape
☐ Duplicate    ☐ Computer Printout
☒ Letter Size    ☐ Microfilm    ☐ Microfiche
☐ Legal Size    ☒ Other (specify) Paper

Inventoried by: Jane Smith

Description: Annual Performance Appraisal of each employee.

| Location | Volume | Inclusive Dates | Retention Period |
|---|---|---|---|
| Office | 5 cu. ft. | 1/3/86 to 1/10/91 | 5 years |
| Storage | 2 cu. ft. | 1/2/81 to 12/31/85 | 5 years |

### REQUIRED RETENTION PERIOD

| APPROVALS | | YEARS |
|---|---|---|
| Originating Office | Charles Johnson | 5 |
| Fiscal Officer | R. T. Greene | 1 |
| General Counsel | M. A. Anders | 5 |
| Executive | Sharon E. Turner | 5 |

### FINALIZED SCHEDULE

| Office  3 | Storage  2 | Destroy After 5 years |
|---|---|---|
| Authorized by:  E. Harrison | | Date  1/31/-- |

Special Instructions

Confidentiality to be maintained in storage location as well as in the office.

P110: 5/86

prevent departmental "clean-ups" which may destroy valuable records.) The schedule cannot be prepared until the project director has determined the locations of records within the organization, decided upon the sequence in which records are to be inventoried, and estimated the time necessary to complete the inventory.

***Locations.*** The number of records locations varies according to the degree of centralization of the organization's records storage facilities. If all or most of the organization's active records are housed in a centralized area and most of the inactive records are housed in a records center, the identification of locations is greatly simplified. In most organizations, however, the identification of storage locations is not so simple.

*Identify file locations*

Records are often retained within each department (sometimes within each office). If this is the procedure, the project director may find it helpful to do a "walk-through" to assure a comprehensive inventory and to approximate the amount of time needed in each area. Unless the project director is familiar with the storage area for inactive records, a "walk-through" of that area is also helpful. The project director may want to sketch the approximate position of records in each location to save time in completing the actual inventory. The project director may find it helpful to note on this sketch a description of the storage equipment housed in each area.

***Sequence.*** The project director must also determine the order in which records are to be inventoried. Many directors prefer to inventory the active records before the inactive records, but both procedures are used.

*Inventory sequence*

***Time.*** Once the order in which records are to be inventoried is determined, the project director must estimate the time to be spent in each location. Familiarity with the locations of records and the space required to contain them improves the accuracy of this estimate. The estimated time for completion should always provide for interruptions which inevitably occur.

*Estimate time required*

When the elements of the schedule have been determined, the schedule can be presented to key managers for approval. After any suggested adjustments are made, key departmental personnel and others whose cooperation is needed should be informed of the schedule. Orientation meetings should be held for those assisting in the actual inventory, and the work can then begin.

## Conducting the Inventory

Three steps must be performed in each records location in order to complete the inventory. These steps are to (1) identify the record series, (2) identify the required space, and (3) categorize the records. In addition, when all locations have been inventoried, someone (usually the project director) must standardize the terminology used on all inventory forms.

*Steps in conducting inventory*

### Identify the Record Series

In each records location, an inventory form is completed for each record series identified. A record series may contain many files (which may be on paper or other media); therefore, care must be exercised in determining the correct title for each record series and which files are to be included in each series.

When working with electronic media, such as computer tapes, one must identify the **data sets** or groups of data or information. It is important to determine the data set type. Is the data set a master file, a backup, or a print format tape? One must also identify the hierarchy of data sets. There may be redundant information as daily, weekly, quarterly, and annual data sets are maintained for sales data, for example. Each type of data set and each level within the hierarchy will have different retention requirements.

### Identify the Required Space

The inventory form shown in Figure 3–1 asks for the volume of the record series in the office and in storage. This information is critical for any facilities and equipment planning which may follow the completion of the records inventory.

Two methods are used to measure the volume of records: a linear measure of the record series or an estimate of volume in cubic feet. A tape measure suffices for providing a linear measure; however, estimates in cubic feet are more common. When estimating the cubic feet filled by a record series, allow 1.5 cubic feet for each letter-size drawer and 2 cubic feet for each legal-size drawer.

*Linear or volume estimates*

### Categorize Records

While estimating the space requirements of a record series, the **records analyst** (a specialist in systems and procedures used in creating, processing, and disposing of records) should identify records as active or inactive. Because of their decreased activity, those records identified as inactive should be moved from the office location to a storage area. Some of the records in storage may no longer be needed. These items within the record series should be

*Active or inactive records*

noted by date, and a brief notation should be made in the "Description" section of the inventory form. The note acts as a reminder to the records analyst for further action to be taken when the inventory is completed. The proper storage and disposal of records allows for more efficient utilization of locations and equipment.

*Vital records*

The records analyst should also be alert to the presence of any vital records within the record series. Vital records, those records essential to the uninterrupted operation of the organization or to the resumption of the organization's activities following a disaster, should be removed immediately from office files and stored with other vital records in a maximum protection area.

## Standardize Terminology

When the records inventory has been completed, the project director or the records analyst must review the inventory forms in order to standardize the terminology used from department to department. Careful orientation before beginning the inventory minimizes this problem; however, unless one person does all of the inventory, some similar record series may have very different titles. This review process also provides an opportunity to identify any record series which have been divided unnecessarily.

## Status Report

The records inventory is often the initial step in organizing a records management program. An inventory is critical in preparing a retention schedule and in planning facilities, equipment, and staff. Before proceeding to any other activities, however, the project director should prepare a status report to be presented to top management. A status report is an interim report prepared to note progress and findings to date. The project director must give careful attention to the data summary and to the preparation of this report.

*Interim report*

## Data Summary

Several options are available for the presentation of data summaries. Usually, the project director summarizes the records inventory findings by department or other subgroup within the organization. Within the department, types, dates, and volume of records should be reported. Quantities of records which can be moved to storage or eliminated and the amount of space which will be available for additional records as a result of these actions may be noted.

**Report Preparation**

Considerations for both oral and written presentations to top management were discussed in Chapter 2. In preparing the status report, the project director should consider presenting departmental data in tabular form and summarizing the data for comparison by departments. A summary allows the top managers to see quickly the results of the records inventory and helps to identify those departments in critical need of records management assistance.

The status report should also contain a proposed plan of action based on the results of the records inventory. Preparing a retention schedule and planning for better utilization of facilities and equipment are two actions which will probably be discussed. The plan of action should include a proposed time schedule, an identification of required personnel, and the steps to be followed in any proposed action.

If certain individuals or departments were especially helpful in completing the records inventory or certain staff members performed exceptionally well, the status report can provide a vehicle for commending these individuals or departments. The status report also provides an opportunity to note suggestions for updating the records status (active to inactive) as needed.

■

## A LOOK AT THE CASE

Gordon Marshall presented the status report of the records inventory at last week's meeting of all department heads. The report included a tabular summary of both active and inactive records for each department. The report also included some organizational totals, such as the total number of cubic feet of records inventoried and the total cubic feet of records which could be destroyed.

How will this information be used in developing a retention program for Spencer Construction Corp.?

■

## RECORDS APPRAISAL

A **records appraisal** is an examination of the data gathered through the records inventory to determine the value of each record series to the organization. The records appraisal process ensures that proper retention and disposal of records are provided. The result of this process should be a records retention schedule.

## Establish Series Value

*Value of record series*

Each of the organization's record series was identified and described as a part of the records inventory. The records manager must determine for each of these series whether its value to the organization is administrative (operational), fiscal, legal, and/or historical (research). These values are the basis for determining the retention period of each series.

### Administrative Value

*Defines operating procedures*

The **administrative value** of a record series is the value it has to the creating office in performing assigned operations within the organization. Records which are used in determining organizational policy or in explaining operating procedures or departmental functions have administrative value. Such records might include an organization chart, policy statements, and procedures manuals.

### Fiscal Value

*Documents use of funds*

A record series has **fiscal value** if it provides documentation of use of governmental funds necessary for audit or operational purposes, data necessary to compile the annual report or to complete the organization's tax return, or documentation of other financial transactions such as purchases and sales. Such records include financial reports and summaries of financial transactions.

### Legal Value

*Documents business transactions*

The **legal value** of a record series is established by the documentation it provides of business transactions. Records having legal value include contracts, financial agreements, titles, and records which provide proof of compliance with regulatory requirements (such as environmental or safety standards).

### Historical Value

*Documents organization's accomplishments*

A record series may also have historical value. **Historical value** is based on the quality or content which causes a record to be valuable today to complete the picture of an organization's accomplishments. Future value to researchers with an interest in that organization, similar organizations, and prominent individuals within that organization is also important. Letters signed by nationally known figures such as politicians or scientists frequently have historical value regardless of their content. Minutes of board meetings have historical value because they document changes in the direction of the organization or implementation of new procedures. Historical records are often housed in the organization's archives. If the organization does not maintain an official archive, historical records are housed in the most protected storage area.

## Establish Retention Periods

Once the records manager has determined the type or types of values for each record series, a retention period is recommended based on these values. This information is placed on the lower half of the records inventory and retention sheet.

### Determine Requirements

Recommended retention periods may be based on the records manager's experience with records of that type, knowledge of the manner in which other organizations are handling similar records, or information from sources such as published retention schedules. Additional requirements can impact on the determination of retention periods. These requirements are usually categorized as organizational, governmental, or archival.

Organizational requirements are of two types: requirements of the originating office and requirements of the administrative policies of the organization. The manager of the originating office indicates the requirements of that office on the line under "Originating Office" on the form in Figure 3–1. An officer of the organization indicates the retention requirements of organizational policies on the line under "Executive" on this form.

*Requirements of originating office and administrative policy*

As a part of the determination of originating office requirements, those records considered vital to the uninterrupted, efficient operation of each department are designated by the department manager. This should be an objective determination. A balance between retaining everything and retaining nothing is desirable. Estimates of the percentage of records that should be considered vital range from four to ten percent. When significantly more than ten percent of the records have been classified as vital, a reevaluation of the records or the process is in order.

*Vital records*

One of the major responsibilities of the records manager is to review the recommendations of the department managers regarding which records are vital and, therefore, must receive maximum protection. When the records manager reviews the departmental reports, there may be disagreement with the recommendations of a department manager. On these occasions, the department manager should be asked to meet with the records manager and to justify his or her position. If the disagreement is not resolved by either the records manager's acceptance of the recommendations of the department manager or by the manager's agreement with the position of the records manager, the records manager has the authority and the responsibility for the final decision. (Procedures for protecting vital records are discussed in Chapter 20, Records Safety and Security.)

*Fiscal requirements*

Prior to submission to the executive officer of the organization, the form should be submitted to the fiscal officer and to the organization's general counsel. The fiscal officer is responsible for noting retention requirements related to taxes or other financial reports. These notations are made on the line under "Fiscal Officer." (See Figure 3–1.) The general counsel is responsible for noting any requirements for retaining these records to support possible litigation and/or to meet statutory requirements at any level of government. Counsel notes these requirements on the line under "General Counsel" on the records inventory and retention sheet. (See Figure 3–1.)

*Legal requirements*

*Archival requirements*

Archival requirements (requirements for long-term retention) usually are identified by the records manager. If records have not been labeled for long-term retention, this requirement may be noted by one or all of the reviewers of the records manager's recommendations.

## Finalize Retention Periods

When the records manager receives the records inventory and retention sheets with all the required signatures (or secures the same information using other forms), a records retention schedule can be finalized. Retention periods include the length of time records are to remain in the originating office, the length of time they are to be housed in the records storage area, and the date the records are scheduled for destruction. To maintain efficient operations, every effort is made to retain records in the originating office as long as the records are active — referred to more than once per month per drawer. When records are no longer active, they should be transferred to the storage area. The records inventory and retention sheet shown in Figure 3–1 includes space to designate each of these dates — in office, in storage, and destruction.

Final retention periods may include the amount of time the record will remain on its original media, the media to which it should be transferred for further retention, and the time on the new media. For example, most magnetic tapes must be recopied every two or three years even with proper maintenance in order to maintain readability. If lengthy retention of information on magnetic tape is necessary, a special note such as "Dump to computer output microfiche and retain ten years" may appear on the retention schedule.

## A LOOK AT THE CASE

Gordon Marshall has used the data from the records inventory to appraise Spencer's records and establish series values and retention periods for each record series. These suggested retention periods were submitted for administrative, fiscal, and legal review and, with a few adjustments, have been finalized.

What additional steps must be completed in the implementation of a records retention program?

## PROGRAM IMPLEMENTATION

After records retention periods have been determined, several steps must be completed to implement the retention program. These steps include schedule preparation, schedule dissemination, schedule review and revision, and the development of a manual of retention policies.

### Schedule Preparation

The established retention periods must be summarized in a list or a retention schedule for distribution within the organization. Record series are usually listed in alphabetic order or alphabetic order by division or function on the retention schedule (also referred to as the retention timetable) along with the number of years the record series is to be retained. Some organizations also include an indication of the authority which established that particular retention period. Many formats can be used; however, the retention schedule must include at least the name of the record series and the retention period. One retention schedule is shown in Figure 3–2.

*Retention timetable*

Figure 3–2
Records Retention Schedule

```
                        LOCKHEED CORPORATION RETENTION SCHEDULE                           PAGE    1
                                    DATE: 10/09/86                                              CRC038
                                  DIVISION - CORLAC

DEPT 02-10 DIRECTOR-ACCOUNTING                SCHED COR04              REVISION 11 EFF DATE 07/15/86
```

| ITEM | DESCRIPTION | FORM/REPORT | OFF | INT | CRC | DES | REMARKS | REC COPY | VR CODE |
|------|-------------|-------------|-----|-----|-----|-----|---------|----------|---------|
| 001 | ACCOUNTING-MANUALS | | CUR. | | | SUPR. | VR 916A | | 916A |
| 002 | CORLAC CHARTS/TEXT OF ACCT - HIST | | 6 | | | 5 | | | |
| 002A | CORRES.-READING/CHRON FILE | | 1 | 2 | 12 | 15 | | | |
| 003 | CHECKS, DIVIDEND-CASHED | 54-062 | | | 10 | 10 | | | |
| 003A | CHECKS-CANCELLED-GEN ACCTS | | | 2 | 5 | 7 | *RECONCILED-CORP VAULT | | |
| 004 | XAR REPORT FILE | | A | | | AR | | | |
| 004A | XAR REPORT FILE-COMMISSIONS | | 1 | 1 | P | | | | |
| 005 | FINANCE POLICY MANUAL HISTORY | | A | | | AR | | | |
| 007A | FINANCIAL STATEMENTS-COMPANY MONTHLY | | 10 | | | 10* | *Y/E, OTHERS 2-5 YEARS | | |
| 007B | FINANCIAL STATEMENTS-CONSOLIDATED | | 10 | | | 10* | *Y/E, OTHERS 2-5 YEARS | | |
| 007C | FINANCIAL STATEMENTS-NOTES TO FIN. STATEMENTS | | 15 | | | 15 | | | |
| 007D | FINANCIAL STATEMENTS-VUGRAPHS | | A | | | AR | | | |
| 007E | FINANCIAL STATEMENTS-SLIDE FORMS | | 2 | | | 2 | | | |
| 007F | FINANCIAL STATEMENTS-W/P, SET 1 | | * | | 5 | 5 | *Y/E SENT ANNUALLY-OTHERS DESTROYED BY DEPARTMENT | | |
| 007G | AY&CO REPRESENTATION/RECOM LTRS | | 1 | 2 | 12 | 15 | | | |
| 007H | FINANCIAL STATEMENTS-W/P, SET 2 | | 2 | 2 | P | | | | |
| 008 | FINANCIAL STATISTICS OF AIRFRAME C | | 10 | | | 10 | | | |
| 009A | GOVERNMENT REPORTS | | A | | 15 | 15 | | | |
| 010 | HISTORICAL STATISTICS-WORKPAPERS | | *A | | 20 | 20 | *SELECTIVE BASIS TO CRC | | |

```
RETENTION  | A-ACTIVE              | CRR-CONTRACT RETENTION | D-DAYS      | NUMBERS-INDICATE YEARS | T-TERMINATED-----
SCHEDULE   | AR-ANNUAL REVIEW      |     REQUIREMENTS        | I-INACTIVE  | P-PERMANENT            | VR-VITAL RECORDS |
LEGEND     | C-COMPLETION OR CLOSE | CUR-CURRENT            | M-MONTHS    | SUPR-SUPERSEDED        | W-WEEKS          |
```
1) FINAL SETTLEMENT OF A TERMINATED CONTRACT: (2) FINAL PAYMENT OF A COMPLETED CONTRACT QUOTE - SUBCONTRACT RECORDS TO BE RETAINED
BASIS OF RELATED PRIME CONTRACT: (3) TERMINATION OF EMPLOYMENT.

*Source: Lockheed Corporation.*

## Schedule Dissemination

The records retention schedule cannot be used and the retention program cannot function if the organization's employees are not informed. The schedule should be disseminated to each office that deals with records as soon as it is printed. A department may receive the entire schedule or only those sections which apply to that department. Some organizations designate one employee within each office as the records liaison person. The designated individual receives the retention schedule and is responsible for compliance with the established retention periods. This includes responsibility for transferring records when appropriate.

## Schedule Review and Revision

An organization is unlikely to repeat the entire inventory and schedule development process more than once every 20–30 years;

but it is likely that adjustments to the schedule will be required during that time. An effective retention program must provide for review and revision of the retention schedule at planned intervals. Some record series may be subject to immediate revision of their retention periods. Due to changes in governmental regulations, some record series may be destroyed earlier or held longer. Other records need periodic review in order to discover the need for new forms, to accommodate record series which have been added or deleted, or to adjust the retention time for records already in storage. The latter need would be evidenced by the rate of reference as documented by charge-out records. If records are seldom referred to after storage, the organization may be able to destroy them at an earlier time. If the reference rates are heavy until scheduled destruction, the retention periods may need to be extended.

*Periodic review and revision*

## Manual Development

Many organizations develop a records retention manual to disseminate policies and procedures on records retention, transfer, and disposal. Other organizations prefer to have one records policies manual which includes policies and procedures for all aspects of the records program. Regardless of the type of manual used, the policies and procedures of the retention program should be prepared for dissemination and distributed along with the retention schedule. These policies and procedures should also include information on how the schedule was developed, provisions for revision, procedures for transferring records, and procedures for destruction of records. Specific details of manual development are presented in Chapter 8.

## A LOOK AT THE CASE

Retention schedules have been distributed to all offices of Spencer Construction Corp. Along with the schedules, retention policy directives have been distributed which will later be incorporated into a comprehensive records policy manual. At this point, no actions have been taken regarding the physical location of records as a result of the records inventory and the development of a retention schedule.

What procedures should be followed in transferring inactive records to the records storage area?

# RECORDS TRANSFER

*Steps in transfer process*

Records transfer is the physical movement of records from expensive office space to a records center or other designated storage area. The steps in the transfer process are (1) determining when records are to be transferred, (2) determining what records are to be transferred, (3) preparing records for transfer, (4) arranging the transfer, and (5) receiving records in the storage area.

## Determine Transfer Period

*When to transfer*

Transfer periods are usually determined by organizational policy rather than by individual departments or offices. Usually some records are identified as inactive and transferred as a result of the records inventory. After that time, records are transferred on a periodic or perpetual basis. **Periodic transfer** means that records are transferred at regularly scheduled intervals. Many organizations do this at the end of their fiscal year. RCA Corp. has an established policy of designating one week each year as Records Review Week. During this week each office of each division reviews its records, destroys records no longer needed, transfers all inactive records to their records centers, and ensures that all records which were scheduled for destruction at the end of the previous calendar year have been destroyed. This activity is widely publicized and receives support from top executives. (A sample of RCA's publicity materials appears in Figure 3–3.) Each office is required to complete a report indicating the volume of active records reviewed, transferred, and destroyed, as well as the number of drawers or shelves emptied and placed in storage.

**Perpetual transfer** allows the division or office to place records in storage whenever the records become inactive. This method may suffer due to the forgetfulness of the records liaison in that office, neglect, or lack of time.

## Determine Records to Be Transferred

*What to transfer*

Many records will have been identified as inactive during the records inventory and should be transferred as rapidly as possible to the records center or other storage area. After this initial transfer, records to be transferred must be identified from the retention schedule. Regardless of the transfer period, all records eligible for transfer must be transferred. Careful identification of all records scheduled for transfer enhances the effectiveness of the retention program.

Figure 3–3
Records Review Week Publicity Material

**File Review Check List**

● All files have been reviewed and unnecessary papers destroyed.

● Records which must be retained in
active files have been moved to the
rear of the file drawer or to the lower
drawers.

● All records for which the retention
period expired on December 31, 1979,
have been destroyed.

● Inactive records requiring further
retention have been transferred to
the inactive storage area in accordance with the Records Retention
Schedule for the department.

● New folders with labels have been
set up for 1980.

● Questions?  Call The Records
Coordinator.

**Don't destroy records before verifying
against your Records Retention
Schedule.**

6703

**GO FOR THE RECORDS!**

**Records Review Week**

**February 18th–22nd**

Instructions for this event are on the reverse side.

*Source: RCA Corp.*

## Prepare Records for Transfer

There are two steps in preparing records for transfer to the storage area. These steps are completing the necessary forms and
packaging the records for storage.

*How to prepare
for transfer*

### Forms

The originating office should prepare a records transmittal form
to send with the records being transferred to the storage area. In
addition to the records transmittal form, some organizations require detailed labels to be prepared for each transfer carton. Other
organizations simply require boxes to be numbered and their contents to be described on the records transmittal form. A records
transmittal form is shown in Figure 3–4.

### Packaging

Records being packaged for storage should be placed in corrugated fiberboard cartons. The most frequently used size is 15 by 12

Figure 3–4
Records Transmittal Form

PREPARE WITH TYPEWRITER.  FOR ASSISTANCE CONTACT RECORDS MANAGEMENT X-5478

## RECORDS TRANSMITTAL

ASSIGNED BY RECORDS MANAGEMENT
BOX/CONTROL NO. _____

| COMPLETED BY TRANSMITTER | TEMPORARY BOX NUMBER _____ | PAGE _____ OF _____ |
|---|---|---|

DIVISION

DEPARTMENT

GROUP

SECTION

UNIT

SUBUNIT

| SUBJECT | SUPERVISOR'S NAME | SUPERVISOR'S SIGNATURE | DATE |
|---|---|---|---|

| ITEM NO. | DESCRIPTION (EACH ITEM MUST BE LISTED) | DATE | | SEQUENCE | |
|---|---|---|---|---|---|
| | | FROM | TO | FROM | TO |
| | | | | | |
| | | | | | |
| | | | | | |
| | | | | | |
| | | | | | |
| | | | | | |
| | | | | | |
| | | | | | |
| | | | | | |
| | | | | | |
| | | | | | |
| | | | | | |
| | | | | | |
| | | | | | |
| | | | | | |
| | | | | | |
| | | | | | |
| | | | | | |

COMPLETED BY RECORDS MANAGEMENT

| RECEIVED BY | DATE | MEDIUM |
|---|---|---|

| CODE: | DIV | DEPT | GROUP | SECTION | UNIT | SUB | RETENTION PERIOD | DESTRUCTION DATE |
|---|---|---|---|---|---|---|---|---|

DISTRIBUTION:
WHITE – Organization File
GREEN – Control No. File

CANARY – Retention File
PINK – In Box
GOLD – Transmitter (after Control No. Assigned)

C-890 (11/81)

*Source: The Coastal Corporation, Houston, Texas.*

by 10 inches as this size is adaptable to both legal- and letter-size records and fits all standard shelving equipment. The placement of records within these cartons is illustrated in Figure 3–5. A 19-by-$13\frac{1}{4}$-by-10-inch carton is also available for folders with side tabs for open-shelf files. These cartons require special shelving equipment. The storage carton for hanging folders, which is 15 by 12 by 11 inches, also requires special shelving.

Figure 3–5
Standard Records Center Cartons

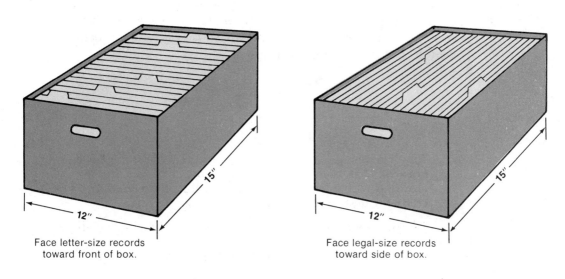

Face letter-size records
toward front of box.

Face legal-size records
toward side of box.

Special attention must be given to identifying and handling confidential records. These records must be protected from unauthorized access while in the storage area and properly disposed of when no longer needed.

## Arrange Transfer

The records storage area may be located offsite, sometimes several miles from the originating office. Advance planning is necessary to ensure that personnel and equipment are available for physically moving the records from one area to another. In addition, the records center personnel must be notified of the planned shipment so that they can coordinate their schedules and be prepared to receive the records upon arrival.

*How to transfer*

## Receive Records

*How to receive records*

Receiving records is the responsibility of personnel in the records storage area. The number and contents of the cartons received must be checked against the records transfer list and any discrepancies noted. Discrepancies must be checked with the originating office immediately. Records may have been left in the office or misplaced between the office and the storage area. Any misplaced records must be located immediately.

Once records have been "checked in," they must be stored in the proper areas of the storage facility and the locations must be noted on the records transmittal form (see Figure 3–4) or in a **locator file** (a special card file or automated index which lists records contents and their locations). This step is crucial to efficient retrieval of records while in storage.

## A LOOK AT THE CASE

The transfer of inactive records to the records storage area at Spencer's has been completed. One corner of this area is now crowded with records which are no longer needed and are ready for destruction.

1. How should Gordon Marshall select a method of records destruction?
2. What documentation should be kept of records destruction?

## RECORDS DESTRUCTION

*Destruction of records*

**Records destruction** is the disposal of records no longer needed by the organization. Disposal may be handled internally by the organization or contracted to a local organization providing this service. Most disposal methods are available either internally or externally; however, the cost of some methods may be prohibitive for in-house operation by all but the largest organizations.

### Methods of Destruction

Tossing papers into the wastebasket is probably the most convenient and least secure method of disposing of unneeded documents. In addition to "tossing," documents may be shredded, incinerated, chemically destroyed, or pulped.

## Shredding

Shredding is a frequently used method of destroying documents and microfilm and is considered to be a secure method of destroying confidential papers. Shredders are available in sizes from those that fit on top of a wastebasket at the side of one's desk to those that shred approximately two tons of paper per hour. These extremes are shown in Figure 3–6. Documents scheduled for destruction may be sold to a paper salvage company with or without having been shredded.

Figure 3–6
Paper Shredders

## Incineration

Incineration was once the most accepted method of document destruction; however, incineration is now considered to be a problem-encumbered method. Although incineration was generally thought to be a secure method of destroying confidential documents, complete documents have occasionally blown out of the incinerator. This creates the possibility of confidential information becoming known to the competition or to the press. In addition, some bits of paper which are not completely burned remain legible, the labor to maintain an incinerator is costly, and in most areas environmental restrictions now weigh heavily in determining whether an organization may use this technique. Incinerators located outside the city limits may meet environmental standards; incinerators that do not meet local environmental standards and are located within the city limits may subject user organizations to criticism by environmentalists, and fines may be imposed. If confidential documents are being destroyed and organizational policy requires that someone witness this destruction, this time-consuming process may be very costly. A service organization may contract to provide a certificate of destruction for a truckload of records; this eliminates the need for a company witness.

### Chemical Destruction

Chemical destruction or maceration is the use of chemicals to soften the paper and obliterate the writing. This method also includes pulverization of records, including microfilm. Pulverizers, like shredders, are available in many sizes depending on the volume of documents to be destroyed. Pulverizing is more efficient than shredding or incineration.

### Pulping

Pulping is an irreversible, safe, clean, convenient, and economical method of destroying confidential documents. Documents are mixed with water and forced through cutters and a screen. The size of the screen may vary according to the security requirements of the material to be pulped. The residue (slurry) which is created is pumped into a hydra-extractor which squeezes out the water. The water is recirculated and the pulp is dumped into trailers for removal from the premises. Pulping is being used increasingly by banks and other organizations which generate a large amount of paper with high security requirements. Depending on the size of the organization, pulping may be done internally or by a contractor.

## Method Selection

After examining the available destruction methods, the records manager should make a final decision, based on the answers to the following questions:

*Criteria for selecting destruction methods*

1. What is the volume of records to be destroyed?
2. Are these records of the same size and type of material? If not, which processes would destroy all types of records?

3. What percentage of the records are confidential?
4. What environmental standards affect the destruction of records in your community?
5. Are bonded contractors available in your area to provide the desired destruction method?
6. Can records be sold to a paper salvage company? Must they be shredded first?
7. What are the comparative costs of an in-house operation versus contracted destruction?

## Destruction Documentation

Many organizations, especially large corporations and governmental units, are required to provide certification of records which have been destroyed. Such certification forms include a description of the records destroyed and the date and method of destruction. Often, the records center supervisor sends a notice to the originating office of impending destruction of records. The originating office then has a final opportunity to retain the records if a need to do so (such as ongoing litigation) exists. The authorization to destroy and the certificate of destruction may be contained on the same form. (See Figure 3–7.)

Some organizations also maintain a records destruction register which lists all destroyed records by date of destruction. This register is a permanent record of when and how records were destroyed.

### A LOOK AT THE CASE

After careful study of the destruction options available to Spencer's, Gordon Marshall proposed that Spencer's contract to have its records pulped. He decided to initiate a records disposition register to document the destruction of records. All elements of Spencer's records retention program were finally in place.

Figure 3–7

Authorization for Destruction of Records

GENERAL INSTRUCTIONS

1. PREPARE AN AUTHORIZATION FOR DESTRUCTION OF RECORDS IN DUPLICATE FOR ALL RECORDS THAT YOU WANT LEGAL AND TAX CONCURRENCE.

2. FORWARD THE ORIGINAL AUTHORIZATION TO THE GENERAL MANAGER OF THE REGION OFFICE FOR APPROVAL. RETAIN THE COPY IN YOUR DEPARTMENT AS A CONTROL FORM UNTIL THE ORIGINAL HAS BEEN APPROVED BY MANAGEMENT.

3. THE GENERAL MANAGER SHOULD APPROVE THE ORIGINAL AUTHORIZATION AND FORWARD IT TO THE COMPANY'S RECORDS MANAGER. HE WILL ASSIGN AN AUTHORIZATION NUMBER, AND CIRCULATE THE FORM TO LEGAL AND TAX FOR THEIR APPROVAL.

4. THE COMPLETED ORIGINAL AUTHORIZATION WILL BE RETURNED TO THE REGION OFFICE. REGION OFFICES SHOULD DESTROY RECORDS BASED ON THE APPROVED AUTHORIZATION FOR DESTRUCTION FORM.

5. THE REGION OFFICE SHOULD RETAIN THE COMPLETED AUTHORIZATION FOR DESTRUCTION FORM.

77-30 (11-85)

AUTHORIZATION FOR DESTRUCTION OF RECORDS
(See Reverse Side For Instructions)

REGION OFFICE AND ADDRESS

DATE      PAGE      OF
AUTHORIZATION NUMBER:

DEPARTMENT      SECTION

RETENTION SCHEDULE NO.      PERSONNEL NAME

RETENTION SCHEDULE ITEM NO.      DESTRUCTION DATE:

TITLE OF RECORDS BY FILING ARRANGEMENT
(TITLE SAME AS USED IN RETENTION SCHEDULE)

DATE OF RECORDS
FROM      TO

OUTSIDE STORAGE LOCATION

NO OTHER RECORDS WERE DESTROYED.

APPROVALS:

REGION OFFICE _____ DATE ____

LEGAL _____ DATE ____

TAX _____ DATE ____

PLEASE EXECUTE - DO NOT INITIAL

DATE DESTROYED _____

HOW DESTROYED _____

DESTROYED BY _____ DATE ____

77-30 (11-85)

**Source:** *Cities Service Oil and Gas Corporation.*

# TERMINOLOGY REVIEW

*Administrative value.* The value of a record series to the creating office in the performance of its assigned operations within the organization.

*Data set.* Groups of data or information stored on magnetic tape.

*Fiscal value.* Value attributed to a record series which documents financial transactions.

*Historical value.* Value attributed to a record which completes the picture of an organization's accomplishments and will aid future researchers with an interest in the organization, industry, or prominent individuals within the organization.

*Legal value.* Value attributed to a record series which documents business ownership, agreements, and transactions.

*Locator file.* A special card file or automated index which lists records contents and their locations.

*Periodic transfer.* The transfer of inactive records to the records center or to another low-cost storage area at regularly scheduled intervals.

*Perpetual transfer.* The transfer of records to the records center or to another low-cost storage area as they become inactive.

*Record series.* A group of records filed together in a unified arrangement which results from, or relates to, the same function or activity.

*Records analyst.* A specialist in systems and procedures used in creating, processing, and disposing of records.

*Records appraisal.* An examination of the data gathered through the records inventory to determine the value of each record series to the organization.

*Records destruction.* The disposal of records no longer needed by the organization.

# COMPETENCY REVIEW

1. What is a records retention program? Explain the goals of a records retention program.
2. What is the function of a records inventory in a records management program?
3. List and explain the steps one should follow in planning a records inventory.
4. What are the choices to be considered in determining who should conduct the records inventory? What factors should be considered in making this determination?
5. What are the two methods of conducting a records inventory? What are the advantages and disadvantages of each?
6. What is a record series? Give at least two examples of record series other than those named in the text.
7. List and explain the procedures for conducting the records inventory.

8. Outline the steps to be followed in preparing a status report at the conclusion of the records inventory. What information should be included?

9. Define records appraisal.

10. Define the four types of values which a record series might have to an organization.

11. Differentiate between organizational, governmental, and archival requirements for records retention.

12. Once a records retention schedule has been developed, what additional steps are necessary to implement a records retention program?

13. What is the importance of timely records transfer to the effectiveness of a records retention program, and what steps must be completed in the transfer process?

14. Define four methods of records destruction.

15. List at least three criteria which affect an organization's selection of a destruction method.

## APPLICATIONS

1. Identify at least five record series within your personal or family records. For each record series establish a series value, suggest a retention period and give a reason for establishing same and identify the appropriate method of destruction.

2. You have just been hired as the records and information manager for the Lasting Shoe Manufacturing Corp., a three-year-old firm in the Northwest which has never had a records and/or information manager or a records or information management program. Outline your presentation to Charles Williams, Chairman of the Board, on the functions of a records inventory and a records retention program.

3. Barbara Guzman, president of Midlands Chemicals, has just given her final approval to your plan for conducting a records inventory. Midlands Chemicals has never had a records inventory. As the records manager, you have chosen two records analysts from your staff to conduct the physical inventory. Outline the important procedures you will present to them in their orientation session on records inventories.

## CONCLUDING CASES

### A. Efficient Power Service, Inc.

Molly Bray is the records manager for Efficient Power Service, Inc. (EPS), an electrical service company based outside San Diego, California. EPS has been in business for 45 years. While some revisions in its retention program have been necessitated by changes in governmental regulations over the years, Molly can find no documentation of when the last records inventory was completed or of any major reconsideration of the retention schedule.

Molly has been employed by EPS for six weeks. During this time she has been familiarizing herself with the records procedures employed by the major divisions of the organization. She decides that before any other aspects of the records management program can be centralized and refined, the retention program must be completely overhauled.

1. What basis can Molly use to convince top executives that such an investment of time and effort is necessary and will produce positive results for the company?
2. How can Molly obtain the support of the other employees for this undertaking?
3. What steps must be completed in planning and conducting the records inventory?
4. What are the major considerations in performing the records appraisal?
5. What additional steps are necessary to revise and implement the retention schedule?
6. What aspects of the records disposal program should be reevaluated?

## B. Brown Manufacturing

Brown Manufacturing is a rapidly expanding corporation with operations in two states. Robert Simms was recently promoted to records manager at Brown's. Robert graduated from the local university two years ago with a bachelor's degree in business administration. Robert has completed several courses in records management, worked summers as a records clerk and a microfilm technician, and has been the records center supervisor for the last two years.

Robert has convinced Brown's top management that a more comprehensive retention program is needed. Robert has obtained approval to conduct a complete physical inventory of Brown's records. Because Robert will serve as project director and has no previous experience in conducting a records inventory, Brown Manufacturing has hired Lucy Higgins, a records consultant, to assist Robert with planning this inventory.

1. How can Lucy help Robert plan the records inventory?
2. What steps must Robert be prepared to take to conduct a physical inventory of Brown's records?

## READINGS AND REFERENCES

Blount, Gail, and Peggy Reid. "Power Packed Records Retention." *Modern Office Technology*, Vol. 31, No. 2 (February, 1986), p. 62.
Brachter, Shayla. "A Basic Manual for Records Retention." *Information Management*, Vol. 19, No. 1 (January, 1985), p. 12.

Canning, Bonnie. "Developing a Retention Schedule." *Administrative Management,* Vol. XLVII, No. 1 (January, 1986), p. 76.

Coker, Kathy Roe. "Records Appraisal: Practice and Procedure." *Records Management Quarterly,* Vol. 19, No. 4 (October, 1985), p. 48.

Crary, Jean K. "The Teeth of the Program — the Records Audit." *Records Management Quarterly,* Vol. 19, No. 3 (July, 1985), p. 12.

Dickinson, A. Litchard. "Retention Schedules — Valuable to Business, But Why Are So Many Ineffective?" *Records Management Quarterly,* Vol. 18, No. 4 (October, 1984), p. 28.

Hancock, W. A., Ed. *Corporate Counsel's Guide #20: Records Retention — The Lawyer's Role.* Business Laws, Inc. (Chesterland, Ohio), 1985.

LaSala, James M., and Robert M. Davidson. "The Headaches of Records Retention and Litigation." *The Office,* Vol. 102, No. 3 (September, 1985), p. 71.

Morgan, Dennis F., and Dennis D. Millican. "A Record Manager's Blueprint for the Inventory and Retention Scheduling of Information in Electronic Form." *Records Management Quarterly,* Vol. 18, No. 3 (July, 1984), p. 43.

Morgan, Dennis F., and Dennis D. Millican. "The Electronic Media Retention Schedule Program: Selling It to Management." *Records Management Quarterly,* Vol. 18, No. 4 (October, 1984), p. 34.

Skupsky, Donald S. "Researching the Legal Requirements for Your Records." *Records Management Quarterly,* Vol. 18, No. 4 (October, 1984), p. 38.

# PROFILE

## Vinson & Elkins

Vinson & Elkins was founded in 1917 by William A. Vinson and James A. Elkins in Houston, Texas. It has grown to be one of the nation's largest law firms with specialized sections to meet the needs of a very broad base of clients, nationally and internationally. These sections include banking, business, corporate, energy, international, intellectual property, litigation, natural resources, public law, and tax, with subsections.

The firm now consists of more than 425 lawyers, 145 legal assistants, and approximately 500 administrative support staff with offices in Houston, Austin, and Dallas, Texas; Washington, D.C.; and London, England.

Vinson & Elkins' manual records management program, created in-house in 1960, served the firm very well until 1980. By that time, the firm had grown and paperwork had increased rapidly, and it was impossible to provide information and services on a timely basis. During the five years preceding this time, the firm's personnel had increased greatly, while the records management staff had remained at eight. Additionally, because of the number of clients and matters being handled by several hundred lawyers in several offices, the possibility of potential client conflicts became apparent. The manual system simply did not yield the type of information necessary to prevent these situations.

After several months of study, the decision was made to automate the existing system in-house, making improvements whenever possible. The database was created from more than four hundred thousand 5" x 3" index cards containing information about every file created at Vinson & Elkins since its inception in 1917. There was a need to capture as much information as possible. The mission was twofold: create an automated records management program from creation to disposition of all files and create a conflict of interest database.

The task involved creating one system that would work with the many different types of law that Vinson & Elkins practiced. Another challenge was that some projects required one file; others, hundreds of files.

The computerized system utilizes an IBM System/38 computer with eight online terminals and one personal computer in records management. The PC functions as a System/38 terminal and a standalone processor for word processing and other PC applications. Offices in Austin, Washington, and Dallas also access the system in Houston by PC, with the smaller London office transmitting information by hard copy, which is keyed into the system.

Before a lawyer accepts a new matter, a conflict of interest check must be made through records management. A computer generated report listing any potential conflicts is prepared and delivered to the requesting lawyer in less than thirty minutes. Once the conflicts are cleared, records management assigns a client/matter number for billing purposes and creates a new file by keying in data on a CRT. A file label is computer generated, a 5" x 3" index card is automatically created for each lawyer working on

the matter, the file is checked out to the requesting lawyer, and a label is attached to the folder, which is then sent to the lawyer. This procedure allows central control with each lawyer maintaining files in the file space directly outside of his or her office. The turnaround time for receiving a new file is less than a half day as compared to five days on the manual system.

When the lawyer has concluded the matter and sends the file to records management to be closed, the information, including retention date, location of the record, and where it will be stored in a commercial records center, is added to the computer data.

Automation has simplified the retrieval system. A request entered on the CRT generates a list at the records center with automatic transmittal lists for retrieval and refiling.

The disposition of files whose retention dates have matured can be handled in several ways. A list of such files can be printed for any lawyer, at any selected interval. The lawyer may choose to mark on the list which files may be destroyed; those that need a longer retention period; and those that can be destroyed, using the usual retention guideline procedures.

While the manual system only allowed data to be retrieved in one way—by client—the computerized system allows the data to be viewed in many different ways. For example, all matters a particular lawyer is handling, or all matters being handled for a particular client, or all litigation, tax matters, or probate matters, can now be retrieved either by printed report or online. Retrieval by computer is limited only by the data stored.

With the aid of the computer, the records management staff of eight, which supported 400 lawyers and legal assistants in 1980, now supports 570 lawyers and legal assistants and can also provide a number of other services, including forms management.

Possible improvements in the near future include microfilming files to decrease the large storage space needed, which, in most cities, continues to rise in cost. Another improvement could include optical disk storage. Either of these systems could prove to be cost-effective, and also would give almost instantaneous retrieval of information for the lawyers. With the present computerization, most of the work has been completed to implement a CAR system for either a micrographics or an optical disk storage system.

Where will Vinson & Elkins go in the future? Vinson & Elkins has information specialists throughout the firm looking at all cost-effective ways of improving the efficient services now provided. Mavis Eppes, a records manager who for a number of years depended upon an excellent manual system, says "To err is human — to be able to blame it on a computer is divine!"

*Contributed by Mavis Eppes*
*Vinson & Elkins, Houston, TX*

# 4
# PLANNING THE FACILITY

## Competencies

After completing this chapter, you should be able to

1. describe the major purposes of records centers.
2. differentiate between the need for records center and active records facilities.
3. discuss the advantages/disadvantages of commercial and company-owned records centers.
4. state factors to be considered when selecting the site for a records center.
5. illustrate and explain the row/space numbering system.
6. compare the physical layout required for a records center with that required of an active records facility.
7. explain the necessity for special purpose storage in a records facility and describe what these special purpose storage facilities might house.

# Introductory Case

The records of Technology, Ltd., founded three years ago, are all stored within the departments generating and receiving the records. All of the records — active, inactive, and archival — are housed together. Technology, Ltd., grew so quickly that other areas took priority, and little attention was given to the increasing number of records as long as space was available for another storage cabinet. However, the cabinets are crowded, and space is not available for expanding the storage area. Department heads are concerned and, as a group, have considered alternatives for solving the increasing problem of departmental storage for records.

1. Should Technology, Ltd., consider
   a. converting basement storage to a records storage area for inactive records?
   b. using offsite storage for inactive records?
   c. storing inactive records in a commercial records center?
2. How should the management of Technology, Ltd., proceed in their consideration of the most appropriate storage for their inactive records?

# RECORDS CENTER FACILITIES

*Active/inactive records*

Facilities must be planned to house two basic types of records—active and inactive. Some practitioners have advocated that, as a general rule,

- 10 percent of an organization's records could be retained for long-term value,
- 25 percent of an organization's records could be maintained in active files,
- 30 percent of an organization's records could be maintained in inactive files, and
- 35 percent of an organization's records may be useless and should be destroyed.

This categorization, then, classifies 40 percent of an organization's records as inactive (30 percent inactive and 10 percent long term—which are usually inactive), and only 25 percent are classified as active. (See Figure 4–1.)

## Purpose

**Records centers** fulfill two major purposes: to serve as low-cost storage centers for inactive records and to serve as reference service centers. When serving in the role of storage center for inactive records, records centers must provide storage that is safe in terms of physical records protection and safe in terms of content security.

Figure 4–1
Distribution of Records Status

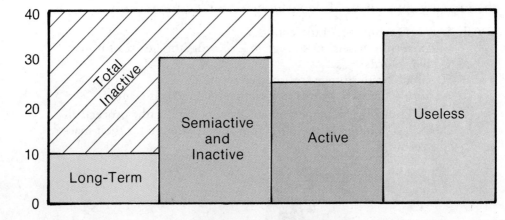

Safety and security are the responsibilities of the records manager and the records center staff.

The amount of savings realized by using records centers to house inactive records was demonstrated in Montgomery County, Ohio. The county's Records Center completed its third year of operations with almost 19,000 cubic feet (50 million documents) of records previously housed in expensive office space. The Center now has shelving and expansion space for about 20,000 cubic feet of records. The Center also houses the county's archival microfilm security vault with about 250,000 master microfiche and 4,500 master microfilm rolls. *Low-cost storage centers*

Any estimated benefits or cost savings must consider the expense of maintaining these records in office space. The costs associated with storing nearly 19,000 cubic feet of records now in the records center would be equivalent to over 1,800 file cabinets occupying over 15,000 square feet of prime space in newer buildings. The annual storage costs avoided by destruction of over 3,000 cubic feet of records is also significant. The storage costs alone for storing more than five million microfilmed documents would include another 300 file cabinets and over 2,000 square feet of prime space in newer offices. A conservative annual savings estimate of $500,000 after operating costs is generally accepted by Montgomery County officials.

Records centers also serve as reference service centers. Requests for semiactive, long-term, or historical records (or copies) are made to the records center staff who then provide the appropriate records or requested information. *Reference service centers*

Records centers should be designed to

- reduce the total volume of records held in office and storage areas,
- establish controls to ensure a continuous flow of records from offices to low-cost storage,
- free space and reduce the need for storage equipment,
- establish an efficient retrieval system,
- develop a cost-justified microfilm program (if appropriate), and
- maintain total security over company records.

## Type

Records centers may be company owned or commercial. Individual circumstances determine which type is the more desirable choice. Each organization must make that decision based on its own needs and available resources.

## Commercial

Commercial records centers may offer a variety of services, ranging from self-service to full-service facilities. A self-service facility, an outgrowth of household storage, is sometimes referred to as a **landlord/tenant agreement.** Under a landlord/tenant agreement, the landlord provides the space and the shelving to house records with charges based on the amount of space or number of cartons required by the tenant. The tenant has the responsibility for maintaining records inventories and for controlling retrievals. This type of offsite storage allows the depositor (tenant) to place any type of records in the space and to remove or add records as needed. The records center (landlord) is obligated to provide "reasonable" care in the maintenance of the storage areas.

Under a landlord/tenant arrangement, the landlord may provide additional services at additional costs. These additional services may include copying, packing records, transferring records, pick up and delivery, facsimile services, and mailing services. A landlord/tenant arrangement provides relatively inexpensive storage due to site location and fewer services offered.

Full-service offsite commercial records centers can generally provide the following services:

- Original records transfer to facility (including transfer boxes and transfer forms)
- Records inventory
- Records security
  fireproof vaults
  sprinkler systems
  burglar and fire alarms
  Halon gas protection
  authorized signature systems
  confidentiality
  back-up water and power systems
  blanket insurance policies covering liability and damage
  bonded employees
- Temperature and humidity controls
- Storage facilities for variety of media
- Pick up and delivery service, scheduled and random basis
- Computerized tracking systems from records receipt to destruction
- Retrieval of box, folder, or document
- Copying services
- Facsimile services
- Destruction services

- Computerized client activity reports providing information concerning costs, retrievals, additions, removals, charge-outs, returns, etc.
- Micrographic services
- Records reconstruction capability
- Consulting services
- Onsite reference and conference rooms
- Communication systems

Commercial offsite records centers may offer services that range from self-service to complete full service and all degrees of service in between.

When the organization does not have or does not wish to allocate the resources necessary to establish and maintain its own records center, the commercial center offers a viable alternative. The organization, when making the decision regarding the commercial records center most suitable for its particular needs, will want to evaluate the desired services in relationship to the cost of providing those services. Five methods are commonly used for computing the costs of using a commercial facility. All of the methods are based on cost per cubic foot of storage space used.

In the first method, the costs of retrieval are included in the storage fee. The retrieval costs are difficult to evaluate because retrieval rates are not necessarily related to required storage space.

*Methods for estimating commercial storage fees*

In the second method, an hourly fee for retrieval is added to the storage fee. This method, of course, relies on the commercial center to provide quick and efficient retrieval and to charge accordingly for that service.

In the third method, fixed fees are charged for various types of services. The pricing is usually based on what the commercial center considers to be "average time" to perform these services.

In the fourth method, a service contract is used. This method is appropriate when companies can accurately predict retrieval requirements. However, if retrievals cannot be accurately predicted or if requests are sporadic, this method may be expensive.

In the fifth method, a combination plan is used. This plan includes a minimum guarantee for a given number of retrievals plus a flat rate for each search above that number. Most commercial centers allow customers the option of changing payment methods after the center and the customer have an opportunity to evaluate the existing payment method. Certainly this item should be negotiated with the commercial records center at the time of the original investigation.

### Company Owned

*Nonprime space*

One of the first options many organizations consider when storing inactive records is nonprime space within their own location — areas such as basement or attic spaces. The use of these areas is dependent on proper heating, lighting, humidity controls, and floor load capacity, as well as the amount of usable space. Usable space depends on ceiling height, minimum obstructions, and odd-shaped spaces that may intrude on the available space. Conversion of these spaces, while an attractive prospect and a possible solution, may also be an expensive, short-term solution. Planning for a records center must include future needs as well as current space pressures.

*Commit resources*

In addition to conversion costs, the organization must be willing to commit resources to purchase appropriate storage tools, to create a system compatible with the existing active records system, and to hire the personnel necessary to operate and maintain the company-owned records center. Resources must also be allocated for the rental costs of the converted space and the energy costs associated with its operation.

Organizations may, of course, go offsite for their records center. A discussion of offsite storage is presented in the following section.

## Location

Although commercial records centers are offsite, company-owned centers may be either onsite or offsite. Often, the organization has little or no control over this decision. If only prime, high-cost space is available, the organization has little choice but to go offsite for records storage space.

### Onsite

*Advantages of onsite location*

If space capable of being converted to a records center on a cost-effective basis is available, the organization may choose an **onsite records center**. Onsite location offers many advantages to the organization. Some managers regard the information availability as a necessary tool for effective performance. Also, a delivery system to get the information from one location to another is not needed. Other managers regard total control over the organization's records/information as important. The application of organizational policies and procedures to records security provides a feeling of confidence to many managers.

## Offsite

Commercial **offsite records centers** offer low-cost storage at locations away from the organizational site. The locations of these records centers may be near or hundreds of miles away from the organizational site. In either case, these facilities provide security for the records.

Company-owned records centers may also be located offsite. Constructing a new facility, renovating an existing building, or locating rental space appropriate for records storage are possible alternatives.

Offsite locations offer two options: aboveground or underground sites. Aboveground facilities are generally less expensive than underground facilities; underground facilities offer greater security than aboveground facilities. Facilities located aboveground may be constructed in a variety of geographic locations while underground site availability is more limited. Underground vaults are located in salt mines, limestone mines, and under mountains and hills. Two centers, one located under the hills of Flora, Mississippi, and one located in a rock salt mine in Hutchinson, Kansas, offer a variety of services, as illustrated by the descriptive advertisements in Figure 4–2.

*Above/ underground sites*

Some experts estimate a cost of $200–300 annually to store a four-drawer file cabinet in buildings in prime locations not including expenses for clerical staff, equipment, and supplies. By comparison, offsite storage companies can store the contents of that same file cabinet for as little as $24 annually.

A cost comparison for a business in New York City that maintained an in-house hard-copy system is shown in Figure 4–3. In this particular case, a sizable savings (53 percent) was realized by selecting commercial offsite storage.

## Site Selection Criteria

A number of factors must be considered when selecting an appropriate site. Major factors to be evaluated include cost, access to records, transportation, and safety and security of records.

## Cost

The costs involved in setting up and maintaining the facility should be taken into consideration when selecting the site for the records center. The cost of using a commercial records center should be compared with that of operating a company-owned center, and the long-term costs of each should be evaluated. The location of the

*Costs of commercial versus company-owned centers*

Figure 4–2
Two Underground Storage Facilities

## SOUTHERN VITAL RECORD CENTER

The company's complex is designed for maximum security from natural and man-made disaster or intrusion. Sixty-one underground vaults are stationed across 600 acres of rolling hills in Flora, Mississippi. Constant security and surveillance is maintained by guards, guard dogs, closed circuit TV, electronic alarm devices, and a six-foot chain link fence. In event of emergency, the Center is served by its own water system and a complete auxiliary electrical generating system.

Each vault is air conditioned with temperature and humidity controls to provide archival conditions for paper records, microfilm, and magnetic tape. The center, reportedly, also maintains the largest and most technically complete underground processing and duplicating lab in the U.S.

In addition, SVRC offers complete information and records management services covering all aspects of analysis, design and implementation of active records, inactive records, vital records and micrographics systems.

## UNDERGROUND VAULTS & STORAGE

Located 650 feet underground in the rock salt mine at Hutchinson, Kansas, the natural temperature of 68° F. and relative humidity in the lower 50% range are ideal for preservation of vital records and information. All ANSI specifications for storage of information are met with optimum storage conditions for any media. More than 300 acres of space are available and facilities can be designed and developed to meet the specific requirements of any client. The location also provides accessible, economical storage for inactive records. UV&S is linked to its depositors in all 50 states and 32 foreign countries by several communications systems. All services connected with storage of records, such as filing, interfiling, referencing, record searches, duplication, destruction, etc., are performed by fully bonded, highly skilled personnel.

*Source: "Underground Vaults,"* Information and Records Management, *Vol. 15, No. 1 (January, 1981), p. 43.*

site will also affect the costs incurred for pickup and delivery service. If the site is in a high-risk area, major expenditures will be required for security and insurance. A lateral view of an underground storage facility is shown in Figure 4–4.

## Access to Records

Regardless of the type or location of the records center, access to the record is of primary interest to the users. An onsite records center obviously allows for ease of access. If the center is located offsite, access is a greater problem. For company-owned centers located offsite, the organization has the responsibility for making the records easily accessible. Commercial centers located nearby may furnish document delivery or allow organizational representatives to come to the records center to obtain necessary information/ records. Often, the customer may exercise both of these options.

*Obtaining information/ records*

Commercial records centers located outside the organization's area have the entire responsibility for document delivery. Records may be delivered via facsimile, special messenger, the U.S. Postal

Figure 4–3
Cost Comparison of Onsite/Offsite Hard-Copy Storage

---

### COST COMPARISON

---

XYZ Company — New York City

Volume of records — 24,000 cubic feet
Activity           — 20,000 retrieval & refiles
                     3,500 new cartons
                     3,500 destructions

| ONSITE | OFFSITE |
|---|---|
| 1. Storage: 7,500 square feet @ $18.75<br>$140,625.00 | 24,000 cubic feet @ $1.25<br>$30,000.00 |
| 2. Accounts Management: 1 supervisor,<br>4 clerks           81,250.00 | Includes pickup and delivery twice per week |
| 3. Courier: –0– | |
| $221,875.00 | 45,000.00<br>$75,000.00 |

*SAVINGS: $146,875.00

*First year savings before initial transfer costs. Estimated transfer costs $30,000.

NET SAVINGS: $116,875.00
53%

(In-house costs include equipment, shelving, and share of utility costs. Above sample estimated according to N.Y.C. rates.)

---

*Source: IMAR Records Center, Inc., Rosendale, NY.*

Figure 4–4
A Lateral View of An Underground Storage Facility

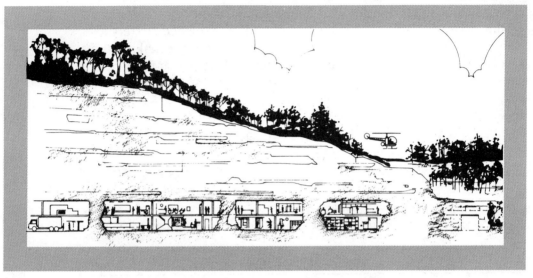

*Source:* *Corporate Headquarters, Iron Mountain Group, Rosendale, NY.*

Service, or other express mail services. The type of delivery depends largely upon the required turnaround time and the size and nature of the records. In general, the original record is retained in storage and a copy of the record is sent to the user. Because 75 percent of all information requests can be answered verbally, telephone service is essential for prompt access to data.

Although most offsite storage centers guarantee 24-hour retrieval and delivery, many managers still fear that they will not have information when they need it. Bekins Records Management Company has installed a new system that will give managers a greater level of control. Their new system, called "The Safekeeper," allows clients to use a personal computer that is connected by a modem to mainframes in Bekins 13 locations, so that the clients can immediately learn the status of their records, place orders for retrieval, delivery, or pickup. As much information as customers choose to provide regarding their files can be entered into the system and cross-referenced under several headings to ensure easy access.

**Transportation**

When evaluating sites for records centers, transportation of records and personnel must be considered. Even if the records center is a company-owned, onsite facility, procedures still have to be established for moving the records as they mature from active status to inactive status. (Transfer procedures were discussed in Chapter 3.) Offsite centers present their own unique challenges for transporting records and personnel. The company-owned, offsite location should have accessible roads that allow easy commuting to the center. Commercial centers should be located in areas that allow prompt delivery by the U.S. Postal Service, special messenger, or other express mail services.

*Transferring records*

### Safety/Security

Records safety and security are of primary concern to management. If records can be accessed by unauthorized persons, lost, destroyed, or stolen, the site under consideration should be immediately discarded as a possible location for a records center. The issue of danger to records in terms of physical records safety and content security is fully discussed in Chapter 20. Safety and security are major factors to be evaluated when selecting a records center site.

*Physical records safety/content security*

## Space Utilization

Once the determination has been made regarding the type of records center most appropriate for the company's needs, careful consideration is then given to maximizing the use of the available space.

### Requirements

The volume of records and kinds of records (paper, fiche, film, disks, maps, and so forth) are determined by the records inventory report. This report identifies all of the organizational records classified as inactive. The space required to house this volume of records is determined by the method in which the records are to be stored.

Most records centers store the records in cartons, and the cartons are placed on steel shelving. The shelving is usually 30 inches deep by 42 inches wide and is placed back to back. This duplexing arrangement allows cartons to be placed back to back on the shelving. If cartons with lids are used, a depth of 32 inches is required for back-to-back placement. Organizations may single or double stack the cartons on the shelves. A maximum of 50 feet of unbroken shelf length is recommended.

*Housing records in a center*

Cartons for microrecords may be single, double, or triple compartmented, depending on the micromedia. Single-compartment boxes 6 by 4 by 24 inches will accommodate 3,000 fiche or 1,500 jackets. A single-compartment box 8 by 4 by 24 inches will accommodate 48 rolls of 16mm film or 24 rolls of 35mm film. Some records centers use pallets stacked on steel frames for rarely referenced records, records with short retention periods, or odd-size material.

Mobile shelving may also be used in the records center. This type of shelving allows for a greater density of records to be stored in the same area. Mobile shelving does, however, limit access to the records when more than one person is shelving or retrieving records.

*Estimating space required*

The amount of space required for records can be determined by applying the general rule that three to four cubic feet of records will take one square foot of space. With multilevel storage, this ratio can be as high as nine cubic feet of records to one square foot of floor space. A documentation measurement guide is shown in Table 4–1.

Of course, ceiling height affects the amount of available storage space. Some organizations are realizing additional storage by using "tall" storage, which makes use of catwalks for access. (See Figure 4–5.) Heights up to 14 feet may be accessed with safety or pulpit ladders; heights over 14 feet require catwalks or a system that uses automated storage and retrieval. Catwalks may be double tiered (placed at levels between shelves eight and nine and shelves fifteen and sixteen).

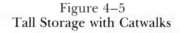

Figure 4–5
Tall Storage with Catwalks

Table 4–1
Documentation Measurement Guide

**CONVERSION TABLE**

| Equipment Type | Equivalents | Cubic Feet* |
|---|---|---|
| Filing Cabinets | One letter-size drawer | 1.50 |
| | One legal-size drawer | 2.00 |
| Filing Cases | One 3″ × 5″ case | .10 |
| | One 4″ × 6″ case | .20 |
| | One 5″ × 8″ case | .25 |
| Shelf Files | Letter-size, 1 linear foot | .80 |
| | Legal-size, 1 linear foot | 1.00 |
| Tabulating Cards | 10,000 cards | 1.00 |
| Magnetic Tape | Seven reels | 1.00 |
| Microfilm | 100 16mm reels (100 feet) | 1.00 |
| | 50 35mm reels (100 feet) | 1.00 |
| Still Pictures | 2,300 35mm, 6 exposure strips | 1.00 |
| | 8,640 2″ × 2″ mounted slides | 1.00 |
| | 2,184 4″ × 5″ film sheets | 1.00 |
| | 5,960 $2\frac{1}{4}$ × $3\frac{1}{4}$ film sheets | 1.00 |
| Machine listings | One linear foot | 1.20 |
| Still Pictures-Prints | 2,350 8″ × 10″ glossies or contact sheets | 1.00 |
| | 9,400 4″ × 5″ glossies | 1.00 |
| Motion Pictures | Six 35mm reels (1,000 feet) | 1.00 |
| | Eleven 16mm reels (1,200 feet) | 1.00 |
| | Fifteen 16mm reels (800 feet) | 1.00 |
| | Thirty-two 16mm reels (400 feet) | 1.00 |
| Sound Recordings | 76 16″ disc recordings | 1.00 |
| | 144 12″ disc recordings | 1.00 |
| | 48 7″ audiotape reels | 1.00 |
| | 32 10″ audiotape reels | 1.00 |
| Video Recordings | Ten $\frac{3}{4}$″ cassettes | 1.00 |
| | Three 2″ reels | 1.00 |
| | Nine 1″ reels | 1.00 |
| | 43 $\frac{1}{2}$″ reels | 1.00 |
| Transfer carton | One 15″ × 12″ × 10″ | 1.00 |
| Transfile (long letter) | One 24″ × 12″ × 10″ | 1.67 |
| Transfile (long legal) | One 24″ × 15″ × 10″ | 2.00 |

*May be rounded.

*Source:* Office Systems 85, *Vol. 2, No. 6 (June, 1985).*

When estimating square footage required to house the volume of records, consider the type of storage container, type of shelving, height of ceiling, and any obstruction that reduces available storage space.

Ceiling heights and stack heights have a major effect on the ratio of cubic feet of records to be housed to square feet of floor space required. As the ceiling/stack heights increase, the ratio of cubic feet of records to square feet of required floor space increases, and the space required to house the records decreases accordingly. This general guideline can be used to determine square foot requirements:

### RATIO OF CUBIC FEET OF RECORDS TO SQUARE FEET OF REQUIRED FLOOR SPACE*

| 8-Foot Stacks | 10-Foot Stacks | 12-Foot Stacks | 14-Foot Stacks | 22-Foot Stacks |
|---|---|---|---|---|
| 2.7 to 1 | 3.3 to 1 | 3.9 to 1 | 4.5 to 1 | 7.1 to 1 |

*excluding aisle space

Applying the formula to a given situation where the stacks are typical eight-foot stacks with 120,000 cartons to be stored (see Table 4–1—one standard carton requires one cubic foot of space) the space required would be 44,444 (120,000 ÷ 2.7) square feet. In this case, if the stacks were 14 feet high, the space requirement would be reduced to 26,666 (120,000 ÷ 4.5).

*Floor load capacity*

Another major consideration is the floor load capacity. **Floor load capacity** is the weight of records and equipment that a floor can safely accommodate. A filled records carton weighs 30–50 pounds. Care must be exercised in planning the records center so that the weight of the current equipment and records does not exceed the floor load capacity and that future additions can be accommodated.

### Physical Layout

The total system of records storage, retrieval, and disposition must be considered when the physical layout of the records center is being planned. The records center must accommodate not only the inactive records storage area but the administrative areas also. (See Figure 4–6.) Plans should include

- Records storage area
- Administrative areas
  Reference area

Office area
Receiving area
Preparation area
Distribution/disposition area

The records storage area should provide feeder aisles of 30 inches to 36 inches with primary aisles 5 feet 8 inches to 6 feet 8 inches depending on the individual needs of the center. Mobile storage equipment reduces the required aisle space. Humidity controls are critical in vault areas reserved for archival, vital, or security-type records. Fluorescent lighting is recommended for all work areas.

*Records storage area*

Figure 4–6
Records Center Layout

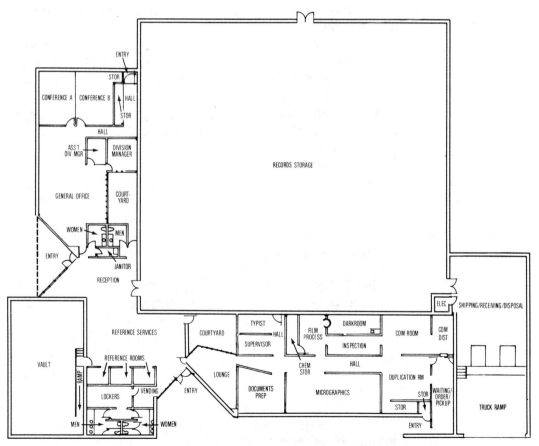

***Source:*** *George Cunningham, Records Management Supervisor, Department of Library Archives and Public Records, Records Management Center, State of Arizona, Phoenix.*

The administrative areas include reference, office, receiving, preparation, and disposition areas. All of these areas are labor intensive and should provide for the comfort of the employees.

*Reference area*

The reference area should be an efficient, comfortable place for users. Tables and chairs, a copier, a microfilm/microfiche reader and, where appropriate, reader printers are minimal requirements. Reference areas generally have limited space; therefore, efficient use must be made of the available area.

*Office area*

The office areas provide the records center supervisor and staff with work space. These office areas should be as suitably furnished as any other administrative area. While the amount of space per worker varies, each staff member (excluding the supervisor) should be provided with a minimum of 100 square feet. The office of the records center supervisor should be larger and provide an attractive, comfortable area in which to work and to confer privately with others.

Since one function of the records center is to serve as a reference area, indexes and controls necessary for prompt retrieval of records are required. The logical place to locate these retrieval tools is in the office area. Space, therefore, must be provided for housing indexes and retrieval equipment so that the records center staff has easy access to them. If noncenter personnel have free access to the indexes and retrieval equipment, a more appropriate location might be the reference area.

*Receiving area*

The receiving area provides a place for records as they come into the center. This area is usually adjacent to the loading dock to facilitate the process. Records (new files and refiles) cannot always be immediately shelved as they are received by the center personnel. In these areas, shelving use, if any, is usually minimal. Because records may be temporarily stored here, appropriate security precautions should be maintained. Forklifts and pallets are often used to deliver records to the receiving area. Doorways, therefore, must be wide enough to accommodate this equipment.

*Preparation area*

The preparation area is where the records center clerks prepare the incoming records for shelving and storage. The size of the preparation area is dependent upon the number and types of activities to be performed and the equipment necessary to accomplish the tasks. Equipment may run the gamut from manual sorters for refiles and interfiles to microfilming equipment for microfilm/microfiche production.

The disposition area should be separated from the receiving area in order to minimize the risk of mistaking accessions for records scheduled for disposition. All records identified for disposal in the records retention and disposition schedule are transferred to the disposition area. If the quantity of records scheduled for disposal is small, the organization may wish to allow the records to accumulate until more are ready for destruction. If the organization is having a commercial company destroy its records, accumulating records is the most economical approach. (Destruction techniques were discussed in Chapter 3.) Organizations with many records to be destroyed may have their own destruction equipment.

*Disposition area*

The disposition area, as well as the receiving area, should be located near (preferably adjacent to) the loading dock. Also, as required in the receiving area, doorways must be wide enough to accommodate forklifts and pallets necessary to move the records.

### Space Numbering Systems

A system is needed for finding the records once they have been shelved. In order to facilitate the location process, each carton is assigned an address (location) designation according to a **space numbering system**. Different organizations use different space numbering systems; however, one generally accepted method serves as a basis for many adaptations. This basic method is the row/space numbering method.

If the row/space numbering method is used, several steps are involved in assigning the numbers to the stack areas. First, each row is assigned a number. This number is posted at the front of each row. If rows are accessible from either front or rear, numbers are posted at each end of the row. The following illustration shows four single rows of shelving, each shelf housing cartons stacked back to back, or two deep.

*Row/space numbering method*

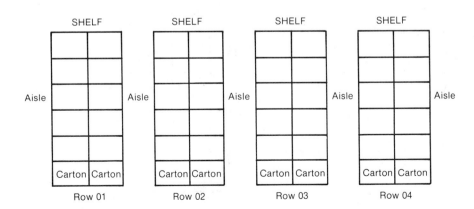

The row number provides the first part of the address. The second part of the address is the assigned space number. Each space accommodates one carton. Even numbers are usually assigned to the right side of the shelf; odd numbers are assigned to the left side. In the following illustration, each shelf in each row houses six boxes; only one shelf (the bottom shelf) in each row of shelves is shown.

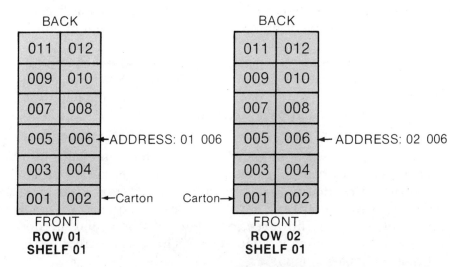

If each row has six shelves, the arrangement of Row 01 would appear as illustrated:

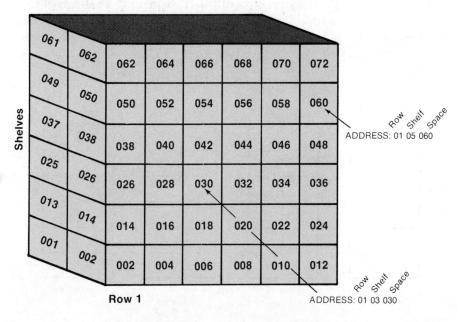

*Row/shelf/space numbering method*

Some records center personnel have found it easier to locate cartons of records if a shelf number is also assigned. In the previous illustration, the address for carton 030 in row 01 would be row number 01, shelf number 03, space number 030, or 01 03 030.

■

## A LOOK AT THE CASE

Technology, Ltd., must recognize the problems presented by the volume of records now housed in its offices. One of the first decisions Technology, Ltd., must make is whether to allocate the necessary resources (personnel, capital outlay, space) to establish and maintain its own records center. The alternative, of course, is for Technology, Ltd., to contract the services of a commercial records center. If the decision of the organization is to contract for this service, the next move is to select the records center that best suits Technology, Ltd.'s needs. Negotiations for the best possible contract should be made with the commercial records center.

If the company elects to operate its own records center, decisions must be made regarding location (onsite or offsite), staffing, equipment, and layout, and policies must be established for the operation of the records center.

1. Should Technology, Ltd., house its active records in a centralized, decentralized, or combination system?
2. How should the company plan the space for its active records?

■

## ACTIVE RECORDS FACILITIES

Twenty-five percent of an organization's records are considered active; these records are used in the daily operation of the organization. It is primarily these active records that provide managers with the necessary information on which to base current business decisions.

### Purpose

Because active records are such a vital part of the decision-making function, they must be available to managers at the time they are

*Rapid retrieval of information required*

needed. Fast turnaround from request to retrieval is essential. Retrieval is facilitated by having the active records housed in close proximity to the people requiring the information.

## Type

Active records may be housed in a centralized, decentralized, or a combination system. Each system has distinct advantages and disadvantages.

*Centralized.* A **centralized records storage system** provides for the housing of all active records in one location within the organization. All records that need to be retained are forwarded by each department to a central records area. Large organizations do not find a totally centralized system efficient because placing the central records in a location convenient for all departments is virtually impossible. For many smaller organizations, however, a centralized records system is appropriate.

*Provides uniform approach*

Centralization provides a uniform approach to the records system. All records are stored by the same rules and retrieved by the same procedures which is advantageous in terms of

- providing consistency in procedures,
- identifying responsibility and accountability,
- keeping related records together,
- training new clerical personnel,
- providing uniform service to all departments,
- minimizing duplicate records,
- providing better utilization of space, equipment, and personnel,
- allowing greater security of records, and
- providing one-stop retrieval of records.

*Decentralized.* A **decentralized records storage system** is one in which the records of each major department or office are housed

**WIZARD OF ID**                    **BY BRANT PARKER & JOHNNY HART**

within that area. Many managers prefer this system because it allows them to retain control over and have immediate access to their own records. Accessible records and total control must be balanced against the problems incurred by allowing each department to operate autonomous records systems. Problems associated with decentralized systems include the following:

*Immediate access/ departmental control*

1. Each department has its own records system; therefore, a lack of uniformity exists in the total records system.
2. Each department houses its own records; not all related records are housed together.
3. Several departments may retain copies of the same record; this practice encourages duplicate records.
4. Departments may duplicate equipment or maintain underutilized equipment; maximum equipment utilization will not be realized.
5. Each department tends to secure records in a different manner; therefore, records security may be haphazard and inadequate.

When information must be immediately available with multiple references to records made by only one department, and when individual departmental records control is necessary, a decentralized system is appropriate.

***Combination.*** The **combination records storage system** is a system that allows many departments to maintain their own records under a centralized system of control. Typical records maintained in a decentralized records system include personnel, payroll, credit, financial, and sales records. Under the combination approach, responsibility for the system is assigned to the records manager or to the person operationally responsible for maintaining the organization's records. This person establishes the network for the control system and for the operational procedures of the system.

*Decentralized file under centralized control*

The combination approach provides the individual control, the accessibility, and the immediacy of a decentralized system as demanded by many managers. It also provides the controls and uniformity of a centralized system. Advantages of centralized control include providing a uniform system of storage and retrieval, minimizing misfiles and lost records, minimizing duplicate records, providing for centralized purchasing which results in better cost efficiency, facilitating records movement according to the records retention and disposition schedules, and having the feeling of management confidence that often accompanies structure.

However, many of the problems inherent in each of the systems are transferred to the combination system. The problems of not having related records housed together and lack of flexibility resulting from uniform, organization-wide procedures still occur. The combination system is used by organizations or companies which own and operate other companies.

The records storage system selected—centralized, decentralized, or combination—should be the system that most closely fits the needs of the particular organization, its subunits, and its personnel.

## Space Planning

Since active records are located in prime office space, the area should be planned for maximum efficiency at least cost. A discussion of the advantages and disadvantages of various types of equipment is presented in Chapter 6. In many instances, the available space dictates the type of equipment and the layout.

*Floor load capacity*

One factor to be considered is the weight of the storage equipment and load stress on floors. This is particularly true in older buildings, although newer construction should also be checked to establish weight capacity. If this is a concern, the use of alternative equipment may produce the storage capacity required at less total weight. Equipment weight is nonproductive; the weight of the contents is productive. Floor load capacity may be expressed by the weight the floor can stand (measured in pounds per square foot) multiplied by the amount of available space (measured in square feet). For example, if a floor is able to stand 50 pounds per square foot and the room contains 300 square feet of floor space, a total weight of 15,000 pounds (50 multiplied by 300) may be safely stored in that room.

Differences exist between the weight of the equipment and the storage capacity per pound of equipment weight. Table 4–2 illustrates this concept.

Let's examine how to use this information to determine the most efficient use of space. Given a room 30 by 18 feet (540 square feet), a requirement of 10,000 linear inches of storage capacity, and a floor load factor of 50 pounds per square foot, the total floor load weight available would be 27,000 pounds (50 × 540 = 27,000).

Productive weight is determined by

$$\frac{\text{Record weight (capacity} \times \text{record weight per filing inch)}}{\text{Hardware weight + record weight}} = \text{Productive weight.}$$

Table 4–2
Comparison of Nonproductive Weight to Productive Weight*

| Type of Equipment | Hardware Weight (pounds) | Capacity (inches) | Weight Per Filing Inch (pounds)** | Productive Weight Per 1,000 Pounds Floor Load (percent) |
|---|---|---|---|---|
| Electro-file (fiche) | 1250 | 700 | 1.78 | 32.8 |
| Elevator file | 3000 | 933 | 3.2 | 38 |
| Four-drawer file | 160 | 100 | 1.6 | 55.6 |
| Roll-out shelves | 300 | 200 | 1.5 | 57 |
| Lateral open shelf | 185 | 204 | .9 | 69 |
| Eight-drawer fiche file (double compartment) | 195 | 424 | .46 | 65.5 |
| Lateral open shelf | 145 | 204 | .7 | 74 |

*Assuming the weight of the paper files is two pounds per filing inch; fiche files, 14 ounces per filing inch (14 ounces is for original film; duplicate film weighs only 9 ounces per filing inch).
**Weight per filing inch in pounds is determined by

$$\frac{\text{Hardware weight (pounds)}}{\text{Capacity (inches)}} = \text{Weight per filing inch}$$

*Source: Mountain Bell Telephone Co., Denver, CO.*

In Table 4–2, the weight of a four-drawer file is shown as 160 pounds; 100-inch capacity at two pounds per filing inch of records is 200 pounds which equals a total weight for records and hardware of 360 pounds. Dividing the total weight of 360 pounds into the record weight of 200 pounds, a productive weight percent of 55.6 is obtained. To determine the productive weight percent for fiche files, the same formula is used substituting fiche weight of 14 ounces per filing inch for the two-pound weight used for paper files.

A number of options are available for selecting the appropriate floor plan for the previous situation.

1. Capacity may be obtained by using 100 four-drawer cabinets (100-inch capacity per cabinet; 10,000 linear inches required).
2. Capacity may be obtained by using 50 roll-out shelf files (200-inch capacity per shelf; 10,000 linear inches required).

3. Capacity may be obtained by using 49 tightly packed lateral files (204-inch capacity per file; 10,000 linear inches required).

4. Capacity may be obtained by using 24 double-compartmented fiche files (424-inch capacity per file; 10,000 linear inches required).

Consider, however, the following information which relates to the requirements and the floor load capacity. (See Table 4–3.)

Table 4–3
File Capacity/Weight

| Type of Equipment | Number of Files | Weight of Files | Weight of Contents | Total Weight |
|---|---|---|---|---|
| Elevator file | 11 | 33,000 | 20,000 | 53,000 pounds |
| Four-drawer file | 100 | 16,000 | 20,000 | 36,000 pounds |
| Roll-out shelf files | 50 | 15,000 | 20,000 | 35,000 pounds |
| Lateral open shelf | 49 | 9,065 | 20,000 | 29,065 pounds |
| Fiche files | 24 | 4,680 | 8,750 | 13,430 pounds |

*Source: Mountain Bell Telephone Co., Denver, CO.*

The problem? In all instances except the fiche files, the choices exceed the 27,000 pound floor load capacity.

Whether four- or five-drawer cabinets, lateral cabinets, open-shelf files, or mobile files are selected will depend on the organizational needs, the selected storage system (decentralized, centralized, or combination), and the available storage space. Some typical cabinet arrangements in a decentralized system follow.

*Guidelines for efficient layout*

Some guidelines for more efficient layout include the following:

1. Avoid opening cabinets into a traffic aisle. If this arrangement is unavoidable, allow four feet for drawer opening and 18–24 inches for aisle traffic (assuming a one-person traffic pattern).

2. Allow four feet for each drawer opening and for one records clerk.

3. Allow four feet for each drawer opening and each records clerk where cabinets on each side of the aisle open facing each other.

Centralized records storage, depending on space available, may be arranged in various ways. Ample aisle space should be al-

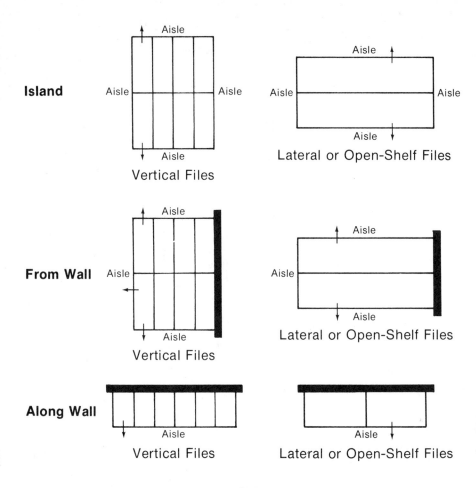

**Island**

Aisle

Vertical Files

Lateral or Open-Shelf Files

**From Wall**

Aisle

Vertical Files

Lateral or Open-Shelf Files

**Along Wall**

Vertical Files

Lateral or Open-Shelf Files

lowed — a minimum of 3 feet; 4 feet if cabinets open into aisle space; 5.5 feet if allowing for cabinet opening and passageway; 8 feet if cabinets open face-to-face; 9.5 feet if cabinets open face-to-face and passageway is required. (See Figure 4–7.)

Note that the wide aisle provides enough room for two workers in a single aisle. With the two-aisle system, four employees can comfortably work in the file system. This means increased speed and efficiency in filing.

Cross aisles should be provided every 25 feet if rows are long. Outlets for convenience, efficiency, and safety in case of an emergency are provided. Several arrangements for centralized records storage are possible. The important point to remember is that these records must be efficiently arranged to save space (because of their high-cost location) and to save time (because of their labor-intensive function).

The following illustrations show three of the many possible central storage arrangements.

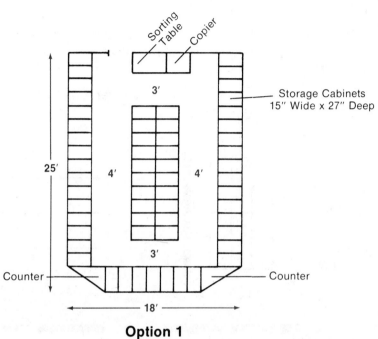

**Option 1**
Vertical Storage

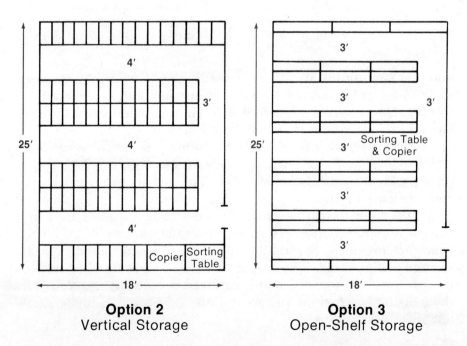

**Option 2**
Vertical Storage

**Option 3**
Open-Shelf Storage

Figure 4–7
Centralized Records Storage

## A LOOK AT THE CASE

Technology, Ltd., having made a decision regarding the inactive records, now turns its attention to the analysis of the active records. The managers begin to consider the advantages and disadvantages of a centralized approach, with all records being housed in a central location; a decentralized approach, with each department maintaining its own records; or a combination approach, with major departments maintaining their own records under a central control system.

Once that basic decision has been made, space layout planning begins. Because the active records are located in Technology, Ltd.'s high-cost office space, efficient space utilization and efficient work flow will be of primary concern.

1. What other types of records should Technology, Ltd., plan for in its facilities program?
2. How should other types of records be housed?

# MEDIA RECORDS STORAGE

## Purpose

*Unique housing requirements*

Many records are not in $8\frac{1}{2}$-by-11-inch paper form and cannot be accommodated in traditional records housing. As organizations review their records and storage needs, many make the transition from paper records to other forms. This transition requires a different type of storage for both records centers and active records facilities.

## Types

The many forms of paper and other media records should be included as plans are made for storage facilities. Some of these include audiovisual materials, cartographic materials, computer output, publications, microforms, and engineering drawings.

### Audiovisual Materials

Plans must be made to accommodate storage of cassette tapes, transparencies, slides, video cassette tapes, phonographic records, and video disks. Cabinets are available to handle the special needs of these audiovisual materials.

### Cartographic Materials

Maps may be housed in roll cabinets, drawer cabinets, or in hanging file cabinets. Hanging cabinets are recommended for active records; this provides for rapid retrieval of material and efficient use of space. Maps classified as inactive may be stored in roll cabinets or in flat drawer cabinets. In records centers, maps may be stored in specially designed containers.

### Computer Output

Computer output may take the form of printouts, magnetic tapes, or microforms. Each of these forms requires storage quite different from standard paper records. Computer printouts may be of varying sizes and may be unable to stand upright for shelf storage. Placing the printouts in hanging folders saves space and facilitates retrieval. Printouts may be placed in hanging folders or they may be hung by the clips that are part of the binding. Either method suspends the carriers on horizontal rods. Folders designed to house computer printouts upright on shelves are another storage option.

Magnetic tapes are placed in dustproof containers and stored upright in racks or suspended on horizontal rods. When planning for storage, one must remember that magnetic media is very sensitive material and must be protected by climate controls. Because electrical and magnetic sources may cause tape erasure, the location of the storage racks is important.

## Publications

Magazines and periodicals present some of the same storage problems as computer printouts; these publications are of varying sizes and lack the support needed to stand alone on shelves. Current issues may be stored in shelf cartons or displayed on specially designed shelves. As the periodicals accumulate, they should be bound and stored in the same manner as books.

## Microforms

Microfiche, roll or cartridge microfilm, microfilm jackets, and aperture cards require special types of storage cabinets. These cabinets are fully discussed in Chapter 6. As plans are made for either records center or active records storage, the special requirements for microforms must be considered.

## Engineering Drawings

Engineering drawings, like cartographic materials, may be stored in roll cabinets, in flat drawer cabinets, or in hanging files. The selection criteria used for engineering drawings is the same as the selection criteria used for maps.

## Mixed Media

Storing mixed media within the same work area is often desirable. Center hook filing allows printouts, microfiche, diskettes, magnetic tape, letter- and legal-size papers, manuals, and audiovisual media to be hung on hanger bars, similar to hangers in a closet. The media are housed in binders, folders, and containers that provide space for labeling. Center hook filing allows related information to be stored together regardless of media used. End hooks also permit conventional drop filing.

Center hooks can be installed in shelved units or on walls over workstations for easy access and to take advantage of vertical space.

■

## A LOOK AT THE CASE

Technology, Ltd.'s records, while primarily traditional paper records, include engineering drawings, computer output, and microforms. In the plans for its records center and the plans for its active records storage, Technology, Ltd., must consider these special needs as well as the storage needs for its paper records.

■

## TERMINOLOGY REVIEW

■ ***Centralized records storage system.*** A system for providing housing for all active records in one location within the organization.

***Combination records storage system.*** A system for housing active records in individual departments under centralized control.

***Decentralized records storage system.*** A system for housing records in individual departments or offices that create or receive the records.

***Floor load capacity.*** The weight of records and equipment that a floor can safely accommodate.

***Landlord/tenant agreement.*** A self-service type of commercial records center operating under a landlord/tenant agreement.

***Offsite records center.*** A storage facility located away from the organization site.

***Onsite records center.*** A storage facility located on the same site as the organization.

***Records centers.*** Storage facilities to house inactive records and to serve as reference service centers.

***Space numbering system.*** A method of designating the storage location of records.

## COMPETENCY REVIEW

■ 1.  What are the major purposes of the records center?
2.  How do needs for a records center differ from needs for active records facilities?
3.  Discuss considerations in making the decision either to employ the services of a commercial records center or to establish a company-owned records center.
4.  What factors must be considered when selecting a site for a records center?

5. Draw and explain an illustration of the row/space numbering system.

6. Compare the physical layout required for a records center with that required for an active records facility.

7. Describe special storage needs for four media forms, excluding $8\frac{1}{2}$-by-11-inch paper records.

## APPLICATIONS

1. Identify the problems in space requirements and layout in the stacks area of the records center sketch shown below:

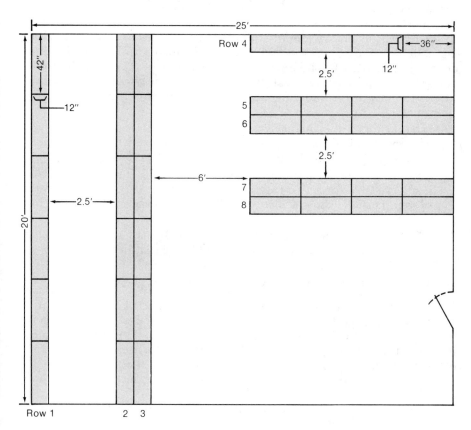

2. Rearrange the layout in Application 1 to eliminate the problems identified. Describe how the new arrangement accomplishes this goal.

3. From the information given about Southern Vital Record Center and Underground Vaults and Storage (page 90), evaluate how well each company meets the site selection criteria shown on pages 89–93.

4. Are Southern Vital Record Center and Underground Vaults and Storage full-service records centers as described on pages 86–87? Explain.

CONCLUDING CASES

## A. Jolly Jelly Beans Candy Company

Jolly Jelly Beans Candy Company is an established candy manufacturer celebrating its 75th anniversary. The company experienced steady growth until 1981 when President Ronald Reagan made jelly beans a popular candy; this factor caused a growth spurt in the industry. The building currently housing Jolly Jelly Beans Candy Company was constructed in 1946, with additions in 1964 and 1981.

The current active records system is decentralized. Each department maintains its own records and uses its own system. Compiling related records has become more difficult, and the number of "lost" records has increased to the point that management decision making is impaired.

A records inventory identified 9,000 linear inches of records now being housed in four-drawer vertical cabinets 15 inches wide and 27 inches deep. The company has investigated the possibility of making a change to open shelves and has indicated its willingness to authorize that expenditure if the task force studying the system documents the need for this change.

1.  What factors will influence your recommendation regarding the type of active records system (centralized, decentralized, or combination) most appropriate for Jolly Jelly Beans Candy Company?

2.  Assuming there is a room measuring 27 by 15 feet that could be made available for active records storage, design a layout for a central storage facility. Also calculate the floor load capacity. The room has been rated at 65 pounds per square foot of space.

3.  State your recommendation for Jolly Jelly Beans Candy Company's active records system, giving the rationale for that decision.

## B. Stereo Factory to You Wholesalers, Inc.

Stereo Factory to You Wholesalers, Inc., has allocated a recently vacated 40-by-50 foot space for use as a records center. Inactive records are now housed in various locations throughout the building. The space allocated for the records center is adjacent to the company offices in the 60-year-old Smythe Building. The engineers have calculated the floor load capacity as 70 pounds per square foot. The ceiling height in the building will allow 14-foot stacks.

The organization currently has the following records that have been recently classified as inactive:

50 4-drawer letter filing cabinets
245 transfer cartons (15″ × 12″ × 10″); letter size
500 linear feet of open-shelf files, letter size
75 100′ 35mm roll microfilm

Given this information, calculate

1.  ratio of cubic feet of records to square feet of space required

2.  cubic feet required for records
3.  floor load capacity

Prepare this information for Jose Martinez, president of Stereo Factory to You Wholesalers, Inc. Include any recommendations you might have regarding how these records should be stored (filing cabinets, boxes, open shelves, etc.).

## READINGS AND REFERENCES

"Advantages of an In-House Records Center." *Information and Records Management*, Vol. 15, No. 2 (February, 1981), p. 24.

Austin, Robert B., and Donald S. Skupsky. "How to Determine Cost Savings for a Records/Files Management Program." *Office Systems Management*, Vol. 7, No. 1 (Fall 1983), p. 4.

Bekins Records Management Company, Los Angeles, California, 1985.

Ciura, Jean. "Managing Inactive Corporate Records." *Information Management*, Vol. 19, No. 6 (June, 1985), p. 19.

"Coping with the Hard-Copy Crunch." *Office Administration and Automation*, Vol. 45 (May, 1984), p. 78.

Diamond, Susan Z. "Save Time and Space with Central Filing." *Office Systems '85*, Vol. 2, No. 2 (February, 1985), p. 62.

Eggert, Al E. "File Management and Micrographics: A Winning Combination." *IMC Journal*, Vol. 19, No. 1 (First Quarter, 1983), p. 37.

"Filing: Cheaper by the Billion." *Modern Office Technology*, Vol. 30 (February, 1985), p. 70.

Haller, Stephen E. "Montgomery County: Our Program Is Successful Because It Works." *Information Management*, Vol. 19, No. 2 (February, 1985), p. 17.

Leaper, Rae. "What's in the Box?" *Records Management Quarterly*, Vol. 18, No. 2 (April, 1984), p. 34.

Mongiovi, Daniel. "Off-Site Records Storage Service." Presentation, Association of Records Managers and Administrators Conference, New York. (September, 1985).

*Mountain Bell Records Management Manual.* Denver, Colorado (Revised February, 1977).

Murphy, Terence. "Taking Control of Your Office Records." Presentation, Association of Records Managers and Administrators Conference, New York. (September, 1985).

National Records Management Council Survey, as cited by Lora L. Smart. "Getting It Together." *Records Management Quarterly*, (October, 1978).

"No Visible Means of Support." *Modern Office Technology*, Vol. 29 (November, 1984), p. 72.

Payne, Marjorie Thomas. "Off-Premises Records Storage: Choosing the Right Approach." *Information and Records Management*, Vol. 13, No. 3 (March, 1979).

"The Role of the Commercial Records Center." *Information and Records Management,* Vol. 15, No. 3 (March, 1981), p. 50.

Russell, Margaret B. "From Catacombs to Records Center in Just Five Months." *Records Management Quarterly,* Vol. 18, No. 3 (July, 1984), p. 58.

Settani, Joseph Andrew. "The Personal Aspects of Records Management." *Office Systems '85,* Vol. 2, No. 6 (June, 1985), p. 84.

Stephens, David O. "How to Plan Your Files Strategy." *Office Systems Management,* Vol. 2, No. 2 (Winter 1982), p. 4.

"Underground Vaults." *Information and Records Management,* Vol. 15, No. 1 (January, 1981), p. 43.

# 5
# CLASSIFICATION SYSTEM SELECTION

## Competencies

After completing this chapter, you should be able to

1. define and identify applications for which an alphabetic classification system—by name, by subject, or by geographic location—is appropriate.
2. define and identify applications for which a numeric classification system—by serial, duplex, or decimal order—is appropriate.
3. explain the differences between middle and terminal digit arrangements.
4. define and identify applications for which an alphanumeric classification system—by subject-numeric order or by phonetic order—is appropriate.
5. define and identify applications for which a chronologic classification system is appropriate.
6. describe the advantages of a Uniform Classification System.
7. explain the importance of determining the basic file groups of an organization's records prior to selecting a classification system.
8. explain the importance of determining the file features and identifying user requirements of an organization's records prior to selecting a classification system.

# Introductory Case

Three months ago, Katherine Dickinson was employed as records manager of Fitness Development, Inc. (FDI). FDI sells and services physical development equipment to gymnasiums, fitness centers, and recreational facilities.

FDI's records are growing at a fast pace, having doubled in the past two years. Records are decentralized according to operating unit, and each unit determines the classification system that best fits its needs. As managers and secretaries are promoted, transferred, or terminated and replacements are employed, frequent changes are made in the types of classification systems used. Changes are determined by the knowledge and experience of the incoming employees. All of FDI's records are in hard-copy form.

As Katherine familiarized herself with the existing records systems within each operating unit, she began to consider the possibility of implementing a centralized system for maintaining active records and establishing a records center for inactive records. Katherine's next move was to conduct an organization-wide records survey. Upon completion of the survey, she compiled the survey data; a portion of the data is shown on page 119.

| Department | Record Volume (linear feet) | Classification System Used | Percent of Active Records to Inactive Records |
|---|---|---|---|
| Accounting | 72 | Numeric | 55% |
| Personnel | 56 | Alphabetic (by name) | 45 |
| Parts/Service | 48 | Numeric | 65 |
| Sales | 80 | Alphabetic (by name) | 50 |
| Administrative Offices | 96 | Subject | 30 |

1. What types of classification systems might Katherine consider?
2. What are some criteria for making her decision on the type of classification system to use?

*"Do you want the personnel file on Mr. Perkins that's in the file cabinet or the one in the shoe box in your closet?"*

## TYPES OF CLASSIFICATION SYSTEMS

There must be a more logical way to classify records than that indicated in this cartoon. By definition, a **classification system** is a logical, systematic ordering of records which uses numbers, letters, or a combination of numbers and letters for records identification.

*Basic systems*

There are four basic systems for classifying records: (1) alphabetic, (2) numeric, (3) alphanumeric, and (4) chronologic. Each of these basic systems has variations; however, the principle of alphabetic, numeric, alphanumeric, and chronologic order is consistent with each system.

## Alphabetic

**Alphabetic classification systems** are those that classify records alphabetically by letter, word, and unit. There are three primary types of ordering within an alphabetic classification system: (1) by name, (2) by subject, and (3) by geographic location.

### Ordering by Name

Records arranged in **name order** are filed according to names of people, organizations, agencies, and businesses. The name filing order is a simple alphabetic system and is the easiest system to create and use. An alpha name filing order groups records pertaining to the same individual or organization, keeping these records together. However, name ordering does not group records of related subjects together. Because alpha name files may be accessed directly, no index is required.

*Small volume*

Records filed in alpha name order are most appropriate for correspondence case files where the volume is small and the need for expansion is limited. In general, if records exceed 1,000 files, alpha name filing is inefficient.

Some problems associated with filing records by name are:

1. Handwritten correspondence/signatures are sometimes difficult to interpret, causing misfiles.
2. Congestion often occurs under common names. For example, in a normally distributed file arranged by name, almost half of the names will be under six letters of the alphabet—S, B, M, H, C, and W.
3. Similar or identical names may cause the person searching the files to go through numerous records to obtain the requested file or information.
4. Larger volumes of records cannot be accommodated.
5. File expansion is difficult.
6. Files are difficult to purge because the alpha system does not correspond to age of record, as compared to straight numeric systems that are in chronologic order.

Alphabetic systems have a built-in provision for general (miscellaneous) files not provided by other classification systems. In Figure 5–1, the general files are the separate A, B, and C folders at the end of each section.

Figure 5–1
Alpha Name Arrangement

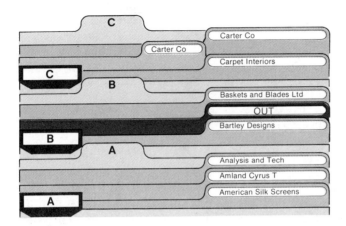

## Ordering by Subject

**Subject order** is an arrangement of records by their content subjects. The subject arrangement is the most difficult to classify because different people tend to "see" records in different ways. One person classifying records involving leased automobiles may conclude that the subject is *Automobiles — Leased* while another may judge *Vehicles — Leased Cars* as the primary subject. In "pure" subject filing, the subject topic is based on the record content. Some organizations do not follow this guideline, and the result is a topic mix of informational content (record subject), record-centered topics (for example, the name of the department originating the record), or a record characteristic (for example, press releases). One method of minimizing this problem is to establish a subject files manual (or incorporate this information into the organization's records management manual) to control general correspondence filing. A subject files manual includes a written reference list, or relative index, of subjects within the files. A **relative index** is a dictionary-type listing of all words and combination of words by which material may be requested. The index is alphabetically arranged and serves as a control list for classifying records. A portion of a subject files relative index is shown in Figure 5–2.

*Topic based on content*

Figure 5–2
Relative Index to Subject Files

| Subject | Filed Under |
|---|---|
| **A** | |
| Account Balances | ACCOUNTING |
| Activities—Employee | PERSONNEL |
| Administrative Issuances | ADMINISTRATION |
| **B** | |
| Benefits Administration | EMPLOYEE BENEFITS |
| Brokers and Agents | INSURANCE |
| **C** | |
| Claims and Loss | INSURANCE |
| Compensation | PERSONNEL |
| Corporate Law | LEGAL |

*Topical arrangement*

Subject files may be arranged in **topical order** in which records are in alphabetic order by subject with no real attempt being made to file related subjects together. Since this system is the one used in dictionaries, topical order is often referred to as dictionary order.

*Encyclopedic arrangement*

Subject files may also be arranged in **encyclopedic order**—filed by subject alphabetically. However, unlike topical or dictionary order, the subjects are grouped as they would be arranged in an encyclopedia—by major subject areas with subgroupings.

A comparison of topical (dictionary) and encyclopedic orders illustrates the difference in handling the same subjects in two subject ordering systems.

| Topical (Dictionary) Order | Encyclopedic Order |
|---|---|
| Bids and Quotes | ADMINISTRATION |
| Employee Activities | Office Services |
| Grievance Procedures | Security |
| Housing Assistance | Visitors |
| Office Services | |
| Purchase Orders | EMPLOYEE RELATIONS |
| Security | Employee Activities |
| Specifications | Grievance Procedures |
| Visitors | Housing Assistance |
| | |
| | PURCHASING |
| | Bids and Quotes |
| | Purchase Orders |
| | Specifications |

Filing arrangements of topical and encyclopedic orders are shown in Figure 5–3.

Figure 5–3
A Comparison of Topical Order and Encyclopedic Order Arrangements

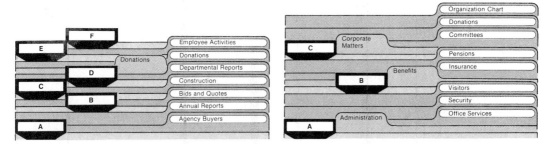

Topical Order                    Encyclopedic Order

Though encyclopedic order is better suited for larger volumes of records than is topical order, it is still limited to small numbers of records that can be processed efficiently. Subject ordering is dependent upon an alphabetic relative index that is both logical and comprehensive. The use of a relative index assures consistency when more than one person handles the records.

Subject filing is particularly suitable for manager/executive individual files. These files, which are based on the records of a particular manager or department, are largely personalized. Subject files save time for executives requiring immediate reference to all information on a particular topic prior to making a decision. Flexibility and expansion are provided by adding subdivisions to a main file. However, unless extreme care is taken, subdivisions may grow until the system becomes inefficient.

*Suitable for individual executive files*

Selection of subject topic is time consuming because each document must be read prior to coding; and topic selection, as mentioned earlier, is sometimes difficult. In theory, subject files should not require the use of general folders because every record has a subject. In application, however, general folders may be used at the end of each primary or secondary topic to collect generally related items. General folders may be used when there are not enough correspondence/subjects to justify individual folders.

**Ordering by Geographic Location**
**Geographic order** is an arrangement of records in alphabetic order by place or location. Locations may be grouped in various arrangements, such as the following:

| County or State | Example |
|---|---|
| State, City | South Carolina, Myrtle Beach |
| Company or Person | Addison-Daniel Manufacturing Company Dan Dorchester, Treasurer |

*Grouping by location or place*

| Region or District | |
|---|---|
| Region | Western Region |
| City | San Diego |
| Company or Person | RV Dealers |

| City | |
|---|---|
| City | Montgomery |
| Company or Person | McAfee Bagpipes |

| Street | |
|---|---|
| Individual Address | Duquesne Avenue, 106 |

Geographic files are particularly appropriate for sales records filed by district; real estate property information filed by address; customer files for specific types of similar institutions or businesses, such as banks, schools, churches; market surveys; branch offices; or other kinds of information that may be referenced according to geographic location.

Figure 5–4 shows a portion of a geographic file arrangement.

*Alphabetic index essential*

An alphabetic index is essential to geographic filing. Reference is commonly made to an individual name or a company name rather than to place or location. The alphabetic file includes the name of the person or organization and the complete address for that correspondent. When an address is unknown or misplaced, the alphabetic index provides a quick reference.

Geographic filing systems have certain advantages. A visual estimate of the file activity within any geographic area can be made quickly. Files may be added, deleted, or rearranged easily. However, more time is required to establish and use a geographic file because two files must be established — the geographic file and the alphabetic file. Also, two locations may have to be referenced when locating an individual file. Misfiles may occur because of similarity of state names and because many cities having the same names are located in several states.

Figure 5–4
Geographic Arrangement

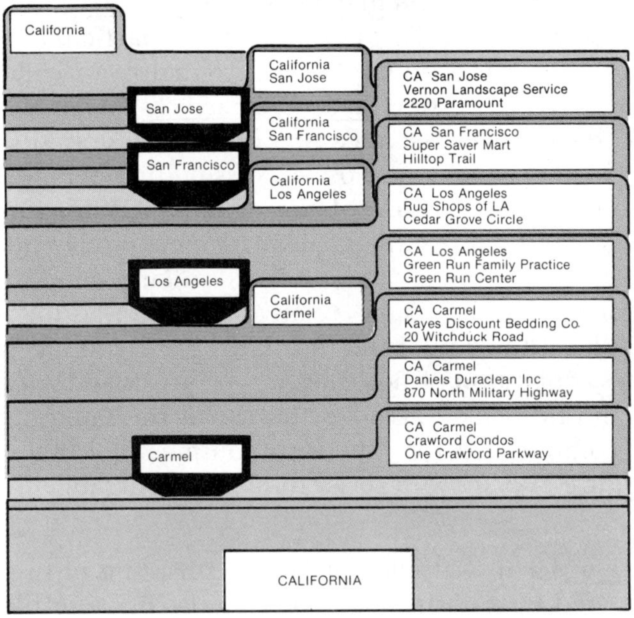

## Numeric

In a **numeric classification system**, records are arranged in order by number rather than by name. Numeric file numbers may originate in several ways: the number is a part of the record itself, as in invoices, checks, or social security numbers; or the number is added to make processing and retrieval easier. When numbers are a part of the original document, reference will generally be made to the document number. When the number has been added to the record internally, reference will usually be made to subject or name. For example, a check has a number that is part of the record (check) itself, and when an inquiry is made regarding the check, that inquiry is usually made by check number. On the other hand, if a number is assigned within the organization to a case history, a person outside the organization would not know the assigned case number, and the inquiry would be made by the name of the individual whose case history was being referenced. Internally, then, reference would be made to an alphabetic index to obtain the case history number.

*Number is part of record*

*Number is added to record*

There are three primary types of ordering within the numeric classification system: (1) serial (consecutive); (2) duplex (numbers separated into parts); and (3) decimal.

## Serial

In a **serial order**, records are arranged consecutively, such as 1, 2, 3, 4, and so forth. Numbers may begin with 01, 10, or 100 and increase consecutively. Serial arrangement is particularly suitable when numbers are preprinted on the original record, such as the numbers on purchase orders, tickets, or checks. When the organization has control over issuance of numbers, a simple sequential numbering system can be developed. Missing numbers within a file allow for quick identification of lost or misfiled documents. Because a serially numbered file is also chronologic (last number issued is most current), files can be purged in large blocks.

Expansion of serial files is relatively simple; additional numbers are added at the end of the file. The ease of adding files, however, creates congestion of new files in one area and slows retrieval if more than one person accesses the file at the same time. Serial order is recommended for files with volumes of 1,000 to 10,000 records. Figure 5–5 shows a serial number file arrangement.

## Duplex

*Provides more even distribution of files*

The **duplex order** uses duplex numbers consisting of two or more parts, separated by a dash, space, or comma. Because files are arranged in sequence by the first part of the number and then by succeeding parts, new files are evenly distributed throughout the

Figure 5–5
Serial Number Arrangement

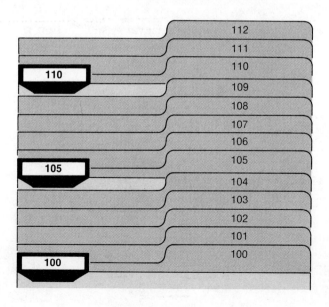

file series. A duplex arrangement is advantageous when large numbers of records—generally more than 10,000 records—are to be filed. Two types of duplex numbers are terminal and middle digit.

In terminal and middle digit filing, a number is divided into three groups. Zeros are added to the left of the number to create three groups; for example, 76214 becomes 07 62 14. These numbers are always read from right to left. The parts or groups of numbers comprising the duplex number are referred to as the primary (first), secondary, and tertiary (final) numbers. The primary number is the guide to the file section, drawer, or shelf; the secondary number indicates the guide location within the file system; and the tertiary number indicates the order in which the file is located behind the secondary guide. Because you are working with pairs of numbers rather than one long number, there is less chance of misfiling.

**Terminal digit order** requires that the groups of numbers be read from right to left. The right group is the primary number, the middle group is the secondary number, and the left group is the tertiary number. The number 04 10 25 is read in this manner:

*Terminal digit*

| 04 | 10 | 25 |
|----|----|----|
| Tertiary<br>(Folder Number) | Secondary<br>(Guide Number) | Primary<br>(File Section, Drawer,<br>or Shelf Number) |

By system design, new files added to a terminal digit system are not clustered in the same area; therefore, congestion of users or records clerks in the file area is reduced. Since folders are divided into groups of two or three numbers, misfiles are also reduced; transpositions are less likely to occur when the number is broken down into shorter groups. Terminal digit arrangement is particularly appropriate for hospitals and other organizations where the volume of records exceeds 10,000 and the incoming records are rapidly turned over to the records department.

*Volume exceeds 10,000*

Figure 5–6 graphically illustrates how terminal digit works. To create a terminal digit system for 40 file drawers, begin labeling the first drawer with the first primary number, 100, through to the last drawer which would be primary number 139. When refiling or removing a folder, always refer to the last digits on the far right side. For example, 000–100–119 would be filed in drawer 119 behind the secondary guide 100, and it would be the first folder behind the guide.

Figure 5–6
How Terminal Digit Works

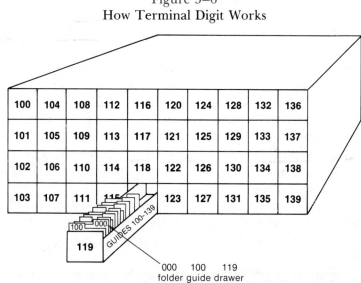

000    100    119
folder guide drawer

Since numbers in the terminal digit system must be read from right to left instead of the usual left-to-right method, training users and records clerks takes longer. When a block of sequentially numbered files is requested, many different locations must be accessed in order to retrieve the records. Purging a terminal digit system takes longer because records are not filed in chronologic order. Figure 5–7 shows an open-shelf terminal digit file arrangement.

*Middle digit*

**Middle digit order** uses the middle numbers as the primary numbers, first numbers as secondary numbers, and the last numbers as tertiary numbers. The number 04 10 25 is read in this manner:

| 04 | 10 | 25 |
|---|---|---|
| Secondary (Guide Number) | Primary (File Section, Drawer, or Shelf Number) | Tertiary (Folder Number) |

Middle digit arrangement distributes records through the files in blocks of 100; records consecutively numbered 702500–702599 would be in the same sequence. Therefore, a user or records clerk must look in only ten places for 1,000 consecutively numbered records in order to purge the files. **Block integrity** — all records related to one subject are filed together — is maintained with middle digit arrangement. For example, a real estate agency may file all

Figure 5–7
Open-Shelf Terminal Digit Arrangement

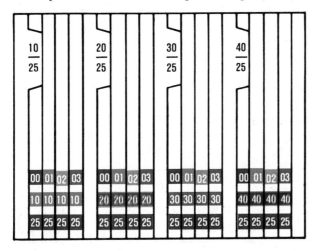

records relating to one tract of properties together, or an insurance company may retain all active policies written by each sales representative in one block. However, training people to read the numbers in a middle digit arrangement requires additional training time before a high level of proficiency is reached. Figure 5–8 shows a middle digit file arrangement.

Figure 5–8
Middle Digit Arrangement

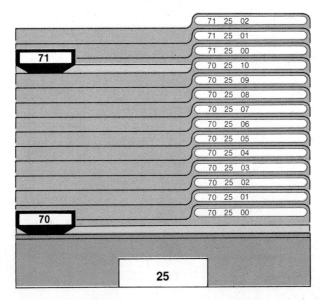

A comparison of serial, middle, and terminal digit file arrangements is shown in Figure 5–9.

There are advantages and disadvantages of each of the three previously described numeric systems—serial, middle, and termi-

Figure 5–9

Comparison of Serial, Middle, and Terminal Digit Arrangements

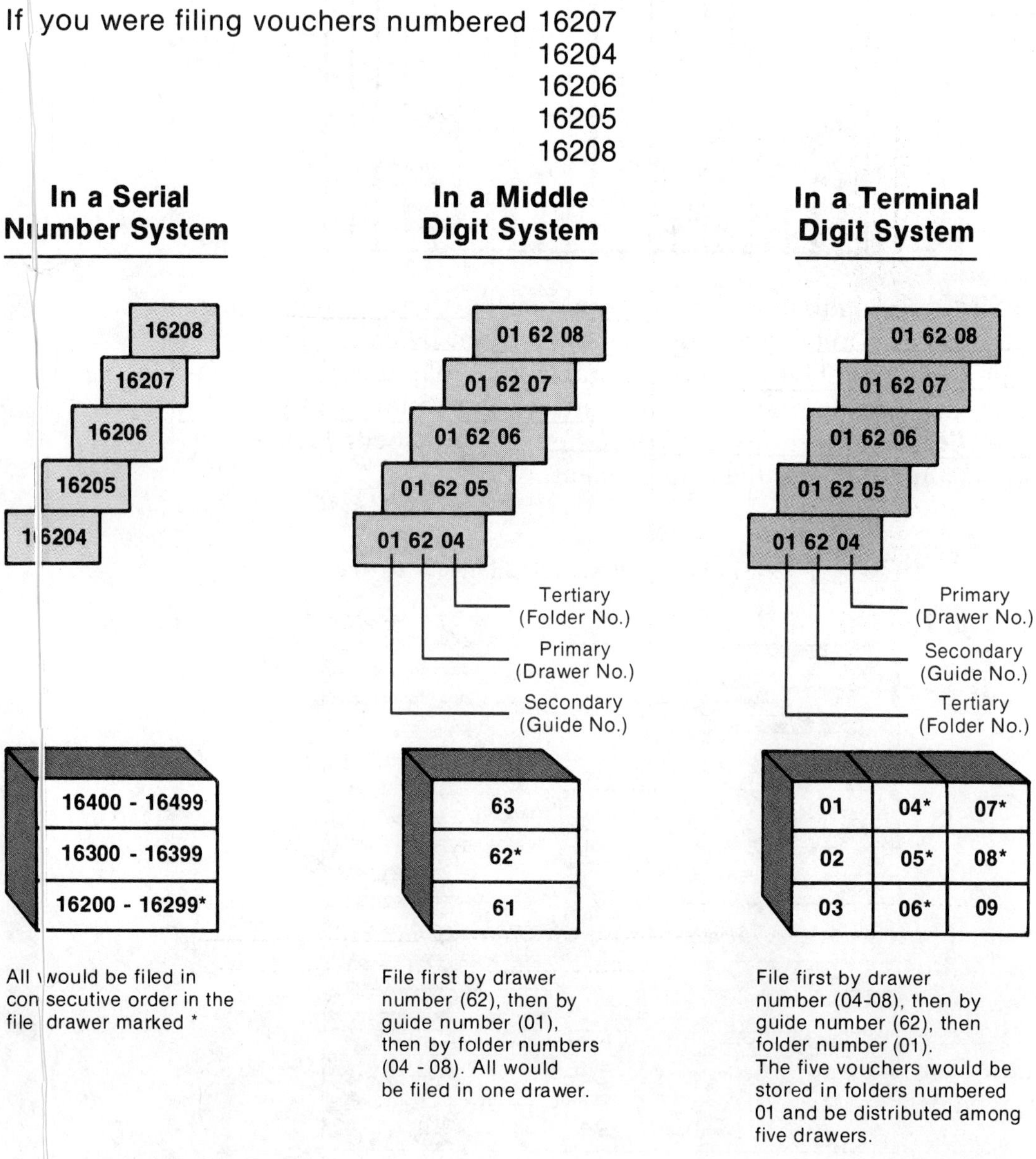

If you were filing vouchers numbered 16207
16204
16206
16205
16208

| In a Serial Number System | In a Middle Digit System | In a Terminal Digit System |
|---|---|---|
| 16208 | 01 62 08 | 01 62 08 |
| 16207 | 01 62 07 | 01 62 07 |
| 16206 | 01 62 06 | 01 62 06 |
| 16205 | 01 62 05 | 01 62 05 |
| 16204 | 01 62 04 | 01 62 04 |
| | Tertiary (Folder No.) | Primary (Drawer No.) |
| | Primary (Drawer No.) | Secondary (Guide No.) |
| | Secondary (Guide No.) | Tertiary (Folder No.) |

| In a Serial Number System | In a Middle Digit System | In a Terminal Digit System | | |
|---|---|---|---|---|
| 16400 - 16499 | 63 | 01 | 04* | 07* |
| 16300 - 16399 | 62* | 02 | 05* | 08* |
| 16200 - 16299* | 61 | 03 | 06* | 09 |

All would be filed in consecutive order in the file drawer marked *

File first by drawer number (62), then by guide number (01), then by folder numbers (04 - 08). All would be filed in one drawer.

File first by drawer number (04-08), then by guide number (62), then folder number (01). The five vouchers would be stored in folders numbered 01 and be distributed among five drawers.

nal digit. These factors should be considered when making a selection of the most appropriate system for your particular needs. The filing tasks for each of the three numeric systems are compared in Figure 5–10.

Figure 5–10
Task Comparisons for Serial, Middle Digit, and Terminal Digit Ordering

| Filing Task | Serial | Middle Digit | Terminal Digit |
|---|---|---|---|
| Sort | Slow | Fast | Fast |
| Work distribution | Difficult to divide work evenly | Easy to divide work evenly | Easy to divide work evenly |
| File guide preparation | Constantly updated | Guides prepared once | Guides prepared once |
| Record transfer and destruction | Easy | Easy | Difficult |
| Pull 100 consecutively numbered records | Easy | Easy | Difficult |
| Place new records in the file | All placed at open end of file | Last 100 records evenly distributed | All evenly distributed |

## Decimal

**Decimal numbering arrangements** are familiar to all who use a library. Ninety percent of all libraries in the United States use the Dewey Decimal System. This arrangement is most appropriate for libraries, governmental agencies, pharmaceutical, and engineering firms.

*Decimal numbering system*

Each of the Dewey system's ten divisions may be divided into ten subdivisions, and each subdivision may be further divided into ten additional subdivisions. The Dewey system, therefore, should be used only in organizations whose files may be limited to ten major headings. This lack of flexibility limits the use of the Dewey Decimal System.

Each numeric system has standard peripheral subsystems that must be in place for efficient use of numeric ordering. Numeric arrangements are **indirect access** systems—the person accessing the files must first consult an alphabetic index to determine the code number for the record, correspondent, or subject. This is in contrast to an alphabetic system, which is a **direct access** system. The person accessing the alphabetic file goes directly to the file without first having to consult an index to determine the location of the file.

*Numeric files*

Numeric files require (1) an accession book, (2) an alphabetic index, (3) a general alphabetic file, and (4) a cross-reference file. The **accession book** contains a listing of numbers assigned to correspondents/subjects and shows the next number to be assigned. When a record is accessed, reference is not made to the accession book to obtain the number; the accession book simply provides information regarding previously assigned numbers and numbers available for assignment to new records. The accession book lists only the name assigned to a particular number. All other pertinent information may be obtained from the alphabetic index. Therefore, to obtain the number assigned to Super Charger Engines, first look in the alphabetic index and then go to the numeric file to pull the record. A partial page from an accession book and a sample card for an alphabetic index are shown in Figures 5–11 and 5–12.

Figure 5–11
Page from Accession Book

| | | Page 105 |
|---|---|---|
| Number | Name | Date |
| 2000 | Super Charger Engines | 8/16/-- |
| 2001 | Marine World | 8/16/-- |
| 2002 | Recreational Vehicles, Inc. | 8/17/-- |
| 2003 | Thomas Martin | 8/17/-- |
| 2004 | Jerome Cozens | 8/17/-- |

In a numeric filing system, a general alphabetic file must be maintained for correspondents/subjects not active enough to warrant a separately numbered folder. Usually when documents for a particular correspondent/subject exceed five, these materials are removed from the general (G) file, assigned a number, and placed in an individual folder. If fewer than five records were filed under the name of Jerome Cozens, the alphabetic index card would have a G in the upper-right corner instead of the 2004 file number.

Figure 5–12
Alphabetic Index Card

Cozens Jerome                    2004


Jerome Cozens
1622 Northwest Station
Dallas, TX  75240-1423

Cross-reference cards/files are prepared for most filing sys-     *Cross-reference*
tems—alphabetic, numeric, or any other system in which a relative     *cards/files*
index is not maintained. The cross-reference card/file merely notes
another place(s) where information might be located. For example,
if Jerome Cozens were president of Recreational Vehicles, Inc., the
cross-reference card would note "See also Recreational Vehicles,
Inc." Cross-referencing makes finding records easier when reference might be made to a record in more than one way.

## Alphanumeric

**Alphanumeric classification systems** are arrangements of records
based on a combination of words and numbers. These alpha codes
should provide some information about the contents of the file. Alphanumeric files may have either subject or phonetic arrangement.
Subject arrangements are the most often used alphanumeric classification system. According to a recent survey, the phonetic arrangement is rarely used.

### Subject
**Subject-numeric order** follows an encyclopedic arrangement; re-     *Subject-numeric*
lated materials are filed under major headings and subheadings.     *order*
Subject titles are assigned numbers that indicate major divisions
and subdivisions. For example, a file on ANIMALS, a major division, might include headings of *Domestic, Farm, Wild*, and *Circus*.
Each major heading would be assigned a number indicating that it
is a major division. Each major division may be divided into subdivisions (*Domestic, Farm, Wild, Circus*) and assigned numbers that indicate these are subdivisions of a major division (ANIMALS).
   One of the difficulties with a subject-numeric arrangement is
that files may be in alphabetic order by letter block (all As, Bs, Cs,
and so forth, together) but not alphabetically within each block.

For example, all subjects beginning with the letter C would remain together, but within the block of Cs, "claims" might follow "construction." Two methods exist for dealing with this problem. One method leaves many unassigned numbers for new files between the assigned numbers: blocks of 50–100 unassigned numbers might be left between each assigned number. The other method sacrifices numeric sequence by filing alphabetically within each letter block. "Construction" would follow "claims," but "construction" might be out of order numerically because it was assigned a number before "claims" received a number. A subject-numeric system is most appropriate for volumes of 1,000 to 5,000 files.

An alphabetic index may be maintained for the assigned numbers of the subject titles. The index allows users who may be unfamiliar with a topic to locate the subject division. Use of an alphabetic index also provides a list of previously assigned numbers; this prevents two subjects from being assigned identical numbers.

Although the captions of most headings and subheadings include both the assigned number and the subject heading, material to be filed may be coded by number only. Number coding is a time-saver for the person responsible for coding material for filing.

A comprehensive method of cross-referencing may be necessary if topics can be referenced in more than one way. As volume increases, cross-referencing becomes essential for efficient retrieval. Figure 5–13 shows a portion of an alphanumeric subject arrangement.

Some subject-numeric systems use numbers for subdivisions only. Abbreviated systems in which primary subject areas are assigned abbreviated titles and the subdivisions are assigned the abbreviated title plus a number are also used. An example of an abbreviated method used by the Georgia Department of Archives and History is shown in Figure 5–14.

### Phonetic

*Phonetic order*

**Phonetic order** is an alphanumeric filing arrangement of records by the sound of the name, regardless of the spelling. A phonetic system can be used more effectively with 10,000 or more individual name files. Many of the problems inherent in other systems—such as misspelling, mispronunciation, poor handwriting, and different spellings of sound-alike names—can be minimized with a phonetic system. However, phonetic arrangements are not frequently used; in part because training users is time consuming, and improperly coded records are difficult to locate. Because of the infrequent use, the phonetic arrangement is only briefly described here.

Figure 5–13
Alphanumeric Subject Arrangement

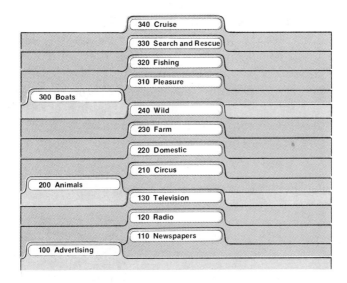

## Chronologic

A **chronologic classification system** is an arrangement in which records are stored in date order. Records are filed in chronologic sequence by day (date) of the month. (See Figure 5–15.) Chronologic arrangements have three accepted applications: (1) suspense

*Chronologic applications*

Figure 5–14
Abbreviated Alphanumeric Subject Arrangement

SP–SUPPLIES

RM–8 Training Program
RM–7 Forms Management
RM–6.2 Storage Vault
RM–6.1 Service Bureau
RM–6 Micrographics
RM–5 Filing Systems
RM–4 Records Center
RM–3 Retention Schedules
RM–2 Legislation
RM–1 Organization

RM– RECORDS MANAGEMENT

files, (2) transaction files, and (3) within individual files. Suspense files are often referred to as pending, or tickler, files. The term "tickler" is used because reference to the file "tickles" your memory, and you are reminded to take certain action. As information that requires future action is received, the record (or a copy) is filed in the folder which corresponds to the date action should be taken. Such material should never be filed in an individual file until action is completed. Similarly, interoffice records that require a response should not be filed in individual files until the response has been received. Placing these records in a suspense file eliminates the need for a "pending list." Each morning the suspense file is checked for possible required action. If action is required, the record is removed from the suspense file, and appropriate action is taken before releasing the record for filing.

Figure 5–15
Chronologic Arrangement

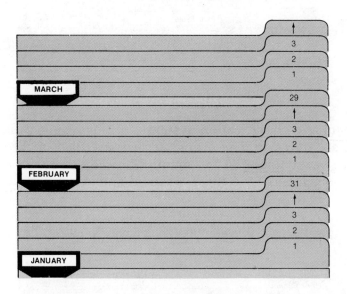

Transaction files organize records by date of transaction. This type of file is most appropriate for documenting transactions that occur on a day-to-day basis. Transaction documents may include purchase and sales records, personnel records, shipping records, and so forth.

*No index required*

A chronologic arrangement does not use an index; therefore, if a record is requested by name, a physical search of the file is required. If frequent reference is made by information other than date, other file systems should be considered.

Within all files, records should be arranged in reverse chronologic order—that is, the most recent (last) record in the front of the folder and the first record at the back of the folder. Records are arranged in the order of their occurrence, with the most recent transaction being the first record the user sees.

A survey of 67 selected companies located in 12 cities throughout the United States was conducted in 1980 by Barbara Christensen. The organizations surveyed varied in size and number of employees; the average number of employees was reported at 3,343. The largest organization had 25,000 company employees in one location; the smallest organization had 18 company employees in one location.

As part of the study, survey recipients were asked to identify the kinds and number of classification systems used in their organizations. Survey results of the types of classification systems used are shown in Table 5–1. Results indicate that alphabetic, straight numeric, and subject classification systems are used within the largest number of organizations, with geographic and subject numeric used by nearly one-third of the organizations surveyed. A follow-up survey conducted in 1985 by the authors validated the Christensen study with almost identical percentages of use.

Table 5–1

Number and Percent of Respondents and the Kinds
of Classification Systems Used Within Their Companies

| Classification System | Number of Respondents | Percent of Respondents |
|---|---|---|
| Alphabetic | 42 | 62.7 |
| Chronologic | 5 | 7.4 |
| Decimal | 1 | 1.5 |
| Duplex numeric | 1 | 1.5 |
| Geographic | 22 | 32.8 |
| Middle digit | 1 | 1.5 |
| Numeric, straight | 42 | 62.7 |
| Phonetic | 1 | 1.5 |
| Subject | 43 | 64.2 |
| Subject numeric | 20 | 29.8 |
| Terminal digit | 8 | 11.9 |

*Source: Barbara Christensen, "An Analysis of Storage Areas, Equipment, and Supplies,"*
Records Management Quarterly, *Vol. 16, No. 2 (April, 1982), p. 55.*

Because most organizations have a variety of types of records which are referenced in different ways, many organizations use more than one classification system. As reported in Table 5–2, the range of different kinds of classification systems used is one through nine. The mode is two and the mean is three. The organization using nine different classification systems employs 5,000 people.

Table 5–2
Number of Classification Systems Within Each Company

| Number of Respondents | Number of Systems | Percent of Respondents |
|:---:|:---:|:---:|
| 11 | 1 | 16.4 |
| 15 | 2 | 22.4 |
| 14 | 3 | 20.9 |
| 11 | 4 | 16.4 |
| 8 | 5 | 11.9 |
| 4 | 6 | 5.9 |
| 1 | 9 | 1.5 |
| 3 | no response | 4.6 |
| 67 | | 100.0 |

*Source:* Barbara Christensen, "An Analysis of Active Storage Areas, Equipment, and Supplies," Records Management Quarterly, Vol. 16, No. 2 (April, 1982), p. 55.

## Uniform Classification System

*"An organization exists only if communication flows between the individuals within it."*

*—Alcan and Alcan Group*

*Uniform Classification System*

Communication cannot flow easily between individuals when inconsistent and non-standard vocabulary is used in the records of an organization. A **Uniform Classification System (UCS)** is an attempt to bridge this gap through the use of standardized business vocabulary in its records classification. Companies that are geographically separated, multilingual, or experience heavy staff turnover suffer particular difficulties when exchanging records and information. A UCS is a way to minimize these difficulties through a consistent and standardized subject classification system that is communicated and used throughout the organization.

In their efforts to implement a UCS, many organizations have developed comprehensive manuals, complete subject indexes, and comprehensive relative indexes. In addition, preprinted folder labels are furnished and used in all departments and units throughout the company. A partial subject-numeric index is shown in Figure 5–16 along with a preprinted folder label corresponding to one of the categories in the index.

*Subject-numeric index*

Figure 5–16
Subject-Numeric Index

```
      ADM 1000 to 1300     ADMINISTRATION              Retention

      ADM 1020             DEPARTMENTAL ISSUES
          ADM 1020-1       Activity Reports            1 year
          ADM 1020-2       Staff Meetings - Eastern    1
          ADM 1020-2-1     Staff Meetings - Southern   1
          ADM 1020-2-2     Staff Meetings - Northern   1
          ADM 1020-3       Annual Reports              4

      ADM 1050             TRAINING PROGRAMS
          ADM 1050-1       Apprenticeship              5
          ADM 1050-2       Employee Development        3
          ADM 1050-3       Management Trainee          5



                   ADM          ADMINISTRATION
                        1050    TRAINING PROGRAMS
                          -2    Employee Development
```

## A LOOK AT THE CASE

Katherine has reviewed the classification systems — alphabetic, numeric, alphanumeric, and chronologic — and has decided that, because of the unique applications in each department, more than one classification system will be necessary even in a centralized system. However, before she can reach a decision on the types of classification systems for Fitness Development, Inc., Katherine realizes that she must consider the needs of the users.

From the records survey, Katherine compiles the following additional information:

| Department | Basic File Groups Used | Referenced By | Additional User Requirements |
|---|---|---|---|
| Accounting | Case Records | Number | |
| Personnel | Case Records, Correspondence | Name | |
| Parts/Service | Technical Reference Cards, Case Records | Number | |
| Sales | Case Records, Correspondence | Name | |
| Administrative Offices | Correspondence | Subject | |

How can this information help Katherine choose the most appropriate type(s) of classification system(s) for Fitness Development, Inc.?

■

## CRITERIA FOR CLASSIFICATION SYSTEM SELECTION

As defined earlier, a classification system is a logical, systematic ordering of records. The basic records groups within the system and the manner in which individual records are most frequently referenced must be determined in order to establish the most appropriate records classification system for the organization.

### Determine Basic File Groups

*Nine basic file groups*

A **file group** consists of a collection of records with similar characteristics that should be separated from other groups of records in the office. There are nine basic types of file groups: general correspondence; transitory correspondence; case records; case working papers; technical reference materials; convenience copies (nonrecords); film, tape, or disk records; cartographic materials and drawings; and cards.

#### General Correspondence
The general correspondence file consists of letters, memorandums, telegrams, enclosures, reports, and miscellaneous materials. Such records are usually arranged by subject.

## Transitory Correspondence

The transitory correspondence file consists of routine materials and may be authorized for disposal within a six-month period or less. If these records account for five percent or more of the correspondence, they should be kept in separate folders for ease of disposition. If fewer than 100 papers a month are involved, they may be kept in a single folder in chronologic order; if the volume is much larger, subject filing may be required to facilitate reference.

## Case Records

Case record files consist of records such as purchase orders, invoices, contracts, investigations, requisitions, loans, research projects, construction projects, and personnel records. The case record file group contains material relating to a specific action, event, person, organization, location, product, or thing. Typically, a case record handles a transaction or relationship from its beginning to end. Case records are always filed by name or number or a combination as in alphanumeric systems.

## Case Working Papers

In order to reduce the size of the case records file, case working papers should be differentiated from case records. Case working papers have short-term use and comprise the background, preliminary papers, drafts, and routine reminders, requests, or correspondence regarding a particular case file. Working papers should be kept in a separate folder from the case records so that later screening for disposal can be avoided. Generally, these two folders (distinguished from one another by labeling) are retained together while the case file is active.

It is important to distinguish between case working papers and transitory correspondence. Working papers are related to case

records; transitory correspondence is related to general correspondence. Intermixing case working papers and transitory correspondence complicates disposal. Transitory correspondence is normally disposed of within six months after preparation or receipt; case working papers are generally disposed of after a specified time following the conclusion of the transaction or working relationship.

### Technical Reference Materials
Technical reference materials include printed reports, periodicals, research studies, and internal instruction and information manuals. As a general rule, when more than one file drawer of the general file contains reference materials, separate filing should be arranged.

### Convenience Copies
Maintaining extra copies results in cluttered, inefficient files. These copies should never be filed unless some action needs to be documented. If extra copies are retained for the convenience of users, the copies should be kept in separate folders identified by the name of the originating office. Copies should not be interfiled with general correspondence or case records.

Many organizations keep a "day file" of letters or memos originating from an office; papers are arranged in date order. This "convenience file" is circulated to allow others within the organization to be informed.

### Tape, Film, Disk, and Microrecords
These records are easily identifiable, unlike some other record groups. Tape, film, disk, or microrecords may require special handling and storage. When sound recordings are converted to paper records, the recording may be discarded or reused.

### Cartographic Materials and Drawings
This file group contains maps (including field survey notes, geodetic surveys, and astronomic readings, as well as what are traditionally called "maps"); charts (including graphic presentations and nautical, weather, and aeronautical charts); and engineering drawings (including blueprints, diazo prints, pencil sketches, and tracings). Many materials may be reduced to a standard $8\frac{1}{2}$-by-11-inch size and filed with related information. If more than ten percent of this category of materials is oversized, separate filing is warranted.

### Cards
Cards have a physical size and format that logically separates them from other file groups. Cards include common sizes used as in-

dexes, catalogs, or summaries; punched cards; and aperture cards.

Separating records into basic types facilitates referencing by reducing the search area. Separation also keeps essential documents apart from short-term papers, allowing more efficient disposition. Different retention periods are accommodated more easily when record groups are established.

The quantity of records involved affects the file grouping. If less than a file drawer of case records or technical reference materials is involved, little advantage is gained by separating them from general correspondence.

## Determine Requested File Feature

Once the basic file groups within the organization have been identified (most often accomplished during the records inventory), a system must be selected for arranging the records for each separate file group. Record series are also identified during the records inventory. Record series indicate groups of records related by content; file groups indicate categories of records by function.

To select an appropriate classification system, first determine how the users will most often request that particular record — which "filing feature" will most likely be used. **Filing features** are characteristics by which records are stored and retrieved.

*Determine file features*

When a user requests correspondence, the request is made according to one of the following features:

1. surname of individual or organization name
2. name (title) of project, product, transaction, or thing — for example, the name of a project (text revision); name of product (IBM typewriter); transaction (blouse returned for credit); or thing (poster)
3. location (geographic or political division — county, state, parish, and so forth)
4. number (symbol) assigned to transaction, commodity, location, project, individual, or organization unit
5. date prepared or used
6. subject/topic describing the content

Forms are usually requested by

1. title of form (subject),
2. surname of individual or organization name,
3. number (symbol assigned for transaction control or other identification), or
4. date.

Because forms are used often in case files, they are usually filed by name or number.

Reports may be requested by

1. title of report (subject),
2. subjects in addition to the main subject,
3. surname of author,
4. name of originating organization,
5. number of project or contract with which identified,
6. number assigned for control, or
7. date of issuance.

Some file systems place recurring or periodic reports under a "Reports" category subarranged by report title or form title (if the report is a form).

The primary task, then, is to identify which filing feature will be requested most frequently by users. Are the users more likely to request information by name, by assigned number, or by other identifying elements?

## Determine Additional User Requirements

*User needs vary*

In addition to determining the file groups within the organizational records and the filing features most often used, consideration must be given to any additional user needs. These requirements vary from organization to organization or from department to department; therefore, any unique needs that were not previously considered must be identified. For example, the need of records users for complete information should not be overlooked. If photographs and correspondence are separated, either both files are searched when records are requested, or the office runs the risk of the users taking action without having complete information. Usually the physical characteristics of papers, such as the size of engineering drawings, require materials that might preferably be filed as a unit to be filed separately.

Should the files be continuous or should they be separated into individual file groups? Figure 5–17 illustrates these options.

A guide to systems for arranging files is shown in Figure 5–18. This guide summarizes operating considerations under each of the filing features of records. It is important that the classification system(s) that best fits the needs of the users be selected and implemented. An efficient records system with logical filing arrangements allowing for fast retrieval will provide the user with the requested information to be used in the decision-making process.

Figure 5–17
One Continuous File or Separate Groups?

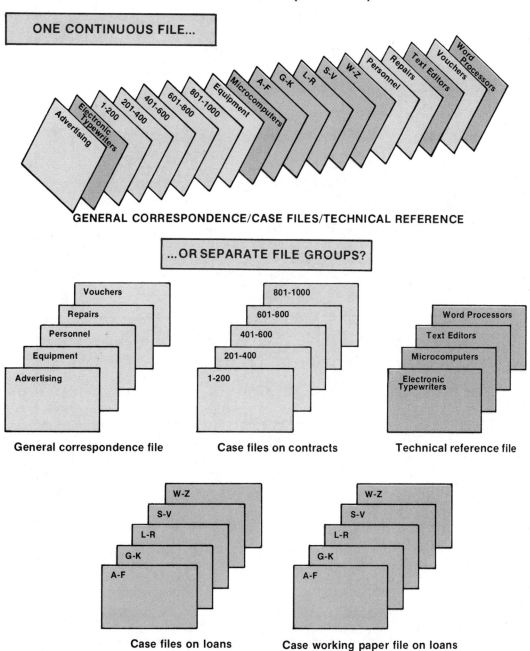

*Source:* Files Operations: Managing Current Records. *General Services Administration, National Archives and Records Service, Office of Federal Records Centers, 1981.*

Figure 5–18
Guide to Classification Systems

| Filing feature of record | Usual filing sequence | Most suitable file groups | Need for index file (by second filing feature) | Need for cross-referencing a record within the file | Likelihood that record description used in request will pinpoint file location | Likelihood of file designation being shown on record when originated | Likelihood of file designation being expressed the same on records to be filed together | Ease and accuracy in marking a record for filing | Ease and accuracy in sorting and filing |
|---|---|---|---|---|---|---|---|---|---|
| Names of people, organizations, or firms. | Alphabetic by name. | Case. Case working papers. Technical reference. | Normally not needed, except for precedent cases. | If more than one name involved. | Usually. Foreign, organization, and unusual names may be troublesome. The larger the file, the greater the problem. | Nearly always. | Usually, except for misspellings. Exchanging personal and organization names causes inconsistency. | Fast and easy, if names can be underlined. Fairly slow if names must be written. Spelling errors may occur in unfamiliar names. Adherence to filing rules required. | Slow and difficult. Eye must scan each letter of each word to determine sequence; words and titles vary widely in length. The larger the file, the greater the problem, and the greater the need for rigid adherence to filing rules. |
| Names or titles of projects, publications, products, or things. | Alphabetic by name. | Case. Case working papers. Technical reference. | Normally not needed, except for precedent cases. | If more than one name or title involved. | Sometimes. Project titles may be troublesome. The longer the name or title, the less chance of agreement. The larger the file, the greater the problem. | Usually. | Usually. Difficulties may occur with project and other long titles. | Fairly slow. Key words to be underlined in long titles. Incomplete titles may have to be completed by handwriting. Adherence to filing rules required. | Slow and difficult. Eye must scan each letter of each word to determine sequence; words and titles vary widely in length. The larger the file, the greater the problem, and the greater the need for rigid adherence to filing rules. |
| Geographic areas or locations. | Alphabetic by name (often subarranged by people, things, etc.) | Case. Case working papers. Technical reference. | Frequently needed as location is not always known. | If more than one area or location involved. | Sometimes. Record may be requested by city but filed by State, or may be requested by people, organizations, or things without the location given. The larger the file, the greater the problem. | Usually. Location is shown, but not subarrangement file designation. | Depends on consistent choice of locational level for each record. | Fast, if location can be underlined. Subarrangements often require handwritten designations. | Fairly difficult, depending on number of breakdowns and subarrangements. Precise filing required. The larger the file, the greater the problem. |
| Numbers or symbols. | By number or symbol. | Case. Case working papers. Technical reference. | Name index needed to obtain number or symbol, not known or incorrectly shown. | If more than one number or symbol involved. | Depends upon widespread use of the numbers or symbols within the office and extent of use on records from the outside. | Nearly always — but sometimes omitted. | Nearly always. | Fast, if numbers or symbols are short or segmented. Numbers or symbols susceptible to transposition and other errors. | Easy, if numbers or symbols are short or segmented. Transposition and other errors likely. |
| Dates. | By date prepared or used. | Convenience. Transitory. Suspense. | Not needed unless large volume filed only by date. | Not needed. | Usually for suspense. For convenience or transitory files, exact date often not known. | Always. | Always. | Fast and accurate. Marking rarely needed. | Easy and accurate. |
| Subject topics. | Alphabetic by subject topic, or by numeric or alphanumeric file code. | General correspondence (may include cases subarranged by names or numbers). Technical reference. | Occasionally an index by names of people, firms, and organizations needed. | If more than one subject involved, or record is brought forward. | Unlikely. Request may be vague, and differing terms may be used to describe same record. Relative index may be needed to determine proper subject topic. | Unlikely, since subject, if shown, rarely matches subject topics of receiving organization. | Unlikely. | Slow, as content must be read. Use of file code speeds writing, but may require reference to subject outline or relative index. Faulty decisions and errors in writing may occur. | Difficult, if alphabetically filed by word topics. Easier if filed by short file codes. The more complex the code the more difficult the accuracy. |

**Source:** Files Operations: Managing Current Records. *General Services Administration, National Archives and Records Service, Office of Federal Records Centers, 1981.*

## A LOOK AT THE CASE

Based on a careful evaluation of the data from the records survey and on interviews with department managers and staff, Katherine has determined that the in-place classification systems are basically serving the needs of the users at this time. The volume of active records is relatively small, and quick user access to the records is important to the managers. Katherine has, however, identified some additional user requirements. The Parts/Service Department could more efficiently serve their customers if a transaction file to follow up on orders were used. The Sales Department could get feedback regarding customer satisfaction with a suspense file as a basis for a follow-up of customer sales.

Katherine has determined that, because a large portion of the records are inactive or useless, active records should be separated and retained in each department under a centralized system of control. The records need to be purged; useless records should be disposed of. If record volume continues to increase with the same rapidity (doubled in the past two years), Katherine plans to recommend the establishment of a records center to house inactive records. She would also reevaluate the efficiency of the classification systems to determine if these systems are still meeting the needs of the users.

## TERMINOLOGY REVIEW

*Accession book.* A book containing a list of numbers previously assigned to correspondents/subjects and numbers available for assignment to new records.

*Alphabetic classification system.* An arrangement of records that classifies records alphabetically by letter, word, or unit.

*Alphanumeric classification system.* An arrangement of records which uses a combination of words and numbers.

*Block integrity.* All records related to one subject are filed together.

*Chronologic classification system.* An arrangement in which records are stored in date order.

*Classification system.* A logical, systematic ordering of records using numbers, letters, or a combination of numbers and letters for record identification.

*Decimal numbering arrangement.* Arrangement used primarily in libraries (Dewey Decimal System) that uses numbers, decimals to classify records into ten major categories.

*Direct access.* A storage system which permits access to records without reference to an index.

*Duplex order.* A classification arrangement using numbers with two or more parts separated by a dash, space, or comma.

*Encyclopedic order.* Records arranged alphabetically by subject, as used in an encyclopedia.

*File group.* A collection of records with similar characteristics that should be separated from other record groups.

*Filing features.* Characteristics, such as name of originator or organization, date, or form number by which records are stored and retrieved.

*Geographic order.* An arrangement in which related records are grouped by place or location.

*Indirect access.* A storage system which requires reference to an index before a record can be accessed.

*Middle digit order.* A type of duplex arrangement in which the middle two digits are primary digits, the first two digits are secondary digits, and the last two digits are tertiary digits.

*Name order.* An arrangement in which records are classified by name of organization or person.

*Numeric classification system.* An arrangement in which records are classified by number rather than by name.

*Phonetic order.* An alphanumeric arrangement of records by sound, regardless of the spelling of the name.

*Relative index.* A dictionary-type listing of all words and combinations of words by which records may be requested.

*Serial order.* An arrangement in which records are stored using consecutive numbers.

*Subject order.* An arrangement of records by the subjects of the records.

*Subject-numeric order.* An alphanumeric arrangement in which records are stored using an encyclopedia arrangement; related materials are stored together under major headings and subheadings.

*Terminal digit order.* A type of duplex numeric arrangement in which the last two digits are the primary digits, the middle two digits are the secondary digits, and the first two digits are the tertiary digits.

*Topical order.* An arrangement of records in alphabetic order by subject.

*Uniform Classification System (UCS).* A standard classification system used throughout an organization.

## COMPETENCY REVIEW

1. Define alphabetic classification system and identify the three common types of ordering used in an alphabetic classification system.
2. Define numeric classification system and identify the three major types of ordering used in a numeric classification system.
3. Explain the differences between middle and terminal digit arrangements.
4. Define alphanumeric classification system and describe its two major types of arrangements.
5. Define chronologic classification system.
6. What are the advantages of a Uniform Classification System?
7. Prior to selecting a classification system, why is it important to
   a. identify basic file groups?
   b. identify file features?
   c. identify additional user requirements?

## APPLICATIONS

1. Given the following limited information, which of the classification systems would you recommend to the users? Justify your recommendation.
   a. small (800) volume of client records
   b. 26,000 insurance policy files in a branch office
   c. patient records in a large medical complex
   d. personal files of the president of Macon University
   e. incoming purchase orders for a grocery wholesaler
   f. routine correspondence—transitory
   g. home office of a large department store with branches in 52 cities
   h. invoices for purchasing department of parts manufacturer
   i. 52,000 records of names of buyers from a catalog house
   j. records on which future action must be taken
2. a. Place the following names in alphabetic order:

   James D. DeLiso
   Delio, Jan
   Donna C. Delsey
   Deleo's Deli
   James, Danielle

   b. Place the following names in topical order; then place the names in encyclopedic order:

   | | |
   |---|---|
   | Rusty Tub | Hairdynamics |
   | Bathroom Boutique | Hairstyles Unlimited |
   | Aspen Tile Company | John's Barber Shop |
   | Mosaic Tiles | Johnson Hairworks |
   | The Bathtub Inc. | The Lion's Mane |

    c. Place the following numbers in correct order using terminal digit, middle digit, and serial arrangements:

      27114, 27119, 27117, 27118, 27115, 27110

    d. Place the following records in chronologic order. This is November.

      Memo dated 11/21/87, received 11/29/87
      Letter dated 8/18/87, received 8/22/87
      Letter dated 11/22/87, received 11/26/87
      Memo dated 8/13/87, received 8/23/87
      Memo dated 8/12/87, received 8/22/87

3. Prepare a suggested relative index for the following records used in a large discount department store.

| | | | | |
|---|---|---|---|---|
| junior dresses | rings | men's sport coats | pearl necklaces | purses |
| junior sportswear | watches | men's suits | shoes | wallets |

## CONCLUDING CASES

### A. Davidson Division, Language Laboratories

Davidson Division of Language Laboratories is a multinational corporation selling both hardware and software to organizations and individuals for use in developing competency in a second language. The company experienced phenomenal growth in the 1970s, and branch offices were established in the United States, France, and Germany. In response to a decrease in business and a general recessionary slump in the early 1980s, the decision was made to consolidate operations in the United States and close four branch offices.

All of the records of the four branch offices will be moved to the home office since customers will now be serviced from this location. The move may make it necessary to recommend a files reorganization. The home office files records in several ways:

- General and transitory correspondence are filed together by client as well as by subject.
- Correspondence and sales reports from the branch offices are filed by branch office location.
- Technical reference manuals and materials are in stacks.
- Case records are filed according to function:
  - Purchase orders are filed serially by prenumbered series.
  - Invoices are filed by vendor name.
- Total volume housed in the home office exceeds 100,000 records.

Branch office records are filed differently at each branch. Branch No. 1 files all records alphabetically by name of individual or organization. Volume of records totals 22,000.

Branch No. 2 files all account records serially by account number. Correspondence is filed with the account record. Volume of records totals 7,000 active accounts.

Branch No. 3 has only been in operation for eight months. Their system is still in the organizational stage because of a turnover of staff. An estimated 4,000 records are in the files.

Branch No. 4 has an office manager who is a stickler for detail. All records have been identified and are filed by file group. Although the volume of some file groups is very small, the office manager requires that the records be separated into the appropriate file groups. Volume of records totals 18,700.

You are asked to recommend a classification system for the consolidated home office records. Provide support for your recommendation.

## B. Superior Leasing

Delores Paine has just signed the preliminary franchise papers for Superior Leasing, an automobile leasing agency in a large metropolitan area. She is confused about which classification system would best serve her needs. Delores has tentatively grouped the records for her agency into these categories: Administrative Correspondence, Client Records, Accounting Records (including purchase orders, accounts receivable, accounts payable), Service Records, Inventory, Insurance, Fiscal Records (including tax records and financial statements), Advertising (including advertisements, advertising agencies, mailing lists), and Personnel Records.

Delores is aware that she has choices among classification systems, but she has not approached those choices in the same systematic, logical way in which her other management decisions have been made. Delores takes out a sheet of paper and begins to make notes. She has completed the following part of a chart when she is called to the telephone for a conference call.

| Types of Records | Possible Classification System(s) | Considerations in Decision |
|---|---|---|
| Administrative Correspondence | Alpha by name of correspondent | Volume—if fewer than 1000, use name<br>Index not required<br>Groups records by organization/individual<br>Provides for general records |
| | Alpha by subject of correspondence | Groups records by topic<br>May need to refer to index<br>Difficulty in deciding on topic<br>Need for liberal cross-referencing |
| Client Records | | |

Complete the chart for Delores.

## READINGS AND REFERENCES

Acton, Patricia. "How to Design A Subject Classification System." Presentation to 30th Annual Conference, Association of Records Managers and Administrators, Inc., New York, New York (September, 1985).

Christensen, Barbara. "An Analysis of Active Storage Areas, Equipment, and Supplies." *Records Management Quarterly*, Vol. 16, No. 2 (April, 1982), p. 55.

Christensen, Barbara. "What's In a Name?" *Records Management Quarterly*, Vol. 15, No. 4 (October, 1981), p. 54.

Daum, Patricia. "Implementing Administrative File Systems." *Records Management Quarterly*, Vol. 19, No. 2 (April, 1985), p. 36.

*Files Operations: Managing Current Records.* General Services Administration, National Archives and Records Service, Office of Federal Records Centers, 1981.

General Services Administration, National Archives and Records Service, Office of Federal Records Centers. *File Operations: Managing Current Records.* Washington, D.C.: U.S. Government Printing Office, 1981.

Georgia Department of Archives and History, Division of the Secretary of State. *Files Management.* Atlanta, Georgia, 1979.

*Mountain Bell Records Management Manual.* Denver, Colorado. (Revised February, 1977).

Perks, Denis G. "Uniform File System for the Multinational, Multilingual Corporation." Presentation to 30th Annual Conference, Association of Records Managers and Administrators, Inc., New York, New York (September, 1985).

Richelsoph, Martin. "Progressive Techniques for Subject Filing." *Records Management Quarterly* (April, 1981).

Westington, Ralph. "Case Records Filing Systems." *Records Management Quarterly* (April, 1976).

# 6
# STORAGE EQUIPMENT AND SUPPLIES

## Competencies

After completing this chapter, you should be able to

1. list selection criteria for storage equipment and explain how each affects the purchasing decision.
2. list selection criteria for storage supplies and explain how each affects the purchasing decision.
3. define and give examples of manual, mechanical, and automated storage equipment.
4. describe appropriate storage equipment for audiovisual materials, magnetic media, maps/engineering drawings, and publications.
5. explain the purpose of guides, folders, labels, and binders in a storage system.
6. explain how color coding increases storage/retrieval efficiency and describe methods in which color may be used.
7. describe the use of color coding in alphabetic, numeric, and alphanumeric classification systems.

# Introductory Case

"I don't know why you're making such a big fuss over the purchase of storage equipment and supplies. Central Transfer & Storage Co. has always used four-drawer cabinets and manila folders, and they've worked just fine," said Paul Greene, executive vice president of Central Transfer & Storage Co.

"I know that has been true in the past," said Carl Stone, Central's records manager. "However, our volume of records has been steadily increasing, and our records no longer consist only of paper records. Our inventory records are on computer output microfiche with weekly summaries on computer printouts. We maintain a card file of customer names, addresses, telephone numbers, and account numbers. Our sales records are maintained in paper form. Because of our varied storage requirements and the many storage equipment options available, I would like to reexamine our equipment and supplies needs."

"Very well, Carl," replied Greene, "but I'm still of the opinion that this is 'much ado about nothing'."

1. What criteria should Central Transfer & Storage Co. use to select storage equipment?
2. What criteria should Central use to select storage supplies?

Storage equipment and supplies are the keys to efficient storage and retrieval of information. Multiple options exist for the storage of all forms of records—documents, cards, microforms, and other media. Vendors are constantly upgrading their products in this very competitive and rapidly changing field. Most vendors offer consultative services to assist in the selection of storage equipment and supplies. A basic knowledge of available options is still, however, essential for selection of equipment to meet the needs of the individual organization.

## SELECTION CRITERIA

Selection criteria vary in importance with each organization. Certain criteria are important and should be considered (then eliminated if not appropriate for specific needs) before any purchases are made. Some criteria apply to both equipment and supplies. Because of differences in the way the criterion is applied or in the importance of each criterion, selection criteria for equipment and supplies will be discussed separately.

### Equipment

Equipment selection criteria can be summarized into five categories: (1) storage/retrieval requirements, (2) space requirements, (3) security requirements, (4) equipment costs, and (5) operation costs.

#### Storage/Retrieval Requirements

Determining storage/retrieval requirements involves defining the basic storage needs of the organization. The types of records to be stored—paper, cards, microforms, oversize documents, audiovisual materials, or other media—need to be considered. Equipment may need to be mobile or adaptable to more than one location or function. The storage/retrieval speed required by the organization should also be taken into consideration. The speeds obtainable with various types of manual equipment vary from 100 to 400 pieces per hour; with some automated equipment, a record can be stored or retrieved in three seconds. Faster speeds are usually required for more active records or where a large volume of records must be stored or retrieved.

*Basic storage needs*

*Storage/retrieval speeds*

## Space Requirements

*Floor space ratios*

Office space is an expensive item; therefore, the amount of space required for various types of storage equipment is an important consideration. Compare floor space ratios when evaluating equipment space requirements. Floor space ratios represent the storage capacity per square foot of floor space occupied by the storage equipment. For example, the vertical storage cabinet in Figure 6–1 has a storage capacity of 6 cubic feet (or 100 filing inches) and requires 7 square feet of floor space. The lateral storage cabinet has a storage capacity of 14 cubic feet (168 filing inches) and requires 12.6 square feet of floor space. The vertical cabinet stores 0.86 cubic feet of records per square foot; the lateral cabinet stores 1.1 cubic feet of records per square foot.

Figure 6–1
Space Requirements of Vertical and Lateral Storage Cabinets

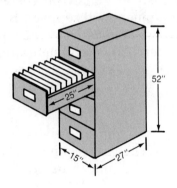 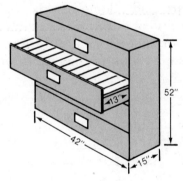

Aisle space required = 15″

Sq. ft. = 25″ + 27″ + 15″ = 67″ (5.6 ft.)
x 15″ (1.25 ft.) = 7.0 sq. ft.

Aisle space required = 15″

Sq. ft. = 13″ + 15″ + 15″ = 43″ (3.6 ft.)
x 42″ (3.5 ft.) = 12.6 sq. ft.

## Security Requirements

Security requirements will vary within an organization. Some records may be accessed by all employees; others, such as personnel records protected by the Freedom of Information and Privacy Act, must have very limited access. Storage equipment may have no security features (open shelves) or may have various security features, such as locks or security codes, for access. Because of the higher cost, secure equipment should not be purchased except as needed.

## Equipment Costs

For most organizations, cost should not be the overriding factor in the equipment selection process. All types of equipment which meet the first three selection criteria and are available from local vendors should first be identified. Then the costs of these types of equipment should be compared. Item costs should be adjusted so that equal volumes of storage space are being compared in price. For example, if one four-drawer cabinet with a lock costs $285 and a five-drawer cabinet with a lock costs $365, the five-drawer cabinet which costs 22 percent more is actually less expensive because it provides 25 percent more storage capacity in the same floor space. *Storage capacity* Storage capacity may be measured in cubic feet (1.5 cubic feet per letter-size drawer or 2.0 cubic feet per legal-size drawer) or in linear filing inches (using a tape measure to determine actual storage inches available). Storage capacity is most often measured in cubic feet for inactive records and linear filing inches for active records. The calculations for the storage capacity of a vertical storage cabinet drawer are illustrated in Figure 6–2.

## Operation Costs

Operation costs include the costs of personnel to store and retrieve information, the cost of compatible supplies, and the cost of the space required to house the equipment. Personnel costs will be determined by the volume of records, the frequency of requests for materials or information, and the storage/retrieval speed of the *Personnel, supplies, additional space*

Figure 6–2
Storage Capacity of a Letter-Size Vertical Storage Cabinet Drawer

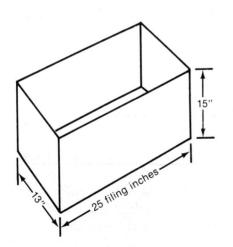

Height of stored documents:     9.0"
Width of stored documents:     11.5"
Length of stored documents:    25.0"
Volume of records drawer:

9.0" x 11.5" x 25.0" = 2587.5"
÷ 1728" = 1.5 cu. ft.

equipment. The cost of compatible supplies may be a very important consideration if the equipment vendor is the sole source of these supplies. If the equipment is adaptable to standard sizes of supplies, cost of supplies becomes a much less important consideration. It is, however, important to determine whether special supplies are required before equipment is purchased. If additional space must be purchased or leased to accommodate additional equipment, this cost is considered to be an operational cost. Because of such additional costs, space requirements are a priority consideration in equipment selection.

# Supplies

There are four selection criteria for supplies. These are (1) equipment compatibility, (2) efficiency, (3) quality, and (4) economy.

## Equipment Compatibility

*Supplies selection criteria*

Supplies such as guides and folders must be compatible with the equipment purchased. For example, open-shelf files require guides and folders with side tabs rather than top tabs; visible index or other card files may accommodate cards of only one size. Any such restrictions should be considered before the equipment is purchased in order to avoid higher operating costs. The individual responsible for purchasing supplies must be aware of any restrictions to avoid stocking quantities of unusable supplies or work slowdowns because needed supplies are not in stock.

## Efficiency

Manufacturers are conscious of increasing storage and retrieval efficiency through special features of their supplies. For example, preprinted folders are available for alphabetic, numeric, and alphanumeric classification systems. These folders are especially helpful when an organization or department establishes its records system or converts to a new type of storage equipment. The use of color coding (discussed later in this chapter) also contributes to the efficiency of a records system through rapid identification of records locations and misplaced records.

## Quality

Quality of supplies may be determined by weight or type of materials used in construction. File guides need to be of heavier material than file folders because of their more frequent use and greater length of time within the drawer or on the shelf. Selection should be based on the quality necessary to do the job economically.

**Economy**

Minimizing costs is a consideration in most of an organization's operations. Buying a lesser grade of material for file guides or folders (which will be in active use for long periods of time) often results in costly replacement purchases. Savings can often be realized through quantity supplies purchases. First, purchase small lots of supplies from a vendor to determine the quality of supplies and the ability of the vendor to provide needed sizes and weights. If the initial purchase is satisfactory, then larger quantities should be considered for frequently used items or for supplies with long shelf lives.

## A LOOK AT THE CASE

Carl Stone considered the appropriate criteria for the selection of storage equipment and supplies. His primary concerns with regard to equipment were storage/retrieval speed, space requirements, security requirements of the records to be stored, equipment costs, and operation costs. Carl determined that the appropriate selection criteria for supplies were equipment compatibility, their contribution to the efficiency of storing and retrieving records, quality of supplies, and economy.

1. What are the storage equipment options?
2. How should these criteria be applied to Central's storage equipment purchases?

## EQUIPMENT

Storage equipment may be classified as manual, mechanical, or automated. Equipment options will be presented for all forms of records: documents (records in paper form), cards, microforms, magnetic media, audiovisual records, publications, and maps and engineering drawings.

*Equipment selection criteria*

### Manual

Manual storage equipment provides a stationary storage space for records; the records user must go to the files to store or retrieve records. Types of manual storage equipment described in this section are (1) conventional (vertical) cabinets, (2) shelf files, (3) lateral files, (4) unit box lateral files, (5) card files, (6) microrecord files, and (7) other media files.

### Conventional (Vertical) Cabinets

Conventional storage cabinets are available in one- to five-drawer sizes. One-drawer units may be on casters to provide mobility. Two-drawer cabinets are often used at desk side so that the user can remain seated. Three-drawer units are frequently used as counter areas and may have a simulated wood top to provide attractive working space. The four-drawer cabinet has traditionally been the most frequently used piece of equipment for document storage; however, the five-drawer unit is gaining in popularity because of the 25 percent increase in storage capacity in the same floor space. Typical storage/retrieval speeds achieved in conventional drawer equipment range from 100 to 200 items per hour.

### Shelf Files

Shelf units are usually 36 inches wide (width may vary from 32 to 42 inches) and may be from two to eight tiers high. Although many shelf files are open, both large and small units are available with roll-back fronts. Documents are stored in folders which are placed on shelves in the same manner as in drawer files (bottom edge of the folder down). However, guides and folders with side tabs are necessary for proper identification. Because there are no drawers to open or close, storage/retrieval speeds are much faster with shelf files. Typical storage/retrieval speeds range from 150 to 350 items per hour.

### Lateral Files

With lateral files, documents are filed from the side rather than from the top. The most frequently used type of lateral file is the roll-out cabinet. Lateral file cabinets are similar to conventional cabinets except that lateral drawers are wider and not as deep. Because of this construction, less aisle space is consumed by the open lateral drawer—about 13 inches compared to 25 inches for the vertical drawer cabinet. Lateral files are available in two to five-drawer sizes. Frequently the upper tiers of a large lateral unit are used for less active records prior to their transfer to the records center. Normal storage/retrieval speeds with this type of equipment are from 150 to 250 items per hour.

## Unit Box Lateral Files

**Unit box lateral files** utilize specially designed boxes to hold file folders. The boxes hang from rails which are affixed to heavy posts along the shelves. Each box holds about four inches of material and hangs at a slight angle. (See Figure 6–3). The slant of the boxes provides fast reference and usually eliminates the need to completely remove a folder from the box before storing or retrieving information. Typical storage/retrieval speeds using unit box lateral files range from 200 to 400 items per hour.

Figure 6–3
Unit Box Lateral Files

## Card Files

Card files are used in many organizations to provide (1) quick reference to frequently used information; (2) an index of specific items or of other files; and (3) a record of activities (such as accounts receivable payments and charges). Cards used in card files are usually one of three types: (1) index cards (5 by 3, 6 by 4, or 8 by 5 inches); (2) aperture cards ($7\frac{3}{8}$ by $3\frac{1}{4}$ inches); and (3) ledger cards ($5\frac{1}{2}$ by $8\frac{1}{2}$ inches) used to record accounts receivable and accounts payable activities. *Types of cards*

   Special types of manual storage equipment are available for cards. These types of equipment include cabinets with drawers of special heights (sometimes partitioned to store two rows of cards per drawer), boxes, trays, and card visible cabinets which allow one edge of each card to be viewed to identify the information found on the card. (See Figure 6–4.)

Figure 6–4
Card Visible Cabinet

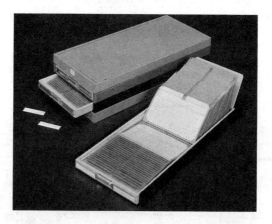

## Microrecord Files

*Microform storage*

Microforms are frequently stored in cabinets similar to conventional vertical cabinets, although the drawers are not as deep. With the use of drawer dividers, the same cabinet can be used to house microfiche, aperture cards, or microfilm. (See Figure 6–5.) These cabinets are constructed of various materials and may contain from four to eleven drawers.

Figure 6–5
Microforms Storage

Trays constructed in various sizes and of materials ranging from high-impact plastic to metal are also used to store microrecords. Most trays have optional protective covers. Frequently fiche trays are stored in specially designed cabinets which may be modular, mobile, or permanent units. (See Figure 6–6.)

Microfiche are also stored in ring binders with loose-leaf pages; each of these pages will house from four to ten microfiche. Many of these are easel binders, which stand on the desk for easy use.

Figure 6–6
Microfiche Tray

## Center Hook Files

Increased use of information stored on multi-media has increased the need for equipment which allows information which is used together to be stored together. Center hook filing equipment allows printouts, microfiche, diskettes, magnetic tapes, letter- and legal-size papers, and audio-visual media to be hung on hanger bars. (See Figure 6–7.)

*Multi-media storage*

Center hook filing can be installed in shelf units or on walls over workstations for easy access and efficient space utilization. The media filed are housed in binders, folders, or containers that provide space for labeling contents.

## Other Media Files

Many organizations also need to store and retrieve information from other media, such as audiovisual media, magnetic media, maps/engineering drawings, and publications. Each of these media types has some special storage requirements.

Figure 6–7
Center Hook Filing Equipment

*Audiovisual media*

Films, filmstrips, tape recordings, records, and optical disks may be housed in cabinets similar to those used for roll microfilm stored in cartridges. Canisters of film are usually stored on open shelves; filmstrips and tape recordings are usually stored in cabinets. Records and optical disks are placed in protective envelopes and then stored in boxes or trays.

*Magnetic media*

Floppy disks and diskettes used in word processing applications, and computer tape reels, cartridges, and disks must be protected from dust. Floppy disks are placed in protective pockets to minimize dangers from handling or environmental factors. These pockets may then be stored in boxes, albums, or binders. (See Figure 6–8.) Computer tapes may be stored in lateral files or in open-shelf files which use canister racks or hanging racks. (See Figure 6–9.)

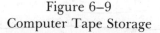

| Figure 6–8 | Figure 6–9 |
| --- | --- |
| Floppy Disk Storage | Computer Tape Storage |

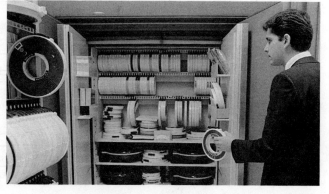

Maps and engineering drawings present unique storage requirements because of their large size. These media may be stored flat in specially designed cabinets (see Figure 6–10), roll stored in either vertical or horizontal units (see Figure 6–11), or placed in hanging files (see Figure 6–12). Documents in flat or roll files are usually numbered and indexed by location for easy reference. Oversize documents in hanging files may be identified by a clip attached to the rod; these documents should also be indexed for efficient access.

*Maps/ engineering drawings*

Figure 6–10
Maps/Engineering Drawings Storage

Figure 6–11
Roll Unit

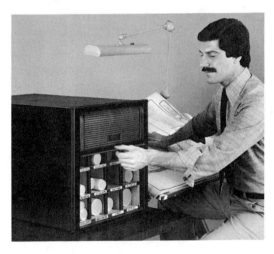

Figure 6–12
Hanging File

*Publications*          Publications include all types of printed matter prepared for distribution; however, periodicals present unique storage requirements. Periodicals require open, slanted shelves or literature racks (see Figure 6–13) for the display of current issues, and open shelves or unit boxes are used to display past issues until they are bound. Books and bound copies of periodicals may be stored on open shelves.

Figure 6–13
Periodicals Displayers

## Mechanical

Mechanical storage equipment is equipment which moves to speed access to records. Most mechanical storage equipment saves space and reduces storage/retrieval time. Types of mechanical storage equipment described in this section are (1) mobile aisle systems, (2) rotary files, (3) power elevator lateral equipment, and (4) conveyor systems.

### Mobile Aisle Systems

*Saves aisle space*

**Mobile aisle systems** are space-conserving cabinets of shelves or trays which move on track (either manually or electrically) to create aisles for accessing records. (See Figure 6–14.) Much of the space in central records locations has traditionally been consumed by the aisles which provide access to conventional cabinets or shelves. Rapidly increasing lease/purchase costs for office space have caused many organizations to seek ways to eliminate the unproductive space consumed by aisles.

Figure 6–14
Mobile Aisle Storage

Mobile aisle systems offer a storage alternative which can increase the storage capacity of existing space 100 percent or more or can accommodate existing records in 50 percent or less of the space required for conventional cabinets. The floor space required to house comparable filing inches of records in conventional vertical cabinets, static shelves, and a mobile aisle system are compared in Figure 6–15. The reduced floor space requirement and the subsequent reduction in cost of floor space for records storage significantly reduce records system operating costs.

Figure 6–15
Floor Space Savings with Mobile Aisle Storage

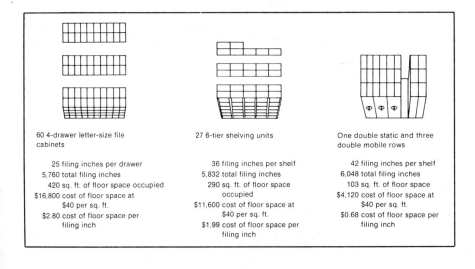

| 60 4-drawer letter-size file cabinets | 27 6-tier shelving units | One double static and three double mobile rows |
|---|---|---|
| 25 filing inches per drawer | 36 filing inches per shelf | 42 filing inches per shelf |
| 5,760 total filing inches | 5,832 total filing inches | 6,048 total filing inches |
| 420 sq. ft. of floor space occupied | 290 sq. ft. of floor space occupied | 103 sq. ft. of floor space |
| $16,800 cost of floor space at $40 per sq. ft. | $11,600 cost of floor space at $40 per sq. ft. | $4,120 cost of floor space at $40 per sq. ft. |
| $2.80 cost of floor space per filing inch | $1.99 cost of floor space per filing inch | $0.68 cost of floor space per filing inch |

### Rotary Files

Rotary files are circular single- or multiple-tier units in which each tier turns individually for rapid storage and retrieval of records. Rotary files allow multiple access to stored materials and provide efficient use of storage space. Rotary files are used to house documents, cards, and microforms. One multiple-tier unit designed to house several types of media is shown in Figure 6–16.

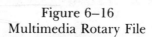

Figure 6–16
Multimedia Rotary File

### Power Elevator Lateral Files

*Shelf comes to records clerk*

**Power elevator lateral files** are multiple-tier units which utilize a Ferris wheel approach to electrically bring the desired shelf to the user when needed. The shelves may be constructed to employ the sideways position of files used in other lateral storage equipment; however, the conventional forward position is also widely used. Power elevator lateral files may house documents, cards, or microforms.

A primary feature of this equipment is improved efficiency in storing and retrieving documents or other media because the shelf or drawer comes to the user as needed. (See Figure 6–17.) Many systems have a numeric keypad for directing the appropriate shelf to the access position. The operator may perform all filing functions from a seated position; this eliminates time lost in walking from the desk to the files and back.

Figure 6–17
Power Elevator Lateral File

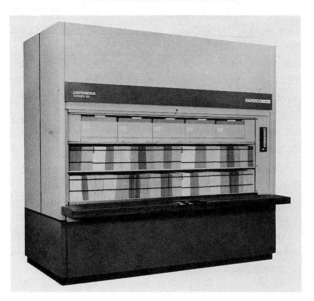

## Conveyor Systems

Conveyor systems are mechanical storage systems which, like power elevator lateral files, bring the desired folder to the user in response to dialing or keying in the folder number. A conveyor system is similar to the conveyor system found in many dry cleaning businesses where an attendant pushes a button and a rack of clothes turns to the desired location. Similarly, the records user pushes a button and a rack of records moves around to the desired location for access.

*Folder comes to user*

## Automated

Automated records storage systems provide computer-assisted file controls, storage, and retrieval. Types of automated records storage equipment discussed in this section are (1) document tracking systems, (2) microforms storage/retrieval systems, and (3) magnetic storage systems.

### Document Tracking Systems

A **document tracking system** is a computerized system which tracks the location of file folders as they move between departments or individuals. Document tracking systems represent a marriage of microprocessing equipment and color-coded storage.

These systems have an expandable database with disk memory. Essential data in each active and inactive folder stored in a central location are recorded in memory. This enables the system to track folders as they leave storage or are passed from person to person.

*Machine-readable codes*

Document tracking systems identify folders through their machine-readable color codes. Numeric systems are bar coded for identification; alphabetic systems have labels printed using an OCR (Optical Character Recognition) typeface. A typical file control station consists of a CRT (cathode ray tube) terminal, a wand for reading OCR or a wand and a laser scanner for reading bar codes, and an optional printer for printing copies of information from the files.

In addition to the file control station in the central storage area, similar units may also be placed in major departments or divisions of the organization. These additional control stations allow for the tracking of folders as they move from person to person within the office. (See Figure 6–18.)

Figure 6–18
Document Tracking System

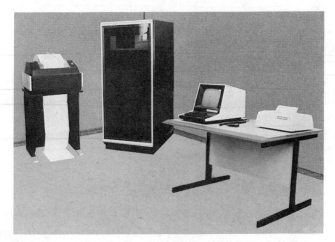

## Microforms Storage/Retrieval Systems

Automated microforms storage/retrieval systems provide computer-assisted file controls, storage, and retrieval. This equipment may be a manual filing system with an online computer index. It may also be a fully automated system which produces COM (computer output microfilm or microfiche), which is coded for computer-assisted retrieval in addition to a contents index (which may be online or stored on disks). The contents index may be based on key words, or it may be a numeric index in-which part of the number refers to the type of document to be retrieved.

Microforms retrieval systems rely on the logic of a computer or microprocessor. In addition to the logic system, such a system usually contains a selector keyboard (which the operator uses to direct the functioning of the equipment and to indicate the particular document or frame to be viewed), a viewing system, and a mechanism for printing a copy of the document, if needed. (See Figure 6–19.)

*Computer logic*

Figure 6–19
Automated Microforms Retrieval System

## Magnetic Storage Systems

Magnetic tape systems employ a scanning and storing technology in which documents are digitized (converted into binary code) and stored on magnetic tape or tape cartridges and retrieved as needed in paper copy or on a CRT screen. Each document is indexed as it enters the system so that it may be accessed as needed. Magnetic tape systems provide speedy access, eliminate charge-outs, update rapidly, require less space, and increase file security. Viewing documents in a magnetic tape system is essentially the same as viewing microfilm.

## Laser-Optic™ Filing Systems

Optical disk systems were first developed in the late 1920s, but they had very limited storage capacity. In recent years the storage , capacity of optical disks has increased to the point (54,000 frames/ documents per disk) that manufacturers are developing extensive storage and retrieval applications.

One of the most recent developments is Tab Products' Laser-Optic™ Filing System. This system (using a document feeder) can read 50 pages and file them on an optical disk in less than five minutes. (See Figure 6–20.) Paper records are scanned by a semiconductor laser and stored on a Tellurium Selenium photoelectric disk. The fidelity and accuracy of this process is such that users can retrieve copies which are as clear as the original documents.

The Laser-Optic™ system can retrieve documents at the rate of a page per second. Documents may be viewed on the screen, paper copies may be reproduced by a laser printer, or an optional facsimile function is available to send copies electronically to other locations. As many as eight workstations located up to a mile away from the base unit can be accommodated, permitting a great deal of flexibility in system uses.

■

## A LOOK AT THE CASE

Carl Stone examined manual, mechanical, and automated storage equipment options and evaluated each option on its speed of operation, space requirements, ability to provide required records security, cost, and operation cost. After the evaluation, Carl recommended the following:

1. Sales records, such as purchase orders and invoices, which continue to be maintained in paper form could be more efficiently accessed and more economically housed in open shelves.
2. Special microfiche cabinets should be purchased.
3. The customer card file should continue to be maintained.
4. Equipment utilization should be reviewed biannually.

Carl is now ready to evaluate the supplies used in Central's records program.

1. What are the supplies options?
2. What supplies will be necessary to implement the recommended equipment purchases?

■

Figure 6–20
Tab Products' Laser-Optic™ Filing System

## SUPPLIES

**Supplies** are consumable items which assist in storing and retrieving records. Supplies used in document storage include guides, folders, labels, and binders. The use of color-coding supplies has gained wide acceptance because it leads to greater efficiency in document storage and retrieval.

*Supplies are consumable*

## Guides

**Guides** are used for separating records into sections to facilitate storage and retrieval and for supporting folders by keeping them upright in a cabinet or on a shelf. A **tab** projecting from the top or side edge of the guide provides for easy identification of file sections or of special folders. Although other tab cuts are available, guide tabs are usually one-third or one-fifth cut. (Tabs may also be purchased separately and attached to hanging folders.) Type and weight of the paper stock are the important qualities to consider in selecting and purchasing guides. Guides may be constructed from fiber, pressboard, manila, bristol board, plastic, light metal, and mylar (used for punched tab card files). The weight of a guide describes the thickness of the material and is expressed in points (one point equals 1/1,000 of an inch). File guides made of 25-point pressboard are more commonly used.

## Folders

**Folders** are containers for documents within the storage equipment. Folders used in drawer files will have tabs in the top position; folders used in shelf files will have tabs on the side. Tab cuts may be full, half, third, or fifth. (See Figure 6–21.) Manila is most frequently used in the construction of folders; however, pressboard, kraft (comparable in quality to manila but darker in color), and red rope or fiber (made from sulphite with a tough jute and hemp) may also be used. Scoring lines near the bottom edge allow for expansion as additional documents accumulate in the folder.

Figure 6–21
Top and Side Tab Folders

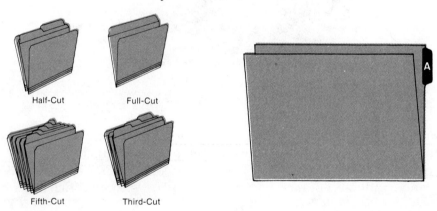

Half-Cut    Full-Cut

Fifth-Cut    Third-Cut

Folders are also available in three special styles: bellows folded, pocket, and hanging or suspension. Bellows-folded folders are designed to flatten out on the bottom to make a more solid base as the papers accumulate and the folder expands. Pocket folders have bellows folds on the sides as well as bottom edges to allow for expansion. Hanging or suspension folders are made of heavy-weight but flexible materials designed to house several folders and to hang from suspension rods. (See Figure 6–22.)

## Labels

**Labels** are used to identify the contents of folders, drawers, shelves, binders, trays, and boxes. Labels are available in sheets, rolls, and pads. Color labels or labels with color stripes may be used to code a records system.

Figure 6–22
Special File Folder Styles

a. Bellows folded                    b. Pocket                    c. Hanging/Suspension

## Binders

Binders are available to house records in a variety of media—printed documents, cassettes, floppy disks, microfiche, microfilm jackets, and computer printouts. Binders are available in familiar ring types or post types (most often used with accounting records).

## Color-Coding Supplies

Color coding has gained wide acceptance for improving efficiency for records storage and retrieval and aiding in the identification of misfiles. Color may be added to the system through color file folders, color labels, color bars or bands on labels or folders, color OUT cards, or color signals.

*Uses of color coding*

The substitution of color file folders for manila folders is particularly useful in designating files by date or identifying specific departments or functions. For example, red folders might identify the finance department, blue folders the human resource department, green folders the planning department, and so forth. Color folders are not limited to these applications, however.

Color labels may have a stripe across the top edge or be all of one color. Solid colors are usually fairly light in tint to allow printed information to be readable.

Color bars or bands are placed uniformly on folders. A misplaced folder labeled with a color bar or band is quite evident with even a cursory inspection.

Color OUT cards are vivid reminders that a file has been borrowed and not returned. These cards may also be used to denote day, week, or month of the out-of-file material.

Color signals are usually plastic clip ons or pressure sensitive signals. These signals are attached to records that require special attention.

In alphabetic systems, color coding is assigned to the first and second letters of the surname. The second letter is coded because that is where most misfiles occur. Most color-coded alphabetic systems use between 10 and 13 colors.

In numeric systems, color may be used to speed storage and retrieval by using ten colors to represent the 0 to 9 digits. By adding color labels (which represent the digits in a numeric file), a band of color is produced throughout the storage system. When a folder is out of place, this band will be interrupted with a different color, which will easily identify the misfiled folder.

Color coding is equally as effective in enhancing alphanumeric systems. In this type of arrangement, letters are assigned a numeric value and each number, or both letter and numeral, is color coded. Figure 6–23 illustrates alphanumeric color coding.

Using color to aid storage and retrieval speed and efficiency is not limited to paper copy. Color may be used for all types of record media. Microfilm rolls, jackets, magnetic tapes, and disks can be color coded. (See Figure 6–9.) Color coding is available for nearly all styles and types of records.

Figure 6–23
Color Coding with Alphanumeric Arrangement

## A LOOK AT THE CASE

Carl Stone reviewed various types of supplies available for use in Central's records program. After evaluating the compatibility, efficiency, quality, and economy of each option, Carl made the following recommendations:

1. Pressboard guides and manila folders with side tabs should be purchased for use with the open-shelf equipment.
2. Pressboard guides should be purchased for the microfiche cabinets.
3. Color labels should be applied to the folders used on the open shelves, and efficiency and accuracy of storing/retrieving records should be studied to determine if other color label applications should be developed.

## TERMINOLOGY REVIEW

*Document tracking system.* A computerized system which tracks the location of file folders as they move between departments or individuals.

*Folders.* Containers for documents within the storage system.

*Guides.* Items used for separating records into sections to facilitate storage and retrieval and for supporting folders by keeping them upright in a cabinet or on a shelf.

*Labels.* Items used to identify the contents of folders, drawers, shelves, binders, trays, and boxes.

*Mobile aisle systems.* Space-conserving cabinets of shelves or trays which move on track (either manually or electrically) to create aisles for accessing records.

*Power elevator lateral files.* Multiple-tier units which utilize a Ferris wheel approach to electrically bring the desired shelf to the user when needed.

*Supplies.* Consumable items which assist in storing and retrieving records.

*Tab.* A projection from the top or side of a guide or folder used to identify the contents.

*Unit box lateral files.* A shelf filing system which uses specially designed boxes which hang from rails to hold file folders.

## COMPETENCY REVIEW

1. List four selection criteria for storage equipment and explain how each affects the purchasing decision.
2. State three selection criteria for supplies and explain how each affects the purchasing decision.
3. Define and give at least two examples of manual, mechanical, and automated document storage equipment.
4. Describe two storage equipment options for each of the following:
   a. audiovisual materials
   b. magnetic media
   c. maps/engineering drawings
   d. publications
5. Explain the purpose of guides, folders, labels, and binders in a document storage system.
6. How does the use of color coding increase storage/retrieval efficiency? Describe two methods for using color.
7. Describe the use of color coding in alphabetic, numeric, and alphanumeric classification systems.

## APPLICATIONS

1. Divide the class into at least four groups. Have a two- to four-page written summary of one of the following topics prepared by each group: manual storage equipment, mechanical storage equipment, automated storage equipment, or records storage supplies. Each summary should be accompanied by several brochures and cost data. On the assignment due date, each group should be prepared to make a three- to five-minute oral report summarizing its findings.
2. Compare the cost of floor space to store 4,536 filing inches of paper documents in (a) four-drawer letter-size file cabinets, (b) six-tier shelving units, and (c) six-tier double mobile rows. The cost of floor space is $45.00 per square foot. (The information in Figure 6–15 may be helpful.)

## CONCLUDING CASES

### A. Stafford Academy

Stafford Academy's enrollment for the current school year is 5,250 students. Enrollment has been steadily increasing during 15 years of operation.

Student records are maintained in 60 four-drawer vertical files in the registrar's office. The registrar is concerned about the volume of records and the slow retrieval of information from student files. There is no space to add additional storage cabinets, and the demand for retrieval of information is increasing. Dr. Brenton, Stafford's president, ordered a freeze on hiring six months ago, and the current staff cannot process requests for information efficiently.

1.  What types of data should the registrar employ to convince Stafford's records manager that new records storage equipment is needed?
2.  What are two options the records manager might be asked to consider? Explain briefly the advantages/disadvantages of each of these options.

## B. Bayview Dental Clinic

Bayview Dental Clinic has maintained patient records by patient number arranged in a terminal digit system since it opened eight years ago. The records are stored on open shelves. Misfiles have become an increasing problem as the numbers of dentists and patients increase.

Pat Franklin, Bayview's records manager, must do something to control the number of misfiles. Her first thought was to hire another records clerk; however, Pat would like to avoid the ongoing cost of additional personnel.

1.  Should Pat consider other equipment options? Explain.
2.  Should Pat consider other supplies options? Explain.

## READINGS AND REFERENCES

Siragusa, Gail. "A Manager's Guide to Document Filing Systems." *Administrative Management,* Vol. XLVI, No. 11 (November, 1985), p. 26.

"High Density Mobile Files: A Place for Everything." *Today's Office,* Vol. 20, No. 6 (September, 1985).

# 7
# MICROGRAPHICS

## Competencies

After completing this chapter, you should be able to

1. define microforms, microrecords, and micrographics.
2. state the advantages and limitations of using microrecords.
3. list the steps in conducting a feasibility study for the conversion of paper records to microrecords and describe the categories of data which are essential to this study.
4. list and define the types of microforms.
5. describe the preparation of documents for filming.
6. describe standard camera film.
7. define reduction ratio.
8. define the modes of microfilm image orientation.
9. describe the types of microform cameras and list an application of each type.
10. describe the types of microfilm coding.
11. describe the types of film processors.
12. explain reversal processing and state the most frequent reason for its use.
13. list the factors which affect film development and explain how these factors may be controlled by the operator.
14. state the need for inspection of microforms and explain the inspection techniques.
15. define the types of film used in duplicating microforms.
16. explain the importance of readers and reader printers to the use of microrecords.
17. outline the contents of a report to management on the results of a feasibility study of a conversion to microrecords.

# Introductory Case

Nationwide Auto Wholesalers, Inc., is a national distributor of auto parts. For product distribution, the country has been divided into ten regions. Each month, Nationwide prepares computer-generated reports of sales by region and product group. Currently, this information is being keyboarded into the computer daily.

Bernard Seay, Nationwide's records and information manager, has been asked by Maria Rodriguez, executive vice president, to explore ways in which the use of microforms might improve Nationwide's sales records and the reporting of sales data.

1. What are the advantages and limitations of microrecords?
2. What types of information should be gathered in determining the feasibility of a microrecords application?

Demand for rapid storage and retrieval speeds and spiraling costs of storage space have resulted in microforms becoming an increasingly popular media for storing records. A **microform** is any medium which contains miniature or "micro" images. The records stored on microforms are often called **microrecords. Micrographics** is the term which refers to the procedures for creating, using, and storing microrecords.

## FEASIBILITY OF MICRORECORDS APPLICATIONS

The decision to use microrecords must be based on an organization's specific needs and records applications. Consideration of a new microrecords application usually arises from a specific records problem, such as limited storage space or the need for faster storage and retrieval speeds. When a conversion to microrecords seems to be an appropriate solution to a records problem, the organization must examine the advantages and limitations of using microrecords and complete a feasibility study to determine whether the benefits outweigh the costs of such a conversion.

### Advantages and Limitations

As with every records management tool, the use of microrecords has both advantages and limitations. Each of these should be weighed carefully in evaluating the potential benefits of using microrecords within an organization.

**Advantages**

The most obvious advantage of using microrecords is the floor space saved for uses other than for records storage. Records reduced to microimages may require as little as two percent of the storage space the original records required. The reduction in records size also requires fewer storage cabinets which will produce savings in storage equipment and supplies purchased.

Microrecords improve file integrity; individual film images cannot be separated or misplaced as sheets of paper might be. This advantage increases in significance as the number of pieces of paper per file increases.

As the demand for up-to-date information increases, improved productivity resulting from the use of microrecords becomes more important. Information stored as microimages can often be retrieved in a few seconds from an automated file system.

No longer is valuable time wasted in walking to the file room while customers or managers wait for a response.

Storing records in microform is an excellent means of protecting vital and archival records. The original microfilm can be stored offsite while copies are stored in the office. The low cost of making diazo duplicates and of mailing duplicate microrecords also enhances the practicality of their use. In addition, producing paper copies of microimages when required is easy. Microrecords are (in most cases) admissible as primary evidence in court, also.

**Limitations**

One major limitation of using microrecords continues to be that microimages are unfamiliar to many users. Users' familiarity with microrecords is increasing; however, users need to be trained in the use of readers and reader printers and in how to locate the desired image. Providing readers and training users are additional costs in converting to the use of microrecords. The floor space required and the energy used by readers add additional costs.

Microrecords use is also limited by the turnaround time needed to produce microimages. During preparation and filming, the original records are inaccessible. Further, the inability to annotate or change information on microrecords makes the production of microrecords impractical for "high activity" records (any record that is modified frequently).

## Considerations in a Microrecords Feasibility Study

The feasibility study describes the current and proposed systems and compares the costs of storing and retrieving records in these systems. The feasibility study may compare the costs of several alternative solutions to the records problem. A form for collecting comparative data must be designed to meet the needs of the organization. A request for micrographic services form is shown in Figure 7–1. Regardless of the form, a thorough examination of the records to be converted, the equipment needed, the supplies required, and the labor costs is essential.

**Records**

The feasibility study should begin with information about the record series in which the problem exists. It should answer questions such as the following:

1. Who uses the records?
2. How are the records used?

Figure 7–1
Request for Micrographic Services Form

| Amtrak ⟩⟩ | **REQUEST FOR MICROGRAPHIC SERVICES** | |
|---|---|---|
| | **1. DATE** | |
| **NOTE: ONE REQUEST PER RECORD SERIES** | | |
| **2. REQUESTOR/TITLE** | **3. PHONE** | |
| **4. DEPARTMENT** | **5. LOCATION** | |
| **6. REC. MGMT. APPROVED RETENTION SCHEDULE PERIOD**  □ NONE ASSIGNED | **7. REC. MGMT. APPROVED CORPORATE FILE CLASSIFICATION NUMBER(S)**  □ NONE ASSIGNED | |
| **8. RECORD SERIES TITLE   AND DATES** | | |
| **9. CURRENT STORAGE LOCATION**  □ OFFICE  □ WAREHOUSE  □ RECORDS CENTER  □ LIBRARY  □ OTHER ____ | | |

**10. PRESENT FILING EQUIPMENT USED**

| | **GUIDE FOR ESTIMATING CUBIC FEET PER DRAWER** | | | |
|---|---|---|---|---|
| **FILING CABINET** | | | | |
| **VERTICAL** | **FULL** | **¾ FULL** | **½ FULL** | **¼ FULL** |
| LETTER | 1.50 | 1.13 | .75 | .38 |
| LEGAL | 2.00 | 1.50 | 1.00 | .50 |
| **LATERAL   (ALSO OPEN SHELF)** | | | | |
| 30" WIDE | 2.07 | 1.55 | 1.04 | .52 |
| 42" WIDE | 2.89 | 2.17 | 1.45 | .72 |
| **DRAWINGS OR MAPS - 1.00 CU. FT. PER 75 DOCUMENTS** | | | | |

**11. FLOOR SPACE MADE AVAILABLE FOR REUSE**

**12. ESTIMATED RECORD VOLUME** _____ Cubic Feet

**13. PHYSICAL CHARACTERISTICS OF RECORD SERIES [Check all appropriate boxes]**

a. **NO. OF PAPERS PER FILE** □ 0-25 □ 25-50 □ 50-75 □ 75-100 □ Other _____

b. **FORMAT** □ LETTER SIZE □ LEGAL SIZE □ MAGNETIC TAPE □ DRAWINGS □ PHOTOGRAPHS □ OTHER _____

c. **PRINT** □ HANDWRITTEN □ TYPED □ TYPESET □ COMPUTER PRINTOUT

d. **COLOR** □ WHITE □ YELLOW □ PINK □ BLUE □ GREEN □ OTHER _____

e. **REPRODUCTION** □ ORIGINAL □ COPY □ FACSIMILE TRANSMISSION □ OTHER _____
    □ PRINTING ON ONE SIDE □ PERCENTAGE OF PRINTING ON TWO SIDES _____ %

f. **INK** □ BLACK □ COLOR _____

g. **PAPER FASTENERS** □ STAPLES □ CLIPS □ PASTE □ OTHER _____

**14. FILE INDEX**
    □ CHRONOLOGIC □ ALPHABETIC □ NUMERIC □ ALPHANUMERIC □ BATCH □ MULTIPLE □ OTHER _____

**15. CURRENT FILE REFERENCE RATE PER DAY, WEEK, MONTH OR YEAR**
    □ NONE    NO. OF TIMES _____ PER _____

**16. FREQUENCY OF REFERENCE GREATEST** □ DOES NOT VARY
    1st □ 30 DAYS □ 60 DAYS □ 90 DAYS □ 6 MONTHS □ 1 YEAR □ OTHER _____

**17. DISTRIBUTION OF FILE INFORMATION**
    □ NONE  **METHOD:** □ ORIGINAL □ COPY TO □ OTHER DEPT(S) _____

**18. COPY OF DOCUMENT MADE UPON RETRIEVAL**
    □ NEVER □ 25% □ 50% □ 75% □ 100% □ OTHER _____

**19. FREQUENCY OF FILING ADDITIONS TO FILE [PER HOUR, DAY, WEEK OR MONTH]**
    □ NONE    NO. OF TIMES _____ PER _____

**20. FREQUENCY OF ALTERATIONS TO RECORD AFTER FILING [PER DAY, WEEK, MONTH OR YEAR]**
    □ NONE    NO. OF TIMES _____ PER _____

**21. FREQUENCY OF PURGING UNNECESSARY DOCUMENTS [PER DAY, WEEK, MONTH OR YEAR]**
    □ NONE    NO. OF TIMES _____ PER _____

**22. FILE CROSS-REFERENCED TO PROVIDE MULTIPLE ACCESS POINTS** □ YES □ NO
    IF YES — REFERENCED BY □ NAME □ SERIAL NO. □ SUBJECT □ OTHER _____

| **23. □ DISAPPROVED** | **24. □ APPROVED** | **25. SIGNATURE** |
|---|---|---|
| | | _____  _____ |
| | | MANAGER RECORDS MANAGEMENT        DATE |

NRPC - 1916

**ORIGINATOR RETAIN PINK COPY**

*Note:* The name "Amtrak" and the accompanying arrow design are both registered service marks of the National Railroad Passenger Corporation.

*Source:* Journal of Micrographics, *(October, 1982), p. 51.*

3. Where are the records located?
4. Where are the users located?
5. How many records per day are out of file when requested?
6. What are the size, condition, and color of the documents?
7. What are the nature and frequency of additions, deletions, and changes to these records?
8. How long are the records scheduled for retention?
9. How many pages per average document? Is any information placed on the back of the document?
10. How many documents are sorted, stored, or retrieved per day?
11. What indexing system is used?

The answers to questions 1–5 will determine the type of microform which might be considered and the need for multiple copies and viewing stations. The characteristics of the documents and the need to retain and update the information (questions 6–8) will determine the practicality of converting to microrecords. (Short retention periods and frequent need to update information reduce the desirability of this conversion.) This information may also narrow the filming equipment options. Questions 9 and 10 are important in establishing the cost of operating the current system and estimating the operation costs of a microrecords system. In calculating labor costs, consider the varying salaries of records users who perform storage and retrieval activities. The time a manager spends searching for an out-of-file document is more costly than the time a records clerk spends searching for the same document. Identifying the current indexing system (question 11) will assist in establishing current system cost and in determining the design and coding requirements of a microrecords system.

*Practicality of converting to microrecords*

*Establishing cost of current system and microrecords system*

## Equipment

Data on equipment should include the cost of continuing the current system (such as additional storage cabinets or shelves) and the cost of equipment for the conversion to microrecords. In determining the cost of equipment for conversion to a microrecords system, consideration must be given to existing in-house filming capacity. If adequate equipment and personnel are available to perform the filming, coding, processing, inspecting, and duplicating functions or if the image conversion is to be contracted to a service bureau, the equipment consideration may be reduced to the need for special storage equipment and additional readers or reader printers. If the application under consideration will be the first conversion

*Existing filming capacity*

to microrecords or if the existing equipment is being used to capacity, equipment costs must include cameras, processors, inspection equipment, and duplicators in addition to readers, reader printers, and storage equipment. The cost of such equipment should be

*Amortize equipment costs*

amortized over the useful life of the equipment. The cost of equipment also includes the floor space it consumes.

## Supplies

The cost of filming, processing, duplicating, and storage supplies for the microrecords application must be compared to the cost of the supplies necessary to continue existing storage/retrieval procedures. Conversion (onetime) costs must be separated from operating (ongoing) costs of the microrecords system.

## Labor

*Training for technicians and users*

Operating a microrecords system requires specially trained technicians. The additional training cost to prepare these employees must be considered a conversion cost. Subsequent increases in salaries or salaries of additional employees, if any are required, are increased operating costs. In addition, some training should be provided to all microrecord users; this training will also be a conversion cost.

## Cost Comparison

The cost data on records, equipment, supplies, and labor gathered during the feasibility study should be totaled to provide the operating cost of the present records system, the cost of converting to a microrecords system, and the operating cost of a microrecords system. The capital outlay for conversion and the comparative costs are important factors in determining the practicality of a conversion to microrecords.

■

### A LOOK AT THE CASE

Bernard Seay has reviewed the types of information which should be included in a feasibility study. In order to identify an appropriate microform for auto parts inventory records, Bernard feels he should become more familiar with the types of microforms which are available.

What formats are available for microrecords?

■

## MICROFORMS

Seven types of microforms will be discussed in this section. These are (1) roll film, (2) microfiche, (3) jackets, (4) aperture cards, (5) micro-opaques, (6) nonstandard microforms, and (7) computer input microfilm. (See Figure 7–2.)

Figure 7–2
Microforms

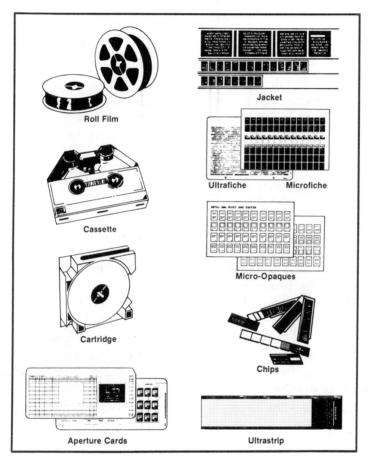

### Roll Film

Roll film may be 16mm, 35mm, or 105mm and may be made from filming source documents or from computer output. Roll film may be stored on an open reel or encased in a cartridge or cassette. Documents such as correspondence, checks, and sales records are filmed on 16mm film; oversize documents such as maps and engineering drawings are filmed on 35mm or 105mm film. Computer

*Computer output microfilm*

output microfilm (COM) is imaged directly from the magnetic computer tape; the electronic impulses on the tape are converted to visual images and stored on the microfilm 10 to 20 times faster than line printing. Some COM recorders allow the film to be imaged without the intermediate step of recording on magnetic tape.

## Microfiche

A **microfiche** is a sheet of film containing multiple miniature images in a grid pattern. Microfiche are available in various sizes; however, the most common size is 6 × 4 inches. This size accommodates 98 document pages per fiche (using a 24x reduction ratio). Fiche which are manually stored and retrieved have an eye-readable header (line containing title information) that identifies the content. Fiche which have very high redution ratios (90x or greater) are referred to as **ultrafiche**. One 6-by-4-inch ultrafiche may contain 4,000 or more pages. The lower right corner frame (or frames) of the grid usually contains an index of either that particular fiche or an entire set of fiche. Microfiche (105mm film) may also be imaged directly from computer tapes or online from electronic impulses producing another form of COM.

## Jackets

A **jacket** is a transparent plastic carrier for strips of microfilm cut from reels. The horizontal area into which the strip of film is placed is called a channel. Jackets may be of several sizes and may contain either 16mm or 35mm film. Individual frames or additional strips of microfilm may be added to the jacket at any time.

Some organizations are now using card jackets. These cards are often preprinted to request specific information (such as for personnel files or bank accounts) and provide channels for one or more strips of microfilm as may be necessary to keep the file current.

## Aperture Cards

An **aperture card** is a $7\frac{3}{8}$ by $3\frac{1}{4}$ inch card into which an opening(s) has been cut to accommodate the insertion of a frame(s) of microfilm. Aperture cards are widely used for a single large item, such as a blueprint or map on 35mm film or multiple images on 16mm film. Indexing information may be punched into the card and printed across the top.

## Micro-Opaques

A **micro-opaque** is a sheet of opaque paper stock containing multiple miniature images in a grid pattern very similar to microfiche. The advantage of using micro-opaques is that each side of the micro-opaque can contain a separate set of images. Micro-opaques are, however, almost impossible to duplicate and require high-intensity illumination for viewing.

## Nonstandard Microforms

Some additional microforms (chips, scrolls, and strips) are in limited use in custom-designed microrecords systems. A **chip** is a piece of film containing a microimage and optical or magnetic coding for automated retrieval. A **scroll** is a roll of extra-wide film (105mm) found in some automated retrieval systems. **Strips** are short lengths of film (105mm) which are containerized and coded for use in an automated retrieval system.

## Computer Input Microfilm

**Computer input microfilm** (CIM) is microfilm containing images which are converted to electronic signals for storage on magnetic tape to be used as input to a computer. CIM has great potential as a low-cost method of rapidly introducing information from large microfilm files (such as medical, insurance, or census data) into a computer for processing.

## A LOOK AT THE CASE

Bernard's review of available microforms was quite helpful. As he examines the cost of converting to and operating a microrecords system, Bernard realizes he must know more about equipment options and the required operating procedures in order to select the best solution for handling Nationwide's parts inventory and accurately determining the cost of the selected system.

1. What equipment options are available for filming, coding, processing, inspecting, duplicating, and reading microforms?
2. What procedures are required in filming, coding, processing, inspecting, and duplicating microforms?

# PROCEDURES AND EQUIPMENT

Each of the steps in producing and using microrecords requires special procedures and equipment. Required procedures and equipment options are discussed in this section.

## Filming

When the records to be filmed have been identified, the documents must be prepared. Then film, image size, image orientation, and type of camera must be selected.

### Document Preparation

Before documents can be filmed, all paper clips and staples must be removed since these will cause camera malfunctions. Torn papers should be mended with transparent tape, and small papers should be attached to standard-size paper by using transparent tape or rubber cement. Unnecessary attachments such as envelopes, routing slips, receipt acknowledgments, or duplicate copies (unless considered a part of the record) should be destroyed. Computer printouts can be processed in batches by using a pin-fed method (pins on a machine fit into the punched holes on the sides of the computer printouts) to feed the printouts onto the camera bed. Forms do not need to be separated for filming.

### Camera Film

*Base side, emulsion side*

Microfilm is either camera film or copy film. (Copy film is discussed in the duplicating section of this chapter.) Microfilm has two distinct sides — a base side and an emulsion side. All microfilm has either an acetate, triacetate, or polyester base material. The emulsion is the coating that captures the image. Standard camera film has a silver halide emulsion and is often called "silver film." This film is specially designed to capture the detail essential to microimages.

### Image Size

*Reduction ratio*

The use of microforms requires reduction of document size to a miniature image on film and the magnification of that image for reading. Image size is usually stated as a reduction ratio. A **reduction ratio** is the size of the film image as compared to the size of the original document. Reduction ratios are expressed as 24x, 30x, or 24:1, 30:1, and so forth. A reduction ratio of 24x, for example, means that the film image is $\frac{1}{24}$th the size of the original document.

## Image Orientation

**Image orientation** is the positioning of images on the film. Single images may be placed across the width of the film in either the cine or comic modes. (See Figure 7–3.) The **cine mode**, which takes its name from cinema film, is achieved by feeding the document into the camera horizontally, with the heading or top of each sheet entering the camera first. The **comic mode** of image orientation, which takes its name from the manner in which frames of a comic strip are presented, is achieved by feeding the document into the camera with the heading to the left or to the right.

Two images may be placed across the width of the film in either the duplex or the duo mode. (See Figure 7–3.) The **duplex mode** is a method of microfilming both sides of the document simultaneously with the images presented side by side. The **duo mode** is a method of microfilming in which images are placed in consecutive order down one half of a strip of film and back the other half. Duo mode filming allows the filming of more documents per roll of film when using high reduction ratios.

Figure 7–3
Modes of Image Orientation

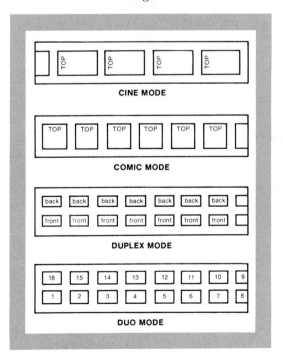

### Types of Cameras

Several types of cameras are used in microfilming source documents. Special filming equipment is required to produce computer output microfilm or microfiche.

A **rotary camera** uses rotating belts to transport documents through the machine and advances the film at the same speed to create the effect of a stationary image. (See Figure 7–4.) A rotary camera is used to film high-volume records (such as checks, invoices, and sales slips) which require fast, efficient, and economical procedures. Filming rates depend upon the skill of the operator and the condition of the documents to be filmed. An experienced operator using an automatic feed can film at the rate of 3,000 documents per hour if the documents are letter size, of uniform thickness, and in good condition.

*High-volume records*

Figure 7–4
Rotary Camera

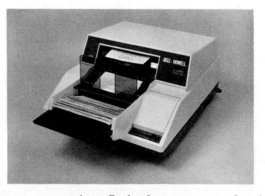

A **planetary camera** is a flatbed camera used primarily to microfilm stationary engineering drawings and other large documents. The document is positioned in the "bed" of the camera. The film unit above the document may be raised or lowered to vary the reduction ratio. Smaller planetary cameras are available for filming smaller documents which are bound, are of varying sizes, or are too brittle to feed through a rotary camera.

*Oversize documents*

A **step and repeat camera** is also a flatbed camera with an overhead film unit. The step and repeat camera is designed to expose images in unifrom rows and columns for preparing microfiche. (See Figure 7–5.) Images are positioned on the microfiche by the programmed movement of the film over a stationary aperture. The film is stationary when the exposure is made.

Figure 7–5
Step and Repeat Camera

The step and repeat camera is used in micropublishing books, catalogs, parts lists, and specifications. A step and repeat camera is particularly appropriate for these applications because of the simplicity of its operation and because it allows the precision alignment necessary to prepare an index of images and to locate a particular frame.

*Micropublishing applications*

An **updatable microfiche camera** is a step and repeat camera which allows additional images to be added to the microfiche at any time (if space for these additional images exists). Bell & Howell has developed such a camera. (See Figure 7–6.) This record processor is a film-based and electrostatic image-fusing system that permits

*Alteration of images*

Figure 7–6
Updatable Microfiche Camera

the alteration of images at any time by adding such words as VOID and PAID with an overprint system. The film may be repositioned and additional images added in any unexposed position(s). The master fiche may be filed in envelopes near the camera. When additions or changes are made, the fiche is repositioned in the camera, imaged, and then refiled. Records users receive duplicates of the original fiche; these duplicates may be discarded after use.

A **COM recorder** is a unit which records electronic data from computer output on microfilm or microfiche. (See Figure 7–7.) Most COM recorders use standard COM film which must be processed outside the recorder in a separate processing unit; however, recorders are available which use dry silver film (which provides instantaneous in-machine processing) or provide in-machine processing using containerized chemistry and washing. COM recorders may be either online or offline units. Online units interface with the host computer; they do not require the intermediate step of computer tape input. Offline units operate only with computer tape input.

Figure 7–7
Offline COM Recorder

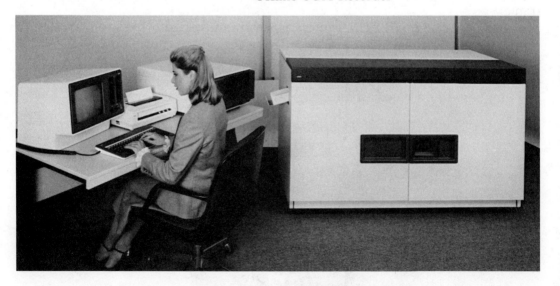

## Coding

During the filming process, microforms may be coded or indexed for automated retrieval. The coding may utilize either (1) flash targets, (2) bar coding, (3) odometer indexing, or (4) blip coding.

## Flash Targets

**Flash targets** are used to divide a roll of film into batches of information. A flash card, which indentifies a batch, may be used as a title page to begin a roll of film, a section of roll film, or a row or channel of a microfiche. Such a target would be positioned to indicate each change in subject matter. When such a coding system is used in producing computer output microfiche, the final frame of the microfiche may contain an index of its contents.

## Bar Coding

Bar coding is another method of coding microforms. **Bar coding** is a pattern of clear and opaque bars between images on roll film. Its appearance is similar to that of the pricing code on many food items. Bar coding requires additional space on the film and a special terminal to advance the film, interpret the code, and stop the film at the desired group of images. The operator must then advance the film frame by frame to the desired image. One simplified version places the code beneath the image on the film.

## Odometer Indexing

**Odometer indexing** indicates the distance of each image from the beginning of the roll of film. Some COM recorders will simultaneously record the odometer index along with the images. Other systems require that processed film pass through a viewer with an odometer to record these index codes. A contents index will usually appear on the first frame of the roll of film.

## Blip Coding

Image-count marking or **blip coding** is accomplished by placing a blip (an opaque, optical rectangle) below each image to identify it. A viewer (with logic) counts blips until it reaches the requested frame. Microforms coding techniques are shown in Figure 7–8.

# Processing

Noncommercial processors available today process film to archival quality standards, do not require darkrooms, and are relatively simple to operate. These processors develop 16mm or 35mm film at a rate of five to ten feet per minute.

## Types of Processors

The three types of processors—deep tank, roller transport, and straight film path—are shown in Figure 7–9. In a deep tank processor, the film is supported by bottom and top rollers and is

*Deep tank processor*

*Roller transport
processor*

*Straight film
path processor*

pulled through the developing chemicals by a lead document moving in a serpentine path. A roller transport processor uses rollers to move the film in a serpentine path through the developer. A straight film path processor uses rollers to move the film in a straight line through the developing solution.

Figure 7–8
Microforms Coding Techniques

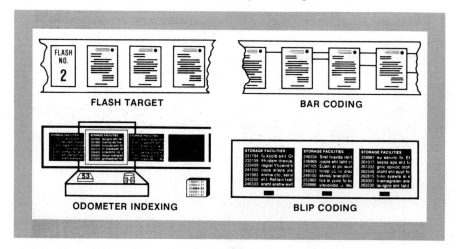

## Reversal Processing

**Reversal processing** is a procedure which changes the polarity of the film. Film has either positive or negative polarity. Film which has **positive polarity** (image) produces black characters on a clear background; film which has **negative polarity** produces clear characters on a black background.

Reversal processing was developed for use in conjunction with COM, which has positive polarity. In a reader, a positive image produces a glare from light passing through the clear background. Positive polarity also magnifies dirt and dust on the film. These traits make the positive image undesirable to many, thus creating a need for reversal processing.

Reversal processing may take either of two forms—full reversal or partial reversal. Full reversal is used when the original will be viewed in the reader. Partial reversal is used when diazo duplicates are made from the original, and the original will not be viewed. Partial reversal eliminates the re-exposure, second developer, and fixer steps required in full reversal processing.

Figure 7–9
Types of Processors

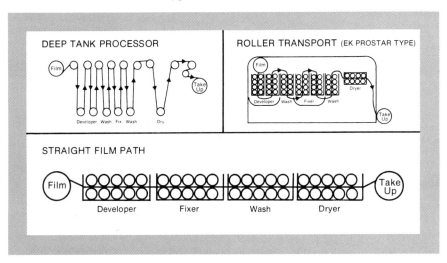

## Developing

The four factors affecting film development are (1) the temperature of the developer, (2) the length of time the film is in the solution, (3) the condition of the developer, and (4) the agitation of the
film. The higher the temperature of the developer, the less time    *Temperature*
the film is required to be in the solution. If the film is transported
through the solution at a fixed speed, the only way to control development is to control the temperature.

Developer becomes less effective with repeated use. Consequently, developer must be replaced as used and in accordance
with the manufacturer's recommendations. Film agitation is pro-    *Film agitation*
vided automatically as the film moves through the processor. Upon
leaving the developer, the film is submerged in a fixing (hypo) solution to stop development and harden the emulsion. This fixing    *Fixing solution*
solution dissolves any silver bromine that was not reduced to metal-
lic silver during processing. (Some organizations find it advantageous to reclaim this silver from the fixing solution for resale.)
After being submerged in the fixing solution, the film is washed
and dried.

## Inspecting

Established quality standards for microfilm can only be maintained
through frequent inspections. Inspections may include checking

with a light box, taking densitometer readings, making comparisons with a resolution test chart, and performing a methylene blue test.

### Light Box

The initial piece of equipment used in film inspection is a light box. Film is cranked over the glass top of the light box and read with a magnifying glass or jeweler's loupe. The purpose of this initial inspection is to determine that the documents were captured on the film without any distortion, such as improper positioning or a blurred image.

### Density

**Density** is a numeric measurement of the amount of light which passes through the black background of negative microfilm. This measurement is obtained by using a densitometer. The standard density measurement for film is 1.0 to 1.2. Measurements outside this range indicate that the film images have poor contrast. Lower readings indicate that insufficient light was used in filming; higher readings indicate that too much light was used in filming or that the film was overexposed.

### Resolution

The **resolution** or sharpness of the image becomes increasingly important with enlargement since any blurred image will become increasingly fuzzy. Good resolution results from good film and lens quality.

The National Bureau of Standards Resolution Test Chart 1010, the most frequently used test chart, consists of 21 identical test patterns in varying sizes. Each pattern on the chart is assigned a numeric value from 1.0 (largest pattern) to 18 (smallest pattern). The resolution test consists of determining the smallest pattern that can be distinctly recognized under the microscope. This pattern number's numeric value is multiplied by the reduction used to determine the lines per millimeter (LPM). For example, if the pattern number is 5.0 and the reduction is 24x, the resolution is 120 LPM ($5.0 \times 24 = 120$ LPM)—the generally used standard. Values below 120 LPM indicate substandard resolution.

### Methylene Blue Test

Because hypo residue affects the longevity of film images, a methylene blue test is performed to test for this residue. Commercial processors perform this test routinely once a day or every other day on each processor. The test can be performed in-house by trained personnel using test kits and following the manufacturer's instructions.

# Duplicating

Duplicating is the process of producing multiple copies of microforms. The process and the types of copy film used are discussed in this section.

## Duplicating Process

Duplication of microfilm can be accomplished by simultaneously exposing two rolls of film in the film unit of the camera. Multiple copies of microfilm are, however, most frequently made by contact printing. **Contact printing** is achieved by placing the emulsion side of the original developed camera film in contact with the emulsion side of the copy film and directing a light beam through the original image to the copy. The copy film is then developed to produce the duplicate microfilm.

## Types of Copy Film

There are three types of copy film: (1) silver print film, (2) diazo film, and (3) vesicular film. Silver print film may be either reversal or nonreversal film. Reversal film will produce a positive copy from a negative-image original; nonreversal film produces a copy with the same polarity as the original film. (If the original film has a positive image, the copy will have a positive image.) Duplication of silver print film requires darkroom conditions. After exposure, the film is developed using the same procedures as for the original film.

*Silver print film*

Diazo film is a nonsilver film. Diazo film consists of an acetate or polyester base coated with diazonium salts and a dye. This coating is light sensitive. Diazo film is developed through exposure to ammonia vapors in a development chamber. If the film is underdeveloped, the process can be repeated until the film is fully developed. Thermal diazo film, which can be developed by heat in the same type of equipment used to process vesicular film, is also available. Diazo duplicates always have the same polarity as the original film.

*Diazo film*

Vesicular film is developed by a heat process. Most vesicular film will produce duplicates having the reverse polarity of the origi-

*Vesicular film*

nal film. The development of vesicular duplicates does not require darkroom conditions.

## Reading

*Magnification matches reduction*

Utilization of microforms depends upon the ease with which the stored information can be read. Microimages are usually read using a reader (viewer) which magnifies the microimages to eye-readable sizes. When the magnification of the reader matches the reduction of the camera used in filming, an image will fill the viewing screen and, consequently, be easier to read. If the reader magnification is less than the reduction, the image will be smaller than the screen, may be difficult to read, and may cause eyestrain. If the magnification is greater than the reduction, only a part of the image will be visible on the screen at any given time.

Some microform readers have screens which allow the simultaneous viewing of two pages. Readers are available in varying sizes from free-standing models to hand-held models. (See Figure 7–10.) Reader printers have the ability to produce a hard copy of a document shown on the screen.

Figure 7–10
Microforms Reading Equipment

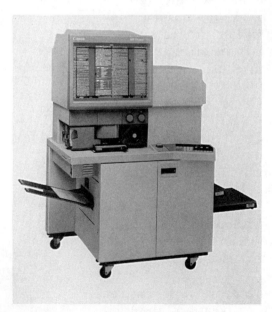 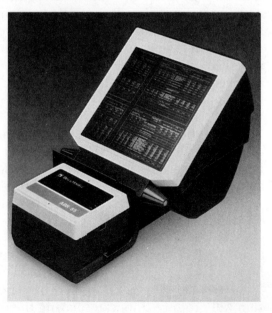

■

## A LOOK AT THE CASE

After Bernard Seay carefully examined the required procedures and the equipment options for a microrecords system, he wanted to summarize the data he had collected and present his recommendations to Maria Rodriguez, executive vice president.

What format should be used to present the results of the feasibility study to management?

■

## REPORT TO MANAGEMENT

When the data collected during the feasibility study have been analyzed, recommendations should be presented to management. (The preparation of oral and written presentations to management was discussed in Chapter 2.) The report to management, whether written or oral, should follow an outline such as the one shown in Figure 7–11.

The cover letter should state the purpose of the report and the existing support for it. The management summary restates the purpose of the report, summarizes the costs and benefits, suggests an appropriate time or schedule for implementation, and requests action by management. The present system should be described, including how the system works and why it needs to be changed. A description of how the proposed system will work, what its benefits will be, and how it will affect employees and the operations of other departments should follow. The description of the proposed system must clearly address how this system will alleviate weaknesses in the present system.

Cost is a crucial element of any proposal. The cost analysis section of this report should include an itemized summary of implementation costs and a comparison of the cost of operating the present and proposed systems. The cost analysis might be presented as a table such as the one shown in Table 7–1. This table allows one to compare the costs of storing documents and microfilm (or other appropriate microforms) in prime office space to the costs of storing them in a records center. The costs of filming in-house or contracting with a service bureau to do the filming (discussed further in Chapter 19) can also be compared.

Figure 7–11
Outline of Report to Management

---

### MANAGEMENT PROPOSAL AND COST JUSTIFICATION FOR A MICROGRAPHIC SYSTEM

**COVER LETTER**

—WHAT DO YOU WANT?
—DO THE MANAGERS AFFECTED BY THIS PLAN AGREE WITH YOU?

**MANAGEMENT SUMMARY**

—WHY ARE YOU WRITING THIS PROPOSAL?
—CAN YOU SUMMARIZE YOUR FINDINGS?
—WHAT WILL THIS PLAN COST?
—WHAT IS THE TIMING ON THIS PLAN?
—WHAT DO YOU WANT ME TO DO?

**PRESENT SYSTEM**

—WHAT IS HAPPENING TODAY?
—WHAT IS WRONG WITH WHAT WE'RE DOING?
—WHY SHOULD WE CHANGE?

**PROPOSED SYSTEM**

—WHAT CAN I EXPECT FROM THE MICROGRAPHIC SYSTEM?
—HOW WILL IT WORK?
—HOW WILL I BE BETTER OFF THAN I AM NOW?
—HOW WILL THIS AFFECT MY STAFF AND OTHER DEPARTMENTS?

**COST ANALYSIS**

—WHAT WILL THIS PROPOSAL SAVE THE ORGANIZATION?
—WHAT WILL THIS PROPOSAL SAVE MY UNIT?
—HOW DOES THE COST OF THE PROPOSED SYSTEM COMPARE WITH THE PREVIOUS SYSTEM?
—PREPARE AN ITEMIZED SUMMARY OF ALL COSTS ASSOCIATED WITH THIS PROPOSED SYSTEM

---

*Source:* RCA Corp.

Table 7–1
Cost Analysis

SOURCE DOCUMENT VS. MICROFILM DOCUMENT
One Storage Cabinet — One Year

| Storage Costs | Office | | Records Center | |
|---|---|---|---|---|
| | Paper | Microfilm | Paper | Microfilm |
| Floor Space Required | ___ | ___ | ___ | ___ |
| Rental/Square Feet | ___ | ___ | ___ | ___ |
| Floor Space Costs | ___ | ___ | ___ | ___ |
| Storage Equipment (Amortized) | ___ | ___ | ___ | ___ |
| Labor | ___ | ___ | ___ | ___ |
| TOTAL | ___ | ___ | ___ | ___ |

| Filming Costs | In-House | Service Bureau |
|---|---|---|
| Document Preparation | ___ | ___ |
| Filming Equipment (Amortized) | ___ | ___ |
| Supplies | ___ | ___ |
| Filming Labor | ___ | ___ |
| Service Bureau Cost Per Image | ___ | ___ |
| TOTAL | ___ | ___ |

The section concerning system implementation should indicate the number and type of positions to be filled, the training required, and the effect on current organizational structure; a suggested implementation schedule should also be included. Systems improvement opportunities might include better utilization of resources (personnel, equipment, and space) and an enhanced competitive position. The report should emphasize how the proposed system will contribute to the improved utilization of resources and competitive position of the organization.

No report is complete without supporting documents. Some exhibits which strengthen this type of report are a list of assumptions on which the report is based, specifications and brochures for equipment, job descriptions for new positions or positions where duties will change significantly, and an organization chart, if basic reporting procedures need to be changed.

## A LOOK AT THE CASE

Bernard Seay prepared a written report for Mrs. Rodriguez. The analysis of the data demonstrated that the parts inventory records were an excellent choice for conversion to microrecords. Equipment would need to be purchased and employees would need special training. Despite these costs, savings would be realized in time, space required to store records, and employees needed to store and retrieve records; and the response time for handling customer inquiries would be substantially reduced.

In his report to Mrs. Rodriguez, Bernard recommended the conversion of the parts inventory records to microfilm and suggested a schedule for this conversion. Mrs. Rodriguez obtained the approval of the board of directors, and Bernard and his staff began to implement the conversion schedule.

## TERMINOLOGY REVIEW

*Aperture card.* An 80-column keypunch card ($7\frac{3}{8}''$ by $3\frac{1}{4}''$) into which an opening(s) has been cut to accommodate the insertion of a frame(s) of microfilm.

*Bar coding.* A pattern of clear and opaque bars between images on roll film.

*Blip coding.* A method of coding accomplished by placing a blip (an opaque, optical rectangle) below each image to identify it. Also called "image count marking."

*Chip.* A piece of film containing a microimage and optical or magnetic coding for automated retrieval.

*Cine mode.* The positioning of microimages on film which takes its name from cinema film and is achieved by feeding documents into the camera with the headings or tops of each sheet entering the camera first.

*Comic mode.* The positioning of microimages on film which takes its name from the manner in which frames of a comic strip are presented and is achieved by feeding the document into the camera with the heading to the left or to the right.

*Computer input microfilm (CIM).* Microfilm containing images which are converted to electronic signals for storage on magnetic tape to be used as input to a computer.

*COM recorder.* A microfilm unit which converts data from a computer into human-readable language and records it on microfilm.

**Contact printing.** Method of duplication achieved by placing the emulsion side of the original developed camera film in contact with the emulsion side of the copy film and directing a light beam through the original image to the copy. The copy film is then developed.

**Density.** A numeric measurement of the amount of light which passes through a black background of negative microfilm.

**Duo mode.** A method of microfilming in which images are placed in consecutive order down one half of a strip of film and then back down the other half.

**Duplex mode.** A method of microfilming both sides of a document simultaneously with the images presented side by side.

**Flash targets.** Method used to divide a roll of film into batches of information.

**Image orientation.** The positioning of images on film.

**Jacket.** A transparent plastic carrier for strips of microfilm.

**Microfiche.** A sheet of film containing multiple miniature images in a grid pattern.

**Microform.** Any medium which contains miniature images.

**Micrographics.** The procedures for creating, using, and storing microforms.

**Micro-opaque.** A sheet of opaque paper stock containing multiple miniature images in a grid pattern similar to a microfiche.

**Microrecords.** Records stored on microforms.

**Negative polarity.** The light to dark relationship of a film image in which clear characters are produced on a black background.

**Odometer indexing.** Method of indexing which indicates the distance of each image from the beginning of the roll of film.

**Planetary camera.** A flatbed camera used primarily to film stationary engineering drawings and other large documents.

**Positive polarity.** The light to dark relationship of a film image in which black characters are produced on a clear background.

**Reduction ratio.** The size of a microimage as compared to the size of the original document, usually expressed as 24x, 30x, or 24:1, 30:1, and so forth.

**Resolution.** The sharpness of a microimage.

**Reversal processing.** A procedure which changes the polarity of film.

**Rotary camera.** A type of microfilm camera that photographs documents while the documents and film are being moved by transport mechanisms at the same speed.

**Scroll.** A roll of extra-wide film (105mm) used in some automated retrieval systems.

**Step and repeat camera.** A flatbed camera designed to expose images in uniform rows and columns for the preparation of microfiche.

**Strips.** Short lengths of film containing microimages which are containerized and coded for use in automated retrieval systems.

*Ultrafiche.* A microfiche produced at a reduction ratio of 90x or greater and containing microimages of 4,000 or more pages.

*Updatable microfiche camera.* A step and repeat camera which allows additional images to be added to the microfiche at any time (if space for these additional images exists).

## COMPETENCY REVIEW

1. Define the terms microforms, microrecords, and micrographics.
2. State three advantages and three limitations of using microrecords.
3. List the procedures in conducting a feasibility study for the conversion of paper records to microrecords and describe four categories of data which are essential to this study.
4. List and define five types of microforms.
5. What preparation must be done before filming documents?
6. Describe standard camera film.
7. Define reduction ratio.
8. Define four modes of microfilm image orientation.
9. Describe five types of microform cameras and list one application for each type.
10. Describe four types of microfilm coding.
11. Describe three types of film processors.
12. Explain reversal processing and state the most frequent reason for its use.
13. List four factors which affect film development and explain how three of these may be controlled by the operator.
14. State the need for inspection of microforms and explain three inspection techniques.
15. Define three types of film used in duplicating microforms.
16. Explain the importance of readers and reader printers to the utilization of microrecords.
17. Outline the contents of a report to management on the results of a feasibility study of a conversion to microrecords.

## APPLICATIONS

1. If costs were not a factor, which would be the most desirable microform for each of the following record series?
   a. Personnel records
   b. Invoices (Accounts Receivable)
   c. The Congressional Record
   d. Bank copies of customer checks
   e. Inventory records

2.  Using ads in periodicals in your school library, compare the advertised features of three brands of one of the following types of equipment: microfilm cameras, COM recorders, readers, reader/printers, duplicators. Prepare a chart (similar to the one below) to report your findings.

| Feature | Brand Name & Model No. | Brand Name & Model No. | Brand Name & Model No. |
|---|---|---|---|
|  |  |  |  |
|  |  |  |  |
|  |  |  |  |

## CONCLUDING CASES

### A. Johnston Insurance Company

Leonard Greenfield, micrographics supervisor of Johnston Insurance Company, was familiar with many uses of 16mm film for records storage. Leonard has just been approached by Gail LaChance, director of marketing, about a low-cost way to microfilm and duplicate policyholder records for simultaneous use by a number of departments. Leonard approaches you with his dilemma—roll microfilm is not a good solution for this application.

What form of microrecord would you suggest to Leonard? Justify your choice.

### B. Arthur Simpson, Records Consultant

Arthur Simpson is a records consultant specializing in microrecords applications. Arthur has been contacted by the assistant superintendent of the local school system who asked him to make a 20-minute presentation at the next school board meeting. The topic for Arthur's presentation is "Criteria for Determining the Feasibility of Filming Students' Permanent Records."

You work for Arthur on a part-time basis. When you came in today you found the following message on your desk:

"Please help me plan this presentation to the school board. List 8–10 of the criteria you feel are most important (be sure to include all four areas of concern). Make any other suggestions you feel will be helpful in organizing this presentation."

## READINGS AND REFERENCES

Avedon, Don M. "Selecting a Microform Reader Is a Matter of Application," *Office Systems,* Vol. 2, No. 8 (August, 1985), p. 66.

Costigan, Daniel M. *Micrographic Systems.* 2nd ed. Silver Spring, Maryland: National Micrographics Association, 1980.

Darvin, Herb. "Production Up, Costs Down with Microfiche System." *The Office,* Vol. 102, No. 6 (December, 1985), p. 36.

Fruscione, James. "A Blueprint for the Evaluation of Computer Output Microfilm Applications," *Records Management Quarterly,* Vol. 19, No. 3 (July, 1985), p. 44.

Hallerman, Dennis M. "Why Microfilm?," *Records Management Quarterly,* Vol. 19, No. 2 (April, 1985), p. 30.

Hensel, John. "Micrographics: Where We Go From Here," *IMC Journal,* Vol. 21, No. 1 (First Quarter, 1985), p. 5.

*Journal of Micrographics,* (October, 1982), p. 51.

Ker, Neil R. "The Vital Role of Front-End Microfilming," *IMC Journal,* Vol. 21, No. 1 (First Quarter, 1985), p. 35.

Klein, Henry J. "Microfilm, the Computer and the Small Company," *Records Management Quarterly,* Vol. 18, No. 4 (October, 1984), p. 45.

Oris, Michael. "A Case for Micrographics," *The Office,* Vol. 102, No. 3 (September, 1985), p. 84.

Rudnitsky, Andrea. "The Use of Micrographics and Electronic Technology in Records Management Status and Trends," *Records Management Quarterly,* Vol. 18, No. 1 (January, 1984), p. 42.

Siragusa, Gail. "Archival Records Storage — Microfilm vs. Paper," *Administrative Management,* Vol. 46, No. 12 (December, 1985), p. 56.

Soat, John. "Computer Output Microfilm: Where, Why and How," *Administrative Management,* Vol. 46, No. 11 (November, 1985), p. 54.

Tanner, Eric C. "Quality-Control Procedures Can Put Micrographics Over," *Office Systems,* Vol. 2, No. 9 (September, 1985), p. 83.

Williams, Robert F. "Electronic Document Management: The Coming Revolution in Records Management," *IMC Journal,* Vol. 21, No. 4 (Fourth Quarter, 1985), p. 33.

Wise, Joseph. "Micrographics: When Is It Right for You?" *Administrative Management,* Vol. 47, No. 1 (January, 1986), p. 59.

Wolf, David R. "The Technologies and Role of Directly Updatable Micrographics Systems," *IMC Journal,* Vol. 21, No. 1 (First Quarter, 1985), p. 19.

## COMPREHENSIVE CASE, PART I

The Powell Sales and Service Company is a large-volume dealer of personal computers. PSS sells and services personal computers from six different manufacturers; each manufacturer offers at least three models.

PSS has been very successful in its marketing effort and, as a result, has gained a large share of the personal computer market.

The market for personal computers has expanded three times the projected growth. When PSS was organized, only three major investors were active in the management of the organization—Jason Powell, president and in charge of administration; Sue Powell Floyd, vice president in charge of sales and service (and the only salesperson for the first several months of operation); and Lu Chiang, vice president for personnel and overall jack-of-all-trades. As the organization expanded, the need for additional personnel became evident and employees were added in all departments.

Powell Sales and Service Company has a decentralized system of active records throughout its organization. The fast growth of the company in volume of sales and in service calls and contracts has resulted in an even greater growth in volume of records required. The sales and service growth has been received positively by management; the record growth has not. The primary reasons for the negative reception are that it is often difficult to have fast record access and that there is a tremendous duplication of records throughout the organization. All of this has caused the records manager to review the decentralization of records and to recommend to the vice president for administration that a study of the current system be conducted.

The following information was obtained from the records inventory and from the records retention schedule:

|  | Records Volume | Housed In | Record Series | Records Media |
|---|---|---|---|---|
| **Adm. Offices** | 1,200 linear inches | 5-drawer vertical cabinets | Reports Correspondence | Paper |
| **Sales** | 720 linear inches | Open shelves | Sales records | Paper |
| **Service** | 210 lin. in., cards 10 lin. in., fiche | Card cabinets Fiche cabinets | Service manuals Customer records | Cards Microfiche |
| **Accounting** | 420 lin. in., open shelves 576 lin. in., lateral cabinets | Lateral cab. Open shelves | Financial records | Computer printouts Forms |
| **Personnel** | 50 lin. in., fiche | Fiche cabinets | Personnel records | Microfiche |

The records retention program has just been implemented. No records have been purged. You may assume that the general rule of one-third records remaining in active files, one-third transferred to inactive files, and one-third remaining in each department will allow the organization to function effectively. If you believe other assumptions must be made, list them on a separate sheet.

From the information provided and the assumptions you make,

1. recommend records to be transferred to inactive storage or discarded.
2. determine the area needed for an active records facility. If, in your opinion, certain records should be retained in designated departments, indicate which departments, which records, and provide a rationale statement for your recommendation.
3. recommend types of equipment to be used in the active records facility.
4. determine floor load capacity required by using information from 1, 2, and 3 above.
5. design a centralized active records facility.

# PART TWO
## Organizing the System

# 8
# RECORDS MANAGEMENT MANUAL

## Competencies

After completing this chapter, you should be able to

1. describe the components of the organizing subsystem and explain its role within the records management system.
2. define a records management manual.
3. list the purposes of a records management manual.
4. explain the types of records management manuals.
5. list and describe the steps in preparing a records management manual.
6. describe the procedures for distribution and maintenance of a records management manual.

# Introductory Case

Tanaka Appliances has four manufacturing plants in the western part of the United States; these four plants employ more than 3,500 people. Each plant employing a total of 275 people has a sales division. Plants and sales divisions maintain individual records systems in a rather haphazard fashion.

Three months ago, Carlos Lopez was hired as the records manager for Tanaka Appliances. In his previous company, which employed fewer than 600 people, the records system was well organized. Each department followed a few written directives which were kept within the department and updated as needed. At Tanaka Appliances, written records procedures are minimal and are distributed only within the records department. Carlos feels that these procedures should be more widely distributed, perhaps through the development of a records management manual.

1. What is a records management manual?
2. What purposes could it serve within the records management system?

*Organizing subsystem*

A records management system contains four subsystems — planning, organizing, staffing, and controlling. The function of the organizing subsystem is to coordinate the records management system to assure its efficient operation. Each of the four processes in the organizing subsystem — developing the records management manual, establishing a retrieval system, integrating information technologies, and developing special records applications — contributes to the efficiency of the records management system. Developing a records management manual is the first process in the organizing subsystem of the records management system. (See Figure 8–1.)

## NEED

Most functional units within an organization use the services of the records unit. Many organizations find the use of a records management manual increases the efficiency of the records unit and expedites requests for records unit services.

## Definition

*Who, what, when, where, and how of records management*

A **records management manual** is a guide to how the records management system works. Information on the who, what, when, where, and how of the records management system (for employees of the records unit and for others in the organization who may need to use the services of the records unit) is provided in the manual.

Large organizations find comprehensive records management manuals indispensable to the functioning of their records units. The comprehensiveness and formality of the manual generally increase as the size of the organization increases. Small organizations may need only a few pages of operating procedures to achieve the desired results; however, every organization needs a records management manual in some form.

## Purposes

The development and utilization of a records management manual serves four specific purposes: (1) standardizes procedures, (2) establishes responsibility, (3) assists in employee training, and (4) provides for updates of procedures.

Figure 8–1

Relationship Between the Records Management System and the
Organizing Subsystem

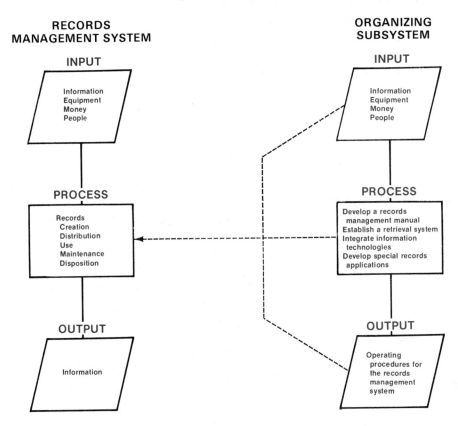

## Standardizes Procedures

Whether an organization has a centralized or decentralized records system, certain procedures need to be performed consistently by each unit. Some of these procedures are establishing records retention periods, selecting equipment and supplies, and transferring records to the records center. An organization with a centralized records system has an even greater need for standardized procedures: records sent to the active files area need to be properly coded. Records center clerks can then respond to requests for information or retrieve files more efficiently.

Oral instructions are frequently forgotten or misinterpreted. Written instructions are more likely to elicit consistent correct performance. In addition, establishing written procedures minimizes questions concerning how to perform a task. Questions of this kind

*Questions
are costly*

are very costly to the organization since they cause the inefficient use of two employees' time—the one who must ask what to do and the one who must provide an answer.

### Establishes Responsibility

When the organization establishes responsibility for the performance of certain records-related tasks, it determines who—which individual, group of individuals, or department—is responsible for completing the tasks. Specific instructions for responsibility prevent employees or departments from "passing the buck" when a job is not done properly or on time. Establishing the "who" also allows users of records unit services to determine with whom to discuss a records problem or whom to ask to perform a certain service.

*Prevents "passing the buck"*

### Assists in Employee Training

Records management manuals usually contain detailed job descriptions for members of the records unit staff. Complete procedures for performing the duties of each position are included in these job descriptions. Flowcharts illustrating the flow of work within the records unit and into the records unit from other units within the organization may also be included in the manual. The flow of records to and within Tenneco's records division is shown in Figure 8–2.

*Detailed job descriptions including instructions on task completion*

A list of procedures to follow in completing each assigned task, illustrations of the source of each task, and locations of documents to be filed or forms or reports to be delivered are valuable tools for newcomers to the records unit, those promoted to new positions within the unit, or other employees of the organization. These procedures do not replace experience in the performance of assigned duties or on-the-job training. However, they provide a ready reference until procedures become familiar; this will prevent additional time from being lost in asking and answering the same questions.

### Provides for Updates of Procedures

Records policies may be updated through the issuance of new directives. Sometimes, however, not everyone is notified or someone fails to dispose of the old directive when the new one is issued. Many times, procedures are not examined at regular intervals to determine if more efficient methods or tools are available. A records management manual can alleviate these difficulties by providing a complete set of written procedures, a format which can be easily updated, and a procedure for regular review and revision of records policies.

*Provides for regular review and revision*

## Figure 8–2
## Records Management Flowchart

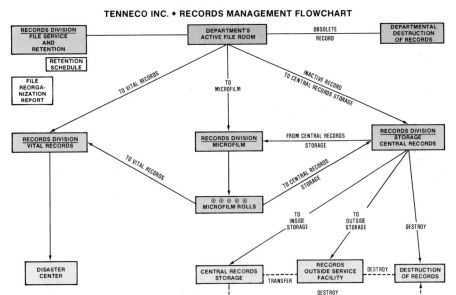

**TENNECO INC. • RECORDS MANAGEMENT FLOWCHART**

*Source:* Tenneco Inc.

## A LOOK AT THE CASE

Carlos Lopez has prepared a presentation for the executive committee of Tanaka Appliances which explains the need for a guide—a manual—to the records management system. He is prepared to discuss with the committee the purposes such a manual would serve—standardize procedures, establish responsibility, assist in employee training, and provide for updates of procedures. In explaining each aspect of the manual's use, Carlos plans to emphasize the increased efficiency of records operations that can be expected once the manual is in use. Carlos will then ask the executive committee for its approval and support in completing this project.

1. If support of the executive committee is forthcoming, what other steps must be completed in preparing a records management manual?
2. In what order should these steps be completed?

# PREPARATION

Preparing a records management manual is an extensive task which demands a thorough knowledge of the organization, its goals, and the manner in which the records unit is organized to help achieve these goals. Manual preparation demands careful planning and consistent attention to detail. The preparation process involves completing the following steps:

1. Obtain the approval of top executives for preparing a manual.
2. Determine the type of manual needed.
3. Assign authorship responsibility.
4. Identify sources of information for the manual.
5. Determine the content of the manual.
6. Collect and analyze data.
7. Write the manual.
8. Publish the manual.

## Obtain Approval of Top Executives

No task affecting the operation of the entire organization should be undertaken without the approval and support of the top executives. The details for planning a presentation to top executives were discussed in Chapter 2. Specific data to be included in a presentation on the need for developing a records management manual should include the definition and purposes of such a manual (as discussed earlier in this chapter) and the expectation of increased efficiency in the operation of the records unit as a result of the implementation of a manual.

*Communicate support of top executives to all employees*

Once top executives have approved the development of a records management manual, their support should be communicated to those individuals who will be required to provide information or other support to this project. Department heads, division heads, records liaison persons, and records unit staff members will be asked to perform extra tasks to assist in the preparation of this manual. Cooperation may be more readily offered if all participants are aware that the top executives consider this project important to the overall functioning and success of the organization.

## Determine Type

Records management manuals may be classified as one of five types. These types are (1) policy, (2) organizational, (3) administrative, (4) operational, and (5) combination.

## Policy Manual

A **policy manual** establishes general guidelines for consistent decision making. Establishing written policies requires managers to anticipate needed actions. A manual based on these guidelines provides a framework for day-to-day procedures and operations. Employees are responsible for working and making decisions within the established framework. (See Figure 8–3.) The major disadvantage of this type of manual is the possibility of multiple interpretations of some guidelines because of the general framework described.

*Guidelines for decision making*

## Organizational Manual

An **organizational manual** describes the structure, duties, and responsibilities of each unit and explains the relationships between other units and the records unit. Each section of the organizational manual contains an organization chart and a description of the duties and responsibilities of each position within that section of the records unit. A separate listing is often made of managers of those units of the organization using records unit services.

An organizational manual provides the opportunity to place proper emphasis on line and staff relationships within the unit and within the organization. Careful thought in preparing such a manual may eliminate overlapping responsibilities or gaps in responsibilities. The major disadvantage of this type of manual is that it usually does not illustrate the informal relationships within the records unit and the organization which contribute to the smooth functioning of the records unit. In addition, once the relationships are established and published, the organization may find the published structure to be inflexible in dealing with changing needs.

*Emphasis on line and staff relationships*

## Administrative Manual

An **administrative manual** includes standard operating procedures that facilitate the completion of tasks requiring the work of more than one unit of the organization. Procedures are prescribed courses of action for stated conditions, and their publication clearly establishes authority and responsibility. Administrative manuals for a records management system would include guidelines for preparation and distribution of correspondence and directives; approval, printing, and use of forms; and transfer of records to the records center.

*Prescribed courses of action*

## Operational Manual

An **operational manual** contains detailed information on the structure, policies, and procedures of one unit of an organization. An

Figure 8–3
Policies of a Records Management Program

---

### TENNECO INC.

SUBJECT: Corporate Records Management

GENERAL POLICY

　　All records management services for Tenneco's Houston based companies are provided by the Corporate Records Management Section of the Tenneco Inc. Office Services Department. In addition, Corporate Records Management provides advice and assistance to Tenneco's non-Houston based companies in establishing and implementing effective records management programs, and is responsible for insuring that these programs comply with established Tenneco standards.

GENERAL

Corporate Records Management is responsible for the following:

- Establishing standard filing procedures; organizing and reorganizing files to assure conformity with standard filing practices.
- Conducting reviews of departmental files and records management operations.
- Training company personnel responsible for handling departmental records.
- Assisting with selection of new file personnel, upon request.
- Assisting with design, layout, and requirements for file rooms, as well as supervising the relocation of file areas.
- Selecting standard filing supplies and equipment.
- Establishing and maintaining retention schedules.
- Disposing of records obtained through the acquisition of additional entities.
- Reviewing and approving or disapproving records destruction forms.
- Storing records (received from other departments) in accordance with established retention schedules.
- Controlling onsite and off-premise records facilities.
- Coordinating the transfer of records to records storage areas.
- Coordinating the destruction of records by Central Records Storage.
- Receiving and filing notifications of the destruction of records by departments.
- Microfilming company records as outlined by retention schedules.
- Establishing and maintaining a vital records program.
- Storing and controlling the original executed copy of certain contracts.

---

*Source:* Tenneco Inc.

operational manual is used only in the unit for which it was prepared.

Examples of frequently used operational manuals include a records retention manual, a filing manual, and a correspondence manual. A **records retention manual** includes the records retention schedule, procedures for establishing retention periods, procedures for transferring inactive records to the records center, and procedures for the destruction of records.

A **correspondence manual** contains policies on the creation and distribution of correspondence, guidelines on efficient and effective document creation, form letters, formats for letters and other communications, guidelines for selecting the most effective type of communication, and guidelines on effective dictation techniques. A **filing manual** contains rules and regulations for filing which standardize procedures, assist in training personnel, and make storage/retrieval more efficient.

### Combination Manual

A **combination manual** includes information on records policies, the structure and responsibilities of the records unit in relation to other units, administrative procedures, and operating procedures. Many organizations have found that a manual which brings together all four elements of administering and operating the records management system can be more effectively used by all organization employees. Having all the information in one manual eliminates having time lost in determining which manual contains the needed information. When policies and procedures are presented in a combination manual, some organizations use different colors of paper to distinguish between them.

*Policies, structure, and procedures*

Distribution of a combination manual may include supplying the complete manual or separate sections to different levels of personnel—managers and administrative support personnel. When a combination manual is distributed by sections, a complete copy of the manual should be available to each unit and to each user who has a need for a complete manual.

## Assign Authorship Responsibility

Preparing a records management manual is seldom considered to be a one-person task. A committee of employees from the records unit and other units in the organization can provide a broader input source. Through delegation of information gathering and writing responsibilities, the preparation time can be reduced. All

*Establish manual committee*

employees should be notified that a manual is being prepared and encouraged to make suggestions to the manual committee.

Successful completion of the preparation process requires a thorough knowledge of all aspects of the records management system as well as familiarity with the organization and the special records requirements of various units. Because of these requirements, the records manager will usually chair the committee and direct the completion of this project. Consideration should be given to appointing to the committee those managers and supervisors who will be involved in the implementation and use of the manual.

## Identify Sources

Many records management manuals are seldom used because of poor selection or presentation of material. Therefore, the manual committee should identify all possible sources of information before beginning to write.

*Review manuals of other organizations*

One of the most readily identified sources of information is the records management manuals of other organizations. An examination of these manuals will suggest topics to be included, methods for presenting information, and printing formats. Often this examination process will reveal as much about what to avoid as about what to include. Committee members may notice wordy or unclear instructions, improper sequencing of instructions, information which is hard to find, and/or unnecessary contents. Observing these faults in other manuals may make committee members more conscious of avoiding them in preparing their own manual.

Additional sources of information for the manual are organizational directives that include items about records; surveys of employees within each unit that will be using the manual; vendors of records management equipment and supplies; records management and other professional organizations and publications; and grievance records concerning past problems with records management policies and procedures. The organization's legal counsel and auditor should also be consulted for input on meeting legal and fiscal requirements. In addition, the committee may wish to consider hiring a records management consultant to make suggestions or to direct the committee in its manual preparation efforts.

## Determine Content

The records management manual will be only as effective as the information it contains. The manual should contain all information necessary to the efficient functioning of the records unit. Contents of the manual can be divided into three sections: (1) introduction, (2) body, and (3) closing.

## Introduction

Introductory material should include title page, preface, and table of contents. The title of the manual, organization name, authorship of the manual, and publication date should appear on the title page. Authorship should give recognition to all personnel who assisted in the preparation of the manual. The preface should explain the reason for the manual, define records management, and describe the scope of material included in the manual. Some organizations also include information on the authorization of the manual and the signatures of those who gave this authorization. The table of contents lists the subjects covered in the manual and their locations by page number.

*Title page, preface, table of contents*

## Body

The body of the records management manual contains organization charts of the structure of the records unit and of other units which depend upon its services. This section also includes policies and procedures for each task performed within the records unit. Other policies and procedures which affect the creation, distribution, use, maintenance, storage, or destruction of records in all other units are also included. Typically policies and procedures are included for the following topics: creation and distribution of correspondence; creation and distribution of directives; creation, distribution, and use of forms and reports; storage/retrieval of records (see Figure 8–4); retention of records; destruction of records; selection of storage equipment and supplies; microrecords applications; and use of telecommunications. Policies and procedures may be communicated in narrative form, in lists of step-by-step instructions, in flowcharts, or in playscript form (see section on "Write the Manual").

*Structure, policies, and procedure*

## Closing

Closing material includes a glossary of terms used within the manual and an index to the contents. The glossary should include definitions of all technical and records-related terms, such as record, nonrecord, long-term record, temporary record, active record, inactive record, vital record, and microrecord. The names of various microforms and filming equipment should also be included.

*Glossary*

## Figure 8–4
## Information Retrieval Procedures

Records Management Manual
Part 1

Mountain Bell

I.M. 140

Form 5076
(Rev. 10/81)

### REQUEST FOR INFORMATION, WITHDRAWAL, OR EXAMINATION OF RECORDS

**TO:** Records Center Supervisor
1585 Allison Street
Lakewood, Colorado 80215-1025

DATE _July 16, 19--_

**REQUESTED DATA**
(TO BE COMPLETED BY RECORDS CENTER)

**REQUESTED BY:**
NAME _J. A. Barton_ DEPARTMENT _Accounting_
ADDRESS _601 East 8th Ave._ CITY _Denver_ STATE _Colorado_
ROOM NO. _____ TEL. NO. _555-1617_

**REQUEST TAKEN BY:**
_V. A. Clark_

**REQUESTED BY:**
TELEPHONE [X] TWX □ FORM 5075 □

| ROOM NO. | DESCRIPTION | PERIOD Beginning | Ending |
|---|---|---|---|
| SN 865 | Routine Estimates - Colorado | 1-1-80 | 12-1-80 |
| | | | |
| | | | |
| | | | |
| | | | |
| | | | |

INFORMATION OR RECORDS REQUESTED

**TRANSMIT DATA BY:    DATE**
TELEPHONE □
CO. MAIL [X] _July 26, 19--_
U.S. MAIL □
PREPAID EXP. □
DUPL. COPY □

**QUANTITY:**
BOXES _____
PACKAGES _1_
ITEMS _____

RECORDS RECEIVED BY _____ DATE _____

RECORDS RETURNED TO RECORDS CENTER
BY _____ VIA _____ DATE _____

RECORDS RECEIVED AT RECORDS CENTER
BY _____ DATE _____

**LOCATED IN RECORDS CENTER**
SECTION NUMBER _3_
SHELF NUMBER _4_

**ESTIMATED DATE RECORDS WILL BE RETURNED:**
_July 30, 19--_

### INSTRUCTIONS FOR PREPARING FORM 5076

1. In general the data required to prepare the form is self-explanatory. The Records Center will enter the data in the blocked area.

2. If the request is made by Form 5076, the "estimated date records will be returned" should be entered by the person preparing the form.

3. Requests may be made by telephone or TWX. In these instances the Form 5076 will be prepared by the Records Center. An alternate method is to originate Form 5076 in triplicate and send all copies to the Records Center.

4. Upon receipt of the request, the Records Center will secure and forward the records to the requester, returning the original and duplicate copies of Form 5076 by separate mail.

5. Upon receipt of the records, the original copy of Form 5076 should be signed and returned to the Records Center.

6. When the records are returned, the manner and date of the return should be shown on the duplicate copy of Form 5076 and returned to the Records Center by separate mail.

7. Upon receipt of the records in the Records Center the manner and date of the return should be shown on the original copy of Form 5076.

*Source: Mountain Bell Telephone Co.*

An alphabetic index is essential for efficient access to the information within the manual. When the writing is completed, a thorough search should be made of each page of the manual for key words to include in the index. To minimize the omission of key words and/or page numbers, two people should independently prepare indexes. The index should be placed in the front of the manual for quick, easy access.

*Index*

## Collect and Analyze Data

Once the content has been determined, the manual committee must begin the task of collecting information. The committee may wish to have the records manager meet with unit heads to "sell the program" and encourage their cooperation and that of their staffs. A brief explanation of the benefits to be derived in terms of more efficient operations will emphasize the importance of having a records management manual. Unit heads or members of their staffs may be asked to write or review existing procedures for inclusion in the manual. Involvement in this stage of the development process will increase the likelihood of widespread usage of the completed manual.

The task of collecting information should be divided among the manual committee members. Deadlines should be established for the collection process so that the work of the manual committee can proceed in a timely manner.

All of the data gathered must be categorized according to function within the records unit, such as micrographics, forms and reports, active records, and so forth. The number and types of categories will vary with the size of the organization (particularly the size of the records unit).

The information which has been sorted into categories must then be analyzed to determine appropriateness and importance in the manual. Because it is a time-consuming task, this analysis is usually done by subcommittees of the manual committee, with each subcommittee making determinations for the different elements of the records management program. Each subcommittee will make suggestions to the manual committee regarding information to be included in the manual. The manual committee may accept, reject, or make changes in these recommendations before the material is accepted for inclusion and presented to the manual writers.

*Data are analyzed by subcommittees*

## Write the Manual

After content decisions have been made, the actual writing of the manual may begin. The writing is usually done by the records manager and supervisors of the sections of the records unit. These individuals are more qualified to write the manual because of their knowledge of the organization and their experience in the records management program.

*Writing must be easily understood*

The major objective of the writing phase is to write in a manner that will be easily understood. The manual may not be used unless this objective is achieved for all potential users. For this to be accomplished, the level of writing should be appropriate so that it will be understood by all users.

Understanding will be more easily achieved if the writers remember three essential elements — simplicity, strength, and conciseness. Simplicity is achieved by using simple terms and short sentences and paragraphs to convey information or procedures. Build on basic concepts.

Strength comes from a positive style of writing. Use specific, active verbs to state actions to be taken. Instructions should be given in positive rather than negative terms; use "*do*s" rather than "*don't*s."

Conciseness is achieved by avoiding unnecessary information or repetition of information. If users need the same information in two or more types of circumstances, state the procedures once and refer users to that page(s). Limit qualifying statements and prepositional phrases to provide only essential descriptions.

In addition to these three elements, correct grammar, spelling, and punctuation are also essential. A careless presentation of information makes it appear less important to users. Presentation of the information is also enhanced by the use of major and minor headings to organize the material. Use bullets to make items in a list stand out, and state listed items in one or two words where possible.

Manuals may be written in narrative style, contain lists or flowcharts of step-by-step procedures, or be written in playscript format. The narrative style is the most commonly used style, although it requires the most reading to determine the action to be taken. Some organizations compile lists of step-by-step procedures from existing directives on records management and republish them in a manual.

Many organizations have found the playscript format effective in presenting procedures. (See Figure 8–5.) The playscript style of

Figure 8–5
Procedures Written in Playscript Format

**SUBJECT:** Transferring Inactive Records to the Records Center

| Position | | Action |
|---|---|---|
| Active Records Clerk | 1. | Determines which records have achieved inactive status according to the retention schedule and should be transferred to the Records Center. |
| | 2. | Prepares a transfer list to accompany records sent to the Records Center. |
| | 3. | Packages records in storage cartons. |
| | 4. | Notifies the Records Center of the planned shipment of records. |
| | 5. | Arranges the physical movement of records (within the building or offsite). |
| Records Center Clerk | 6. | Receives records cartons and checks contents against transfer list. |
| | 7. | Stores records in the appropriate area of the Records Center and notes locations on the transfer list. |
| | 8. | Returns a copy of the transfer list with locations to the originating office/unit. |

writing uses two columns. The left column designates the position title of the person responsible for completing a certain task or making a certain decision; the right column describes the task to be performed or the decision to be made.

*Use illustrations*

Consideration should be given to the inclusion of charts, cartoons, and photographs wherever these might contribute to the clarity of the material in the manual. Appropriate examples should also be included when discussing correspondence styles or forms design.

*Distribute first draft for review*

A limited number of copies of the first draft of the records management manual should be distributed to selected managers, supervisors, and users for review. This process usually results in several suggestions for clarity or presentation improvement and may result in the addition of overlooked information. Suggestions should be reviewed by the manual committee. Those suggestions which will improve the manual should be incorporated into a second draft and be presented to the executive committee or top executives for approval before the manual proceeds to final draft stage.

## Publish the Manual

The approved records management manual may be published in several ways. Photocopy and offset printing are the two most commonly used procedures. Selection of the printing method will be affected by the needed quantity, unit cost, and desired appearance.

The quantity of required copies is frequently determined at the beginning of the preparation process through the identification of all employees who will be using the manual. Unit costs of the manual are affected by quantity, size, paper weight, number of ink colors used, and type of binding selected. These factors determine the appearance of the manual and will reflect the importance the organization places on this manual.

*Appearance reflects importance*

The $8\frac{1}{2}$-by-11-inch size is most convenient for use as a reference book and is preferable if the manual is prepared in typed form. Other page sizes may be considered if the manual is to be printed. Many organizations select a loose-leaf format for quick and easy updating. If the manual is very thick, printing on both sides of the paper will make it easier to handle. Tabs (along the open side of the manual) which indicate the beginning of each section allow more efficient usage.

Covers or binders should reflect the importance of this manual to the organization. If the organization has other published manuals, the color of the cover/binder of this manual should be different to make it easily distinguishable. The title should be printed or imprinted in a manner indicative of importance. Too much cost cutting in the printing process will increase costs later through decreased manual use.

■

## A LOOK AT THE CASE

Carlos Lopez obtained the approval and support of the executive committee of Tanaka Appliances for the preparation of a records management manual. He appointed a manual committee which decided to prepare an organizational manual. The committee then assigned authorship responsibility to Carlos and the supervisors in his division, identified sources of information, determined content areas, and collected and analyzed material. A draft of the manual was then prepared and distributed for review. Several suggestions for improving readability were incorporated into a second draft, which was presented to the executive committee for their approval. The approved manual was then published in $8\frac{1}{2}$-by-11-inch, loose-leaf form in blue three-ring binders. The title and company name were imprinted in gold on the manual covers.

Carlos is now concerned about the use of the manual.

1. How should the manual be distributed?
2. How should the manual be maintained?

## USE

Maximum use of records management manuals is a primary consideration throughout the preparation process. When the manual is published, wider usage can be assured through distribution to the most likely users and through continuous maintenance.

### Distribution

Determination of which employees should receive copies of the records management manual should be made early in the preparation process. The number of manuals needed should also include copies for designated executives. A list of manual recipients should be maintained by the records manager for control purposes. Manuals may be numbered and assigned to specific recipients, or each manual may be personalized with the recipient's name printed on the cover. Although personalizing manuals may encourage usage, the added expense may not be justified.

*Maintain a list of manual recipients*

Many organizations find it helpful to distribute manuals at a training session. Such a session should be designed to familiarize users with the manual. Instruction in the use of the records management manual should also be included in subsequent orientation sessions for new employees.

### Maintenance

Maintaining the records management manual includes determining the amount of usage and usefulness of the information in the manual; it also includes updating the contents to enhance the manual's value to users. During the early preparation phase, provisions should be made for the maintenance process to include regular audits, quick updates, periodic revisions, and prompt revision distribution.

### Regular Audits

*Use survey*

The audits in the maintenance process are surveys of manual usage conducted at planned intervals. Such audits should be conducted at least annually, preferably more frequently. The survey results will reveal how frequently the manual is referred to; who refers to it; and what, if any, material is out of date.

### Quick Updates

Because procedures are not static, procedures manuals are soon unusable if no provision is made for updating information. Some procedures will change in response to new equipment, government regulations, or organizational needs. An updatable format allows these changes to be made quickly on an as-needed basis. This need to alter procedures is the reason many organizations select the loose-leaf format for their manuals. When the loose-leaf format is used, only the affected pages need to be revised, reprinted, and replaced within the manual. Otherwise, changes must be written around current printed information or new manuals must be prepared. If an employee must consult another source — such as a new directive — for procedural information, the manual soon loses its significance.

### Periodic Revisions

*Comprehensive review*

To keep the manual properly maintained, a schedule for reviewing the entire manual at regular intervals should be established. Such a comprehensive review should be conducted every two years. This review cycle will help maintain continuity within the manual through updates of particular procedures and will ensure that interdepartmental relationships affected by changes are reflected in the manual.

### Prompt Revision Distribution

Little is accomplished by revisions if employees are not aware of the changes. Some organizations assign one individual the task of inserting revised pages in all manuals throughout the company. If revised pages are distributed to manual holders for insertion into their manuals, a checklist of procedures which have been added or deleted should accompany the revised pages. Confusion about which update is most recent can be eliminated by dating each revised page.

Some organizations require users to initial a memo which accompanies the revised pages and return it with the outdated manual pages to a central location. The user's name is checked off the
distribution list as the pages are returned. Users who fail to return
outdated pages by the deadline are contacted again.

*Check revision
distribution/
insertion*

## A LOOK AT THE CASE

Carlos Lopez has determined that each designated employee
received a copy of the records management manual. Carlos has
also established controls for maintaining this manual. Use audits will be conducted annually, revised pages will be distributed as needed, and a comprehensive review of the manual
will be conducted every two years.

Carlos now feels that the records management manual development has been successfully completed and that the manual's usefulness will be maintained.

## TERMINOLOGY REVIEW

**Administrative manual.** Contains standard operating procedures that facilitate the completion of tasks requiring the work of more than one unit
of the organization.

**Combination manual.** Contains information on records policies, the structure and responsibilities of the records unit in relation to other units,
administrative procedures, and operating procedures.

**Correspondence manual.** Contains policies on the creation and distribution
of correspondence, guidelines on efficient and effective document
creation, form letters, formats for letters and other communications,
guidelines for selecting the most effective type of communication,
and guidelines on effective dictation techniques.

**Filing manual.** Contains rules and regulations for filing which standardize
procedures, assist in training personnel, and make storage/retrieval
more efficient.

**Operational manual.** Contains detailed information on the structure, policies, and procedures of one department/division of an organization.

**Organizational manual.** Describes the structure, duties, and responsibilities of each department/division and explains the relationships between other departments/divisions and the records unit.

*Policy manual.* Contains written general guidelines used for consistent decision making.

*Records management manual.* A guide to how the records management system works.

*Records retention manual.* Contains the records retention schedule, procedures for establishing retention periods, procedures for transferring inactive records to the records center, and procedures for the destruction of records.

## COMPETENCY REVIEW

1.  Describe the components of the organizing subsystem and explain its role within the records management system.
2.  What is a records management manual?
3.  What purposes does a records management manual serve?
4.  List and explain five types of records management manuals.
5.  List and describe the steps in preparing a records management manual.
6.  Describe the distribution procedures which are essential for a records management manual.
7.  Describe the maintenance procedures which are essential for a records management manual.

## APPLICATIONS

1.  Procedures may be written in many styles. The playscript format is illustrated in Figure 8–5. Write the procedures in Figure 8–5 in narrative format. Compare the advantages and limitations of each format.
2.  You have been hired as a consultant for Brown Shampoo Company to direct the revision of their records management manual while Brown's records manager is recovering from surgery. Administrative approval has been obtained for his project. List and explain the other steps which will be necessary to determine the usefulness of the existing manual and to make the revision more of an asset to Brown's employees.

## CONCLUDING CASES

### A. Security Finance Co.

Linda Gallagher is the records manager for Security Finance Co. in Meadowpoint. Security's records program has operated in accordance with a few administrative directives throughout its 25-year history.

Eighteen months ago a large office equipment manufacturer opened a plant in Meadowpoint. Since then, the town's population has nearly tripled, and Security's customers have increased proportionately. In addition, recent legislation has created new retention requirements for some finance company records.

Linda Gallagher has decided to seek administrative support for the development of a records management manual. Linda is scheduled to make a presentation to the executive committee next week to obtain approval.

1. How should Linda explain the need/benefits of a records management manual to the executive committee?

2. At what steps in the preparation of a records management manual should Linda report to the executive committee?

3. How will the executive committee be involved in maintaining the usefulness of the records management manual?

## B. Haynes Manufacturing

Haynes Manufacturing is a national manufacturer and distributor of furniture and home appliances. Julie Asano, Haynes' records manager, has just completed a use audit of Haynes' records management manual. This was the first audit since the manual was published two years ago. The audit revealed that the records management manual was seldom referred to because many of its procedures were out of date.

1. What steps should Julie take to make the records management manual more useful?

2. What steps can Julie take to ensure that the records management manual does not become unusable in the future?

## READINGS AND REFERENCES

Ellman, Edgar S. "How to Write a Personnel Manual." *Administrative Management,* Vol. 43, No. 7 (July, 1982), p. 28.

Hogan, Kathryn C. "Office Management Manuals." *Records Management Quarterly,* Vol. 14, No. 2 (April, 1980), p. 32.

Lunine, Leo R. "How to Write a Manual: Part II." *Today's Office,* Vol. 18, No. 2 (July, 1983), p. 19.

# 9
# SYSTEMS OPERATION AND RETRIEVAL

## Competencies

After completing this chapter, you should be able to

1. define the storage procedures applicable for most records systems (manual, mechanical, or automated).
2. describe specific procedures for maintaining manual file operations.
3. identify major similarities/differences between manual and mechanical operations.
4. explain the differences in information capture among internal storage, magnetic storage, microimage storage, and hard-copy automated storage.
5. differentiate between information retrieval processes for the four categories of automated retrieval.
6. describe control methods for manual, mechanical, and automated operations.
7. explain specific activity reports and procedures for obtaining the information.
8. describe status reports and explain the procedures for obtaining the information.
9. describe types of information obtained through activity and status reports and explain how this information is useful in improving records management.

# Introductory Case

When Deluxe Paper Clips Manufacturing Company opened its doors in 1944, business was good, primarily due to government orders. As Deluxe became known for its prompt delivery and excellent service, they began to get large orders from private industry and public institutions. In five years, business had exceeded their expectations by 150 percent. Business continued to grow, and Deluxe continued to prosper as new types of paper fasteners were added to the product line. They continued to maintain their reputation for promptly filling and delivering orders and for friendly service.

In the early 1980s, business began to decline and complaints became common.

*"I placed our company's order over a month ago, and we have not even received acknowledgment."*

*"We received our order late, and it was less than 75 percent complete."*

*"Our receiving department has notified us that when you finally send our orders, they are incomplete, and you don't even send back order notices. We don't know if you made a mistake, or if you are out of a particular stock number."*

*"Your billing is incorrect. You bill us for goods not ordered or not received."*

After reviewing a number of these complaints, Vincent Mazzaro, vice president for administration, has called a meeting to discuss the problems, their effect on profits, and to try to identify possible solutions. Present at the meeting are the marketing manager, records manager, and the operations manager.

Vincent begins the meeting with a review of the types of problems that are shown in the complaints and a description of the seriousness of the business decline. He asks each manager to consider how his/her department might contribute to solving these serious problems and to be prepared to give Vincent an oral report in one week.

1. What areas should the records manager examine?
2. What should be included in the record manager's report?

*"Nothing is lost until you look for it"*

The universal principle of retrieval is illustrated in "The Hazards of Filing" as shown below.

---

### THE HAZARDS OF FILING

The time it takes to find something in the files depends on how urgently it is needed: the greater the urgency, the longer the time.

You are more likely to find what you really aren't looking for.

You won't need an item you once filed until two days after you have thrown it away.

The item you can't find in your files will always be the one your employer wants.

The person who is given the task of reclassifying and refiling in the department will be transferred the day after the task is completed.

The only time your employer will take the wrong file is when leaving on a business trip, and the mistake will not be discovered until the plane is 30,000 feet over Nashville.

You'll never misfile anything you won't need at some future date.

Paper clips were deliberately designed to clip together documents that weren't meant to be filed together.

For a comprehensive filing system to work, it has to be too complicated to be understood.

The more you file away, the less likely you are to find the item you are looking for.

If material is to be saved for legal, tax, financial, or other esoteric reasons, no one will remember what those reasons were after the material has been filed.

People who look for something in your files will automatically refile that material under the wrong heading.

The only time people won't be able to find things in your files is when you are out sick.

---

*Source: Atlanta Chapter, Association of Records Managers and Administrators, Inc.*

## STORAGE PROCEDURES

"It's not my filing, it's my finding..." is a familiar saying when problems are experienced in locating records. The saying is inaccurate because the storage procedures affect the finding: records properly stored according to established procedures will be easily retrievable by anyone familiar with the system. Records may be stored or retrieved by manual, mechanical, or automated methods. Regardless of the selected method, general procedures are applicable to all methods; specific procedures differ according to the system used. The general procedures for records storage include

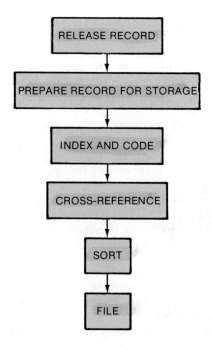

## Release Record

The first step in the procedure is to check for a release mark on the record. A **release mark** is a notation that the immediate need for the record has passed and the record may now be stored. The record recipient has the responsibility for making that decision. The release mark may be an initial or the simple notation "file." The mark is usually made on the upper right corner of the document, if hard copy. In any case, the release mark authorizes the record to be stored.

## Prepare Record for Storage

*Check for condition*

Paper records should be checked for filing condition. Paper clips are removed; related records are stapled together or punched so that they may be fastened to folders; torn papers are mended with transparent tape; and small papers are taped or attached by rubber cement on standard-size paper. Oversize material to be filed must be folded separately; this reduces the amount of filing space required and allows each record to be retrieved individually. Unnecessary attachments such as envelopes, routing slips, receipt acknowledgments, or duplicate copies (unless considered a part of the record) should be destroyed.

*Remove attachments*

Prepare source documents that are to be microfilmed or stored on other media. The documents should be unfolded, paper clips and staples removed, and wrinkled papers straightened.

Magnetic media must be handled and stored with care. Floppy disks must not be bent, folded, creased, or mutilated in any way. Manufacturers of floppy disks will not guarantee performance of the disks unless measures are taken to file each floppy disk completely pressure free. Hair, dust, or fingerprints on the read-write head may damage or erase stored data. Magnetic media exposed to extreme heat, cold, or light may also result in lost data. To avoid data loss on magnetic media, keep disks in their jackets when not in use, store diskettes on edge, handle diskettes by jackets only, and write on labels *before* placing them on the disks. Also, when storing magnetic disks, avoid stacking diskettes, attaching paper clips or rubber bands to diskettes, or placing magnets near diskettes. Diskettes should not be placed near motors, transformers, power cords, chemicals, or liquids.

## Index and Code

**Indexing** is deciding where a record is to be filed based on the classification system used. Determining the name, subject, or caption by which a record is to be stored is a mental process that takes place prior to coding.

**Coding** is indicating on a record where it is to be stored. Proper coding follows alphabetic rules and the procedures for the specific classification system used. There are various methods of coding, depending on the record medium. Complete coding of magnetic and film media is essential. Paper documents contain visible information and, if misplaced, a reasonable chance of locating and identifying the record still exists. Disks, tapes, and film do not have this visible advantage. The contents of disks, tapes, and film should be identified on the media as well as on the storage containers. Each disk, tape, or film medium may be identified with a code that corresponds to a matching code on the storage container. This code is repeated on the locator index.

*Code all media*

## Cross-Reference

If records may be requested in more than one way, indicate that fact and prepare a cross-reference for the record. Cross-referencing is accomplished at the same time as the indexing and coding procedure. A **cross-reference** directs the person looking for the record to another location where the record or information may be found. Cross-referencing is also used when related material is in another location or when the location of the record within the system has been changed.

## Sort

**Sorting** is arranging records in filing order according to the classification system used. Records to be microfilmed, as well as records that are manually or mechanically placed in files, must be in the desired sequence. Records placed in an automated system do not require sorting prior to storage.

*Sorting procedures*

If large numbers of records are to be sorted, a rough sort is made first. Depending on the number of items to be sorted, the rough sort may first be block sorted. **Block sorting** is the process of rough sorting records into groups of alphabetic letters (A, B, C, D, E, F) or in groups of numbers (1–10, 11–20), and so forth. If a numeric system is used, block sorting is done in multiples of 10 or 20. Geographic sorting is first done by state. If the number of records to be sorted is small, rough sorting is usually accomplished by placing all the As, 10s, or cities alphabetically (depending on the system) in one stack; Bs or 20s in another stack; and so on. Fine sorting is then done by putting the records in order within the alphabet, digits within the numeric system, and cities alphabetically within the state.

## File

**Filing** is the action of storing the record. The record may be stored in hard copy in an appropriate storage area; on microfilm, microfiche, magnetic tape/disks, or optical disks; or within the memory of a computer or word processor.

■

## A LOOK AT THE CASE

The records manager for Deluxe Paper Clips Manufacturing Company needs to evaluate the efficiency of the company's general procedures for storage and retrieval. The result of this evaluation should be a determination of areas in which specific procedural problems exist.

   If the company is using manual storage and retrieval techniques,

1. What specific considerations should be given to files maintenance?
2. What specific considerations should be given to files control?

■

## MANUAL OPERATION AND RETRIEVAL

**Manual operation and retrieval** refers to the process of storing and retrieving records without the aid of mechanical or automated devices. Anyone placing a record in its appropriate folder in a storage cabinet or on a shelf or in a disk box is using a manual system. Studies indicate that, although many organizations are using more automated retrieval systems, the majority of small and mid-size organizations still rely on manual retrieval. The trend, however, is toward more efficient, less labor-intensive systems of records operations and retrieval.

### Prepare Record for Storage

The storage procedures previously described are applicable in a manual system. Records are screened for release marks, filing condition, coding, and cross-referencing, if necessary, and are sorted to expedite the storage process. The entire name, subject, or number that is used for filing purposes is called the **filing segment**. Methods of coding include underlining or circling key words, names, or subjects and writing a subject or numeric code at the top of (or other prominent place on) the record. The cross-reference notation appears on the document if it is a paper document. The person doing the coding may mark an "x" next to the related name

*Coding procedures*

or subject within the document to indicate a cross-reference. If the related subject (cross-reference topic) is inconsistent with the relative index to subject files, an "x" is written at the top of the record followed by the subject under which the cross-reference should be made. Figure 9–1 shows these cross-reference notations.

Figure 9–1
Cross-Reference Notations

Cross-Reference Within Document          Cross-Reference Written on Document

The cross-reference may take several forms: (1) photocopy of the original record, (2) cross-reference sheet, (3) long-term cross-reference, or (4) index card. (See Figure 9–2.)

*Provides record trail*

**Long-term cross-references** are used to provide a trail or forwarding address for the record when one or more of the following factors are present:

- Names of people or organizations are filed in more than one place.
- Related material is stored in multiple locations.
- Filing is contrary to standard filing rules.
- Names have been changed.
- Entire file is moved to a new location.
- Records are reclassified from one file arrangement to another.
- Divisions and subsidiaries of a large corporation are to be identified.

Figure 9–2
Cross-Reference Forms

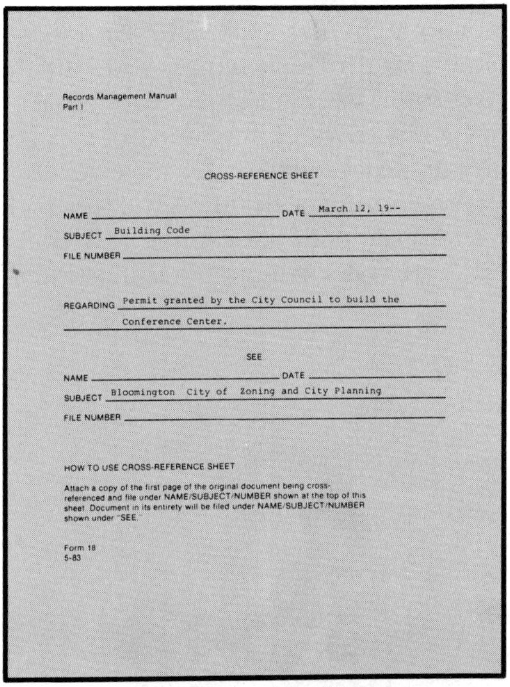

Records Management Manual
Part I

CROSS-REFERENCE SHEET

NAME _____ DATE __March 12, 19--__

SUBJECT _Building Code_____

FILE NUMBER _____

REGARDING _Permit granted by the City Council to build the_____

__Conference Center.__

SEE

NAME _____ DATE _____

SUBJECT _Bloomington City of Zoning and City Planning_____

FILE NUMBER _____

HOW TO USE CROSS-REFERENCE SHEET

Attach a copy of the first page of the original document being cross-
referenced and file under NAME/SUBJECT/NUMBER shown at the top of this
sheet. Document in its entirety will be filed under NAME/SUBJECT/NUMBER
shown under "SEE."

Form 18
5-83

**Cross-Reference Sheet**

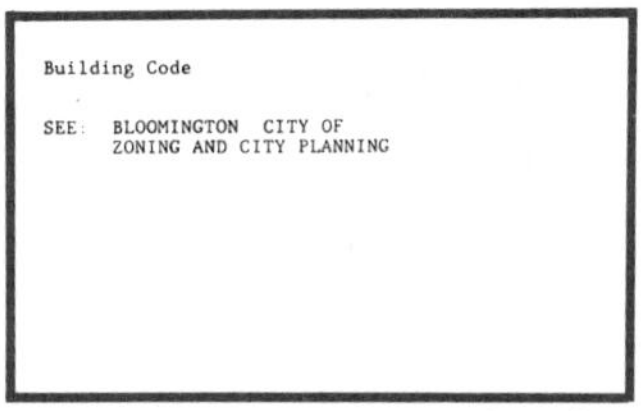

Building Code

SEE:   BLOOMINGTON   CITY OF
       ZONING AND CITY PLANNING

**Cross-Reference Card**

*Long-term
cross-reference*

A long-term cross-reference is made from a file folder or fiche envelope with the cross-reference information typed on the label. Long-term cross-references are an integral part of the records system. Long-term cross-references are microfilmed if the records are filmed or transferred with the other folders to inactive storage at the appropriate interval. Long-term cross-reference folders should be marked with a shoulder label or other labeling device, such as a distinctive color or type style, to facilitate replacement of the cross-reference when the existing cross-reference is microfilmed or transferred. (See Figure 9–3.)

Figure 9–3
Long-Term Cross-Reference with Shoulder Label

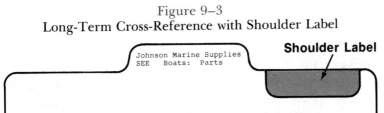

Johnson Marine Supplies
SEE   Boats:  Parts

**Shoulder Label**

*Sort*

When sorting is performed manually, devices may be used to aid the sorting process. The most commonly used sorters are horizontal sorters and vertical sorters. Horizontal sorters are flat, in either a long, narrow style or in a circular style. They are most efficient for sorting single papers and offer savings of as much as 60 percent over desktop sorting. Vertical sorters have self-supporting dividers on an adjusting track. These sorters can be used for folders, jackets, and single documents. Because several inches of material can be placed behind a divider, the vertical sorter is appropriate in cases where the material cannot be accommodated in a horizontal sorter. A special sorting table is illustrated in Figure 9–4.

Figure 9–4
Sorting Table

## Files Maintenance

Filing systems remain efficient only if they are properly maintained. Established maintenance procedures should be followed on a regular basis.

### Drawer/Shelf Files

Overcrowded storage cabinet drawers cause slowed records retrieval. A properly maintained vertical file drawer should use 23 to 24 of the 27 available storage inches, allowing 3 to 4 inches for work space. Microfiche filed in drawer cabinets should have 1 to 2 inches of work space. Shelf files should be full enough to allow files to stand upright but loose enough to allow folders to be easily stored and retrieved. All drawers/shelves should be clearly labeled *Label file* to include the records title, years covered, the arrangement fol- *drawers/shelves* lowed, and the segment of the particular file included in that drawer/shelf. Labels should be typewritten or computer generated with uniform format and should provide current information. For example, if the drawer label reads

```
        Invoices              #1200-1650
July 1-Dec. 31, 19--      7/1 - 12/31, 19--
        #1200-1650               INVOICES
```

but the drawer contents were transferred to a records center and the drawer now houses invoices for the period beginning January 1, 19—, storage and retrieval are slowed. Drawer labels narrow the search to one drawer.

## Guides

Guides or dividers allow storage and retrieval to be accomplished more quickly by providing eye targets. Guides narrow the search to *File guides* several folders. Too few guides are inefficient; too many guides *provide eye* waste storage space. Guides should be provided for every 6 to 8 *targets* folders in a very active drawer/shelf file and for every 10 to 15 folders in a less active drawer/shelf file. This translates to 15 to 25 guides per file drawer/shelf for very active files and 10 to 15 guides per file drawer/shelf for less active files. Card files require a file guide for every 20 cards in very active files; for less active card files, one guide per 30 cards is sufficient.

## Folders

Folders must be clearly labeled to reduce retrieval time. Like drawer labels, folder labels should be typed or computer generated using a uniform format. Folder labels narrow the search to the *Labels identify* contents of one folder. Labels and folders must be replaced when *folder contents* their condition slows storage or retrieval. In order to minimize wear, folders should be handled by the sides—not by the tabs. All folder labels should be clearly visible. When folders become filled with papers, the scoring at the bottom of the front folder leaf should be creased to allow papers to rest squarely on the bottom of the file drawer. Folders should not be overcrowded—three-fourths inch of material is the maximum one folder should house, even if the folder is scored. Noticeably thick folders should be subdivided into separate folders by either date or subtopic.

*Guide/folder arrangements*

When a paper record is filed, the record is inserted facing forward with the top of the page to the left. Documents should be arranged chronologically within the folder; the latest record should be placed on top. This placement makes the most recent information available first.

A straight-line guide/folder arrangement (all guides at left and all folder labels at right) allows additional guides and folders to be inserted without causing a confusing arrangement. If the file arrangement is consecutive and fixed, with no additional guides or folders to be added, staggered positions may be used. Guides and folders are usually not staggered in the same arrangement. Guides may be staggered with folders in a straight line, or folders may be staggered with guides in a straight-line arrangement.

## Accessing the Files

To maintain files efficiently and to provide ready access to records, the person accessing the files must have knowledge of the record system (whether it is direct or indirect access) and must follow established steps for requisitioning and charging out records.

### Direct/Indirect Access

*Indirect access requires index*

Records may be accessed directly or indirectly. Direct access requires no intermediary steps — one goes directly to the storage area and retrieves the record. Indirect access requires the use of an index to direct the person accessing the record to the appropriate storage area.

### Developing the Index

*Index is location tool and guide for code selection*

An index is a location tool. Just as an index in a book directs the reader to a page within the book, a records index directs the researcher or records clerk to a particular file where the required information may be located. The index also provides the person coding documents with a guide for code selection. The manual index is based upon the classification system used by the organization and the manner in which information is normally requested.

The indexes may be comprehensive, sophisticated systems or simple listings as required to meet the needs of the organization and the user. Essential in most offices is a **basic classification index**, a categorical grouping of subjects with appropriate subheadings. In addition, a relative index is maintained to show, in dictionary-type listing, all possible words and word combinations by which the material may be requested. Each index to stored material should be kept current by making new entries for additional classifications as they occur. An example of one type of index is shown in Figure 5–2 on page 122.

*Types of indexes*

## Record Retrieval

Manual retrieval refers to finding and retrieving records without the aid of mechanical or automated devices. Paper records are stored in folders and housed in cabinets or shelves. Anyone requiring the record must go to the cabinet or shelf and, with the aid of guides and labels, retrieve the record from its folder. Microfiche, roll film in jackets, and aperture cards are retrieved similarly. Codes or identification numbers on the fiche headers, fiche envelopes (if used), jackets, and aperture cards are used to locate these records. Roll film, cartridges, and cassettes may be manually located by referring to their indexes for location information. These microforms are then manually placed on readers or reader-printers to obtain the required information.

*Retrieving paper records*

*Retrieving microrecords*

Roll film may be manually retrieved from storage. A reel of film that fits in the palm of your hand is more easily misplaced than a drawer of paper records. Care must be exercised to replace film in the proper carton, particularly when several reels are used at the same time. Using color signals on film cartons and reels is one way of preventing misfiling. Reels of different series can be assigned different colors. A diagonal line drawn end to end across the tops of all the cartons in a drawer or on a shelf is particularly effective for cartons maintained in numeric sequence. A visual scan quickly reveals missing or misfiled cartons.

*Using color signals*

## Control

A method for tracking records and recording activity is essential to the total records management system. The method includes procedures for requesting records/data, for charging out requested records, and for follow-up and return of the records.

*Tracking records and recording activity*

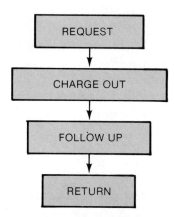

## Requisition

Records may be requested in either written form or by telephone. Telephone requests, however, should be recorded. If the organizational policy allows telephone record requisitions, the documentation responsibility rests with the records clerk who receives the telephone call. The same format may be used for either telephoned or written requests. (See Figure 9–5.)

*Document all record requests*

Figure 9–5
Records Retrieval Request

| RECORDS RETRIEVAL REQUISITION | | | | | |
|---|---|---|---|---|---|
| REQUESTED BY | | EXT. | DATE REQUESTED | | |
| DEPARTMENT | | LOCATION | RECEIVED (DATE/TIME) | | |
| RECORD TYPE    □ BOX    □ FILE    □ OTHER: | | | | | |
| TITLE | | | ROW | SECTION | SHELF |
| | | | | | |
| | | | | | |
| | | | | | |
| | | | | | |
| REQUEST TAKEN BY | | | | | |
| Form 55 5/31/87 | | | | | |

## Charge-Out

The procedure for checking out records for use by a requester is called **charge-out**. After completion or receipt of the record requisition, the record is then charged out to the requester. A charge-out is like an IOU, and the person borrowing the record is responsible for its return. A multiple-part requisition form may be used for charging out a record as well. When a multiple-part requi-

*Multiple-part requisition forms*

sition form is used, one copy of the form is inserted in the pocket on the plastic OUT guide (see Figure 9–6); the second copy is inserted in the tickler file; the third copy is attached to the folder. One copy of this form may be used to prepare management re-

Figure 9–6
OUT Guide with Insertion

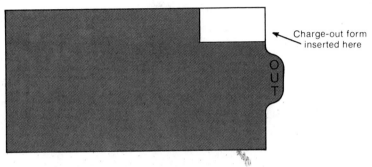

Charge-out form inserted here

O
U
T

ports, as discussed later in this chapter. An OUT guide, OUT folder, or OUT sheet may also be used to indicate that a file/record has been removed. An OUT guide replaces a folder removed from the files when other documents will not need to be filed in the folder during its absence from the file. An OUT guide provides space to fill in information regarding the name of the folder, the date the folder was removed, who requested the folder, and the date the folder should be returned. Of course, if the system of inserting a copy of the requisition or charge-out form in the pocket of the guide is used, the necessary information will be included on that form and not on the OUT guide. (See Figure 9–7.)

*OUT guide*

Figure 9–7
OUT Guide

| OUT | | | |
|---|---|---|---|
| Subject | Charged To | Date | Return Date |
| Marshall file | Todd | 6/24/-- | 6/26/-- |
| Tompson file | Patterson | 6/24/-- | 6/26/-- |
| Car Rental file | Simpson | 7/3/-- | |
| | | | |
| | | | |
| | | | |

*OUT folder*

An OUT folder replaces the requested folder as it is removed from the files and serves as a holding device for incoming papers until the return of the original folder to the file. Folder name, date removed, and requester name should be filled in on the form printed on the outside of the OUT folder. An OUT sheet is used to replace a document that has been removed from a folder. An

*OUT sheet*

OUT sheet identifies the document (by subject, date, and originator when applicable), who requested the document, when the document was requested, and date(s) the document is to be returned. Since an OUT sheet is placed within the folder as a substitute for a removed document, it should be placed in the same chronologic position within the folder as the removed document. The charge-out form must be removed from the files upon return of the charged out material. A line is drawn through the notation on the OUT form or OUT folder (as shown in Figure 9–7), and the form or folder is ready to be reused.

## Follow-Up

Records are not always returned on the specified date, and follow-up is often necessary to maintain complete files. It is reasonable to allow records to be charged out for a week to ten days; however, any period extending beyond two weeks is unacceptable. Confidential records usually may not leave the premises. If the policy of the organization allows confidential material to be borrowed, this material may not be charged out for longer than overnight.

*Follow-up procedures*

The mechanism for follow-up is usually a "tickler" or suspense file. This file is arranged chronologically with current month guide in front followed by 31 day guides. Guides for the remaining months are at the back of the file. One efficient way to indicate records that have been charged out and require follow-up is to place a copy of the requisition form behind the month guide to show the due date. Another efficient follow-up method is the use of follow-up folders. These folders have a plastic protected edge with a visible sliding signal which can be set to indicate the date of follow-up. One form of a request for return of records is shown in Figure 9–8.

Each day the file is checked for records charged out and not yet returned. Records still outstanding require a follow-up which may take the form of a phone call or a fill-in form (see Figure 9–8) sent to the person who charged out the material. The longer the time that files are allowed to remain out, the more difficult they are to recover.

Figure 9–8
Request for Return of Records

| REQUEST FOR RETURN OF RECORDS | | NO. | |
|---|---|---|---|
| To: *Miss Jane Matsumi* | Mail Sta.<br>*148* | Date:<br>*2/17/--* | |
| We like to give good service to everyone. Please cooperate with us by returning either the material listed below or this form showing the expected date of return. Thank you.<br><div align="right">Records Center Supervisor</div> | | | |
| Record Title/Description<br>*Cash Voucher*<br><br>*CV 14763* | | Charge – Out Date<br>*2/2/--* | |
| Remarks: | | Expected Return<br>Date:<br>*2/16/--* | |
| ☐ Continued Over | By<br>*Trudy Masters* | | Date<br>*2/17/--* |
| FORM 32-3/15/86 | | | |

■

## A LOOK AT THE CASE

In the investigation of the problems of information availability and timely retrieval, Deluxe Paper Clips Manufacturing Company's records manager began to study the manual operation and retrieval system in use in the organization. The records manager looked specifically at the procedures for record preparation, file maintenance, files access, and file control. Obvious deficiencies were noted in the areas of file maintenance and control.

1. Should the records manager investigate the possibility of mechanical or automated records operations and retrieval?
2. Will a change to a different system eliminate the identified deficiencies?

■

## MECHANICAL OPERATION AND RETRIEVAL

**Mechanical operation and retrieval** is the use of mechanized equipment to store and retrieve records. Mechanical devices speed retrieval and reduce worker fatigue. Mechanized equipment, as il-

lustrated in Chapter 6, includes mobile aisle systems, power elevator lateral equipment, rotary files, and conveyor systems. The last
three systems eliminate much of the nonproductive time normally
consumed by walking to the files.

## Record Retrieval

The preparation of records, from screening to sorting, is the same
for mechanized operation and retrieval systems as for manual systems. The difference occurs not in record preparation nor in storage but in retrieval. Records are manually placed in the files, even
with a mechanical system. The mechanized file does, however,
*Brings record*
*to operator*
bring the record to the operator for retrieval. The operator first
consults an index to determine the shelf on which the record is located. For example, using a power elevator lateral file, a requisition
is received for the Marshall file. The operator checks the index and
finds that the Marshall file is located on shelf 01. The operator
pushes the 01 number on the keypad, and the mechanized shelf
file rotates to a position in front of the operator; the operator scans
the shelf to find the Marshall file and retrieves it. There is no direct access to the mechanical files arrangement. In all cases, an index must be consulted to determine the location of the record.

Generally, the record is filed manually in a mechanical file: it
is placed in its appropriate location by the operator. Some systems
allow random placement, but these systems use a microprocessor
and are more automated than mechanical. Such systems are discussed under "Automated Operation and Retrieval."

*Sorting*
*aperture cards*
Aperture cards can be sorted by using a mechanical sorter—
the type used to sort punched cards. When the information is
punched into the aperture card (with holes representing numeric
or alphabetic characters), this same information can also be printed
along the top of the card. A mechanical sorter reads the punched
holes, sorts the cards, and aids in retrieval of the aperture cards.
This printed information (card header) provides the information
from which the index may be compiled.

## Control

Control procedures for mechanical operation and retrieval systems
are the same as for manual systems. Applicable methods must be in
place for requisitioning records/data, for charging out records, and
for following up and returning records. In all systems, these procedures are vital for maintaining complete records.

■

## A LOOK AT THE CASE

Deluxe Paper Clips' records manager has looked at various mechanical systems for storage and retrieval and, although the equipment may speed retrieval and reduce worker fatigue, it is not clear that the change to a mechanized system will solve the problems described by Vincent Mazzaro, vice president for administration.

1. Why will the addition of mechanical equipment not solve the problems?
2. Will an automated system solve the problems?

■

## AUTOMATED OPERATION AND RETRIEVAL

**Automated operation and retrieval** uses a computer or microprocessor to store, retrieve, and control information. Internal or external storage media may be used to store, retrieve, or control information in an automated system.

### Internal Storage and Retrieval

Internal memory is information deposited and stored in computer or word processing memory. **Memory** is the capacity to retain data within the system to form a database. Memory is normally used for temporary retention of information or data. Data is usually transferred to external media for long-term retention. The memory capacity differs according to the manufacturer and the level of machine capability.

*Memory*

#### Information Capture

Information may be captured and stored internally through keystrokes, through optical character recognition (OCR), through bar code wands or laser scanners, touch-tone telephones, or through computer input microfilm (CIM). Keystrokes are made on a terminal directly into the computer, or into the word processor through the keyboard. Optical character recognition equipment, through optical readers, bypasses the keyboard and feeds large volumes of pretyped data directly into the data or word processing

*Optical character recognition*

equipment. A document may be typed using an element with an OCR font. The document is fed into an optical character reader where it is read by the scanner and stored on a floppy disk or in memory. The information may then be manipulated by the data or word processor and a final copy is produced. Optical character recognition may also be achieved through an OCR wand. Table 9–1 illustrates some data entry alternatives.

Table 9–1
Data Entry Alternatives

| Entry Method | Human Factors (Operator Position) | Special Machine-Readable Label Required | Entry Speed (10–12 Digit I.D.) | Entry Errors (to total entries) |
|---|---|---|---|---|
| Keyboard/ CRT | Sit, 1 or 2 hands | No | 10–20 sec. | 1/30 |
| Bar Code/ Wand | Sit/Stand 1 hand | Yes | 2– 3 sec. | 1/300,000 |
| Bar Code/ Laser Scanner | Sit/Stand no hands | Yes | 1– 2 sec. | 1/300,000 |
| OCR Wand | Sit/Stand 1 hand | Yes | 3– 5 sec. | 1/1,000 |
| Touch-Tone Telephone | Sit/Stand 1 hand | No | 20–40 sec. | 1/30 |

*Source: Adapted from "Computer Speeds Records Retrieval," Office Systems Management, Vol. 1 , No. 4 (Spring, 1983), p. 12.*

## Indexing

An index provides information to aid in locating a record. Information (numbers and/or text) stored in computer memory is assigned addresses as the information is captured. When this index is recalled to the screen, these addresses (location codes or record identifiers) allow the searcher to determine where the information is stored. Word processing operators classify and index documents as the documents are created so that the index may be called back up on the screen to identify the location of the record. Some systems automatically index a document as it is created and may assign as many as twenty different identifiers (key words or descriptors) to each document. Accessing information stored in

*Accessing the index*

memory requires knowledge of where the information is stored [the address(es)] and how to transfer the information from internal memory to an external form. The information may be called up on a CRT screen, printed, or transferred to external storage (magnetic or film media).

## Information Retrieval

Automated systems make use of a computer to aid in retrieving information. Basically, **computer-assisted retrieval (CAR)** uses various technologies involving automation to assist in timely location and retrieval of information. CAR can be used with manual, semiautomated, and fully automated systems.

When a specific document is requested, the operator calls up the address and supporting information on the CRT terminal. Sometimes the information displayed will answer any questions the user may have without a need to go any further. If, however, the information required is not shown on the screen, the operator then reads the address from the screen, selects the appropriate file, and inserts it into an intelligent retrieval terminal.

Retrieving information from internal storage to eye-readable form is accomplished by calling up information on a CRT screen or by giving commands to a printer which then provides a copy of the stored information. High-speed printers attached to a computer or a word processor provide the user with hard-copy output. The same information may be shown on a screen in those instances when hard copy is not required. Some experts predict that 35 percent of the office work force will be using electronic "file cabinets" by 1991. Automated systems allow users to retrieve online or offline documents by calling up a key word or words from the text. Users can also obtain a listing of all documents containing these words. Searching can be done by title, author, type of document, operator, department, user-defined words, or last date stored.

*Increased use of electronic files*

Xerox's 6085 System is modeled after traditional paper file organization, using "file drawers," "file folders," and "records files." A "file drawer" contains "file folders," and the user is provided a listing of the contents of a particular drawer. The list of contents of a drawer, as well as a directory of the contents of a particular folder, can be shown on the screen.

Storage within the computer or word processor memory has a limited capacity and is primarily used to store information temporarily. For longer term storage, the information is transferred from memory to an external form of storage. A comparison of a system of manual and automated retrieval is shown in Figure 9–9.

Figure 9–9
Comparison of Manual and Automated Retrieval Systems

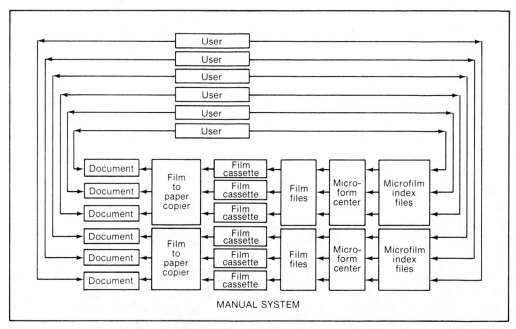

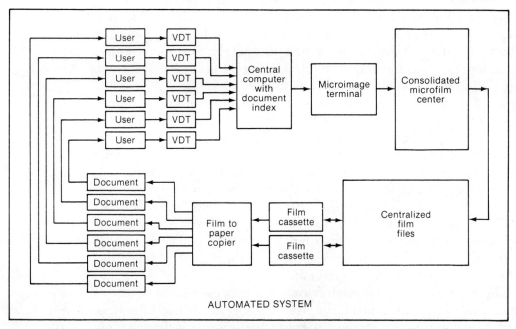

*Source:* *Reprinted from the February issue of* **Modern Office Technology** *and copyrighted 1985 by Penton Publishing, subsidiary of Pittway Corporation.*

In the manual system illustrated in Figure 9–9, users looking for a microfilmed document first went to the files to look up the document's identification. Once found, the user would then go to the microfilm center where the film cassettes containing the document would be retrieved. The cassette containing the filmed document was removed from the files so that a paper copy of the document could be made. Users either waited for the document to be copied to paper, or went back to the microfilm center to get the copy at a later time.

In the automated system in Figure 9–9, users who want documents now determine the document's identification through a computerized index. Once the identification is made, the computer finds the document's location in the film files. The request for a copy of the document is forwarded to the microimage terminal. The microfilm center then extracts the requests for document copies using the terminal. Different requests for documents on the same film cassette are consolidated, and the images are then transferred to paper. When the copy of the filmed document is made, it is sent to the requesting user.

## Magnetic Storage and Retrieval

Storage on **magnetic media** is depositing information offline (externally) from the computer database or word processor memory. Magnetic media storage may take the form of computer tapes or disks, word processor disks, or optical disks. Documents created electronically are most often stored that way too, at least for the short term.

*Stored on magnetic media*

### Information Capture

As discussed in internal memory storage, information is captured by keystroke, optical character recognition, bar code wands, laser scanners, touch-tone telephone, or by computer input microfilm. Once the information is in the system, it may be stored on magnetic media. Magnetic computer storage takes the form of tape or disk. Magnetic tape media uses rolls of magnetized film similar to that used with cassette recorders. Magnetic disks (floppy disks, hard disks, or optical disks) are similar in appearance to phonograph records; information is stored on magnetic spots located on the disk tracks.

Optical disks store digital information by using lasers. A single optical disk the size of a 12-inch phonograph record has the capacity to store 100 times more than a similar size magnetic media disk.

*Optical disks*

Once data is stored on optical disks, it cannot be changed. With the exception of writing over information to destroy it, data can only be read, not re-recorded. Because of this inflexibility, these disks are used for long-term storage of information that does not need to be updated or changed. Several U.S. and international companies have developed an erasable optical disk which will soon be available for demonstration.

## Indexing

*Generating
an index*

Indexing information on magnetic media is accomplished in the same way as is internal indexing—by using key words from the stored information. The index may be maintained on a disk or other magnetic form and can be viewed on a CRT screen. A printed index may be generated from the computer or word processor. The optical disk index may also be maintained on a disk and viewed on a screen. The index may be generated from the optical disk system and printed if needed.

## Information Retrieval

*Label magnetic
media housing*

Although the information is retrieved through automated systems, the magnetic media on which the information is stored is usually retrieved manually. For that reason, disks, diskettes, or tapes must be clearly labeled. Each should be labeled to indicate its contents, just as a file folder is labeled. And, just as a file drawer is labeled, the magnetic media storage equipment should be labeled to indicate its contents. Once the magnetic media are retrieved and entered into or placed onto the equipment, the file number or key word(s) are entered on the keyboard, and the information may be printed or viewed on the screen. This is true for optical disks as well as other magnetic media, such as tapes, disks, and diskettes. Optical disks, however, use a high-speed printer that works like a photocopier. The information is stored as complete pages rather than as individual encoded characters and is retrieved as photographic facsimiles of entire pages, including illustrations.

## Microimage Storage and Retrieval

*Sources of
microimages*

**Microimage storage and retrieval** is the process of storing and retrieving records that have been reduced in size and stored on roll film, fiche, aperture cards, jackets, and opaques. These are described in Chapter 7. Today, there are a wide range of approaches offered for automated storage and retrieval of information in microform format. All require physically coding the film, fiche, jacket, or aperture card in some way. The generic term for these approaches is Automated Document Storage and Retrieval (ADSTAR) Systems.

## Information Capture

Information is captured on microforms by filming source documents or computer printouts, by converting machine-readable computer tapes to microimages by input from a word processor into the computer, or by direct input from a computer's memory. When source documents are filmed, an operator prepares the documents for the camera, using the same techniques that are used to prepare documents for filing. Special care, however, must be taken to remove all clips and staples prior to filming. Computer printouts can be processed in batches by using a pin-fed method (pins on a machine fit into the punched holes on the sides of the computer printouts) to feed the printouts onto the camera bed.

*COM*

**Computer output microfilm (COM)** is an integration of computer and microform technology that converts the information on computer tapes or from computer memory to a microform. The output may be roll film or fiche, whichever is the more appropriate medium for the particular organization.

Since aperture cards and jackets use roll film, information capture is the same as for roll film. Information is captured on opaques in the same manner as on fiche.

Some sophisticated word processors have the capability of providing input to COM. Word processing disks are translated into computer tapes which the COM recorder converts into computer output microfilm (COM). This provides paper copies for the general public and microfilm copies for internal use or record storage. Figure 9–10 illustrates an integrated micrographics system.

## Indexing

Records that are filmed are assigned descriptors (date, author, recipient, key words) along with their film addresses. The film addresses usually include roll number, frame number, and any other identifying number that will assist in locating the records. A sequential number may be assigned to provide a visual verification that the located record is the one that was requested. Indexing may be accomplished in several ways. Source document indexing may be accomplished at the time of filming by placing an indexing CRT next to the microfilmer to assign the descriptors from the hard copy during the filming process. Source document indexing may also be accomplished after filming. The operator places the roll of

*Methods of indexing*

Figure 9–10
Integrated Micrographics System

# MICROGRAPHIC SYSTEMS

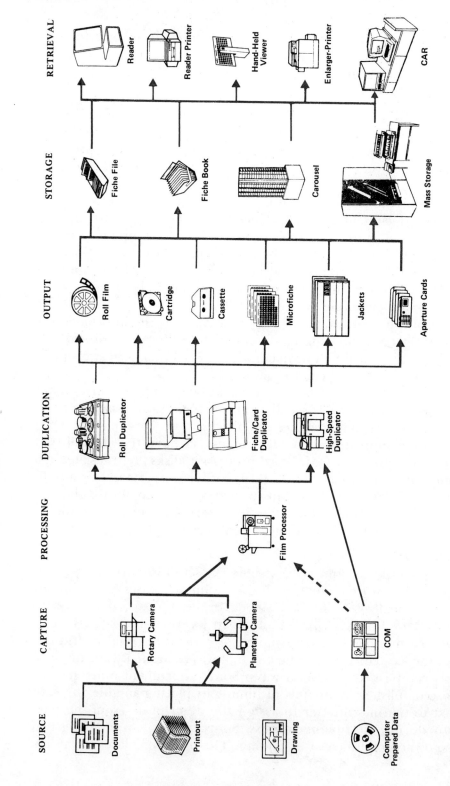

*Source: International Information Management Congress, Bethesda, MD.*

microfilm into a retrieval terminal and advances to the first document image. From this image, the operator assigns descriptors which are keyed into disk memory along with the sequential number assigned to the record. Indexing may also be accomplished automatically with very sophisticated computer equipment and software.

Each computer-generated microfiche includes an index frame which allows the operator to select the specific frame(s) on the fiche on which the information appears. (See Figure 9–11.) The index frame contains an index key to each frame of the fiche and the position of each frame on the fiche. The index frame usually appears in the corner of the fiche, but it may also appear as column indexing (index frame appears at top or bottom of each column). A master index may also be provided. Eye-readable column indexing is generated by the computer (COM) and cannot be used in source document microfilming.

*Microfiche index*

With computerized indexing, records may be filed randomly. The computer can automatically cross-reference, with some systems incorporating dictionaries that automatically reference documents under appropriate synonyms. These complex systems allow

Figure 9–11
Corner Index

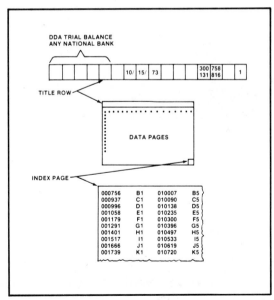

**Source:** *Rick Rager and Judd Smith, "COM Software,"* Information and Records Management, *Vol. 11, No. 4 (April, 1977).*

indexes to be updated and, at the same time, retain the old index (identified as such) as an audit trail.

### Information Retrieval

Computer-assisted retrieval (CAR), using microforms, capitalizes on strengths of two technologies—the ability to store images on microforms at low cost and the ability of the computer to make logical decisions under programmed control. CAR serves all types of microforms, both roll film and unitized formats (jackets, fiche, opaques).

*Offline or online retrieval*

Computer-assisted retrieval can be operated either offline or online to the computer. Offline has indexing and retrieval as separate functions. The operator, using the computer terminal, keys in information to begin the search for the record. In response to the operator-provided information, the CRT screen will display the location of the record. The operator is then responsible for finding that record. Figure 9–12 shows an index displayed on a CRT screen.

Figure 9–12
Computer-Generated Index

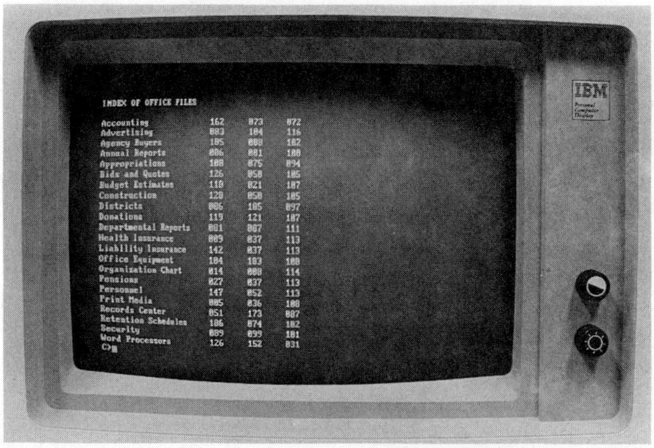

Online CAR has retrieval connected to the computer. The computer may respond in several ways, depending upon the level of assistance given by the computer program. Minimum computer assistance is given when the operator keys in information and the computer responds by displaying the roll of film that the operator should insert. After the operator inserts the appropriate roll of film, the computer then advances the film until it finds the information that has been requested. The maximum level of computer assistance is given when the operator keys in the search parameters and the record image is displayed on the CRT without further operator intervention.

Fiche may be retrieved through automated systems such as the Kodak Image Management System (KIMS). KIMS combines a computer database, image processing, and communications technologies to capture, store, manipulate, and retrieve both computer-based and microfilmed source document information. Information may be delivered to users stationed at multi-purpose workstations.

*Fiche retrieval*

Central to the system is the robotic autoloader, which can store up to 240 Kodak Ektamate film magazines, the equivalent of 1.5 to 3.5 million paper images. Up to six autoloaders can be linked to each system. Under computer control, the autoloader retrieves the requested magazine, loads it at one of four scanning stations, threads and advances the film to the desired frame. The image is then scanned and digitized for transmission to a workstation.

Other systems are available to retrieve fiche automatically through electronic sensing equipment. These systems use optical scanners to locate fiche that have been filed randomly. The operator uses a keypad to enter the descriptor, and the microprocessor scans the fiche or fiche carrier to locate the record.

*Optical scanners*

Charge-out cards should be used for fiche or reels to maintain file integrity. The charge-out card should be a distinctive color to flag the absent reel or fiche and large enough to write the user's name, location of the reel, and date the film was removed. Automated document retrieval and control systems (as shown in Figure 9–13) are also used to maintain file integrity.

Figure 9–13
Automated Document Retrieval System

## Hard-Copy Storage and Retrieval

Hard copy (paper) has traditionally been stored manually. New applications combining a mechanical device with a minicomputer allow automated hard-copy storage and retrieval.

### Document Storage

*Random storage and access*

Documents are stored randomly in automated files; that is, there is no requirement for correct placement of documents in the classification system. Systems such as LEKTRIEVER can accommodate a variety of media from microfilm stored in trays to file folders and computer tapes stored laterally on shelves.

The Kardex Record Control System interfaced with the automated storage and retrieval unit, LEKTRIEVER, provides control with automated storage and retrieval. The LEKTRIEVER is an electric vertical carousel filing system that rotates from floor to ceiling, bringing the desired document to eye level within easy reach within seven seconds. Other document tracking systems (shown in Figure 6–18) are available that use a computer-assisted locator (CAL) system to provide information regarding folder locations, routings, and reservations.

*Using bar code wands*

Automated systems that use bar code wands to read identifying codes eliminate rekeyboarding file numbers and drastically reduce the incidence of misfiles. These optical wands read a bar code or optical characters that have been preprinted or prelabeled on the record jacket or document. The codes are read by moving the light sensor's tip over the codes. This optical scanner is the same system as is used in supermarkets at checkout counters. Figure 9–14 shows an operator using a bar code wand to read coded labels to enter documents into computer memory.

Figure 9–14
Bar Code Wand Usage

## Indexing

Automated hard-copy document storage allows indexes to be created electronically from information keyboarded into the system. The file can be identified from the index list and commanded to move to the access position. The indexing process is similar to the process used in any other automated system.

## Document Retrieval

Hard-copy source documents are usually filed in folders that have optically coded markers. An electronically controlled transport mechanism moves between facing banks of electro-optically coded shelving on which metal file containers are stored. Upon a keyboarded command, the transport mechanism tracks the desired container and delivers it to a workstation. The container automatically returns to its assigned storage place when the proper code is keyboarded into the system.

*Optically coded folders*

An automated records management system that provides retrieval of documents stored by several different methods is shown in Figure 9–15. Note that the system can retrieve images from microfilm, microfiche, paper, aperture cards, and optical disk systems, then send the electronic image of the document to the requester.

Charge-out and follow-up controls may be a part of the retrieval system. Automated charge-out controls may be provided by recording the date and the name of the authorized requester of records removed from the system. Information for follow-up may be compiled from the charge-out data.

*Charge-out and follow-up controls*

The Kardex Record Control System, interfaced with LEK-TRIEVER, provides control with automated storage and retrieval. For each record, the computer stores two types of records—a long-term record and a temporary record. The long-term record includes information such as file I.D. code, status, storage location, last transaction date, and an open field for additional data. The temporary record is used for charge-outs, and includes the requester's I.D. code, date, and department or location the file was charged out to. When the record is returned, this file is deleted. Because the system keeps track of all files at all times, it can provide information about records activity within a given period. Management reports covering everything from items with overdue requests, number of items charged out, departmental usage, and so on are easily generated. Audit trails are provided for all transactions automatically.

Figure 9-15
Automated Document Retrieval System

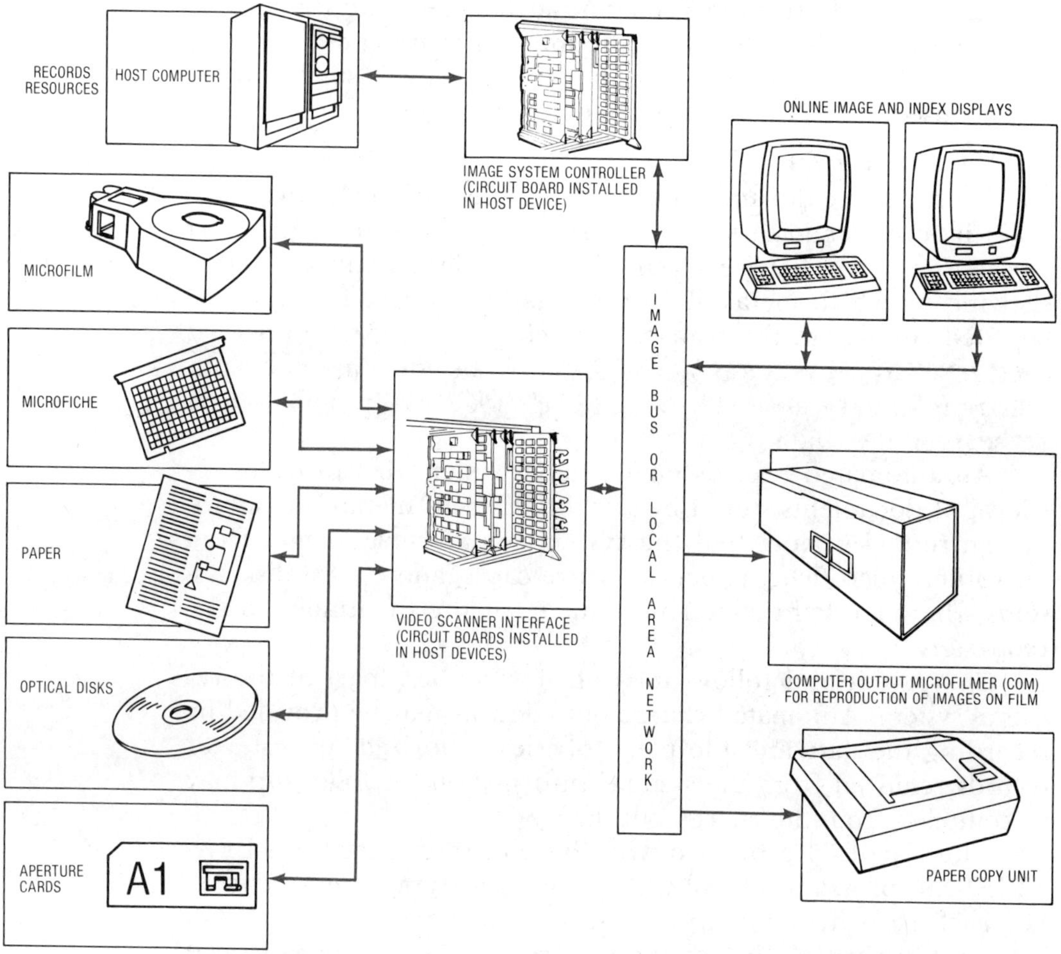

RECORDS RESOURCES | HOST COMPUTER

IMAGE SYSTEM CONTROLLER
(CIRCUIT BOARD INSTALLED
IN HOST DEVICE)

ONLINE IMAGE AND INDEX DISPLAYS

MICROFILM

MICROFICHE

PAPER

OPTICAL DISKS

APERTURE CARDS    A1

VIDEO SCANNER INTERFACE
(CIRCUIT BOARDS INSTALLED
IN HOST DEVICES)

IMAGE BUS OR LOCAL AREA NETWORK

COMPUTER OUTPUT MICROFILMER (COM)
FOR REPRODUCTION OF IMAGES ON FILM

PAPER COPY UNIT

Another method of providing charge-out and follow-up controls uses a bar code reader. Under this system, record numbers are translated into bar code representations and printed or taped onto the file folders or jackets. A hand-held lightpen scans the bar code, instantly transmitting the data to a computer. With lightpen stations in user locations throughout the facility, the movement of records can be tracked, both in- and out-of-file, and needed files can be located quickly. To request a record, the operator keyboards the record number on a terminal; this activates a printer located in the file room. The printer generates a record request slip which shows the file's current location.

A comparison of the relative capabilities of three major media is shown in Figure 9–16. Factors are identified that may affect the decision regarding the selection of paper, electronic/magnetic media, or microforms as a storage and retrieval system.

Figure 9–16
Comparison of Three Major Storage Media

| Factor | Paper | Elect/Mag | Microfilm |
|---|---|---|---|
| Quantity stored | Fair to poor | Excellent | Excellent |
| Visual quality | Excellent | Good to fair | Good to fair |
| Archival quality | Excellent to fair | Fair to poor | Excellent to fair |
| Durability of media | Excellent to fair | Good to poor | Excellent to fair |
| Security | Excellent to good | Excellent to fair | Excellent to good |
| Ability to capture photographs | Excellent | Poor | Excellent |
| Ability to capture handwriting | Excellent | Fair to poor | Excellent |
| Ease of annotation and updating | Fair to good | Excellent to fair | Fair to poor |
| Ease of information correction | Fair | Excellent | Poor |
| Transmission ease | Excellent to poor | Excellent to poor | Excellent to fair |
| Transmission speed | Good to poor | Excellent to fair | Good to fair |
| Transmission cost | Good to poor | Excellent to fair | Good |
| Duplication ease | Good | Excellent to fair | Excellent to good |
| Duplication speed | Good to poor | Excellent to good | Excellent to good |
| Duplication cost | Poor | Excellent to good | Excellent to good |
| Simplicity of storage system | Excellent | Good to poor | Excellent |
| Ease of maintenance | Good | Fair | Good |
| Ability to purge file | Good to poor | Excellent to fair | Good to poor |
| File integrity | Poor | Excellent | Excellent to good |
| Retrieval speed | Good to poor | Excellent to good | Excellent to good |
| Ease of conversion from | | | |
|    microfilm to | Good to fair | Fair to poor | NA |
|    paper to | NA | Good to poor | Good to poor |
|    elect/mag to | Good | NA | Excellent |
| Compatibility with other systems | Excellent to fair | Excellent to poor | Excellent to poor |
| Familiarity of users with system | Excellent | Fair to poor | Good to poor |
| Human-eye readability | Excellent | Poor | Fair |
| Scanning ease | Excellent | Good | Good |
| Equipment durability | Excellent to good | Good to poor | Excellent to fair |
| Cost | Excellent to poor | Excellent to poor | Excellent to poor |

*Source:* Dr. W. H. Baker, Associate Professor of Information Management, Brigham Young University, Provo, UT.

■

## A LOOK AT THE CASE

Since the noted deficiencies are in the areas of files maintenance and control, a change to either a mechanized or automated system will not solve the problems. The records manager should address the identified problems before giving any consideration to changing the system.

How may the records manager obtain additional information?

■

## EVALUATION AND REPORTS

*Determine effectiveness and productivity*

Measuring storage and retrieval activity provides information from which managers can determine the effectiveness and the productivity of the operation and retrieval system. Some questions that should be asked include the following:

- How many times was requested information not located?
- How long does it take, on the average, to locate a record?
- What is the ratio of unlocated records to total record requests?
- Are standards in place for measuring storage/retrieval effectiveness?
- Are procedures in place for reporting the number of items filed and the number of requests received?

Documentation provides this baseline data for evaluation and assessment. The best measurement of storage operations and retrieval is how quickly requested information can be retrieved and provided to the person requiring the information. Several factors affect the speed with which information may be retrieved — the number of records that are misfiled, the number of records that cannot be located, and the number of places that must be searched before locating the requested information.

### Activity Reports

*Establish activity database*

To establish a database for records activity and retrieval efficiency, the records manager must have the total cooperation of the records clerks and records supervisor(s). Accurate information must be obtained regarding the number of records filed, number of misfiles and unlocated records, record preparation time, number of requests for retrieval, and retrieval time.

Information necessary to determine storage efficiency and retrieval effectiveness may be obtained by having persons responsible for those activities keep records similar to those shown in Figure 9–17. For small file volume, such as might be kept by a department secretary, recording several weeks' retrieval data three of four times a year would be sufficient to establish a database. Other organizations might desire detailed information to include storage and retrieval efficiency on a periodic basis. Large organizations using central file facilities may wish to keep a daily record of storage/retrieval efficiency. Some companies have their retrieval system programmed to count automatically the number of searches and to print a report each month.

Figure 9–17
Storage and Retrieval Efficiency

| EFFECTIVENESS IN FILING RECORDS | | | Type of File *Case* | |
|---|---|---|---|---|
| Date | No. Hours Filing | No. Pieces Received | No. Cross-References | |
| | | | Forms | Extra Copies |
| (a) | (b) | (c) | (d) | (e) |
| 7/3 | 3 | 145 | 10 | 15 |

| EFFECTIVENESS IN FINDING RECORDS | | | Type of File *Subject* |
|---|---|---|---|
| Date | No. Requests Rec'd. | No. Not Found | No. Requiring a Search in Three or More Folders |
| (a) | (b) | (c) | (d) |
| 7/3 | 23 | 4 | 9 |

Records should be maintained for each request for either information or records retrieval. Number of pieces received refers to the number of separate papers (memos, letters, forms, and so forth). If a letter is multipage, it still represents one piece; if a memo is stapled to several documents to be stored together, that also counts as one piece. The number of pieces per inch can be estimated if a physical count has previously established the average number of sheets per piece; that is, on the average, how many sheets of paper are filed together as one piece. A one-inch stack of material normally contains 200 sheets, though not necessarily 200 pieces. Divide 200 by the average number of sheets as previously established to determine the average number of pieces per inch. An estimate can easily be made of the number of pieces received by measuring in inches the stack of incoming material. In Figure 9–17, the number of pieces received for storage, not the number of sheets received, is provided on the form.

*Pieces versus sheets*

If file activity needs to be determined by department, this information can be obtained at the same time as the previous information. Some programs using a database stored in a mainframe computer will automatically count, store, and print an annual report of all searches by department; by type of record; by age of material requested. One type of computer-generated report of records activity is shown in Figure 9–18.

Figure 9–18
Records Search Analysis

```
+-----------------------------------------------------------------------------------------------+
| DATE: 01/02/86                 CITIES SERVICE OIL AND GAS CORPORATION                          |
| TIME: 02.10.42                        CORPORATE RECORDS                          PAGE       8  |
|                                    RECORDS SEARCH ANALYSIS                   REPORT ID: G4FAA  |
| DEPARTMENT: NATURAL GAS LIQUIDS                                                                |
|             TECHNOLOGY                                            SCHEDULE NO.  RS-   8        |
|             ENGINEERING                                                                        |
|             ENGINEERING SERVICES/HISTORICAL                                                    |
|                                                                                                |
| PERIOD COVERED: 01/01/85 TO 12/31/85                       TOTAL ITEMS ON SCHEDULE:            |
+-----------------------------------------------------------------------------------------------+
```

| RECORD TITLE | ITEM NO. | CURRENT YEAR | 1 | 2 | 3 | 4 | 5-9 | 10-14 | 15+ | TOTAL SEARCHES |
|---|---|---|---|---|---|---|---|---|---|---|
| | | | | | YEARS SEARCHED | | | | | |
| LAKE CHARLES PROJECTS | 1209 | | | | | | | | | 0 |
| CONSTRUCTION PROJECTS (CONTRACTUAL AGREEMENT) | 1265 | | | | 3 | 4 | 1 | | | 8 |
| CONSTRUCTION PROJECT (CORRESPONDENCE) | 1266 | | 2 | 1 | 2 | | 11 | 3 | 33 | 52 |
| CONSTRUCTION PROJECTS (COST CARDS) | 1267 | | | | | | | | | 0 |
| CONSTRUCTION PROJECTS (COST/AFE) | 1268 | | | | | | 1 | | | 1 |
| CONSTRUCTION SPECIFICATIONS (TERMINALS/PIPELINES/ PUMP STATIONS) | 1270 | | | | | | | | | 0 |
| X-RAY FILES (PIPELINE WELDS) | 1286 | | | | | | | | | 0 |

*Source: Cities Service Oil and Gas Corporation, Tulsa, OK.*

## Status Reports

*Summary of effectiveness and efficiency*

Status reports summarize the activity reports on the effectiveness and efficiency of storage and retrieval functions. These activity report figures are then compared to established individual organizational standards or to industry standards. The comparisons reveal areas which need improvement.

### Reference Ratios

Reference ratios, which measure file activity, can be determined by dividing the number of retrieval requests by the number of pieces stored. The formula

$$\text{reference ratio} = \frac{\text{number of retrieval requests}}{\text{number of pieces stored}}$$

is applied to data supplied through reporting. A ratio of less than five percent is considered low and indicates that the records are inactive and should be transferred to inactive storage or destroyed.

## Accuracy Ratios

Accuracy ratios, which measure the effectiveness of the records system and records personnel, can be determined by dividing the number of records located by the number of records requested. This provides an overall accuracy ratio. Many organizations operate with a 99 percent ratio. The formula

$$\text{accuracy ratio} = \frac{\text{number of records located}}{\text{number of records requested}}$$

is applied to the data supplied through reporting. Even one percent unlocated records is unacceptable in most instances. More specific breakdowns may also be made by determining the ratio of misfiles to total requests as well as determining the ratio of records unlocated to total requests. Misfiles represent three percent of files. This figure, though typical, is high and causes a decline in productivity.

*Determine misfiles ratio*

Further accuracy information may be provided by determining the ratio of records requiring a search in more than one location before retrieval to total records located. The latter statistics may indicate poor indexing or inadequate cross-referencing.

## Personnel Ratios

Personnel ratios, which measure the adequacy of the records staff to perform specific functions, may be determined by analyzing the staff requirements for particular tasks. One employee is required for each 5,200 cubic feet of records received; one employee is required to handle reference activity for each 7,000 cubic feet of records stored annually; one employee is required for each 4,700 cubic feet of records destroyed. The results of personnel ratios will suggest overstaffing or understaffing and provide information regarding the specific area requiring staff adjustment.

## Filing and Retrieval Time

Filing time spent per item may be obtained by dividing the total time used to file (shown in hours, but converted to minutes) by the number of items filed. **Retrieval time** may be obtained by dividing the time used to retrieve items (shown in hours, but converted to minutes) by the total number of requests received.

A status report may also include data regarding the file activity of particular departments or users. This information provides a

*File activity of particular users*

basis for analyzing overutilization or underutilization of records by departments.

Because the information obtained is already identified by classification system in use (subject, numeric, and so forth), statistics may be generated that reflect the efficiency of the particular classification system. For example, if most of the misfiles or unlocated records are identified in the subject classification system, this information could suggest that a careful evaluation be made of the procedures within that system or of the appropriateness of that classification system to the filed material.

Status reports may be generated to include whatever information will be helpful in analyzing the effectiveness and efficiency of the files operation and retrieval system. Reports may be used to identify strengths and weaknesses of the system and to recommend improved retrieval procedures and systems.

## A LOOK AT THE CASE

To provide documentation regarding the filing and retrieval efficiency of the system in use, Deluxe Paper Clips' records manager should conduct files activity analyses through a reporting system. The information gained from the activity reports will provide the basis for status reports. The status reports may then be used to make comparisons between the efficiency of the system in use at Deluxe Paper Clips and established industry standards.

## TERMINOLOGY REVIEW

*Automated operation and retrieval.* Storing, retrieving, and controlling information using a computer or microprocessor.

*Basic classification index.* A categorical grouping of subjects with appropriate subheadings.

*Block sorting.* Rough sorting records into groups of alphabetic letters (A, B, C, D, E, F) or in groups of numbers (1–10, 11–20), and so forth.

*Charge-out.* Procedure for checking out records for use by requester.

*Coding.* Indicating on a record where it is to be stored.

*Computer output microfilm (COM).* An integration of computer and micro-form technology that converts information on computer tapes or from computer memory to a microform.

*Computer-assisted retrieval (CAR).* Using the computer to aid in locating and retrieving records.

*Cross-reference.* An additional notation that directs the user to another lo-cation where the record or information may be found.

*Filing.* The action of storing a record.

*Filing segment.* The entire name, subject, or number that is used for filing purposes.

*Indexing.* The mental process of deciding where a record is to be stored.

*Long-term cross-reference.* An additional notation that is used to provide a trail or forwarding address for a record.

*Magnetic storage and retrieval.* Depositing and retrieving information off-line from the computer database or word processing memory.

*Manual operation and retrieval.* The process of storing and retrieving records without the aid of mechanical or automated devices.

*Mechanical operation and retrieval.* The use of mechanized equipment to store and retrieve records.

*Memory.* The capacity to retain data within the system to form a database.

*Microimage storage and retrieval.* The process of storing and retrieving records that have been reduced in size and stored on roll film, fiche, aperture cards, jackets, and opaques.

*Release mark.* A notation that the immediate need for the record has passed and that the record may now be stored.

*Retrieval time.* The time required to locate a record is determined by di-viding the time used to retrieve items (shown in hours but converted to minutes) by total number of requests received.

*Sorting.* Arranging records in filing order according to the classification system used.

## COMPETENCY REVIEW

1. What storage procedures are applicable for most records systems whether manual, mechanical, or automated?
2. Describe specific procedures for maintaining manual file operations.
3. What are the major similarities/differences between manual and me-chanical operations?
4. How is information captured for
   a. internal storage?
   b. magnetic storage?
   c. microimage storage?
   d. hard-copy automated storage?

5.  How is information retrieved from
    a.  internal storage?
    b.  magnetic storage?
    c.  microimage storage?
    d.  hard-copy automated storage?
6.  Describe control methods for manual, mechanical, and automated operations.
7.  Explain three activity reports and the procedures for obtaining the information for the reports.
8.  Describe two status reports and explain how information is obtained for these reports.
9.  Describe types of information gained through activity and status reports and explain how this information is useful in improving records management.

## APPLICATIONS

1.  Given the following activity reports, compute reference ratios, accuracy ratios, and filing time.

| EFFECTIVENESS IN FILING RECORDS | | | Type of File *Case* | |
|---|---|---|---|---|
| Date | No. Hours Filing | No. Pieces Received | No. Cross-References | |
| | | | Forms | Extra Copies |
| (a) | (b) | (c) | (d) | (e) |
| 7/3 | 3 | 145 | 10 | 15 |
| 7/4 | 7 | 322 | 15 | 29 |
| 7/5 | 5 | 267 | 20 | 16 |
| 7/8 | 6 | 310 | 6 | 21 |
| 7/9 | 5.5 | 292 | 12 | 16 |

| EFFECTIVENESS IN FINDING RECORDS | | | Type of File *Subject* |
|---|---|---|---|
| Date | No. Requests Rec'd. | No. Not Found | No. Requiring a Search in Three or More Folders |
| (a) | (b) | (c) | (d) |
| 7/3 | 23 | 4 | 9 |
| 7/4 | 37 | 2 | 6 |
| 7/5 | 19 | 6 | 1 |
| 7/8 | 52 | 9 | 4 |
| 7/9 | 42 | 4 | 7 |

2.  Prepare a status report including conclusions that may be drawn for the activity reports in Application 1.

## CONCLUDING CASES

### A. Software Distributor

Jo Downing, office manager for a large software distributor to both retail and commercial outlets, has just returned to her office from a highly frustrating meeting with Douglas McAfee, vice president for planning and analysis. Jo has been trying to "sell" Mr. McAfee on the idea of changing the manual operations and retrieval system currently in use to a mechanized or even an automated system. Mr. McAfee is not easily convinced by either subjective arguments or emotional pleas. He has told Jo that if she wants him to consider any changes, she must return with a logical presentation that will specifically address these issues:

1. What are the advantages/disadvantages of the systems, both current and under consideration?
2. How do the systems differ in the way information is stored and retrieved?
3. What is the difference in the way information is indexed?
4. Are there differences in efficiency?

As Jo left Mr. McAfee's office, Mr. McAfee's parting shot was "and prepare this for me in the form of a chart so that I don't have to waste my time reading a voluminous report."

Prepare the chart.

## B. Canadian Industries

Doris Goade is a new employee at Canadian Industries where you have been employed for five years. Your current position is assistant supervisor of central files. Central files is organized as a service function and houses all of the active files for the organization. The records, which are paper and microfiche, are stored and retrieved manually. The records for which Doris will be responsible are stored according to a subject classification system.

The central files supervisor, Eileen Barton, has asked you to train Doris in her new job. To begin the training, you need to explain the procedures for storing and retrieving records to Doris. Describe the procedures as you would explain them to Doris. Present each procedure in logical order.

## READINGS AND REFERENCES

Anderson, Lewis L. "The Challenges of Selecting, Procuring, and Implementing a CAR Microfilm System." Presentation, Association of Records Managers and Administrators, Inc., New York, New York. (September, 1985).

Association of Records Managers and Administrators, Inc., Atlanta Chapter *Newsletter,* February, 1981.

Baker, W. T. Associate Professor of Administrative Management, Brigham Young University, Provo, Utah.

Banks, Richard. "COM vs Optical Disk — Which Way to the Future?" *Information Management,* Vol. 19, No. 4 (April, 1985), p. 1.

Benedon, William. "Computer Records Management." Presentation, Association of Records Managers and Administrators, Inc., New York, New York. (September, 1985).

Canning, Bonnie. "Automated Document Management—Assessing the Need." *IMC Journal,* Vol. 21, No. 2 (Second Quarter, 1985), p. 9.

Canning, Bonnie. "Options in Electronic Records Management." *Office Administration and Automation,* Vol. 45, No. 1 (January, 1984), p. 48.

"Computer Speeds Records Retrieval," *Office Systems Management,* Vol. 1, No. 4 (Spring, 1983), p. 12.

General Services Administration, National Archives and Records Service, Office of Federal Records Centers. *File Operations: Managing Current Records.* Washington, D.C.: U.S. Government Printing Office, 1981.

Johnson, Mina M., and Norman F. Kallaus. *Records Management.* Cincinnati: South-Western Publishing Co., 1986.

Keegan, Allen. "The Automation of a Records Program." Presentation, Association of Records Managers and Administrators, Inc., Calgary, Canada. (October, 1984).

Lacey, John A. "The Expanding Role of Micrographics in Information Management." *Information Management,* Vol. 17, No. 4 (April, 1983), p. 18.

"A Marriage Made in Charleston." *Modern Office Technology,* Vol. 30, No. 2 (February, 1985) p. 94.

Miller, Barbara A. "Charge-Out Control and Retrieval." Presentation, Association of Records Managers and Administrators, Inc., Calgary, Canada. (October, 1984).

Naukam, Lawrence W. "Buying a CAR and Making It Run." *Records Management Quarterly,* Vol. 19, No. 4 (October, 1985), p. 36.

Rager, Rick, and Judd Smith. "COM Software." *Information and Records Management,* Vol. 11, No. 4 (April, 1977).

Raudenbush, Jeanne C., and Robert B. Shaklee. "Computerized Solutions for Records Management." *Office Systems '85,* Vol. 2, No. 8 (August, 1985), p. 44.

Sample, Robert L. "Mathematics of Filing—Cabinets vs. Electronics." *Administrative Management,* Vol. 43, No. 1 (January, 1982), p. 38.

Sleight, Wicky. "Automated Systems: Planning and Implementation." Presentation, Association of Records Managers and Administrators, Inc., New York, New York. (September, 1985).

Sowney, Karen L. "Meeting Mass-Storage Needs of Word and Data Processing." *Office Systems '84,* Vol. 1, No. 11 (November, 1984), p. 36.

# 10
# THE INTEGRATED INFORMATION SYSTEM

## Competencies

After completing this chapter, you should be able to

1. describe an integrated information system.
2. summarize the goals of an integrated information system.
3. describe each of the steps in the implementation process.
4. define the originating subsystem and describe how it is different in the integrated system than it is in a traditional office.
5. define the processing subsystem.
6. define data processing and explain how distributed data processing contributes to the functioning of an integrated information system.
7. define word processing and describe its time-saving applications.
8. list the methods of inputting information into a word processor.
9. define the communication subsystem.
10. describe the types of internal communication services.
11. describe the types of communication services to remote locations.
12. describe the remote conferencing techniques and compare the use of these techniques to single-site meetings.
13. define the storage subsystem.
14. define the types of storage media.
15. explain the role of the records manager in the integrated information system.
16. summarize the effect of each subsystem within the integrated information system on records functions.

# Introductory Case

Major Marketing Consultants (MMC) is a large national firm of marketing consultants who specialize in national marketing campaigns for major manufacturers. MMC has 12 regional offices to handle its 1,200 clients.

Shortly after its initial formation in the early 1970s, MMC purchased a large mainframe computer system with batch processing capabilities. Each regional office established a word processing center using magnetic card typewriters. While these equipment purchases met MMC's needs at the time, the lack of communication capability between offices has begun to infringe upon MMC's ability to serve clients with multiple offices. For the first time, Martin Tedrick, MMC's president and chief executive officer, feels that MMC, despite its excellent personnel, may be losing its competitive edge.

Lynne Finding, MMC's records manager, is called to Mr. Tedrick's office. Mr. Tedrick asks Lynne for her suggestions on how to improve the productivity of information processing and communication functions in each office and between offices. Lynne told Mr. Tedrick that she believed they should explore the feasibility of implementing an integrated information system. Mr. Tedrick asked Lynne to appoint a task force of five to design a system and prepare an implementation plan.

1. What is an integrated information system?
2. What goals can be accomplished by using an integrated information system?
3. What are the steps in implementing such a system?

*There is nothing more difficult to take in hand, more perilous to conduct, or more uncertain in its success, than to take the lead in the introduction of a new order of things....[People] do not truly believe in anything new until they have had actual experience of it.*
                                                            *—Machiavelli*

Discussions of the "automated office," the "office of the future," and the "paperless office" continue. Yet many organizations still do not accept these concepts. Some organizations are waiting to see how these concepts will be employed by others and with what degree of success, and some of the decision makers involved find it hard to believe that an integrated information system is possible or can be very beneficial. However, the integrated information system has become a reality in many organizations.

## OVERVIEW OF THE INTEGRATED INFORMATION SYSTEM

A system (as discussed in Chapter 1) is a group of separate but interrelated parts acting together to accomplish a goal. An **integrated information system** is a group of automated subsystems working together and communicating with each other to process information, distribute it to the appropriate persons in a timely manner, store information (records) for efficient retrieval, and dispose of stored information (records) when it is no longer needed. Four *Four subsystems* subsystems comprise the integrated information system—the originating subsystem, the processing subsystem, the communications subsystem, and the storage subsystem. (See Figure 10–1.)

### Goals

The goals of an integrated information system are specific to the organization which implements the system. These goals can usually be summarized as a desire to implement technological resources which will enhance the productivity of human resources—managerial and support personnel—in achieving the organization's overall goals.

*Enhance productivity of human resources*

Direct costs of office operations are rapidly increasing. The high cost of office operations has forced top executives to focus on improving the productivity of office employees. One obvious technique for improving productivity of human resources is to provide better tools (equipment) to assist them in performing their duties. For this reason, many organizations examine the option of implementing an integrated information system.

Figure 10–1
The Network of Subsystems Comprising the Integrated
Information System

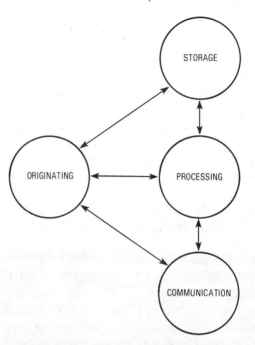

*Decrease costs*

Decreasing the costs of office operations may be one organizational goal which can be achieved by implementing an integrated information system, but it is not the only goal. Many organizations look to improved office technology to decrease the duplication of effort existing in many office tasks. Duplication may exist in repetitive keyboarding to achieve a final copy of an item of correspondence or a report, or duplication may be as simple as the time wasted in "telephone tag" as executives or support staff re-dial the same telephone number to obtain information or confirm meeting dates and times. Increased efficiency not only decreases overall costs of operations, but it also eliminates a great deal of worker frustration.

*Decrease duplication of effort*

Few organizations, however, are willing to devote time and resources to planning and implementing an integrated information system unless they determine that such a system will be a cost-effective method of achieving the organization's overall goals. Organizational goals are usually determined by top executives. These individuals must be convinced that an integrated information system is potentially advantageous before any serious steps can be taken to implement such a system.

*Assist in achieving organizational goals*

## Implementation Process

The four steps in the implementation process are (1) approval, (2) system design, (3) installation, and (4) maintenance.

### Approval

An organization's top executives are not likely to approve any expenditure of time and financial resources that cannot be demonstrated to produce a significant and desirable return on investment. In preparing a presentation to these executives, one must consider how an integrated information system will assist in achieving the organizational goals these individuals have established. An integrated information system should not be presented as something nice to have; it should be presented as an integral part of a profitable, efficient organization.

In seeking top administrative approval to design and implement an integrated information system, one must also be mindful that in the past the strategy for improving efficiency of information operations has been to move certain tasks out of the office. For example, data processing tasks went to the data processing center, word processing tasks went to the word processing center, and microfilming was done in the micrographics center. The concept of an integrated information system in which a network is established to allow these tasks to be done in the office and communicated from one area of the office to another is still futuristic to many organizations. To those who have never seen an integrated information system in action, tailoring each technology so that it works in tandem with others in the system may seem impossible. Because of this, one important presentation strategy is to present examples of similar organizations in which such systems are working effectively. (Specific strategies of making oral and written presentations are presented in Chapter 2.)

*Present examples of effective integrated systems*

Overplan for this step. Anticipate the questions and concerns of top executives and carefully research the responses. Be sure to discuss with top executives not only required technological changes, but also changes in work procedures and role changes for various staff members which must be a part of the new system. The approval and publicized support of the organization's top executives is important not only to the successful implementation of an integrated information system but to its continued effective functioning as well.

## System Design

The first step in designing the integrated information system is to determine who has the responsibility for designing the system. A task force appointed for this purpose can provide a wide range of experience and knowledge. The task force should include members from all levels of workers who will be affected by the implementation of the system and should actively seek input from other workers. Greater involvement of employees in the planning stages will decrease resistance to the new system when it is installed.

*Seek employee input*

The integrated information system task force must determine where technology can enhance productivity and assist in achieving organizational goals. In making this determination, the task force may find it useful to survey employees to ascertain where they perceive bottlenecks in the existing procedures and what suggestions they may have for improving these procedures. The task force must also make a comparative examination of available equipment. Equipment options should be evaluated based on how well they meet the organization's needs, compatibility with other types of equipment needed to complete the integrated information system, ergonomics, and cost (including hardware, software, and maintenance). Many expanding organizations are especially interested in the modularity of equipment—the ability to expand the capabilities of the equipment as the organization's needs expand. Equipment is too expensive to replace when increased capabilities are needed.

One step which may be helpful in evaluating equipment options is to participate in equipment demonstrations. The most informative demonstrations usually take place at another user's location. This permits a more realistic assessment of performance and an opportunity to question current users.

## Installation

Approaches to the installation of equipment for an integrated information system have been categorized as "revolutionary" or "evolutionary." In general, the revolutionary approach of installing all the new equipment throughout the organization at one time has been found to create a great deal of user resistance and chaos in office operations. Employees feel their offices have been taken over by the new equipment, and everyone is learning new procedures and debugging software at the same time. An evolutionary approach allows some employees to become familiar with the equipment and to be able to help others adjust more quickly.

The evolutionary installation approach uses a test site to evaluate software and user acceptance of the selected equipment. Software may need to be adjusted to meet the needs of a specific organization or may be determined to simply be a poor choice for one organization's applications. The appropriateness of the software should be determined before purchasing large quantities of equipment and software. If problems can be satisfactorily addressed, then employee frustrations with equipment that seems inefficient or unworkable are minimized because they are experienced at only one location. An additional benefit of using a test site is that those employees who use the system and see its benefits will help promote the installation of system equipment in other locations throughout the organization. Most organizations find it beneficial to select a department whose employees have demonstrated enthusiasm for the system, a department which will experience dramatic increases in efficiency, or a department with high visibility as a test site.

*Select installation test site*

The performance of the test site should be evaluated before additional installations are considered. This evaluation should encompass questions such as the following:

- Was the site preparation (wiring, temperature control, and so forth) adequate?
- Did the hardware (equipment) and the software perform as anticipated?
- Did the hardware and the software demonstrate the capability of meeting the organization's needs?
- What adjustments/replacements are needed in the software?
- What difficulties were encountered in operator training? How can these difficulties be minimized or eliminated?
- Was there a satisfactory level of user acceptance? If not, what can be done to improve user acceptance?
- Was there an increase in productivity? If not, would other hardware or software options be more likely to improve productivity? Would more or better training improve productivity?

## Maintenance

Once the installation is completed, the integrated information system task force may be disbanded, or it may continue to function as an advisory group for issues relating to the integrated information system. The integrated information system operation is assigned to one manager who is responsible for its maintenance and expansion.

Successful maintenance of an integrated information system has four elements: (1) continuous review, (2) upgrading as needed, (3) employee feedback, and (4) education and training. Organizations are not static; their needs change. Consequently, the best technology for meeting their needs may also change. Work loads may shift; departments may expand their functions and need additional technological support. Someone must be in a position to review and respond to these changing needs.

*Adapt system to changing organizational needs*

Upgrading the integrated information system may become necessary as a result of changing needs within the department, or it may be the result of technological innovations which better address existing needs. Proposed upgrading of equipment should be evaluated in much the same way that original equipment purchases were evaluated: How will the new technology better meet the organization's needs? Is it compatible with existing equipment in the integrated information system? What are the comparative costs of upgrading options versus continuing with the existing system?

*Evaluate proposed upgrading of equipment*

A feedback system is important in avoiding user resistance. Employees must have a suggestion box or an open door to approach the manager with problems or suggestions for improving the system or procedures for using the system. Often, employee feedback is the first indication that the system may need to be upgraded. The system was implemented to enhance the productivity of human resources; if employees find its operation cumbersome or confusing, this goal will not be achieved. These employees must have a means of communicating concerns in order for problems to be corrected and employee satisfaction to be maintained. When system problems are identified, the integrated information system task force may be called upon to develop solutions.

*Encourage employee feedback*

The need for education and training of employees when a new system is installed must be recognized. This need will continue to exist as employees are moved to new positions in which they will use other equipment or new employees are hired. Several training options available to an organization are discussed in Chapter 13.

*Provide continuous education and training*

■

## A LOOK AT THE CASE

Mr. Tedrick called Lynne Finding and the members of the integrated information system task force to his office to congratulate them for their efficient design and smooth installation of MMC's new integrated information system. The involvement of all employees in providing suggestions for system design and equipment selections especially pleased Mr. Tedrick. Each person had a contact on the task force with whom to communicate; consequently, there was no noticeable resistance to the new equipment and the procedural changes it necessitated. Mr. Tedrick also complimented Lynne on the use of a test installation and the subsequent system modification.

Lynne was just beaming as she prepared to leave Mr. Tedrick's office "Just a minute Lynne," Mr. Tedrick said. "I want to be sure I understand exactly what effect this new information system has on the performance of our office functions. Beginning next Friday, I'd like to have a detailed report from you each Friday on one of four subsystems. Let's begin with the origination subsystem next Friday, shall we?"

1. What is the role of the origination subsystem in the integrated information system?
2. Are origination tasks performed more productively in an integrated information system?

■

## ORIGINATING SUBSYSTEM

The **originating subsystem**, the means of putting information into the integrated information system, is the first of four subsystems in the integrated information system. (See Figure 10–2.) The manner in which tasks are performed in each subsystem is significantly changed when the organization implements an integrated information system; however, many possible combinations of options can constitute an integrated information system. Because of this, the descriptions will be of the options, not of "the solution" to implementing an integrated information system.

### Creation Phase

Much of the originating or creation phase of correspondence, reports, and agendas and the initiation of voice communications is performed at the executive, administrative, and managerial levels of an organization, with similar tasks of a more routine nature being performed by administrative support personnel. Often the top level of the organizational structure perceives the most dramatic changes in methodology when an organization implements an integrated information system.

Figure 10–2
The Role of the Originating Subsystem Within the Integrated
Information System

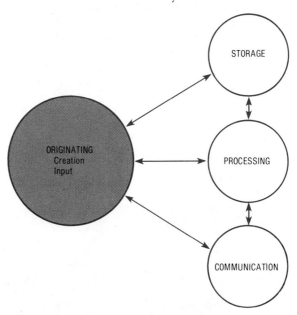

A completely paperless office is not in the foreseeable future for most organizations. Executives will still make notes in longhand, some mail will continue to be received in the familiar format through the postal services, and telephone message notes will exist for some time. The amount of paper appearing on "the boss's" desk will, however, undoubtedly decrease.

## Input Methods

In an integrated information system, input devices may range from longhand notes on the yellow legal pad to keyboarding or voice input into an executive workstation. Those individuals with no keyboarding skills usually prefer to write their notes and let their support personnel put the information into the system. Many executives still rely on dictation as a means of producing correspondence and reports. This may be accomplished by dictating directly to a secretary, by using a dictation recording machine, or by dialing a special number to dictate directly to the word processing center through a telephone.

*Composition in response to previous correspondence or previously received data*

Although some dictation initiates new actions, much dictation is in response to previous correspondence, meetings, or personal encounters or to summarize previously collected data. The executive workstation can significantly expedite the latter type of origination through the ability to recall previous documents to the viewing screen. In many instances, the document can be annotated on the screen. If the executive is to compose a report, the summary data can be recalled to the screen for review and manipulation before preparing the report. The ability of the executive workstation to retrieve information from electronic files or data storage banks is dependent upon the capability of the workstation's microprocessor and, of course, upon these components of the integrated office being connected through a communication network which allows information exchange. (Networks will be discussed further in the communication subsystem section.)

## A LOOK AT THE CASE

Lynne brought Mr. Tedrick a report on the originating subsystem. Her report demonstrates savings of composition time and of file-search time through the direct access to the computer database which includes file location indexes. Mr. Tedrick said he would study the report and would look forward to hearing about the processing subsystem next Friday.

1. What functions are performed in the processing subsystem?
2. How is productivity in the processing subsystem improved in the integrated information system?

## PROCESSING SUBSYSTEM

The **processing subsystem** is the means of manipulating data within the information system to achieve desired results. This subsystem consists of two previously separate elements: data processing and word processing. (See Figure 10–3.) In the integrated information system, these two elements are brought together to achieve increased office productivity.

Figure 10–3
The Role of the Processing Subsystem Within the Integrated
Information System

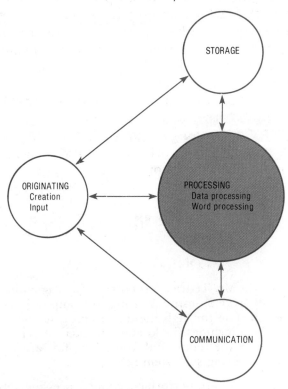

## Data Processing

**Data** are symbols which represent people, objects, events, or concepts; they are raw facts. **Data processing** is the use of a computer to manipulate data to achieve a desired result. When data is placed into a meaningful context for a user it becomes **information.**

### Applications

*Data processing applications*

While computer-directed printers can print items such as mailing labels, variable data on grade reports for students, and report titles, the use of data processing is most frequently associated with the manipulation of numbers. Typically, data processing has been used to perform accounting functions such as computing payroll and printing checks; preparing comparative sales figures by product, sales division, or geographic area; or customer billing. Many of the new computers, even in the personal computer category, are able to produce graphic representations of this data; some can even do this in color. (See Figure 10–4.)

## Distributed Data Processing

Many organizations have found it inefficient to have all their information and processing power in one location and have moved to distributed data processing (DDP). DDP does not eliminate the mainframe computer but brings information and the ability to retrieve and manipulate it to users within the office. This step has brought many organizations closer to an integrated information system. An additional step needed to complete the transformation to the integrated information system is to acquire other automated equipment and communications networks so that the equipment can work together.

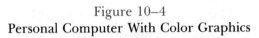

Figure 10–4
Personal Computer With Color Graphics

## Word Processing

Word processing is the manipulation of ideas and data to produce a desired result. Word processing operators work with very sophisticated equipment. (See Figure 10–5.) A keyboard may be used to record information which appears on a video screen. This information can be moved or edited; it can also be printed or stored on a magnetic disk. The most frequent "desired results" of word processing are error-free copies of correspondence, legal documents, and reports.

## Applications

Office productivity can be greatly improved by automating repetitive tasks. Before the evolution of word processing, several draft

Figure 10–5
Word Processing Equipment Components

copies of a report would usually be necessary before the originator was completely satisfied and would allow the final typing of the document. Each draft required the typist to re-keyboard paragraphs which had no changes as well as those in which changes were made. With the text-editing feature available on word processors, the report can be recalled to the screen. The operator can scan the report for those paragraphs in which changes are to be made, make the changes, and print an error-free copy on a high-quality printer which prints at speeds of from 20 to 55 cps (characters per second). Many word processors now have the ability to send the document directly to a photocopier if several copies are to be made.

Additional time savings can be realized when forms, contracts, form letters, and form paragraphs are stored on disks to be recalled when needed. This eliminates any retyping of standard documents or portions of documents while allowing the operator to personalize the document with names, addresses, account numbers, dates, and so forth. Another application which saves time is the ability of most word processors to merge lists of names and addresses with a form letter and print the necessary personalized copies of the letter while the operator is inputting a new document.

*Interface with phototypesetters*     Many currently available word processors are able to interface with phototypesetters. This capability allows the copy for newsletters, brochures, manuals, and so forth, to be prepared by utilizing the text-editing feature of the word processor and to be typeset and printed without re-keyboarding. A tremendous savings in keyboarding is achieved, and the need for a second proofreading is eliminated as well.

## Input Methods

All word processors accept input from their keyboards. When finalized, information may be stored on magnetic disks if the word processor is directed to do so.

Disks can be reinserted into the word processor so that stored information can once again be manipulated. Manipulation of stored data and inputting new information may be necessary for minor changes in standard documents, such as enrollment figures in last year's alumni letter, dates, or policy changes for the employee manual, or the organization's telephone directory.

A third input method is from optical character readers. Optical character readers can read printed information and digitize it so that the word processor can transform it to printed words on its screen. Optical character readers are commonly used for identifying account numbers on checks; however, computer printouts are prepared more and more frequently with machine-readable fonts so that repetitive keyboarding is eliminated.

## A LOOK AT THE CASE

On Friday afternoon Lynne Finding delivered her report on the processing subsystem to Mr. Tedrick. "Our processing speed has greatly increased in all departments," Lynne said. "Each department can now perform most of its own paperwork processing functions. No one is waiting for someone else's work to be completed before his or hers can be done at the data or word processing centers. All reports are being completed on time."

"That's wonderful news, Lynne," said Mr. Tedrick. "I hope next week's report on communications is equally bright!"

1. What are the functions of the communication subsystem?
2. How is the productivity of the communication subsystem improved in the integrated information system?

## COMMUNICATION SUBSYSTEM

The **communication subsystem** is the means of getting information to users in a timely manner. This subsystem is comprised of two types of communications: communications within the organization and communications to remote locations. (See Figure 10–6.)

Figure 10–6
The Role of the Communication Subsystem Within the Integrated
Information System

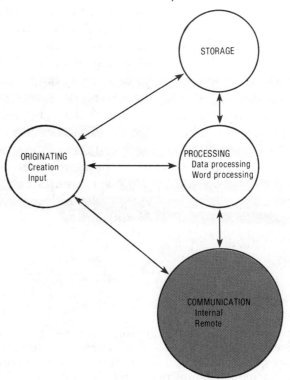

## Communications Within the Organization

*Communication networks*

The sharing of information and processing ability which allows an office to become an integrated system is created by communication networks which join various technologies as well as terminals (workstations) employing the same technology. This is referred to as interactive communication. The diagrams in Figure 10–7 illustrate three approaches to networking. Diagram A illustrates equipment connected to a common, open-ended coaxial cable. Diagram B illustrates equipment linked by a cable loop. In this type of network, the equipment itself may be a part of the loop. Central computer control of equipment components is illustrated in Diagram C.

### Electronic Mail Services

One application of the communications network within the office is the ability to provide electronic mail service. Electronic mail service uses the computer or a communicating word processor as a mailbox and allows each user to access mail through a terminal and to respond by using the terminal's keyboard. This service eliminates "telephone tag." Messages can be composed, edited, distributed, and filed at the user terminal. The mailbox holds the message until the recipient calls for it; the sender does not need to wait until the recipient can be reached by telephone to relay a message. Additional time savings are realized for those applications in which the same message is to be distributed to several locations within the organization; these messages can be sent simultaneously. Prepared distribution lists allow the originator to indicate that the message is to be sent to a designated category of people (such as department heads), and the message is delivered to each designee's mailbox. Electronic mail services have the additional advantage of being noninterruptive. The user may easily check the terminal to determine if messages are waiting, but no buzzing or ringing interrupts important conversations or composition.

*Simultaneous electronic distribution of messages*

### Voice Mail

Voice mail is an alternative to the electronic mail networks that are tied to the typewritten word. Many executives would prefer to deliver some messages orally and bypass the time-consuming ele-

Figure 10–7
Types of Communication Networks

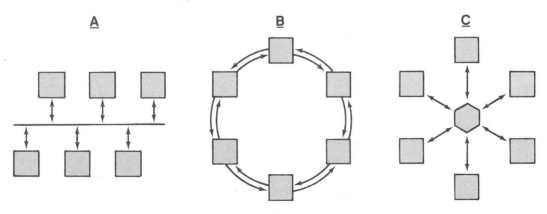

ments of dictating the message and having it transcribed. This is particularly true when the message is to be delivered internally or to a branch of the organization. Voice mail should not be thought of as a replacement for telephone conversation. Telephone contact provides a two-way communication bridge, while voice mail allows only one-way communication. It does, however, end the game of "telephone tag." Voice mail provides the ability to communicate a message to an individual or to groups of people. The user dials an assigned number to enter the voice mail system, relays the message, and the system then attempts to deliver the message to all recipients immediately. If the recipient is not available to receive the message, it is filed in memory. Later, when the recipient dials the voice mailbox, the voice mail is received in its original form—the sender's voice. For priority messages, originators can instruct the system to "keep trying" to reach the recipient at specified intervals. Voice mail systems can also deliver messages at a specific time and on a future date.

*Eliminates "telephone tag"*

### Time Management Services

Internal communications also allow for time management services not previously possible. One important time management application is scheduling meetings. Without an integrated information system, scheduling meetings may frequently require many hours of various support personnel's time in checking "the boss's" schedule. If the meeting was for ten department heads, inevitably nine would be able to come at the first choice time; eight could come at the second choice time, and so forth. The internal communications network allows access to personal calendars so that meetings can be scheduled without talking to each attendee. Once a convenient time is determined, each attendee receives a message that a meeting has been added to her or his calendar.

*Scheduling meetings*

Calendars can also be maintained at user terminals. Users can see appointments scheduled on a particular date on the screens at their desks. Appointments can be canceled or rescheduled with a few simple motions, and the calendar is always up-to-date.

*Calendar maintenance*

## Communications to Remote Locations

Time means money to today's business organizations. The speed with which communications can be transmitted to branch locations or to customers and associates outside the organization continues to increase in importance.

## Telecommunications

**Telecommunications** are those communications sent over telephone lines. The most well-established type of telecommunications is that available through Western Union's TWX and TELEX services. These services use a punched paper tape to send messages to remote locations where they are printed for the recipients. TWX and TELEX are subscriber services. The necessary equipment is leased from Western Union, and a directory of all subscribers and their numbers (much like a telephone directory) is distributed to each subscriber.

Another form of telecommunication is an electronic mail subscriber service. Organizations which do not have their own electronic mail capability may subscribe to a commercial service such as those provided by GTE's Telemail or Tymnet's On-Tyme II. The U.S. Postal Service also offers a commercial service called ECOM, electronic computer-originated mail. ECOM messages are transmitted by common carrier to one of the 25 post offices with receiving equipment, then printed, put into envelopes, and delivered with the mail. Delivery is promised anywhere in the United States within two business days. Mailers pay an advance fee and must send at least 200 messages per transmission.

**Facsimile transmission** is the electronic transmission of hard-copy data over telephone lines. A similar hard copy is produced at the recipient's location. Facsimile equipment (see Figure 10–8) has vastly improved in speed and quality of communication in the last several years. Much of this equipment can transmit unattended after regular business hours for savings in transmission costs or to

Figure 10–8
Facsimile Equipment

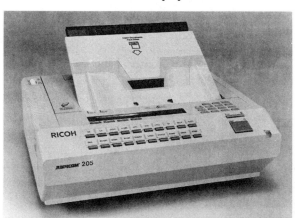

reach recipients in other time zones. Some organizations are now using microfacsimile transmission—the electronic transmission of microrecords—which reproduces microrecords at the recipient's location.

*Interactive communications through telephone modems*

Terminals which have interactive communications may also be connected to communications (telephone) lines through the use of a modem. The modem converts digital data from the sending machine into signals which can be transmitted over telephone lines. These signals are reconverted to digital data at the receiving terminal. To use the modem, a call is placed to the receiving location. When a connection is made, the telephone receiver is placed in the modem and transmission begins. Many terminals can be programmed to transmit unattended.

Several types of conferencing using telecommunication technology are also available. Computer conferencing is possible when interactive terminals are connected via telephone lines. Conference participants may be at their terminals simultaneously, or the information may be stored electronically and accessed at the recipient's convenience. If all participants are at their terminals simultaneously, information is received on their screens, and they may "talk" via their terminal keyboards.

Audio teleconferencing is the most familiar type of conference conducted via telephone connections. **Audio teleconferencing** is voice communication over telephone lines between two or more remote locations. Participants in several locations can talk with each other in a conference call, which may be arranged through an operator or established by the participants. If several people are to participate at each location, all parties are present in the same room and a speakerphone projects the voice so that all may hear and enables each to speak.

*Electronic blackboards*

A teleconferencing technique which is especially useful in relaying graphic illustrations to remote locations in situations where the participants do not need to see each other is the electronic blackboard. (See Figure 10–9.) This blackboard has a pressure-sensitive surface. Chalk strokes are converted to digital data which can be transmitted via telephone lines, and recipients view the blackboard on a monitor. When the blackboard is erased, the monitor is erased. If several illustrations need to be viewed simultaneously, two or three blackboards can transmit over the same telephone line; however, a separate monitor is required for viewing the contents of each blackboard. A separate telephone line is required for audio transmission.

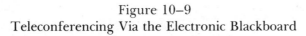

Figure 10–9
Teleconferencing Via the Electronic Blackboard

A similar application uses an electronic pen. Pen strokes made *Electronic pens*
on an electronic pad are converted to signals which are sent via
telephone lines to the remote location. At the receiving location,
another pen records the message. This device produces a hard
copy of whatever is transmitted.

Three forms of video teleconferencing are also possible. The
first of these is slow-scan video which requires separate phone lines *Slow-scan video*
for audio and video transmissions. The video transmission is sent
from a camera which scans the image from top to bottom in about
60 seconds. Receiving systems may store the image until the entire
frame is received. This type of video teleconferencing is best suited
to the transmission of blueprints and other documents.

Another form of video teleconferencing is freeze-frame video. *Freeze-frame*
This form allows one to freeze a single frame from the camera and *video*
transmit it. Although the transmission time remains the same as
with slow scan, the potential problem of blurred images is eliminated. Freeze-frame systems with additional memory capacity can
store multiple frames to allow forward or reverse image retrieval.

The most natural (and expensive) form of video teleconferencing is live, full-motion video. This option allows the camera to *Live,*
focus on the speaker and transmits a visual image as well as the *full-motion*
speaker's voice. These visual images are stored and transmitted as *video*
three-dimensional images.

## Satellite Communications

*Video-conferencing*

Satellite beams are being used by large, geographically dispersed organizations to transmit videoconferences. A videoconference is similar to a live, full-motion video teleconference, except for the method of transmission. Both videoconferencing and video teleconferencing require heavy financial investments to equip the conference rooms; however, many organizations have found these applications to be cost effective because of the savings in executives' time and travel expenses. For organizations unable or unwilling to make this investment, AT&T provides rental teleconferencing facilities in 38 U.S. cities.

Satellites are also used by independent telephone companies to transmit telephone conversations using microwaves. Some communications companies are offering all digital integrated voice, data, and image transmission through satellites.

## Fiber Optics

**Fiber optics** are transparent glass fibers which conduct light (usually in the form of a laser) that may transmit both analog (tonal) and digital signals. The use of optical cables is increasing rapidly in the late 1980s and is expected to continue to increase because of the greater transmission speed provided. Transmission through fiber-optic cables also offers the advantage of immunity to electromagnetic and radio interference, which is particularly important in some industrial environments (such as steelworks) and for cars and aircraft. Other advantages include significantly less signal loss; the insulating quality of glass provides better security; less weight and size; and the potential to carry 10,000 times as much information as the same diameter of copper wire.

■

## A LOOK AT THE CASE

Martin Tedrick welcomes Lynne Finding to his office on Friday afternoon. "Well, Lynne, what good news have you brought today?"

Lynne is more enthusiastic than ever. "Because we can share information among departments through our interactive terminals, our reports are being processed faster than ever. The most exciting thing, though, is that we had our first teleconference among branches this week. The electronic blackboard provided visuals which clarified the presentation of new reports control procedures. We got very positive feedback from all the branches."

"That's just fine, Lynne. So far, this system seems to work as well as you said it would. I look forward to your report on the storage subsystem next week."

1. What are the functions of the storage subsystem?
2. How is the productivity of the storage subsystem improved in the integrated information system?

## STORAGE SUBSYSTEM

The **storage subsystem** is the means of storing, retrieving, and disposing of information according to the organization's needs. (See Figure 10–10.)

Figure 10–10
The Role of the Storage Subsystem Within the Integrated
Information System

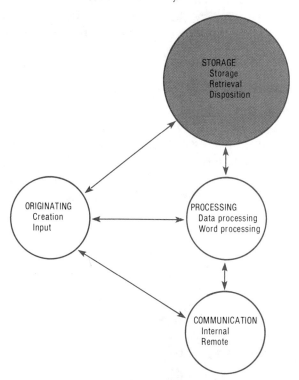

## Storage

Stored information becomes the records of the organization. In an integrated information system, information may be stored through several media.

### Electronic Storage

**Electronic storage** is the depositing of information in an online computer database or in the memory of a word or data processor. Information stored in an online computer database may be quickly accessed from any terminal connected with the computer. This information may then be further manipulated, printed for distribution, or distributed through an electronic mail service. Information stored in the memory of a word or data processor may also be further manipulated, printed, or distributed through an electronic mail service. If this information will be needed for future use, it should be transferred to a magnetic storage medium.

### Magnetic Storage

Information which is to be stored on magnetic media is digitized and stored on computer hard disks, computer tapes, or on floppy disks. This information may also be readily viewed and manipulated once the appropriate tape or disk is located. Another magnetic medium is the optical disk (see Chapter 6). The use of optical disks is expected to continue to increase in the late 1980s and in the 1990s as costs become more competitive.

### Microrecord Storage

Hard-copy documents may be reduced to microimages and stored on microfilm or microfiche. Microrecords may also be computer generated (COM). Microrecords may be duplicated very inexpensively and distributed through the postal services (saving significantly over mailing hard copy) or be distributed through facsimile transmissions. Microrecords may be viewed on a reader printer which will also produce a hard copy of the information, if needed.

## Retrieval

Retrieval is the process of locating stored information and getting it to users in an efficient manner. In an integrated information system, retrieval is usually accomplished with an automated system. Various retrieval systems were discussed in Chapter 9.

## Disposition

Disposition is the elimination of records (stored information) no longer needed by the organization. The timing of records disposition is determined by the retention schedule (discussed in Chapter 3). Methods of disposition vary from organization to organization and with the confidentiality of records (also discussed in Chapter 3).

■

### A LOOK AT THE CASE

Lynne delivered her report on the storage subsystem to Mr. Tedrick on Friday. "Mr. Tedrick, the storage subsystem has produced significant space savings for us through the drastic reduction of paper files. When you examine these figures, I think you'll agree that we may no longer need to plan for expansion of our records center in the next two years."

"Again you've brought good news, Lynne. There is, however, one more report I'd like you to prepare—a report on how this new integrated information system affects your role as records manager. I'll see you again next Friday."

1. What is the role of the records manager in the integrated information system?
2. How does the integrated information system affect each records function?

■

### RECORDS MANAGEMENT IN THE INTEGRATED INFORMATION SYSTEM

Records management is the systematic control of records from their creation to their final disposition. Within an integrated information system, the manner in which records are processed, communicated, stored, and retrieved may change significantly from procedures used in a more traditional office. These changes affect the role of the records manager in the office and the performance of many records functions.

## Role of the Records Manager

Much has been written about who will be in charge of the integrated information system. Will it be the data processing manager? The word processing manager? A committee of managers of data processing, word processing, and communications processing? Each of these choices shares a limiting characteristic. These individuals, while quite competent in their own areas, are accustomed to managing equipment to produce results.

*Knowledgeable about information needs of all departments*

Within the integrated information system, someone must manage information. The individual best prepared to perform this function is usually the records manager. This individual is familiar with the information needs of all divisions and departments of the organization. The records manager knows what records are kept in each office, what the distribution patterns are, what the retention requirements are, and when records may be destroyed. This is a background that no other manager within the organizational hierarchy has.

*Thorough knowledge of each technology*

Records managers must not assume that the integrated information system will be under their control. In order to be given this responsibility, records managers must demonstrate a thorough knowledge of each technology to be employed in the integrated information system and how each will affect overall office efficiency. Records managers must demonstrate leadership qualities which would allow them to lead in the implementation of new technology without alienating other employees and with minimal disruption of office routines.

Even if records managers are knowledgeable and well prepared to assume these responsibilities, it cannot be assumed that they will be appointed to these positions. Office politics often enter into the decision of who will be in control of the integrated information system. However, if the efficient origination, processing, communication, and storage of information is the goal of the integrated information system, there can be no better prepared individual to direct the implementation and maintenance of this system than the records manager.

## Records Functions

Integrated information systems contribute to the speed and accuracy of input, processing, and output of information. The use of an integrated information system changes the manner in which many records functions are performed.

## Origination

As previously discussed, the origination of records will frequently be done at an electronic terminal. This not only allows more rapid composition, but it also prevents misplacing incomplete documents. If the originator must leave the work before completion, the information is simply placed in storage to be recalled later. The availability of access to computer data banks and other automated retrieval systems speeds the accessing of previously stored information which may be important to the composition of correspondence and reports.

## Processing

Processing, both data and words, is also completed at electronic terminals. This equipment continues to be upgraded to provide additional operations and to improve speed of existing operations. Printer speeds are vastly improved over those of the best typists, and much keyboarding is eliminated in the revision stage.

## Communication

Communications used to be written or oral (face to face or by telephone). Now there are numerous other options. Electronic mail and facsimile services allow recipients at remote locations to receive hard-copy data without waiting for the postal services. Electronic mail has also eliminated a great deal of interoffice mail. Teleconferencing, electronic blackboards, and videoconferencing via satellite, though still quite expensive, allow some organizations to have participatory meetings of individuals in several locations and save executive time and travel costs.

## Storage

The integrated information system is much less dependent on paper and paper files. Manually searching paper files to locate information is too slow and too costly. New storage media allow automated access, which reduces retrieval time from several minutes to a few seconds.

The integrated information system offers the opportunity for increased managerial and administrative support productivity within the organization and improved communication speeds, both internally and externally. The organization's needs should be carefully examined before beginning any implementation process. Employee involvement in each stage, from planning to installation, increases the probability of implementing the best combination of options for each subsystem and of minimizing employee resistance to the new equipment and procedures. A thorough knowledge of the organization's information needs makes the records manager the likely choice to manage this new system.

■

## A LOOK AT THE CASE

Friday afternoon Lynne delivered her final report to Mr. Tedrick. "Mr. Tedrick, my role as records manager is much more comprehensive than it was previously. Our productivity is so greatly improved that we have larger volumes of information to process, distribute, store, and retrieve. However, now that all our information functions are automated, each function seems to work more efficiently; and the employees seem to enjoy their work. I continue to get good feedback from all branches and departments. I'm very pleased with our integrated information system."

"I'm very pleased, too, Lynne. So pleased, in fact, that I'm giving you a raise. You'll see it reflected in your next paycheck."

■

## TERMINOLOGY REVIEW

*Audio teleconferencing.* Voice communication over telephone lines between two or more remote locations.

*Communication subsystem.* The means of getting information to users in a timely manner.

*Data.* Symbols which represent people, objects, events, or concepts.

*Data processing.* The use of a computer to manipulate data to achieve a desired result.

*Electronic storage.* The depositing of information in an online computer database or in the memory of a word processor.

*Facsimile transmission.* The electronic transmission of hard-copy data over telephone lines.

*Fiber optics.* Transparent glass fibers which may transmit both analog (tonal) and digital signals by lasers.

*Information.* Data placed into a meaningful context for users.

*Integrated information system.* A group of automated subsystems working together and communicating with each other to process information, distribute it in a timely manner to the appropriate persons, store information (records) for efficient retrieval, and dispose of stored information (records) when it is no longer needed.

*Originating subsystem.* The means of putting information into the integrated information system.

*Processing subsystem.* The means of manipulating data within the information system to achieve desired results.

*Storage subsystem.* The means of storing, retrieving, and disposing of information according to the organization's needs.

*Telecommunications.* Those communications sent over telephone lines.


## COMPETENCY REVIEW

1. What is an integrated information system and what are its goals?
2. Describe the steps in the implementation process.
3. What is the originating subsystem and how is it different in the integrated information system than it is in a traditional office?
4. Define the processing subsystem.
5. What is data processing and how has distributed data processing contributed to the functioning of an integrated information system?
6. Define word processing and describe two of its time-saving applications.
7. List three methods of inputting information into a word processor.
8. What is the communication subsystem?
9. Describe two types of internal communication services and three types of communication services to remote locations.
10. Describe at least three remote conferencing techniques and compare their use to single-site meetings.
11. What is the storage subsystem?
12. Define three types of storage media.
13. Explain the role of the records manager in the integrated information system.
14. Summarize the effect of each subsystem within the integrated information system on records functions.


## APPLICATIONS

1. Trace the path through the integrated information system of (a) an incoming invoice and (b) an outgoing item of correspondence.
2. a. Which technique would be most desirable for inputting the following into the integrated information system?
      (1) Sales data
      (2) Internal reports
      (3) Legal documents from other offices

   b. Which storage technique would be most desirable for each of the following:

(1)  Reports
(2)  Weekly sales data
(3)  Correspondence

## CONCLUDING CASES

### A. Information Enterprises

Information Enterprises (IE) publishes trade journals in the fields of information systems and management. Each of the seven journals has a national readership, and getting them out on time from Information Enterprises' word processing center to the printer is becoming more difficult. Someone is always late! In addition, IE's computer no longer has sufficient processing capability to handle advertisers' accounts, subscription notices and billings, reports of readership and industry surveys, and other business functions, such as payroll.

Betty Wilson, chairman of the board of Information Enterprises, has asked that a consultant be hired to design and direct the implementation of an integrated information system for IE. Ms. Wilson emphasized to the board her concern that any system implemented should continue to provide the records needed for efficient, successful operations.

You have been hired as an information systems consultant to Information Enterprises.

1.  What types of information would be required to prepare a cost justification for an integrated information system?
2.  Outline the steps in the implementation process.

### B. James Wyman

James Wyman, a noted office systems consultant, has been invited to make a presentation on minimizing employee resistance to integrated information systems at an office automation conference three months from today. His audience will be office, word processing, data processing, and information managers.

James has asked you, one of his junior associates, to briefly describe three techniques for minimizing employee resistance to integrated information systems which he might use as the basis of his presentation.

## READINGS AND REFERENCES

Avedon, Don. "Avedon on Office Automation." *Information and Records Management,* Vol. 16, No. 1 (January, 1982), p. 40.

Canning, Bonnie. "A Decade of Development." *IMC Journal,* Vol. 22, No. 1 (First Quarter, 1986), p. 7.

Doyle, Lee W. "Understanding Misunderstood Electronic Mail." *Today's Office,* Vol. 20, No. 8 (January, 1986), p. 35.

Jenkins, Tom. "Take Audio Teleconferencing and Meet Without Traveling." *Office Systems '85,* Vol. 2, No. 4 (April, 1985), p. 100.

Mueller, Robert R. "Integrating Information Processing Technologies." *Information and Records Management,* Vol. 16, No. 1 (January, 1982), p. 18.

Pomerantz, David. "The Ins and Outs of Teleconferencing." *Today's Office,* Vol. 17, No. 2 (July, 1982), p. 66.

Ruprecht, Mary M. "Is Your Organization Ready for Systems Integration?" *Office Systems '86,* Vol. 3, No. 4 (April, 1986), p. 67.

Settanni, Joseph Andrew. "Information Systems Management Values." *Administrative Management,* Vol. 47, No. 4 (April, 1986), p. 32.

Seymour, Jim. "The Adventures of Store-and-Forward Facsimile." *Today's Office,* Vol. 19, No. 2 (July, 1984), p. 56.

Spiller, Rex, and Thomas J. Housel. "Video Teleconferencing — A New Training Tool." *Sloan Management Review,* Vol. 27, No. 1 (Fall, 1985), p. 57.

Thomas, Linda. "Word Processing: Keeping Pace With the Nuclear Age." *IMC Journal,* Vol. 21, No. 1 (First Quarter, 1985), p. 39.

Udler, Allan S. "Effective Implementation of Automated Office Systems: Your Guide to Success." *IMC Journal,* Vol. 21, No. 1 (First Quarter, 1985), p. 14.

Vernon, Robert E. "The Ideal Integrated Office." *Today's Office,* Vol. 19, No. 2 (July, 1984), p. 27.

# PROFILE

## United Telephone of Florida

United Telephone of Florida is one of nine operating companies owned by United Telecommunications, Inc., based in Kansas City, Missouri. United Telephone of Florida's headquarters office in Altamonte Springs and its eight district and two division offices serve 800,000 customers in a territory covering one-third of the state of Florida.

In 1982 William (Ike) Gainey, director of data services, began developing United Telephone's integrated information system. An information network was needed to provide an integrated communications link between the company's executives, their support staffs, and the host computers in the company's various offices. The most important requirement of the proposed system's hardware and software was that it be totally integrated; secondary emphasis was placed on ease of use. Integration was important to avoid a piecemeal, department-by-department approach to determining and addressing information requirements, which would be very expensive.

A committee of managers from five key user departments — accounting, human resources, data services, engineering, and general services — was created to select an organization-wide system. The committee developed a list of major functions which the new system needed to address and interface into the corporate IBM network. These functions were word processing, electronic mail, and calendar management.

Once the goals of the integrated information system were established, the committee began its search for vendors who could provide software and hardware to handle the needed functions. The choice was narrowed to five vendors; then the systems were tested. Each department manager evaluated each critical item by assigning a numeric value to how well each system met the established goals. The final hardware/software decision was based on these evaluations. The selected system integrates software as well as hardware. This is particularly beneficial because users need to learn only one set of commands.

When the system was initiated in March, 1984, Mr. Gainey's staff provided a terminal to all department heads, officers, and each of their secretaries. Senior executives were then surveyed to determine who they talked with most frequently, what kind of information was exchanged with those individuals, and which five business reports they referred to most frequently. The information providers where then supplied with terminals.

A company training center offers formal half-day or one-day classes in all facets of the system. Senior management can either attend classes at the training center or make appointments for training sessions at their own terminals.

The information network has improved communications and increased access to information. The electronic mail feature has allowed executives to decrease the number of face-to-face meetings. When meetings are necessary, calendar management makes arranging the meetings easier. *Administrative Management*'s 1986 First Place Gold Award for Office Automation to United Telephone demonstrates the success of the system.

Dick Brown, vice president of operations, describes the success of the program as follows:

*Paper memos still provide a great deal of information, but I am becoming more and more dependent on my computer terminal for the information I need quickly. Once people gain confidence and take time to learn how to use the system, especially with the help of fine teachers such as we have on our staff, they reap the benefits of the new technology. Management should be confident that computerized networks are the wave of the future.*

Contributed by William Gainey
United Telephone of Florida
Altamonte Springs, FL

# 11
# SPECIALIZED
# APPLICATIONS

## Competencies

After completing this chapter, you should be able to

1. differentiate among the organizational functions of each of the following types of organizations:
   a. banks
   b. governmental agencies
   c. insurance organizations
   d. medical facilities
   e. libraries
   f. multinational organizations
2. state at least one unique requirement of the records management system for each of the following types of organizations:
   a. banks
   b. governmental agencies
   c. insurance organizations
   d. medical facilities
   e. libraries
   f. multinational organizations

There are many specialized applications of records management systems; a few of these systems are discussed in this chapter. Applications within different environments use different systems as dictated by the particular needs of that organization.

Banks, governmental agencies, insurance companies, medical facilities, libraries, and multinational organizations are among those organizations whose records management systems are specialized. Organizational functions, records management systems, and profiles of organizations that exemplify these specialized applications are presented in this chapter.

# BANKS

Banks are unique because their business is money. Banking institutions serve in the capacities of repository, lender, investor, and adviser in financial matters. As a repository, banks provide a safe place for their customers to deposit their funds. As a lender, banks make funds available to borrowers. In their investor capacity, banks invest deposited funds in profit-making ventures; this provides a return on investment to their stockholders. Banks also provide financial advice to their customers. In these various capacities, billions of dollars flow through banking institutions annually. The responsibility for this volume of money necessitates accurate information combined with speedy data retrieval.

## Records Management System

The records of banks include correspondence, customer credit histories, customer account records, internal financial documentation, interbank and intrabank transaction records, legal documents, and personnel records. Most of the records of banks are requested by account number, name, or transaction date.

The first major users of microrecords were banks whose operations have continued to offer a major application for microrecords. Banks use both roll film and fiche for their applications; microforms production is by COM and by source document filming. Retrieval may be manual, mechanical, or computer assisted.

The largest number of records in daily banking activities are in demand deposits—in the volume of source documents (deposits, checks) and reports associated with demand deposits. Checks are processed by item address. Following proof encoding (imprinting of numeric magnetic characters that can be interpreted by high-speed recording equipment), checks are grouped, and each group is assigned a number. The microfilm operator enters the control information into a sequential imprinter on the microfilmer; each item is imprinted with the control and sequence information and receives its microfilm address. After the microfilming has been completed, the checks are forwarded to the data capture area where the computer assigns the same control information as was stamped by the microfilmer.

Many banks also use microfilm to enable each branch office to maintain copies of all customers' signature cards for ready reference and verification by tellers.

An online cumulative transaction journal accommodates 90 to 95 percent of customer inquiries, including what checks have been paid, the amount, date, and number. Other inquiries are addressed through a CRT terminal displaying the microfilm address of the item. The magazine and frame numbers are located, and the image is displayed in seconds. If necessary, a copy can be made immediately.

Distribution of daily reports (trial balances update, drawn on today's deposit report, new accounts report, and so forth) to all branches is facilitated by programming the data into the distribution system and indicating which branches are to receive which reports and in what quantity. The reports are then automatically duplicated in microfiche format and sorted by branch number. Distribution in microfiche form is less expensive in terms of time required to reproduce the reports and postage required to mail the reports to the branches.

# PROFILE

## Citicorp

Citicorp is a $73.8 billion organization serving the financial needs of individuals, businesses, and governments at 1,937 locations in 95 countries. Through its various subsidiaries and affiliates, it engages in commercial banking and trust services, mortgage banking, consumer finance, credit card services, equipment leasing, factoring, payment mechanism research, and the sale of traveler's checks and other variable denominated payment instruments.

Citicorp, through its records management program, provides necessary information to its customers, to governmental agencies, and to Citicorp employees. As Citicorp expanded into new businesses and new locations, its organization became more and more complex, and the backup paperwork required to do business increased accordingly. In the early 1970s, Citicorp officers undertook a long-range program of records management with an emphasis on paperwork reduction and cost savings.

Citicorp's records management program is a total one, encompassing all technologies. This includes micrographics, computer/CRT online systems, telecommunications, word processing, forms management, reports control, facsimile, and centralized storage of inactive records. Through the program, Citicorp and its major banking subsidiary, Citibank, have eliminated billions of documents, thereby reducing floor space, storage equipment, and the number of people needed. The result has been greater efficiency and phenomenal dollar savings.

Citicorp's program of records management received the prestigious William Olsten Award for Excellence in Records Management in 1978. Key factors in its selection were the creativity, innovative qualities, forward planning, implementation of high technology, staff training, and cost effectiveness of the records management program.

In presenting the award, William Olsten, chairman of the board of the Olsten Corporation, cited these savings:

> *Records management demonstrably is one of the most important areas for efficiency and savings in modern business. It is because of the Olsten Corporation's belief in the importance and future of records management and micrographics, and our support of these areas, that we are proud to honor an organization like Citicorp which has made such an outstanding contribution.*

The initial step in developing the program was a records survey. This inventory identified all records by filing units, volumes, and annual accumulations. It also established retention periods for all records; identified vital records; proposed appropriate microfilm applications for both source documents and COM; identified records that could be destroyed; and identified types and volumes of inactive records to be retired from prime space to a records center.

Records retention periods were established based on operational, historical, research, tax, comptroller, and legal requirements. All retention periods were approved by the appropriate supervisor, bank officer, comptroller, tax officer, and legal counsel.

The operating aspects of the program include

...use of a functional classification system which provides for the standardization of one record code number, one description, and one retention period for the same type of record throughout the various locations of Citicorp. Records are grouped under eleven functional categories. This categorization, developed in the early 1970s, remains unchanged despite the major reorganizations within the organization.

...an online computerized system that produces a variety of records, including weekly, monthly, quarterly, and annual summaries.

...a computerized inventory system for Citicorp's approximately 18,000 forms.

...a uniform filing system for the corporate administrative offices.

...an ongoing reports reduction program.

...the first phase of an electronic mail system designed to process, store, and transfer 90 percent of the paper-based applications related to division heads and their particular function.

...an ongoing vital records program in which records are microfilmed, computerized, and stored in a commercial underground facility.

...operational word processing stations throughout various banking groups.

...a mail study at the Citibank center which resulted in Citibank receiving its own ZIP Code from the U.S. Postal Service.

...a facsimile system to provide fast access to data at distant locations.

As a result of its records management program, Citicorp has achieved ten major objectives.

1. Storage of inactive records has been centralized (from five buildings into one), resulting in a $568,000 savings in annual rental costs.

2. Standardization of records cartons from thirteen configurations to three saved $253,000.

3. An average 156,000 cubic feet of inactive records is transferred annually from prime office space to the information center at a space savings worth $312,000.

4. Ten records management positions have been eliminated, resulting in a salary savings of $175,000.

5. Transfer of vital records from in-house to a commercial underground center saves $60,000 annually.

6. Replacement of 20 million computer printouts monthly with 240 million COM frames annually produced a savings of $7.2 million and savings of $1.8 million in storage space.

7. Forms and envelope consolidation and standardization resulted in savings of $588,000.

8. A reports reduction program provides continuing savings in labor hours and storage space.

9. Savings also result from daily microfilm processing of 2.5 million checks and the annual filming of nine million source documents.

10. Implementation of an electronic funds transfer system eliminated millions of hardcopy documents.

The total savings attributed to the records management program is $10,956,000.

Citicorp, an organization whose stature in banking is recognized throughout the industry, implemented a records management system which resulted in paperwork reduction and cost savings. An equally important result has been the ability of the records management system to provide "the right record to the right person at the right time and at the lowest possible cost."

*Contributed by Stuart Shilling*
*Citicorp, Staten Island, NY*

# GOVERNMENTAL AGENCIES

Governmental agencies have an obligation and a responsibility to serve their constituents. Regardless of the level of the agency — local, state, or federal — governmental agencies exist to provide service to the public. The service should be provided as efficiently and economically as possible. To achieve this goal, records managers operating in a governmental environment have the same need to stay current with regard to equipment, staffing, and methods as any other manager of records systems.

## Records Management System

The need to record information and to have that information available is not new. In 1691 in Princess Anne County, Virginia, the city clerk recorded a description of John Vaughan's livestock. The description read "His mark, crop both ears two slits in the right ear and one in the left ear." From this kind of record has evolved the recording of virtually every legal transaction for over three centuries; this has resulted in massive volumes of recorded data.

Federal agencies have recognized the problems that exist with regard to the paperwork explosion. Commissions have been established to study these concerns and to make recommendations for reducing the burden. Legislation has been passed to address the problem. Recognition has been given to the problems of proliferation of sophisticated equipment in a largely uncoordinated system of information management within federal agencies.

Many governmental agencies now use microforms to combat the growing problem of records storage space. In addition to the filming of inactive records, some governmental agencies (such as USDA) have developed COM applications for more efficient processing of billings from suppliers. Suppliers mail computer tapes with itemized billings and microfilm of individual purchase tickets to USDA for processing. This substantially reduces the supplier's mailing costs and USDA's processing time.

Each governmental agency has established unique records management policies which are communicated via directives or manuals. All federal government agencies are responsive to review of the records programs by the General Services Administration.

# PROFILE

## County Clerk's Office
## Laramie County, Wyoming

Laramie County in southeastern Wyoming has a population of about 68,000, based on the 1980 census. The county seat is Cheyenne, which is also the state capitol.

The County Clerk is charged with keeping many of the county's vital records such as real estate deeds, liens, and plats. Also under the Clerk's jurisdiction are auto titles, uniform credit information, marriage records, election records, and budgetary/personnel records. The Clerk also acts as secretary and recorder to the Board of County Commissioners. As such she is responsible for taking and publishing minutes of proceedings and for storing all agendas and accompanying material.

When the present county clerk came into office 12 years ago, there were no records management practices in effect. In fact, stacks of miscellaneous files cluttered the floor of her office. Until 1981, all information management was handled manually with standard alpha or numeric filing. Many of the historic records were hand-written in books weighing as much as 35 pounds each.

In 1981, the Clerk installed the first mainframe CPU and created an in-house data processing center. In just six years, all information and record-keeping processes have been totally automated. All information management systems have been created in-house, so specific systems could be tailored to specific needs. The County Clerk has set up a complete records center to house Clerk's records and election equipment and, as space allows, the records of other county departments.

One major concern in automating was the historic hand-written real estate records. The Clerk's office established a microfilm center and filmed all records, which, due to the volumes of information to be filmed, was a cost/time effective measure. Furthermore, once the filming was current within the Clerk's departments, the Clerk could offer filming services to other governmental entities, thereby generating revenue for the county.

Once filming of the Clerk's material was complete, the original books were vaulted in state archives to preserve their historic quality, while their information is still available on film for working use. Precise, automatic indexing and cross-referencing affords easy access to any needed record.

All real estate information from 1974 on has been entered into a multi-indexed online computer system for easy access and manipulability. Each single record may be accessed by reception number, grantor, grantee, and book/page. Addendums and appendices to records are automatically cross-referenced and "attached" to the parent record as they are entered into the system. A complex network of standards and edits check each entry for validity, and each entry must go through two data entry operators — one for entry and another for verification.

This unique system is so complete that a special computer program allows research access only to private abstractors tracing property boundaries and histories.

One of the main problems encountered in setting up the automated systems was that each set of records had unique handling requirements. No single set of rules applied to all records. Also, because these are considered legal records, accuracy was imperative. And, finally, many of the guidelines had to be set up according to state statute; and, in the case of election records, for example, the county system had to be compatible with the state system.

The elections registration system had to be set up to be especially manipulable and multi-functional as information is continually being added, changed, purged, and put to a variety of uses. From one master file, for example, poll lists, judges lists, absentee labels, master lists, or any designated portions thereof must be run. This is achieved through strict entry coding.

The county employs a full-time technical writer, and complete user documentation is written as each system is written. These documentation manuals enable the staff to use the automated systems accurately and efficiently while cutting training time of new employees.

Laramie County has no records management manual. Rather, each department and each system has procedural and documentation manuals. All manuals are maintained and edited as necessary to achieve consistency. Basically, this is done through a staff of one technical writer and two programmer/analysts under the educated assistance of the Clerk, a Certified Records Manager.

Within the last year, five IBM-PCs have been added to the equipment list and have been interfaced with the Burroughs mainframe. The advantages of networking are now being explored.

The Clerk's office employs a staff of 30, including seven managers. Many of the staff are cross-trained to function in more than one position, and all staff members are familiar with elections material and proficient in data entry. The number of staff has not changed appreciably in the 12 years that the present County Clerk has been in office, though two new departments—microfilm and records center—have been added.

*Contributed by DiAnn Conyers*
*County Clerk's Office*
*Laramie County, WY*

# INSURANCE ORGANIZATIONS

Insurance organizations provide policyholders protection from financial losses caused by health expenses, automobile accidents, fire, theft, and death. Many insurance companies offer their policyholders additional services, such as low-interest loans against the cash value of life insurance policies.

Some insurance companies offer a full range of insurance policies—home, auto, life, and health. Some companies specialize in only one or two areas of insurance coverage. All insurance companies have large volumes of paperwork which begin with the application form.

## Records Management System

Policyholder records are essential to the functioning of any insurance company. These records reveal who is insured, when the policyholder was insured, what type of coverage the policyholder has, what amounts of coverage the policyholder has, what was charged for providing the coverage, and what payments have been made. The policyholder's record is initiated with an application form. If coverage is extended, the record will also contain a copy of the policy, correspondence related to the policy, and records of payments, claims, and loans.

Because of the large volume of paper involved in policyholder records, many large insurance companies have begun to microfilm these records. Jackets are the most commonly used application because they can be updated as needed. Documents are usually filmed 30 days after they are received. The jackets are maintained in the central files area. If the policyholder file is needed, a diazo duplicate of the jacket file is made and sent to the company personnel requesting the file. Using this system, the file is never "out." Copies of the file can be made for all personnel who need the file simultaneously.

Some insurance companies are using microfilm systems in which documents are filmed daily in random order and coded for computer-assisted retrieval. These systems also produce an index of documents for each roll of film. Insurance companies find this microfilm application especially useful for loan application files.

All insurance policies are assigned policy numbers as they are issued. Most policyholder records are filed numerically by policy number. Most companies cross-reference these files alphabetically by policyholder name. Individual agents may find it easier to maintain alphabetic files of policyholders by name and to cross-reference them by policy number.

# PROFILE

# Northwestern Mutual Life Insurance Company

Founded in 1857, Northwestern Mutual Life Insurance Company of Milwaukee, Wisconsin, is the tenth largest life insurance company and the 72d largest business enterprise in the United States. Northwestern has assets of over $19 billion. Its more than 3 million policies are of three major types—life insurance, disability income, and retirement annuities. Additional policies are being added at the rate of approximately 300,000 annually.

The large volume of paperwork required to initiate and service its many policies caused Northwestern to examine the filming of records as a file control tool in the late 1930s. At that time, no microfilming camera existed that could film both sides of their card files simultaneously; however, a determined employee, Elgin Fassel (later to become head actuary), developed and patented a microfilm camera to meet this need. The initial microfilming application reduced 750 cubic feet of records to one and one-half cubic feet of film—a space savings of 99 percent.

A formal records management program was established in 1974 as a part of Northwestern's Administrative Services Department. Walter Riese was appointed to the new position of manager of records. Riese's responsibilities include records storage, retention schedules, retrieval, and vital records security with emphasis on micrographic techniques and forms.

One of the first projects undertaken by the records management team in 1974 was a study of how to efficiently manage the underwriting life insurance application file. The application file was already a part of Northwestern's microfilming program. These files were purged and roll filmed six years after creation. There were still a number of problems similar to those experienced in almost any large file: (1) too many personal visits to the file room; (2) the unit was not informed of transfers of files among users; (3) misfiles; (4) increases in staff; (5) unproductive time spent logging files in and out of the file area; (6) 20 percent of the folders were out of file for referral or updating or were misplaced on any given day; and (7) security was becoming a problem. In addition, Northwestern was trying to maximize use of the file area by putting the most recent policy issues in automatic files. This procedure for maintaining recency of policy issues in automatic files caused seemingly endless shifting of files.

The study of the application file was done by a task force of users and records management personnel. Proposals were solicited from area micrographics vendors and service bureaus for a new micrographic filing system. The task force selected a microfiche jacket system. The application file is filmed when it is 90 days old. Processed film is checked and loaded into previously titled jackets (now printed by high-speed computer). Requests for files are serviced within one hour by dispatch of a diazo copy of the microfiche. Users are required to return the diazo copy to the conversion area for proper destruction.

Since the successful conversion of life application files to microfiche jackets, Northwestern has converted other major files as well. The conversion unit which once filmed 800 applications per day now films over 1,500. Daily requests for fiche have increased from 300 to 1,000. In addition, when the demand for policy loans jumped to over 1,500 per day, a microfilming system with automated retrieval was developed to accommodate this growing file. Loan documents are filmed daily in random order. The loan number and the location on the film is entered on a miniterminal interfaced with a micrographic reader/printer. There is now instant access to loan documents without having to batch requests. This system has proved so effective that it will be expanded to randomly process other files, too.

In 1976, a decision was made to build an addition to Northwestern's Home Office adjacent to the existing building. The new building would house about 75 percent of the company's 2,000 employees. Because of the volume and space consumption, it was decided early in the planning stages that the Policy Title File of over 1,500,000 paper folders would stay in the old building. The distance between most users and the title file area was so great that turnaround time increased to 24 hours.

This situation caused Northwestern to explore alternative methods of filing and sending for title files. First, the files were assigned a unique number (by life), consolidated, and color coded. Title files were then refiled by terminal digit in movable shelving units. Then, a system was custom-designed by Northwestern and an outside engineering firm; the system used the touch dialing of the telephone as the input device and a telephone answering device which established connections with a printer.

To use the system, the user dials the title file extension number; the telephone rings once and then gives a tone. The tone, which is the signal to proceed, is given after the user has entered the information correctly. The user then enters two symbols and a three-digit routing code. Another tone is given, and the user then enters the seven-digit file number. Several files can be requested with one phone call.

The printer prints out the information received over the telephone. At the bottom of each request is the number of requisitions received thus far and the time and date the request was received. These printouts become charge-outs in the file. A corresponding list of names is also kept so that there is a record of who has the file.

When the title file extension is busy, the user enters a two-digit access code and hangs up the telephone. When the extension number is free, the user's phone will ring, and the title file extension will ring when the handset is lifted.

The electronic telephone file request system reduced turnaround time to 12 hours. The title file unit itself has more flexibility in handling requests coming in throughout the day, and personnel do not have to deal with peak loads.

Northwestern has also recognized the need to control the massive paper flow resulting from the wide range of data produced by high-speed computers. Terminal inquiry and computer output microfilm (COM) are two methods used. An offline minicomputer-controlled COM unit was installed at the Home Office to provide a cost-effective alternative to paper.

In early 1981, Northwestern undertook an office automation project to improve management productivity. This system provides many functions through a single terminal workstation. It has a network capable of communicating with Northwestern's computer systems and major data files. It provides computer power for persons who could not previously utilize it—managers, professionals, and administrative support personnel.

A typical workstation includes a minicomputer, a terminal, and a printer. The relationship is not one to one. One minicomputer may support 18 to 30 terminals, and the ratio of terminals to printers might be three or four to one. This new system performs word processing, may provide an electronic index for the Legal Department's massive hard-copy files, and handles electronic messages, calendar management, report generation, and graphics functions.

Northwestern Mutual Life Insurance Company received the Fifth Annual William Olsten Award for Excellence in Records Management Programs at the 26th Annual Conference of the Association of Records Managers and Administra-

tors, Inc., in October, 1981. This prestigious award was established to recognize significant advances in the field of records management. The streamlined records management system Northwestern has achieved through microfilming and its electronic telephone file request system were cited as the achievements being recognized by this award.

*Contributed by Walter W. Riese*
*Northwestern Mutual Life Insurance Company,*
*Milwaukee, WI*

## MEDICAL FACILITIES

Medical organizations provide health services—preventive and restorative—to users (patients). Proper diagnosis and treatment depend upon complete health records.

Medical organizations include single doctors' offices, clinics, health maintenance organizations, nursing homes, hospitals, and research facilities. Each type of medical organization requires accessible and up-to-date patient records for effective functioning.

## Records Management System

### Patient Records

The patient record provides documentation of the medical history, examination findings, prescribed treatments, and results for that individual. These records are necessary for present and future care and may become the basis for research. For example, a patient's record may reveal allergies to drugs so that the physician can avoid prescribing them. The patient record may also contain correspondence or consent forms for surgery or special treatments which have legal significance.

Patient records are assigned a patient number (frequently the social security number) and are filed numerically. Medical records departments frequently use open shelves, color-coded files, and terminal digit filing systems. Most medical records departments cross-reference patient files by name in a card file.

Patient records must be maintained for 20 years. In practice, these records are frequently held much longer, especially if the same doctor or hospital is treating an individual over a normal life span of 70-plus years. Because of the length of time records are held, space becomes a severe problem for many medical records departments. Some medical records departments have begun to microfilm their records. Others are still encountering strong resistance from doctors against the use of microfilm. In some instances, color photographs are an important part of the patient record (especially in research facilities) and this makes microfilming undesirable.

### Transcription

The transcription of medical reports is still a large part of the work of many medical records departments. Dictation systems which are accessed by telephone and which utilize dictation holding tanks are necessary. Transcriptionists are frequently on duty around the clock.

### Professional Certification

The American Medical Records Association (AMRA, 875 North Michigan Avenue, Chicago, IL 60611) provides professional certification by examination to Accredited Record Technicians (ART) and Registered Record Administrators (RRA). One may qualify for the ART examination by completing special college courses or by completing a correspondence course available through AMRA. One must complete a four-year program at an accredited college or university to qualify to sit for the RRA certification examination. Both certifications require the completion of continuing education units to maintain one's credentials.

# PROFILE

## University of Maryland Medical System

The University of Maryland Medical System (UMMS), a private, nonprofit corporation, includes University Hospital, Montebello Center, the James Lawrence Kernan Hospital, the University of Maryland Cancer Center, and the clinical component of the Shock Trauma Center. Visiting professors from all over the world come here to learn and teach, and faculty members are invited to teach all over the world. The Medical System is internationally known as a referral center for desperately ill patients who need the highest level of medical care.

The University of Maryland Medical School, established in 1807, was the fifth medical school founded in the U.S. In 1823, its hospital—the Baltimore Infirmary, forerunner of University Hospital—became the first hospital specifically built for a medical school. The hospital has been in continuous use since then, treating Maryland's patients and training the physicians who serve the state.

The Medical System's illustrious history is matched by its recent record of achievements, including:

- Microwave surgery on brain tumors
- One of the area's first pancreas transplants
- Nationally recognized open-heart surgery
- Research and community outreach at the Hypertension Center
- The Maryland Cancer Registry, a computerized system containing information on every cancer patient diagnosed at every hospital in the state
- The Cancer Center, with new cancer drugs developed here that are unavailable at most hospitals

- High-level trauma care that has saved lives and won international recognition. The new Shock Trauma building will house the premier — and only — multidisciplinary shock trauma center in the U.S.
- Specialized treatments such as radioactive brain implants and a CAT scan/computer treatment plan
- High-risk pregnancy center
- High-risk neonatal care
- Nationally known work in staging and restaging (recurrent imaging) of Phase 3 cancer patients
- Nationally acclaimed programs in teenage pregnancy and behavioral pediatrics

Of the roughly 6,500 hospitals in the country, less than 150 are university medical centers. Academic hospitals labor under a special three-pronged charge: They must emphasize patient care, research, and education. The Medical System's outstanding achievement is the success with which it integrates these responsibilities.

The UMMS professors are also attending staff physicians. They practice what they teach, so they never lose sight of their basic responsibility to patients.

As a teaching hospital, UMMS must maintain medical knowledge and technology that are absolutely up-to-date. Drugs and equipment are available at UMMS that were unheard of a generation ago.

Tomorrow's physicians are trained to think critically, to make proper diagnoses, and to distinguish what is valuable amid the glut of medical research. Ten years ago, for example, who would have believed that we would be able to clone genes, implant hearing aids into temple bones, or use lasers to operate on eyes and brains. What residents learn today may be totally irrelevant five years from now, so UMMS teaches them to be receptive to and discriminating about change. Doctors are not a finished product. The most important thing UMMS physicians can teach a student is the value of self-education.

Research is a very important aspect at the University of Maryland Medical System. Research enables physicians to give good answers to patients — answers based on more than just personal experience. Research at the Medical System includes:

- Major studies on maternal and child health
- The effects of smoking on disease and on newborns
- Magnetic resonance imaging (MRI), diagnostic imaging using a powerful, sensitive magnet
- Work on schizophrenia, psycho physiology, and violent behaviors
- Brain imaging
- New computer-based techniques to evaluate and direct

care of patients with traumatic lung injuries

- Studies on monoclonal antibodies
- Labs on pharmacology, immunology, and basic enzymology
- Interferon and cancer research
- Leading investigations in unconventional fractionation of radiotherapy
- One of the pioneer hyperthermia departments in the U.S.
- The most active academic department in the U.S. in research on new methods of therapy for multiple sclerosis
- Pioneering studies on alpha- and beta-interferon (made by recombiant DNA technology) and cyclosporine A for M.S.
- Pediatric research such as Ketone metabolism of brain receptor sites, sudden infant death syndrome (SIDS), growth hormone receptors, and hypertension in children
- Perinatal research, including ICU nursery, fetal cardiology, and in-utero imaging

The UMMS philosophy of research strengthens patient care. When a patient is treated at the Medical System, information is contributed to a database that will help treat other patients.

Patient care is of the utmost importance. According to R. Adams Cowley, MD, Shock Trauma, the best expression of UMMS philosophy is the quote by Abraham Lincoln, who said, "The only thing greater than giving a life is saving one."

The medical record plays a vital role in patient care. It is of value to the patient, the hospital, the physician, and for research and teaching.

The medical records department at the University of Maryland Medical System consists of 55 employees, including administrative staff. It is staffed 24 hours a day, 7 days a week. The chain of command includes the following: director, associate director, assistant director, and office manager. There are nine supervisors throughout the department, three of whom are Accredited Records Technicians (ART). The directors, themselves, maintain the credentials of Registered Records Administrators (RRA).

The medical records department recognizes the importance of continuity of patient care. When patients return for clinic visits, the medical record is available for the physician. A special flagging system alerts the physician that a chart is available. UMMS was the first hospital in the state to develop its own inhouse abstracting system. These abstracts are extremely important in the research aspect. The medical records department staffs three full-time employees for the statistics and research program. The goal of all research is to improve patient care, and the medical records department is very much involved. The department's Tumor Registry, which abstracts information from the Cancer Center, is used statewide and by various physicians outside of Maryland.

The medical records department utilizes a Unit Number, Terminal Digit Filing System. The unit numbering system provides a single record, which is a formulation of all data gathered on a patient, whether as an inpatient, ambulatory care patient, or emergency patient. A patient entering the hospital is assigned a permanent number and maintains this number for each return visit.

At UMMS, medical records are microfilmed annually. The medical records department maintains two years of records in hard-copy version. Records beyond that time are condensed onto a 6 × 4 microfilm. A date is set each year for the purging of records before the microfilming process. Records are prepared and microfilmed by an outside agency. Therefore, records are removed from the hospital premises. However, they are always made available upon request so that patient care is never jeopardized. It is the responsibility of the department to check each piece of microfilm for accuracy. Although UMMS has a University Health Center, all medical records are centrally located and stored onsite.

In the medical records department, the patient registration area controls any duplication of medical records numbers. The supervisor of this area corrects duplications and notifies all affected patient contact areas. Since this area is automated, the creation of duplications is minimal.

The medical records department has a policy and procedure manual. The manual was developed by the director of the department. Revisions, which are made annually, or as necessary, are performed by the administrative staff. Those service areas affected by revisions are informed through circulation and explanation.

*Contributed by Linda M. Shurites and*
*Elizabeth A. Sontum*
*University of Maryland Medical System,*
*Baltimore, MD*

# LIBRARIES

Libraries are most frequently thought of as lending institutions. One may go to the library and borrow periodicals, books, recordings, maps, art objects, paintings, or photographs. Libraries are also the repositories of historical data, archival data, and special collections such as presidential papers or the personal papers of other prominent individuals.

There are many types of libraries. Libraries may be national (the Library of Congress), state, local (city/county), school (elementary to university), corporate, individual, or special (medical, legal, scientific, and so forth). Many special libraries are housed at individual schools within a university or at research facilities.

## Records Management System

At least two records requirements of libraries are shared universally. The library must maintain a catalog of all the materials in its collection, and the library must maintain records of materials on loan.

Materials are listed in the catalog of resources according to the classification system used in the library. Most libraries use the Library of Congress classification system, the Dewey Decimal System, or a combination of the two. In universities and large cities, the familiar card catalog is being replaced by the COM catalog. The COM catalog provides faster access to information and is usually maintained by participation in a central database.

The familiar "Date Due" cards are also disappearing from the backs of books in some libraries. Many large libraries have installed a computerized system in which an optical scanning wand "reads" an identification code on the book and the identification number on the patron's ID card and records the information in a master file. This system speeds up the check-out process and eliminates the filing and retrieving of the "Date Due" cards.

Increasingly, libraries are finding that they do not have the resources to maintain and increase the number of titles available for circulation. Many libraries have begun to participate in networks as a cost-effective way of expanding their services. One such network is the Southeastern Library Network, Inc., which includes 260 libraries from Virginia to Louisiana, and Online Computer Library Center, Inc. (ONLC), which links 2,400 libraries across the United States. Materials can often be accessed from remote locations by computer or can be transmitted through facsimile transceivers.

Many libraries are further extending their services by subscribing to online databases such as the New York Times Information Bank and Lockheed Missile & Space Co.'s Dialog. These data banks provide a wealth of information.

Some libraries (the public library in Columbus, Ohio, and the one at Warner Amex Cable Communications, Inc., New York, New York) are experimenting with searches of the library catalog via cable television. This system allows users to identify the books they would like to read and push a button to have them mailed to their homes. Many public libraries feel that this type of service would be more cost effective than maintaining branch libraries.

The extended use of computers and micrographic technologies has increased the need for librarians with technological expertise. The American Library Association and other specialized professional groups provide inservice training through their conferences and publications.

# PROFILE

## Library of Congress

Created in 1800 as a reference library for the Congress, the Library of Congress is now also the nation's library. Its services extend not only to members and committees of the Congress, but to the executive and judicial branches of government, to libraries throughout the nation and the world, and to the scholars, researchers, artists, and scientists who use its resources.

Collections of the Library of Congress include over 80 million items covering virtually every subject in formats that vary from papyrus to microform. These materials stretch along 532 miles of shelves and are being acquired at a rate of 10 items per minute. The Library has 20 million books and pamphlets in some 60 languages and more than 35 million manuscripts, among them such treasures of American history and culture as the papers of U.S. Presidents, notable families, writers, artists, and sci-

entists. The library has the world's largest and most comprehensive cartographic collection — almost 4 million maps and atlases, dating back to the middle of the fourteenth century — and a 6-million-piece music collection that includes books, autographed scores, correspondence of composers and musicians, flutes from throughout the world, and rare Stradivarius instruments with Tourte bows.

The Library's 10 million prints and photographs provide a visual record of people, places, and events in the United States and in many foreign countries. Master photos, fine prints, works of popular and applied graphic arts, and documentary photographs are included. Approximately 75,000 serial titles are received annually; 1,200 newspapers are held in the Library's permanent collections, with some dating back to the seventeenth century. There are also 750,000 sound recordings, more than 250,000 reels of motion pictures, and over 3 million microforms.

Throughout each of the three Library buildings, manuscripts, rare books, prints, and maps from collections are exhibited. On permanent display are such priceless treasures as the Library's copy of the Gutenberg Bible, one of three surviving examples printed on vellum and perfect in all respects, and the Giant Bible of Mainz, an illuminated manuscript executed by hand at about the time the Gutenberg Bible was printed.

Through the Congressional Research Service (CRS), a department established over 60 years ago, the Library provides legislators with the information they need to govern wisely and effectively. The staff of CRS answers more than 350,000 inquiries a year, ranging from simple requests for data to highly complex in-depth studies. In addition, CRS prepares bill digests, summaries of major legislation, and other reference tools to help members and their committees stay abreast of the daily flow of legislation.

In the mid-1970s the Information Systems Office for the CRS developed Subject-Content-Oriented-Retriever-for-Processing-Information-Online (SCORPIO). SCORPIO was designed for researchers with little or no computer experience, and the number of commands required to use the system was deliberately limited. Today, SCORPIO offers access to numerous online files.

The Copyright Office in the Library of Congress administers the operation of the United States copyright law, a major force for the encouragement of literary and artistic endeavors. The protection afforded by copyright extends to works of the nation's creative community, including authors, composers, artists, and filmmakers. The copyright registration record maintained by the office provides a valuable record of American cultural growth and innovation. The Copyright Office also provides information about copyright protection, the copyright law, and copyright registrations, renewals, and documents of transfer and reassignments, and distributes copies and certificates of official documents relating to Copyright Office records and deposits.

Records of more than 16 million copyright registrations and copyright transfers are maintained by the Copyright Office. In 1974 the first major online cataloging system, Copyright Office Publication and Interface Cataloging System (COPICS), was introduced. COPICS eliminated the time-consuming task of manually preparing pages for the printed copyright catalog. All registrations after January 1, 1978, are now available to the public through the computerized filing system.

In 1979, the Copyright Office established a Records Management Division. This division maintains an automated inventory system of copyrighted materials stored in an offsite location and is developing new retention criteria for these deposits.

Besides maintaining the Dewey Decimal Classification System, the Library continually expands and develops its Library of Congress Classification system, devised at the end of the nineteenth century and adopted by most academic and special libraries.

Since 1900 many libraries have depended on cataloging information produced by the Library of Congress in forms that have changed from books and printed cards to machine-readable tapes. Such information saves the libraries both time and money.

The Paperwork Management Section of the Central Services Division of the Library of Congress has established an extensive program for the control of the creation, maintenance, and disposition of correspondence, forms, and reports. An agency-wide General Records Schedule is maintained, and once a year each major office is sent a reminder to transfer or dispose of records as scheduled. In addition, offices are audited at regular intervals to determine their compliance with this schedule.

A correspondence manual is available which provides guidelines for the preparation and distribution of Library documents. New administrative support personnel are provided in-house training which includes the use of this manual; procedures for creating, printing, or eliminating forms; and records maintenance procedures.

One of the Library's major concerns is, of course, the preservation of its collection. To achieve this goal, the Library has undertaken an Optical Disk Pilot Program. This pilot program will store up to 500,000 images of print materials (periodicals, maps, manuscripts, microforms, and sheet music) per year on digital optical disks with an online computer index and automated retrieval from a jukebox carousel. Analog optical disks (commonly known as videodisks) are being used to store the Library's image material (slides, photonegatives, transparencies). The disks will allow significant use of the collection without resultant physical deterioration of the original items.

*Contributed by Jean E. Tucker*
*The Library of Congress, Washington, DC*

# MULTINATIONAL ORGANIZATIONS

Multinational organizations conduct their business in two or more countries. Unlike banks, insurance companies, medical facilities, or libraries, multinational organizations do not specialize in any one type of business. Instead, they represent a broad range of industries from the manufacture of jeans to automobiles, from computer software to cameras.

## Records Management System

Just as the organizations differ in their products or services, they also differ in their records management systems. Each organization selects the system that is most appropriate to its individual product/service and to the needs of the organization. Multinational organizations do, however, have one need in common — the need to establish a records management system that is uniform throughout the organization and that can provide information as needed, regardless of the location of the operation. The uniformity desired extends from classification systems to retention schedules to records storage and retrieval systems.

Experiences of records managers in multinational environments that include the United States and European countries have shown that the initiative for uniform systems development, implementation, and control must come from the United States. Companies such as International Business Machines, Squibb Corporation, Avis, Inc., and Tetley, Inc., have found that "turnkey" programs (complete systems that are installed and ready for immediate use) developed by American multinational organizations provide the fastest, most economical, and most efficient approach. The alternative is to educate a team of European personnel and have them develop their own system. This approach has not been as successful as the "turnkey" approach.

Records must meet requirements of each country in which the organization operates and document compliance with all "watch dog" agencies such as the one which monitors trade activities within the European Economic Community. If an organization does not have a comprehensive records management program uniformly implemented, it would be difficult for an organization charged with a violation to properly defend itself with documentation.

In the U.S., legislation often provides the legal requirements for keeping certain records. U.S. businesses have no liability for keeping records indefinitely. In the event of litigation involving such records, businesses operating within the U.S. could not be held responsible for material dating prior to the limits established by law. Not all countries have laws that provide this protection, so businesses operating on a multinational basis have more liability for maintaining records for a longer period. The Federal Register provides information regarding the required retention periods for certain classifications of records and is used within the U.S. to determine basic records retention schedules. Multinational organizations must look beyond the guidelines provided by the Federal Register to determine retention schedules that will meet the needs of the organizations as they operate in different countries having different and often contradictory requirements.

# PROFILE

## Alcan Aluminum Limited

Alcan Aluminum Limited was incorporated in Canada on May 31, 1928. With headquarters in Montreal, Alcan is a multinational enterprise engaged, through subsidiary and related companies, in all major segments of the aluminum business on an international scale. Alcan mines bauxite in seven countries, refines bauxite into alumina in eight, produces primary aluminum in eight, operates fabricating plants in more than twenty, and sells its aluminum and related products throughout the world. Alcan is a publicly owned company with some 59,000 shareholders. The company's shares are broadly held, predominantly in Canada and the United States and to a lesser extent in Europe and other countries. Alcan's management is international in composition consistent with its worldwide activities. Total assets are $7 billion (U.S.).

Alcan's records management program was first introduced in 1979 with full approval of senior management. The initial start up of the program was implemented by a team of consultants from New York. The consultants clearly defined a plan of action which included:

1. Introduce the program in the head office in Montreal.
2. Hold familiarization sessions for every employee.
3. Complete an inventory of all records held in the active offices.
4. Evaluate records to determine retention requirements.
5. Reduce the paper burden in offices by sending inactive records to cheaper storage facility.
6. Help design company forms and develop proper policies and work methods for transferring and destroying forms.
7. Recommend that Alcan hire a full-time records manager to

carry on the full-time activity of records management.

8. Aid the new records manager in publishing and distributing a complete Records Management Manual in the two official operating languages.

During the first two years of the records management program, records in the active office area were reduced 50 percent. Continual control by records management made a recent move to a new world headquarters building a success in terms of space planning since only essential equipment and required records were moved.

Records management helped play a role in the physical layout of each floor in the new headquarters, whereby the problem of stationary hoarding by individuals and need for various types of office equipment was solved. Each floor now has a central work and stationary room containing stationary items, photocopy machine, facsimile telecopier, telex terminal, paper shredder, microfilm reader-printer, and paper cutter table.

The records management structure in Alcan is basic since it was never the intention of senior management to create a vast department of records managers and inhouse analysts. The choice was made to have one records manager reporting directly to the company corporate secretary and responsible for a complete records management program throughout the organization. The records manager in turn would train one existing employee in every department who would don the added role of coordinator responsible for the implementation of the various records management plans in the department.

This method has proven successful since the corporate records manager maintains a continual liaison with all coordinators. In the event of a large project, temporary help is used.

A major cornerstone of the records management program was the development of the Alcan Standard File Classification System. The Alcan Standard File Classification System was devised taking special consideration for the need to communicate and be effective in two official languages used at headquarters: English and French. A numeric subject system was chosen and included major and subfile divisions derived from the initial inventory taken from the active file offices. The numeric system allows users to work and file in either official language while maintaining the same numeric number for subjects with the same theme. Benefits to Alcan and all users include:

1. Improved filing time.
2. Improved retrieval time.
3. Reductions in misfiles.
4. Ability to easily transfer staff from one department to another since staff will be famil-

iar with the existing filing system.

The individual filing systems, although tailormade to special needs, always conform to the master guidelines set out in the Alcan Standard File Classification System. File index systems produced for individuals will also include specific retention periods for each file; the length of time to be held in the active office, and the period of time to be kept in storage. The corporate records manager maintains a duplicate set of all individual file index systems. The information will provide the records manager a means to evaluate:

1. Are the records vital?
2. If vital, are they secured?
3. Are the records held for the proper retention period?
4. Are the records copies or originals?
5. What is the office of record?
6. Which other office has the same information and why?

The records management manuals were initially distributed to all secretarial staff since they are responsible for the filing function. Manuals were also sent to outside subsidiary companies for further distribution and use within their own organizations. Updates to the manuals are done yearly and usually include additions to the numeric codes.

Alcan has decentralized filing systems with centralized control.

The use of an in-house records center for semiactive and dormant material has saved the company $2.5 million a year when one considers the cost of floor space in the active office area. The records center contains over 13,000 boxes of material with retentions ranging from six months to permanent.

In 1984–85 Alcan approved the complete automation of the records center. All records are now maintained on a personal computer which replaced the old manual system. The automated system allows for searches and report generations that were previously impossible to produce. Some of the system's highlights are:

1. Generation of three-part charge-out forms.
2. Searches by box contents, by individual departments, or global searches.
3. User security control.
4. Records retention control.
5. Automatic box assignment (location).
6. Report generation of retention period, requests, box contents, vital records, destroyed boxes, cost allocation, and so forth.

The records retention report and the departmental destruction reports are most useful to the records coordinators. Each list must be reviewed and signed by approving officers. A copy of the signed retention schedule is kept by the department, and the original is held by the records manager. Signed destruction lists are kept by the supervisor of the records center which allows for the final destruction of records. The method of destruction used at Alcan is shred and recycle. All material destined for destruction, including large volumes in the active office, must be sent to the records center.

Two other areas of concern were placed on records management: a centralized contract system and microfilming projects. The implementation of a centralized contract system was established to control, protect, retrieve, and maintain all contracts and agreements between Alcan, its subsidiaries, affiliates, worldwide holdings, governments, and clients. To date Alcan has over 7,000 contracts.

Requests for microfilming are now forwarded to the records manager where each project is studied for cost justification, distribution requirements, the need to preserve or duplicate information, as well as space constraints. Outside microfilming services are called upon to provide prices. Contracts may not necessarily be given to the lowest bidder.

Although records management is somewhat new in Alcan, advances are continually being made in other areas of concern such as forms control, mail management, disaster recovery plans, and uses of office automation and integration.

*Contributed by Denis G. Perks*
*Alcan Aluminum Limited*
*Montreal, Quebec, Canada*

## COMPETENCY REVIEW

1.  Differentiate among the organizational functions of each of the following types of organizations:
    a.  banks
    b.  governmental agencies
    c.  insurance organizations
    d.  medical facilities
    e.  libraries
    f.  multinational organizations
2.  State one unique requirement of the records management system for each of the following types of organizations:
    a.  banks
    b.  governmental agencies
    c.  insurance organizations
    d.  medical facilities
    e.  libraries
    f.  multinational organizations

## COMPREHENSIVE CASE, PART II

Albemarle Life Insurance Company has just expanded the integration of its automated systems to include an offline CAR system. New systems, of course, mean new procedures. Gregory Garcia, Albemarle's records manager, recognizes the need to develop new procedures for accessing policy loan applications (the first application of the new CAR system) through the CAR system. These procedures are to be placed in Albemarle's records management manual.

Gregory has asked you, the active records supervisor, to draft these procedures.

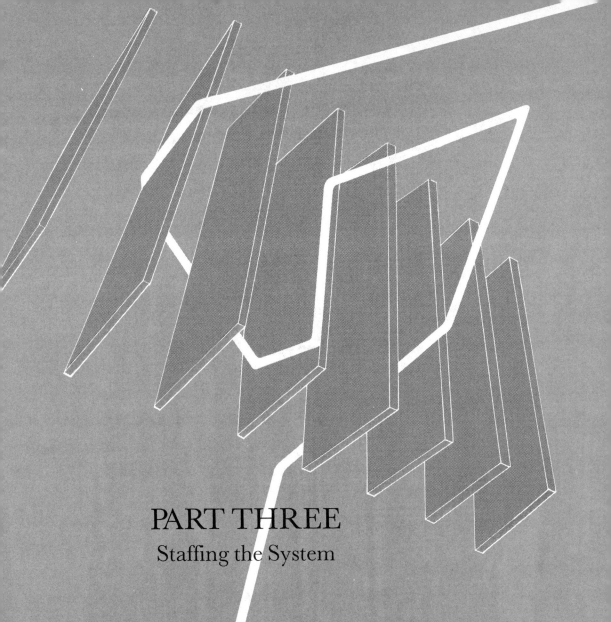

# PART THREE
Staffing the System

# 12
# THE RECORDS MANAGER

## Competencies

After completing this chapter, you should be able to

1. describe organizational staffing patterns that include a records manager and differentiate between the roles established by these patterns.
2. match individual job specifications of potential records managers to job descriptions for records managers.
3. cite the requirements a person must meet to become a Certified Records Manager.
4. list the duties of a records manager and explain how the size of the organization affects these duties.
5. discuss changes in the role of the records manager due to technological developments.
6. plan and describe a self-development program for a records manager under simulated conditions.

# Introductory Case

Sylvia King and Jack Laird are completing the last week of their records management course before final exams. Both are juniors majoring in business administration at the university. Their records management course has awakened in them an interest in pursuing careers in this particular management area.

While discussing their mutual interest in records management before class one afternoon, Sylvia suggests that they make an appointment to visit their city records manager to gain additional insights into the responsibilities and opportunities for careers in records management. Jack agrees to call Mavis Evans, the city records manager, immediately after class to make an appointment for the following week.

1. What should Sylvia and Jack do to prepare for this meeting?
2. What specific questions should they be prepared to ask?
3. What should they hope to gain from their meeting with Mavis Evans?

RECORDS MANAGER: At least 1 year experience in micrographics operation and at least 2 years experience in records management supervision or other administrative function. Will evaluate, design, and develop a method to convert the existing contractor-furnished document control system to a comprehensive records management system in accord with corporate and regulatory policy guidelines. Will provide for the collection, protection, retrieval, distribution and/or disposition of reports, forms, correspondence, and other required documents.

Selecting the records manager and determining the role of that individual within the organization are the first processes in the staffing subsystem. The staffing subsystem is illustrated in Figure 12–1. The function of the staffing subsystem is to provide a well-trained staff to ensure the efficient functioning of the records management system. Achieving this goal is the responsibility of the records manager.

Figure 12–1
Relationship Between the Records Management System
and the Staffing Subsystem

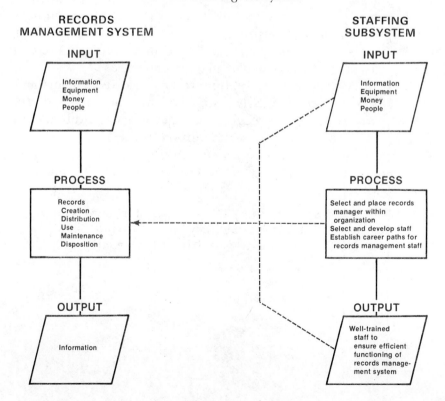

The records manager's position is a challenging one; the position requires many and diverse skills. A careful examination of this position should begin with the role of the records manager within the organization.

## ROLE IN THE ORGANIZATION

Every organization operates within an established structure which is usually outlined on an **organization chart**. This chart is a formal representation of the firm's organizational structure—a diagram of who reports to whom within an organization. Placement on this chart is indicative of the level of responsibility and authority of the records manager and influences the ease with which those responsibilities can be accomplished.

## Placement in Organization

There are many organizational structures which include the position of records manager. The position designations (records manager, director of records management, and records and information manager) and patterns reflected in Figures 12–2, 12–3, and 12–4 demonstrate the influence of organization size on the concept of the best operating structure, whether it is the most

*Organization size affects scope of responsibilities*

Figure 12–2
Organizational Structure—Retail Business

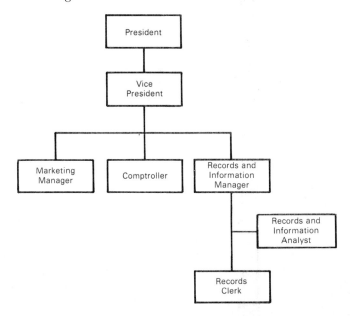

Figure 12–3
Organizational Structure — Municipal Government

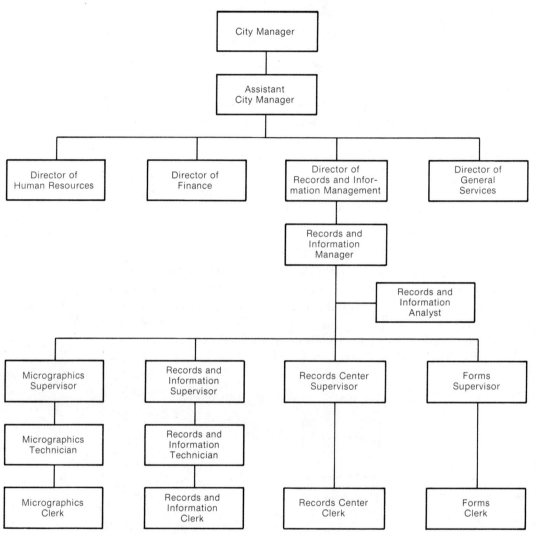

streamlined or the most specialized. Smaller organizations tend to have more streamlined operations — fewer employees with each one performing a wider range of tasks. Larger organizations frequently have more specialized operations — more employees with each one performing only one task or a group of related tasks.

In many small organizations the smaller volume of records and the necessity for minimizing managerial positions allow records management to be one of several tasks performed by a single manager. Some organizations may have records managers who perform some specific tasks of the records management program (such as forms analysis and management or the supervision of active and inactive records) in addition to their management duties. While small organizations may not find it cost-effective to employ a manager whose sole responsibility is the management of records, caution must be exercised to ensure that this important function receives adequate attention. No organization can afford to have its records—its memory—lost in the shuffle of administrative tasks.

Large organizations, because of the volume of records they generate and receive, have more specialized records operations. Each employee within the records unit has a particular task or group of related tasks to accomplish, and this specialization allows for faster, more accurate handling of records. The records manager's responsibilities increase with the degree of specialization; the manager must be familiar with the requirements and procedures of each position and be able to supervise all phases of the records program.

Frequently in a large organization, the records manager will report to the vice president of administration. Such placement al-

Figure 12–4
Organizational Structure—Manufacturing Business

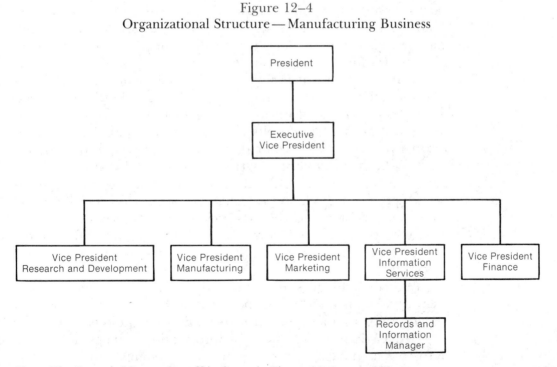

**Note:** The Records Manager's staff is shown in Figure 14–1, page 392.

lows access to top management and usually reflects recognition of the importance of a strong, cost-effective records program to the organization. When such placement exists, the records manager will benefit from participation in the planning of new organizational programs and procedures. Necessary changes in the records program can be planned and implemented simultaneously, thereby increasing organizational efficiency.

## Importance to Organization

Effective management of the records program is the key to cost-effective management and use of information resources within the organization. Because lost records may mean lost business or increased legal liability, the records manager is a key employee.

*Determine information needs*

To fulfill this critical role within the organization, the records manager must develop a thorough knowledge and understanding of the organization's information needs. A general overview knowledge of the nature of the organization's business activities is necessary, as well as specific knowledge of how the organization conducts its affairs. This knowledge can be developed through contact with key individuals (department heads, supervisors, and officers) within the organization and through familiarity with or compilation of a records inventory (see Chapter 3). Combining information gathered in these ways with a previously developed thorough knowledge of records management principles and procedures will allow the records manager to evaluate the existing

*Recognize needed changes*

records program and recommend changes perceived to be necessary to the improvement of this program. The ability of the records manager to recognize needed changes in a consistent manner; to present logical, cost-effective proposals for achieving these improvements; and to maintain efficient records services to the organization will increase the organization's recognition of the importance of the records manager's role to its overall operating efficiency.

Records managers and others involved in records management agree that the records manager must be recognized by top management as an expert in information technology systems — knowledgeable in every aspect of information management from hard-copy manual systems to automated systems and integrated networks.

## A LOOK AT THE CASE

In preparing for their interview with Mavis Evans, Sylvia and Jack have reviewed various organizational structures and how each structure affects the records manager's position. They plan to ask Mavis Evans to explain the organizational structure within the city and to explain what she perceives to be its advantages and disadvantages.

Their research leads Sylvia and Jack to examine several job descriptions for records managers.

1. What specific information will Sylvia and Jack want to obtain from Mavis Evans regarding the qualifications and duties of her position?
2. What specific information will Jack and Sylvia want to obtain about opportunities for advancement?

## JOB ANALYSIS

A **job analysis** is the systematic study of a job to determine its characteristics—its function, specific duties, and qualifications.

A sample job analysis for the records management manager for Chevron Corporation is presented in Figure 12–5.

### Qualifications

Job qualifications generally can be summarized into three categories: education/training, experience, and personal characteristics. Each of these aspects of the records manager's position will vary somewhat with the organization; however, typical requirements are discussed briefly in this section.

**Education/Training**

Education/training considerations include formal education requirements, such as a high school diploma or a college degree; specific course completion requirements—records management, computer science/data processing, automated systems, accounting, business law, and human relations; and specific skills required for the position. Many organizations now seek candidates for the

*Formal education required*

Figure 12–5
Job Analysis — Manager, Records Management, Chevron Corporation

## Title

Manager — Records Management

## Function

The primary responsibility of this function is to provide the corporation with efficient, cost-effective management and control of records in all forms (both hard copy and magnetic media) from creation through active and inactive maintenance to ultimate timely destruction on a worldwide basis. This includes, in coordination with the Corporate Secretary's office, ensuring that effective procedures are established to identify, maintain, and preserve information and vital records needed to protect the interests of the company, employees, and shareholders as required by law, contract, and business prudence.

In carrying out this responsibility, the manager directs and coordinates activities of the Records Management staff in the activities which are listed below.

## Duties

1. Records Retention Schedule Development. Develop, publish, and implement records retention guidelines to ensure the proper identification and retention classification of all Chevron records. Records Management works with the Corporate Secretary Department on defining retention policy and guidelines.

2. Records Transfers. Coordinate records transfers to ensure orderly and proper transition from one location to another when an operation ceases and/or relocates.

3. Active File Systems. Develop active file systems, including both microfilm and paper/hardcopy, to enhance employee productivity and to promote costs and space savings for the corporation.

4. Inactive Records Systems. Develop guidelines and implement procedures for the proper identification and handling of inactive records including their transfer, storage, and retrieval in records center facilities.

5. Vital Records. Coordinate implementation of vital records protection guidelines developed by the Corporate Secretary Department.

records manager's position who have a bachelor's degree in business administration or a related field. Preference is given to those who have an MBA degree and five years' experience in records management. Some organizations with less sophisticated records programs may not require completion of a four-year program, but there is a trend toward a minimum educational requirement of the bachelor's degree for the position of records manager.

All organizations are interested in potential records managers who can demonstrate, through education or practical experience,

Figure 12–5, continued

6. Records Destruction. Develop procedures to identify and control the timely destruction of obsolete and eligible records.

7. Magnetic/Electronic Record Systems. Develop and implement guidelines for the management of magnetic and electronic records including retention, destruction, and archival storage requirements. Records Management will work with the Computer Services Department in the development and implementation of this program.

8. Training, Education and Technology. Coordinate all Records Management educational and training programs within the corporation and include the dissemination of new records technology principles and the evaluation of new techniques and equipment by conducting pilot programs.

9. Litigation Support/File Searches. Assist the Corporate Secretary Department in conducting file searches for responsive records using a network of Records Management personnel located in the various operating elements.

10. Records Management Program Compliance Review. Assure compliance of operating departments with established records management procedures by maintaining a liaison with the Internal Audit Department. Based upon information obtained as a result of their operational review, conduct follow-up measures with the necessary departments.

(NOTE: Pending recommendations of other studies in progress, this function may assume direct responsibility for actual operation of major inactive records storage facilities; i.e., Dublin, Houston, etc.)

<u>Qualifications</u>

Graduation from an accredited college or university with a minimum of a BS degree; well-rounded background in and thorough understanding of records management; an interest in and appreciation for records management. Certified Records Manager recognition considered important. Overall knowledge of the company (oil industry); particular knowledge of international tax peculiarities; legal knowledge of organization structure; knowledge of data processing—structure of documents.

knowledge of each area of the records program. Companies are also interested in obtaining the services of professionals—those who conduct their activities in accordance with established standards developed by a recognized professional organization in the field of records and information management such as the Association of Records Managers and Administrators, Inc. (ARMA).

The **Institute of Certified Records Managers (ICRM)** administers and evaluates the Certified Records Manager (CRM) examination. The ICRM is composed of individuals who have passed the

*Certification by examination*

**Certified Records Manager (CRM)** examination or who were grandfathered (accepted under an earlier system). A Board of Regents elected from the membership serves as the policymaking body for the Institute.

Members of the Institute (CRMs) meet and share common interests and concerns; they share their experience and knowledge through writing, teaching, and speaking. Some CRMs join in research projects and serve on committees to further the profession. New technologies and administrative technicalities are complicating the selection of competent managers. More and more business and government offices are using the CRM as a professional standard by which they measure the competence of applicants seeking records management positions.

To become a Certified Records Manager (CRM), an individual must meet experience and education requirements established by the ICRM and pass a six-part examination within a consecutive five-year period. Prerequisites for taking the examination include three years of full-time or equivalent experience in three or more areas of records management and a baccalaureate degree from an accredited college. If a candidate does not have a college degree, the ICRM Board of Regents may authorize substitution of additional qualifying professional experience for some of the required education. All education and experience qualifications must be met prior to sitting for the examination. Further information on this examination is presented in *Preparing for the CRM Examination: A Handbook*, 3d edition, available from ARMA.

*Effective communications skills*

The records manager must possess effective oral and written communications skills. Poor communications skills may antagonize those whose cooperation is essential to the efficient operation of the records unit or impede the approval and implementation of needed changes. While the effectiveness of communications skills is difficult to determine from one's education/training or experience, many organizations will be especially alert to the demonstration of these skills in the application letter and the job interview. Some organizations require candidates for the records manager's position to submit examples of their writing as part of the application process. The level of skill demonstrated in the writing is weighted heavily in the selection criteria.

### Experience

*Development through related work experience*

Experience requirements may vary from none for an entry-level position within the records unit to several years of on-the-job experience in one or more areas for more advanced positions. For the candidate for the position of records manager, these requirements usually include at least one year of experience in each of one or more specific areas, such as micrographics or forms design/control, and two or three years of experience in a supervisory position. Experience requirements generally increase as the responsibilities of the position increase. Because the records manager must supervise the many varied functions of the records unit, candidates for this position must demonstrate excellent leadership skills, as well as strong organization and planning skills.

## Personal Characteristics

Most positions have certain requirements in terms of personal characteristics. For the records manager, one of the most important personal characteristics is the ability to work effectively with all levels of personnel in the organization. The records manager must work with top management and other department heads as well as employees within the records unit. Awareness of the role of each individual within the organization, the unique personal characteristics of each, and the importance of cooperating and of making requests easy to accept and complete are essential.

*Ability to work with others*

Other requirements include the ability to motivate employees to be efficient, careful, and cheerful in the performance of their duties; to delegate responsibility and authority; and to evaluate performance. Basic to motivation is a records manager who understands his/her employees and encourages them to work toward achieving their aspirations. Any attempt to motivate a person to perform at a high level must be tailored to the needs of that individual. Motivation methods include providing in-service training for employees, replacing inefficient employees or equipment, or acting on complaints of ineffectiveness to design and implement new procedures.

*Ability to motivate others*

The records manager must be a self-starter — one who has the ability to identify and analyze problems, to determine alternative courses of action, and to implement solutions based on sound judgment and a thorough understanding of the records management profession.

## Job Description

A **job description** is a written summary of the job which states (or lists) duties to be performed by the employee. The records manager's job description will vary with the placement in the organization structure and the degree of specialization existing within the records unit. Each job description will include areas of responsibility and specific duties.

*Areas of responsibility*

Areas of responsibility frequently include supervision of records storage, retrieval, and security; forms and reports control; systems design for current records; floor plans/layouts, equipment selection, moving, and conversion; audit and litigation support; reprographics control; microrecords processing and control; development of technical manuals; human resource development; evaluation of performance and procedures; planning, negotiating, and implementing changes based on better utilization of existing resources. Organizational structure may dictate that some of these responsibilities, all of these responsibilities, or more than these responsibilities be included in a particular records manager's position.

*Specific duties*

The specific duties of the records manager will vary with the organization. These may, however, be expected to include planning records center facilities; conducting or supervising the records inventory; planning or coordinating the development and revisions of the retention and disposition program; selecting the classification system(s); evaluating and selecting equipment and supplies; developing the records management manual; selecting, training, and evaluating the staff; working with department heads to establish controls on correspondence, reports, and copies; working with department heads to design forms; and establishing a records security program. Each of these specific tasks is covered in some detail in other chapters of this book. Note, once again, the diversity of these tasks and the broad base of knowledge required to perform them successfully.

## Advancement Opportunities

*Within the organization*

Because the records manager is knowledgeable about the information requirements of each department within the organization and must work with each department to ensure the successful functioning of the records management system, this individual is in an excellent position to advance to Director or Vice President of Information Services, Vice President of Information Resources, or to an equivalent position depending upon the organizational structure.

The records manager with the desire to advance must continuously excel in the performance of assigned responsibilities and demonstrate the desire to increase his or her knowledge of records management and of the organization for which she or he works.

Many records managers participate in professional organizations such as the Association of Records Managers and Administrators, Inc. (ARMA), and the Association for Information and Image Management (AIIM). These organizations provide monthly or bimonthly programs of technical interest to records managers and opportunities to meet other professionals and exchange ideas. Professional publications from these organizations keep managers up-to-date on current technology and procedures. Annual conferences provide opportunities for experts to share new ideas and procedures. Vendors representing U.S. companies and international organizations exhibit equipment, furniture, and supplies at these conferences in an effort to provide records managers with the latest information upon which to base purchasing decisions.

*Professional development activities*

## A LOOK AT THE CASE

Sylvia King and Jack Laird have carefully reviewed information on the records manager's position. This review included the records manager's placement in the organization, importance to the organization, qualifications, duties, and opportunities for advancement. They have prepared a list of questions to ask Mavis Evans when they interview her next week.

The information Sylvia and Jack have uncovered so far has increased their interest in records management. After the interview, they will carefully consider Mavis Evans' comments and perhaps do additional research before deciding on their careers.

## TERMINOLOGY REVIEW

*Certified Records Manager (CRM).* The designation awarded to an individual who has met the experience and education requirements established by the Board of Regents of the ICRM and has satisfactorily passed a six-part examination.

*Institute of Certified Records Managers (ICRM).* A group of CRMs who administer and evaluate the Certified Records Manager examination.

*Job analysis.* The systematic study of a job to determine its characteristics — its function, specific duties, and qualifications.

*Job description.* A written summary of the job which states (or lists) duties to be performed by the employee; the description will include areas of responsibility and specific duties.

*Organization chart.* A formal representation of the firm's organizational structure—a diagram of who reports to whom within an organization.

## COMPETENCY REVIEW

1. Describe two organizational staffing patterns that include a records manager and differentiate between the roles established by these patterns.

2. Name and discuss the education and experience qualifications a potential records manager must possess to satisfy requirements prescribed in job descriptions for records managers.

3. List the requirements a person must meet to become a Certified Records Manager (CRM).

4. Select three duties performed by a records manager and explain how the size of the organization might affect these duties.

5. Cite three problems the records manager may be confronted with as the rate of technological advancement accelerates.

6. Outline the elements of a personal program of self-development for a records manager. Justify the inclusion of each element.

## APPLICATIONS

1. Obtain an organization chart which shows the placement of the records manager of your institution, or local or state government. Explain what the placement of the records manager reveals about the importance of that position within the organization you selected. Give a rationale for your comments.

2. Ralph Woods will graduate from the Modern University with a bachelor's degree in business administration in three months. For the last two years he has worked part-time in the registrar's office where he has become familiar with all aspects of handling student records. Ralph is interested in becoming a records manager. On the bulletin board by the placement office, Ralph sees the job description shown in Figure 12–5. Should Ralph apply for this job? Explain your decision.

## CONCLUDING CASES

### A. Jacobean Corporation

C. M. Hardwick has been employed by the Jacobean Corporation for ten years. C. M. has acquired experience in records center operation, micrographics, forms analysis and design, and correspondence and reports management. Two years ago, C. M. was promoted to the position of records administrator and joined ARMA. C. M.'s education includes a two-year Associate of Applied Science degree in Data Processing from Moore Junior College.

The records manager, to whom C. M. reports, was critically injured in an automobile accident last week and will not be returning to Jacobean Corporation. The vice president of information services has formed a committee to find a qualified individual to serve as records manager.

1. Assume that you are C. M. Hardwick. Based on the information given in the case and any reasonable assumptions you may wish to make, draft a resume for submission to the Search Committee. Emphasize your strengths for the position of records manager.

2. Assume the role of a member of the Search Committee charged with the responsibility of finding a corporate records manager. List weaknesses you find in this candidate's credentials for records manager. For each weakness identified, recommend a course of action that C. M. could pursue to overcome the deficiency.

## B. Sun States Solariums

Sun States Solariums has expanded its sales territory into three southwestern states. Organizational goals call for expansion into ten additional states over the next three years. Currently, records are maintained in each division by the secretaries. The president of Sun States Solariums thinks that this expansion will require a more formal records program. The current organizational structure is illustrated.

1. Prepare a job analysis which highlights the function and qualifications which will be required for the position of records manager.

2. Assign a position on the organizaton chart for the records manager. Explain the placement you selected.

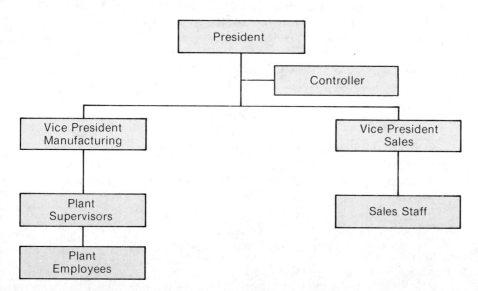

## READINGS AND REFERENCES

■ *ARMA Job Descriptions Guidelines,* 2d ed. Prairie Village, Kansas: Association of Records Managers and Administrators, Inc., 1985, pp. 26–28.

Diamond, Susan Z. "Developing and Staffing the Records Management Program," Chapter 1, *Records Management: A Practical Guide.* New York, New York: American Management Association, 1983, pp. 13–21.

Diers, Fred V. "Records Managers in the Age of Information," *The Office,* Vol. 101, No. 1 (January, 1985), p. 116.

Galitz, Wilbert O. "The Office Environment—Automation's Impact on Tomorrow's Workplace," Part Two of a four-part study based on *Managing the Office—1990 and Beyond,* Willow Grove, Pennsylvania: Administrative Management Society Foundation, Spring, 1984.

Galitz, Wilbert O. "Technological Opportunities," Part Three of a four-part study based on *Managing the Office—1990 and Beyond.* Willow Grove, Pennsylvania: Administrative Management Society Foundation, Spring, 1985.

Homon, Irene. "Records Management Trends," *Records Management Quarterly,* Vol. 18, No. 1 (January, 1984), p. 56.

Johnson, D. S. "The Records Manager's Paradox—Using Technology to Cope With Problems Caused by Technology," *Administrative Management,* Vol. 46, No. 11 (November, 1985), p. 7.

Kennedy, R. E., Manager-Records Management, Chevron Corporation (San Francisco, California). Interviews, September, 1986.

LaMontagne, Alva G., Supervisor Services, and Susan M. Boyd, Information Systems Specialist, Tennessee Valley Authority (Chattanooga, Tennessee). Interviews, May, 1986.

Langemo, Mark. "The Future of Information and Records Management," *Records Management Quarterly,* Vol. 19, No. 4 (October, 1985), p. 28.

Langemo, Mark. "Motivating Toward Excellence and Productivity," *Records Management Quarterly,* Vol. 19, No. 2 (April, 1985), p. 24.

O'Riordan, P. Declan. "Trends in Information Technology 1985," *Information Management,* Vol. 19, No. 1 (January, 1985), p. 1.

*Preparing for the CRM Examination: A Handbook.* 3d ed. Prairie Village, Kansas: Association of Records Managers and Administrators, Inc., 1985.

Rike, Barbara A. "Records Managers and the Age of Information," *The Office,* Vol. 102, No. 3 (September, 1985), p. 109.

Waegemann, C. Peter. *Handbook of Record Storage and Space Management,* Westport, Connecticut: Quorum Books, 1983, pp. 119–127.

Ward, Mary, Systems Administrator, Honeywell, Inc. (Houston, Texas). Interview, May, 1986.

# PROFILE

## Dennis F. Morgan

Manager, Corporate Records Services
Florida Power & Light Company

Dennis F. Morgan has been actively involved in promoting effective records and information management programs and systems for the past six years. He is recognized locally and nationally for his leadership efforts, publications, and, most importantly, for the records management programs he has initiated at Florida Power & Light Company (FPL). Dennis has been employed at FPL for 20 years, has held several supervisory positions in the company's accounting department, and, in 1979, became administrator of the corporate records services department. Soon thereafter he was promoted to department manager, a position he currently maintains.

Florida Power & Light Company is the major subsidiary of FPL Group, Inc., and one of the largest investor-owned utilities in the nation. It is a company committed to programs that concentrate on customers and their needs. FPL, with more than 13,000 employees, serves an average of 2.6 million customers with a service territory that covers 35 counties. Power is provided to customers through more than 50,000 miles of transmission and distribution lines that link more than 375 electrical substations.

Dennis heads a staff of 13 professional and 45 support employees. These department members are located at multiple locations, including the General Office, nuclear, and fossil site facilities. In aggregate, the corporate records services department handles about 350 million documents through a mix of microfilm, microfiche, hard copy, and COM operations. Department accountabilities include: records retention, files management, corporate records center, micrographics, nuclear and technical records computer support, and power plant document control.

The Corporate Records Services staff works closely with user departments, as well as the legal and internal auditing departments, to ensure that records are managed in the best interests of the company. Staff members are available to respond to company requests for individual assistance, provide consultation and training in the design and implementation of manual and automated information systems, and be involved with the coordination of records management programs of FPL's holding and subsidiary companies.

The records retention program is one of the most significant services provided by Corporate Records Services. Begun as a pilot project in the accounting department in 1979, individual retention schedules continue to be developed for every department in FPL. To develop each schedule, analysts meet with each department manager and appropriate staff liaisons to identify and discuss their records types, records use, and regulatory and administrative requirements. After all research and analyses have been completed, finalized retention schedules are routed to appropriate departments for authorization. Over 300 schedules have already been developed.

One of the salient features of the records retention program is the establishment of "Office of Record." As analysts meet with individual departments, they identify and/or verify those departments that are functionally responsible for specific corporate records. The department which is designated as 'Office of Record' for a particular record or record series maintains responsibility for that record for the duration of the required retention period. Other departments having copies of the same record may then appropriately reduce the time frame that they retain the copy, or even eliminate it completely. In effect, duplication of record copies is minimized.

Partner to the records retention program is the files management program. The files management program is a uniform subject filing system in which the codes are based on subjects or functions of FPL's operations. Forty-eight subject filing patterns have been designed for company use. The uniform filing system allows for each employee to access uniformly, thus speeding retrieval time. The uniform system also eliminates time required for employees to learn new file systems if they transfer to another department.

Records analysts inventory a department's records and assist in determining records use and establishing proper file categories. Because of the degree of flexibility of this system, departments can adapt the system to meet their particular needs. For instance, departments that retain a large volume of accounting records may easily use primary, secondary, or tertiary headings to retrieve their records. Other departments with fewer accounting records may find that the major category itself serves as a suitable breakdown.

The newest service addition of the records management department is the Corporate Records Center (CRC). Put into operation in 1984, the CRC measures 8,400 square feet with a 43,000 box capacity in the stacks area. The built-in vault area is 2,300 square feet and houses magnetic tapes, microforms, nuclear quality assurance records and radiographs in a temperature- and humidity-controlled environment. The records center is operated by a supervisor and three clerical employees.

Currently, a computer-assisted box retrieval system is used at the Corporate Records Center. The database contains the box number, its location in the center, a general description of the box contents, retention period, and destruction date. Using this system, requesters can expect a 24-hour turnaround time.

FPL's micrographic operations, under the centralized control of Corporate Records Services, affords cost-effective alternatives to hardcopy maintenance and storage. When a department requests microfilm service, a records analyst meets with the appropriate department personnel to discuss application requirements, use, and records inventory. The analyst then performs a feasibility study to examine the cost involved. After the cost is justified, directions are developed, film tests are completed to assure user satisfaction, implementation is coordinated, and production is monitored. The Corporate Records Center houses all archival microforms in the Corporate Records Center vault facility under proper temperature and humidity controls.

Another aspect of FPL's records management program involves nuclear records keeping. Unique to the nuclear utility industry is the demand for effective records management programs that specifically address nuclear quality assurance documents. The role of Corporate Records Services is to establish and provide necessary services required to support the modification, operation, and maintenance of the power plants. The nuclear records management programs include micrographics, computerized indexing, retentions, filing systems, and training personnel in records management techniques.

Essentially there are two areas requiring Corporate Records Services involvement. The first area is that of assuring that nuclear and technical records programs are designed, developed, implemented, and maintained according to the FPL quality program and regulatory requirements. In conjunction with this, Corporate Records Services assists with quality assurance records indexing and computer hardware and software systems.

In the second area of involvement, Corporate Records Services provides the supervision and training necessary to achieve the efficient control of technical and quality documentation relating to the modification of an operating nuclear plant. Corporate Records Services provides a central location for the collection and verification of drawings, specifications, procedures, and engineering documentation associated with plant change modifications. Corporate Records Services also provides for the reproduction and controls distribution of information used in the construction efforts using computerized tracking/statusing of data. Computer output affords detailed information tailored to each department's needs. Related data is disseminated to user departments onsite to assist in planning, scheduling, and implementing modifications. These printouts reference revision listings and all affected documents, thus assuring an up-to-date status of governing documents. Corporate Records Services provides for the consolidation, review, and turnover of quality records generated as a result of plant change modifications.

Dennis was recognized by ARMA with the 1985 Award of Merit. In 1982 he was awarded Chapter Member of the Year of the South Florida chapter of ARMA, where he has served as president. He is on the Nuclear Information and Records Management Association (NIRMA) Board of Directors and is a recent past president of that organization. For both ARMA and NIRMA affiliations, he has served as a speaker at national conferences. His name appeared in the publication *Who's Who in the South and Southeast*, 1980–1981 and

1982–1983 editions. Dennis Morgan's combined expertise in the areas of accounting and records management has contributed to the successful development of FPL's cost-effective, comprehensive records program—a program that won for the company the 1983 Olsten Award. Because of company-wide quality improvements such as the Records Management Program, FPL received the second annual "Office 10" Award in 1984.

When called upon to offer advice to records managers, Dennis frequently takes this position:

*The records management profession offers an individual unlimited opportunities to contribute to the effective operations of a company. Records managers must be skilled in oral and written communications, organization and strategic planning, accounting/finance, systems development, state-of-the-art technology, and interpersonal communication. At the same time, records professionals must be willing to accept that the working environment of the records management profession is often one of invisible control. The job, if done well, should not draw attention to itself. As such, recognition for a job well done may also be proportionately invisible.*

*Contributed by Dennis F. Morgan*
*Florida Power & Light Company*
*West Palm Beach, FL*

# 13
# HUMAN RESOURCES DEVELOPMENT

## Competencies

After completing this chapter, you should be able to

1. explain the nature and scope of human resources development.
2. determine the personnel needs of a records management unit.
3. analyze the costs and benefits of various types of training.
4. describe the essential elements of effective performance appraisal as an integral part of a human resources development program.
5. outline the process of establishing a human resources development program.
6. recommend appropriate human resources development measures for identified organizational environments, situations, and objectives.

# Introductory Case

Catherine Sargent has just been appointed by the board of trustees of Paul Young University to the newly created position of records manager. After much study, directed by Catherine, the members of the board could see clearly the need for a more efficient means of storing and retrieving university records. The basic design of the system, which was approved as a recommendation of the study, is in place. Now it is time to staff the records management operation. Catherine's focus has turned to the issue of how critical staffing is to the success of the system.

1. What considerations are involved in staff selection?
2. What plans must be made to meet the training needs of the staff?
3. What supervision must be provided for the staff?

*The economic reality of the future will be that each company's growth and success will be in direct proportion to — if not contingent upon — the growth and development of its employees.*

## STAFF SELECTION

In order to realize growth and success through staff development, the organization must select those employees with potential for growth and development. A well-planned staff recruitment and selection process is essential for a successful records management program. The **human resources development plan** is a comprehensive, systematic plan for the recruitment, selection, training, and evaluation of personnel.

*Determine personnel needs*

Successful staff selection results from carefully identified sources of employees and systematically determined personnel needs. The manager examines the work load and the specific skills and personal characteristics needed by employees in order to have a successful records management operation. This examination yields a database to use to determine job functions, job design, and the number of employees needed. After the required job functions are identified, staffing recommendations should also address the constraints of space, budget, and training for the proposed staff. Close coordination and communication with human resources and training and development units are essential at all steps of the process if a comprehensive and effective staff is to be acquired and maintained.

### Job Functions Required

*Relationship of records to staff requirements*

In determining the required job functions, the records manager must consider the types and volume of records to be stored, the number of retrieval requests, and the types of services to be provided. If active or inactive records are to be microfilmed, a microfilm technician may be needed, unless a micrographics service bureau can provide the service more economically. Questions regarding the appropriateness of microfilm can usually be answered as a result of a feasibility study as outlined in Chapter 2.

The number of records to be stored, the number of records to be destroyed, and the resulting growth rate in records has a direct impact on the number of records clerks to be employed. Likewise, the number of clerks, analysts, and technicians needed, the breadth of services to be provided, the operational procedures of the records facility, and the organizational structure of the records unit have a bearing on the number of supervisors needed.

A typical records unit might employ persons in many or most of the positions shown in Figure 14–1 on page 392. The volume of records may cause the number of positions to be expanded or reduced. The larger the records unit, the more highly specialized each position is likely to be. A smaller staff requires each employee to perform more job functions.

## Limitations

A well-developed human resources plan includes the job functions, the rationale for their inclusion, the work load, the number of employees in each function, and growth projections. The human resources plan must also address factors such as space, budget, and the need/availability of training, each of which may limit the implementation of an optimum staffing plan.

### Space

If the records manager participates in the original planning of the organization offices and a long-range plan for facilities, space may not be a problem. Continuous monitoring of organization and records growth may provide a rationale for expanded staffing. Often, however, updating a records program or installing an entirely new system means planning for improved utilization of existing space (see Chapter 4), which may present more of a challenge. Consideration must be given to the current arrangement of space as it relates to the efficient movement of records, to the efficient traffic of records personnel, and to the total work space available. If offsite records storage is to be utilized, employee time must be planned for the transfer, control, and retrieval of documents.

*Determine space requirements/ arrangement*

### Budget

If budget constraints prevent implementation of an optimum staffing plan, the manager may have to explore alternatives such as (1) a phased staffing approach, (2) redistribution of work loads to achieve a more efficient use of existing personnel, (3) a plan to use part-time or temporary employees during peak work loads, (4) providing fewer types of services until financial circumstances allow a fully staffed operation, or (5) the use of interns from work/ study programs at local educational institutions where records management is taught. These programs are also excellent staff recruitment sources for future employees, especially since evaluation

*Determine budgetary needs*

of their skills, attitudes, and compatibility with the organization will have been evaluated during their internship period.

### Need/Availability of Training

If the local pool of job applicants does not contain persons with specialized skills in records management, the records manager has to consider where and in what time frame training is available for needed skills. Factors which contribute to success in training also have to be determined so that the best candidates for training can be selected. Attention must then be turned to selecting the best training option. These options are discussed later in the chapter.

## The Selection Process

The selection process consists of four steps. These steps are (1) preparing job analyses, (2) recruiting employees, (3) making decisions regarding the use and/or development of pre-employment tests, and (4) interviewing the applicants.

### Job Analyses

*Job requirements/ tasks*

Each position within the records unit should have a job analysis which would yield a job description, including tasks to be performed, reporting relationships, tools used, work load, and so forth. The job analysis would also provide information for a job specification, including many or most of the following: educational requirements, any specific knowledge requirements such as computer language(s), physical requirements for the job and work environment, types and amount of experience required, and any special certification requirements, such as a CRM (Certified Records Manager) designation.

The job analysis and writing of job descriptions and specifications should be done by the manager and/or human resources personnel, and extreme caution should be taken to assure accuracy of information gathered. If the job in question does not presently exist within the organization, current literature can provide the base for the development of job descriptions and specifications. Employment agencies can also be excellent resources for current job information. In addition to being an excellent source for information on what types of employees are needed, the job analysis information can also be used in the advertising portion of the recruitment process.

## Recruitment

A number of sources of employees are available to the records manager. For positions considered as advancement opportunities, most organizations prefer to advertise among their own employees first. This is frequently done through the organization's bulletin boards or newsletters. Human resources inventories or individual personnel records provide a source of candidates for in-house promotion. Some organizations maintain a management development program or index which tracks potential managers and executives and estimates the time when these employees will be ready for their next promotion.

*Internal promotion*

Employees also serve as excellent sources for job applicants. They may have friends or family who are interested in new positions with clear career paths. Many excellent prospective employees can be identified through employee recommendations.

The records manager or the human resources director may also consider a number of other sources for employees. The organization may use direct advertising in newspapers or trade journals. Available positions may be listed with either public or private employment services. Public employment agencies, such as the state employment commission, provide their services free to the public. Private employment agencies charge a fee for their services. This fee may be paid by either the employer or the employee.

*External recruitment*

Most colleges, universities, community colleges, proprietary business schools, and vocational-technical schools offer placement services to their graduates. If a local educational institution has a records management program, exploring internship arrangements or listing job openings with their placement office may be beneficial.

## Testing

As a part of the selection process, the records manager must determine whether tests should be used in selecting employees. If tests are to be used, what kinds of tests—keyboarding skills, general clerical, aptitude, personality inventory, general intelligence, or one of many others? Often the complexity of the testing program increases as the size of the organization increases. The records manager should evaluate what a test will reveal about the job performance of a potential employee and use only those tests that provide information relevant to the job in question. Because of legal constraints, tests must be validated (shown to test actual job skills) and administered uniformly to all applicants; therefore, the development of pre-employment tests is a lengthy and costly procedure, often best left to professionals.

*Tests as a selection tool*

## Applicant Interviews

*Interviews as a selection tool*

The interview is a powerful selection tool. A study completed by the Research Committee of the Milwaukee Chapter of the Association of Records Managers and Administrators, Inc., found the interview by the records supervisor to be the most effective selection tool for records personnel. While the interview may take many forms, it should strive to clarify information on the applicant's resume or application form. The interview may also be used to acquire or develop information on items of particular interest. The records manager may wish to control the interview through the use of an interview schedule that would allow each person to answer the same questions in the same order. Or the records manager may wish to keep a record of interview form for each job candidate. The record of interview form allows the interviewer to note for future reference the information acquired during the interview and is especially helpful if the applicant must complete a series of interviews within the company.

■

## A LOOK AT THE CASE

Careful consideration of the information in the feasibility study, including space and budget constraints, and the training requirements, has led Catherine Sargent to determine that the records division needs six additional staff members. She has determined that the positions to be filled are micrographics supervisor, records analyst, two records clerks, and two microfilm clerks.

After determining the positions to be filled, what training options should Catherine consider?

■

## STAFF TRAINING

*Training needs/options*

Staff training needs consist of those competencies staff members need to learn before they can perform their jobs and those competencies needed to advance in their present positions. These needs may be served through on-the-job training, purchased training, or in-house training programs. As a part of evaluating these training options, the records manager will want to determine the benefits and costs of each type of training, as well as make a broad assessment of the total costs and benefits of a comprehensive training and development program for the records management staff.

## Benefits/Costs of Training

Before embarking on any new training program, the organization will want to evaluate program benefits and costs. The records manager must consider these factors in recommending a training program to management. Four major areas of training costs have been identified:

1. time costs, due to time lost when an employee is off the job
2. preparation costs of training materials for the instructor
3. transportation costs to bring personnel together for training
4. miscellaneous costs (meals, lodging, and facilities rental)

*Training costs*

These costs must be compared to the benefits to be derived from training. Benefits for comparison are:

1. increased productivity
2. more accurate information to management
3. improved quality of existing staff
4. more current information on improved methods.

*Benefits of training*

In addition, training contributes to employee satisfaction and may, consequently, help to minimize employee turnover.

## On-the-Job Training

On-the-job training may take many forms. Two of the most common types of on-the-job training are job aids and training by other employees.

### Job Aids

For some positions, especially entry level positions, employees will have the necessary basic skills when they are hired. New employees will need to learn procedures for performing tasks using these skills. For example, the micrographics clerk will need to learn the procedures for preparing documents for filming. (See Figure 13–1.) Procedural information can often be best presented on a printed card or typed sheet to which the new employee can refer until the procedures become familiar. Flowcharts for handling certain types of documents are another type of job aid. Job aids may be a part of the records management manual.

*List of procedures*

Figure 13–1
Job Aid for Preparing Documents for Microfilming

---

**POSITION:** Micrographics Clerk

    **TASK:** Preparing Documents for Microfilming

        1. Check to be sure each file is complete
        2. Repair any tears in documents
        3. Remove any stains or smudges
        4. Remove paper clips and staples
        5. Arrange documents to all face the same direction
        6. Prepare and insert indices where needed

---

## Training by Other Employees

Frequently employees provide training for other employees. This may occur as (1) an employee leaving a position provides training for a replacement; (2) employees having similar job experience provide training; or (3) supervisors provide training to existing or new employees within their supervisory area.

*Difficulties in employees training other employees*

Some managers find the practice of employees providing training to other employees helpful. Others, however, find it frustrating and difficult. If no job procedures manual exists, the experienced employee may forget to explain infrequently used procedures. Some employees may perform well on their jobs but have great difficulty demonstrating to another person how a task should be completed. If informal training by other employees is to be utilized in staff training, specific guidelines for tasks to be included in the training for each position should be developed. The employee providing training should also have some suggested measure to determine whether the new employee has attained competence in performing the tasks described.

## Purchased Training

Purchased training can take the form of consultant services purchased by and designed for an organization, employee participation in professional seminars, or training at any of a number of post-secondary institutions. Each has advantages and disadvantages.

## Consultant Services

If several employees need one-time training in similar or identical tasks, hiring a training consultant to design, conduct, and evaluate this training for the organization may be considered. The consultant determines the organization's needs, defines these needs in terms of competencies and performance standards, selects appropriate methods and materials for providing the needed training, prepares the training facility, conducts the training, and evaluates the results. Having a well-chosen training specialist design and conduct training to fit the organization's specific needs is a major advantage. The disadvantages are the possibility of the consultant's being unavailable when additional training is needed, the lack of training specialists in some fields in which training is desired, and the lack of continuous training.

*Organization-specific training*

## Professional Seminars

Seminars which address many areas of records management are offered by professional associations and training organizations. These seminars are designed to cover topics which are relevant to many organizations. Some of these seminars are offered only in predetermined locations; others may be brought to an individual organization if a minimum number of participants is available. Professional seminars vary in length from one to five days. A fee is charged for each participant, and travel costs and arrangements are the participant's responsibility. Some organizations pay employees' expenses to professional seminars in lieu of providing in-house training or as part of an ongoing staff development program.

Local chapters of the Association of Records Managers and Administrators, Inc., often have active education committees, which have as their charter duties an assessment of local training needs, and subsequently, the development of training seminars to meet those needs. Records managers should inquire about possible communication with or service on such committees. ARMA education committees can be an effective vehicle for obtaining the needed training in a local community.

*ARMA education committees*

## Institutional Training

Among the types of educational institutions offering training related to records management are proprietary business schools, community colleges, and colleges and universities. A directory of such programs is published by the Association of Records Managers and Administrators, Inc. If an educational institution that

*Formal education programs*

regularly offers a program of courses in records management is located in the organization's geographic area, the records manager may wish to develop the staff training program around these courses and relieve the organization of staff training responsibilities. More likely, however, the records manager will find that these courses are a helpful supplement to other training activities. They are often more appropriate for employees preparing for advancement or for those taking the Certified Records Manager Examination than for new employees. The new employees more likely need intensive training immediately in order to function in an unfamiliar position.

The records manager should explore the development of a working relationship with local educational institutions that offer courses in records management through serving on curriculum advisory committees. If advisory committees do not exist, the records manager should encourage their development. These committees serve as an excellent channel for input in the development of needed courses at local institutions.

## In-House Training Programs

*Staff-conducted internal training*

**In-house training** is training which is offered within the organization by its own personnel, as compared with that which might be developed and presented by special consultants or outside firms, or offered to the public by educational institutions. Operating in-house training programs offers the records manager tailor-made, consistent, and effective training programs but also challenges the records manager with the additional responsibilities of planning, conducting, and evaluating training.

### Advantages

*Content control*

From the records manager's point of view, one of the distinct advantages of in-house training programs is content control. The training is designed specifically for each position and includes the organization's policies and procedures. The manager/supervisor knows that each employee who trains for a particular position receives the same training. In addition, the specific content can be updated immediately when equipment or procedures change.

*Availability of training*

A second advantage of in-house training programs is the availability of training. Because the program, materials, and facilities are in-house, they can be used at the manager's discretion. Understudies can be trained continuously to prevent "downtime" resulting from employee absences or promotions. New employees can be trained immediately.

A third advantage of in-house training programs is that they can be competency-based. A competency-based training program includes a list of competencies the employee must acquire to be successful on the job, prescribes activities or exercises for learning these competencies, and provides criterion-referenced measures to determine if the competencies have been acquired. The criterion-referenced measure establishes a performance standard for use in employee evaluation. If a competency is not sufficiently developed, the employee can complete additional activities to improve performance on the competency. If a new employee has already achieved a competency, a pretest can allow the employee to demonstrate this competency and proceed to the next training activity. In this manner, the rate of progress through the training program is determined by the trainee. By contrast, most purchased training at educational institutions is still time based. The student must spend a prescribed amount of time in class in order to meet the criteria for successful completion of the course.

*Competency-based programs*

## Disadvantages

Establishing an effective in-house training program will require a great deal of the records manager's time. A determination of the unit's training needs — the competencies required for each position for which training is provided — must precede any training program planning. Unless the organization has its own training and development unit, consultants who are training specialists may be called in to design the training program and to develop or recommend training materials. However, the records manager must still evaluate the recommendations and make the final decisions. If the organization is not large enough to justify a full-time training staff, the records manager or records unit supervisors must have time to devote to supervising the training.

*Time required*

## Establishing the Program

Although a detailed description of the procedures for establishing an in-house training program is beyond the scope of this book, the steps shown in Figure 13–2 may serve as guidelines. Before starting to develop a training program, obtain top management support for the concept of in-house training. The records manager must be prepared to demonstrate to top management that in-house training is cost-effective, superior to other available training, or necessary because other training is unavailable. Data on program

*Management support*

results should be kept, analyzed, and reported to maintain the support of top management.

A second step in establishing an in-house training program is to determine the position(s) for which training is to be provided. Then the competencies required for each position must be identified through detailed task analyses whenever possible. The next step is to determine the need for instructional materials and to examine commercially prepared packages which might be suitable. If published materials meet the training program needs, a great deal of time can be saved. Some job aids, especially organization procedures, will have to be prepared for employee training if not available in a published procedures manual.

*Select positions for training*

Figure 13–2
Steps in Establishing an In-House Training Program

1. Obtain top management support for the in-house training approach.
2. Determine positions for which in-house programs are the most desirable option.
3. Identify the competencies required for each position.
4. Select the instructor.
5. Determine the instructional materials needed and purchase or develop those which are most appropriate.
6. Establish performance standards for each competency.
7. Schedule periodic evaluations of the training program.
8. Modify the program on an as-needed basis.

*Establish performance standards*

Realistic performance standards, based on previous and present employees' performance, must be established for each competency the employee is to demonstrate. Standards should prescribe the quantity and quality of work to be performed and include time standards where applicable. Plan to evaluate the training program periodically and to update the program as equipment and procedures change. Regular feedback from the training program participants and their supervisors will provide a basis for desirable modifications of the training program. The training program should be responsive to needed change on a continuing basis.

## A LOOK AT THE CASE

The board of trustees of Paul Young University has asked Catherine Sargent to make a presentation at their next meeting concerning the advantages and disadvantages of each of their options for providing employee training. The board is intrigued by the idea of an in-house training program, but they are very conservative with university dollars. Catherine's presentation includes projected training costs and indicates that the necessary training is not available within a fifty-mile radius of the campus. She recommends an in-house training program. The board approves this recommendation unanimously.

In addition to effective training, what other factors can Catherine use to motivate the records unit staff?

## SUPERVISION

Supervision has been defined as working with and through people to achieve the goals of the organization. Effective supervision contributes to effective performance from any staff. An overview of some supervisory responsibilities within a records unit is given in this section.

### Staff Motivation

The manager/supervisor can control many factors in the work environment which contribute to staff motivation. Some of these factors are the physical environment, rules to govern employee behavior, and rewards for extra effort.

### Physical Environment

The trend toward office landscaping to provide more pleasant work environments continues at a rapid pace. The physical environment should be free of obstructions and safety hazards, maintained at a comfortable temperature, planned to provide adequate lighting without eyestrain or glare, decorated attractively with carefully chosen colors, and may include background music. An attractive, pleasant environment contributes to an employee's pride in being associated with the organization and with a particular depart-

*Provide safe, attractive surroundings*

ment. Employee satisfaction with the environment, as evidenced by research studies commissioned by Steelcase, Inc., has an impact upon an employee's feelings of satisfaction, and subsequently upon productivity.

### Rules for Employee Behavior

*Establish appropriate rules*

Rules for employee behavior should be kept to a minimum. Every effort must be made to avoid those rules which are arbitrary and cause negative feelings. Each rule should contribute to effective and efficient employee performance.

### Rewards for Extra Effort

*Reward superior performance*

Some organizations provide bonuses or merit pay increases for their employees who have demonstrated superior performance or who have contributed to developing and implementing more efficient procedures. Many supervisors have also found nonfinancial rewards to be excellent motivators. One of the simplest forms of nonfinancial reward for extra effort is to implement an employee suggestion for improving a procedure and to be sure that the employee receives recognition for the contribution. However, unless such programs are administered effectively, they can have negative effects and become demotivators.

## Employee Development

Each manager/supervisor has some responsibility for the development of the potential of the staff, collectively and as individuals. Several suggestions for encouraging employee development through individual initiative and through the delegation of responsibility are discussed in this section.

### Encourage Self-Development

The manager/supervisor must encourage employees to develop to their full potential on the job. One approach to promoting professional growth is to encourage attendance at meetings/conferences of professional organizations by awarding compensatory time, paying dues for employees, or paying employee travel expenses. Employees might also be encouraged to read professional journals available at the work place or through individually paid subscriptions. Incentive programs with one or more of the incentives being

*Establish incentives*

earned through consistent, measured improvement are another alternative.

The records manager should set an example by active participation in professional activities and by a continuous program of self-development. Membership and participation in local and national activities of professional organizations such as the Association of Records Managers and Administrators, Inc., provide excellent opportunities for self-development. ARMA Industry Action Committees, which serve as resource vehicles for specific types of industries, along with seminars and conferences, provide excellent opportunities for professional growth. A lack of personal committment to professional growth on the part of the employee will, however, negate managerial/supervisory efforts to stimulate self-development.

### Delegate Responsibility

Many opportunities exist for challenging employees with new activities if the manager/supervisor is alert to discovering and utilizing them. Employees may be encouraged to improve a procedure for handling certain documents where a current procedure seems awkward. An employee may be asked to assist in research into new types of equipment or supplies or may assist in preparing special reports. In addition, those employees who have demonstrated superior performance of their own job tasks may begin to serve as coaches for other employees or train as understudies for the next position on their career ladder within the records unit.

*Encourage employee involvement*

Opportunities to delegate responsibility and to "show off" exceptional employees may come through invitations to make presentations to management. If the presentation is made by an exceptional employee, management may not only get the correct information, but they may also get the idea that the records unit is training some very capable employees and future managers. As frequently as possible, the manager/supervisor should involve employees in making decisions relating to their work environment and procedures. The manager/supervisor should be cautioned, however, that participatory decision making will not work unless employees perceive that their suggestions are considered objectively, implemented when appropriate, and credited to the contributor.

## Staff Evaluation

Many managers regard staff evaluation as the most difficult part of their jobs. Evaluation can be made more manageable through carefully established performance standards, regular measurements of performance, and standard procedures for resolving personnel problems.

### Establish Performance Standards

Performance standards for entry-level competence in each position are established when preparing job descriptions and used when evaluating training programs. These same standards should be used to measure employee improvement in job performance. Lack of consistency and conformity of expectations and standards throughout the total staff development process results in confusion, conflict, and poor relationships between employees and supervisors. Poor supervisor-subordinate relationships affect the quality and quantity of work performance. Expected improvement in quantity or quality of work should be established and noted at periodic intervals.

### Measure Performance

Each employee should expect some informal work observation as well as periodic formal evaluation of performance. Performance must be measured against established standards. Employees who have equal experience and who are assigned similar tasks must be measured against the same performance standards. Although the primary objectives of performance appraisal should be employee development and improved performance, employees should understand that these performance evaluations will be used to determine continuance in their present positions, merit pay increases, and potential for advancement. Feedback is provided to the employee after each evaluation so that the employee can note progress toward standards and focus on areas where improvement is needed.

### Resolve Personnel Problems

As with every other position, some difficult tasks are among those required of the records manager. One of the more difficult tasks is maintaining records unit efficiency despite employee turnover. However, if the records manager is conscientious in providing training for employees, motivating them, and encouraging self-development, this problem should be minimized. There will always be, unless the organization is growing very rapidly, some employees for whom opportunities to advance do not occur quickly enough. These employees will continue to seek advancement through different organizations. Employee turnover must be expected. By training understudies and providing in-house training, the records management unit will continue to function smoothly.

*Loss of personnel*

Unchecked tardiness and absenteeism are contagious and seriously affect the efficient operation of any division. Most organizations resolve these problems by not tolerating tardiness or absen-

*Tardiness and absenteeism*

teeism except under emergency conditions. Usually these situations can be handled on an individual basis; however, a consistent policy with regard to excusing absence from the job must be formulated and followed.

Employee dishonesty is a widespread and costly problem and takes many forms. It may include personal/home use of office supplies, working less than a full work day, extending break periods or lunch hours, abusing sick leave benefits, using company phones for personal long distance calls, or embezzling cash. Appropriate inventory control systems of supplies, proper orientation to breaks and lunch periods, employee accountability for work performed, equitable work load distribution, adequate pre-employment screening of job applicants, proper control systems for accessible cash, and the creation of a satisfying and effective work environment through proper supervision all contribute to the reduction of employee dishonesty.

*Dishonesty*

Surveys of factors contributing to the success of beginning office workers have identified the ability to get along with others as one of the most important abilities an office worker can possess. Most records management positions require extensive interaction with clients and co-workers. The amount of human interaction should be given consideration in the development of job descriptions, performance criteria, and performance appraisal programs. A consistent example of positive approaches to dealing with people may encourage some employees to improve their own interpersonal skills. Some employees may need to participate in communication workshops or other activities designed to cultivate these skills.

*Ability to interact with others*

Resolving a problem of unsatisfactory performance is an unpleasant task. When a performance problem is identified, the records manager must carefully analyze the problem before taking any action. A decision tree for locating appropriate solutions to performance problems is presented in Figure 13–3.

Before approaching the employee, the records manager must be sure the employee had the proper opportunity for job training, that the employee's performance was measured against performance standards that were fair and consistent with those used to evaluate other employees, and that the employee was informed of the need to improve his or her performance and failed to do so. Termination decisions are made through consistent application of organizational policies. Employees to be terminated should be informed of this decision by their immediate supervisor and must be given cause for the termination.

*Termination*

Figure 13–3
Decision Tree for Determining Solutions to Performance Problems

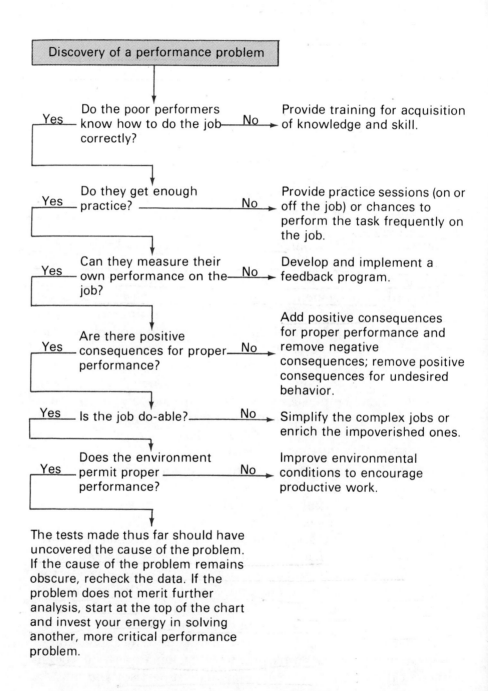

Discovery of a performance problem

Yes — Do the poor performers know how to do the job correctly? — No → Provide training for acquisition of knowledge and skill.

Yes — Do they get enough practice? — No → Provide practice sessions (on or off the job) or chances to perform the task frequently on the job.

Yes — Can they measure their own performance on the job? — No → Develop and implement a feedback program.

Yes — Are there positive consequences for proper performance? — No → Add positive consequences for proper performance and remove negative consequences; remove positive consequences for undesired behavior.

Yes — Is the job do-able? — No → Simplify the complex jobs or enrich the impoverished ones.

Yes — Does the environment permit proper performance? — No → Improve environmental conditions to encourage productive work.

The tests made thus far should have uncovered the cause of the problem. If the cause of the problem remains obscure, recheck the data. If the problem does not merit further analysis, start at the top of the chart and invest your energy in solving another, more critical performance problem.

## A LOOK AT THE CASE

Catherine Sargent now has a fully staffed records unit and is implementing a specially designed training program for records personnel. Her thoughts now turn to the management of the division to ensure its success and efficiency. In order to accomplish this, Catherine has planned and implemented a program of staff motivation, development, and evaluation procedures.

## TERMINOLOGY REVIEW

*Human resources development plan.* A comprehensive, systematic plan for the recruitment, selection, training, and evaluation of personnel.

*In-house training.* That training which is offered within the organization by its own personnel, as compared with that which might be developed and presented by special consultants or outside firms, or offered to the public by educational institutions.

## COMPETENCY REVIEW

1.  Describe the nature and scope of human resources development as it relates to records management personnel.
2.  List the types of information needed to make a decision regarding the records management positions needed in an organization.
3.  Compare and contrast available staff training options and give an example of when each would be most appropriate.
4.  Explain the role that performance appraisal plays in a total human resources development program.
5.  Prepare an outline of the steps necessary to establish a human resources development program.
6.  Identify the criteria and/or rationale needed for deciding to develop an in-house training program for records unit personnel.

## APPLICATIONS

1.  List and describe a program of incentives that records supervisors might implement to motivate records unit employees to improve their productivity/performance.

2.  Describe the actions you would take in:
    a.  conducting a supervisory interview with an employee whose tardiness and absenteeism have become frequent.
    b.  conducting a supervisory interview with an employee who is not meeting performance standards.

# CONCLUDING CASES

## A. Parker Sporting Goods

Wayne Stewart, the new manager of Parker Sporting Goods, is concerned about employee performance in all areas of his operation, but has decided to focus on the records management staff as the first training priority.

He has asked you as the records manager to make an assessment of the competence and performance of your staff, identify the sources of the problems, and recommend a plan for the development and evaluation of records management personnel.

Be certain that your report to Mr. Stewart includes the following:
1.  An outline of your total staff development program
2.  An assessment of current staff recruitment and selection, with recommendations for improvements
3.  An update of current staff needs of the records management unit
4.  A recommendation for performance criteria and appraisal forms.

## B. Tamara Training School

Two owners of Tamara Training School, Aaron Pedley and Michael Garry, have recently hired you to work with the micrographics clerks they plan to hire within the next six months. Your job is to assist Julian Soto, the micrographics analyst, in developing a job description, job specifications, and performance standards for their work.
1.  What type of study process would you recommend to Julian Soto as a data gathering vehicle for acquiring the information needed to prepare the job description, job specifications, and performance standards for the micrographics clerk position?
2.  Since you do not have a micrographics clerk position in the Tamara Training School organization at the present time, where do you suggest that Julian Soto look for information?

# READINGS AND REFERENCES

Association of Records Managers and Administrators, Inc. *Directory of Collegiate Schools Teaching Records Management.*

Association of Records Managers and Administrators, Inc., Greater Seattle Chapter, Library Committee, "The Public Library as an Arm of ARMA," *Records Management Quarterly*, Vol. 18, No. 4 (October, 1984), p. 68.

Boylen, Mary E. "The Four Costs of Employee Training." *Administrative Management,* Vol. 41, No. 3 (March, 1980), p. 40.

Carlberg, Scott. "Using Videotape for Records Management Training," *Records Management Quarterly,* Vol. 18, No. 2 (April, 1984), p. 30.

Cullivan, Kathryn Gould. "Taught Any Good Classes Lately?" *Records Management Quarterly,* Vol. 18, No. 4 (October, 1984), p. 66.

Deming, Basil S. *Evaluating Job-Related Training,* Prentice Hall and American Society for Training and Development, 1983.

Gammie, Gayle. "Records Management Training — Your Company Needs It." *Records Management Quarterly,* Vol. 6, No. 4 (October, 1972), p. 73.

Goodman, David G. "Selection and Training of Records Personnel." *Records Management Quarterly,* Vol. 14, No. 4 (October, 1980), p. 49.

Laird, Dugan. *Approaches to Training and Development.* 2d ed. Reading, Massachusetts: Addison-Wesley Publishing Co., Inc., 1985.

Langemo, Mark. "Motivating Toward Excellence and Productivity," *Records Management Quarterly,* Vol. 19, No. 2 (April, 1985), p. 24.

Miller, Sharon R. "IRM Education — A Joint Effort," *Records Management Quarterly,* Vol. 18, No. 4 (October, 1984), p. 62.

Pennix, Gail B., and Jan Schouw. "When All Else Fails — Smile!" *Records Management Quarterly,* Vol. 19, No. 4 (October, 1985), p. 40.

Robek, Mary F. "ARMA Chapter Activities Promoting the CRM Program," *Records Management Quarterly,* Vol. 18, No. 4 (October, 1984), p. 70.

Scherer, W. T. "How to Get Management's Commitment for Training." *Training and Development Journal,* Vol. 32, No. 1 (January, 1978), p. 3.

Steelcase, Inc. *White Collar Productivity: The National Challenge,* A Study Compiled by The American Productivity Center, 1982.

*The Steelcase National Study of Office Environments: Do They Work?* Conducted by Louis Harris & Associates, Inc., 1978.

*The Steelcase National Study of Office Environments, No. 11: Comfort and Productivity in the Office of the 80's,* Conducted by Louis Harris & Associates, Inc., 1980.

# 14
# CAREERS IN
# RECORDS MANAGEMENT

## Competencies

After completing this chapter, you should be able to

1. match job responsibilities and job titles in the field of records management.
2. list methods of professional development in the field of records management and explain the benefits of each.
3. select a career path which is appropriate to your interests, education upon entering full-time employment, previous experience (if any), and career goals.

# Introductory Case

Marty Grange has just completed the first year of the two-year program in administrative services at Jackson Community College. One of the courses he took during the third quarter was records management. Marty really enjoyed the classwork.

In this course he studied the importance of information to management and the overall viability of a business. He was especially interested in how the use of recent technologies, such as electronic databases and optical disk storage, are improving the efficiency with which records are stored and controlled. In addition, he observed that records management is a field supported by strong professional organizations. As a result, Marty began to reconsider his choice of administrative assistant as a career goal. Marty decides to investigate the following questions:

1. What positions are available in the field of records management?
2. What preparation is required?

Career choice can be a very important influence on success and happiness. The importance of this decision should cause an individual to examine carefully the future of the industry/position to which he or she aspires and to examine the interests, aptitudes, and abilities which could be brought to the chosen position.

The United States Bureau of Labor Statistics documents that white-collar workers make up over 53 percent of the work force. This percentage is expected to grow to 65 percent by 1990 and to 90 percent by the year 2000. The shift from an industrial society to an information society has caused records management to become an expanding technical information field, which is rapidly becoming more specialized. As organizations become more dependent upon information and its rapid processing, effective proliferation control and efficient storage and retrieval become increasingly important. These factors have greatly enhanced career opportunities in records management. Not only do the number of positions in the information field continue to increase, but the opportunities to advance within and from these positions also increase.

*Rapidly expanding technical field*

## PREPARATION

Entry into the records management field may be made at several levels and in several specific areas of expertise. While most positions in records management share some requirements, each has its own specialized requirements as well. The first step in successful preparation for a career in records management is to investigate types of positions available and qualifications required for each.

*Investigate positions/ qualifications*

The size and structure of the organization determine the degree of specialization within records management positions. Large, highly structured organizations usually have very specialized positions which offer many career opportunities. Smaller, less structured organizations usually have fewer positions and they are less specialized and more inclusive of the overall records management responsibilities. These positions typically offer more limited career opportunities. The discussion in this chapter covers positions which may be found in a large organization's records unit under the direction of a records manager (as represented in Figure 14–1). A smaller organization which employs only a records manager and one or two records clerks may assign very different responsibilities to these individuals; however, those responsibilities are among those presented in this discussion.

## Qualifications

As was discussed in Chapter 12, job qualifications are usually divided into three categories: education/training, experience, and personal characteristics. Each of these requirements varies somewhat from position to position and with the employing organization.

### Education/Training

Formal education (such as graduation from high school and/or college), specific course completion, and specific skills for each position may be required. In large organizations, most positions require a college degree and some experience in the field or some college course work and extensive experience. Most of the positions on the bottom lines of the organization chart require a high school diploma.

*Specific knowledge/skills*

### Experience

Experience requirements vary from none for an entry-level position within the records unit to several years of related on-the-job experience for more advanced positions. Specific requirements for each position are outlined in another section of this chapter.

*Knowledge and skills acquired on the job*

### Personal Characteristics

Personal characteristics contribute to success in any position. Most positions within the records unit require staff members who can relate well to other people, analyze data, and organize work.

*Individual attributes*

## Career Paths

There are five major career paths in the field of records management: active records, records center, micrographics, forms, and reports. Each of these career areas contains both entry-level and advanced positions. In addition, beyond these career paths are the positions of records and information analyst and senior records and information analyst and the position of records and information administrator, as illustrated in Figure 14–1. This section gives a brief overview of the responsibilities and qualifications of positions in each area. The position of records manager is discussed in Chapter 12.

### Active Records

The **active records staff** is responsible for controlling all records that are accessed at least once a month and for the determination of when records should be transferred to inactive status. The active

Figure 14–1
Records and Information Management Career Ladder

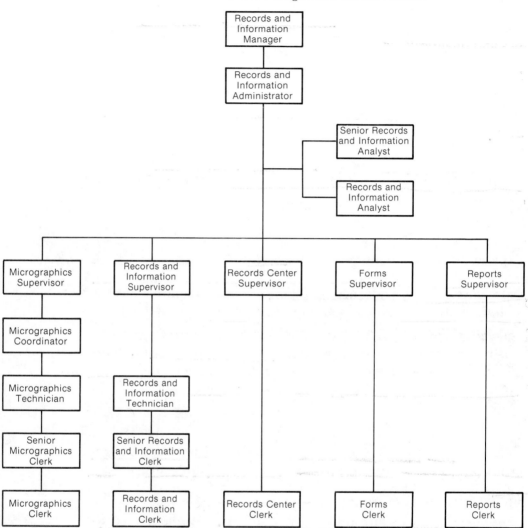

records supervisor, sometimes called the records and information supervisor, is responsible for efficiency and uniformity of filing procedures throughout the organization. Two or three levels of employees may report to the active records supervisor. Typical job responsibilities and qualifications in the active records department are outlined in Figure 14–2.

## Records Center

The records center staff is responsible for controlling all inactive records of the organization. The center staff receives records which are transferred from the active records department and is responsible for the maintenance of the organization's vital records. The responsibilities of the records center supervisor are very similar to those of the active records supervisor. Position responsibilities and qualifications in the records center are described briefly in Figure 14–3.

Figure 14–2
Careers in the Active Records Department

| Job Title | Duties and Responsibilities | Personal Characteristics | Education/ Experience | Advancement Opportunities |
|---|---|---|---|---|
| Records and Information Supervisor | Maintains uniform active records system and procedures throughout the organization<br>Develops more efficient and economical methods of records maintenance<br>Plans and conducts special active records projects<br>Administers vital records program<br>Selects and supervises staff | Works effectively with all levels of personnel<br>Supervises effectively<br>Coordinates available resources<br>Has good organizational skills<br>Has developed analytical skills | Minimum of 2 years college in records systems related work or equivalent work experience | Records and Information Analyst<br>Senior Records and Information Analyst<br>Other staff position |
| Records and Information Technician | Maintains specialized records systems, such as medical or engineering records<br>Conducts systems analysis in specialized area<br>Assists in designing records retention schedules and monitors adherence to establish schedule | Relates well to people<br>Plans and organizes well<br>Has developed analytical skills | High school diploma<br>2 years experience in records management or equivalent academic training | Records and Information Supervisor<br>Other records management staff position |
| Senior Records and Information Clerk | Coordinates with records center and other records areas to monitor files according to established standards<br>Retrieves information for users<br>Maintains logs and indexes summarizing status of information<br>Oversees transfer of records according to retention schedule | Relates well to people<br>Comprehends difficult questions and derives answers from records<br>Plans and organizes well<br>Possesses clerical typing skills | High school diploma<br>1 year experience at Records and Information Clerk level | Records and Information Supervisor<br>Records and Information Technician |
| Records and Information Clerk | Sorts, indexes, files, and retrieves all types of records<br>Searches and investigates information in files<br>Classifies materials and records<br>Maintains charge-out system for records removed from files | Relates well to people<br>Possesses mechanical aptitude<br>Is able to analyze data for answers to questions | High school diploma which includes some training in filing and retrieval<br>Entry-level position | Senior Records and Information Clerk |

Figure 14–3
Careers in the Records Center

| Job Title | Duties and Responsibilities | Personal Characteristics | Education/ Experience | Advancement Opportunities |
|---|---|---|---|---|
| Records Center Supervisor | Operates and maintains the records center Is responsible for vital records protection, storage, and disposition Selects and supervises staff | Works effectively with all levels of personnel Supervises effectively Coordinates available resources Has good organizational skills | Minimum of 2 years college in records systems related work or equivalent work experience | Records and Information Analyst Records and Information Administrator Higher staff position |
| Records Center Clerk | Assists in accession, reference, retrieval, and disposal activities of center Assists with vital records Searches, sorts, and files records as required by users Maintains charge-out system for records removed from files | Relates well to people Possesses clerical typing skills Possesses mechanical aptitude Is able to analyze data for answers to questions | High school diploma which includes work in filing and retrieval May be entry-level position | Records Center Supervisor Records and Information Technician |

## Micrographics

The **micrographics staff** is responsible for converting certain records or types of records to microforms. The procedures used in this conversion and the microrecords control program are the responsibility of the micrographics supervisor. Usually both technicians and clerks serve as staff members. The number of persons employed in each position varies with the size of the organization and the number of micrographic applications used. Typical responsibilities and qualifications for employees of the micrographics department are outlined in Figure 14–4.

## Forms

Forms are an integral part of collecting and processing data. The **forms staff** is responsible for establishing forms operating procedures, analysis procedures, and design and specification standards, and for controlling forms throughout the organization. The supervisor is assisted by the forms clerk. The responsibilities and qualifications for members of the forms department are described in Figure 14–5.

## Reports

The **reports staff** is responsible for the development, implementation, and control of reports throughout the organization. Only large organizations have a separate reports department. Many smaller organizations have only one reports position.

Figure 14–4
Careers in the Micrographics Department

| Job Title | Duties and Responsibilities | Personal Characteristics | Education/ Experience | Advancement Opportunities |
|---|---|---|---|---|
| Micrographics Supervisor | Plans and controls central micrographics program Works closely with records and information analyst and other corporate members in development of micrographics applications Selects and supervises staff | Has ability to communicate effectively Has developed analytical and organizational skills Supervises effectively | 2 years micrographic systems work experience 4 years progressive related work experience | Records and Information Analyst |
| Micrographics Coordinator | Sets priorities and schedules daily work Monitors human and operations resources Ensures quality control Trains micrographics personnel | Communicates effectively Has ability to develop performance goals Has ability to supervise technical personnel | High school diploma or equivalent 3 years experience in micrographics | Micrographics Supervisor |
| Micrographics Technician | Provides technical advice regarding new projects, equipment, and quality control Operates microfilming equipment Develops and maintains indexing and retrieval aids Monitors micrographics procedures manual and production statistics Monitors micrographics clerks | Relates well to people Plans and organizes work well Possesses mechanical aptitude Possesses knowledge of office procedures | High school diploma or equivalent 2 years experience in micrographics | Micrographics Coordinator Micrographics Supervisor |
| Senior Micrographics Clerk | Receives and logs documents to be filmed Prepares documents for filming and operates equipment Handles special projects Monitors quality control Conducts routine equipment maintenance | Relates well to people Possesses mechanical ability Possesses filing and clerical typing skills Analyzes problems well | High school diploma or equivalent 1 year experience in micrographics and/or training in micrographics | Micrographics Technician |
| Micrographics Clerk | Prepares documents for microfilming Operates microfilming equipment Prepares indexes and targets Searches, sorts, and files microforms | Relates well to people Possesses mechanical aptitude Possesses filing and clerical typing skills | High school diploma Entry-level position | Senior Micrographics Clerk |

The reports supervisor is responsible for the development and implementation of all organization reports, management policies, and procedures. Maintaining the reports catalog and operating the central reports library are the primary responsibilities of the reports clerk. Typical responsibilities and qualifications for members of the reports department are outlined in Figure 14–6.

Figure 14–5
Careers in the Forms Department

| Job Title | Duties and Responsibilities | Personal Characteristics | Education/ Experience | Advancement Opportunities |
|---|---|---|---|---|
| Forms Supervisor | Plans, implements, and coordinates forms control program throughout organization<br>Provides technical assistance regarding design, use, specifications, cost, and procurement of forms<br>Selects and supervises staff | Communicates effectively<br>Has high aptitude for identifying problems | Minimum of 2 years of college in records systems related work or equivalent work experience | Records and Information Analyst<br>Other staff position |
| Forms Clerk | Maintains records required to document and control all company forms<br>Calculates reorder points for each form and coordinates orders | Relates well to people<br>Is attentive to detail | High school diploma with training in office procedures<br>May be entry-level position | Forms Supervisor |

## Records and Information Analyst and Administrator Positions

The **records and information analyst** and **senior analyst** are staff personnel responsible for providing assistance in reviewing existing records systems and preparing revisions for improvement, as shown in Figure 14–7. Through systems analysis, new procedures are designed for special projects involving active and inactive records, micrographics, forms, and report management. The **records and information administrator** is the middle-management

Figure 14–6
Careers in the Reports Department

| Job Title | Duties and Responsibilities | Personal Characteristics | Education/ Experience | Advancement Opportunities |
|---|---|---|---|---|
| Reports Supervisor | Has responsibility for development and implementation of all organizational reports, management policies, and procedures<br>Selects and supervises staff | Relates well to people<br>Has high aptitude for identifying problems | Minimum of 2 years college in records systems related work | Records and Information Analyst<br>Other staff position |
| Reports Clerk | Maintains central reports catalog and library<br>Retrieves reports as needed by users | Relates well to people<br>Maintains confidentiality of data | High school diploma with training in filing and office procedures<br>Entry-level position | Reports Supervisor |

position immediately below the position of records and information manager. The administrator is responsible for translating organizational plans for implementation by the individual records divisions. Organization assets are protected through the systematic review and control of information from this level of the hierarchy.

Figure 14–7
Careers as Records and Information Analysts and Administrators

| Job Title | Duties and Responsibilities | Personal Characteristics | Education/ Experience | Advancement Opportunities |
|---|---|---|---|---|
| Records and Information Administrator | Designs policies and procedures for records and information management and directs their implementation<br>Establishes short-range objectives to carry out long-range goals of management<br>Coordinates personnel resources for the records and information system<br>Prepares periodic reports used in controlling the records and information system<br>Ensures adherence to laws affecting the control of information | Relates well to people<br>Possesses organization, planning, and leadership skills<br>Demonstrates ability to perceive, analyze, and solve problems | College degree or equivalent work experience<br>5 years experience in records systems | Records and Information Manager |
| Senior Records and Information Analyst | Analyzes existing records systems and prepares proposals for change<br>Designs manual and/or automated records systems<br>Monitors retention programs<br>Directs the establishment of a vital records protection program<br>Directs and/or supervises other systems analysts | Relates well to people<br>Has well-developed supervisory skills<br>Has ability to analyze problems and seek solutions | College degree; or 2 years college with specialized courses in records systems and a minimum of 2 years work experience as a records and information analyst; or 4-6 years experience in records systems with knowledge of automated technologies plus 2 years work experience as a records and information analyst | Records and Information Administrator |
| Records and Information Analyst | Analyzes existing records systems and prepares proposals for change<br>Designs manual and/or automated records systems<br>Prepares or assists in preparing retention schedules<br>Writes procedures<br>Provides records staff training<br>Assists in establishing a vital records protection program | Relates well to people<br>Possesses organizational, planning, and motivational skills<br>Has ability to analyze problems and seek solutions | College degree or 2 years college plus courses in records systems; or 4-6 years experience in records systems with knowledge of automated technologies | Senior Records and Information Analyst<br>Records and Information Administrator |

■

## A LOOK AT THE CASE

Marty's investigation convinces him that he would like to enter the records management field as a records technician. He feels that the remainder of his program at the community college will prepare him for this step; however, he realizes that he may have to begin as a records clerk. Knowing this, he is eager to learn what he can do to advance rapidly within the field once he is employed.

How can an employee in the field of records management pursue professional development?

■

## PROFESSIONAL DEVELOPMENT

Four major methods of professional development are available for those in the field of records management: institutional and in-house training, professional organizations, professional publications, and the Certified Records Manager examination. Each of these methods has been discussed previously as a part of the professional development program of the records manager or as a part of a staff development program initiated by the records manager. Each method is reviewed in this chapter from the perspective of choices available to individual staff members.

### Institutional and In-House Training

*Training provided by educational institutions*

Educational institutions (both two-year and four-year) offer a variety of courses which may be helpful to the records management professional. Courses in records management, business administration, and human relations should be considered. These courses may be particularly helpful to those starting at levels which do not require a college degree. Courses which earn credit toward a degree may not only add specific knowledge, but also help fulfill a requirement for advancement.

*Training provided by the organization*

Many large organizations offer special in-house training programs. These programs are taught by the records manager, by other qualified personnel (such as the forms supervisor teaching a course in forms management), or by outside consultants hired for this specific purpose. If in-house training is offered, it is often free to the employee and provides an excellent opportunity to acquire specific skills which can open doors to new opportunities. Some organizations also fund participation in professional seminars for employees who wish to develop new or improved job skills.

## Professional Organizations

Participation in professional organizations such as the **Association of Records Managers and Administrators, Inc. (ARMA)**, and the **Association for Information and Image Management (AIIM)** offers many opportunities for professional growth. Organization members have the opportunity to meet others in similar positions and to exchange ideas on resolving problems or making operations more efficient. Professional organizations also promote excellence in performance through suggested performance standards. Comparing personal performance with suggested standards provides an additional incentive for those seeking to advance within the profession. Many professional organizations also encourage and coordinate research into specific problems or procedures important to professionals in that field. Often the results of this research and the development and implementation of innovative procedures are presented in annual conferences or published in the organization's periodicals. For example, Project ELF, Eliminate Legal-size Files, was initiated at the 1980 ARMA Conference. Since that time, the Judicial Conference of the United States has decided to eliminate legal-size files in federal courts and a number of state courts have also adopted letter-size paper.

*Growth through professional activities*

## Professional Publications

Several journals and newsletters are published by professional organizations and by specialists in records management, as illustrated in Figure 14–8. Often these publications are available in the organization's library or public libraries. Members, of course, receive these publications with their membership. The *Records Management Quarterly*, an ARMA publication, and *Inform*, an AIIM publication, report studies of importance to records management personnel.

*Growth through professional reading*

Professional publications are excellent sources of information on technical innovations or improvements in the records management field. In addition to the product information presented, a forum for discussing new techniques and procedures which can

Figure 14–8
Selected Professional Publications

increase efficiency of operations is also provided. The interest which an individual demonstrates by reviewing these publications and applying these innovations to the organization's records procedures (as appropriate) will often cause an immediate supervisor to notice initiative and interest in professional growth. These characteristics are important for promotion within the organization or for obtaining advancement opportunities outside the organization.

## Certified Records Manager Examination

*Growth through professional certification*

The Certified Records Manager (CRM) designation is conferred by the Institute of Certified Records Managers (ICRM) upon successful completion of a six-part examination. Those who aspire to the top level of records management may want to prepare for this examination as a part of their professional development program.

## A LOOK AT THE CASE

Having familiarized himself with the methods of professional development, Marty is more convinced than ever that a career in records management is the right choice for him. In addition to pursuing the second year of his program at the community college, Marty begins to make a point of setting aside time every other week to visit the local library to read records management publications. He also begins to investigate the opportunities in records management in local firms. As a part of his investigation, Marty plans to learn as much as he can about the professional development programs within those organizations which offer the positions in which he is interested.

## TERMINOLOGY REVIEW

*Active records staff.* Personnel responsible for controlling all records that are accessed at least once a month and for the determination of when records should be transferred to inactive status.

*Association for Information and Image Management (AIIM).* A professional organization for records and information management professionals.

*Association of Records Managers and Administrators, Inc. (ARMA).* A professional organization for records and information management professionals.

*Forms staff.* Personnel responsible for establishing forms operating procedures, analysis procedures, and design and specification standards, and for controlling forms throughout the organization.

*Micrographics staff.* Personnel responsible for converting certain records or types of records to microforms.

*Records analyst staff.* Personnel responsible for providing assistance in reviewing existing records systems and preparing revisions for improvement.

*Records and information administrator.* Manager responsible for translating organizational records and information plans for implementation by the individual records divisions and for controlling the records information system throughout the organization.

*Records center staff.* Personnel responsible for controlling all inactive records of the organization.

*Reports staff.* Personnel responsible for the development, implementation, and control of reports throughout the organization.

## COMPETENCY REVIEW

1. Match each of the job responsibilities in Column B with the job titles in Column A. The items in Column B may be used as many times as appropriate.

| A | B |
|---|---|
| 1. Records and Information Supervisor | a. Sorts, indexes, and retrieves all types of records |
| 2. Forms Clerk | b. Maintains micrographics procedural manual |
| 3. Reports Clerk | c. Prepares documents for microfilming |
| 4. Micrographics Clerk | d. Maintains uniform filing systems and procedures throughout the organization |
| 5. Records and Information Clerk | e. Selects and supervises staff |
| 6. Forms Supervisor | f. Determines when forms should be recorded |
| 7. Records and Information Technician | g. Maintains catalog of reports available for access |
| 8. Micrographics Technician | h. Plans, implements, and coordinates a forms control program throughout the organization |
| | i. Monitors adherence to records retention schedule |
| 9. Records and Information Analyst | j. Analyzes records system and designs proposal for improvement |

2. Explain how a records and information analyst would assist the forms supervisor and the records and information supervisor.
3. List four methods of professional development in the field of records management and explain the benefits of each.

## APPLICATIONS

1. Select a career path in records management according to your interest, education upon entering full-time employment, previous experience (if any), and career goals. Explain your choice. Identify each intermediate step along this path and explain the methods (other than hard work and excellent performance) by which you might hope to advance.

2.  As records and information administrator, you have the immediate responsibility of hiring a new micrographics supervisor. You must make your choice from among the following three applicants for the position:

|  | **Educational Preparation** | **Work Experience** |
|---|---|---|
| Applicant A | 4-year degree in business management from local university | 2 years as a reports clerk (while completing college) |
| Applicant B | high school diploma | 4 years as a records and information clerk |
|  |  | 8 years as a senior records and information clerk (in your organization) |
| Applicant C | 2-year degree in office management from area university | 3 years as a records and information clerk |
|  |  | 1 year as a micrographics clerk |

a.  Which applicant would you choose?
b.  Why did you choose this applicant over the other applicants?

## CONCLUDING CASES

### A. The College of Business Administration

Sheryl Stoner and Rosemary Keith are both students in the college of business administration at the local university. Sheryl has enrolled in a records management course for the next term; Rosemary has just completed the course. Sheryl and Rosemary meet each other in the bookstore one day and part of their conversation is as follows:

Sheryl: I'm really looking forward to the records management course I'm taking next semester.

Rosemary: I'm sure you'll learn a lot. I found the course quite challenging.

Sheryl: I'm seriously thinking about a career in records management. What are the career options and what can one do to prepare for advancement?

Answer Sheryl's question.

### B. Duncan Service Agency

Becki Adams is the records manager for Duncan Service Agency. She is responsible for all records management duties in the organization. As the agency has grown to include a main branch office and three regional offices, the control of records has become a challenging responsibility. She is not only responsible for sorting, indexing, coding, storing, and retrieving all records but also for making sure certain vital records are permanently secure.

Because of a tremendous increase in work during the past year, Becki has hired two assistants. She is now training them. In addition, her employer and owner of the company told Becki last week that she feels the use of micrographic records may soon be necessary.

Becki knows that she must begin some long-range planning for the records management department. She foresees a time when the company will require a separate active records department, a records center, and a micrographics department. She feels now is the time to begin planning to specialize the records management functions. A first priority is to prepare herself and her assistants for such a change.

1. What are some ways Becki and her two assistants can prepare for careers in specialized records departments, such as a records center or a micrographics department?

2. What personal factors may play an important role in determining whether Becki's assistants would be capable of assuming a leadership role in one of the new departments?

3. Do you feel the organization may have to look outside for personnel to fill the supervisory positions in the specialized departments? Explain why.

## READINGS AND REFERENCES

*ARMA Job Descriptions Guidelines,* 2d ed. Prairie Village, Kansas: Association of Records Managers and Administrators, Inc., 1985.

Bailey, Robert L. "Information and Records Management as a Career," *Records Management Quarterly,* Vol. 17, No. 2 (April, 1983), p. 43.

Benedon, William, CRM. "Professional Status Through Certification," *Records Management Quarterly,* Vol. 12, No. 1 (January, 1978), p. 30.

Bronder, Susan M. "Gaining Professional Status: The Leadership Role of the Institute of Certified Records Managers," *Records Management Quarterly,* Vol. 18, No. 1 (January, 1984), p. 20.

Deutsch, R. Eden. "Tomorrow's Work Force," *The Futurist,* Vol. 19, No. 6 (December, 1985), p. 8.

Ebner, Hans, Jr. "In-House Training Program Produces Records Managers," *The Office,* Vol. 102, No. 9 (September, 1985), p. 19.

Langemo, Mark. "The Future of Information and Records Management," *Records Management Quarterly,* Vol. 19, No. 4 (October, 1985), p. 28.

"Outline for Certified Records Manager Examination," *Records Management Quarterly,* Vol. 19, No. 4 (October, 1985), p. 63.

## COMPREHENSIVE CASE, PART III

Jon Hunter is the records manager of Music Merchandise Marts, Inc. (MMM), a nationwide retailing organization. MMM's board of directors has recently approved Jon's request to begin in-house microfilming of several records applications. Jon has planned the use of existing space for filming activities and for storage of microforms. Two rotary cameras with automatic feed and other essential equipment and supplies have been ordered.

Jon has projected that the micrographics department will be filming an average of 32,000 documents per day. Since not all documents will be uniform in size or in a condition which would allow automatic feeding, Jon projects that each technician will be able to film an average of 2,500 documents per hour. Jon has also projected that each clerk will be able to prepare an average of 2,000 documents per hour. Jon anticipates that the micrographics department will receive an average of 65 requests daily for information or microforms. Since requests for information require more time than retrieving a microform, Jon projects that the average request will consume five minutes.

1. Based on Jon's projections, what would be the optimum number of employees for the micrographics department? Specify the positions to which they should be assigned and give a rationale for your answer.

2. If Jon's budget does not allow for the optimum number of employees, what positions could be combined or added later? Explain.

3. What will be Jon's initial and ongoing staff development responsibilities with the addition of a micrographics department?

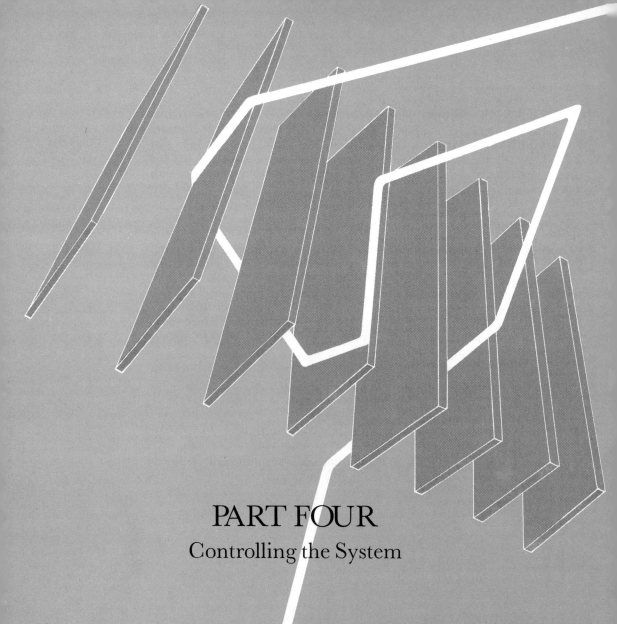

# PART FOUR
## Controlling the System

# 15
# THE CONTROL FUNCTION

## Competencies

After completing this chapter, you should be able to

1. describe the role of the control subsystem and its relationship to the records management system.
2. identify types of control and apply these controls to specific examples of each.
3. justify instituting a records control system.
4. describe links in the scope of control and describe the relationships between the links.
5. assign control responsibilities to appropriate records personnel and users.
6. describe an administrative audit and the types of problems an administrative audit may reveal.
7. describe an operational audit and the types of problems that may be revealed in an operational audit.

# Introductory Case

Beauty Image, Inc., is a small manufacturer and distributor of hair care products in Texas. Although there is another major producer within the sales territory, Beauty Image's pricing and aggressive promotion have allowed them to capture a large share of the market (40 percent during the last six-month period).

Despite the sales success, their profits are decreasing. While the rate of decrease is not alarmingly high, the fact that the decline is a steady one is cause for concern.

Mark O'Connor, director of information systems, just completed a task force study to identify areas in which the increases in costs are disproportionately high. The following table summarizes by major category of expenditure the findings of the task force:

| Category | Prior Year | Current Year | Percent of Increase or Decrease |
|---|---|---|---|
| | (Costs expressed in thousands) | | |
| Materials costs | $450 | $499 | +11% |
| Personnel costs | | | |
| Management | 210 | 246 | +17 |
| Administrative support | 100 | 116 | +16 |
| Production | 250 | 275 | +10 |
| Transportation costs | 90 | 95 | + 6 |
| Advertising/promotional costs | 100 | 112 | +12 |
| Administrative (office) costs | 75 | 105 | +40 |

1. Allowing for an inflationary factor of 5 percent, what categories appear disproportionately high?
2. What factors might have caused the excessive rise in costs?
3. What actions should Beauty Image, Inc., consider in its effort to curb costs?
4. What is the function of control in this case?

*Seventy-five percent of all information available was developed within the past two decades, and information is generated at the rate of seventy billion new pieces per year.*
*What are the implications of this staggering statistic for records management?*

**Control** is the function that compares achieved results with planned goals. The control function is the process of ordering, evaluating, and providing feedback to the records management system. Control is a subsystem of the overall records management system and should be viewed as a part of the process function of that system. As with all systems, the control subsystem is composed of interdependent parts operating as a whole to accomplish a given purpose. An illustration of the relationship between the total records management system and the control subsystem is shown in Figure 15–1.

*Control subsystem*

## THE CONTROLLING PROCESS

The purpose of the control subsystem is to establish and maintain order in the records management system. Three types of control are used in the process portion of the control subsystem—precontrol, concurrent control, and feedback control.

**Precontrol** takes place before work is performed. Precontrol attempts to eliminate potential problems before they occur. In order to accomplish this, management creates policies, procedures, and rules that will reduce the possibility of problems occurring. For example, a policy may be established that allows only key manage-

*Precontrol*

Figure 15–1
Relationship Between the Records Management System
and the Control Subsystem

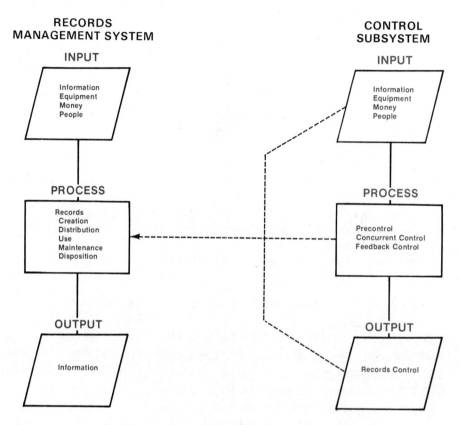

RECORDS
MANAGEMENT SYSTEM

INPUT

Information
Equipment
Money
People

PROCESS

Records
Creation
Distribution
Use
Maintenance
Disposition

OUTPUT

Information

CONTROL
SUBSYSTEM

INPUT

Information
Equipment
Money
People

PROCESS

Precontrol
Concurrent Control
Feedback Control

OUTPUT

Records Control

ment personnel to issue directives. This is a type of precontrol that addresses the potential problems of too many directives or directives that are conflicting. Another form of precontrol is the establishment of a uniform records system. Precontrol determines the most orderly and appropriate method of establishing and maintaining a records system for a particular organization.

*Concurrent control*

**Concurrent control** takes place as work is being performed. Concurrent control affects personnel, equipment, procedures, and performance. One form of concurrent control is demonstrated by the requirement that all retrieved records must be charged out and followed up for prompt return. Security measures used on a daily basis are another form of concurrent control. Reports, correspondence, and forms control programs exercise both precontrol and concurrent control as they establish policies for creation and distribution of the various forms of communication; and concurrent control is exercised in the use, maintenance, and update of the communications.

**Feedback control** concentrates on past performance. The basis of feedback control is a comparison of historical data with current performance data. For example, data may be compiled regarding the number of misfiles in an organization. These misfile statistics may then be compared to previous years' records to determine the need for corrective action. Cost analysis of forms design and production is another type of feedback control. So is the provision for receiving comments from users of any of the established procedures.

*Feedback control*

All aspects of the control subsystem should be used to establish (precontrol) and maintain (concurrent and feedback control) order in the records management system.

There are many other examples of control in a records management system. Control applications range from simple to complex and from short- to long-term; each application contributes to establishing and maintaining order in the system. Many of the procedures discussed in previous chapters are types of control. For example, the records retention and disposition procedures combine precontrol, concurrent control, and feedback control. Precontrol is applied by the establishment of a timetable for retaining records and policies for records disposition; concurrent control is applied by adhering to the established schedule and by preparing records for disposition; feedback control is applied by monitoring the system and providing corrective action.

*Control applications*

## Need

The necessity for control in information processing is broadly based. Included are the need to

- control proliferation of information,
- provide uniform procedures,
- minimize information duplication,
- provide timely information,
- control varied media sizes and forms,
- establish cost-effective information processing, and
- establish standards of performance.

All other functional areas of management—planning, organizing, staffing, and directing—are affected by and integrated with the control function.

## Control Proliferation of Information

The need to control records is growing, as is the quantity of information available to users. An organized system must be established to handle the increasingly available information, as well as soft- and hard-copy records. One of the major concerns of managers is information overload. So much information is generated and so little effort is expended to screen and select appropriate information that managers are deluged with information; not enough time is available to discriminate between essential information, useful information, interesting information, or trivia. Over 50 percent of the workers in this country produce and process information rather than material goods. Further, predictions for the future are for information to grow four times faster than the population. Another example of the staggering future paperwork explosion is the statement that one million pages of new records are created every minute of every day in the United States alone — twenty pounds per year for every person in the country! For this amount of available information, there must be consistent control of paperwork generation. Without these controls, the information overload will provide managers with so much information as to render them ineffective.

*Information overload*

## Provide Uniformity

Some systematic control is necessary for providing a uniform approach to records creation, distribution, use, maintenance, and disposition. As the number of people involved in each of the records stages increases, the need for uniformity also increases. Imagine the confusion in an organization where each person creates records in a different way, stores the records according to his or her own eccentric method, distributes records at will, retains records that each wishes to retain, and disposes of records based on whim. Envision, if you can, the time, effort, and frustration of trying to find a record processed in this way. Uniformity also provides rules to minimize the effect of one-person files that no one else understands or can use. Uniformity, therefore, is necessary if records are going to be available in appropriate quantity and quality and at least cost.

*Consistent approach to records handling*

## Minimize Duplication

Controls in place tend to minimize records duplication. As controls are established, implemented, and evaluated, duplication should decrease. Original record proliferation is enough of a battle to conquer without the additional problems created by copies. Duplicates

*Costly duplication*

are not only costly to create but also require just as much storage space and processing effort as original records.

## Provide Timely Information

Information, to be effective, must be current and easily accessible to the user when needed. A manager who needs information for a report due next week is not going to be able to use information that arrives too late to incorporate into the report. Information gathered too soon may not accurately assess current status and may not be helpful. Therefore, a control system is necessary to provide checks on the accessibility of the information managers require.

*Information accessibility*

## Control Varied Media Sizes and Forms

One of the problems facing records managers is the creation of records of varying sizes and in various forms. This problem was recognized and addressed by the federal government when the conversion from "government-size" paper to standard letter-size paper was made in January, 1983. **Project ELF** (Eliminate Legal-size Files) was introduced by the Association of Records Managers and Administrators in 1980 and has had a substantial impact on reducing the number of legal-size files. Project ELF is supported by the international board of the Business Forms Management Association and by the Association for Information and Image Management. In September of 1981, the Judicial Conference of the United States met and decided to eliminate legal-size requirements for all federal courts. The effective date for conversion to standard-size paper was January, 1983. Although this is not legislation, it is an administrative decision made by the federal judiciary and is binding on all persons who choose to do business with the federal courts. In addition, many state court systems have made the conversion to letter-size paper.

*Project ELF*

The General Services Administration issued two Federal Property Management Regulations (FPMR 120 and FPMR 122) which serve to discourage the use of legal-size file cabinets in all government agencies. FPMR 120 discourages their use by requiring that agencies requesting cabinets for existing systems must obtain these cabinets from surplus, rather than through purchase. FPMR 122 calls for the redesign of forms to letter size unless it is not economically feasible.

In organizations using several paper sizes, consideration should be given to the numerous costs incurred as a result of this policy. Most information can be accommodated on standard-size ($8\frac{1}{2}$ by 11 inches) paper. There is little documented evidence to

*Use standard-size paper*

support the need for legal-size ($8\frac{1}{2}$ by 14 inches) paper. However, documented evidence that legal-size paper increases the cost of records does exist. Legal-size storage cabinets cost more to purchase, occupy more floor space, house no more records than regular-size cabinets, and cost more to maintain. Additionally, the use of legal-size cabinets requires stocking two sizes of supplies, i.e., folders, guides, file pockets, hanging folders, and paper. Consideration of this need for dual paper accommodation must be given in the lease or purchase of copy and microfilm equipment. Records carton use should be limited to 10-by-12-by-25-inch size, or storage cartons, too, must be purchased in two sizes. The trend is to provide uniformity in size and form to manage records more efficiently.

*Reduce forms of media*

Records control minimizes the number of forms of media used within an organization. Computer tapes, microfilm, COM, jackets, aperture cards, microfiche, paper, printouts, floppy disks, optical disks, tapes, videotapes, hard disks, and so forth, all present unique storage and retrieval challenges. Therefore, established controls on the types of media used in records creation and storage are necessary. These controls are established only after careful consideration of the needs of the organization, of current and future compatibility, of equipment and systems availability, and of user requirements. The final selection is made on a cost-effective basis. An organization rarely requires all of the various media forms. Most organizations do, however, use several types of media. If properly evaluated and controlled, multimedia forms are compatible and effective.

## Establish Cost Effectiveness

*Cost of paperwork*

Paperwork costs are increasing at unbelievable rates. Overall, 84.4 percent of the cost of business relates to paperwork. The cost of preparing letters is an illustration of the inflated cost of paperwork. In 1930, the Dartnell Institute of Business Research initiated its program of annually studying the cost of a business letter. In that initial year, the average cost to produce a letter was 29.6 cents. In 1986, the average cost had risen to $8.92, an increase of 3,014 percent! Not many businesses can continue to absorb costs that are spiraling at such unprecedented rates. It is essential that paperwork/information processing be made cost effective.

## Establish Performance Standards

*Objective performance evaluation*

Employee standards of performance must be established, and procedures must be developed for measuring performance and for making comparisons of measured performance against established standards. Judgments can then be made objectively regarding the performance of the employees in relation to the expectations of the standards. Additionally, provisions must be in place to allow corrective action to be taken when needed. Controls of employee performance provide the manager with the necessary tools to measure employee productivity and to take appropriate steps to control unsatisfactory performance.

## A LOOK AT THE CASE

The categories that Mark O'Connor should be concerned with are costs of management personnel (up 17 percent), costs of administrative support personnel (up 16 percent), and costs of office operations (up 40 percent). The costs of materials (up 11 percent), advertising/promotional costs (up 12 percent), and production personnel costs (up 10 percent) also deserve some scrutiny. However, Mark needs to make a detailed analysis to determine the cause(s) of the dramatic increase in office costs and the significantly higher-than-average increases in management and administrative support personnel costs. He should carefully consider the types of control systems in place (precontrol, concurrent, and feedback control). His analysis should also include a determination of the effectiveness of the control function in minimizing information proliferation, providing procedural uniformity, reducing information duplication, providing timely information, controlling varied media sizes and forms, providing cost-effective information processing, and establishing employee performance standards.

## Scope

The control function addresses three major areas of records management: information quality and quantity, supplies and equipment use, and employee performance. The result of an effective system of control will be an information network that provides the manager with the information necessary to make management decisions. In order to accomplish this, systems must be established that are appropriate and individually tailored to satisfy the unique needs of each organization. The linkage of the three elements that comprise the scope of the records management control system is shown in Figure 15–2.

## Information Quality and Quantity

*Information to enhance decision making*

The goal of records management is to provide the "right record to the right person at the right time and at the lowest possible cost." Implicit in this statement is the assumption that information will be provided to the manager in a quantity and quality that will increase the probability that managerial decisions will be substantially correct for the situation. Information, however, cannot compensate for poor decision-making skills, replace common sense, nor guarantee correct decisions. Appropriate information can, however, enhance the skills of the manager and provide the quality and quantity of data necessary to make objective evaluations and reach a decision from the available alternatives. This is the central and primary link in the scope of the control subsystem.

Figure 15–2
Linkage of Elements of the Scope of the Control Subsystem

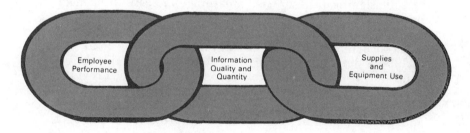

## Supplies and Equipment Use

*Establish materials and equipment control*

The scope of the control subsystem must include an evaluation of the efficient use of supplies and equipment. Misuse of materials and supplies may occur routinely unless this aspect of control is monitored carefully. Duplicate folders, too many copies, careless records handling, and excessive purchases of materials with a limited shelf life are all examples of ways in which waste can occur. A program should be established for materials control which would include a regular review of all office supplies and inventory needs. Random checks on individual use rates are advisable. Feedback should be provided to those persons who are responsible for and concerned with supplies control.

Idle equipment is a costly waste, as is equipment whose use is poorly scheduled. Equipment selected without regard to its compatibility with current office equipment is a waste of the organization's funds and results in inefficient use of both equipment and personnel. The control system should provide for appropriate selection, effective use, and reduced downtime of equipment.

**Employee Performance**
The third link in the chain is the effectiveness of employee performance. This performance evaluation encompasses all levels of employees who are involved in the creation, distribution, use, maintenance, and disposition of records. The performance of employees is reflected in administrative costs and in productivity. Under no circumstances should one believe that only clerical workers comprise this link; that judgment is far too narrow. While consideration of individual performance is a major element, consideration should also be given to the sequencing and scheduling of office services.

The linkage of the scope of the control subsystem shows an interdependency among the elements, with the central link — information quality and quantity — dependent upon the other two elements — effective employee performance and use of supplies and equipment. With the primary objective of providing the "right record to the right person at the right time and at the lowest possible cost," the end links of this chain are crucial ones.

*Elements are interdependent*

## A LOOK AT THE CASE

As Mark is conducting the detailed analysis of the control system, he should determine if the scope of the system includes an evaluation of the quality and quantity of the information available, of the use of supplies and equipment, and of the performance of the employees.

1. Does the system provide the right person with the right record at the right time and at the lowest possible cost?
2. Does the system provide for the efficient use of supplies and equipment?
3. Does the system provide for an effective procedure for employee performance evaluation?

## RESPONSIBILITIES FOR RECORDS CONTROL

Responsibilities for records control are shared by two groups: those involved in the preparation and use of records and those involved in processing records.

### Records Preparation and Use

Those persons responsible for the preparation and use phases are the originator, the recipient, and the administrative support staff. The originator of the record has the primary role in controlling. Seventy-five percent of the cost of a record is incurred at the creation phase. At the creation level, then, special restraint should be exercised.

*Creation costs*

### Originator

The use of good judgment by the originator is essential. Written requests or replies are often unnecessary. A phone call may not only meet the need but also provide a quicker response. Therefore, the first rule of good judgment is to write only those messages that require documentation. Second, the request or response should be made in a concise manner. Lengthy letters, with their accompanying jargon and rhetoric, are expensive luxuries that few organizations need or can afford. For interoffice correspondence, replies written or typed on the original letter are appropriate and reduce costs.

The originator should designate the number of copies to be made. The number should reflect only essential copies. The number of courtesy copies should be limited to those persons who really need them. In the case of routine replies or inquiry letters, no copy need be made. Some managers have "security blanket" copies made of all outgoing correspondence. This is not necessary.

*Role of originator*

Depending on the system used, the originator may be the appropriate person to indicate the filing preference and cross-reference notations. This is particularly appropriate where there are no centralized records, where there is high staff turnover, or when the manager is the sole person using the office file. Whether this is the ase or whether there is a coding clerk, all persons should abide by an established, uniform procedure for coding documents for filing.

In a centralized records system, one person responsible for designating and marking (coding) each document or record is more efficient. Uniformity that may not be present when each originator is responsible for coding can be achieved when one person is assigned this responsibility.

## Recipient

The recipient, too, has an opportunity to share in the control of records. Once the particular piece of correspondence has been acted upon, the recipient follows the same procedure as the record originator. Incoming junk mail should be thrown away after its use; routine response letters and requests should be thrown away after action has been taken. Only those documents that may be required later should be stored. If the recipient is aware that the original document or copy is retained elsewhere and is available upon request, the document can be thrown away upon completion of all related work.

*Role of recipient*

## Administrative Support Staff

The administrative support staff plays a major role in records control. The primary responsibility for the preparation of records is performed by staff personnel. Efficient use of supplies and equipment is essential during the preparation phase.

*Role of administrative support staff*

Many secretaries assume the responsibility for deciding the disposition of the records, as well as for preparing and distributing any copies. The manner in which these decisions are made will be reflected in the effectiveness of the system of control. In fact, and in practice, it is at this level that the system either succeeds or fails—is effective or ineffective. Therefore, the administrative support staff must understand the importance of records control and support the control system.

## Records Processing

A number of people share the responsibility for processing records. These people include the records manager, department heads and supervisors, the records center staff, and the administrative support staff.

## Records Manager

The records manager is the person ultimately responsible for the development, implementation, and evaluation of the total records control system. Under the direction of the records manager, persons involved in the preparation and use, as well as in the processing phase of records, perform their responsibilities relating to records control. The records manager must have the authority to establish and require a system of records creation control, set the standards, and establish the procedures for implementation and follow-up on compliance by others within the organization.

*Role of records manager*

Requests for records flow through the office of the records manager. Decisions that affect all levels of management are made by the records manager regarding correspondence, directives, reports, forms, printing, and micrographics.

What, specifically, can the records manager do to control the creation and retention of records? The records manager

1. approves requests for new reports. These requests must be channeled through the records manager, and new or revised reports will not be prepared until and unless they have been approved.
2. approves requests for new or revised forms. As with reports, no new or revised forms will be prepared until approval has been obtained.
3. establishes guidelines for use by all originators for an efficient flow of correspondence and directives.
4. evaluates all requests for printing. In order for this procedure to be effective, the in-house printing operation must be under the direction of the records manager. When contract printing is used, requests for each contract must be channeled through the office of the records manager.

The records manager provides guidance, assistance, and advice regarding all aspects of the creation, distribution, use, maintenance, and disposition of all records.

A 1985 survey of records professionals conducted by the authors revealed that many organizations recognize the need for records control in the form of documented policies and procedures provided in records management manuals. Table 15–1 shows the responses regarding the percentage of use of control programs.

Table 15–1
Records Control Programs

| Type | Percent in Use |
|------|----------------|
| Records Management Manual | 92.86% |
| Microrecords Control Program | 57.14 |
| Vital Records Protection Program | 50.00 |
| Forms Control Program | 42.86 |
| Correspondence Control Program | 28.57 |
| Copy Control Program | 28.57 |
| Reports Control Program | 21.43 |
| Directives Control Program | 10.71 |

The percentage of use of correspondence, copy, reports, and directives control programs is especially low. The need for controls in these areas is critical to an efficient records management system. These issues are discussed in detail in the chapters that follow.

## Department Heads and Supervisors

The responsibilities of heads of departments and supervisory personnel are largely in the area of follow-through and follow-up—follow through with procedures established by the records manager and follow up on adherence to procedures by personnel within their departments. Supervisors and department heads are vested with authority over employees. This authority should be exercised in a positive way to ensure that employees under their supervision know and follow the control procedures. Supervisors and department heads also have a responsibility to their immediate supervisors to carry out the procedures established for supervisors and department heads. For example, department heads and supervisors must adhere to the records retention schedule in order to have an effective system of records retention and disposition. At the same time, the persons they supervise must use the established procedures for maintaining records to be kept and for disposing of records in the manner and at the time prescribed.

*Role of department heads and supervisors*

## Records Center Staff

Records center personnel are responsible for the major portion of records processing procedures. This staff receives the records, prepares the records for storage, checks out records to users, and prepares the records for disposition. The total records system is really tested in the records center. It is important, even critical, that the records center staff fully understand its responsibilities for control, understand and implement the control procedures, and provide feedback to the records manager if procedures are inappropriate or difficult to maintain.

*Role of records center staff*

## Administrative Support Staff

In many small and medium-size offices where there are no records centers and where all records are decentralized, the administrative support staff has the same responsibility for records as the records center staff has in a centralized system. The administrative support staff receives records, prepares records for storage, finds records upon request, and prepares records for disposition. The quantity of records may differ, specialization of individual employees may differ, and the system may differ because of the level of sophistication employed, but the responsibilities remain the same.

*Role of administrative support staff*

■

## A LOOK AT THE CASE

The disproportionately large increases in management costs, administrative support personnel costs, and office costs should provide Mark with "food for thought" as he examines Beauty Image's control system. Managers and administrative support staff may not be exercising their control responsibilities. A hard look should be directed toward the records originators to determine the extent to which control is maintained in the creation and distribution of written communications. Further, the same careful scrutiny should be given to the managers as recipients of written communications. Mark should determine if the administrative support staff is performing the control functions of their jobs.

Mark cannot stop with the people involved in the preparation and use of the records. He must also examine the performance of the people who process the records.

■

## EVALUATION OF THE CONTROL SYSTEM

Evaluation of the effectiveness of the control subsystem is accomplished by scheduled audits of the system. Audits should determine if the system provides for the information needs of managers in their decision-making processes and if the operational system is effective.

**Audit** is defined as a regular examination and verification of a specific activity. An **audit trail**, then, is a procedure which provides documentation for regular examination and verification. In the case of records management controls, audits and audit trails may be either administrative or operational.

### Administrative Audit

*Value analysis*

An **administrative audit** is a review of the effectiveness of the system in terms of the functional quality and quantity of the records available. The administrative audit may begin with a value analysis. Does the system accomplish the function efficiently at the lowest possible cost? This analysis can be made only by participation and involvement of all users. If a substantive number of responses to the value analysis are negative, then an administrative audit is needed. Questions should be asked regarding the use of information and the quality and quantity necessary to make business decisions.

- What specific information/reports are currently received?
- What information is needed in more detail? What information is needed in summary form?
- What information on the above list is received but never used? What information is seldom used?
- What information is needed but not currently available for decision making?
- How long does it take to receive requested information?

Questions should also be asked addressing the role of the manager in the creation and distribution of information. This audit data would then be correlated with the use data and appropriate changes made. Such questions might include

- What records/documents are created?
- What records/documents are distributed? To whom are these records/documents distributed?

A final set of questions should be asked regarding the functional quality of the system. Because these elements affect the effectiveness of the decision-making process, they are included in the administrative audit. Information derived from these types of questions, however, would be used in the operational audit. These questions might include

*Functional quality*

- What records are stored?
- What records are maintained?
- How often are records referenced?
- How long does it take to receive requested records?
- How many misfiles are encountered on a monthly basis?

The administrative audit looks closely at the entire records management system in relation to its effectiveness as a tool for management decision making. This audit should include regular monitoring and review processes and should identify the areas where there are administrative breakdowns or bottlenecks in the records control system.

## Operational Audit

The **operational audit** looks at the system's effectiveness as a process of ensuring that specific tasks are performed effectively and efficiently. The administrative audit identifies the effectiveness of

*Task performance*

SHOE

the system as a whole in providing managers with necessary information with which to make decisions.

Operational audits attempt to identify the origin of the current control system (where problems exist) to establish why things are done the way they are. To make this determination, it may be necessary to diagram the flow of information and list specific persons and routing procedures. The purpose of this diagram is to identify all of the persons involved in the flow of information and to isolate particular problem areas. After identification of persons involved has been made, the operational audit then addresses specific tasks. At this stage the obvious procedural problems emerge. Not-so-obvious problems may require more investigation, for symptoms may be mistaken for problems.

When looking at specific tasks, the auditor identifies who performs the task, when it is performed, why it is performed, where it is performed, and what method is used to accomplish the task. Figure 15–3 shows the types of questions to be asked in an operational audit.

## A LOOK AT THE CASE

Mark will perform an audit on the control system at Beauty Image, Inc. He should include both an administrative audit to establish the effectiveness of the system in the decision-making process and an operational audit to determine the efficiency of the system in ensuring that specific tasks are performed in an effective manner. The results of these audits should provide information regarding the cause(s) for the disproportionately large increases in costs incurred for some of the operations of the organization.

Figure 15–3
Guide for Task Analysis for Operational Audit

| Initiating Records | Why | Reevaluating Records |
|---|---|---|
| **NEED** | | **NEED** |
| What do the records in this procedure accomplish that justifies their existence?<br>What other records are related or duplicate in whole or in part the same information?<br>What inadequacies are there in the records in the procedure? | Why this need? | Does the cost exceed the worth?<br>Is the information needed?<br>Is there a better source or a better way to keep this information?<br>Can the record be combined?<br>Can the record be eliminated?<br>Can the record be simplified or resequenced?<br>Can the record be added to another procedure? |
| **PEOPLE** | | **PEOPLE** |
| Who requires the data?<br>Who enters the information?<br>Who extracts the information? | Why by these people? | Can the work be assigned to other units or clerks to simplify the work or combine its handling?<br>Can the records in the procedure be resequenced to simplify the entering or extracting of the information? |
| **PLACE** | | **PLACE** |
| Where are the records in this procedure written and processed?<br>Where are the records sent?<br>Where are the records stored? | Why here? | Can the writing and processing be combined with similar work done by another unit?<br>Does the design of the record aid in storage, retrieval, and disposition? |
| **TIME** | | **TIME** |
| When are the records in the procedure written?<br>When are these records processed?<br>When are the records stored? | Why at this time? | Are the various processing steps in their proper order?<br>Can the peak load be leveled off by better scheduling of the flow?<br>Can information be requested so it can be processed during a slack period? |
| **METHOD** | | **METHOD** |
| How are the records in this procedure written?<br>How is the information processed?<br>How is the information transmitted?<br>How is the information stored? | Why this method? | Can the writing method be improved?<br>Can the routing or mailing method be changed?<br>Have the records been geared to the most efficient use of office equipment/systems? |

## TERMINOLOGY REVIEW

*Administrative audit.* A review of the effectiveness of the system in terms of the functional quality and quantity of the records available.

*Audit.* A regular examination and verification of a specific activity.

*Audit trail.* A procedure which provides documentation for regular examination and verification.

*Concurrent control.* A type of control that takes place as work is being performed.

*Control.* The function that compares achieved results with planned goals.

*Feedback control.* A type of control that concentrates on past performance as compared to current performance data.

*Operational audit.* A review of the effectiveness of the system as a process to ensure that specific tasks are performed effectively and efficiently.

*Precontrol.* A type of control that takes place before work is performed and concentrates on preventing problems before they occur.

*Project ELF.* A project (Eliminate Legal-size Files) focused on eliminating legal-size files from offices and converting to standard-size paper files.

## COMPETENCY REVIEW

1. Describe the role of the control subsystem and its relationship to the records management system.
2. Define the three types of control, giving an example not cited in the text of each type of control.
3. Why is an efficient and effective system of records control important?
4. What are the three links in the scope of control and what is the relationship between and among the links?
5. How would you determine whether an administrative or operational audit is more appropriate?
6. Discuss three problems that might be discovered during (a) an administrative audit and (b) an operational audit.

## APPLICATIONS

1. Select one record that is processed either through your workplace (if employed) or through your educational system (if not employed). Then take this record through the task analysis for an operational audit as shown in Figure 15–3.
2. Identify the type(s) of control represented by each of the following:
   a. personnel selection
   b. performance appraisal
   c. retention schedule

    d.   records activity report
    e.   records center design
    f.   records management manual
    g.   central files supervisor
    h.   forms design
    i.   reports, in general
    j.   vital records protection program

3.   Justify your selection of the types of control for each of the items in No. 2.

4.   Assign two control responsibilities to each of the following categories of users or processors: originator, recipient, administrative support staff, records manager, records center staff, department heads, and supervisors. Where there may be dual responsibility, specify.

## CONCLUDING CASES

### A. Utilities Company

Toni Chinn is supervisor of the records center of a major utilities company. She is an ambitious, intelligent employee whose goal is to become the records manager of the company, a position that has director status in her company.

As the supervisor of the records center, Toni has noticed that the bulk of the records delivered to the center originate from one division. As she checks into the situation, she further notes that most of the records originate with Jim Schmidt, division chief of the research and development division.

The records center is becoming crowded. When Toni checks the volume of records from the R & D division, she discovers the following:

- When the records are to be destroyed, Jim Schmidt always either asks for an extension of time, asks for copies for his personal file, or refuses to authorize destruction.

- Jim seems to keep copies of all correspondence, reports, and interoffice communications, as well as flyers and routine notices.

- Jim has been quoted as saying "I always document everything. I do not believe in this informal telephone communication. I have a secretary and he is paid to type my documents."

Toni has mentioned the problem to the records manager, but Martha DeSilva is 64 years old, almost ready to retire, and doesn't want to deal with this problem. She tells Toni to "handle it" with Jim Schmidt personally.

1.   What specific concerns should Toni address with Jim?

2.   What recommendations should Toni make to (a) Jim Schmidt? (b) Martha DeSilva?

3.   Why is this a particularly sensitive problem? What are some of the possible ramifications?

## B. S & L Company

During lunch in the S & L company cafeteria, a number of the employees were discussing their pet peeves. Their conversation was overheard by Ted Duncan, the records manager.

Carlota (records center clerk): Records don't come to us on any systematic basis. For several months we will receive no records; the next month we are swamped with records. We just can't handle them.

Iris (secretary): The letters I type are so long; I rarely type a letter that is less than two pages with at least one "p.s."

Roman (clerk): It seems that we send copies to everyone, even the custodian!

Victor (central files clerk): Letters we get for filing from one department are always coded—wrong. The coding never matches the ones we are supposed to use.

Tim (secretary): My department files everything—including memos that are no longer of interest—like the one about the Christmas party.

Sam (management trainee): We seem to generate reports for everything. We must have a report on reports!

Iris: Carlota, I don't mean to be personal about this, but the last three times we requested records from the records center, we had to wait a long time to get them. By the time the records were received, they were not as useful as they should have been.

What control responsibilities should Ted examine, based on the comments he overheard?

## READINGS AND REFERENCES

Aschner, Katherine, ed. *Taking Control of Your Office Records: A Manager's Guide*. New York: John Wiley & Sons, Inc., 1984.

*Dartnell Target Survey*. Chicago: Dartnell Institute of Business Research, 1986.

Gunther, H. Michael, and Barbara Lang. "Conducting an Operational Audit of Active Files." *Records Management Quarterly*, Vol. 17, No. 4. (October, 1983) p. 5.

———. "Planning for an Operational Audit of Active Files." *Records Management Quarterly*, Vol. 17, No. 3 (July, 1983), p. 30.

"Office Productivity: Challenge of the 80s." *Business Week*, No. 2677 (March 2, 1981), p. 49.

Varga, Roberta M. "Computer Assisted Record Control Systems for Financial Records." *Records Management Quarterly*, Vol. 17, No. 1 (January, 1983) p. 13.

# 16
# CORRESPONDENCE AND COPY CONTROL

## Competencies

After completing this chapter, you should be able to

1. identify the goals of a correspondence control program.
2. describe the procedures for establishing a correspondence control program.
3. describe methods for achieving each of the goals of a correspondence control program.
4. identify alternatives to hard-copy correspondence.
5. explain methods of evaluating a program of correspondence control.
6. describe the importance of a correspondence manual to correspondence control.
7. distinguish among copy practices, procedures, and devices.
8. describe considerations in the selection of copy methods and printing methods.
9. identify cost factors associated with correspondence and copy functions.

# Introductory Case

Sandy Reynolds is the administrative assistant to Tom Milton, president of Ames Oil Company, a large refinery with an annual income exceeding $10 million. Sandy is waiting to talk with Tom regarding one of her assignments. Tom asked Sandy several weeks ago to investigate some of the complaints that he has received about processing correspondence.

A word processing center was installed over a year ago, but many of the managers are not using it at all; some managers use the center on a very limited basis. There have been complaints from the word processing supervisor about the number of revisions required before a document is considered acceptable by the managers. The word processing operators have expressed concern about the quality of the correspondence they are given to process. Further, the managers are not satisfied with the turnaround time when materials are sent to the word processing center.

In addition, Sandy has discovered that almost every department has exceeded its budget for copying, and there are still two months left in the fiscal year. Everyone seems to use the copiers located on each floor for all copying needs—whether one document or several hundred documents need to be copied. There is no control over the copying equipment.

Sandy wants Tom to give her the authority to go into each department and conduct a survey to determine if the problems are organization-wide or isolated. As she waits for Tom, Sandy mentally prepares her case for conducting the survey.

1. What areas should Sandy investigate?
2. What specific questions should she ask?

Correspondence management includes establishing goals, policies, and procedures for written communications; implementing the goals, policies, and procedures; monitoring, following up, and measuring the effectiveness of the program; and making changes based on identified needs.

According to the Dartnell Corporation, Inc., offices in the United States generate more than 76 million letters and 234 million photocopies daily. This volume of correspondence generation, combined with a lack of writing skills and indiscriminate copy distribution, may cause managers to make poor decisions or take incorrect action because the written communications were misunderstood.

*More than 76 million letters a day*

## CORRESPONDENCE CONTROL

Correspondence management tends to be very loosely structured; therefore, written communication has grown at unprecedented rates. As the cost of management time has increased, the cost of other office personnel time has also increased. When these costs are combined with the expenses of paper, materials, storage and retrieval equipment, and all of the other peripheral costs of correspondence, correspondence creation control is essential. It is important to establish and implement an ongoing program of correspondence control.

*Increasing costs*

## Establish Program Framework

*Formalize process*

Establishing an effective program of correspondence control requires a formalization process. This process includes defining authority, assigning responsibility, and promoting the program within the organization.

### Define Program Authority

One of the first steps in establishing a correspondence control program is to define authority for the program. Authority is granted by top management and communicated to all management levels. This communication is usually in the form of a directive that clearly identifies the objectives and goals of the program, the person(s) responsible, and the specific responsibilities.

*Gain support*

As discussed in previous chapters, the approval, support, and commitment of top management to a new program is essential if the program is to succeed. To gain this level of commitment, upper level managers must be convinced that the new program provides additional avenues to reach organizational objectives and that the program offers positive cost benefits. The job of the records manager and the records management staff is to provide this supporting data when approval of the program is requested.

### Assign Program Responsibility

Responsibility for a program of correspondence control should be assigned to the records manager and the records management staff. The responsibilities include

1. providing guidance in correspondence writing techniques so that correspondence is clear and easy to understand.
2. standardizing correspondence style and format by using a correspondence manual.
3. encouraging use of preprinted form letters and aiding in their development.
4. providing leadership in the development of guide letters and guide paragraphs and the mechanics of using both.
5. promoting training in correspondence management techniques, including copy control, dictation, and the use of readability formulas.
6. cooperating in developing standards for automating correspondence.
7. conducting or assisting in correspondence work measurement studies.
8. establishing a clearinghouse for shortcuts that offer more efficient production of correspondence.

## Promote the Program

Any new program needs advertising and promotion to get it under way. Cooperation and coordination with those who are to be affected by the change are important in establishing and implementing the correspondence control program. The interest of potential users must be aroused and continued through a planned program of information dissemination. There is less resistance to change when those who are to be affected by the change have an opportunity to contribute to the planning, development, and implementation of the program. When a correspondence control program is in the planning and development phases, input should be solicited from all management levels and from the administrative staff who support them.

*Obtain user input*

## Determine Program Goals

Once the framework for the program has been established, program goals for the organization need to be determined. Goals of a program of correspondence control usually include

- improving correspondence quality,
- improving correspondence productivity,
- reducing correspondence costs, and
- facilitating correspondence storage and retrieval.

Depending on specific needs, the emphasis placed on each goal will vary from organization to organization. One organization may need to place more attention on improving the quality of its correspondence and facilitating correspondence storage and retrieval; another may concentrate on improving productivity and reducing correspondence costs. Other organizations may find it necessary to focus on developing a program of correspondence control that encompasses all of the goals. This determination of emphasis on goals has to be made within each organization. Primary consideration should be given to the contribution this program will make toward meeting the overall objectives of the organization.

*Determine organizational needs*

## Improve Correspondence Quality

Letters, memorandums, and other written communications must be constructed in a way that clearly communicates the information and action desired. Correspondence should be written in such a way that the person receiving it should not have to guess at the meaning, draw inferences, or make assumptions about the intent of the writer. Nor should the correspondence present the recipient with additional questions to be answered before the requested action can be taken.

**Improve Correspondence Productivity**

Typically, there has been little improvement in the time required to produce correspondence. Also, the emphasis on productivity improvement has been in the administrative support arena, with little attention given to the need for managers to increase correspondence productivity. Since managers earn 74 cents of each white-collar dollar, focus on management productivity would result in greater productivity returns.

**Reduce Correspondence Costs**

The costs of producing letters have increased dramatically—from 29.6 cents in 1930 to $8.92 in 1986. The acceleration of correspondence costs, along with the increased volume of correspondence, makes reduction of costs essential.

**Facilitate Correspondence Storage and Retrieval**

A link exists between the creation of quality correspondence and the ability to properly store and efficiently retrieve correspondence. Clearly written, concise letters facilitate easier and faster identification both in the storage process and in retrieval.

## Determine Present Procedures

Prior to making any change in the correspondence control program, the present procedures should be examined and evaluated. This examination and evaluation may lead to the determination that no formal procedures are in place; that the present procedures are effective; that the present procedures, with modifications, will be effective; or that new procedures need to be developed and implemented.

**Survey Present Correspondence Procedures**

*Identify strengths and weaknesses*

One of the ways to determine the present procedures is to conduct a survey to identify current correspondence practices and strengths and weaknesses within the present system. Some of the questions that provide data for the identification of strengths and weaknesses include the following:

- What percentage of the originator's time is spent in composing correspondence?
- What percentage of correspondence is dictated to a secretary?
- What percentage of correspondence is dictated to a machine?

- What percentage of correspondence is composed in longhand?
- If the originator is not using machine dictation, what is the reason?
- How is the correspondence produced (automated equipment, typewriters, electronic mail)?
- How many hours a day is the dictation and word processing equipment in use?
- How many copies are normally made of outgoing correspondence?
- What is the average number of pages for letters and memorandums?
- What is the usual turnaround time? Is current turnaround adequate?
- What percentage of correspondence does the originator require in rough-draft form?
- What percentage of correspondence is returned to the typist for revision?
- To what extent are form letters used?
- To what extent are guide letters or guide paragraphs used?

In addition to conducting a survey, the records manager and the records staff may review a large sample of the organization's correspondence to determine the quality of the correspondence. This review allows identification of organization-wide problems in correspondence quality as well as individual weaknesses in correspondence creation.

*Sample correspondence*

Another approach to reviewing organizational correspondence is to require an extra copy of all correspondence to be forwarded to the records manager; this should be done for a short period of time—perhaps two weeks. The copies should be forwarded on a daily basis to allow the records manager and the records staff time to review the correspondence in small quantities. Either approach allows the records manager to obtain the kind of information needed to begin the evaluation of the present correspondence control program.

*Review correspondence*

### Evaluate Current Correspondence Procedures

An analysis of the responses to the survey and of the sampling of the correspondence provides information from which judgments may be made regarding correspondence quality and the efficiency of the correspondence control program. The results of this evaluation should be used as the basis for recommendations regarding the program.

## Analyze Cost Factors

Communications costs associated with correspondence are an important consideration for any organization as it attempts to meet

*Correspondence costs*

the information needs of its managers in a cost-effective manner. Correspondence costs can be categorized as origination, processing, maintenance, distribution, and user time costs.

**Correspondence origination costs** are those costs directly related to the writing and research time necessary to draft correspondence. Origination costs are difficult to determine accurately as most originators make little effort to clearly define actual time spent in document creation.

**Correspondence processing costs** are the costs involved in actual preparation of the document; these costs include equipment, materials, supplies, and administrative support.

**Correspondence maintenance costs** are the costs associated with storing and retrieving correspondence.

**Correspondence distribution costs** are the costs related to distributing correspondence to appropriate recipients.

**Correspondence user costs** are those costs that represent user time — the time necessary for the recipient to efficiently interpret and use the information. User costs are directly related to the quality and timeliness of the information. For example, a poorly written letter will require more of the user's time to interpret, extract, and follow through on requested action than a clearly written letter that leads the user directly to the action required.

An analysis of each of the correspondence costs factors identifies areas in which the records manager and staff should focus their attention in their efforts to improve the organization's correspondence management program. The chart in Figure 16–1, from Dartnell Corporation, illustrates one method of determining letter costs.

## Develop Plan for Accomplishing Goals

*Specific actions to achieve goals*

After the correspondence program goals have been clearly identified, a plan for accomplishing these goals must be developed. Specific actions that lead to reaching the established goals should be included in the plan. These recommendations become a part of the working plan and are incorporated into the total package when it is presented to top management for endorsement.

### Improve Correspondence Quality

*Provide guidelines*

The development of guidelines for effective writing and a program of assistance for developing writing skills are used to improve the quality of an organization's correspondence. The records manager

Figure 16–1
Letter Costs

## Determining The Cost Of One Letter

| Cost Factor | Average Cost | Your Cost | Determining Cost |
|---|---|---|---|
| Dictator's Time . . .<br>For this cost, it was established that the executive received an average weekly salary of $738 and takes approximately 8 minutes to dictate a single business letter. | $2.46 | | Based on a 40-hour week, this cost is determined by calculating an executive's salary for 8 minutes.<br>($738 ÷ 40 hrs. = $18.45 per hour)<br>($18.45 ÷ 60 min. = 30.7¢ per min.)<br>(30.7¢ × 8 min. = $2.46 per letter) |
| Secretarial Time . . .<br>Based on a salary of $331 for the secretary, this figure includes all the time involved from dictation through filing of the letter. | $2.48 | | This cost is obtained in the same manner as the dictator's cost, using 18 minutes for all time involved. |
| Nonproductive Labor . . .<br>This is the time consumed by both dictator and secretary that is not directly productive when a letter is being prepared. It has been set at 15% of labor costs for both. | $0.74 | | This cost is arrived at from the use of previous studies. It is especially aimed at interruptions during dictation or transcription and time lost when participants are involved in producing a letter. |
| Fixed Charges . . .<br>A catchall charge that wraps up the share of overhead, depreciation, taxes, heating, etc. given to the letter. It also includes the fringe benefits share for the time consumed by letter preparers. Set at 52% of total labor costs. | $2.57 | | This is a hard cost to pinpoint but it is necessary to cover those regularly running or recurring costs of doing business. It is the letter's share (18 minutes of time for a secretary and 8 minutes of manager's time). |
| Materials Costs . . .<br>Stationery, envelopes, carbon paper, copy machine paper, typewriter ribbons and cartridges and other supplies needed to get out a letter. | $0.26 | | This cost is easily arrived at if you maintain records covering your supplies and basic equipment expenses. Multiple copies cost extra money. |
| Mailing Cost . . .<br>First class postage (22¢) added to cost of labor for gathering, sealing, stamping, sorting done by personnel other than the secretary. | $0.41 | | If you are using more express mail for your correspondence, this cost could go much higher. Otherwise it is easy to determine. |
| **TOTAL COST**<br>**$8.92** | **YOUR COST**<br>_____ | | |

It should be pointed out that the figures presented here are based on a formula to determine the cost of a single, traditional boss-secretary type of letter dictated face-to-face with the secretary completing the transcribing and connected filing. Communications with repetitive copy, lengthy reports and/or bids are not represented in this survey.

*Source:* Dartnell's Target Survey, *Dartnell Institute of Business Research, 1986.*

and staff provide the originator with guidelines that allow for more efficient achievement of correspondence responsibilities. In order for these guidelines to be accepted, managers must regard them as beneficial rather than as additional red tape or rules that must be followed. Standard procedures can be more efficiently presented in a correspondence manual or guide.

Typical guidelines focusing on improving writing style and quality include an emphasis on the four C's of good writing; writing should be clear, concise, correct, and complete. All of the generally accepted rules of good writing apply: Know your reader; write for the reader; use simple, direct language; use short sentences; break up long paragraphs; get to the point immediately; request the action desired, and so on.

*Readability formulas*

To maintain ease of reading and plain writing, readability formulas may be applied to the correspondence. Originators should be familiar with at least one method for determining readability level and should be encouraged to apply the formula to their correspondence. The two most widely accepted readability formulas are the "Reading Ease Formula" as revised and simplified by Rudolph F. Flesch and the "Fog Index" by Robert Gunning. An occasional application of one of the formulas to a sample of a manager's correspondence will maintain an awareness of readability.

*Writing aids*

A program of assistance for developing the writing skills of the originators is another way to improve correspondence quality. Writing workshops may be organized to sharpen the writing ability of anyone who generates correspondence and who recognizes the need for improvement. Writing handbooks should be available for reference, and follow-up workshop sessions should be provided when needed. Slide/tape or videotape presentations may be used for individualized assistance. Though lacking the structure of a workshop, individualized aids allow managers to work at their own speed, address their individual problems, and use their discretionary time for self-improvement. Whatever format is chosen to strengthen writing skills, provisions should be made to allow opportunities to practice writing various types of correspondence and for evaluative sessions to provide feedback to the participants.

## Improve Correspondence Productivity

There are a number of practical ways in which the production of letters, memorandums, and other forms of correspondence can be improved and the quality of the output enhanced. Some of these methods include the use of

**machine dictation.** Dictation of correspondence into a recording machine as opposed to face-to-face dictation to a secretary is known as **machine dictation**. According to the Dartnell Study, the 1986 cost of a machine-dictated letter is $6.55 as compared to the $8.92 cost of face-to-face dictation. Figure 16–2 shows the comparison between the costs of two types of dictation.

Figure 16–2
Cost Comparison of Face-to-Face and Machine-Dictated Letters

| COST FACTOR | FACE-TO-FACE LETTER | MACHINE-DICTATED LETTER |
|---|---|---|
| Dictator's Time | $2.46 (8 minutes) | $2.15 (7 minutes) |
| Secretary's Time | $2.48 (18 minutes) | $1.37 (10 minutes) |
| Non-productive Labor (15% total labor) | $0.74 | $0.53 |
| Fixed Charges (52% total labor) | $2.57 | $1.83 |
| Materials | $0.26 | $0.26 |
| Mailing (including postage) | $0.41 | $0.41 |
| | TOTAL COST $8.92 | TOTAL COST $6.55 |

*Source:* Dartnell's Target Survey, *Dartnell Institute of Business Research, 1986.*

**preprinted form letters.** Preprinted form letters save time both in origination and in preparation. Using preprinted form letters is the most economical method for mass mailings. In organizations where similar requests and inquiries are frequent and where similar responses are used, a file of form letters is a cost-saving device. The originator simply indicates pertinent information to be included and the appropriate form letter number; the typist follows the instructions. The result is a preprinted letter that may contain selected added information unique to the recipient. When fill-ins are used, type style should be consistent with print style and, when possible, the name of the recipient should be used to minimize the impersonal feeling often generated by form letters.

**guide letters and paragraphs. Guide letters** provide a suggested pattern of responses for routine letters and project a more personalized appearance. Guide letters are individually prepared by use of a typewriter or a word processor. Guide letters can be stored in the word processing system and merged automatically with a list of names and addresses. As with preprinted form letters, a file of guide letters should be maintained. Originators indicate guide letter number and name and address of recipient; the typist or word processor operator produces an individually typed letter.

In cases where a guide letter in its entirety is inappropriate, guide paragraphs can be used. Guide paragraphs contain information that is used frequently in preparing correspondence. The originator refers to paragraph number or numbers and provides any variable information to the typist or word processor operator who prepares the letter.

**alternatives to hard-copy correspondence.** Hard copy (paper) has been the primary mode of correspondence for most organizations. Only in the past few years have other alternatives become feasible. Despite the "paperless" office concept which has been touted for years, many organizations still prefer the security of paper documents. However, as technological advances become more economical and integrated systems more prevalent, it may be possible to minimize dependence on hard copy and to maximize other options. Alternative methods of correspondence fall into three major categories: electronic mail networks; telecommunications, including telephone, wire and satellite services, teleconferencing, facsimile transmission, voice mail, and communicating computers and word processors; and microforms.

*"Paperless" office*

Each of these alternatives to hard-copy correspondence is available and in use. Many of the policies and procedures established for hard-copy correspondence creation and distribution are also applicable to other forms of correspondence. It is important to note, too, the necessity for controls for all correspondence forms. While the controls may differ in format, the basic philosophy and guidelines for controlling correspondence creation and distribution are similar.

**use of word processing equipment.** As the costs of personnel have increased, a corresponding decrease in the cost of technology has been noted. As a result of this cost reversal, managers have begun to look more closely at ways to increase productivity and retain cost effectiveness. One of the alternatives is to implement a word processing system and to take advantage of the benefits of the decreased cost of technology while improving productivity.

*Increased use of word processors*

Productivity increases may be reflected by both originators and processors of correspondence. The revision capabilities of word processors allow more freedom in making required changes, and the simplicity of making changes encourages revisions that result in more clear and concise correspondence. Revisions can be made without retyping the entire document which increases the productivity of the word processing operator.

**standardized format.** A standard format for letters, memos, and other written correspondence provides for more efficient production of the correspondence. A standard format saves time. The processor is familiar with the format; therefore, decisions about placement of letter parts, margins, tabs, and other variables, do not have to be made. A standard format saves motion; the processor does not have to change margins, tabs, and so forth. A standard format also assures acceptable letter and memorandum formats.

**productivity standards.** To schedule and control routine work effectively, a manager should know how much work the employees are capable of performing (work standards), the status of work in progress and scheduled (work load), how much work is received (volume), and how much employees are doing in relation to work scheduled (work performance). The first step is to establish the unit of work against which performance will be judged. An ongoing program can aid in determining how many people are needed to perform certain functions, how to cope with peak work loads, and how to evaluate the performance of individual workers. Some typical writing, dictating, and typewriting rates are shown in Figure 16–3.

*Establish standards of work*

Figure 16–3
Typical Writing, Dictating, and Typewriting Rates

| For a Standard Page of 30–40 Lines | Time Required |
| --- | --- |
| Dictating time per page | 15 minutes |
| Transcribing time per page | 25 minutes |
| Dictating and transcribing time | 1.5 pages per hour |
| Preparing longhand copy and transcribing time | 3 pages per hour |
| Addressing envelopes | 140 per hour |
| Writing longhand drafts (175–word letter) | 2 letters per hour |
| Typing from longhand drafts | 1.5 letters per hour |
| Typing letters from shorthand notes | 2 letters per hour |
| Typing letters from machine dictation | 2.4 letters per hour |
| Typing guide letters | 6.7 letters per hour |
| Typing form letters | 20 letters per hour |

It should be noted that these are typical industry standards and should be adapted to fit the situation within the organization.

## Reduce Correspondence Costs

There is a reverse correlation between reducing correspondence costs and increasing correspondence productivity. Therefore, as the productivity increases through use of a combination of the previously discussed methods, correspondence costs decrease.

*Productivity increases/costs decrease*

Additional reductions in costs may be obtained by providing training and making information available to managers so that they are more skilled in correspondence creation. Then managers would spend less time in planning, writing, reviewing, and revising documents. Training and information should also be made available to those who process the correspondence so that they spend less time in producing, revising, distributing, storing, and retrieving correspondence.

### Facilitate Correspondence Storage and Retrieval

A clear writing style makes it easier to index and code records. Properly coded records are easier to store and to retrieve. Therefore, letters, memorandums, and other correspondence must be written in a style that facilitates the storage and retrieval processes. The person coding the records should be able to quickly identify where the record should be stored. Anyone wishing to retrieve the record should be able to do so quickly if the record has been properly coded and stored.

## Disseminate New Procedures

*Correspondence manual*

Written policies, procedures, and guidelines are essential for establishing and maintaining uniform procedures for correspondence control. The correspondence manual is one tool for providing information regarding standardization in preparation and distribution of letters, memorandums, and other written communications.

The correspondence manual may be a part of a comprehensive records management manual, be integrated in a communications manual, or be a separate publication. In any case, the manual should include

- organization policies regarding correspondence creation and distribution;
- guidelines for efficient correspondence creation, including methods of maximizing use of the word processing system;
- guidelines for effective correspondence creation, including letter-writing principles and formats;
- form letters, guide letters and paragraphs, and guidelines for using the formats;
- effective dictation techniques;
- guidelines for selecting the most appropriate and cost-effective communication media; and
- guidelines for correspondence distribution.

The manual should be distributed to all persons who originate correspondence. To be effective on a continuing basis, the distribution list should be updated as a part of the routine control system. Manual preparation and utilization procedures were discussed in Chapter 8.

A system for monitoring use of the manual is helpful. This system may use observations, formal surveys, or requests for feedback from users. Part of the system should include comments from users regarding the effectiveness of the content of the manual and suggestions for improvement.

*Monitor use of manual*

Based on the feedback obtained from monitoring and on new developments that would improve correspondence effectiveness and efficiency, regular revisions and updates should be made. As revisions are made, they are coded to indicate that the material is a revision; the date of the revision is included in the code. This information usually appears at the top or bottom corner of the page. For example, Rev. 1/87 or Rev (2) 1/87 indicates that the second revision was made in January, 1987.

*Revise manual*

It is highly recommended that correspondence manuals be in loose-leaf format. Adding or deleting pages/sections is easy. Changes are distributed along with a memo stating what revisions have been made and that the revised content replaces the outdated section(s). In some smaller organizations where the logistics of revisions are relatively simple, the records manager may recall the correspondence manuals and the staff will make appropriate insertions/deletions centrally.

Along with distribution of the correspondence manual, the records manager may wish to schedule training sessions. These sessions provide the opportunity for explanations concerning how to use the manual most effectively and how revisions will be made and feedback requested. This also provides an opportunity for the manual users to ask any questions about the manual and its use. One of the additional benefits gained from these training sessions is that the records manager is given immediate feedback regarding the clarity and completeness of the manual.

*Training sessions on manual use*

## Establish Correspondence Evaluation Program

Procedures should be established for monitoring the total correspondence control program so that this very important function is not left to chance. Decisions should be made regarding how often a program review should be made, how extensive the review should be, who should conduct the review, and what methods should be used to obtain the information.

*Conduct*
*in-depth reviews*    An in-depth review should be conducted at least every three years for an ongoing, effective program. A new program would require more frequent monitoring, perhaps annually. It is not desirable, however, to allow a new program to operate through the entire year without frequent progress checks. The progress checks could be made quarterly.

Several methods may be used to evaluate the correspondence control program. These methods include monitoring the standards, using program checklists, and obtaining feedback.

## Monitor Standards

Established standards of performance should be monitored on a regular basis to determine whether the standards are reasonable, whether the standards are being adhered to, and whether the standards need to be revised to reflect more realistic performance expectations.

## Use Checklists

Checklists may be developed to assist the records manager and staff in determining the strengths and weaknesses of the correspondence control program. Figure 16–4 shows a checklist designed to evaluate the major factors of quality, cost, and productivity.

Figure 16–4
Correspondence Control Checklist

|  | Yes | No |
|---|---|---|
| 1. Correspondence Directives and Instructions | | |
| A. Are directives and instructions for preparing correspondence included in a manual or similar format for convenient reference? | ____ | ____ |
| B. Are there time limits for disposing of action correspondence? | ____ | ____ |
| C. Do the limits conform with standards for correspondence set by other organizational policies? | ____ | ____ |
| D. Are there standards for simplicity and uniformity of correspondence? | ____ | ____ |
| 2. Correspondence Volume and Cost | | |
| A. Is there a system for determining correspondence work load? | ____ | ____ |
| B. Is the average time required to prepare dictated letters 25 or fewer minutes? | ____ | ____ |
| C. Is the average time required to prepare a guide letter 8 or fewer minutes? | ____ | ____ |

|  | Yes | No |
|---|---|---|

D. Is the average time to prepare a form letter 3 or fewer minutes? _____ _____

3. Correspondence Handling
   A. Is the average number of revisions per letter 1 or none? _____ _____
   B. Are outgoing letters mailed in window envelopes when appropriate? _____ _____
   C. Is the number of copies prepared for routine correspondence 3 or fewer? _____ _____
   D. Have criteria for purchasing equipment such as typewriters, dictating machines, word processors, and copiers been adopted? _____ _____

4. Correspondence Quality
   A. Within the past year, have originators who need assistance attended a correspondence workshop or had similar training to develop writing skills? _____ _____
   B. In a readability sample of correspondence, did the majority of letters have less than 10 percent of words of 3 or more syllables? _____ _____
   C. Did sentences average fewer than 21 words? _____ _____
   D. Did the paragraphs average 7 lines? _____ _____
   E. Was the amount of correspondence that was returned for rewriting because of violations of plain letter writing less than 10 percent? _____ _____

5. Form and Guide Letters
   A. Are form letters, guide letters, and paragraphs assembled in an orderly system? _____ _____
   B. Are form letters, guide letters, and paragraphs indexed by subject? _____ _____
   C. Is the most recent review of form and guide letters more than 2 years old? _____ _____

6. Evaluation
   A. Is there a system of ongoing review of the correspondence control program? _____ _____
   B. Is the last program review no more than 3 years old? _____ _____

## Obtain Feedback

Feedback may be obtained through both formal and informal, structured or unstructured methods. On a formal, structured basis, scheduled observations and interviews, formal surveys, and correspondence sampling may be conducted with conclusions drawn from the information obtained. On an informal, unstructured basis, feedback may be obtained from interviews with users and from informal observation of the effectiveness of the program. Information gained from both types of feedback is valuable and the methods are usually complementary.

*Formal, structured feedback*

*Informal, unstructured feedback*

## A LOOK AT THE CASE

Sandy Reynolds and her staff would require information from the departments regarding current correspondence policies and procedures. Questions might include

- Are you providing assistance to correspondence originators? If yes, in what form?
- What percentage of the originators use the word processing system?
- For what type of correspondence is the system used?
- What is the current policy regarding correspondence creation and distribution?

What other questions might provide Sandy with information that would help her better understand the correspondence control problems of each department?

## COPY CONTROL

The concept of copy control is relatively new. In the past several years, a rather remarkable phenomenon has occurred. While the cost per copy has decreased, total expenditures for copying have increased. Copying volume is, therefore, rising at a much greater rate than copying costs.

*Duplicate record*

A **copy** is a duplicate record—a reproduction of the original. The introduction to the office environment of relatively inexpensive and simple-to-operate copying equipment has resulted in a dramatic increase in the number of copies produced. Figure 16–5 shows the enormous number of copies that are produced monthly by organizations.

*Copy control*

**Copy management** may be defined as the management of copying practices, procedures, and control devices to ensure the effective and economical creation of copies. Copy control is more than a bookkeeping procedure that keeps track of equipment use; it is a total system of management. Consideration is given to how people use the equipment (practices), to the requirements for duplicate records (procedures), and to the management and control of the copiers and duplicators (devices).

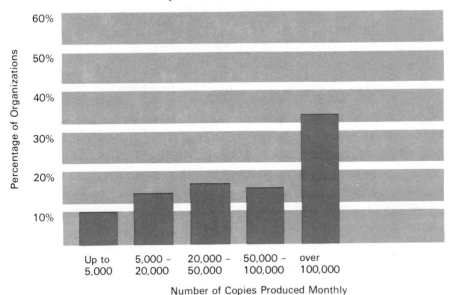

Figure 16–5
Copies Produced Monthly

*Source: Lou Pilla, "Committee of 500: The Rising Tide,"* Management World *(September, 1982).*

## Practices, Procedures, and Devices

Copies should contribute to the decision-making process by providing the right information to the right people, at the right time, in the right quantity, and at the least cost. Economical creation refers not only to the cost per copy but also to the need to limit creation (or re-creation) to necessary business copies. A system must be designed to provide comprehensive copying service which coordinates the three elements of the program—practices, procedures, and devices.

### Copy Practices

Good **copy practices** require instruction in equipment use and application of common sense. New employees often are given no instruction in machine operation; this results in improper and sometimes damaging use of the equipment, wasted supplies, and poor copies. Employees familiar with efficient machine operation may be guilty of making "one more copy just in case" or rounding off the requested number. Many of the copies produced are unusable because of operator error or neglect. Good practice is to check for

*Efficient equipment use*

**acceptable copy.** When multiple copies are to be made of a document, a test copy should be made to see if it is acceptable instead of running 50 copies only to discover they are unusable.

**copy destination.** If the copy is for internal use and quality is not critical, legible copy should be accepted instead of discarding legible copy to attempt perfect copy.

**quantity indicator.** After copies are made, the quantity indicator should be returned to "1." If the person who previously used the machine left the indicator at "50" and the next person to use the machine needs only 1 copy but neglects to check the quantity indicator, multiple unneeded copies will result before the error is detected.

**type of paper in the feeder.** As in the case of the quantity indicator, failure to check the type of paper in the feeder will result in a legal-size document being copied on standard-size paper, or vice versa; this will require another run and create waste.

**staples, paper clips, and so forth.** Foreign objects cause the equipment to malfunction. The operator needs a work surface other than the copier for taking apart or assembling documents to avoid the possibility of objects falling into the mechanism.

**machine malfunction.** If the machine is not functioning properly, a note should be left on the copier so that the next user will not waste time and supplies.

## Copy Procedures

**Copy procedures** for controlling the making of duplicate copies must be developed based on the unique needs of each office or department, focusing on copy creation rather than copy production. In order to determine basic copy requirements, attention should be given to developing a current copying activity profile. The profile should include

*Copying activity profile*

- kinds of documents routinely copied (including personal and unauthorized copies),
- purpose served by copies (information copy; copies of forms, directives, and other documents that should be obtained through supply channels; and so forth),
- urgency of copying requirements,
- copying requiring special handling for either copy quality, confidentiality of documents, or other unique requirements,
- volume of copying,
- composition of copying (one copy of 75 documents or 75 copies of one document), and
- procedure for validating need prior to copying.

Based on the profile, each office or department should be analyzed and ways of improving information distribution and eliminating copying costs resulting from inefficient practices and procedures should be recommended.

Consideration must also be given to procedures necessary to prevent copyright violations. The copyright law effective January 1, 1978, is more definitive and more inclusive than previous copyright laws. Many publications have the following statement printed on the copyright page:

*Copyright law*

> All rights reserved. *The text of this publication, or any part thereof, may not be reproduced or transmitted in any form or by any means, electronic or mechanical, including photocopying, recording, storage in an information retrieval system, or otherwise, without the prior written permission of the publisher.*

Note that the copyright law extends beyond hard copy to include other types of media. Anyone responsible for requesting or processing copies should be familiar with the restrictions included in the copyright law regarding what can be copied, how many copies may be made, and the purposes for which authorized copies may be reproduced.

## Copy Control Devices

**Copy control devices** are attached to copy machines to limit access to authorized users. More sophisticated versions of the mechanisms are available which not only control access but also provide an accountability system. With this system a transaction recorder unit controls, records, and accounts for use of copiers. Users identify themselves with access cards or "keys" to unlock the machine. Recorded data includes the copier station, number of copies, the user, department code, and job category. The copies are then run and the data is recorded on a digital tape cassette. Cassettes are processed by computer to produce usage reports that are given to the person responsible for copy control. The reports are also available in summary form to be distributed to department heads for their analyses. An additional function allows for "charge-back" to the user. Information provided through this report allows for a more objective evaluation of the current copying activity than a simple recording of the number of copies produced by each department in the aggregate. This information, combined with the procedural analyses previously discussed, provides the basic data for the development of a comprehensive copy control system that is designed to meet the needs of individual users. Figure 16–6 shows one type of copy control device.

*Control mechanisms*

Figure 16–6
Copy Control Device

## Selection of Method

Copies may be produced in facilities ranging from convenience copiers to contracted services, from quick copy centers to in-house printing plants. The facility should be matched to the copying needs of the organization—the number of copies required of a single document, the complexity of the job, the quality required, and the cost related to each alternative method.

### In-House Facilities

*Centralized versus decentralized*

Services can be categorized as in-house or contracted. **In-house copy facilities** are located within an organization as either a centralized or decentralized operation. A centralized operation is one in which all copying is produced in one place—a copy center or a printing plant. A decentralized operation provides copying capabilities in locations throughout the organization; access is usually controlled by an access key or code. Decentralized operations are usually more convenient and provide quicker turnaround time than centralized systems. Turnaround time is controlled by the availability of personnel to make the copies and the availability and accessability of the equipment. Centralized operations generally require a greater turnaround time, and the paperwork involved in requesting any form of centralized copying is greater than that required in a decentralized operation. Decentralized operations, however, are more difficult to control than centralized operations. More people have freer access to the equipment, and the operation itself is far less formal than in a centralized operation.

### Self-Service Copiers

Unattended, self-service copiers are often referred to as **convenience copiers** because they are located throughout the facility to provide for *convenient* copies. Each office makes its own copies by using an access key or code to operate the machine. Convenience copiers range from desktop machines to floor models that perform multiple tasks. Desktop models are often restricted to one copy at a time and may be limited to single sheets of paper; there may be no capacity for copying bound pages. At the other end of the range is the large floor model that copies in black and white and color, makes transparencies, collates, duplexes, reduces, enlarges, and feeds automatically.

*Unattended copiers*

    The copier should be matched to the use. Cost to make one copy of a document may vary widely from machine to machine because high-capacity, multiple-task machines are used to make too few copies. Self-service unattended copiers are usually recommended for runs of less than 50 copies; some organizations recommend only 25 copies as the upper limit for convenience copiers.

*Match equipment to use*

### Attended Multi-Function Copiers

The more sophisticated attended floor model copiers that are centrally located perform more functions than self-service copiers. In addition to the multi-functions possible with self-service copiers, the attended copiers may pad, staple, fold, cut, bind, slipsheet, and add covers. They may also offer more than one size reduction or enlargement, and accept continuous unburst computer printouts. For some organizations, attended copiers fill the quick copy needs of 50–250 copies.

*Attended copiers*

    Control of equipment purchase should be centralized, and criteria for selection of machines should be based on the proposed use of the copiers. The Department of the Army has issued criteria based largely on the number of copies per minute the machine can produce, as shown in Figure 16–7. The number of copies per minute (first criterion in the chart) determines the group in which a copier is placed. The recommended volume ranges, average monthly volumes, and ratio figures are for guidance only and intended as reasonable limits. Depending on the particular application, actual production or ratio may vary.

Figure 16–7
Office Copier Categories

| CRITERIA | AUTOMATIC MODEL COPIERS | | | | MANUAL/SEMIAUTOMATIC MODEL COPIERS |
|---|---|---|---|---|---|
| | GROUP 1 | GROUP 2 | GROUP 3 | GROUP 4 | GROUP 5 |
| Letter-Size Multiple Copies Per Minute (Group Determinant) | 50 – 99 | 25 – 49 | 11 – 24 | 1 – 10 | Dependent on Speed of Operator |
| Copy Paper Loading Facility | Yes | Yes | Yes | Yes | Normally |
| Multiple Copy Dial-Up | Yes | Yes | Yes | Yes | No—Requires Manual Insertion of Original |
| Ratio of Copies to Original | Maximum 25 | Recommended 20 | Recommended 15 | Recommended 10 | Recommended 5 |
| Produces Black and White Copies Only | Yes | Yes | Yes | Yes | Yes |
| Recommended Range of Monthly Volume of Reproduction | 25,000 to 150,000 | 10,000 to 50,000 | 3,000 to 25,000 | 1,000 to 10,000 | None |
| Average Monthly Volume of Reproduction | 75,000 | 25,000 | 10,000 | 5,000 | None |

*Source: Army Regulation 340–20 (Washington, D.C.: Department of the Army, 1985).*

Centralized copy control not only allows for uniformity in selection, but also minimizes the proliferation of printing and copying centers. Responsibility for monitoring facilities and equipment selection to assure that capacities are matched to requirements should be vested in the office of the records manager. High-volume use of convenience copiers reduces the cost per copy but results in higher total copying costs. As discussed earlier, this is a major trend and one that must be controlled.

## Quick Copy

**Quick copy** is a centralized system representing one of the forms of in-house copying. A paper master is produced on equipment that resembles a copier. To produce the copies, the paper master is placed on a printing press—an offset printing operation. Copies made via quick copy are of high quality—usually higher quality than copies made on convenience copiers. Economically, it is not feasible to run fewer than 50 copies by using the quick copy method. Because of the breakdown of the image on the master, quick copying is generally not recommended for more than 700 copies.

*50–700 copies*

Turnaround time varies according to the capacity of the in-house printing facility, the schedule, and the demand on the system. Most organizations aim for 24-hour turnaround. Because this is a centralized operation, completed paperwork must accompany the material to be copied.

## Printing

Self-service copiers are used for up to 50 copies and produce copies of varying quality. Some organizations use attended, multi-function copiers for 50–250 copies. Quick copy is appropriate for 50 to 700 copies of high quality. Self-service and attended copiers and quick copy are used for relatively simple copying. When more than 700 copies are needed or when the job is a complex one that uses a number of photographs, illustrations, or colors, then printing is the appropriate method. The decision should be based on size, content, complexity, and cost of the material to be copied. Phototypesetting equipment, compatible with copiers and word processing equipment, is available so that direct transfer from the copier or word processor may be made to the phototypesetting equipment.

*700 or more copies or complex jobs*

## Contracted Services

Organizations with minimal copying needs that will not justify equipping, staffing, and operating an in-house printing system must use the services of outside printing contractors. Some organizations, while maintaining their own in-house printing facility, may still find it necessary to contract some jobs that their own operation cannot accommodate because of the size, complexity, or urgency of the printing job. Many firms, however, have found that operating their own print facility has produced very positive results.

*Use of contracted services*

Prior to selecting a printer to whom a contract will be awarded, the organization should carefully evaluate these factors:

*Selection of printing services*

- quality of the output produced by the printer
- total cost of the job
- turnaround time promised/fulfilled
- reputation of the printer

Advantages and disadvantages of the three printing alternatives—in-house copy, quick copy, and commercial printer—are shown in Figure 16–8.

While the preceding discussion has divided reprographic services into two major categories—in-house and contracted—it is not an either/or decision. In fact, many organizations use a combination of services. Convenience copiers may be strategically located for making a minimal number of copies; a quick copy center may be operated to accommodate multiple copies when quality copy is important; a print shop may be located within the facility; and outside printing services may be contracted. Any combination of these services may meet the needs of the organization.

Figure 16–8
Three Printing Alternatives: Pros and Cons

| INPLANT COPIER/ AUTOMATED DUPLICATOR | QUICK COPY SHOP | COMMERCIAL PRINTER |
|---|---|---|
| Most convenient. | Very convenient. | Least convenient. |
| Low-to-medium quality. | Low-to-medium quality. | Highest quality. |
| Low cost on short runs. | Medium cost on short runs. | Highest cost on short runs. |
| Inefficient for long runs. | Costly for long runs. | Efficient for long runs. |
| Poor reproduction of illustrations. | Acceptable reproduction of illustrations. | Best reproduction of illustrations. |
| Poor quality on screened material. | Acceptable quality on screened material. | Best quality on screened material. |
| Limited to 8½ × 11, 8½ × 14, and some 11 × 17. | Limited range of sizes, usually to 11 × 17. | Large presses for maximum size flexibility. |
| Bindery limited to collating, some stitching. | Moderate selection of bindery services. | Full range of bindery. |
| Ideal for under 500 runs. | Competitive up to 2500 runs. | Competitive at longer runs, 2500 plus. |
| No color capability. | Color at a premium. | Color at a premium, including process color. |
| Limited paper stock in copier. | Wider range of papers on duplicator-size presses, including cover stock. | Full range of papers, cover stock, envelopes, etc. |
| Space, overhead, and labor commitment. | No overhead or space. | No overhead or space. |
| Supervision required. | Service usually on a retail, walk-in basis. | Salesman will call on you. |

*Source: Brett Rutherford, "I Need a Thousand Copies of This," Administrative Management, Vol. 43, No. 9 (September, 1982), p. 45.*

## Cost Factors

*Cost categories*

The cost factors associated with copies are important to any organization as it attempts to provide information to users within the imposed budget constraints. Costs of copying can be categorized as processing, maintenance, distribution, and user time costs.

**Copy processing costs** are the costs involved in making necessary copies; these costs include equipment and equipment maintenance, materials, supplies, and administrative support time.

**Copy maintenance costs** are the costs related to storing and retrieving the copies.

**Copy distribution costs** are the costs associated with distributing the copies to the appropriate recipients.

**Copy user costs** are those costs that represent user time—the time necessary for the recipient to efficiently interpret and use the information. User costs are directly related to the quality and timeliness of the information. A poorly reproduced copy will require more of the user's time to interpret, extract, and follow through on requested action than a copy that is clear and easy to read.

## Responsibility

Responsibility for copy control rests with the person requesting the copy. Unless he or she accepts that responsibility and is accountable for his or her actions, the control program will probably not succeed. While administrative support personnel must assume the responsibility for using correct copying practices and be accountable in that regard, procedural decisions must be made at a higher management level. Full support and demand for compliance for the copy program must come from top management.

*User accountability*

## Evaluation

In the final analysis, success will be based on the degree to which the objectives of the program are met. If the objectives are to ensure effective and economical creation of necessary copies, then the success of the control program must be measured by the degree to which these objectives are achieved.

*Objectives*

## A LOOK AT THE CASE

Sandy Reynolds will want information regarding the current copying practices, procedures, and devices used. She will request any data that is available to provide her with an overview of the copying requirements by department, as well as usage records by department. Each manager should make available the rationale for selection of copying methods and an analysis of how well the methods match the needs of the users. Organizational objectives and cost figures will be helpful to Sandy's evaluation of the effectiveness and efficiency of the current system of producing duplicate records.

# TERMINOLOGY REVIEW

*Convenience copiers.* Self-service, unattended copiers that are located throughout the facility to provide for convenient copies.

*Copy.* A duplicate of the original record.

*Copy control device.* Mechanism attached to copy machines to limit access to authorized users.

*Copy distribution costs.* Costs associated with distributing the copies to the appropriate recipients.

*Copy maintenance costs.* Costs related to storing and retrieving copies.

*Copy management.* The management of copying practices, procedures, and devices to ensure the effective and economical creation of copies.

*Copy practices.* How the copying equipment is used.

*Copy procedures.* The requirements for making duplicate records.

*Copy processing costs.* Costs involved in making necessary copies, including equipment and equipment maintenance, materials, supplies, and clerical time.

*Copy user costs.* Costs that represent the time the user must take to interpret and use the information.

*Correspondence distribution costs.* Costs associated with distributing correspondence to the appropriate recipients.

*Correspondence maintenance costs.* Costs associated with storing and retrieving correspondence.

*Correspondence origination costs.* Costs directly related to writing and research time necessary to draft correspondence.

*Correspondence processing costs.* Costs involved in actual preparation of documents including equipment, materials, supplies, and administrative support.

*Correspondence user costs.* Costs that represent user time to correctly interpret and use the information contained in the correspondence.

*Guide letters.* Letters that provide a suggested pattern of responses for routine letters.

*In-house copy facilities.* Copying facilities located within an organization as either centralized or decentralized operations.

*Machine dictation.* Dictation of correspondence into a recording machine as opposed to face-to-face dictation to a secretary.

*Quick copy.* Centralized copying facility representing one of the forms of in-house copying.

# COMPETENCY REVIEW

1. Identify the four major goals of a correspondence control program.
2. What procedures should be followed to establish a correspondence control program?

3. Describe two methods for achieving each of the goals of a correspondence control program.

4. Identify three alternatives to hard-copy correspondence.

5. Describe three methods of evaluating a program of correspondence control.

6. Explain the importance of a good correspondence manual to correspondence control.

7. Distinguish among copy practices, procedures, and control devices.

8. What should be considered in making a decision regarding the appropriate copying method? What should be considered in making a decision regarding the appropriate printing method?

9. Describe the cost factors associated with correspondence and copy functions.

## APPLICATIONS

1. Compose guide paragraphs that you, as a resort complex employee, may use to prepare responses to the following situations:

    a. to respond to a request for a brochure of a resort complex
    b. to confirm a hotel reservation
    c. to say that the hotel is booked for the date requested
    d. to say thank you for asking about the resort complex
    e. to ask to change hotel reservations to another date
    f. to respond to an inquiry about the costs of hotel rooms
    g. a friendly closing

2. Put the paragraphs together to form a letter

    a. saying that the hotel has no available accommodations for the date requested
    b. confirming a reservation
    c. sending a brochure

3. As director of printing and publications, you have been asked to recommend the most appropriate method for copying the following materials:

    a. 150 copies of a memo
    b. 22 copies of a letter having intra-company distribution
    c. 800 copies of a questionnaire
    d. 350 copies of a color brochure
    e. 15 copies of an advertisement including several photographs
    f. 10 very high quality copies of a proposal to be submitted for funding a $2.4 million contract

CONCLUDING CASES

## ■ A. Quality Merchandise Distributors, Inc.

Sara Thompson is manager of the administrative services division of Quality Merchandise Distributors, Inc. One of Sara's responsibilities is to approve all expenditures for office equipment and supplies.

Sara has just received purchase requisitions for 45 new five-drawer cabinets. These requests represent an increase of 50 percent over the previous year. Sara is surprised by the increase and concerned about the cause(s) for the increase.

1.  What steps might Sara take to determine the cause(s) of this increase in requisitions for storage equipment?
2.  What steps can be taken to curtail future requests for storage equipment?

## B. Leggett Company

Mike O'Leary has just received the following memo to be typed and distributed. As he reviews the memo and prepares to type, he is concerned about the quality of the memo.

Mike has checked his calendar, and he finds that January 10 is on Wednesday. What other concerns would you have regarding the quality of the correspondence? What specific recommendations would you make to improve the quality?

---

**Leggett Company**                                    INTEROFFICE COMMUNICATION

TO: Department Heads
FROM: Jo Simmons, Vice President for Administrative Services
DATE: January 3, 19--
SUBJECT: Departmental Concerns

We need to resolve some problems within and among departments. Please be prepared to discuss the existing problems and to recommend solutions when we meet on Monday, January 10.

If it is impossible for you to meet at that time, notify me at least one week prior.

---

## READINGS AND REFERENCES

Army Regulation 340–20. Washington, D.C.: Headquarters, Department of the Army, December 22, 1985.

Avedon, Don M. "Electronic Mail Systems." *Information and Records Management,* Vol. 15, No. 1 (January, 1981), p. 12.

Dartnell's Target Survey. "1986 Cost of Business Letter Remains Under $9.00." Dartnell Institute of Business Research, Chicago, Illinois. 1986.

Department of Transportation. *Transportation Automated Office System.* Washington, D.C.: U.S. Government Printing Office, undated.

Fernberg, Patricia M. "Auditing Copier Costs." *Modern Office Technology,* Vol. 30, No. 9 (September, 1985), p. 110.

General Accounting Office, *Federal Records Management: A History of Neglect.* Washington, D.C.: U.S. Government Printing Office, February 24, 1981.

General Services Administration, National Archives and Records Service, Office of Records Management. *Correspondence Management.* Washington, D.C.: U.S. Government Printing Office, 1973.

Hanson, Richard E. "Highlights on Copier Usage." *Office Systems '84,* Vol. 1, No. 1 (July/August 1984), p. 90.

Hanson, Richard E. "Fast-Changing Copier Technology Provides User Ease and Convenience." *Office Systems '85,* Vol. 2, No. 7 (July, 1985), p. 42.

"In-House Duplicating System Cuts Firm's Turnaround Time," *The Office,* Vol. 93, No.3 (March, 1981), p. 126.

Keer, Karen. "Technology is Redefining Copying Machine Functions." *Office Systems '86,* Vol. 3, No. 3 (March, 1986), p. 34.

Marking, B. Thomas. "Copy Management: An Emerging Program." *Records Management Quarterly,* Vol. 14, No. 1 (January, 1980), p. 20.

Meth, Clifford. "Write With Light." *Administrative Management,* Vol. 47, No. 3 (March, 1986), p. 39.

Metzner, Kermit. "Consider Your Needs in Copier Selection." *Office Systems '86,* Vol. 3, No. 3 (March, 1986), p. 41.

Miller, Dennis. Supervisor of Printing and Publications, Old Dominion University (Norfolk, Virginia). Interview, July, 1981.

Pilla, Lou. "Committee of 500: The Rising Tide." *Management World* (September, 1982).

Rutherford, Brett. "I Need a Thousand Copies of This." *Administrative Management,* Vol. 43, No. 9 (September, 1982), p. 45.

# 17

# DIRECTIVES CONTROL

## Competencies

After completing this chapter, you should be able to

1. define directive.
2. explain the benefits derived from a directives control program.
3. relate the importance of a classification system to directives control.
4. describe the format of a directive.
5. explain the rationale for a directives distribution system.
6. determine the most effective directives distribution system.
7. evaluate a directives control program.

# Introductory Case

Unique Jewelry, Inc., is a family-owned business that manufactures many different types of unique jewelry, much of it special order. When the company was first organized, everything was operated on a very informal basis. Joyce Holloway, the owner, was responsible for the design and production process; Stan Holloway was responsible for sales; and Taylor, their daughter, ran the office.

Over the years they have expanded their operations so that Unique Jewelry, Inc., is no longer a family operation. The company now employs over one hundred factory workers, ten salespersons, four designers, and three office employees. Business has improved so much that Joyce is seriously considering building a second plant geared for retail sales only.

Now that the company is expanding its operations,

1. How can Joyce Holloway help ensure consistency in future operations of the business?
2. What is the best method for communicating organizational policies, procedures, and rules to the employees?

*Downward communication*

A **directive** is an instruction from management—a form of downward communication—usually addressing policy or procedure. A directive serves as the vehicle for communicating information from managers to individuals who have a need to know or are required to act. Directives may include policies, procedures, notices, orders, guidelines, rules, and regulations—any of the many formal communications that provide direction from upper management about what, why, how, when, and by whom action is to be taken.

Controlling directives creation, distribution, maintenance, and disposition through a well-developed directives control program is essential. A directives control program includes policies and procedures for establishing, implementing, maintaining, and evaluating the total directives control program. The directives system relates to the operational aspects of the delivery system itself.

*Employee benefits*

Experience has shown that an effective directives control system is an essential element of administrative/subordinate working relationships. Directives which are not clear may cause confusion for affected employees. Directives may be issued too late, and deadlines may be missed; conflicting directives may cause conflicting actions. Directives may be amended and supplemented in a disorganized way, resulting in a combination of the errors described. Due to incomplete or obsolete instructions, directives distribution may not be systematic.

*Administrative benefits*

In addition to providing timely directives written in appropriate language and uniform format and revised and supplemented in a systematic way, a directives control program provides other administrative benefits by

- establishing specific responsibility and accountability;
- eliminating repetitive judgments on routine matters;
- encouraging employee cooperation by describing work relationships;
- instructing supervisors and employees in routine tasks;
- reducing confusion, conflict, and doubt by explaining work procedures;
- conditioning for change by presenting the plan in writing prior to its implementation; and
- reducing costs.

## PLAN DIRECTIVES CONTROL PROGRAM

A plan must be developed for the **directives control program**—a systematic method for establishing, implementing, maintaining, and evaluating the directives of an organization. A well-developed plan maximizes the opportunity for program success and minimizes the opportunity for failure.

## Establish Program Framework

Establishing the directives control program requires a formalization process. This process includes defining authority for the program, establishing staff responsibilities, establishing a central clearing point, and selecting contact persons.

*Formalization process*

### Define Authority

Support of top management is essential, as it is with any new program. Management support must be communicated to all organization members. Authority for the program must be defined, granted, and communicated to all levels of management. This authority is communicated through a directive on directives. The **directive on directives** describes the framework for the program (policies and procedures) and the philosophy of the program (establishing a single control system for issuing and distributing directives within the organization).

*Directive on directives*

### Establish Staff Responsibilities

Responsibility for operating the directives program should be placed in a single, specific unit of the organization. In a large organization, a separate directives unit may be needed. The supervisor of the directives unit would be responsible to the records manager. In small organizations, the responsibility for directives control may be assigned to the records management staff. A central clearing point for directives must be designated, whether the responsibility is placed within a separate unit or within the records management unit.

### Establish Central Clearing Point

A **central clearing point** within the organization provides coordination for the directives program. The central clearing point, staffed by a professional and as many employees as the size of the program warrants, can provide consulting services for directives control to all affected offices/departments. Central clearing point staff should have a thorough knowledge of the functions of the organization, organizational structure, effective writing and presentation skills, subject classification systems, reprographics, indexing, distribution practices, and methods of maintaining a current directives control program.

*Provide consultation and coordination*

### Select Contact Persons

*Establish working relationship*

A contact person should be selected within each user department. The contact person is an important element in the directives control program. This contact person is responsible for coordinating the work of the central clearing point staff and the user department. The contact person also sets the tone of cooperation within the department and establishes good working relationships with the central clearing point staff.

## Inventory Current Directives

A determination must be made of the volume, content, currentness, and distribution of organizational directives in place in order to plan an effective directives control program.

### Collect and Analyze Directives

*Collect copies of all directives*

An inventory of all directives should be conducted. The inventory should include a copy of each directive issued by a department/unit. The contact persons in each unit can be very helpful in the inventory process by securing copies of the directives and forwarding the copies along with an inventory to the central clearing point. The central clearing point staff should then begin an analysis of the directives, grouping them into broad subject categories. Obsolete directives should be separated from current directives.

### Return to Originating Unit

*Review and revise directives*

After the sample directives are divided into subject groupings, they are returned to the contact person in the **originating unit**—the department creating the directive or office responsible for the function or subject described in the directive. The originating office reviews the directives for possible revisions or deletions. Obsolete material is deleted; the deletion can range from a word to eliminating the entire directive. Other directives may be condensed, consolidated, rearranged, or rewritten. The originating office may suggest more descriptive or concise subjects and alphabetic index entries. The sample directives, including revised and deleted materials, and other necessary information are returned to the central clearing point. Central clearing point staff then decides which directives need substantial revisions and which will be integrated later according to a conversion schedule.

### Develop Conversion Schedule

After the directives and their revisions and deletions are returned to the central clearing point, the central clearing point staff then decides which directives to incorporate into the program immediately. Some of the directives may need substantial revision that would prevent incorporating them into the program at this point. A conversion schedule must be developed to show at what point additional directives will be integrated into the program.

## Develop Directives Control Program

The plan for developing the directives control program includes determining the content to provide complete information, establishing the format to provide uniformity, and developing a classification system to expedite storing and retrieving directives.

### Determine Directive Content

Directives may be classified as long-term or temporary. Long-term directives remain in effect until canceled or revised. Temporary directives have a short life, designated by the specific time of effectiveness on the directive. Immediately upon date of expiration, destroy the temporary directive. By carefully following this procedure, obsolete directives are not confused with long-term ones.

*Long-term or temporary*

Directives usually address policy and/or procedure. **Policy** statements provide guidelines for making decisions; **procedure** statements tell how to implement the policies. A policy might state that "each user should have access to appropriate records in a timely manner to promote efficient and effective decision making at the lowest cost." The procedures statements would define the steps for accomplishing this policy. While it is often suggested that policy and procedural directives be separate, issuing a directive that states both purpose (policy) and implementation (procedures) may be more practical.

*Policy or procedure*

The subject of a directive is determined by the originating unit. The originating unit also assures that content is complete, accurate, and appropriate; does not duplicate or conflict with existing directives; and complies with program controls. For example, if a directive requires completing a form, the originating office should review the form with a forms analyst to ensure that the form is properly designed and economically printed and that adequate supplies of the form are available.

Actual writing of the directive is also the responsibility of the originating office. Each directive should be prepared in correct format and in accordance with writing and editorial guidelines established by the organization. A standard practice for directive development, coordination, and issue should be developed. A printed

*Responsibilities of originator*

directive coordination sheet should be used where feasible. Using an illustrated sample to explain preparing forms, reports, or other documents addressed by the directive is helpful. Hundreds of words can be replaced with an illustration of a properly completed form with annotated instructions for its preparation.

*Review directive*

Primary responsibility for securing input and approval from the departments concerned with the subject of the directive lies with the originator. Conflicts in content or in methods of work should be eliminated before the directive is issued. Each directive should be reviewed in advance by every department concerned with the functions the directive addresses. Review of the directive with accompanying comments and approval is accomplished by simultaneous circulation to each affected office. When copies of the directive are returned, the originating office reviews the comments, makes desired changes, ensures that all necessary approvals have been obtained, and then submits the information to the central clearing point. After verifying the approvals, the central clearing staff confirms that the directive is nonconflictive and nonduplicative, and that it conforms to program regulations and controls.

Editorial assistance may be provided by the central clearing staff, but the editing responsibility rests with the originator of the directive. Final approval and signatures are obtained for each directive by the central clearing point staff. The effective date is assigned by the central clearing staff after confirmation from the originating office has been obtained.

## Establish Directive Format

*Standardize format*

A standard format should be used for all directives. If originators are required to put their thoughts in an organized, logical format, the directive is better organized. Users receive a directive that contains all the necessary information, and they know that vital information is always found in the same place on the directive.

All directives should include the following information (see Figure 17–1):

The *name of the issuing or originating unit* appears at the top of the directive; the name or an abbreviation appears at the top of each succeeding page.

The *directive number* appears in the upper right corner of the first page and on all succeeding pages. If back and front pages are used, the directive number appears in the upper left corner of

Figure 17–1
Directives Format

---

HUMAN RESOURCES DEPARTMENT (issuing unit)


844 (directive number)
January 14, 19—(effective date)



To:   All Human Resources Department Employees

Subject:   Payroll Deductions


A.   (purpose)


B.   (forms required)


C.   (explanatory primary paragraph)


1.   (subparagraph)

(a)   (subordinating paragraph)

(i)   (further delineation)

(ii)

(b)

2.   (second subparagraph)


D.   (additional information)

Distribution: 1C

---

even numbered pages and in the upper right corner of odd numbered pages.

The *date the directive takes effect* is shown just below the directive number. Usually the effective date is the same as the issue date. However, the directive may be retroactive or future dated, if appropriate.

The *addressees* are indicated just below the issuing organization. Addressee identification must correspond with that used in the distribution list.

The *subject* appears just below the addressee. This wording should agree with the approved subject classification list.

The *content* follows an established pattern which allows for subdivisions. A suggested pattern is A. 1. (a) (i); each of the four symbols represents a finer subdivision of the paragraphs. All major paragraphs carry a heading; subparagraphs may carry headings to assist the reader. Generally, a directive follows this pattern: purpose; forms, reports, records required by the directive; narrative or text; and list of attachments or exhibits.

The *distribution code* appears as the last item on the first page. Some organizations prefer to use a distribution list. A code, however, is more efficient in large organizations.

Figure 17–1 illustrates the content and format of a directive. Other formats may be used as long as all necessary directive components are included and uniformity for the creator and the reader is provided.

The page numbering system omits numbering the first page. Succeeding page numbers are centered at the bottom of each page.

For ease of reading when material is placed in binders, use a left margin of $1\frac{1}{4}$ to $1\frac{1}{2}$ inches. In either case, use standard margins for all directives. Indentions show the degree of subordination of topics within the directive.

*Technical considerations*    Some technical considerations are type and paper size, and style of presentation of material. Standard-size ($8\frac{1}{2}$ by 11 inches) paper is recommended because it costs less and is less expensive to copy and store. Binders to house directives are also less expensive to purchase in standard size. Paper should be the lightest weight that provides sufficient strength to prevent tearing when it is filed in the directives manual, yet have sufficient opacity to prevent "bleeding through" (copy showing through on the reverse side of the paper). Some organizations use colored paper to distinguish between policy and procedures. For example, green paper for all policy statements or yellow paper for all procedures. Although this seems a reasonable method, directives are more expensive to produce and sometimes more difficult to read on colored paper. Several colors of paper must be stocked, and policy and procedure statements must be separated in the manual. White paper is more practical for all directives because a less expensive printing and binding process is required. Also, a policy statement and the implementation procedures can be placed on the same page of the directive.

The most commonly used presentation style for policy statements is narrative form. Procedures are best presented in outline style. Outline form shows the separate procedural steps with appropriate subdivisions. This style allows an employee to select a particular procedure that is applicable to a particular situation. Some special formats such as playscript, text table (in which there are both text and tables), and decision logic tables or decision trees (in which patterns of relationships are graphically shown) are based on outline form and may be especially suitable for instructional directives.

*Narrative/outline style*

## Develop Classification System

A subject classification system for directives allows all directives relating to one subject to be filed together. This eliminates the necessity for looking in more than one place for related information.

The classification system should be based on the subject of the directive — not on whom the directive affects, whom it is from, or to whom it is addressed. The preliminary basis for establishing the classification system is from the directives inventory conducted during the planning phase. When the central clearing staff originally categorized the directives, the directives were divided into broad subject areas. Subject classification for each directive is assigned by the originating office so the central clearing point staff can verify the subject and the classification number.

*Subject classification*

The classification system uses a primary subject and secondary or tertiary subject designators if appropriate. The words chosen for the subjects must be short, simple, and commonly used and understood by the users. For example, a section of a subject classification system for directives about the broad human resources category might have a secondary subject, such as compensation. Compensation may have tertiary subject designators similar to those listed below:

HUMAN RESOURCES

Compensation
  Salary guidelines
  Salary advancement
  Reserved
  Payroll deductions
  Insurance
  Travel expenses
    Travel expenses: Applicants for employment
  Contracts
  Termination pay
  Reserved

Note that two areas are marked "Reserved." Reserved entries may be used to reflect topic areas for which no policy or regulation is currently required or to allow for orderly future expansion of the series.

*Subject/numeric classification*

Once subjects have been determined, select a numbering system. The selected numbering pattern must permit expansion and distinguish between consecutive directives on the same subject. Application of a numeric system to the subject classification previously shown may be as follows:

| | |
|---|---|
| HUMAN RESOURCES | 800 |
| Compensation | 840 |
| Salary guidelines | 841 |
| Salary advancement | 842 |
| Reserved | 843 |
| Payroll deductions | 844 |
| Insurance | 845 |
| Travel expenses | 846 |
| Travel expenses: Applicants for employment | 846.1 |
| Contracts | 847 |
| Termination pay | 848 |
| Reserved | 849 |

Expansion is provided by the addition of a decimal number as directives are added to a subject category. The preceding example uses a three digit pattern; large organizations may use four or more digits in their numbering systems. The system, however, should not become too cumbersome for a practical application.

■

## A LOOK AT THE CASE

Because Unique Jewelry, Inc., began as a small, family-owned and -operated company, organizational decisions were made and communicated on a very informal basis. The past informal communication system did not require a directives system. Now that Unique Jewelry, Inc., has expanded, Joyce Holloway needs to initiate a system to inform all employees of company policies, procedures, and rules. Although unwritten, many policies, procedures, and rules have become a part of the system through tradition—"that's the way we've always done it."

Policies, procedures, and rules are best communicated through a directives system. Joyce, therefore, must begin by formalizing the policies, procedures, and rules by which she wishes to continue to operate in a directives system.

1. What steps should be taken to implement a directives system?
2. What kind of directives distribution system should be in place?

■

## IMPLEMENT DIRECTIVES CONTROL PROGRAM

Implementation of the directives control program includes preparing the directives manual and determining a distribution system for directives.

### Prepare Directives Manual

The **directives manual** consolidates all the organizational directives, including the directive on directives, in one place. The directives manual may be a separate publication or may be a part of the records management manual. Employees may reference any current directive without having to refer to a number of sources. All directives referring to any one subject are placed together in the directives manual.

*Purpose*

Preparation of the directives manual is a function of the central clearing point staff. Decisions must be made regarding the information to be included in the manual. Only information which provides the most assistance to originators and users of the directives manual should be considered. Information should also be included regarding procedures for making changes and revisions within the directives manual.

### Content

The directives manual contains a title page, a table of contents, an alphabetic/subject index, a numeric index, the directive on directives, and a copy of each current directive.

*Title page*

The title page includes the manual title (Directives Manual) and date completed. A list of persons involved in the preparation of the manual may be included.

*Table of contents*

The table of contents shows major divisions of the directives manual and the page numbers of these sections.

*Indexes*

Indexes are numeric and alphabetic subject listings. The numeric index, prepared by the central clearing point staff, is a list of all directives in effect on a given date. Each entry includes the directive number and subject title. Revisions must also be listed. Entries are arranged by directive number — the same order in which the directives are arranged in the directives manual. Generally a separate index for each major distribution code is issued. Major distribution codes relate to the major classifications of distribution — i.e., Headquarters Only. Other distribution codes may be assigned for individuals within the major distribution code. Separate indexes often require less paper than a single, consolidated index for all users. The index is issued as part of the directives manual when the directives control program is introduced.

A portion of a numeric index is shown below:

| Directive Number | Subject |
|---|---|
| 320 | Administrators and supervisors new to system, salary schedule guidelines |
| 440 | Hazardous work |
| 514 | Gifts to employees |
| 811 | Employee health examinations |
| 830 | Firearms, carrying of |
| 840 | Grievance procedures |
| 844 | Hospitalization plans |
| 850 | Employee leave — general |
| 852 | Jury Duty |
| 853 | Employee leave for illness/death in family |
| 853 | Employee disability benefits, long term |
| 854 | Employee annual leave |
| 857 | Employee educational leave |
| 880 | Employment of relatives |

Before the quantity of directives makes finding directives and using the manual a time-consuming task, create an alphabetic subject index. This index is created by the central clearing point staff in consultation with the originators. The alphabetic subject index is an alphabetic listing of words and terms by which an employee may reference the directives. Each index entry includes the index word or term selected and the subject classification number. A separate index entry should be made for each key word when the classification contains two or more key words. This index is similar to the index in the back of a book. A copy of the index must be maintained in all manuals. Generally a separate alphabetic subject index is developed for each major distribution code, just as the numeric index is separated. A portion of an alphabetic subject index is shown below:

*Alphabetic subject index*

EMPLOYEES

| | |
|---|---|
| Administrators and supervisors new to system, salary | |
|    schedule guidelines | 320 |
| Disability benefits, long term | 853 |
| Employment of relatives | 880 |
| Firearms, carrying of | 830 |
| Gifts to employees | 514 |
| Grievance procedures | 840 |
| Health examinations | 811 |
| Hospitalization plans | 844 |
| Hazardous work | 440 |
| Leave | |
|    annual | 854 |
|    educational | 857 |
|    general | 850 |
|    illness/death in family | 853 |
|    jury duty | 852 |

Originating offices recommend index entries for each directive prepared, while the central clearing point approves the entries, maintains, and updates the index.

The first directive in the directives manual is the one that provides authorization for the program—the directive on directives. This directive, in addition to providing authorization, provides originators with information regarding when directives should be written, how they should be written, how to obtain approval, and the procedures for distribution. The directive on directives also provides the basic information necessary to aid the originator and the user. Since the directive on directives establishes the policy and procedures for all directives that follow, it must be carefully written, using all the guidelines for effective communication. The im-

*Directive on directives*

portance of this directive cannot be minimized. The remaining portion of the directives manual contains all of the current organizational directives.

## Changes and Revisions

*Maintain currentness*

An essential part of directives control is maintaining current contents. Directives, to be effective, must offer users up-to-date information so that they will be aware of current requirements and will not operate under obsolete instructions. When current content is not maintained, confidence in the directives program is impaired.

When a minor portion of a directive is changed, reissue only the applicable pages. Users insert revised pages into their directives manuals and remove superceded pages. Each revision date is noted on the appropriate page. If an additional page is needed for a revision, adjust the page numbering by adding a number or a letter to the original page number. For example, 12, 12a, 13, 14, 14a, 14b. Renumber the pages when the directive is revised in its entirety. For the user's convenience, flag changes by asterisks, an arrow on the left margin pointing to the new material, or some other means. Comparison of old and new versions is then possible.

*Revising directives*

If major changes must be made in a directive, rewrite and reissue the entire directive as a revised directive. Major revisions affect 40 percent or more of the directive. A checklist of current directives is prepared and distributed by the central clearing point staff. A simple comparison should be made of directives in the directives manual and the current listing.

Some organizations have tried the procedure of having changes written in by directives users. This is not recommended, for the cost of an employee's time to write in the changes far exceeds the cost of issuing a revised directive. Pasting in changes, publishing notices to correct a directive, or issuing a single revised paragraph also are not economical procedures for broadcasting revisions. Revised pages require no more paper than the notice of revision, and a simple change is maintained.

*Revising indexes/tables of contents*

Revised tables of contents and indexes for directives should be issued periodically or at least once a year. In organizations where revisions/changes are frequent, issue indexes reflecting revisions/changes semiannually. The first page of each directive should state clearly what to do with policies or procedures made obsolete by the directive.

## Format

Most directives manuals are housed in some type of loose-leaf binding. This allows additions and deletions to be made with minimal effort and maintains grouping of directives according to subject. Use tabbed divider sheets to indicate the primary subject classification number and key word(s); this allows quicker reference to the manual. All directives should be preassembled by the central clearing point staff. Prepunch directives to fit the standard binders provided.

*Directives manual aids*

The directives that are included in the directives manual must be standard in size and format. Printing the directives on both sides of a sheet of paper (rather than on a single side) reduces the bulk of the directives manual and facilitates its use.

## Determine Distribution

Distribution of the right directives to the right employees is critical to the effectiveness of the directive control program. Distribution is usually made according to a pattern established along organizational lines. Distribution codes are assigned for each category of recipients. Distribution lists are prepared according to the established organization patterns. A control number is assigned to each directives manual as it is charged out to a particular individual. Circulate directives as broadly as possible, yet be selective so that each employee is provided with the exact directive guidance needed to perform the job.

*Distribution patterns*

Distribution may be made according to organizational, functional, or organizational/functional lines. The following is an organizational distribution pattern in which operations are geographically dispersed.

### Distribution by Organization

Distribution may be made by organizational pattern. This is particularly appropriate when organizations have offices that are geographically dispersed.

| Organization | Code |
| --- | --- |
| All locations | 1 |
| Headquarters only | 2 |
| Headquarters and regional offices | 2, 3 |
| Regional offices only | 3 |
| Regional and district offices | 3, 4 |
| District offices only | 4 |

### Distribution by Function

Because the organizational distribution pattern is often not as specific as desirable, distribution may be made by function. An illustration of a functional distribution pattern is as follows:

| Function | Code |
|---|---|
| Administrative services | A |
| Financial services | B |
| Human resources services | C |

## Distribution by Organization and Function

A combination approach along both organizational and functional patterns is sometimes desirable. The organizational/functional approach is as follows:

| Organization/Function | Code |
|---|---|
| All locations, administrative services | 1A |
| Headquarters only, financial services | 2B |
| Headquarters and regional offices, human resources services | 2C, 3C |
| Regional and district offices, administrative services | 3A, 4A |

*Assign responsibility*

Distribution lists, like directives, must be kept up-to-date. The list is composed of titles and company addresses of those who receive directives, revisions, and cancellations. At the central clearing point, a list is maintained for each distribution code. Although people within the organization may change, the directives manual is assigned to a particular title or function. Individual offices are responsible for seeing that the manual is placed in the hands of the right person(s). Assign one person in each office responsibility for maintaining directives. This employee inserts any new directives in binders; removes and destroys canceled material; circulates notices and transmittal sheets and then destroys them; checks the directives in the binder whenever a new numeric index is issued; posts changes to the numeric index when required; and obtains necessary copies of directives for replacement when an older copy is torn or damaged in some way.

*Directives information*

Transmittal sheets sometimes accompany directives. The transmittal sheet gives a summary of the contents of the directive, outlines changes which have occurred in a revision, or cancels a directive. Transmittal sheets may be issued either by the originator or by the central clearing point staff. Uniformity is more easily achieved if the central clearing point staff prepares the transmittal sheets to accompany the distribution of the directives.

■

## A LOOK AT THE CASE

Even though Unique Jewelry, Inc., is a relatively small company, Joyce Holloway still needs to implement a system of distributing the directives that could be continued as the company grows. In the present organizational structure, a very simple distribution system is appropriate.

1. How can the directives control program be evaluated?
2. How can the directives system be evaluated?

■

## EVALUATE DIRECTIVES CONTROL PROGRAM

An essential component of the directives control program is evaluation. The evaluation program provides the information necessary to determine how effective the directives are in supporting and contributing to management decision making and employee productivity. In addition, information gathered in the evaluation identifies needed improvements in the directives control program.

### Obtain Feedback

Feedback from the central clearing point staff and from user groups, combined with the good judgment of the records manager, forms the foundation for evaluation of the directives control program.

### Central Clearing Point Staff

As the central clearing point staff receives directives for processing, an ongoing evaluation of the quality of the directives, an assessment of the need for the directives, and a check on distribution should be maintained. However, compliance with directives requirements does not guarantee program effectiveness. For example, an audit of originators and users might reveal that directives are being created, approved, and distributed but are not received, not properly understood, or simply not implemented by the user groups.

> *Directives effectiveness*

The central clearing point staff should conduct a formal review of the directives files to determine (1) obsolete material; (2)

*In-depth review*

the procedures for preparing, distributing, coordinating and approving directives; (3) material to include in the directives manual; and (4) staffing, facilities, and work processes within the central clearing point staff. This in-depth review should be conducted at least every three years. In addition, a self-evaluation should be a continuing, monitoring activity to ensure optimum performance of various directives control components.

## User Groups

*User appraisal*

User groups must provide information regarding both the program appraisal and the system appraisal. The **directives program appraisal** addresses the policies and procedures for establishing, implementing, maintaining, and evaluating the total directives control program. The **directives system appraisal** addresses the operational aspects of the delivery system itself. One method of obtaining program and system appraisals is through a comprehensive checklist such as the one shown in Figure 17–2.

*Conduct interviews*

An additional method of obtaining user information is through interviews with those who write directives and those who use directives. These interviews, conducted by the central clearing point staff and the records manager, provide information regarding attitudes toward the directives control program—information not obtained through a checklist type of feedback.

Figure 17–2
Directives Control Checklist

**Directives Program Checklist**

|  | Yes | No |
|---|---|---|
| 1. Is overall responsibility for managing the directives program assigned to an upper management level office? | | |
| 2. Is an official assigned responsibility for managing the directives program? | | |
| 3. Are these assignments spelled out in a formal directive? | | |
| 4. Are there provisions for delegating directives management functions to lower organizational levels, if necessary? | | |
| 5. Is there a current directive on directives? | | |
| 6. Is the directive on directives clearly written and understandable? | | |
| 7. Does the directive on directives cover the program's purpose, responsibilities, types of issuances, classification system, clearance, and coordination requirements? | | |
| 8. Is there a requirement to periodically review the directives program for effectiveness and compliance with established procedures? | | |
| 9. Is there a requirement to ensure that recommendations resulting from such reviews are implemented? | | |

|  | Yes | No |
|---|---|---|

10. Has there been a systematic effort within the past two years to have program and administrative offices evaluate and comment on the program?

11. Do policymaking officials understand the purpose of the directives management program?

12. Are directives used to communicate all policy?

13. Do program managers use directives to prescribe program procedures and standards?

14. Do officials who issue policy directives know if their directives have been received and are being implemented?

15. Do supervisors understand and use directives as a means of directing the actions of employees?

16. Are procedures for preparing directives available and being followed by persons who need to communicate policy and procedures?

17. Are procedures available and being followed to ensure that directives are reviewed at least every two years by originators to see if they are still needed?

18. Is the distribution of directives determined by their originators?

19. Do originators of directives obtain comments on proposed directives from those who will be affected?

20. Do organizational units receive only the directives they need?

21. Can directives be easily located when they are needed, and are they current?

22. Are departments that receive directives:
    ○ Filing new directives immediately?
    ○ Removing and destroying canceled directives promptly?

23. Do directives writers receive training and technical assistance on how to write directives in clear and concise language?

24. Is there a directive for each of the programs and administrative functions?

25. Is there a plan and schedule for the start and completion of directives for each program and administrative function not covered?

## Directives System Checklist

1. Directives procedures
    (a) Are procedures established and being followed to distinguish between directives of long-term significance and those of a temporary or one-time nature?
    (b) Does the directives system allow regional and branch offices to initiate or supplement directives?
    (c) Are provisions made for issuing directives that require immediate action?
    (d) Are all proposed directives checked for compliance with applicable statutes, other administrative regulations, and existing policies and procedures?
    (e) Are joint issuances (directives developed by two or more organizational units) provided for within the system?
    (f) Is there a schedule for reviewing, updating, and canceling existing directives?

|  | Yes | No |
|---|---|---|

2. Directives staff
   (a) Does the directives function have sufficient staff to effectively manage the directives program?
   (b) Is the staff sufficiently trained and experienced?
   (c) Does the staff provide training to management and operating units on the need for directives and how to develop and prepare directives?
   (d) Does the staff provide, as a minimum, editorial services such as editing for grammar, punctuation, capitalization, and use of abbreviations and symbols?
   (e) Are the clearance and coordination of directives accomplished within a reasonable time frame, such as 10 to 15 days for internal issuances and 60 to 90 days for external issuances?
   (f) Does the staff maintain a historical file of all directives?
   (g) Does the historical file contain complete background information on every directive issued?
   (h) Does the staff have a complete set of administrative regulations?
   (i) Do directives comply with these administrative regulations?
3. Writing directives
   (a) Are most directives written using active verbs and short words?
   (b) Do most directives use short sentences (about 15 words), limit the use of qualifying statements, and list conditions and exceptions separately?
   (c) Do most directives state the main point in the first sentence, tie sentences together, and use short paragraphs (10 or fewer lines)?
   (d) Is the Fog Index or some similar guide used to help measure readability?
4. Format
   (a) Does the directives format provide for
       ○ easy reading?
       ○ distinctive topic presentation and emphasis?
       ○ logical paragraph sequencing and identification?
       ○ adequate margins?
   (b) Are the name and short address of the originating office shown on the first page of the directive?
   (c) Is the name of the originating office or its abbreviation shown on each succeeding page of the directive?
5. Classifying and coding
   (a) Is there a subject classification system (a series of primary subjects with secondary and, perhaps, tertiary subdivisions pertaining to the programs and functions of the agency) for the directives system?
   (b) Is the existing subject classification system flexible enough to cover all the major functions of the organization?
   (c) Does the subject classification system employ terms commonly understood and used throughout the organization?
   (d) Does the classification system avoid splitting primary subjects?
   (e) Can subordinate subjects be added to or removed from the classification system without disturbing the arrangement of primary subjects?
   (f) Are cross-references kept current?
   (g) Are code numbers assigned to the subject classification terms?
   (h) Is the classification numbering pattern flexible enough to cover different aspects of the subject?

|  | Yes | No |
|---|---|---|

(i) Is there a list by classification code number sequence of all directives in the system? ____ ____

(j) Is the classification code number list updated or supplemented at least annually? ____ ____

(k) Are directives identified by classification symbols? ____ ____

(l) Do the classification symbols for directives contain the appropriate subject classification code number? ____ ____

(m) Does the classification symbol appear on all pages of directives? ____ ____

(n) Is an appropriate date shown below the classification symbol on each page? ____ ____

6. Indexes and finding aids

(a) Is there an alphabetic index (a listing in alphabetic order by subject) of all directives in the system? ____ ____

(b) Is the alphabetic index easy to read and use? ____ ____

(c) Is the alphabetic subject index updated at least annually? ____ ____

7. Publication

(a) Are there provisions for the economical publication of directives? ____ ____

(b) Is the scheduling of publication done by the directives staff? ____ ____

(c) Are directives put into the publication process within one week after their approval? ____ ____

8. Distribution

(a) Is the distribution system explained in a directive? ____ ____

(b) Is a distribution coding system used? ____ ____

(c) Does the distribution system provide a means for directing material to different organization levels and to different subunits within each level? ____ ____

(d) Are distribution lists and the quantities sent to each addressee reviewed semiannually? ____ ____

(e) Is there an established procedure followed for requesting and approving changes in the distribution list? ____ ____

(f) Is the distribution of directives made within five days after publication? ____ ____

(g) Are revisions and changes given the same distribution as the directives they amend? ____ ____

(h) Does the system allow for special handling (such as transmission by means of telecommunications) of directives when immediate action is required? ____ ____

(i) Does the distribution system have a procedure for efficiently addressing envelopes and labels? ____ ____

9. Changes and revisions

(a) Is there a prescribed method for identifying changes and revisions to existing directives? ____ ____

(b) When revised directives are issued, are changes "flagged" by asterisks, arrows, or some other means? ____ ____

(c) When a substantial part of a directive, 40 percent or more, is to be changed, is the entire directive reissued as a revision? ____ ____

(d) Is an appropriate revision date shown on revised directives? ____ ____

*Source:* Evaluating Directives Management. *General Services Administration, National Archives and Records Service, Office of Records Management (Washington, D. C.: U. S. Government Printing Office, 1980), pp. 3–9.*

## Take Corrective Action

*Identify and correct weaknesses*

The purpose of any evaluation program is to provide information that will strengthen and improve performance. Use the data and information obtained through the various evaluative methods to identify areas of the directives control program that need strengthening to improve performance.

The records manager, along with the central clearing point staff, should analyze the information obtained, identify areas needing attention, and plan and implement corrective action.

## A LOOK AT THE CASE

Now that Joyce Holloway has established the directives control program, she needs to determine the effectiveness of the system. Joyce may accomplish this evaluation by using verbal feedback from user groups and by using checklists to identify specific areas of the program that need improvement. Once these areas have been identified, plans to take corrective action should be made and implemented.

## TERMINOLOGY REVIEW

**Central clearing point.** Unit whose function is to provide coordination for the directives program.

**Directive.** An instruction from management, usually addressing policy and/or procedure.

**Directive on directives.** A document describing the framework and philosophy of the directives control program.

**Directives control program.** Systematic method for establishing, implementing, maintaining, and evaluating an organization's directives.

**Directives manual.** Handbook containing all of the organizational directives and the directive on directives.

**Directives program appraisal.** A directives evaluation addressing the policies and procedures for establishing, implementing, maintaining, and evaluating the total directives control program.

**Directives system appraisal.** A directives evaluation addressing the operational aspects of the delivery system itself.

**Originating unit.** Department creating the directive or responsible for the function or subject described in the directive.

*Policy.* Guideline for decision making.
*Procedure.* Statements of how to implement a policy.

## COMPETENCY REVIEW

1.  What is a directive and what communication direction does it represent?
2.  What are the benefits derived from using a directives control program?
3.  Explain the importance of an appropriate classification system to directives control.
4.  Describe the format of a directive.
5.  Explain the rationale for a directives distribution system.
6.  Which of the three distribution systems do you think is most effective? Why?
7.  What are the major categories to be considered when evaluating a directives control program?

## APPLICATIONS

1.  Draw the format for a directive.
2.  Using the format shown in this chapter, write a directive to establish a policy, procedure, or regulation regarding an issue that your instructor assigns. Suggested issues might include establishing a dress code, tardiness policy, class attendance policy, procedure for writing a directive, or a policy regarding smoking.

## CONCLUDING CASES

### A. Gott Associates

Mary Gott, after serving for a number of years as a records manager in a major utilities company, has opened her own very successful consulting business—Gott Associates. Mary employs ten additional consultants who have expertise in areas ranging from technical writing to management information systems. She has been more than satisfied with their performances until recently; there appear to be major misunderstandings among the staff. Mary, believing in the importance of employee participation in decision making, has allowed a high level of decentralization. In an effort to determine the source(s) of the staff misunderstandings, Mary has the following conversation with Murray Stein, one of the consultants.

Mary: There appears to be some communication problem within the company, and I'd like your thoughts on what the problem is.

Murray: Well, Mary, to be honest with you, I simply do not know what the policies of this company are. It seems that when I make a decision, someone says "That's not company policy." I find that I've violated something I didn't even realize existed!

Mary: Are there other problems?

Murray: Yes, often when I am working on a consulting job, the client simply doesn't understand our company's procedures. I'm not sure of the company's policies or procedures, and it's difficult to offer an explanation.

1. Identify two major problems that Mary must recognize.
2. What would you suggest as Mary's first action?
3. What other actions must she take?
4. With whom does the responsibility for poor communications reside?

## B. Consulting Firm

Lynn Rosso, a partner in a consulting firm, has contracted with a large metropolitan school system to evaluate their directives manual. The correspondence Lynn has received from James Donetti, the school system's assistant superintendent for administration, indicates that there are numerous policy statements originating at all levels, from department heads within schools to the school board. Procedures for implementing the policies do not accompany the policies, and the regulations are issued separately.

Lynn has also contacted a number of individuals within the school system to determine the type of directives distribution and directives manual maintenance procedures currently in place. The conclusion is that there are no established procedures for creation, maintenance, or distribution of directives. Lynn asked to have a copy of the directive on directives; the response was "We don't have one."

1. Where should Lynn begin in the evaluation of the directives manual?
2. What specific areas should Lynn examine based on the communications with the representatives of the school system?

## READINGS AND REFERENCES

General Services Administration, National Archives and Records Service, Office of Records Management. *Communicating Policy and Procedure*. Washington, D.C.: U.S. Government Printing Office, 1967.

General Services Administration, National Archives and Records Service, Office of Records and Information Management. *Evaluating Directives Management*. Washington, D.C.: U.S. Government Printing Office, September, 1980.

McMaster, John B. "The Case for Written Procedures." Problem Clinic, Dartnell. Chicago, Illinois (May 23, 1983).

Westington, Ralph. "Directives Management." Address given at ARMA Conference, Boston, Massachusetts, October 20, 1980.

# 18

# FORMS AND REPORTS CONTROL

## Competencies

After completing this chapter, you should be able to

1. define the function of forms within an organization.
2. list and explain the benefits of a forms control program.
3. explain the importance of top management support for forms control.
4. describe the steps to be taken in completing a forms analysis.
5. differentiate among the types of forms files.
6. list and explain the guidelines for forms design.
7. define the function of reports within an organization.
8. differentiate between the responsibilities of the records manager and those of other managers for reports management.
9. outline the procedures to be followed in establishing a reports management program.
10. explain the importance of a report review request form (or similar form) in the reports management program.
11. list and explain the criteria which should be applied when establishing or reviewing report requirements.
12. differentiate between the types of reports files.
13. explain the need for periodic report evaluation.
14. describe how the use of computer technology can result in more efficient distribution of reports within an organization

# Introductory Case

SYST Manufacturing, Inc., is a southern company which manufactures and sells promotional items ranging from pencils to chairs—anything on which an organization's name and/or logo can be printed. In the last three years, SYST has experienced rapid growth; its gross sales have increased from $500,000 to $2 million annually.

Necessity has forced many new procedures for sales and plant operations. However, the types and volume of forms and reports in use and being generated have not been controlled. SYST has a new records manager, Rhonda Murray, who has suggested that forms and reports control programs be instituted. Rhonda has noted that there were only 65 official forms in existence two years ago. With the rapid growth in sales has come an increase in personnel, products, sales territories, materials suppliers, customers, and forms.

1. What is a forms control program?
2. What benefits can SYST expect to receive from a forms control program?

Information gathering and processing is a critical task in every organization. The quality, completeness, and usability of the information gathered affect the productivity of administrative support personnel; the accuracy of many business operations, such as accounting and personnel functions; and the quality of most business decisions.

Forms and reports are the two types of business documents used in gathering, processing, and distributing information. Forms are primarily used for information gathering and processing. Reports present data to management for use in decision making. Because each is very important to information processing within every organization, forms and reports control functions are essential in records management.

*Information gathering and presentation*

## PROCESSING INFORMATION WITH FORMS

**Forms** are carefully designed documents used to gather and transmit information necessary for operational functions and for historical records. For example, an invoice received by an organization is a record of a purchase which is used to make a payment. Once paid, the invoice becomes part of the organization's historical records and provides documentation of items purchased, total amount of purchases, total amount of purchases by category for a month or year, or total purchases from a particular vendor. Traditionally, forms have been preprinted on paper media. Today many organizations with computerized electronic information systems are using electronic forms. These forms, called **templates**, are blank forms stored electronically in an information processing system. They are displayed on a terminal, such as a microcomputer, for "fill-in."

### Definition

A **forms control program** is a records management function designed to achieve the efficient collection and distribution of information through the use of forms. The forms control program should ensure that all necessary information (and only necessary information) is collected in the most efficient manner and distributed to those who need the information.

*Efficient data collection*

## Objectives

An efficient forms control program should produce time and cost savings in information processing for the organization. These benefits are achieved through the accomplishment of four objectives: (1) forms creation control, (2) elimination of obsolete forms, (3) standardized format, and (4) standardized and streamlined information distribution.

### Control Creation of Forms

There is a great temptation within every department or division of an organization to create a new form to collect information for each task as a need is perceived. Often the required information is already being collected for another purpose in the same department or in another department. The organization must pay not only for the cost to design and print new forms but also for additional personnel costs for processing. To control this problem, many organizations assign control of forms creation to one individual. The forms supervisor receives and reviews all requests for new forms to determine the need for the form and the most economical method of producing it.

### Eliminate Obsolete Forms

Organizations without forms control programs often retain old forms that have not been used in years. Perhaps a new form has taken the place of the obsolete one, or there is no longer a need for the form. These old or unusable forms should be destroyed to make room for those forms which are in use. The space occupied by obsolete forms is very costly. In addition, someone may use the obsolete forms still retained.

### Standardize Formats

Most organizations have several forms which require some of the same information. Standardizing the order in which that information is requested increases the efficiency with which those forms can be completed and processed. Also, standardizing the manner in which fixed data, such as the organization name, appear on a printed form may result in printing economies.

### Standardize and Streamline Distribution

A final benefit of a forms control program is that careful review of forms allows the distribution of information to be standardized and streamlined. The number of copies of each form must be justified so that those persons or departments who were receiving nonessential information merely because it is "nice to know" will no longer receive that information. Those persons or departments who receive essentially the same information from two or more forms will no longer have to deal with this duplication.

■

## A LOOK AT THE CASE

Rhonda Murray has carefully examined the benefits to SYST Manufacturing, Inc., of establishing a forms control program. In planning how to proceed, Rhonda must answer these questions:

1.  How can I present this information to top management in a manner that will ensure their support?
2.  Once I have gained top management support, what additional steps will be necessary to establish a forms control program?

■

## ESTABLISHING FORMS CONTROL

If an organization has no forms control program, the records manager must carefully assess the benefits of such a program to the organization and present these to top management. This presentation is a critical task, as the support of top management is essential to the success of the program.

### Top Management Support

In preparing to approach top management, the records manager must collect data to support the need for the program and present the data in a logical, businesslike manner. Before making a presentation to top management, the records manager should critique the material to be presented. The following questions may be helpful in determining the completeness and choice of data and the presentation methods:

* Is top management familiar with the concept of forms control?
* What concerns about forms have been expressed by management? (Remember, fewer forms are used in executive offices than in most other offices of the organization.)

- What concerns about forms have been expressed by users?
- What information does top management need to make a decision on the appropriateness of and need for a forms control program?
- Is the presentation of information clear, concise, and logical?

*Secure managerial support*

The goals of the presentation to top management on the need for a forms control program are to gain approval and to have top management communicate this approval to all departments of the organization. This communication will usually take the form of a directive which firmly establishes which individual has responsibility and authority for forms control. Top management support should be communicated in writing to ensure the recognition of the new forms control program and the individual responsible for it. Further communication of specific procedures in the forms control program should be left to the responsible party.

## Forms Analysis

A new forms control program cannot be undertaken without a thorough knowledge of the current status of forms within the organization. **Forms analysis** is the process of determining whether a form is necessary and, if so, how it should be designed to assure maximum efficiency. The first step in completing this analysis is to conduct a forms survey. Information obtained from the survey should include what forms are being used, what the purposes of these forms are, who is using the forms, what forms are no longer being used, and how effectively the forms are designed.

### Survey Current Forms

*Inventory departmental forms*

A **forms survey** is an inventory, by department, of the forms currently in use or in stock. A survey form such as the one in Figure 18–1 is distributed to each department head. In addition to requesting copies of forms originated in that department, the survey form should request information which identifies the form, its purpose, type, the number of copies distributed, the persons/departments receiving copies, frequency of use, the date it was last used, the date it was last revised, and its retention period.

*Eliminate duplicative forms*

This inventory provides the forms supervisor with a good overview of the current status of forms within the organization. Missing, duplicate, or inconsistent form numbers should identify unauthorized forms within each department. After being identified, unauthorized forms can be eliminated or replaced with legitimate forms. The forms survey also identifies the distribution path of each form. Analysis of these paths often reveals that copies are

Figure 18–1
Forms Survey Form

| Form No. | Title | Purpose | Type** | Frequency of Use | No. of Copies Distributed | Persons/ Departments Receiving Copies | Date of Last Use | Date of Last Revision | Retention Period |
|---|---|---|---|---|---|---|---|---|---|
| P201 | Purchase Requisition | Order Supplies | U | UF | 2 | sender purchasing | Daily | 1/80 | 1 yr. |

FORMS SURVEY*

DEPARTMENT _Finance_   DIVISION _Purchasing_   DATE OF SURVEY _1/13/--_
PREPARED BY _Robert Jones_   APPROVED BY _Alice Ray_

*Please attach three copies of each form listed.

**Identify the type of form as follows:
C – carbon interleaved unit sets
D – duplexed
F – continuous feed
S – single sheet
U – carbonless unit sets

F100-1
Rev. 9/86

being distributed unnecessarily. Controlling distribution assists in controlling printing costs of the form and, more importantly, minimizes the indirect costs of time to complete and process the forms.

**Evaluate Flow of Forms**

A minimum amount of time should be spent in transferring a form from one location to another. At least 75 percent of the time required to process a form should be working time. Consultation with users of forms will reveal if forms reach their destinations in a timely manner; for example, at off-peak work periods when the forms can be quickly processed.

**Eliminate Inactive Forms**

If the forms survey indicates that a particular form has not been used for a year or more, consideration should be given to eliminating that form from stock and from users' files or to combining the form with another form. Further consultation with the department head should be undertaken before this decision is reached.

**Establish Forms Files**

At the time of the forms survey, three copies of each form inventoried should be collected to be used in establishing the necessary forms files. Three files should be established—numeric, functional, and specifications.

*Numeric file*

A **numeric forms file** is established for each form in use. The numeric forms file becomes a historical record of that form and should contain such information as the original request for the form, a sample of the original form and each subsequent revision, a reorder record, and any correspondence related to that form.

*Functional file*

The **functional forms file** groups forms according to function. This grouping allows ready recognition of duplicate forms. Classification titles must be carefully selected for functional forms files. Each title should denote clearly the purpose of the forms contained in that file so that there can be no misinterpretation of the contents. Any lack of clarity results in lost forms and may contribute to the design of new forms when forms are already available for a particular function.

*Specifications file*

A **specifications forms file** groups forms according to the manner in which they are printed. Consequently, all carbon interleaved forms are filed together as are all single sheet forms, continuous feed forms, and so forth. Having these forms grouped together may contribute to printing economies if several forms of the same type can be reordered at the same time.

## Consolidate Forms

Organizing all forms into functional files allows the forms analyst to easily identify those forms which serve the same function. If very small differences occur on two or more forms in terms of the information requested, it should be determined whether one of the duplicative forms could serve for both purposes or whether one form could be designed to serve two or more similar purposes. Such consolidations of forms may be numerous in large organizations which have had no previous forms control, as each department may have designed its own form for a common purpose.

## Evaluate Forms Design

A final step in forms analysis is the evaluation of forms design. Specific guidelines for designing new forms are discussed later in this chapter. At this point, the forms analyst will want to evaluate how well each existing form works from the standpoint of the originator and the user. The following questions may assist in this evaluation:

- Does the form request the required information in a concise, unambiguous manner?
- Is the information requested in a logical sequence?
- Is sufficient space provided to record the requested information?

## Establish Staff Responsibilities

Assignment of staff responsibilities varies greatly with the size of the organization. In a very small organization, the forms control program, along with the control of all other written communications and documents, may be the responsibility of the office manager. The office manager may find it advantageous to have the forms vendor assume some responsibilities, such as design and inventory maintenance. A somewhat larger organization may have a records manager directly responsible for forms control. Most medium-to-large organizations, however, have a designated forms supervisor and perhaps several persons who are directly responsible to this person. Typical job titles and responsibilities for a forms control program were outlined in Chapter 14.

*Organization size affects scope of responsibilities*

## Publicize Forms Control Procedures

After the forms analysis has been completed and the forms department is organized, other departments should be informed of the operating procedures that have been established. Specific procedures differ from organization to organization; however, policies must cover at least three areas—originating forms, ordering forms, and evaluating forms.

### Originate Forms

Department heads need to be informed that they must discuss any perceived need for a new form with the forms analyst. Department heads must know whether to contact the forms analyst or, if there are several analysts, to contact the forms supervisor so that someone can be assigned to review their forms needs with them. Department heads must submit a form request (see Figure 18–2) that describes the purpose and justification for a new form. Comparison of the proposed form with forms in the functional files is essential to ensure that no form which could meet this need is presently available. Once it has been determined that there is no existing form for this purpose, the forms analyst can work with the department head in designing the required form.

*Determine need for form*

### Order Forms

Several procedures for ordering forms need to be clearly defined. The first of these procedures is to establish printing specifications and quantities for initial orders. These determinations are usually made by the forms analyst and form originator during the design phase. Type and size of the form are determined by cost consider-

Figure 18–2
Form Request

| | | 1. Date of request June 1, 19-- | 2. Form No. BC-487 |
|---|---|---|---|
| **REQUEST FOR A NEW OR REVISED FORM** | | 3. Date required July 4, 19-- | 4. Cost Project No. BC 68-007 |
| Complete all applicable items. Facts not known at time of request should be submitted as soon as available. | | 5. Department Programs Management | |

| 6. TITLE OR DESCRIPTION Monthly Programs Schedule | 7. Forms superseded BC-228 | 8. EDITION ☐ New   ☐ Other ☒ Revised |
|---|---|---|

| **9. TYPE OF FORM** | a. Category ☒ Administrative ☐ Processing ☐ Letter or memo ☐ Other ——————— | b. Number and/or title of prescribing directive OR ☒ None | c. Related forms none |
|---|---|---|---|
| | | d. Budget number and expiration date N/A | (Attach correct confidential statement when required.) |

| **10. USAGE** | a. Frequency of use ☐ One time ☐ When required ☐ Daily ☒ Monthly ☐ Quarterly ☐ Annually | b. Point of usage ☐ Single department ☒ Multiple departments ☐ Regional office ☐ Other ——————— | c. How data will be filled in (all or part) ☒ Typewriter ☐ Hand ☐ High Speed Printer ☐ Other ——————— | d. Number of copies prepared at one writing<br><br>e. Estimated monthly usage 125 copies<br><br>f. Total number required 1,000 |
|---|---|---|---|---|

| **11. REPORTING, ADDRESSING AND MAILING METHODS** | a. ☐ Personal interview ——→ : Starting date | b. ☒ Mail ——————→ : Mailing date July 30, 19-- |
|---|---|---|
| | (1) Description of portfolios, binders, etc., to be used<br><br>N/A | (2) How forms are to be addressed ☒ Typewriter ☐ High Speed Printer ☐ Other _____<br><br>(3) Description of envelopes to be used *Enter form numbers or attach sample(s)* plain white ☐ Self-mailer |

| **12. DESIGN SPECIFI-CATIONS** | a. Size of form 10 1/2" X 8" | b. Paper stock 24 lb. Hammermill | **13. STOCKING AND DISPOSITION** | |
|---|---|---|---|---|
| | c. Other specifications<br><br>N/A | | a. Where forms will be stocked ☐ Department ☒ Central ☐ Mail service ☐ Other _____ | b. Disposition of revised or superseded forms ☐ Use ☐ Dispose of when revision received ☒ Dispose of immediately |

| 14. Purpose of form<br><br>to furnish progress information on scheduled programs | c. Number of forms on hand ——————→ 200 | |
|---|---|---|
| | 15. Person to contact regarding this form Mary Way | |
| | Building No. Annex Q | Room No. 480 | Telephone Ext. 6547 |

| | **16. APPROVALS** | | |
|---|---|---|---|
| Form B13 12/86 | a. Department Manager *Lee Allen* | Date June 2 | b. Records and Information Administrator *R.J. Miller* | Date copy released June 4 |

SUBMIT TWO (2) COPIES TO:   Records Management Division

ations as well as by the originator's needs. At this time, a determination is also made as to whether this form will be printed in-house (if in-house printing facilities are available) or contracted out. Printing specifications are indicated on a form such as the one shown in Figure 18–3 and sent with a sample copy to the printer or print shop. Inventory procedures must also be established. Forms may be stored in the department from which they will originate or in a central location. Once reorder points have been established for each form, it must be clearly established whether the department is to reorder or to notify the forms department (usually the forms clerk) that the form should be reprinted. Without clearly defined inventory procedures, user departments may be tempted to order new unauthorized forms as well as to reorder authorized forms.

*Printing,
inventorying,
and ordering
procedures*

### Evaluate Forms

Procedures for forms control should clearly establish the intervals at which each form is to be evaluated for continued use. Any form which has not been used in over a year should be considered for discontinuance. Periodic evaluation also offers an opportunity to revise forms if the need for the data they collect should change. This could mean additions, deletions, or new arrangements of sections of the form to accommodate changing needs.

## A LOOK AT THE CASE

Once the forms control program had been established, Rhonda Murray directed her attention to one specific aspect of the program—forms design.

What design principles will facilitate the collection and use of data through forms?

## FORMS DESIGN

Efficient and cost-effective information collection and processing can only be achieved with well-designed forms. Forms design affects the accuracy and efficiency with which forms can be completed and processed. Because the design of the form affects its

Figure 18–3
Forms Specification Form

# Forms Specifications

(TO BE COMPLETELY FILLED OUT and SUBMITTED WITH EACH FORM ORDERED FROM THE PRINT SHOP)

| Department | Account Number | Date Ordered |
|---|---|---|
| *Micrographics* | *87-320* | *9/18/--* |

| Person Requesting Material | Signature of Supervising Authority | Telephone Number |
|---|---|---|
| *Martin Thomas* | *Jan Wilmot* | *3861* |

| Brief Description of Form or Form No. | No. of Copies Per Page | Size of Form |
|---|---|---|
| *11-M* | *100* | *4¼x14* |

| Number of Pages | Check Appropriate Box: |
|---|---|
| *1* | ☐ New Form (Make metal plate & store)    ☐ Quick copy    ☒ Rerun of Form Previously Printed |

| Color of Paper | Color of Ink | Miscellaneous Information |
|---|---|---|
| *white* | *black* | |

## CHECK APPROPRIATE BOXES

☐ FORM PRINTS ON ONE SIDE ONLY                ☒ PUNCH HOLES:        ☐ 2 Across top

☐ FORM PRINTS ON BOTH SIDES                                        ☒ 3 Down side

☐ RESET TYPE                ☐ COLLATE IN SETS        ☐ STAPLE

☒ PAD IN TABLETS                ☐ PERFORATE

☐ WRAP IN PACKAGES                ☐ NUMBER: Red Ink        ☐ Start . . . . . . . . . . .

Black Ink    ☐ End . . . . . . . . . . . .

(DO  NOT  WRITE  BELOW  THIS  LINE)

# For Reproduction Services Use Only

| Job Number | Date Completed | Date Promised | Date Received | Initials |
|---|---|---|---|---|

| STOCK | $ | CLEANUP | $ | Miscellaneous Information: |
|---|---|---|---|---|
| PLATEMAKING | | COLLATE | | . . . . . . . . . . . |
| PRESSWORK | | PERFORATING | | . . . . . . . . . . . |
| WRAP | | PUNCHING | | . . . . . . . . . . . |
| PADDING | | NUMBERING | | . . . . . . . . . . . |
| FINISHING CUTS | | STAPLING | | . . . . . . . . . . . |
| CUTTING DOWN LARGE STOCK | | FOLDING | | . . . . . . . . . . . |
| TYPESETTING | | TOTAL CHARGES | $ | Impressions |

| NUMBER of SHEETS | SIZE and DESCRIPTION |
|---|---|
| | |
| | |
| | |
| | |

WHITE COPY — Reproduction Services   ●   CANARY COPY — Retain for Your Records success in collecting information, careful attention must be given to this element of a forms control program.

## Goals of Forms Design

The basic goal of forms design is to facilitate the collection and use of data. In addition, forms design should seek to achieve printing economies.

### Facilitate Collection and Use of Data

If a form meets the goal of facilitating collection and use of data, the forms user should find it easy to determine what information is being requested and to complete the form. The form's originator (individual/department requesting information) should also be able to rapidly extract the needed data from the form. Specific design guidelines are discussed in the paragraphs which follow; however, three general principles contribute to meeting the goal of facilitating collection and use of data. First, each form should present a good visual effect. A form which has a jumbled or crowded appearance contributes to a poor attitude and a haphazard response on the part of the individual(s) who must complete it. An attractive, professional appearance is more conducive to care in the completion of the form. Second, the writing required should be minimized. This not only contributes to the ease of completion, but it also provides more uniform responses that are subject to minimal misinterpretation. Uniformity of responses allows for more efficient processing of the information on the forms.

*Design contributes to better collection and use of data*

Third, items should be placed on the form in logical sequence. This aids the user in completing the form and, again, aids in the processing function. If the same information is requested on more than one form, it should be requested in the same order on each form to assist in processing and in transferring the information from one form to another. The principle of consistent sequencing is particularly important if information from several forms is to be summarized on another form. The information should be placed on the summary form in the same order in which it appears on the forms being summarized.

### Achieve Printing Economies

At least three areas should be examined in order to meet the goal of printing economies. The first area is the size of the form. Forms should be designed on standard paper sizes whenever possible. These sizes are shown in Table 18–1. Using standard paper sizes saves in printing costs because of better use of paper and fewer pa-

*Standardize paper sizes*

per cuts. An added benefit of standard paper sizes is ease of filing and finding forms.

Table 18–1
Standard Forms Sizes

| (Column 1)<br><br><br><br>Size of Form<br>(in Inches*) | (Column 2)<br>Standard Sheet That<br>Permits Form in<br>Column 1 to be Cut<br>Without Waste<br>(in Inches) | (Column 3)<br><br>Number of<br>Forms Obtained<br>from Single<br>Standard Sheet | (Column 4)<br>Number of<br>Single Forms<br>Obtained from<br>One Ream<br>of Paper |
|---|---|---|---|
| $2\frac{3}{4} \times 4\frac{1}{4}$ | $8\frac{1}{2} \times 11$ | 8 | 4,000 |
| $2\frac{3}{4} \times 8\frac{1}{2}$ | $17 \times 22$ | 16 | 8,000 |
| $5\frac{1}{2} \times 8\frac{1}{2}$ | $8\frac{1}{2} \times 11$ | 2 | 1,000 |
| $5\frac{1}{2} \times 8\frac{1}{2}$ | $17 \times 22$ | 8 | 4,000 |
| $8\frac{1}{2} \times 11$ | $17 \times 22$ | 4 | 2,000 |
| $8\frac{1}{2} \times 14$ | $17 \times 28$ | 4 | 2,000 |
| $11 \times 17$ | $17 \times 22$ | 2 | 1,000 |

*The equivalent metric sizes are available from the American Paper Institute and from forms manufacturers.

*Source: B. Lewis Keeling and Norman F. Kallaus, Administrative Office Management, 9th ed. (Cincinnati: South-Western Publishing Co., 1987), p. 552.*

*Order appropriate quantities*

A second area which should be carefully considered is the number of copies ordered. Before printing decisions are made, consideration must be given to the number of copies of the form which will be used and to the quantities at which printing costs decrease. A final consideration is the color, quality, and weight of the paper to be used. These characteristics should be determined after considering the life and use of the form and, in the case of unit sets, the number of copies in the set. Forms which are routed through several departments and are, therefore, subject to much handling must be on better quality paper than those which are used once briefly and are not retained more than a few weeks. Color is an especially important consideration if documents are to be microfilmed. For example, blue paper will not reproduce well on microfilm.

*Select appropriate paper color, quality, and weight*

## Guidelines For Forms Design

Large organizations may develop a very specific set of guidelines for use in forms design. The guidelines contained in the following paragraphs should be helpful to organizations of all sizes.

### Divide Form into Parts

Every form can be divided into two parts: the facilitative area and the working area (see Figure 18–4). The **facilitative area** is usually at the top of the form and provides information which, although necessary, is peripheral to the main purpose of the form. Examples of information which may be contained in this area are the organization name and address, form title, form number, form revision date, instructions for completing the form, and routing instructions. Some of this information may be indicated in the bottom margin (either corner), thus splitting the facilitative area of the form. The location of form numbers and revision dates should be consistent within the organization. The **working area** of the form is that portion which requests information necessary to achieve the purpose for which the form was designed.

Figure 18–4
Parts of Forms

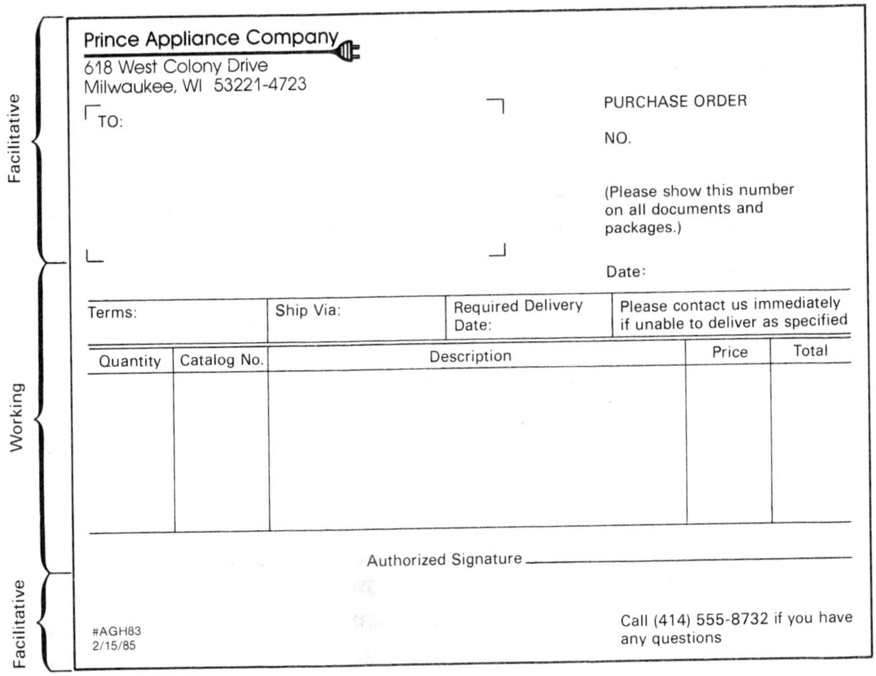

Prince Appliance Company
618 West Colony Drive
Milwaukee, WI 53221-4723
TO:
PURCHASE ORDER
NO.
(Please show this number on all documents and packages.)
Date:

| Terms: | Ship Via: | Required Delivery Date: | Please contact us immediately if unable to deliver as specified |
|---|---|---|---|

| Quantity | Catalog No. | Description | Price | Total |
|---|---|---|---|---|
| | | | | |

Authorized Signature

#AGH83
2/15/85

Call (414) 555-8732 if you have any questions

## Allow Adequate Spacing

The spacing of items and lines on a form contributes much to the good visual effect, ease of completion, and efficient processing of the information collected. Spacing must accommodate the characteristics of the method of completion. Forms are generally completed in one of three ways: handwritten, typewritten, or completed by computer. The spacing of the form should accommodate the most likely completion tool. Most forms are completed in handwriting or by using a typewriter; therefore, the form design must accommodate both methods of completion. The spacing used most frequently to accommodate both is 3-by-5 spacing, which allows three writing lines to a vertical inch (double spacing on most typewriters) and five characters to a horizontal inch to provide sufficient space for handwritten responses. Forms which are designed for the typewriter only should allow ten spaces to a horizontal inch to accommodate pica type. The arrangement of space for each item can then be determined by the length of the expected response.

## Use Upper Left Captions

Many forms are designed by using a typewriter, and the captions are simply placed at the left of the item. More efficient use of space is achieved when upper left captions (ULC) are used. (See Figure 18–5.) When forms are completed by using a typewriter, responses can be clearly distinguished from the upper left captions; the result is more efficient extraction of information.

## Use Captions Which Clearly Designate Desired Information

Captions should be brief but, more importantly, they should be very specific in the information they request. The form user should not have to question the intent of the form designer when responding. Captions should be carefully chosen and used consistently with all forms when the same or similar information is requested.

## Place Ballot Boxes in Front of Responses

This guideline applies whenever it is possible to predetermine all responses and to have the respondent select the appropriate response. Ballot boxes should be used whenever possible to improve the accuracy and efficiency of completing and processing the form. Respondents should be instructed to place an "x" in the appropriate box rather than a "✔" to minimize misinterpretations of responses. Yes or No choices should appear at the end of the

Figure 18–5
Upper Left Captions

AVOID THIS:

| REQUEST FOR COMPANY PARKING STICKER |
|---|
| Name_____ Social Security Number_____ |
| Department _____ Office Phone_____ |
| Home Address_____ |
| City, State_____ ZIP Code_____ |
| Make of Auto_____ Year_____ Color_____ License No._____ |

USE UPPER LEFT CAPTIONS:

| REQUEST FOR COMPANY PARKING STICKER | | | |
|---|---|---|---|
| Name | | Social Security Number | |
| Department | | Office Phone | |
| Home Address | City, State | | ZIP Code |
| Make of Auto | Year | Color | License Number |
| T-3<br>12/1/85 | | | |

question where the respondent would logically choose the proper response.

## Make Forms Self-Instructing

Instructions for completing forms should be clear and concise and placed near where they are needed. Those who read the instructions should not be subjected to a laborious discourse which insults their intelligence. Unless instructions are very lengthy, they should not be printed on the back of the form or on a separate sheet, as this increases the probability that they will not be read.

## Identify Organization on All External Forms

On forms which have interoffice functions, printing the organization's name and address or displaying its logo is often superfluous. However, when forms such as purchase orders, invoices, and customer surveys are sent to persons outside the organization, organization name and address are essential. This identification provides information critical to the processing of the form by the recipient and its proper return to the organization. In addition, this identification becomes an advertising tool for the organization.

### Display Forms Number and Identifying Title

This guideline may seem obvious, but it should not be overlooked. Having the form number and title printed in the same location on each form provides immediate identification of the form and alerts the recipient as to its purpose. In addition, it is necessary to the maintenance of inventory and the forms files and for user identification.

### Display Date

Each form should display its original date of printing or most recent revision date. This information usually appears with the form number. Its placement may appear in any location; however, placement on the form should be consistent within the organization. Printing the date on the forms ensures the use of current forms and identifies obsolete forms which should be purged from inventory and users' files.

### Show Distribution and Routing on Forms

The individual who completes a form should know where the form is to be sent and who will have access to the information contained on that form. Including distribution information at the top or bottom of the form is recommended.

## Computer Forms Design

Computer software packages may be used to design business forms. Templates, or blank forms which include lines, type, artwork, and logos, can be created and stored. These forms may be produced in color if appropriate printers are available. A user may enter the variable information into the template directly from a terminal and have the completed electronic form transmitted to another workstation or printed onto paper. Blank forms may be printed and then filled in. The same principles of form design apply to forms created by hand or electronically.

## Forms Design Checklist

Forms design is a multistep process. At the completion of the design process and before the form is released for printing, reviewing the form by using a forms design checklist is helpful. The checklist shown on the following pages demonstrates the types of items which should be checked and provides a beginning checklist for those organizations that do not already have one.

# FORMS DESIGN CHECKLIST

|  | Yes | No |
|---|---|---|

**Arrangement**

1. Considering the source of the information, its use, and the way users normally write or read it, are all items and groups of items arranged in the right sequence? ___ ___

2. Considering the type of storage equipment used, is the key information (data used to retrieve the form from a file) in the most visible location? ___ ___

Spacing

3. Considering the preparation method, has the proper amount of space been provided for each piece of requested information? ___ ___

4. Is the horizontal spacing adjusted to provide a minimum number of typewriter tab stops? ___ ___

5. Is the vertical spacing set so that the typist can always use the carriage return lever or key to move the carriage to the next line? ___ ___

6. Is all extra space used properly for emphasis, separation, and balance instead of looking leftover? ___ ___

Captions

7. Will all captions be understood by everyone who might use the form? ___ ___

8. Are captions placed in the upper left corner of each fill-in area? ___ ___

9. Will abbreviations be readily understood? ___ ___

10. Are group captions or headings used to identify major areas? ___ ___

Multiple-Choice Answers

11. Are possible answers given (including checkboxes) whenever they would help the users provide better answers in less time? ___ ___

12. Are the answers and check boxes arranged properly for the most productive and accurate fill-in? ___ ___

Instructions and Distribution

13. Can someone unfamiliar with the form complete it without referring to any other source for help? ___ ___

14. Have all unnecessary instructions and explanations been left off the form so that the user's intelligence will not be insulted? ___ ___

15. Are the distribution instructions shown on the form in the most effective way for its usage pattern and construction? ___ ___

16. If an interior copy is to be removed from the set before the others, is that copy slightly longer so that it can be easily identified and removed? ___ ___

## FORMS DESIGN CHECKLIST, continued

|  | Yes | No |
|---|---|---|
| 17. Is the self-mailer format used whenever applicable? | | |
| 18. Is the form designed to fit a window envelope whenever appropriate? | | |

### Margins
| | | |
|---|---|---|
| 19. Does the form have adequate margins for the required lock-up (gripper) space on the press? | | |
| 20. Are the margins adequate for any binding technique to be used, such as hole punches for notebooks and post binders? | | |
| 21. Are the margins adequate for other handling characteristics, such as filing, copying, stapling, and so on? | | |

### Type, Lines, and Screens
| | | |
|---|---|---|
| 22. Do all of the lines on the form do what they are supposed to do? (Some guide, some separate, some stop.) | | |
| 23. Is screening (shading) used where helpful to separate, highlight, or identify fields or zones, and not just to decorate the form? | | |
| 24. Within the same typeface, is there variation in the size of type, its boldness, and use of capital and small letters and italics to enhance the appearance and legibility of the form? | | |

### Construction
| | | |
|---|---|---|
| 25. Is the size appropriate for the printer, all users, and storage equipment? | | |
| 26. Is the construction right for the way the form will be handled? | | |
| 27. Is the paper right for the form's use and retention needs? | | |
| 28. Is the color of ink appropriate? | | |
| 29. Are all appropriate holes, perforations, scores, and so forth, shown on the layout and not interfered with by the copy? | | |

### Identification
| | | |
|---|---|---|
| 30. Is the title meaningful? | | |
| 31. Is the form properly identified with a number and date for ease in referencing, ordering, inventorying, and so on? | | |
| 32. Is the organization properly identified? | | |

### General
| | | |
|---|---|---|
| 33. Will this form accomplish its purpose with the minimum amount of effort by all users? | | |
| 34. Is this the best possible tool to do this job? | | |

## A LOOK AT THE CASE

Having successfully implemented a forms control program within SYST Manufacturing, Inc., Rhonda Murray now examines the need for a reports management program. SYST produces weekly, monthly, and annual reports of sales by region, product, and salesperson. In addition, numerous reports are prepared each year on the feasibility of new products, markets, sales techniques, manufacturing techniques, and other organizational procedures.

1. How do reports differ from forms?
2. What are the objectives of a reports control program?

## PROCESSING INFORMATION WITH REPORTS

Reports are generally upward communications to management. Reports control is necessary for managing reports proliferation and providing managers with the information resources necessary for responsible decision making.

A **report** is a written presentation of information useful in the decision-making process. A report may be narrative, tabular, or graphic; it may be on paper, microfilm, or on a computer screen. A report should be presented in the format that is most appropriate for the information presented and the audience to which it is presented.

*Upward communication to management*

### Types of Reports

Reports may be manually prepared or machine generated; they may be one-time occurrences, or they may be provided on a recurring basis. A variety of report types may be used in defining policy and in planning, controlling, and evaluating organizational operations. Among the most frequently occurring types of reports which should be included in the reports control program are

1. activity reports which reflect participation of personnel in special activities,
2. feeder reports which reflect contribution (as in a production report),

3. forecasts which provide projections,
4. status reports which reflect existing conditions,
5. summary reports which provide a recapitulation of activities,
6. consolidated reports which provide a compilation of existing data,
7. onetime reports which provide information required for one time only or by one or more departments, and
8. special studies reports which show results of research, development, and operational testing concerning a particular program or problem.

Many routine documents should be excluded from the reports control program. Among these are minutes of meetings, administrative procedures, and technical manuals.

## Objectives

Special needs of an organization must be incorporated into the objectives of its reports control program. Among those objectives common to most programs are the following:

1. Identify reports production and the need for these reports.
2. Provide visibility of report volume and its costs.
3. Control creation of new reports.
4. Establish a method for purging unnecessary reports from the system.
5. Determine the number of hours expended in report preparation.
6. Control distribution and provide audit controls.
7. Improve the quality and true effectiveness of reports.
8. Promote exception reporting where appropriate.
9. Reduce the number of items in reports through content analysis.
10. Consolidate, simplify, and standardize reports.

## A LOOK AT THE CASE

A reexamination of the objectives of a reports control program convinced Rhonda Murray of the need to establish such a program at SYST Manufacturing, Inc.

1. What procedures should be followed in establishing the program?
2. What criteria should be used in establishing report requirements?
3. How should reports be evaluated?

## ESTABLISHING REPORTS CONTROL

Obtaining top management support for reports control is vital to its success. When the management of an organization makes the decision to include a reports control program as an integral part of its total system of records control, the organization commits a portion of its resources to the reports control program. In order for the program to succeed, responsibilities, procedures, distribution, and evaluation must be clearly defined.

## Responsibilities

The first step in establishing a reports control program is to define responsibilities for the implementation and maintenance of the program. Reports control should be a responsibility of the records manager and staff. However, certain segments of reports control rest with other management levels. Management at all levels is responsible for reports generation. Therefore, management is also obligated to ensure that reports are limited to those essential to efficient operations, are produced in the most economical manner, and are distributed only to those with a need to know. Managers may also play a significant role in the initial and periodic inventories of recurring reports as requested by the records manager.

*Define implementation and maintenance responsibilities*

The reports originators and recipients have a responsibility beyond the generation and use of reports. They coordinate the completion of an inventory and report questionnaire as required by the records manager. The report originator and recipient also effect action to cancel a report or to reduce the number of copies distributed as indicated by the questionnaire findings.

The purpose of reports control is to provide a continuous advisory control over the ever-growing reports proliferation. However, since reports are operational tools, the final control remains with the individual/department requiring the report. The reports control system provides overall surveillance of reports. It initiates actions for conducting inventory and audit functions; it provides planning, implementation, and audit of machine-generated reports, in cooperation with word processing and data processing personnel. Finally, the reports control program staff prepares annual summaries which identify cost savings, reduction, or containment of reporting for management's review.

## Procedures

After the decision to control reports has been made and before implementation begins, policy is established for the program. This policy is communicated by outlining the scope of the reports information program and clearly enumerating procedures, including approval procedures of all report requests and reviews, output formats and layout, final report approval, and evaluation and follow-up.

### Reports Inventory

*Survey existing reports*

The first step in the development of the program is to conduct an inventory of existing reports. A reports inventory form, along with a letter of instruction and a listing of reports to be included or excluded from the inventory, is routed to all department heads. (See Figure 18–6.) Data requested on the reports inventory form includes department, location, account number, report title, number of pages, originator, and method of preparation. The completed inventory form is returned to the reports control staff.

Figure 18–6
Reports Inventory Form

**REPORTS INVENTORY**

| 1. DEPARTMENT | | | | 2. LOCATION | |
|---|---|---|---|---|---|
| *Industrial Research* | | | | *Building A, Rm. 37* | |
| 3. DATE *6/20/--* | | 4. ACCOUNT NO. *451-033* | | 5. TELEPHONE *8300* | |

| 6. REPORT TITLE | 7. NO. OF PAGES | 8. SECURITY CLASSIFICATION | 9. ORIGINATING DEPARTMENT | 10. PREPARATION | |
|---|---|---|---|---|---|
| | | | | MANUAL | DP |
| *Budget Status-X1* | *6* | *S-E* | *I Research* | | *X* |

CE15
11/86

The reports inventory is followed by reports questionnaires. (See Figure 18–7.) The report questionnaire is distributed to each report's originator. A questionnaire is completed for each report. The questionnaire is accompanied by a letter of instruction, which also includes completion dates. Completed forms (Section I only) are returned to the reports control staff; the originator retains a copy. One copy of each form is then reproduced for each name on

Figure 18–7
Report Questionnaire

| REPORT QUESTIONNAIRE | | | |
|---|---|---|---|
| **SECTION I** TO BE COMPLETED BY REPORT ORIGINATOR | | 1. REPORTS CONTROL NUMBER | |
| 2. REPORT TITLE | 3. REPORT DOCUMENT NO. | 4. DATE OF PREPARATION | |
| 5. REPORT ORIGINATOR AND DEPARTMENT | 6. ACCOUNT NUMBER | 7. TELEPHONE | |

| 8. REPORT SECURITY CLASSIFICATION ☐ S/RD  ☐ C/RD  ☐ UNCL.  ☐ OTHER _____   ☐ AWD SIGMA _____ |
|---|

| 9. DISTRIBUTION | | |
|---|---|---|
| COPY | RECIPIENT'S NAME | DEPARTMENT |
| | | |
| | | |
| | | |
| | | |
| | | |
| | | |
| | | |
| | | |
| | | |
| | | |
| | | |
| | | |

10. REPORT OBJECTIVE _____     11. METHOD OF PREPARATION ☐ MANUAL   ☐ DP

12. REPORT PREPARATION REQUIRES _____ HOURS     13. FILE CODE

14. REPORT IS PREPARED     ☐ DAILY ☐ WEEKLY ☐ MONTHLY ☐ _____

15. PRESCRIBING DIRECTIVE ON FILE?     ☐ YES ☐ NO  IF YES, CITE _____

**SECTION II** TO BE COMPLETED BY REPORT RECIPIENT

A. IS THE REPORT STILL REQUIRED?     ☐ YES (EXPLAIN BRIEFLY) _____
☐ NO (REMOVE FROM DISTRIBUTION)

B. ☐ REDUCE NUMBER OF COPIES TO _____ (WHEN APPLICABLE)

C. CAN THE FREQUENCY BE LESS OFTEN FOR YOUR PURPOSE?     ☐ YES  ☐ NO     IF YES, WHAT INTERVAL? _____

D. HOW CAN THIS REPORT BE IMPROVED? _____
_____
_____

| CI36 7/83 | E. RECIPIENT'S SIGNATURE | TELEPHONE | DEPARTMENT | ACCOUNT NO. |
|---|---|---|---|---|

the distribution list and then forwarded to these individuals. Section II of the report questionnaire is then completed by each recipient, who is asked to evaluate the report by answering questions relating to whether the report is still required, if the report can be improved, and so forth. Finally, the recipient signs the report questionnaire and returns it to the reports control staff.

*Evaluate existing reports*

The records manager reviews the completed questionnaires to

- delete from the distribution list the names of individuals no longer requiring the report,
- delete from the distribution list the names of individuals who fail to reply within 20 days,
- eliminate the report if distribution is reduced to zero,
- take follow-up actions to update distribution lists and improve reports based on comments made by recipients, and
- prepare a report inventory log. (See Figure 18–8.)

*Summarize survey data*

The report inventory log provides a summary of the report questionnaire data. Information gained from Section I of the report questionnaire provides a one-line entry reflecting the title of each report, its frequency, the number of pages, copies distributed, and the hours spent annually in preparation. Section II provides the number of copies eliminated and hours saved. The report inventory log is a "before-and-after" picture of the results of the report questionnaire.

Figure 18–8
Report Inventory Logs

| REPORTS INVENTORY LOG | | | | | | | | | | | |
|---|---|---|---|---|---|---|---|---|---|---|---|
| DEPARTMENT | | | | LOCATION | | | | | DATE | | |
| REPORT TITLE | SECURITY STATUS | | PREPARATION METHOD | | REPORT ACTIVITY | | | REPORT SAVINGS | | | REPORTS CONTROL NUMBER |
| | CLASSIFIED | UNCL | MANUAL | DP | ISSUE FREQUENCY | NO. OF COPIES DISTRIBUTED ANNUALLY | NO. OF HOURS USED IN PREP. ANNUALLY | NO. OF COPIES CANCELED | REPORTS REDUCED IN FREQUENCY | NO. OF COPIES ELIMINATED ANNUALLY / NO. OF HOURS SAVED ANNUALLY | |

CJ20
7/87

## New Reports

Each new report request must be evaluated in order for control to be maintained over new reports. A report review request is completed for each new report in order to ensure uniformity of review. (See Figure 18–9.) This report review form serves several purposes. It provides authorization, forms a nucleus for a functional file, and provides for review at regular intervals.

## Reports Criteria

Some of the criteria which should be applied when establishing or evaluating report requirements are

1. **use.** The use of the report should justify the cost of preparing, submitting, and distributing the report.

Figure 18–9
Report Review Request

| REPORT REVIEW REQUEST | | | 1. Date *12/10/--* |
|---|---|---|---|

**2. Report Title** *Progress Report - Inventory*  **3. From (Originator)** *Phillips*  **4. Report Due Date** *2/1/--*

**5. Report Security Classification**  ☐ S/RD  ☐ C/RD  ☒ Uncl  ☐ Other _____  ☐ AWD  Sigma _____

**6. Report Objectives**

*Monitor effect of new computerized inventory control procedure.*

**7. Identifying Authority for Report** (Procedure, Policy Letter, Reference, Memo, etc.)  *memo from Executive Vice President of Finance*

**8. DISTRIBUTION**

| Copy | Recipient's Name | Department |
|---|---|---|
| *1* | *J. Walsh* | *Finance* |
| *2* | *Ann Brehm* | *Production* |
| *3* | *Phil Lance* | *MIS* |
| | | |
| | | |
| | | |
| | | |
| | | |
| | | |

**9. Preparer's Name** *Patty Smith*  Account Number *883*  Date *11/15/--*

**10. Authorizer's Name** *Anne Phillips*  Account Number *434*  Date *11/15/--*

**11. Report Submitted on Form?** ☐ Yes ☒ No  If Yes, Give Form Number _____  Title of Form

**12. Number of Pages** *2*  **13. Report Frequency** *bimonthly*  **14. Method of Preparation** ☐ Manual ☒ DP

**15. Cost of Preparing Report Annually**

Preparation ___*15*___ x ___*20*___ = $ *300.00*
　　　　　　　　Hours 　　　Cost per Hour

Routing ___*3*___ x ___*1*___ = $ *3.00*
　　　　　No. of Copies 　Cost per Copy
　　　　　Dist.

Total $ *303.00*

**16. File Code** *AF 37*

**17. Estimated Length of Time Report Will Be Published**  Months *12*  Years

**18. Do You Retain Master or a Copy of This Report?** ☒ Yes ☐ No  If Yes, for How Many Years? *long-term*

**19. Reviewed by Reports Control**  Reports Control Number

CF16 8/84  Date _____  Signature _____

2. **essentiality.** Reports should be instituted or continued only as a means to maintain essential data. A report is not directed merely as a device to verify the accuracy of another report.
3. **economical procedures.** Data should be collected, processed, and transmitted by the most economical means; the means should be consistent with any established priorities. This includes sampling, change reporting, and reporting by exception.
4. **utilization of data.** Data submitted to an office should be used to the maximum extent by other offices within that group. Data collection and storage must be limited to users for which a valid need exists.
5. **coordination.** Requests for reports should be fully coordinated with preparation and process activities.
6. **combined reports.** The redesign of reporting requirements should be a continual process to provide efficient compilation of essential data. Duplication of data collection and transmission should be held to the minimum and be consistent with the need to identify information in separate reports.
7. **summarization.** Reports should be briefly summarized. Only information that is essential should be incorporated.
8. **deadlines.** Deadlines should be realistic. Attempting to meet impossible or impractical deadlines can result in additional costs, inaccuracies, and the need to resubmit.
9. **levels of organizations.** In order to be monitored for accuracy, reports should flow through established levels of organizations.
10. **frequency.** Frequency of the report should be dictated by the rate of data change.
11. **simplicity.** Data should be prepared and processed by the most direct method.
12. **applicability.** Reports should include only that information deemed essential to a specific activity.

## Reports Files

Reports files are helpful in maintaining a sound reports control program. A file which includes the written procedures for use of the report, a copy of the report, and a report control form should be established for each report. The report control form includes a description of the report, the initiator, frequency of report, distribution, analysis of cost, and a date for annual review. Some organizations prefer to maintain two files — a functional reports file and a historical reports file. The **functional reports file** maintains information about reports with a like function. This file helps to minimize duplication, as each new request for a report would be checked against the functional reports file. In instances where an

*Functional reports file*

existing report contains much of the information that is requested on the new report, an examination of the functional reports file makes that comparison relatively easy. It may be that information not included could be incorporated into an existing report; this would eliminate the need for an additional report. The **historical reports file** maintains a history of each report. When questions arise regarding the origination or purpose of a report, reference should be made to the historical reports file.

*Historical reports file*

### Reports Catalog

Large organizations often issue a reports catalog. This is helpful in making organization members aware of information available to them in report form. A reports catalog often curtails the need to print large numbers of copies of reports; employees receive reports catalogs and know that these reports are available to them in a central location.

## Distribution

The method of distribution for reports can be the same procedure as that for directives distribution (see Chapter 17). This system provides control, verification, and an audit trail.

## Evaluation

Report evaluation is provided via feedback from originators, users, and recipients. Unless firm control is exercised, all recipients are not users. Several methods are available for establishing usage. One method is to request feedback by using a questionnaire such as the one shown in Figure 18–10. The problem with this approach is that many managers think they must have copies of all reports whether the reports are used or merely filed. Answers to this type of questionnaire are often less than accurate. A different approach, and usually more effective (though less forthright), is to bury the same questionnaire deep within the report. You will notice that the notation is made that "If you wish to continue to receive this report, you must respond within 10 days." This is highly effective.

*Feedback from originators, users, and recipients*

A more comprehensive analysis of each report should be made on its anniversary date. This analysis is an in-depth review of all aspects of the report from the viewpoints of the users and of the preparers. A sample reports review guide is shown in Figure 18–11.

Figure 18–10
Report Evaluation Form

---

## REPORT EVALUATION FORM

TO: Report Recipient                                      DATE:

To assist in reducing the volume of paperwork, your evaluation of this report is needed. Please check the item below that, for you, best describes the attached report copy —

☐ 1. I don't really need this report; please discontinue it.

☐ 5. I need the report as is; please continue it. (I keep it on hand for ___ months.)

☐ 2. I need the information in the report but could obtain it from a reference copy if one were made available in my general area.

Additional comments on Item No.:

1._____

2._____

3._____

☐ 3. I need the information, but a less frequent copy would serve my purposes. I would like a copy (circle one): weekly, monthly, quarterly, annually.

4._____

5._____

☐ 4. I need this report, but it would be much more useful if the report could be modified in format or content.

| Date | Your Name | Department |
|------|-----------|------------|
|      |           |            |

Note: If you wish to continue to receive this report, you must respond within 10 days.

F80
1/85

Figure 18–11
Reports Review Guide

| REPORTS REVIEW GUIDE | DATE | FILE NUMBER | | |
|---|---|---|---|---|
| TITLE OF REPORT | | | | |
| Note to Reviewing Officers—Check appropriate column. If "Questionable" is checked, use separate sheet for recording changes or observations. | | | Ques-tion-able | Satis-fac-tory |
| PART I: To be completed by the using office<br><br>1. USEFULNESS | | | | |
| 1. THE REPORT AS A WHOLE. Who uses it? How is it used? What is its purpose? Should it be continued? | | | | |
| 2. USE OF EACH ITEM. Is every item used? Are there any items missing? | | | | |
| 3. USE OF EACH COPY. Are all distributed copies used to good purpose? | | | | |
| 4. USE OF NEGATIVE REPORTS. Are negative reports required? What use is made of them? | | | | |
| 5. FREQUENCY. Is frequency adequate? Is a lower or diminishing frequency feasible? | | | | |
| 6. VALUE VERSUS COST. Is the value of the report worth its cost? | | | | |
| 7. EFFECTIVENESS. How effective a management tool has this been? | | | | |
| 8. CONTENT. Do the contents develop trends by properly mixing historical, current, and projected conditions? | | | | |
| 2. QUALITY | | | | |
| 1. ADEQUACY AND SUITABILITY. Are scope and content of the report tailored to needs? | | | | |
| 2. COMPARISONS. Are comparisons provided against goals, standards of past performance, or some other known factor? | | | | |
| 3. REPORTING UNITS. Are units proper for meaningful interpretations? | | | | |
| 4. SIGNATURE AUTHENTICATION. Are signatures of verifying and approving officials included when necessary? | | | | |
| 5. ACCURACY. Is source data accurate? What is its record of dependability? | | | | |
| 3. TECHNIQUES | | | | |
| 1. INTEGRATED REPORTING. Are data needs of other levels and offices tied in? | | | | |
| 2. EXCEPTION REPORTING. Would it be appropriate to report conditions only when other than normal? | | | | |
| 3. SAMPLING. Would the sampling of a few offices provide representative and reliable data? | | | | |
| 4. STANDARDIZATION. If forms are used, do all offices use the same form? If narrative is used, is there a standard of acceptability? | | | | |
| 4. EASE OF USE | | | | |
| 1. STYLE OF PRESENTATION. Does the style of presentation provide clarity and finding ease? Is it condensed? Are graphics used well? | | | | |
| 2. SUMMARY INFORMATION. Would just a summary be better? | | | | |

Reports Review Guide, continued

| PART II: To be completed by the preparing office | Ques-tion-able | Satis-fac-tory |
|---|---|---|
| **1. POLICY** | | |
| 1. PREPARATION. Has a procedure been written for the preparation of the report? | | |
| 2. REVIEW. Are the report and the preparation procedures regularly reviewed? | | |
| **2. SHORT CUTS** | | |
| 1. ANOTHER AVAILABLE SOURCE. Is the data in some other report? Is the data more accessible from another office? | | |
| 2. COMBINATION. Could this report be combined with another report? | | |
| 3. BY-PRODUCT. Is it possible to get the report as a by-product of some other process (i.e., multicopy form set)? | | |
| 4. DISTRIBUTION. Are all copies distributed essential? | | |
| **3. TIMING** | | |
| 1. ADEQUATE TIME. Do due dates give enough time for preparation and review? | | |
| 2. OFFICE WORKLOAD. Has preparing office workload been considered? Could end of month or end of year reports be avoided? | | |
| 3. REPORTING PERIODS. Are there periodic conflicts among respondents or between feeder and summary reports? | | |
| 4. SUBMISSION. Has complete and/or timely submission of this report been a problem? | | |
| **4. FORMAT** | | |
| 1. PRESENTATION. Does the type of presentation—narrative, graphic, tabular—best portray the information? | | |
| 2. STRIP REPORTING. Is it possible to match feeder reports from several sources and compile by stripping? | | |
| 3. ARRANGEMENTS AND SIZE. Are items grouped and sequenced to work flow? Is spacing adequate for responses? | | |
| 4. LAYOUT. Does the layout lead the reader to prompt and accurate conclusions? | | |
| 5. ARRANGEMENT OF RECORDS. Should records be arranged differently to simplify reporting? | | |
| **5. SOURCES** | | |
| 1. FEEDER REPORTS. Are procedures for feeder reports provided to ensure uniformity and simplicity? | | |
| 2. DIRECT USE OF RECORDS. Could actual records or copies be sent instead of prepared report? | | |
| 3. CUMULATIVE DATA. Can fiscal or statistical data be kept on a cumulative basis in order to eliminate last minute workloads? | | |

JA 13620
1/86

## USING COMPUTER TECHNOLOGY

Computer technology is having a significant impact on preparing, transmitting, and controlling reports. Report writers and users can use word processing, graphics, and database software to improve efficiency and to expedite the reporting process.

### Document Preparation

Word processing software assists the report writer in writing and editing reports quickly and efficiently. Software is available which checks for grammatical, punctuation, and spelling errors as well as word choice. When reports are stored electronically, they are easily corrected and ready for reuse.

In many information processing systems, the user can access data from a company database and incorporate it into a report. Graphics software makes possible the conversion of tabular and numeric information into graphic displays, such as charts and graphs.

### Document Transmission

Reports stored electronically may be transmitted over communication lines from one terminal to another rather than being sent manually in paper form. Also, they may be stored in a database until accessed by a user. In electronic storage systems, reports are available in a more timely manner, yet time and money are not wasted in distributing reports unnecessarily.

### Document Control

Databases may be used to store indexes of reports prepared within the organization. In addition, catalogs describing available reports may be stored. Such a system may also record who accesses reports and should restrict the access of reports to authorized users. Also, functional and historical report files may be stored electronically for improved access.

■

## A LOOK AT THE CASE

Rhonda Murray has implemented forms and reports control programs at SYST Manufacturing, Inc. During the next six months, she will observe the success of the procedures which have been established and adjust them as needed.

■

## TERMINOLOGY REVIEW

■ *Facilitative area.* The section of a form, usually at the top, which provides printed information that, although necessary, is peripheral to the main purpose of the form, such as organization name, form number, and instructions.

*Forms.* Carefully designed documents used to gather and transmit information necessary for operational functions and for historical records.

*Forms analysis.* The process of determining whether a form is necessary and, if so, how it should be designed to assure maximum efficiency.

*Forms control program.* A records management function designed to achieve the efficient collection and distribution of information through the use of forms.

*Forms survey.* An inventory, by department, of the forms currently in use or in stock.

*Functional forms file.* A forms control file which groups forms according to their purpose.

*Functional reports file.* A reports control file which maintains information about reports with a like function.

*Historical reports file.* A reports control file which maintains a history of each report.

*Numeric forms file.* A forms control file which documents the history of each form and which contains such information as the original request for the form, a sample of the original form and each subsequent revision, a reorder record, and any correspondence related to that form.

*Report.* A written presentation of information useful in the decision-making process.

*Specifications forms file.* A forms control file which groups forms according to the manner in which they are printed.

*Templates.* Blank forms stored electronically in a computerized information processing system.

*Working area.* The section of a form which requests information necessary to achieve the purpose for which the form was designed.

## COMPETENCY REVIEW

1. Define the function of forms within an organization.
2. Define a forms control program. What benefits does it offer an organization? What is the importance of top management support?
3. What is forms analysis? Describe the steps to be undertaken in completing a forms analysis.
4. Many organizations maintain three types of forms files. Define each in a manner that clearly differentiates its function.
5. Which two types of files are also maintained for reports? What is the purpose of each?
6. List at least five guidelines for forms design and state the importance of each.
7. What are reports? What is their function within an organization?
8. Differentiate between the responsibilities of the records manager and those of other managers for reports management.
9. How can the use of computer technology result in more efficient distribution of reports within an organization?

## APPLICATIONS

1. Prepare a one-page application for employment form. Include the following categories of information:

   a. name
   b. address
   c. form number/revision date
   d. date of birth
   e. education and training
   f. work experience

   g. form title
   h. current date
   i. social security number
   j. references
   k. company name and address
   l. title of job applied for

2. Jones Enterprises has never had a reports control program. Alex Smith, the new records manager, has obtained top management approval for such a program.
   a. Outline the procedures to be followed in establishing this program.
   b. Explain the importance of a report review request form (see Figure 18–9) or a similar form in this program.
   c. List and explain at least five criteria which should be applied when report requirements are established.
   d. Explain the importance of periodic report evaluation to the success of the reports management program.

## CONCLUDING CASES

### A. Vocations United

Erin Watkins has just been hired as the reports supervisor of Vocations United, a large educational association. Erin was hired to develop and implement a reports control program for the association. In accordance with current procedures, each department now gets an information copy of every report generated by the association staff. Since the organization now has a staff of 500 and generates an average of 20 reports each month, this distribution is presenting processing cost and storage problems.

Erin decides to finalize her plans for controlling reports. List the steps to be completed in developing and implementing the reports control program.

## B. The Royals Corporation

Ralph Peters has just been hired as the forms manager for Royals Corporation, a philanthropic organization whose primary goal is the support and encouragement of community theaters. The Royals Corporation employs 3,000 workers at its headquarters in Washington, D.C.

One of Ralph's first duties is to design a forms control program. He feels that he must conduct a forms survey first. But when Ralph mentioned this to his records manager, Andrea Martin, he received this reply, "Our employees will never take the time to complete a survey form; they will never see the value in it." Ralph's job of convincing Andrea Martin to support a forms survey is not going to be easy. Prepare Ralph's defense.

1. How does the forms survey relate to forms analysis?
2. When the forms survey is completed, how can the information be used?
3. After obtaining Ms. Martin's support, what is Ralph's next step?

## READINGS AND REFERENCES

### ▪ Forms Management

Bubnash, George. "Obtaining Maximum Benefits from Forms Management." *Records Management Quarterly,* Vol. 2, No. 1 (January, 1968), p. 37.

"Electronic Publishing—A Boon for Forms Management," *The Office,* Vol. 101, No. 12 (December, 1985), p. 76.

"Forms Management Survey," *Records Management Quarterly,* Vol. 17, No. 2 (April, 1983), p. 54.

Horton, Forest W., Jr. "The Formless Form," *Records Management Quarterly,* Vol. 18, No. 3 (July, 1984), p. 48.

Jacob, Marvin. *Form Design: The Basic Course-Plus!,* Cleveland, Ohio: Formsman, Inc., 1980.

Keeling, B. Lewis, and Norman F. Kallaus. *Administrative Office Management.* 9th ed. Cincinnati: South-Western Publishing Co., 1987.

Kerrigan, Douglas. "Gaining Control Over the Cost of Business Forms," *Office Administration and Automation,* Vol. 46, No. 6 (June, 1985), p. 27.

Matthies, Leslie H. "Coordinating Changes on Forms," *Journal of Systems Management,* Vol. 38, No. 8 (August, 1985), p. 41.

McCoy, Michael J. "Selling Forms Management to Top Management: A Consultant's View." *Information and Records Management,* Vol. 13, No. 8 (August, 1979), p. 14.

Myers, Gibbs, and Joseph M. Cherico. "Forms Design in the Fast Lane," *Journal of Systems Management,* Vol. 36, No. 4 (April, 1985), p. 30.

Myers, Gibbs, and Leslie H. Matthies. "Pen and Pencil Forms," *Journal of Systems Management,* Vol. 35, No. 7 (July, 1984), p. 40.

Osteen, Carl E. *Forms Analysis: A Management Tool for Design & Control,* Stamford, Conn.: Office Publications, 1969.

Raines, Gar, ed. *Forms for the 80's: How to Design and Produce Them,* Philadelphia: North American Publishing Company, 1980.

Russell, W. James. "Good Forms Management Improves Productivity," *The Office,* Vol. 99, No. 5 (May, 1984), p. 78.

Zitzner, John. "Forms Management: How to Find the Right Package," *The Office,* Vol. 101, No. 12. (December, 1985), p. 132.

## Reports Management

Hayes, Kenneth V. "Creating a Reports Catalog or Inventory," *Records Management Quarterly,* Vol. 17, No. 1 (January, 1983), p. 21.

_____. "Developing a Standard Practice or Procedure on a Reports Program," *Records Management Quarterly,* Vol. 18, No. 2 (April, 1984), p. 44.

_____. "Documenting the Results from a Reports Improvement Program," *Records Management Quarterly,* Vol. 18, No. 1 (January, 1984), p. 38.

_____. "Improvement of Reports and Implications for Information Management," *Records Management Quarterly,* Vol. 18, No. 3 (July, 1984), p. 54.

_____. "Organizing a Reports Program in a Large Company," *Records Management Quarterly,* Vol. 16, No. 4 (October, 1982), p. 20.

_____. "Procedures for Analyzing Reports Part I — The Quantitative Approach," *Records Management Quarterly,* Vol. 17, No. 3 (July, 1983), p. 42.

_____. "Procedures for Analyzing Reports Part II — The Qualitative Approach," *Records Management Quarterly,* Vol. 17, No. 4 (October, 1983), p. 24.

_____. "Staffing a Reports Improvement Program," *Records Management Quarterly,* Vol. 17, No. 2 (April, 1983), p. 33.

Schiell, Chuck. "Reports Control and Evaluation." *Records Management Quarterly,* Vol. 12, No. 3 (July, 1978), p. 24.

# 19
# MICRORECORDS CONTROL

## Competencies

After completing this chapter, you should be able to

1. describe general microform production requirements.
2. list and explain additional criteria to be used in the selection of a service bureau.
3. compare in-house microfilm production with service bureau contracted production.
4. describe an objective way in which service bureau selection may be made.
5. describe measures that may be used to control unnecessary microforms distribution.
6. explain how updatable microfiche is a form of control.
7. describe factors that should be evaluated to determine the effectiveness of a microrecords program.

# Introductory Case

A major records management consulting firm has just submitted a microforms feasibility study to the management of Design Associates, Inc., an international architectural design firm. The study showed a positive cost benefit curve; both short- and long-term benefits could be realized with microforms usage. The consultants recommended that Design Associates, Inc., contract with a service bureau to perform the operations.

1. What are some of the considerations that Design Associates' managers should examine before making the decision to contract with a service bureau?
2. Why do you think the consultants did not recommend an in-house operation?
3. What types of controls should management exercise regarding the microrecords system?

Microrecords have become an increasingly popular form of records storage. The increased usage demands a careful evaluation of the control system that monitors the creation and use of microforms.

# PLAN MICRORECORDS CONTROL PROGRAM

*After the*
*feasibility study*

After a micrographics feasibility study has been completed (see Chapter 7) and reviewed, and the decision has been made to implement a micrographics program, consideration must be given to a microrecords control program. If the feasibility study only addresses whether it would be viable to convert from a paper-based system to a micrographics system, then control decisions must be made regarding where to locate the new micrographics system and how to control the microfilming operation.

## Examine Microforms Production Requirements

*In-house*
*or offsite*

Microforms can be produced either in-house or offsite. An in-house facility is operated within the company location; offsite locations are usually operated by a service bureau. Regardless of where the microfilm production takes place, certain general requirements for production efficiency and effective use must be met. These requirements are discussed in the following paragraphs.

### Quality Assurance

*Quality criteria*

The quality of the output is one of the most important considerations in the production of microfilm. Quality may be measured in terms of clarity, density, eye-readable headers, and film thickness. Poor quality film that is difficult to read or deteriorates is unacceptable regardless of the superiority of any or all other criteria.

### Legal Acceptability

Quality of the original film and all copies must be maintained. Specific legal requirements must be met; the requirements differ

*Original*
*film/copy quality*

according to the application to be filmed. Admissibility of microfilm records in federal courts is contingent upon meeting the following requirements:

1. the microfilm was made in the regular course of doing business;
2. filming was accomplished in a manner which accurately produced a durable copy of the original document; and
3. the copy was satisfactorily identified.

Inferior quality of either the original or the copies is unacceptable and should not be tolerated. Minimum quality standards must be established, monitored, and enforced. This is often more easily accomplished by an in-house operation.

## Production Turnaround Time

Turnaround time requirements differ according to the needs of the individual users within the organization. For some applications, fast turnaround time is not essential. It may be necessary to know only that the microform will be delivered at the requested specified intervals. Other applications, however, may require very quick turnaround in order for employees to perform their jobs in a timely manner. In either case, users should expect to receive microforms within the same time frame as they currently receive hard copy.

*Time required for processing*

The microfilming production schedule in an in-house operation is made within the organization by persons knowledgeable about the needs of the individual users. Priority requests may be given preference, and consideration does not have to be given to scheduling other users who are outside the company. When an off-premises service bureau is contracted to perform the processing, equal consideration must be given to each client. A service bureau off-premises cannot afford to be as responsive to the needs of the individual user as can an in-house staff operation.

## File Integrity

**File integrity** refers to the accuracy and completeness of the file. In an in-house operation, responsibility for lost or misfiled records lies with the organization's staff. When an outside agency is employed to produce microfilm, "tracking" misplaced records is more difficult because more people are handling the records. Organizational control over the integrity of the files, if not lost, may be considerably diminished.

## Information Control

In an in-house operation, data never leaves the premises for processing. Any required information is always accessible to users; there is no dependence on an outside agency. Many users see this complete control over information as vital to the information processing function.

## Data Security

Information security is a major concern to all organizations. The current emphasis on legislation and enforcement of individual privacy/freedom of information forces organizations to be especially

*Security control*

careful of the security of their documents. In-house operations provide better control over the physical security of information as well as better control over employees responsible for maintaining information security.

### Standards Consistency

*Standards control*

Quality checks must be made often so that any deviation from the desired standards can be immediately detected and corrective action taken. Service bureaus also actively seek to maintain consistent standards and stress the importance of uniformity to their employees. The fact remains, however, that control over standards is no longer in the hands of the organization. The control has moved to an outside agency, and deviations from company standards must be addressed through communications between the company and the service bureau. Immediacy is lost and corrective action may be delayed.

### Equipment Required

The equipment required in microforms production varies according to the needs of the organization, the input to be processed, and the output desired. Input may be source documents or computer output film; output may be in the form of computer output microfilm or microfiche. Therefore, equipment must be selected after analyzing the needs, input, and desired output. Companies may not wish to spend their resources to properly equip a facility. Additional cost considerations for equipment include maintenance and equipment downtime.

### Training Required

*Refilming costs*

Trained personnel are required to run the microfilm production operation. Consequently, the provision for training and regular updating of the staff is an important consideration.

Many companies do not have the trained microfilm staff, nor do they have the expertise necessary to train inexperienced personnel. An additional cost incurred by inexperienced microfilming staff is the cost of refilming during the learning curve.

### Space Needed for Facility

Some companies do not have the space required to house the equipment and staff for a complete microfilming operation. Other companies may not want to reallocate space currently used for other company operations.

## Determine Production Location

Microforms can be produced in-house as an organizational operation or by a service bureau on a contracted basis. Each approach to microforms production has benefits and limitations. These benefits and limitations must be identified and carefully evaluated prior to making the decision regarding in-house or service bureau microfilming.

### In-House Production

In the organizational operation, the production facility is owned, equipped, staffed, maintained, and controlled by the organization. An in-house operation may be contracted to a service bureau. The microfilming operation, although located on the premises, is set up and staffed by the service bureau. Many companies believe the latter arrangement provides all of the advantages of an in-house operation without the expense involved in the lease/purchase of equipment and hiring and training personnel to staff the facility. A third in-house option is a "turnkey" approach. An outside bureau is contracted to plan and implement the conversion and to supervise its operation until the organizational staff has the capacity to keep the microfilm program running efficiently.

### Contracted Services

**Contracted microforms services** are microforms contracted to a service bureau for processing offsite at the service bureau facility. A service bureau may offer a number of options to an organization. One of their major services, of course, is to convert the organization's documents into microforms. In addition to document conversion, a service bureau may conduct a systems analysis based on the study of the client's records and needs and present a proposal for a microfilming program. The study would identify the types of records most suitable for microfilming. In addition to the identification, a cost comparison of the proposed and present systems would be prepared for the client's consideration.

### Effect of Location

Location affects both costs and turnaround time. If the location of the facility is inconvenient, it will not encourage use and, therefore, not be conducive to growth. Inconvenient or distant locations increase transportation costs, delivery costs, and turnaround time. Carefully orchestrated transportation arrangements, which add to administrative support costs, are also required. Distances up to fifteen miles (if easily accessible) are acceptable.

## Cost Benefit Analysis

A cost benefit analysis should be conducted to determine which microform production location is most appropriate for the individual organization. The benefits must at least equal, if not exceed, costs. Some benefits, however, are not tangible, but they must still be considered in the determination. For example, the confidence and security an executive might feel by having all records processed in-house is an intangible benefit—one that cannot be measured in dollar value.

Service bureaus spread overhead expenses over many users, so the price/cost is often significantly less than for an in-house facility. Long-term costs should be considered as well as initial start-up costs.

## Establish Service Bureau Selection Criteria

In addition to the general microforms production requirements discussed above, other considerations unique to service bureaus are reputation, references, sample work, contractual arrangements, document security, and file integrity.

### Reputation

What is the reputation of the service bureau with regard to the factors discussed as criteria? Does the service bureau have an established reputation within the industry, or is it a new company?

### References

Will the service bureau provide the organization with references so a check may be made with other customers of the bureau? Does the service bureau suggest that other customers should be contacted or do you have to ask for references?

### Sample Work

Will the service bureau provide the organization with microfilm work samples made from the organization's own documents? Or will the service bureau provide samples from previous jobs?

### Contractual Arrangements

Does the contract with the service bureau provide for the interests of the organization? Does the contract provide for penalties if work is late, misplaced, or of poor quality?

### Document Security and File Integrity

How does the service bureau provide for security of the data input and output? Is a system in place to provide necessary document security and file integrity?

## Service Bureau Evaluation

The decision to award a microfilming and processing contract to a service bureau requires satisfactory answers to all of the above questions. In addition, the service bureau must meet requirements for microform production quality and efficiency.

In order to evaluate the service bureaus objectively and to arrive at a decision based on the individual organizational needs and priorities, a table such as Table 19–1 should be developed. The weighted criteria are listed, and space to fill in the evaluation of each bureau is provided. A scale of one to ten is used; however, these weights may be assigned according to the rank of importance assigned by the organization. For example, "Quality of Output" has an assigned weight of 10 (the highest value), while "Education/Training" has an assigned weight of 3 (the least value). In addition to the assigned weights, an optimum should be found against which to measure each criterion. For "Location," as an example, an optimum of 0–15 miles might be used, and any bureau located within the 15-mile radius would be rated a value of 5. Other locations would be ranked from 4 to 0 depending upon their distance

*Weighted evaluation of selection criteria*

Table 19–1
Evaluation Chart

| Criteria | Weight | Service Bureaus | | | | |
|---|---|---|---|---|---|---|
| | | A | B | C | D | E |
| 1. Quality of Output | 10 | 7 | 5 | 10 | 9 | 2 |
| 2. Turnaround Time | 8 | 2 | 7 | 5 | 7 | 3 |
| 3. Document Security | 8 | 5 | 6 | 6 | 5 | 8 |
| 4. Reputation/References | 7 | 6 | 4 | 4 | 6 | 0 |
| 5. Type of Equipment | 6 | 5 | 4 | 4 | 3 | 3 |
| 6. Location | 5 | 4 | 5 | 5 | 4 | 5 |
| 7. Price | 5 | 4 | 4 | 4 | 3 | 5 |
| 8. Contract Conditions | 5 | 0 | 2 | 3 | 4 | 1 |
| 9. Education/Training | 3 | 2 | 0 | 2 | 3 | 0 |
| TOTAL | 57 | 35 | 37 | (43) | (44) | 27 |

***Source:*** *Karen DelVacchio, "How Do You Choose a COM Bureau?"* Information and Records Management, *Vol. 11, No. 11 (November, 1977), p. 40.*

*Obtain samples*

from the organization. "Quality of Output" should be determined from the work samples obtained from the service bureaus—work samples based upon the organizational input. The work samples would then be rated from most acceptable to least acceptable and assigned numeric ratings from 10 to 0.

Once the criteria ratings have been made, each service bureau's ratings are totaled and the selection is made. In cases (such as the example in Table 19–1) when two service bureaus are within one point of each other, an analysis of exactly what the differences are and the importance of each of the particular items to the organization should be examined carefully.

■

## A LOOK AT THE CASE

Design Associates, Inc., should examine their needs and ability to organize an in-house operation. Whether they have the physical facilities to allocate to an in-house operation, whether they wish to allocate resources to buy necessary equipment to begin and maintain a professional operation, and whether they have or can obtain experienced personnel to operate the facility are questions that need to be answered. These considerations must be balanced with the company's need to control the information in terms of production turnaround time, document security, film quality, testing new applications, standards consistency, and file integrity.

If the decision is made, however, to accept the recommendation of the consultants to contract with a service bureau, an objective comparison of service bureaus, made by using weighted criteria specific to the needs of Design Associates, Inc., should be made. The contract would then be awarded based on the evaluation.

■

## IMPLEMENT MICRORECORDS CONTROL PROGRAM

After the decision regarding in-house microrecords operation or service bureau processing is made, the microrecords control system is implemented.

## Analyze Microrecords Conversion Requests

After the original conversion from paper to microforms, any additional requests for a microforms application must be evaluated to
determine if the application is appropriate and within the cost
benefit parameters set by the organization. A formal procedure
should be established for evaluating these requests.

*Evaluate additional requests*

Requests for additional microforms use are referred to the
person charged with the responsibility for micrographics operations. In some instances, the person designated is the records manager; in larger organizations, the person may be the micrographics
supervisor.

Figure 7–1 in Chapter 7 is representative of forms used to request conversion to a microforms system. The purpose of each request for data is to justify the use of a microforms system over the
current document system. Additional information may be requested that projects benefits to be accrued from the proposed
conversion.

Some organizations require far less documentation. The request may be made in the form of a letter application that briefly
describes the need for a new or modified microforms use. The letter is generally followed by a conference with the requester in
which additional information is obtained. Many micrographics departments regard themselves as a service arm of the organization;
consequently, if the application for conversion to microform is justified, it is routinely approved.

*Document need*

## Establish Storage and Retrieval Controls

Any effective records management system, regardless of the
method of storing and retrieving records (manual, mechanical, or
automated) or the form of the record (electronic, magnetic, microform, or hard copy), must have controls for storing and retrieving
records. The general storage procedures described in Chapter 9
are applicable to microforms. In addition to these procedures,
some storage and quality controls are unique to microfilm applications.

### Quality Assurance Procedures

A daily routine should be established for making resolution and
density checks to ensure that all microfilm produced is to specification. The U.S. government has issued a standard specification
which provides both density and resolution standards. The background density for 16mm film is .90 to 1.31, with 35mm film hav-

*Resolution and density standards*

ing a more narrow field of 1.00 to 1.20. A density check should be made daily and/or when the film emulsion number changes. Film characteristics change from batch to batch and, consequently, require varying amounts of light to obtain the proper film density. The government specification also states that the resolution quality of all processed microfilm shall be no less than

113.6 lines/mm at $16\times$,
120.0 lines/mm at $24\times$, or
135.0 lines/mm at $30\times$.

Resolution measures the degree of sharpness or acuity of the film, which refers to the ability of the film to satisfactorily record fine details, such as separate but closely placed lines. Resolution is usually expressed as the maximum number of line-pairs per millimeter the film system (camera, microfilm, and development process) can satisfactorily resolve, with measurement made by a microscope.

A series of resolution patterns, each consisting of five line-pairs in each direction, are photographed. The patterns range from line spacing of 1 line per millimeter to 10 lines per millimeter, with each pattern step increased about 10 percent. When photographed the actual patterns become smaller proportionally to the reduction ratio; i.e., at 10:1, the 4.5 lines per millimeter pattern becomes 45 lines per millimeter on film; at 24:1, the 3.6 pattern produces $24 \times 3.6 = 86$ lines per millimeter on the film. When read under the microscope, the larger patterns are usually clearly readable as five lines in each direction, but with examination of each pattern progressively smaller in size (but with higher line resolutions) a point is reached where the lines are no longer distinct. The resolution is expressed, therefore, as the last pattern that can be clearly discerned as five lines in each direction, and the value is determined by the pattern number multiplied by the reduction ratio used. Figure 19–1 illustrates a National Bureau of Standards chart used for determining film resolution.

A resolution check should also be made daily, and results of both the resolution and density tests should be recorded and kept on file. (See Figures 19–2 and 19–3.)

Additional storage controls are provided through a microfilm preparation document form, a job status log, a microfilm inspection report, and a source document microfiche inspection report.

Figure 19–1
Microcopy Resolution Test Chart

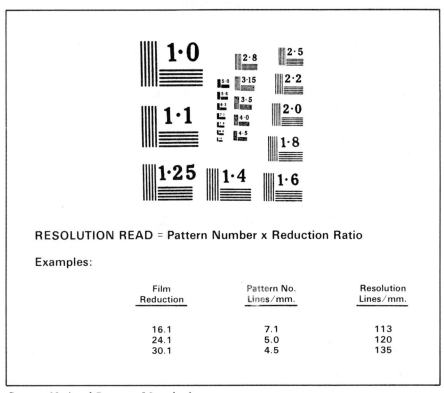

RESOLUTION READ = Pattern Number x Reduction Ratio

Examples:

| Film Reduction | Pattern No. Lines/mm. | Resolution Lines/mm. |
|---|---|---|
| 16.1 | 7.1 | 113 |
| 24.1 | 5.0 | 120 |
| 30.1 | 4.5 | 135 |

*Source: National Bureau of Standards.*

Figure 19–2
Resolution and Density Documentation

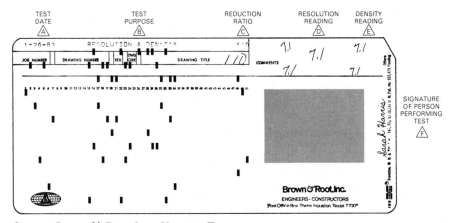

*Source: Brown & Root, Inc., Houston, Texas.*

Figure 19–3
Density Log

| BROWN & ROOT, INC. | | | | | |
|---|---|---|---|---|---|
| RECORDS MANAGEMENT DEPARTMENT | | | | | |
| MICROFILM SERVICES    MS-44 | | | | | |
| ROLL NO. | DEPARTMENT | DOCUMENT TYPE | LOGGED BY | DENSITY | DATE |
| 67 | INDUSTRIAL CIVIL | ARCO VP | JJ | 1.14 | 9/8/-- |
| 20 | INDUSTRIAL CIVIL | ARCO PUR ORD | NH | 1.26 | 9/8/-- |
| 657 | PERSONNEL | UPDATES | NH | 1.18 | 9/8/-- |
| 679 | PAYROLL | FDTS | NH | 1.22 | 9/8/-- |
| 66 | INDUSTRIAL CIVIL | ARCO VP | JD | .95 | 9/8/-- |
| 16 | PAYROLL | UNITED FUND | JJ | 1.22 | 9/8/-- |
| 77-08-01 | ACCOUNTS PAYABLE | VP | JJ | 1.24 | 9/8/-- |

*Source:* Brown & Root, Inc., Houston, Texas.

*Provide audit trail*

These documents provide an audit trail that may be used to

1. help locate any job being processed,
2. identify person responsible for processing,
3. identify defects in the microfilm and identify responsibility, and
4. identify defects in source document microfiche and identify responsibility.

As the jobs are received, they are indexed and entered in a log. As the jobs are processed, each person initials the individual portion for which he or she is responsible. Figure 19–4 is an example of a form used for microfilm preparation control, and Figure 19–5 is a job status log for 35mm filming; Figures 19–6 and 19–7 are a microfilm inspection report and a source document microfiche inspection report.

## Special Film Targets

Special targets are used when filming to indicate unique filming procedures or to identify particular sequences on the film. The targets are the same size as the documents to be filmed. Some of these special targets are

**cross-reference targets** which provide information regarding the location of related records;

**missing document targets** which document the fact that certain records were missing when the records were received for filming;

Figure 19–5
Job Status Log

STATUS OF 35MM JOBS

| Ticket No. Date | Customer Name | Status of Job | Completed |
|---|---|---|---|
| 10257<br>9-12 | Tina Allen<br>19 orig | 1. Index      4. Mount<br>2. Keypunch   5. Dupe<br>3. Film       6. Intersperse | RH<br>9-13 |
| 10291<br>9-12 | Tina Allen<br>12 orig | 1. Index      4. Mount<br>2. Keypunch   5. Dupe<br>3. Film       6. Intersperse | RH<br>9-13 |
| 10256<br>9-12 | Tina Allen<br>34 orig | 1. Index      4. Mount<br>2. Keypunch   5. Dupe<br>3. Film       6. Intersperse | RH<br>9-13 |
| 9241<br>9-12 | Oliver Jones<br>4 orig | 1. Index      4. Mount<br>2. Keypunch   5. Dupe<br>3. Film       6. Intersperse | RH<br>9-13 |

*Source: Brown & Root, Inc., Houston, Texas.*

Figure 19–4
Microfilm Preparation Document

Box or Drawer
Number _____

BROWN & ROOT, INC.
MICROFILM SERVICES

MICROFILM PREPARATION DOCUMENT

NOTE
THESE FILES ARE READY FOR MICROFILMING.
DO NOT REMOVE ANY FILES.

Documents prepared for microfilming. _____ Date prepared _____

By _____ From Document _____ through _____
By _____ From Document _____ through _____
From Department _____ Location _____

Received – Microfilm Department

By _____ Date _____

1. Are documents in proper order?  ☐ Yes  ☐ No
If answer is No, documents are to be returned to originating department for proper preparation.

Returned to Department   Date _____   By _____
Received in Department   Date _____   By _____

2. Were any documents missing from file and not noted as missing?  ☐ Yes  ☐ No
If so, explain _____

3. Comments _____

MS-7 1M R11-74

*Source: Brown & Root, Inc., Houston, Texas.*

Figure 19–6
Microfilm Inspection Report

## COASTAL STATES GAS CORPORATION
### MICROFILM INSPECTION REPORT

Roll No. _____ Camera No. _____ Camera Operator _____

Date Filmed _____ Description of Records _____

**INSTRUCTIONS:**
Check Beginning Affidavit _____
Check Target Sheets _____
Check for items out of order _____
Carefully examine each image _____
Attach prints of errors or
defects if necessary _____
Note nature of defect or error _____
Check Ending Affidavit _____

Resolution Reading — Satisfactory _____
                        Unsatisfactory _____
Density Reading — Satisfactory _____
                     Unsatisfactory _____

**DEFECT CODES:**
1. Blank Film
2. Bleed Through
3. Blurred
4. Dark Streak
5. Double Exposure
6. Dust on film
7. Edge Fog
8. Fog
9. Folded Document
10. Frilling
11. Image off center -
    partial cutoff at
    edge of film
12. Irregular space
    between images
13. Light Streak
14. Overexposure
15. Overlapped Document
16. Scratch
17. Spots
18. Stains
19. Static Marks
20. Stretches
21. Underexposure
22. Other

In the course of my inspection of this roll of film, I have discovered the following:

| ITEM | DEFECT CODE NO. | LOCATION ON ROLL | RETAKE | | OTHER |
|------|------|------|------|------|------|
| | | | YES | NO | |

**COMMENTS:**
I certify that this roll of film is satisfactory, except as specified _____.
This roll of film is unsatisfactory and should be rephotographed _____.

Date _____  Inspector _____
Date _____  Supervisor's Review _____
Retakes Required: Inspected _____  Spliced to this roll _____
Date _____  Inspector _____
Date _____  Supervisor's Final Approval _____
Add-ons Required: Inspected _____  Spliced to this roll _____
Date _____  Inspector _____
Date _____  Supervisor's Final Approval _____

M-9
7/86

***Source:*** *The Coastal Corporation, Houston, Texas.*

Figure 19–7
Source Document Microfiche Inspection Report

## COASTAL STATES GAS CORPORATION
### (M-23)
### SOURCE DOCUMENT MICROFICHE
### INSPECTION REPORT

Job No. _____ Camera No. _____ Camera Operator _____ No. of Sheets _____

Date Filmed _____ Description of Records _____

**INSTRUCTIONS:**
Check Target Sheets _____
Check for items out of order _____
Carefully examine each image _____
Attach prints of errors or
defects if necessary _____
Note nature of defect or error _____

**DEFECT CODES:**
1. Bleed Through
2. Blurred
3. Dark Streak
4. Double Exposure
5. Dust on film
6. Fog
7. Folded Document
8. Frilling
9. Image off center-
   partial cutoff at
   edge of film
10. Light Streak
11. Overexposure
12. Overlapped Document
13. Scratch
14. Spots
15. Stains
16. Static Marks
17. Underexposure
18. Other

In the course of my inspection of this sheet of microfiche, I have discovered the following:

| ITEM | DEFECT CODE NO. | FICHE SHEET # | FRAME COORDINATE | RETAKE | | OTHER |
|------|------|------|------|------|------|------|
| | | | | YES | NO | |

**COMMENTS:**
I certify that this job is satisfactory, except as specified _____.
This job is unsatisfactory as specified and should be rephotographed _____.

Date _____  Inspector _____
Date _____  Supervisor's Review _____
Retakes Required: Completed _____  Inspected _____
Date _____  Inspector _____
Date _____  Supervisor's Final Approval _____

M-23
7/86

***Source:*** *The Coastal Corporation, Houston, Texas.*

**substandard document targets** which show that the original record was not completely legible and that the quality of the microimage is below standards;

**correction targets** which testify that the preceding document has been remicrofilmed to assure legibility;

**camera operator targets** which provide identification of the camera operator and the date of the filming; and

**organization of information targets** which state the order in which the records were received and filmed.

Several of these film targets are shown below in reduced size.

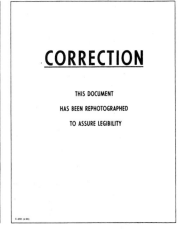

*Source:* *The Coastal Corporation, Houston, Texas.*

## Determine Charge-Back to Users

*Accountability is essential*

One of the controls exercised is a system of accountability for the costs of converting paper documents to microforms. The user is charged for the costs involved in the conversion; however, these charges may be made in several ways.

*Line item charge*

1. A dollar charge is made to the user's line item account in the budget. With this type of charge-back, the user is provided with a listing of each job charged to the department and the basis for the charge. The charges may be on a per page basis, a predetermined charge, or a time charge.

*Information report*

2. The user is provided the same information as in item 1 above; however, no actual charges are made against the user's budget. All charges accrue to the organization. The user, however, receives an information report detailing use and costs.

*Allocation accounting*

3. An allocation accounting is made which indicates percentage of use by department. For example, the finance department may account for 36 percent of the work of the micrographics department; the human resources department may account for only 3 percent of the work.

The method of accountability used by the organization is not so important; what is important is that some method of accountability be provided within the control system. This charge-back system also provides the basis for monitoring and evaluating microforms use. Figure 19–8 is an example of a multipart microfilm request/billing form.

## Maintain File Integrity

File integrity refers to the accuracy and completeness of the record. The development of an updatable form has provided a vehicle for maintaining accurate and complete records by using microfiche or microfilm jackets. **Updatable microfilm/fiche** allows all

*Updatable microforms*

file information to accumulate on one record and for corrections to be made and the file to be updated. Updating the fiche record is a simple procedure that enables the information to be added to the master fiche. Unlike ordinary microfiche, updatable fiche can be reimaged. (See Figure 19–9.) Under the old system of microfiche, each update was processed on a separate fiche. Therefore, in order for users to have a complete file, it was often necessary to distribute numerous microfiche to users. The new technology provides a method of indicating any information previously recorded that is currently invalid. The system does not allow for "erasures"; how-

Figure 19–8
Microfilm Request/Billing Form

**Brown & Root, Inc.**

16 — 4117

**16MM**

MICROFILM REQUEST/BILLING

MICROFILM THE ATTACHED DOCUMENTS AS INSTRUCTED BELOW:

| DATE OF REQUEST | | |
|---|---|---|
| MONTH | DAY | YEAR |

| G/L CODE | JOB/ACCOUNT NUMBER | | | |
|---|---|---|---|---|
| | DEPT. | NUMBER | SUFFIX | COST CODE |
| | | | | |

(CREDIT – 6124-0018)

☐ RETURN ORIGINAL ROLL TO REQUESTOR

☐ MOUNT ORIGINAL ROLL IN JACKETS

☐ KEYPUNCH & PRINT INDEX (NO. OF COPIES _____ )

☐ PLACE SECURITY ROLL IN VAULT

☐ DUPLICATE ROLLS (NO. OF ROLLS PER ORIGINAL _____ )

☐ SPECIAL FILMING INSTRUCTIONS _____

RECORD DESCRIPTION (BE SPECIFIC)

| DELIVERED TO MICROFILM SERVICES BY | ACCEPTED BY |
|---|---|
| TOTAL NUMBER SUBMITTED<br>BOXES | TOTAL NUMBER SUBMITTED<br>DOCUMENTS |

| REQUESTED BY | DIVISION/DEPARTMENT | APPROVED BY |
|---|---|---|
| MAIL LOCATION | PHONE EXTENSION | |

▼     **FOR MICROFILM SERVICES USE ONLY**     ▼

TO: GENERAL ACCOUNTING (BILL THE FOLLOWING CHARGES TO THE JOB/ACCOUNT SHOWN ABOVE)

| | | |
|---|---|---|
| ORIGINAL FILM | _____ ROLLS @ $_____ | /ROLL | $_____ |
| SECURITY FILM | _____ ROLLS @ $_____ | /ROLL | $_____ |
| DUPLICATE FILM | _____ ROLLS @ $_____ | /ROLL | $_____ |
| PRINTS FROM MICROFILM _____ PRINTS @ $_____ | /EACH | $_____ |
| XEROX OR MICROFILM COPIES _____ @ $_____ | /EACH | $_____ |
| PRINT OUT OF INDEX _____ LINES @ $_____ | /EACH PLUS $_____ | $_____ |
| SUPPLIES _____ | | |
| | | $_____ |
| LABOR _____ HOURS @ $_____ | /HOUR | $_____ |

TOTAL $_____

| **MICROFILM SERVICES** | SIGNED BY |
|---|---|

MS-4 (3-82)

GENERAL ACCOUNTING

*Source: Brown & Root, Inc., Houston, Texas.*

Figure 19–9
Updatable Microfilm Record

ever, words like "void" or "superceded" can be superimposed on any previous record. This permits the original image to be read though the record contains the notation that it is no longer valid.

Updatable microfilm jackets also unitize microfilm and provide a master jacket from which copies may be made. This method, like the updatable microfiche, allows all of the file information to accumulate on one record. This eliminates the necessity of sending a number of microfilm records to a user because one single record contains all of the information. (See Figure 19–10.)

Figure 19–10
Updatable Jackets

An additional protection of file integrity is a dated **certificate of authenticity** or **identification**. This target, signed by the operator, may be imaged on each fiche, at the beginning of every roll of film, or at the time a record is voided. If any question arises regarding the record, validation may be made with the operator who processed the record. An example of a certificate of identification is shown in Figure 19–11.

*Operator validation*

Figure 19–11
Certificate of Identification

CERTIFICATE OF IDENTIFICATION

THIS IS TO CERTIFY THAT THE MICROPHOTOGRAPHS APPEARING

ON THIS FILM STARTING WITH_____

_____ AND ENDING

WITH_____

ARE ACCURATE AND COMPLETE REPRODUCTIONS OF THE RECORDS OF

**COASTAL STATES GAS CORPORATION** AS DELIVERED IN THE REGULAR

COURSE OF BUSINESS FOR PHOTOGRAPHING.

IT IS FURTHER CERTIFIED THAT THE MICROPHOTOGRAPHIC

PROCESSES WERE ACCOMPLISHED IN A MANNER ON FILM WHICH MEETS

WITH REQUIREMENTS OF **THE NATIONAL BUREAU OF STANDARDS** FOR

PERMANENT MICROPHOTOGRAPHIC COPY.

DATE PRODUCED_____, 19\_\_\_ _____
                                        CAMERA OPERATOR

PLACE_____
        (CITY)            (STATE)

*Source: The Coastal Corporation, Houston, Texas.*

## Establish Distribution System

*Distribution based on recipient needs*

As with any other information system, the distribution of micro-forms must be based on the recipients' needs to have access to the information. At the time of the request for microforms conversion, the person(s) who should receive copies of the microform should be identified. The needs of the designated recipients should be carefully evaluated; appropriate additions or deletions should be suggested. If the microform is one that requires distribution to several users, a distribution list is prepared. The distribution system may be similar to the system previously described in Chapter 17 in the discussion of the distribution of directives.

Prior approval must be given before providing information belonging to one department to another department. For example, if the production department needs a copy of a microform containing information about the finance department, the finance department must grant approval before the microform can be released.

Master copies are usually maintained in the master file area and never leave this central point. Any changes to the master microform are made centrally. Copies of the master are distributed to users who are on the approved distribution list.

## A LOOK AT THE CASE

The management of Design Associates, Inc., will want to have a formal procedure for requesting additional applications of the microrecords system. They may study forms currently in use by other companies, modify an acceptable form to meet their own needs, or they may design their own form. Another procedure that must be established is one that allows for properly charging users and for providing users with information regarding their costs.

Design Associates, Inc., will also wish to establish a system of distribution and control of copies. This procedure, along with procedures for monitoring and evaluating the system, will allow the company to make the most efficient and effective use of the microrecords system.

What are the procedures for evaluating the microrecords control program?

# EVALUATE THE MICRORECORDS CONTROL PROGRAM

Established procedures must be in place for submission and review of new microforms applications. On a periodic basis, ongoing microforms projects should be assessed to determine that continuance is justified, that procedures and equipment are consistent with operations efficiency, and that the objectives remain consistent with the objectives of the organization. Output quality, information availability, information use, and actual versus projected benefits should be examined.

*Review need for continuing project*

Departments using microforms must maintain adequate system documentation on a continuing basis and make this documentation available for review. The department responsible for microforms control should conduct onsite visits to review the microrecords program and to provide any assistance or advice to the users. Interim requests for information may be made in the form of a memo asking all distribution areas to review their needs. Costs/allocation reports provide another data base that may be used to monitor the system. Comparison of these data over a period of time establishes a pattern of use that is helpful in analysis and evaluation.

## Analyze Procedures for Submission and Review

As applications are submitted for conversion to microforms or as ongoing projects are reviewed for continuance, uniform procedures should be applied to the submission, review, and approval of all applications.

*Uniform procedures for submission*

### Procedures for Submission and Review of New Applications

To monitor the submission and review process of new applications, the guidelines that should be used are as follows:

**Procedures for Submission and Review of New Microforms Applications**

| | Yes | No |
|---|---|---|
| a. Are a directive and a set of written procedures available for submission, review, and approval/disapproval of microforms applications? | ____ | ____ |
| b. Are the procedures known by those who may submit a microforms proposal? | ____ | ____ |
| c. Are the procedures easily understood? Can most individuals follow the procedures without additional aid from the micrographics management staff? | ____ | ____ |

|  | Yes | No |
|---|---|---|

d. Are the procedures specific concerning documentation required?

e. If formats are specified for system descriptions and/or cost benefit analyses, are samples provided?

f. Are the procedures followed? Has every system implemented since the procedures were established been through the review process?
   If the above answer is "no," was an exception justified?
   If "yes," on what basis? _____

g. Do most proposals received contain all required documentation?
   If the answer is "no," has assistance been provided by the micrographics staff?

h. How long does the review procedure take from the time an application is received until it is approved? _____

i. Do the procedures specify a time limit for the review?

j. Do originating offices know the approximate length of time required for review and approval?

k. Can the reviewing office approving the proposal also authorize expenditures?

l. If coordination with several offices is required, is the requirement clearly defined?

m. If applications are reviewed by several offices, are the reviews concurrent when possible?

## Procedures for Review of Ongoing Projects

Ongoing projects should be reviewed to determine their continued value to the company. To monitor ongoing projects, the following guidelines should be followed:

### Procedures for Review of Ongoing Projects

|  | Yes | No |
|---|---|---|

a. Are formal procedures available for evaluating the efficiency and effectiveness of existing microforms projects?

b. Is a review conducted to determine whether projected benefits are being obtained in ongoing projects?

c. Are existing microforms projects regularly reviewed for conformity with established policies, procedures, and standards?

d. Does the review procedure specify a time period for subsequent reviews?

e. Have reviews been conducted as scheduled?
   If the answer is "no," why were schedules not maintained?

|  | Yes | No |
|---|---|---|

f. Have reviews included evaluations of both system effectiveness and compliance with policies and procedures?

g. When a review results in identification of a problem and a change is recommended, is the recommendation documented and followed-up to ensure its implementation?

## Analyze Quality of Output

Samples of microforms should be examined to determine whether they can be read with ease. The legibility of microform images can be affected by a variety of factors, including the resolution, density, contrast, quality, and condition of the document being filmed as well as the quality and condition of the reader being used. Compare several newly created microforms with the original document to determine the degree of legibility loss. To monitor the quality of the output, the following guidelines should be adhered to:

*Compare samples of microforms*

**Analysis of Quality of Output**

|  | Yes | No |
|---|---|---|

1. Resolution
   a. How many lines per mm are required for this application to meet the standard?

   _____

   b. Are resolution tests performed daily?
   c. Do they show that the standard is met consistently?
   d. Are records of resolution tests maintained?
   e. Are resolution tests performed using the National Bureau of Standards test chart?

2. Density
   a. What density range is required for filming documents in this application?

   _____

   b. Are density tests performed daily?
   c. Are records of density tests maintained?
   d. Do they show that the standard is met consistently?

3. General
   a. Does the examination of sample microforms show that the images are legible?
   b. Are users able to read the filmed images with ease?
   c. Are users able to operate the readers with ease?
   d. Have users been trained to operate and maintain the equipment they use?

## Determine Information Availability

*Input must be accurate, current, and complete*

Information is usable only if it can be located quickly and is accurate and complete. Input to the system must follow established controls to assure that the inputs are accurate, current, and complete. All of these factors affect the availability of the information and must be carefully examined. Some of the questions that may be asked regarding the availability of information include

### Information Availability

|  | Yes | No |
|---|---|---|
| **1. General** | | |
| a. Can the user obtain the required information without referring to other reports? | _____ | _____ |
| b. Can the user be sure the information is accurate and reliable? | _____ | _____ |
| c. If not, in what way is the information not reliable? _____ | | |
| d. If the information is considered inaccurate or unreliable, what method does the user use to overcome the problem (keep manual records, look up the source document, inquire by phone, and so forth)? _____ | | |
| e. Is the information current and does it meet the organizational standard for currentness? | _____ | _____ |
| f. If the information is so outdated that it detracts significantly from its usefulness, can the updating cycle be improved? | _____ | _____ |
| g. Is the response to retrieval requests at least as fast as projected in the original system proposal? | _____ | _____ |
| h. If not, has action been taken to examine the problem? | _____ | _____ |
| i. What action has been taken? _____ | | |
| **2. Finding the Information** | | |
| a. Do titles, labels, and other information adequately identify the contents of each microform? | _____ | _____ |
| b. Are titles and labels clearly visible and easy to read? | _____ | _____ |
| c. Do the titles and labels contain all items necessary for locating the correct microrecord? | _____ | _____ |
| d. Are indexes provided where necessary? | _____ | _____ |
| e. Are indexes complete? | _____ | _____ |
| f. Do the indexes contain all items necessary to locate a specific page, frame, record, or report? | _____ | _____ |
| g. Are indexes located in a standard location on all microforms? | _____ | _____ |

|  | Yes | No |
|---|---|---|

h. Is the information presented in the sequence and grouping that best suits the needs of the users? _____ _____

i. If not, what should be changed?

3. Examining the Input
   a. Is all of the input to be filmed provided on time? _____ _____
   b. Do control procedures ensure that all input is processed? _____ _____
   c. Are records adequate to locate the source of any items missing from the final output? _____ _____
   d. Is follow-up action taken promptly if input documents are not received as scheduled? _____ _____
   e. Are logs, records, and processing controls adequate for data control throughout the microform production process? _____ _____
   f. Are retention periods for input sufficient for reference and/or reuse for refilming? _____ _____
   g. Are microrecords verified for completeness and accuracy? _____ _____

## Analyze Information Use

Information is valuable only if it is used. Therefore, a vehicle must be developed for analyzing information use to determine how well the micrographics program meets the needs of the users. Some of the questions that may be asked regarding the use of information include

**Analysis of Information Use**

|  | Yes | No |
|---|---|---|

1. Information Requirements
   a. Do the recipients use the microrecords? _____ _____
   b. For what purposes are the microrecords used?

   c. Are the initial purpose and justification still valid? _____ _____
   d. Is the microform the only available source of this information? _____ _____
   e. Do the microrecords meet all of the users' requirements? _____ _____
   f. If not, what requirements are not met?

   g. Has the user been able to eliminate any paper records and use only microforms? _____ _____

|  | Yes | No |
|---|---|---|

h. Are all data on the microrecord essential?

i. Does the microrecord contain all items of information required by the users?

j. Are users satisfied that the microrecords are adequate substitutes for the original records?

k. What has the user done about deficiencies in the output received?

_____

l. What has been done about complaints or suggestions for improvement?

_____

m. Are periodic surveys scheduled with all users of microrecords?

2. Information Retrieval

a. Are reference copies stored as closely to the users' work locations as requirements for control of access and security permit?

b. If the reference file is centralized, are enough readers or reader printers available for quick reference?

c. Are users permitted to take a duplicate out of the file for extended reference or must the master record be checked out?

d. Is the file up to date? Are filing and retrieval backlogs dealt with promptly?

e. Are retrieval requests batched and ordered in the file sequence for quick retrieval whenever possible?

f. If the reference files are located at or near the users' work stations, has information on the storage of microforms been provided to the users?

g. Have users been provided with both storage equipment and supplies (for example, filing devices and fiche envelopes)?

## Analyze Actual Versus Projected Benefits

If an organization has an effective micrographics program, each microrecord application has been determined to be cost effective before approval and implementation. However, unforeseen problems often occur, and changing program requirements and operating environments may affect the operating costs or benefits realized from the application. A review of the effectiveness of the application is in order. The following considerations should be evaluated.

### Actual Versus Projected Benefits

|  | Yes | No |
|---|---|---|
| a. Did the micrographics management office review and approve the application? | ___ | ___ |
| b. Was a systems analysis conducted? | ___ | ___ |
| c. Was a cost benefit analysis conducted? | ___ | ___ |
| d. Are the assumptions and constraints noted in the original cost benefit analysis still valid? | ___ | ___ |
| e. Are the current system costs within the range of the projected system costs? | ___ | ___ |
| f. Are the projected benefits being realized in the current system? | ___ | ___ |
| g. Is equipment acquired for this system being used to capacity? | ___ | ___ |
| h. If not, has the unused equipment capacity been noted and arrangements for sharing capacity been identified? | ___ | ___ |

i. What arrangements are being implemented? _____

## A LOOK AT THE CASE

Design Associates, Inc., should establish procedures for evaluating the microrecords program to determine that continuance of the program is justified, that procedures and equipment are consistent with operations efficiency, and that the objectives of the program remain consistent with the objectives of Design Associates, Inc. Output quality, information availability, information use, and cost versus benefits should be examined.

## TERMINOLOGY REVIEW

**Camera operator targets.** Frame of microfilm on which the date filmed and the operator are identified.

**Certificate of authenticity/identification.** Frame on each roll of microfilm that identifies the date filmed and the operator, and verifies the accuracy and completeness of the reproductions.

**Contracted microforms services.** Microforms produced through contract with a service bureau.

**Correction target.** Frame of microfilm showing that the preceding document has been refilmed.

*Cross-reference target.* Frame of microfilm that provides information regarding the location of related records.

*File integrity.* Accuracy and completeness of the file.

*Missing document target.* Frame of microfilm documenting records that were missing when records were originally received.

*Organization of information target.* Frame of microfilm showing the order in which the records were received and filmed.

*Substandard document target.* Frame showing that the original record was not completely legible and that the quality of the microimage is below standard.

*Updatable microfilm/fiche.* Form of microrecord that allows all file information to accumulate on one record and for corrections to be made and the file to be updated.

## COMPETENCY REVIEW

1. Describe seven general microform production requirements.
2. Identify five additional criteria unique to service bureau selection.
3. Compare in-house and service bureau contractual microfilm production in terms of benefits and limitations.
4. Describe an objective method for selecting a service bureau.
5. Describe several methods of controlling microforms distribution.
6. How are updatable microfiche a form of records control?
7. Describe factors that should be evaluated to determine the effectiveness of a microrecords program.

## APPLICATIONS

1. Write to three micrographics service bureaus to request information regarding
   a. turnaround time provided
   b. document security/file integrity provided
   c. location in relation to your home or school addresses
   d. costs for processing (1) roll microfilm (2) microfiche
   e. any additional requirements you believe to be important
2. Compile the information you have received in Application 1 into a chart format and make a decision regarding which service bureau you would select based on the information obtained. Include a rationale for selection that indicates additional information required to make a better decision.
3. You are the records manager of Creative Wood Products, Inc., a relatively new company that is not ready to commit resources to equip, staff, and maintain its own microfilm processing operation. After obtaining information from five service bureaus, you have compiled the information shown in Table 19–1, Evaluation Chart. Using the fig-

ures on this chart, determine the following:

a. Which service bureau(s) would you consider for processing the records of Creative Wood Products, Inc.?

b. What factors would influence your final decision?

## CONCLUDING CASES

### A. Dominion College

As the person responsible for the micrographics operations of Dominion College, Murray Einhorn is responsible for evaluating any additional user requests for microforms conversion. He has just received the following preliminary data from the human resources department.

---

**DESCRIPTION OF CURRENT SYSTEM** *(COM PROPOSALS)*
For use of this form, see TM 12-257; the proponent agency is TAGCEN.

1. DOCUMENT DESCRIPTION *(Include explanation in REMARKS block when norms shown by asterisk (*) in 1c, d, and e below are exceeded.)*
Personnel folders

*a.* SUBJECT MATTER

Employee applications, evaluations, leave requests, and other related documents

| *c.* PAPER SIZE *(11x14 7/8)* | *d.* CHARACTERS PER LINE *(135)* | *e.* LINES PER PAGE *(66)* | *f.* NUMBER OF PRE-PRINTED FORMS | *g.* HIGHEST SECURITY CLASSIFICATION |
|---|---|---|---|---|
| 8½ x 11 and 4¼ x 5½ | 102 | 66 and 33 | Various | Confidential |

2. DESCRIPTION OF CURRENT MICROFORM SYSTEM *(Include format (roll, fiche, etc.), size (16mm, 105mm, etc.), type (silver, diazo, vesicular), reduction ratio, copy film image (positive or negative).)*

None

| 3. COMPUTER MAKE AND MODEL USED TO PRODUCE CURRENT OUTPUT | 4. MAGNETIC TAPE |
|---|---|
|  | TRACK          BPI |

5.                                          VOLUME OF PAPER

| *a.* ANNUAL TOTAL OF COMPUTER PAPER CONSUMED *(Include reports not identified for microform conversion.)* | *b.* ANNUAL TOTAL OF PAPER TO BE CONVERTED TO MICROFORM *(Enter annual totals from DA Form 1500-1-R, Current Paper Costs.)* |
|---|---|
| *(Number of Sets)* | *(Number of Sets)* |
| 1 – PART |  |
| 2 – PART |  |
| 3 – PART |  |
| 4 – PART |  |
| 5 – PART |  |
| 6 – PART |  |

*c.* NUMBER OF PAGES REPRODUCED BY OTHER COPY METHOD

6.                                          VOLUME OF MICROFORM

| *a.* TYPE | *b.* ORIGINAL FRAMES/FICHE | *c.* NUMBER OF COPIES |
|---|---|---|

7. STORAGE, INDEXING, AND RETRIEVAL

16-4
12/86

1. What aspects of this request might influence Murray to approve the conversion of this paper system to a microforms system?
2. What aspects of this request might influence Murray to deny the request?
3. What additional information would Murray need to make a final decision?

## B. Color Your Lawn, Inc.

When Marie and Mason Lowe began their part-time flower and seed catalog sales business in 1975, they had no idea that by 1983 the business would become a full-time venture. Mason resigned his position as an accountant, and Marie found that it was no longer possible to work only a few hours each day in their "home office." Color Your Lawn, Inc., is a huge success with catalog sales exceeding $10 million annually.

Mason has been proud of his ability to handle the financial aspects of the business. Marie is largely responsible for the selection of items to be included in the catalog and for catalog printing and distribution. A competent staff has been hired to fill and ship catalog orders and to handle the paperwork involved.

All of Color Your Lawn's records are currently in hard-copy form, but Marie and Mason have been discussing other options. This afternoon they have an appointment with a local vendor of micrographics equipment. Marie turned to Mason and said "What questions should we ask? I'm not sure I know enough to ask the 'right' questions. And this is such an important decision for us."

1. What questions should Marie and Mason ask the vendor?
2. Should they explore both an in-house operation and a contractual arrangement with a service bureau?

## READINGS AND REFERENCES

*Brown and Root, Inc., Records Management Manual.* Houston, Texas, July, 1981.

Burch, Bradford M. "How Records Management Policies Affect the Use of Micrographics Technology." *Journal of Micrographics,* Vol. 15, No. 10 (October, 1982), p. 47.

Burilla, Joanne, State Micrographics Manager, Virginia National Bank (Norfolk, Virginia). Interview, July, 1981.

*The Coastal Corporation, Micrographics Program Procedures Manual.* Houston, Texas, undated.

DelVacchio, Karen. "How Do You Choose a COM Bureau?" *Information and Records Management,* Vol. 11, No. 11 (November, 1977), p. 40.

General Services Administration, National Archives and Records Service, Office of Records Management. *Evaluating Micrographics Management.* Washington D.C.: U. S. Government Printing Office, 1980.

Georgia Department of Archives and History. *Book I: Administrative Procedures, A Basic Guide to Microforms.* Atlanta, Georgia, 1978.

*Microfilming of Records.* Washington D.C.: Headquarters, Department of the Army, 1969 with revisions 1977.

Pomerantz, David. "Managing Information in the Eighties." *Today's Office,* Vol. 18, No. 2 (February, 1983), p. 53.

Rwira, Edward C. "In-House Versus Service Bureau Considerations: The In-House Case." *International Micrographics Congress Journal,* Vol. 18, No. 1 (1982), p. 13.

Settani, Joseph A. "Micrographics Applications: Safe, Secure, & Cost Effective." *Office Systems '86,* Vol. 3, No. 6 (June, 1986), p. 78.

Wise, Joseph. "In-House or Service Bureau? Seven Factors to Consider." *Administrative Management,* Vol. 47, No. 3 (March, 1986), p. 20.

# PROFILE

## Hardee's Food Systems, Inc.

Today, Hardee's Food Systems, Inc., directs the operation of a multi-million dollar fast service family restaurant chain.

The company traces its origin to 1960 when Wilber Hardee began turning out popular 15-cent hamburgers at a small Greenville, North Carolina drive-in. Within a year, Rocky Mount businessmen Leonard Rawls and Jim Gardner formed Hardee's Drive-Ins, Inc.

By 1986, Hardee's Food Systems, now a subsidiary of Imasco Limited of Montreal, Canada, had grown to 2,543 fast service family restaurants in the United States and several foreign countries. Of this number, 877 were company-owned and the remaining 1,666 were operated by Hardee's licensees.

Hardee's new micrographics system solved the massive problems caused by paper-based accounts payable and payroll files. These problems were highly visible. The active accounts payable files required 83 file cabinets, occupying 996 square feet of space. The warehouse facility for inactive files was receiving 200 boxes a month, and it was almost filled to capacity. Total costs to maintain, refile, and purge these files exceeded $67,000 annually. To maintain the company's paper-based file system, additional warehouse space would have to be obtained, more file cabinets purchased, and additional personnel employed.

Instead, Hardee's chose to convert to microfilm tied online to existing computer systems containing vendor history. This $80,000 investment included two document cameras with document locator attachments, three reader-printers, a microfilm processor, and a microfilm duplicator. The payback period was estimated to be .83 years.

From September 1, 1982, until March, 1986, the Records Center produced 2,000 microfilm cartridges of over 5 million accounts payable invoices. The cartridges are stored in cabinets using 20 square feet of floor space. In hard copy form, the documents would require approximately 2,000 boxes or 400 five-drawer file cabinets. An average of 6,000 accounts payable documents are filmed daily by the Records Department.

After the labor intensive document preparation (removing staples, paper clips, etc.), the documents are filmed. The camera, with an attached document locator, uses a two-level blip system. The lead document, usually an invoice, is assigned a large blip and a unique number which is then imprinted on the document. Each succeeding document in the package has the same location number but is identified by a small blip automatically put on by the camera. While the location number is imprinted on the document, a counter inside the camera keeps track of the total number of documents filmed.

After filming, the documents are indexed via a CRT terminal online to the mainframe computer by matching the cartridge and frame number (printed on the document) to the vendor/invoice number. Indexing is done directly from the actual documents to reduce the possibility of indexing error and to improve turnaround time.

Retrieval of a particular invoice has been quick and accurate. Using the vendor/invoice number retrieved from vendor history, an operator accesses the online microfilm index which lists the microfilm cartridge and frame number. The operator then pulls the appropriate microfilm cartridge, inserts it into a Page Search Reader, inputs the frame number, and the film is automatically advanced to the right document. Frequently customer inquiries can be answered directly from information on the screen. If necessary, high-quality prints are available in seconds at the push of a button.

Although there are no statistics comparing the retrieval rates of microfilm versus paper files, Hardee's Data Processing/Records Manager Diane Lyles believes the chances of an invoice being "lost" are practically non-existent. The consensus is that film is more legible and more efficient than paper files and that retrieval is simpler and much faster.

"Hardee's new system has saved us a tremendous amount of storage space and expense," said Bill Burd, vice president of Hardee's Management Information Services. "Also, we have excellent retrieval capabilities. When something is put on microfilm, it is there forever, exactly where it was put."

*Contributed by Henrietta S. Barbour
and Bill Burd
Hardee's Food Systems, Inc.
Rocky Mount, NC*

# 20
# RECORDS SAFETY AND SECURITY

## Competencies

After completing this chapter, you should be able to

1. identify the major responsibilities of the records manager for records safety and security.
2. state the potential natural hazards to records and the actions for minimizing the risk of record loss.
3. identify primary methods of providing safeguards for vital records.
4. relate the changes necessitated in records handling to the 1974 amendments to the Freedom of Information Act and Privacy Act.
5. identify the major responsibilities of the records manager for protecting the security and confidentiality of the contents of records.
6. describe procedures for controlling access to records.
7. describe methods for controlling access to areas/facilities.
8. describe methods for controlling access to equipment.

# Introductory Case

Sue Nordstrom has just been appointed records manager for White Transportation Company. Oscar Benitez, the plant manager, has suggested that Sue begin her work by conducting an appraisal of the physical security of the records. As she approaches the records center, she hears a request being made to the records center clerk. "I need the personnel record of Mark Tsu who was employed from about 1979 to 1984."

1. What specific things should the new records manager check regarding the physical safety of the records?
2. What should she determine regarding the safety and security of the vital records?
3. What responsibility does she have for the security of the content of the records?
4. What procedures should be in place to protect record confidentiality?

.... **Fire Loss over \$1 million in New York High-Rise Office Building—One World Trade Center**

.... **Company Sustains Major Losses of Records in Flood—Ceases Operation**

.... **Company Sued—Ex-Employee Charges Violation of Privacy Act**

These headlines are all too familiar to the public and to persons responsible for the protection of business records. Security is a responsibility that cannot be regarded lightly, and records managers must plan to safeguard records from damage and destruction.

*Need for physical safety and content security*

The importance of records was addressed in Chapter 1. Because records and information are becoming increasingly critical to the continuing successful operation of an organization, more and more attention is being directed toward protecting the physical properties and content integrity of records. Original records that are destroyed cannot be replaced. While attaching a monetary value to a record is difficult, imagining the impossibility of a business continuing to operate without records is not difficult. There would be no sales contracts, no accounts receivable records, no strategic or tactical plans, no correspondence documenting action, no payroll records, no customers' lists, no stockholders' reports— no basis for continuing operation. The paper or media record may have little intrinsic monetary value, but the value of the information contained in the record is incalculable. Records are not generally appraised or insured, and even those that have been appraised often are undervalued. When inventory records are destroyed, collecting insurance is difficult. Organizations exist and prosper based on action taken as a result of the information to which they have access. If records are destroyed, the database is eliminated.

## DEVELOP COMPREHENSIVE SAFETY PROGRAM

Before a comprehensive safety program can be implemented, a thorough study of the records must be made. This study includes determining records classifications, physical volume of records by class, space needed to house the inventoried records, cost to the organization of the loss of each class of records, protection necessary for safe records storage, procedures needed for handling records, and need for a safety education program.

## Determine Records Classification

Records divisions, or classifications, suggested by the National Fire Protection Association are shown in Table 20–1. Much of this classification information may be determined by reference to a previous records inventory or by an actual survey of the records. Following or concurrent with the records classification, steps are taken to develop a comprehensvie safety program. While these are actions specific to protection from fire, they are applicable to records protection from other elements as well.

## Determine the Physical Volume of the Records by Class

How many square feet of shelf space do the records occupy? How many file drawers house records and what is the square footage of these file drawers? Of the total space required, how much is required for Class 1 records? How much of the total space required is needed for Class 2 and Class 3 records? What should be done with Class 4 records?

## Determine Space Needed to House the Inventoried Records

Based on the physical volume of the records by class, how much space should be allocated for each class of records? What is the estimated rate of accession for each class? What is the rate of transfer/disposal for each class? How much space would be needed if the total allocation for each class included accessions and transfers?

## Estimate the Cost to the Organization of the Loss of Each Class of Records

Objectively evaluate the cost to the organization if all records classified as vital were lost. To put this cost in dollar terms, questions such as the following should be considered: If all vital records were destroyed tomorrow, how long would it take to reconstruct the information and how much would it cost? How much time would be unproductive and what would the dollar cost be? How many contracts would be lost and what is their monetary value? How many accounts receivables would not be collected and what is that total cost? All costs incurred by the loss of vital records should be totaled, and the process should be repeated for the other classes of records. All costs incurred by the loss of all records should be totaled; the total will be much higher than anticipated. Of those organizations whose records are destroyed, 35 percent go out of

*Value of records to organization*

business; this fact establishes firm ground for the viability of a records protection program. Not only does the dollar figure provide an appraisal of the value of the records, but it is also a valuable tool for convincing management of the importance of

Table 20–1
Records Classification

| Class | Definition | Example | Recommended Protection |
|-------|-----------|---------|------------------------|
| Class 1 — **Vital** | Records *essential* to the continued life of the business. These records are irreplaceable because they give evidence of legal status, ownership, and financial status. Vital records are generally housed in active records storage. | Accounts receivable Inventory Contracts Creative materials Research documentation | Fire resistant vaults Dispersal Fireproof safes |
| Class 2 -- **Important** | Records *necessary* to the continued life of the business. While these records can be replaced or reproduced, this can be done only at considerable cost in time and money. Important records may be housed in either active or inactive storage. | Accounts payable Directives Payroll records | Safes Vaults |
| Class 3 — **Useful** | Records *useful* to the uninterrupted operation of the business. These records are replaceable although their loss could cause temporary inconvenience. | Bank statements Correspondence | File cabinets |
| Class 4 — **Nonessential** | Records having no present value and should be destroyed. | Requests answered Advertisements Announcements | Use, then destroy |

*Source: Gordon P. McKinnon, editor.* Fire Protection Handbook, *15th ed. (Boston: National Fire Protection Association, 1981).*

records, and it more than justifies any costs involved in their protection.

## Determine Protection Necessary for Safe Records Storage

This determination should be based on the information obtained in the survey. Types of protective storage are rated by tests conducted under standard fire conditions.

Any sizable collection of records not contained in vaults, safes, or insulated cabinets creates a fire hazard regardless of the storage method, the storage location, or the record medium. The trend toward making maximum use of available space through open-shelf housing presents a particular fire hazard. The close proximity of the opposing sides of the aisles could result in rapid fire expansion and increased heat feedback. The higher the stacks and the narrower the aisles, the more severe and rapid is the fire development. *Paper records*

Magnetic media and their containers do not represent a hazard more severe than that of paper. Polystyrene cases and reels, however, present a severe fire hazard because they contain a high Btu content and burn fiercely. The storage systems designed to safeguard materials of cardboard or paper composition are not adequate protection for polystyrene materials; special storage systems are required. *Magnetic media*

## Establish Procedures for Handling Records

Procedures should be established for handling records under ordinary conditions, during hazardous conditions, and under post-hazard conditions. What are the responsibilities of the people who handle the records? Do they have, in writing, what they are expected to do in the event of fire or other natural disasters? Have they had opportunities to practice the established procedures with follow-up and evaluation of the process? If the answer to any of the questions is "no," management should take immediate action to correct the situation. Some procedural considerations in the protection of records under both ordinary and extraordinary conditions include the following: *Procedural considerations*

1. In case of a disaster during working hours, records in use should be returned to their proper places within the files if at all possible. Responsibility for this process should be designated, and one person should oversee the operation and have authority to direct everyone to exit the building for personal safety.

2. Records in use but belonging in vaults should be returned to the safe or vault at the end of each working day. Under no circumstances should the records be left out overnight.

3. Employees should not allow important papers to accumulate on desks or in in-baskets. These records should be returned promptly to a protected area.

4. Records normally protected may be unprotected when temporarily in other hands. For example, important documents may be at an attorney's office; engineering drawings may be at the construction site; records may be in the process stage at another branch office. Whenever possible, originals should be retained for their protection, and copies should be distributed for use.

## Establish Safety Educational Program

Many employees have the attitude toward disaster that "it can't happen here," but disasters do occur in all locales, in all environments, and at all hours. (See pages 564-566 for the story of the Cheyenne, Wyoming, disaster.) Employees should be prepared to deal with the emergency in a planned and careful manner. Procedures for ensuring personal safety, of course, are of highest priority. All employees should know where the fire extinguishers are, how and when to use them, where the alarms are located and how to use them, and how to deal with panic and confusion. Practice should be provided via simulated disaster conditions; assignments should be made for exiting, and responsibilities should be designated for those who may need assistance. Procedures should also be established, as discussed earlier, for the safety of records.

As businesses are becoming more aware of the need for professional records management, they are also being alerted to the necessity of viable, tested disaster planning.

These disaster plans, custom-designed on a business-to-business basis, contain detailed instruction for disaster preparedness, disaster-in-progress, and disaster recovery procedures. In theory and in practice, disaster plans are the ultimate safety educational program for any business.

■

## A LOOK AT THE CASE

Based on the procedures discussed, the new records manager could begin by evaluating the present system of records safety.

Since the building was constructed in 1976, she first checks the date of the latest building inspection. The inspection date is October, 1984. Sue Nordstrom makes a note on her "things-to-do" list to request a fire safety inspection. She then ascertains that the records have been appraised, classified, and protected in accordance with their established value. Sue also makes an informal inquiry of several employees to find out if they are aware of the procedures for daily and emergency handling of records. A few employees appear to be minimally acquainted with what to do in the event of a fire, but most are not even aware that there is a fire alarm, much less where it is or how to use it! Another item is added to Sue's "things-to-do" list — organize an employee safety educational safety program soon.

What other types of hazards to the safety of the records should concern Sue Nordstrom?

■

## PHYSICAL SAFETY HAZARDS

The physical safety of records may be endangered by natural and/or man-made hazards. Hazards that may pose particular threats to records safety include fire, earthquakes, wind and rainstorms, water, mold and mildew, insects and rodents, dust, theft and vandalism.

### Fire

There are a number of potential hazards to records safety; however, the primary hazard is destruction by fire or by the water or chemicals used in fire containment. Each year, more than 25,000 fires occur in office and educational buildings; damages exceed $100 million. The cost of fire losses is rising each year; therefore, protection against fire losses is critical.

When new buildings are constructed, local fire departments inspect and approve both the architectural drawings and the buildings as they progress through the construction stages to completion. New buildings, therefore, are more likely to have greater fire resistance and modern detection systems than older structures. The existing older buildings should be upgraded in terms of fire deterrents, detection systems, and safety alarms. Scheduled inspections should be a part of the total safety protection program in both new and older structures.

*Fire deterrents*

## Other Natural and Man-Made Hazards

In addition to damage by fire, records must be protected from other types of natural or man-made hazards. Consideration, therefore, should be given to possible damage or destruction by elements including earthquakes, wind and rainstorms, mold and mildew, insects and rodents, dust, theft, and vandalism. Figure 20–1 shows the severe damage that flooding can cause to a company's records.

Figure 20–1
Flood Damage

**Cheyenne, Wyoming, Disaster**

On the evening of Thursday, August 1, 1985, a freak storm settled over Cheyenne, Wyoming. In less than three hours, more than six inches of rain were dumped on a community that normally receives little more than that in a whole year. To compound the disaster, great amounts of hail accumulated—in some places drifts up to eight feet were recorded.

Twelve people were killed.

The lower floor of the county court house in downtown Cheyenne was inundated by a tide of water and ice that swept through the halls with enough force to rip away public seating that was bolted to the marble walls. Desks and file cabinets were piled into corners, a full-size refrigerator used to store microfilm and chemicals floated like a boat amidst confidential papers and cartons of film. A thick layer of debris—leaves, tree branches, sludge, and trash—stuck to everything it touched.

The storm ended about 10:00 PM Thursday. By 8:00 PM Friday all but about six inches of the water had been pumped from the basement, the building had been declared structurally sound, gas and electricity had been turned off, and we were able to begin clean-up operations.

The water was ice-cold—uncomfortable to work in, but a plus because such temperatures do not favor growth of bacteria and other contaminants. Offices housed in the basement included county court, treasurer, microfilm, and budget/payroll departments. Some of the records soaked by the flood were more than 100 years old, irreplaceable for their historic value alone. The fiscal and court records were also of primary importance.

Our first concern was to stabilize the damaged record environment so that further damage would not occur. ALL paper records were boxed in standard-size record boxes and transferred to a refrigerated truck loaned to us by Safeway Stores, Inc. As the records were loaded into the truck, a careful inventory was made. The truck, while not reaching temperatures low enough to freeze the records, at least maintained their condition without further deterioration. The truck was used to transport the records to large freezer units on F.E. Warren Air Force Base, in Cheyenne, where they could be frozen.

In our haste to begin recovery, we neglected to use rubber gloves, boots, or other protective gear. This oversight necessitated tetanus shots for everyone on the recovery team.

One phone call arranged the arrival of a mobile environmental drying chamber at F.E. Warren Air Force Base by August 6. The seven-plus TONS of records previously transported were loaded into the chamber, which was then sealed and allowed to process for 17 days. When the records came to light once more, they were crisp, dry, and completely usable. Because of the quick action and this amazing procedure, our paper document recovery rate was 100 percent.

The county clerk was the only county agency equipped with a microfilm lab and therefore did the filming for all departments of the county and for some outside agencies as well. The damaged rolls of microfilm were rinsed gently in clean water, then placed, in their cartons, in large plastic garbage cans of clean, room-temperature water. It was important that the air be forced out of each carton so that all film was kept uniformly saturated. No containers were allowed to float. These containers were then taken to a lab in Fort Collins, Colorado, where the film was reprocessed using ONLY WATER—NO CHEMICALS! Again, using this procedure, our recovery rate was 100 percent.

### Cheyenne, Wyoming, Disaster, continued

Luckily, our main computer center was on the second floor and only peripheral equipment was damaged by the flood. Once more, quick action was the key to recovery. All damaged equipment was taken to a clean, dry room, dismantled as much as possible, and allowed to air-dry. Each piece was then vacuumed carefully, oiled where necessary, and reassembled. This technique afforded us usable equipment until replacements could be shipped in. Wyoming's low relative humidity contributed to the success of this venture.

Many of our floppy diskettes were damaged during the flood, and the soak-to-store then clean-and-dry-to-restore method worked well for these. The diskettes were stored for several days in room-temperature, distilled water. Then the jackets and sleeves were removed carefully, the diskettes were cleaned gently in successive baths of distilled water, and air-dried. The diskettes were then placed in new sleeves and their data recopied to new diskettes. (It was important, we found, to keep contaminated material strictly separated from new or restored material to prevent spread of contamination.)

Remember that in the recovery of automated media, the more technically advanced the medium, the less recoverable the data. For instance, water- or smoke-damaged magnetic tapes can be gently cleaned in distilled water and carefully dried inch-by-inch, but total data recovery is chancey, and such attempts may damage the expensive equipment used to read the tape. Fixed disk recovery presents the same type of risk on an even more expensive scale.

All things considered, we survived our disaster very well, indeed. Our offices were closed only one working day—the day after the flood—and reopened for business on Monday morning. Offices were "dislocated" for more than four months. We are still assessing psychological effects and dealing with the loose ends of insurance, equipment and supply replacement, and so forth.

The things we learned are innumerable and invaluable: a viable disaster plan including vital record identification and analysis, is indispensable! Backup, offsite copies of diskettes, microfilm, mag tapes and disks, is a must! (Don't forget offsite copies of software, operating systems, and documentation.) An alternate "hot site" for automated recovery operations is recommended. The "little" things count, too: Always use indelible black pen for signatures, labels, etc. Colored file folders look nice, but in a water disaster, they "bleed" and add to recovery problems. Paper clips and staples cause rust spots on documents and encourage one more type of contamination.

The most important lesson of the Laramie County disaster was "Yes! It CAN happen to us!" Never again will we be unprepared!

Diann Conyers and Janet Whitehead
Laramie County, Cheyenne, Wyoming

# PREVENTIVE AND RECONSTRUCTION PROCEDURES

Disaster plans should be developed to include procedures for preventing records damage and reconstructing records damaged in a disaster. Methods for preventing damage and reconstructing records differ according to the type of hazard and the record media.

## Fire

Of all the hazards, fire has the potential for the greatest amount of damage to records. Protection from fire is provided by storing records in vaults, safes, cabinets, rooms, and boxes. Fire resistance of records containers is measured in terms of the time it takes for the interior of the storage facility to reach 350 degrees. Paper requires a higher temperature to ignite, but the 350-degree standard provides a safety cushion.

*Paper*

Microfilm and magnetic media are damaged at temperatures lower than 350 degrees. Standard insulated files designed for 350-degree temperature protection must be supplemented for electronic media. Figure 20–2 shows a diskette storage box that is designed to be used with an insulated legal file and has been tested for one hour with temperatures up to 1700 degrees. The storage box maintained an inside temperature below 125 degrees during the hour test and for an additional hour after the test.

*Other media*

Figure 20–2
Insulated Diskette Storage Box

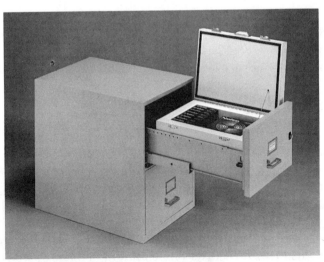

Nine out of ten data processing disasters are caused by fire. All diskettes and tapes not being used in the day's run should be kept in containers where they are not only protected from fire, but also from dust, static electricity, magnetic interference, and unauthorized users.

*Protection provided by equipment*

Fire resistance of records containers varies a great deal — from five minutes for uninsulated steel files or cabinets to up to six hours for insulated vault doors. Insulated, modern safes are rated fire resistant for up to four hours. Steel storage cabinets are not fire resistant. Although it is true that the cabinets will not burn, the fire resistance of the contents is rated at about five minutes. A study of the case records of 2,597 fires, compiled by the Safe Manufacturer's Association, revealed that when four-hour safes were used, 94.6 percent of the contents were saved compared to 34.7 percent for inspected insulated cabinets with a 45-minute rating. Table 20–2 shows the fire resistance of various types of records containers. The type of storage applicable for protection from fire is also applicable to protection from other hazards.

Table 20–2
Fire Resistance of Records Containers

| Container | Fire Resistance Time |
|---|---|
| Insulated record vault doors | 2, 4, and 6 hours |
| Insulated file room doors | $\frac{1}{2}$ and 1 hour |
| Steel plate vault doors (with inner doors) | about 15 minutes |
| Steel plate door (without inner doors) | less than 10 minutes |
| Modern safes | 1, 2, and 4 hours |
| Old Line, Iron, or Cast Iron safes, 2- to 6-inch wall thickness | Uncertain |
| Insulated records containers (storage cabinets and files) | $\frac{1}{2}$, 1, and 2 hours |
| Containers with air space or with cellular or solid insulation less than one inch thick | 10 to 20 minutes |
| Uninsulated steel files, cabinets, wooden files, wooden or steel desks | about 5 minutes |

**Source:** *Gordon P. McKinnon, editor.* Fire Protection Handbook, *16th ed. (Boston: National Fire Protection Association, 1986).*

Some records damaged by fire may be reconstructed. After placing readable pieces together, paper records may be laminated or photocopied. If the condition of the records permits, records may also be microfilmed.

*Halon gas*

Halon gas, a fire fighting agent, is particularly effective and safe when used in a records environment. Halon gas is a nonconductive, no-residue agent that will not affect information stored on magnetic tape or other media. The use of Halon gas minimizes thermal shock, eliminates contamination caused by chemical extinguishers, and is safe when used in enclosed areas. This protection is available in complete built-in systems for large organizations, in small automatic extinguishers for smaller organizations, and in portable fire extinguishers.

Extinguishing fires presents special problems for computers. Water can severely damage electrical or electronic equipment. Carbon dioxide is effective on electrical equipment fires but is toxic and hazardous to people. Cold carbon dioxide sprayed on a hot display screen can cause the CRT to explode.

## Water

Water can be as devastating to records as fire; therefore, precautionary measures should be just as carefully planned. Any signs of leaks from roof or upper floors must be reported immediately and repaired. Personnel who know the procedures for coping with either major or minor emergencies minimize the amount of damage.

Blast freezing is recommended for water-damaged paper records to stabilize record condition and halt contaminant damage. **Blast freezing** is a process by which material is frozen very quickly. The advantage of blast freezing over traditional freezing methods is that it is much faster and forms very tiny bubbles and crystals as opposed to larger ones formed by regular freezing.

*Paper*

Wet paper is fragile and should be handled as little as possible. No effort should be made to separate pages, remove clips or staples, or clean away mud or soot. Records may be frozen in file tubs and file drawers, or, if necessary, packed flat and uncrowded in standard storage boxes.

A careful inventory should be made as records are packed or transferred for freezing, as this will help with relocation of records after drying is accomplished. Records cannot be counted as restored until they are back on the shelves and in use once more.

Ideally, the records should be restored by freeze drying; that is, by evaporation of the moisture before it returns to a liquid state. There are several companies in the United States which provide mobile environmental chambers to dry records in this manner. The phone number of one or more of these companies should be included with every records manager's vital records. Figure 20–3 illustrates one type of commercial restoration.

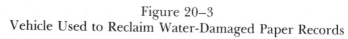

Figure 20–3
Vehicle Used to Reclaim Water-Damaged Paper Records

*Microfilm*      Microfilm should be left in cartons. Sludge on outside of cartons may be rinsed away in a gentle stream of clean, room-temperature water. Film should then be placed in a plastic container filled with clean, room-temperature water for storage until processing. Each carton of film should be pushed under water and turned to force all air out of the carton, as film must be kept uniformly wet to keep one roll from sticking to the one above it.

A one-percent solution of formalin added to the storage water will allow about two weeks of storage time without loss of film quality. During storage or transportation, do not agitate the stored film any more than necessary. If film is agitated, the layers of film may separate.

To reprocess the film, remove all chemicals from the film processor. Rinse chemical recepticals and refill them with clean, room-temperature water. Remove as many brushes, rollers, and screens from the film path as possible. Process as usual. Change water in the processor often to avoid spreading contamination.

Some microfilm companies provide emergency cleaning services, and this is an alternative that should be considered. These companies, of course, have the expertise to handle emergencies as well as normal cleaning services.

Automated records—data stored on floppy diskettes, fixed disks, and magnetic tapes—are subject to the same dangers as are paper and filmed data. While these automated records are more easily duplicated and recreateable, they are the most likely to be unrestorable. Therefore, the best defense against automated record loss is a solid backup and rotation procedure with offsite storage of duplicate data and a pre-arranged "hot site" for restoration activities.

## Earthquakes, Wind, and Rainstorms

If the building housing the records is substantial and watertight, little else can be done in a preventative way to protect the safety of the records. If the location is one where there is a history of earthquakes or where earthquakes are probable, shelving should be adequately, though not severely, braced; this makes allowance for the sway factor. The damage from storms is directly related to either flooding or leakage. When the building location is being considered, careful evaluation should be given to ground absorption and susceptibility to flooding. When there is any doubt, records should be raised at least four inches off the floor and stored in watertight containers at the lower shelf levels. The installation of a pump that operates automatically when moisture is present is an additional precaution.

## Mold and Mildew

Mold and mildew damage can occur on any type of record and are usually caused by poor control of humidity and temperature levels. The temperature should be kept between 65 and 75 degrees, and the relative humidity should be maintained at 50 percent for best preservation of paper records. Microfilm is even more susceptible to growth of mold and mildew than paper and is quite sensitive to temperature changes. A relative humidity level of 40 percent discourages the growth of mold and mildew in film. Magnetic media have somewhat different requirements for relative humidity levels. When these levels exceed 80 percent for a sustained period of more than four hours, fungus growth is accelerated.

*Humidity/ temperature controls*

Periodic inspections and an awareness of mold or mildew and the places that would tend to stimulate the development of those substances are important preventative measures. If records are relatively inactive and housed in an area that has little traffic because of record inactivity, one of the assigned duties of a records clerk should be to take a quick walk through the area and specifically look for signs of mold or mildew. As with other types of damage, one must know how to care for the problem without causing further damage to the record.

*Mold- and mildew-damaged records*

Methods of restoration differ according to the type of record and type and extent of damage. However, one of the first actions should be preventative. Ventilation retards the growth of mold spores. In warm, humid atmospheres, mold growth on water-damaged materials can be expected to appear within 48 hours. When this condition occurs, the air should be kept circulating. In cold weather the heat should be turned off; in hot weather the air conditioning should be turned on. Records should be kept from heat. Papers should be dried in temperatures up to 140 degrees, and each paper should be brushed lightly in the open air to remove mildew. Spores may be removed by a treatment of thymol crystals. The technician should be knowledgeable in this process before attempting the removal. Film and magnetic media have to be carefully wiped or cleaned with a special solution to prevent damage to the records.

It is important that both water-damaged and contaminated material be kept strictly separated from "clean" or restored material. If microfilm was stored in cardboard cartons, for example, get new cartons for the restored film and dispose of the old ones. If film was stored in plastic cartons, sterilize the cartons before replacing restored film in them.

## Insects and Rodents

Insects and rodents can destroy records or make them unusable in a relatively short period of time. Periodic inspections are helpful in preventing damage. Signs of the presence of insects and rodents are usually observable if one is specifically looking for their existence. If insects and rodents are found, an exterminator should be called for an appraisal. Damage to the records should be ascertained. Where portions of the records have actually been destroyed, replacement is not possible. The remaining portions, however, should be repaired or reproduced.

## Dust

Excessive dust also has an effect on the legibility and the rapidity of deterioration of the records. The type of record has an influence on the extent of the damage that can be caused by dust. For example, dust accumulated on computer tapes, on disks, on microfilm, or on floppy disks can be highly damaging and in some cases affect the output. For magnetic tape, relative humidity levels below 45 percent cause static electricity which attracts dust to the tape. The signal density of the tape also makes it especially susceptible to dust collection. Proper control of air conditioning with recirculated filtered air reduces the amount of dust in the air.

## Theft and Vandalism

Theft and vandalism are major concerns to businesses, and these concerns are now expressed in billions of dollars spent annually to protect property, products, and records. This major issue of protection of records from theft and vandalism is discussed in the latter part of this chapter. The safeguards applicable to the security of the records content are also applicable to the protection of the records against unauthorized access.

One of the most important aspects of the protection and restoration program is preplanning. A list of experts to call in case of an emergency and a list of places to obtain necessary supplies are musts for the person responsible for emergency procedures. Table 20–3 summarizes preventive and reconstruction procedures.

Table 20–3
Preventive/Reconstruction Procedures

| Medium | Damage | Cause | What To Do |
|---|---|---|---|
| Paper | Charred | Fire damage | Laminate<br>Paper copy<br>Microfilm |
| Paper | Wet, soggy | Water damage | Freeze dry<br>Blast freeze |
| Paper | Mold/mildew | Humidity | Ventilate<br>Brush lightly<br>Thymol crystal treatment<br>Dry at 140 degrees maximum<br>Keep temperature at 65 to 75 degrees<br>Keep relative humidity at 50 percent |
| Microform | Wet | Water damage | Place in plastic container filled with clean, room-temperature water for storage<br>Freeze if salvage operation takes more than a few days |
| Microform | Mold/mildew | Humidity | Keep relative humidity at 40 percent<br>Relative humidity above 80 percent causes fungus growth |
| Magnetic | Mold/mildew | Humidity | Ventilate<br>Clean carefully with restorative solution |

■

## A LOOK AT THE CASE

In her get-acquainted tour of the records facility, Sue Nord-strom notices that, although the temperature is comfortable for the employees working in the center, the facility seems quite damp. In the rear section of the center, a musty odor causes her to suspect that there may be some existing or potential damage to the records from mold or mildew. Sue asks one of the records center clerks to check for possible existence of either substance. If a problem exists, the clerk is to note both the location and the extent of the damage. Sue will then determine the proper action to take. She sees no apparent signs of any insect or rodent infestation of the records — for that, she breathes a sigh of relief!

Since the vital records protection program is an essential part of the development of the total program of records safety and security, Sue must take the necessary action to strengthen the existing program.

What specific aspects of the present program should be strengthened?

■

## VITAL RECORDS PROTECTION

Vital records, those records necessary for the continued operation and survival of a business, must be protected. A program of safety and security, often time consuming and costly because of its labor-intensive operation, involves the entire corporate structure. Vital records are found in every department that plays a legal, financial, or operational role in an organization. Because the protection program affects so many people and is so critical to the continuation of "business as usual," the program must be an integral part of the total records system. "Why is a vital records protection program more important than insurance?" is a frequently asked question. The answer is that protection of the organization's vital records ensures the continued life of the business, while insurance pays the organization after its death following a disaster.

## Methods of Protection

Protection of the records from loss may be accomplished by several methods. Documents may be duplicated in various forms, or documents may be stored in minimal-risk containers at either onsite or offsite locations. For maximum safety, duplicate records should be made, and these records should be stored in minimal-risk areas. Only vital records are affected; therefore, the volume of records to be duplicated should not exceed ten percent of the total records of the organization.

*Duplicate records*

### Duplication

**Duplication** is a method of providing a copy of an original document. If duplication is selected as the preferred safety measure, other considerations must be addressed. The following questions highlight some of these considerations.

*What form should duplicates take?* Duplicates can take the form of paper copies, roll microfilm, microfiche, magnetic tapes, or other media used by the organization. The selection should be made on the basis of the needs of the organization and the equipment and facilities available. This analysis should include questions such as the following:

1. Will users have ready access to readers for microfilm or fiche?
2. Will printers be available if hard copy is required by the users of tape, film, or fiche?
3. Is there adequate file space for paper copies?
4. Is equipment available to make multiple paper copies?
5. What facilities/equipment are needed for housing any duplicates?

*Do duplicates now exist?* Are duplicates available for records which are already generated? If so, what form are they in and where are they located?

*When should duplicates be made?* Consideration must be given to whether duplication should occur at the time the record is created or at a scheduled time. This decision, of course, affects where the duplicate should be made. If duplication occurs at time of creation, controls are needed to ensure that the duplicates are made. Duplication at the time the record is generated would normally be in paper form.

*Where should duplicates be made?* If offsite storage is provided and duplication occurs at that location, equipment must be provided at the offsite location. Consideration must also be given to providing access to the duplicates, if necessary. In some instances, having a limited quantity of reproduction equipment onsite may be necessary.

***How often should updates be made?*** A schedule for updating the information must be maintained. The amount of time between updates would greatly affect records reconstruction following a disaster; this should be taken into consideration when decisions concerning intervals are made. For example, if records updates are scheduled on an annual basis, data would have to be gathered for an entire twelve-month period in order to reconstruct that record to a current basis.

*Use of original versus duplicate record*

A frequently discussed issue is when to use the original record and when to use a duplicate. If the vital records are active records, the user normally works with the source documents (original record); the duplicates, in whatever form, are stored in another location where they can be safeguarded. Examples of active vital records where originals are used are accounts receivable, current contracts, and creative works in progress. Original inactive vital records, in contrast to active vital records, are stored for protection, and the duplicates are used when the need occurs. Examples of inactive vital records are corporate charters, minutes of stockholders meetings, and completed creative works.

Many organizations recognize the need for and value of the dual protection afforded by the provision of duplicate copies and minimum-risk storage. The term "minimum risk" is used because it is virtually impossible to provide protection that is 100 percent risk free. For example, Virginia laws applicable to state agencies require the submission of microfilm duplicates of records to the Virginia State Library Board, whose responsibility as the records repository is established by law. The financial records of Wall Street are microfilmed and sent for protective storage to the salt flats of Utah, where they are housed in underground vaults. The social security records are housed in an old limestone mine in northwestern Pennsylvania, 260 feet underground. Figure 20–4 shows how records in various media can be efficiently stored under ground.

*Selection criteria for storage facilities*

When decisions are being made concerning the storage facilities necessary to house either the originals or the duplicates (depending on whether the vital record is considered active or inactive), attention should be given to the total volume to be stored and to any special requirements, such as temperature, humidity, size, or shape of the records.

Figure 20–4
Underground Storage

## Dispersal

**Dispersal** is one method of providing a copy of an original docu-<br>
ment for records reconstruction. Dispersal is normally used with<br>
paper copies only. The source receiving the copy can be either in-<br>
ternal or external to the organization. Internally, copies may be<br>
sent to other persons who have interest in the particular document.<br>
This method, however, does not provide a consistent procedure<br>
for ensuring that every document will have a duplicate. A method<br>
of routine dispersal is followed when information is sent to exter-<br>
nal sources. For example, if an organization's federal income tax<br>
forms were destroyed, duplicates could be obtained from the gov-<br>
ernment; if bank records were destroyed, the bank could provide<br>
duplicates; if insurance policies were destroyed, the insurance com-<br>
panies could provide duplicates. In some instances, this form of<br>
records safety is all that is needed.

*Internal/external<br>
dispersal*

## Special Respositories

For maximum protection of original and duplicate records, con-<br>
tainers resistant to natural disasters should be considered. Records<br>
are traditionally stored in vaults, safes, cabinets, rooms, and boxes.<br>
Maximum protection is provided by insulated vaults with heavily<br>
insulated doors. It is important to evaluate the needs of the organi-<br>
zation and the concentration of risk before making a decision re-<br>
garding the type of storage container required. (See Table 20–2.)

## Vital Records Protection Manual

Once all decisions have been made regarding identification of vital records, the procedures to be followed for implementation, and the most appropriate method of protection, a vital records protection manual should be developed. This **vital records protection manual** may be a separate document, part of the records management manual, or part of the records retention and disposition manual; its form depends on the needs of the organization. Whichever course of action is taken, the manual should list all vital records according to department and contain both the vital record code number and the retention date.

## A LOOK AT THE CASE

When Sue Nordstrom began her inspection of the records facility, she determined that the records had been appraised, classified, and protected according to their established value. The system for protection used by White Transportation Company is one dimensional. Records are kept in fire resistant vaults and no system is available for duplication of records other than by nonscheduled dispersal. Sue should consider the cost benefit of establishing a process of records duplication to provide dual protection of the records. An updated vital records protection manual should be a part of the total system of protection, and measures should be taken to ensure its use.

When the case was introduced, Sue Nordstrom overheard a request for a personnel file of a former employee. Should Sue follow up on the procedure used to provide information from the company files?

## CONTENT SECURITY

**Content security** provides protection against intentional destruction, disclosure, modification, or breach of confidentiality of information.

## Need for Security

Since the 1960s, more and more attention has been directed toward the protection of the content of organizational records. In 1974, the passage of the amendments to the **Freedom of Information Act and Privacy Act** provided even greater protection. The two acts combine to ensure the security and integrity of personal information collected by governmental agencies. The objective of the law is to protect individuals from harm, inconvenience, embarrassment, or unfairness by safeguarding the confidentiality and integrity of personal records. Individuals have the right to know what information is collected; to have access to their personal records, either by inspection or copy; to question, refute, and correct information; and to add explanatory statements if desired. Furthermore, safeguards against unauthorized access are to be maintained. Public access to public records is also guaranteed under the law.

*Freedom of Information Act and Privacy Act*

Many states have enacted laws which enhance and strengthen the federal legislation. Subsequent and pending legislation would extend the protection afforded individuals to include the private as well as the public sector.

*State legislation*

In addition to the need for legislated record protection, organizations in the private sector are also recognizing the need to establish their own programs of internal record integrity and security. Voluntary programs are beginning to emerge as businesses accept their responsibilities in this area of records management. Certainly part of the motivation is a genuine concern for records integrity; however, some motivation can be attributed to the desire for voluntary compliance before there is a need for legislated compliance. In this manner, the private sector can adopt protective measures appropriate for its own needs without federal intervention.

The laws were enacted to protect the privacy of personal and financial information concerning employees and customers. If information is released without permission, the organization could be liable for damages. Clearly major factors to be considered are the increasing number of lawsuits being brought against organizations for breach of confidentiality and invasion of privacy and the large court-awarded settlements in favor of the plaintiffs. Thus, organizations have a proprietary interest in protecting themselves from any action that could be construed as a breach of confidentiality or of privacy.

## Effects of Legislation

Organizations are increasingly affected by the impact of both mandatory and voluntary controls of information security. A new law may very well be added to Murphy's Law, Parkinson's Law, and others. The new law is *Ricks' Law of Increasing Paperwork:* "As controls on paperwork increase arithmetically, the paperwork necessary to accomplish the controls increases geometrically."

*Effects on recordkeeping procedures*

One of the impacts of the emphasis on content security is the potential for increased recordkeeping in both strategies of implementation and for accountability. Most legislation requires records to be maintained with such accuracy, timeliness, completeness, and relevance as is reasonably necessary for fairness. In order to accomplish the required documentation, a major overhaul of current recordkeeping procedures may be necessary. New procedures need to conform to the objectives of the individual organization with regard to security as well as with regard to the law and its intent.

The Federal Privacy Protection Study Commission, authorized by the 1974 Act, issued a report in July, 1977. This report, entitled "Personal Privacy in an Information Society," identified eight principles of personal information management practices. Any organization considering the development of a program of record confidentiality should study these principles and incorporate them in its own system.

*Principles of personal information management*

1. *Openness* — There should be a policy of openness about an organization's personal recordkeeping policies, practices, and systems; there should be no secret systems.
2. *Individual access* — An individual about whom information is maintained by a recordkeeping organization in individually identifiable form should have a right to see and copy that information.
3. *Individual participation* — An individual should have the right to correct or amend the substance of personal information maintained by a recordkeeping organization.
4. *Collection limitation* — Internal collection of personal information within a recordkeeping organization should be limited to necessary information.
5. *Use limitation* — Internal uses of personal information within a recordkeeping organization should be limited to those who have a need to know.
6. *Disclosure limitation* — External disclosures of personal information by a recordkeeping organization should be limited.
7. *Information management* — A recordkeeping organization should bear affirmative responsibility for establishing reasonable and

proper information management policies and practices to assure that its collection, maintenance, use, and dissemination of information about an individual are necessary and lawful and that the information itself is current and accurate.

8. *Accountability* — A recordkeeping organization should be accountable for its personal recordkeeping policies, practices, and systems.

## Procedures for Records Access

Once the principles have been clearly established, specific procedures for implementation are developed. To establish these procedures, the records manager may wish to review current procedures for

*Gaining access to records*

1. legitimate access to records,
2. safeguards against unauthorized access, and
3. maintaining the integrity of records.

A careful review should reveal specific areas in which improved procedures are necessary and areas that fully meet all requirements for compliance. Areas that are somewhat questionable may require legal interpretation.

### Document Access

A central source for records access, with one person responsible for compliance with company guidelines, is desirable for ease of control and delegation of responsibility. These guidelines should be written, disseminated, and enforced. All employees at all management levels should be informed regarding the procedures to be followed when requesting information or providing requested information to another.

When access to a record is requested, the person processing the request should follow established procedures. These procedures might include the following:

*Access procedures*

1. If review of a personal record is requested by the individual, two forms of identification should be required if the person is unknown; completion of authorization form is required.
2. If a copy of a personal record is requested by the individual, two forms of identification should be required if the person is unknown; completion of authorization form and a signature for receipt of copy are also required.
3. If the requester is a company employee with a need to review, copy, or log out a record, a signature on a receipt for the copy or a signature on a log identifying the record reviewed or logged out should be required.

4. If the request is made by mail, its legitimacy should be verified and, when necessary, written permission for the release of the information should be obtained.
5. If records are highly confidential, only authorized persons may be allowed to review the records. When this situation exists, an "authorized-to-see" list should be available, and the requester's name must appear on that list to access the record.
6. In all other instances, the records manager or designee must grant authorization on a case-by-case basis. Documentation may be provided by signature on a log or request form. Other controls, as discussed in the following sections, may be appropriate.

Forms may range in complexity from a very detailed form to a simple notation of the name of the person requesting the record, the date, the record requested, and presence of a copy, if applicable. The form required by the General Services Administration for access to personal information is shown in Figure 20–5.

### Area/Facility Access

A system of controlled access to an area or facility must be established to maintain safeguards against unauthorized invasion of records. The primary criterion for entrance should be that only those whose work requires access should be admitted!

Multiple options are available for security control, ranging from old-fashioned keyed locks to computer-controlled card readers. The three primary access controls which do not require checking by guards/security personnel are

*Access controls*

- keys used to unlock doors. Keys are easily duplicated and lost; anyone can use them. The lock itself is vulnerable to entry and cannot distinguish between persons authorized to enter and those who are not.
- electronic or mechanical push button entry controls. These controls require memorizing a series of numbers and/or letters and people often forget the code. Some people record the code where others may find and use it. This form of access is also vulnerable to electronic lock picking.
- plastic cards with coded strips. These cards can control a single door or multiple entry points. The card may be inserted into the reader which controls the lock, or the reader may act as a remote terminal controlled by a central microcomputer. The cards may be coded to include authorized doors and unauthorized doors. A combination of these three controls may be used, such as are shown in Figure 20–6.

Figure 20–5
Privacy Information Act Request Form

| | |
|---|---|
| **PRIVACY ACT INFORMATION REQUEST** | Agency Facility _____<br>Control No. _____ |

◄ *False statements subject to criminal penalties. See Pub. L. 93-579, 88 stat. 1902 (5 D.S.C. 552a(i).* ►
THIS FORM TO BE COMPLETED BY AGENCY

**SECTION I – REQUESTER AND RECORD IDENTIFICATION**

**1. REQUESTER INFORMATION**

| 1. NAME OF REQUESTER *(Please print)*<br>Michael Rutherford | a. ADDRESS *(Street, city, state, ZIP code)*<br>20 Fulton Street<br>Baltimore, Maryland 21224 | b. TELE. NO. *(Include area code)*<br>301-781-7833 |
|---|---|---|

**2. RECORD REQUEST**

a. DESCRIPTION OF RECORD *(Title, index number, etc.)*

Personnel Record

b. LOCATION OF RECORD *(Office, activity, city, organization)*

CINCLANT FORCES    Atlanta, GA

Individual whose record is being sought IF OTHER THAN REQUESTER *(applies to c, d, e and f below)*

| c. NAME | d. ADDRESS *(Street, city, state, ZIP code)* | e. TELE. NO. *(Include area code)* |
|---|---|---|
| | | |

| f. REPRESENTATIVE'S LEGAL CAPACITY *(Copy of authorizing document must be attached, e.g., court's guardianship order, power of attorney, etc.)* | g. ACTION REQUESTED<br>☐ PERSONAL ACCESS    ☐ FILE DISAGREEMENT STATEMENT<br>☒ REVIEW    ☐ AMENDMENT    ☐ COPY<br>☐ OTHER *(Specify)* |
|---|---|

| h. SIGNATURE OF REQUESTER<br>Michael Rutherford | i. DATE<br>1/17/-- |
|---|---|

**SECTION II – AGENCY RESPONSE**

**3. ACTION TAKEN ON RECORD REQUEST** *(Items marked with an "X" apply to your request.)*

| ☐ a. YOUR REQUEST HAS BEEN RECEIVED AND IS BEING PROCESSED. WE WILL RESPOND WITHIN 30 DAYS.<br>☐ b. THE RECORD YOU REQUESTED IS ATTACHED.<br>☐ NO FEE    ☐ SUBMIT $ _____ FEE.<br>☐ c. WE DO HAVE THE RECORD. FOR PERSONAL ACCESS, PLEASE CALL OR WRITE THE PERSON WHOSE NAME APPEARS BELOW, FOR A COPY SUBMIT $ _____ | ☐ d. WE NEED ADDITIONAL INFORMATION TO RESPOND TO YOUR REQUEST. PLEASE PROVIDE THE FOLLOWING INFORMATION *(See remarks)*.<br>☐ e. THE RECORD YOU REQUESTED IS EXEMPT FROM DISCLOSURE UNDER THE LAW. PLEASE SEE ATTACHED EXPLANATION.<br>☐ f. WE DO NOT HAVE YOUR RECORD IN OUR FILES. |
|---|---|

g. REMARKS

| h. SIGNATURE OF OFFICIAL | i. TITLE OF OFFICIAL |
|---|---|
| | |

| j. ADDRESS OF OFFICIAL | k. DATE |
|---|---|
| | |

**SECTION III – FOR AGENCY USE ONLY**

**4. AGENCY INFORMATION**

| a. REQUEST RECEIVED:<br>BY | DATE | b. IDENTITY ESTABLISHED IN PERSON:<br>APPROVED BY | DATE |
|---|---|---|---|
| c. ACTION ASSIGNED TO: | | d. DATE | e. RESPONSE DUE DATE |
| f. FEE DATA<br>AMOUNT DUE<br>$ | DATE RECEIVED | g. NONCOLLECTIBLE COSTS | |

* U.S. GOVERNMENT PRINTING OFFICE, 1975-632-463          OPTIONAL FORM 203-17-75
General Services Administration

*Source:* *General Services Administration (Washington, D.C.: U.S. Government Printing Office, 1975).*

Figure 20–6
Devices for Access to Facilities

*Audit trails*

Electronic access devices provide audit trails through recording employee number, door number, date and time of entry, or attempted entry, and other information the company wishes to include. This information may be printed out as a hard-copy log to be reviewed by the appropriate persons.

According to Larry Grady, Marketing Vice President of Microcard Technologies, Inc., there are three classifications of security

1. what you have—key, card, photopass
2. what you know—password, code, personal identification number (PIN)
3. what you are—unique characteristics that only you possess.

In the first two categories—what you have and what you know—you are issued a method of access. You are given a key, a card, a password, a PIN, or a code. In the last category—what you are—you are enrolled in an access system biometrically. These **biometric devices** measure and record your unique characteristics, such as fingerprints, voice, or retinal eye patterns. These characteristics are matched electronically as you attempt access to an area or to a facility.

Where access controls are in place and enforced, there should be a central place for visitors to apply for entrance. Once inside the facility, the visitors are subject to all of the other access controls; unlimited access is not granted.

## Equipment Access

The need for an additional safeguard is recognized. As more and more organizations turn to a totally integrated system of records management which combines the technologies of word processing, data processing, telecommunications, micrographics, and reprographics, procedures for prohibiting unauthorized access and controlling authorized access to electronic files must be provided. These controls are critical for compliance with external and internal privacy regulations.

*Equipment controls*

Information may be obtained in many ways, including visual call up on the CRT, computer printout from stored data, on a word processor (hard copy from stored documents), or facsimile. Because the possibilities for storing and retrieving information are greater than ever, precautions against misuse must be consistently and constantly exercised.

Controls can be built into the electronic files system. Entry into the system may require a code, a password, or a key. The person desiring information keys in an assigned numerical code, a password, or a combination of the two to gain entry into the system and retrieve the desired information. For additional safety, some systems may require a key to unlock the keyboard. Similar controls for prevention of unauthorized copying of records are necessary. Reproduction equipment should be located in a restricted area where access and use are controlled.

## A LOOK AT THE CASE

Certain procedures must be followed in order to protect the privacy of employee, personal, and financial records and to protect businesses from lawsuits stemming from unauthorized release of information. Therefore, Sue Nordstrom should be concerned about the request for the personnel record of a former White Transportation employee. The file clerk to whom the request was made should establish the legitimacy of the request and follow the procedures for releasing information and documentation. If the person requesting the record has no right to see it, the request must be denied.

## TERMINOLOGY REVIEW

*Biometric devices.* Scanners that measure and record fingerprints, voice, or retinal eye patterns.

*Blast freezing.* A process by which material is frozen very quickly.

*Class 1 records.* See *Vital records.*

*Class 2 records.* See *Important records.*

*Class 3 records.* See *Useful records.*

*Class 4 records.* See *Nonessential records.*

*Content security.* Providing for the protection of the content of records from destruction, disclosure, modification, or breach of confidentiality.

*Dispersal.* A method of providing a copy of an original document by having access to a copy distributed externally or internally.

*Duplication.* A method of providing a copy of an original document by reproducing the original in paper, microfilm, microfiche, magnetic, or other media used by the organization.

*Freedom of Information and Privacy Acts.* Two acts that combine to protect personal information collected by a government agency.

*Important records.* Those records necessary to the continued life of a business; also called Class 2 records.

*Nonessential records.* Those records having no present value to the organization; also called Class 4 records.

*Useful records.* Those records useful to the uninterrupted operation of the business; also called Class 3 records.

*Vital records.* Those records essential to the continued life of a business; also called Class 1 records.

*Vital records protection manual.* A manual listing all vital records of an organization according to department; contains both the vital record code number and the retention date.

## COMPETENCY REVIEW

1.  Identify the major responsibilities of the records manager in the area of records safety and security.
2.  With regard to the natural hazards to records,
    a.  Which one presents the most danger?
    b.  What responsibility does the records manager have for building safety?
    c.  What steps can be taken for minimizing the danger of records destruction?
3.  Why is a vital records protection program essential to the survival of an organization?
4.  Categorize the methods that may be used to protect vital records and evaluate the protection provided by each method.

5.  When evaluating possible methods of protecting vital records, what considerations should be reviewed?
6.  What do you see as the trend toward greater/lesser effects of legislation for records management?
7.  Describe the procedures for controlling access to records.
8.  Describe the methods for controlling access to areas/facilities.
9.  Describe the methods for controlling access to equipment.

## APPLICATIONS

1.  Classify your personal records as Class 1, Vital; Class 2, Important; Class 3, Useful; or Class 4, Nonessential. Provide a rationale for your classification of each item. Your records may include canceled checks, insurance policies, income tax returns, purchase records, bills to be paid, birth certificates, and so on.
2.  Do you agree/disagree that the records management practices have only been minimally affected by recent legislation? Support your answer.
3.  Review another student's response to Competency Review 7 and point out the deficiencies and strengths in his or her procedures.

## CONCLUDING CASES

### A. Kennedy's Consulting Service

Bill Pace has been the records manager at Kennedy's Consulting Service for two years. Kennedy's is a large firm with a high volume of clients whose records contain confidential information. For some time, Bill has been concerned about the safety and security of the client records. The records center is "bulging at the seams"; it is understaffed; records are everywhere. Boxes of accessions are stacked in the receiving area. Neat piles of refiles are stacked on the counters. The desks in the reference area seem to have papers and microfiche scattered all over.

Kennedy's has always had a practice of open access. All consultants have free access to the records center. In fact, everyone seems to have access!

Bill's predecessor, George Wilson, did not believe in a lot of red tape. He always said, "Just go get what you need to do your work. If you sign for something every time you need one little item, we'll be flooded with paper."

1.  What are some specific concerns Bill should address immediately?
2.  How can he solve these problems?
3.  What kinds of long-term planning must he do?

## B. Dodson Time Shares, Inc.

Kim Tokuda, the records manager of Dodson Time Shares, Inc., has been attempting to establish a program to protect the physical safety of Dodson's records. Despite many informal discussions with several of the vice presidents, Kim has been unable to convince top management that a comprehensive safety program is necessary for the continuing success of the organization. Typical responses included "We have insurance to cover disasters"; "Kim said that only four to ten percent of our records are essential anyway"; and "It won't happen to us."

1.  What is the first step Kim should have taken to establish a comprehensive program of safety for Dodson's records?
2.  What steps should be taken next?

## READINGS AND REFERENCES

Betts, Kellyn S. "Electronic Access Controls Always Alert." *Modern Office Technology*, Vol. 31, No. 6 (June, 1986), p. 108.

Bound, William A. J. "Security: Protecting Information Resources and Media." *Information Management*, Vol. 18, No. 8 (August, 1984), p. 18.

Brenner, Robert C. "Developing a Disaster Plan for Your Computer System." *Office Systems '85*, Vol. 2, No. 12 (December, 1985), p. 80.

Carter, Roy. "Management Accountability and Corporate Security." *Administrative Management*, Vol. 47, No. 6 (June, 1986), p. 52.

Chasen, Irving. "Contingency Planning for Automated Systems." *Office Administration and Automation*, Vol. 45, No. 6 (June, 1984), p. 57.

Ciura, Jean M. "Vital Records Protection: Part I, Identifying Essential Information." *Information Management*, Vol. 19, No. 2 (February, 1985), p. 11.

Ciura, Jean M. "Vital Records Protection: Part II, Systems Design and Implementation." *Information Management*, Vol. 19, No. 4 (April, 1985), p. 16.

Gast, Bruce M. "Data Safes Secure Computer Records Against Fire and Other Risks." *Administrative Management*, Vol. 47, No. 6 (June, 1986), p. 56.

Hoffman, Annie, and Bryan Baumann. "Disaster Recovery—A Prevention Plan for NWNL." *Records Management Quarterly*, Vol. 20, No. 2 (April, 1986), p. 40.

Holzman, Henry. "Keeping Your Offices Safe & Sound." *Modern Office Technology*, Vol. 30, No. 5 (May, 1985), p. 92.

"Is Getting In Getting Out of Control?" *Today's Office*, Vol. 20, No. 4 (September, 1985).

*Management of Personal Information Records with System 200*. Chicago, Illinois: A.B. Dick Company (1979).

"Manual for Fire Protection for Archives and Records Centers." National Fire Protection Association, 1986.

McKinnon, Gordon P., editor. *Fire Protection Handbook,* 16th ed. Boston: National Fire Protection Association, 1986.

Minter, W. D. "Managing A Vital Records Program." Presentation, 1985 ARMA Conference, New York (September, 1985).

"Protection of Records." National Fire Protection Association, 1986.

"Report of the General Services Administration Advisory Committee on the Protection of Archives and Records Centers." General Services Administration (April, 1977).

Rofes, William L. "Information Security." Presentation, 1985 ARMA Conference, New York (September, 1985).

Schul, John. "12 Steps in Vital Records Planning." *Information and Records Management* (March, 1977).

Seymour, Jim. "Wanted for Software Theft." *Today's Office,* Vol. 19, No. 3 (August, 1984), p. 20.

Sherman, Lloyd E. "Is Your Vital Information Protected?" *Administrative Management,* Vol. 47, No. 6 (June, 1986), p. 50.

Stafford, Vera K. "The Design of a Vital Records Program." Presentation, 1985 ARMA Conference, New York (September, 1985).

## COMPREHENSIVE CASE, PART IV

You have just been appointed records manager for Super Saver Stores. After several weeks of familiarizing yourself with Super Saver's records management system, you have concluded that an important part of the system is not in place. There seem to be, at best, minimal controls over correspondence, copies, directives, reports, forms, microrecords, or even over the security of records.

As a preliminary to establishing a control system, you have decided to investigate the control systems used by several other organizations. This investigation must take place while you are conducting your other duties as records manager; therefore, you decide to limit your investigation at this time to one of the control programs. Select one of the following control programs for evaluation:

- Correspondence control
- Copy control
- Directives control
- Reports control
- Forms control
- Microrecords control
- Records safety and security controls

For the control program selected:

1. Design a form to collect the information.
2. Write letters to five organizations requesting that they supply the information needed.
3. Analyze the information received.

4. Write follow-up letters as required to obtain the information.

5. Prepare a report that compiles and summarizes the collected information. The report may be in narrative, tabular, or text-table form.

6. Add an evaluation section to the report that identifies strengths and weaknesses of the control programs analyzed. Recommendations may be made regarding the weaknesses. If assumptions are to be made, the assumptions should be stated.

# APPENDIX A
## Archives Management

*History is the witness that testifies to the passing of time; it illuminates reality, vitalizes memory, provides guidance in daily life.*

— *Cicero*

Archival management preserves history and provides the vehicle for using history in a beneficial way in the business environment. Archives house public or private organizational records that have been selected for long-term retention and preservation. Archives have been called "records preserved for reasons other than those for which they were created." The original reason for the creation of the records may no longer exist; the historical value becomes the reason for retaining the records.

## ARCHIVES USE

Records are preserved and maintained in order to provide documentation that will aid managers in their daily activities and will aid the organization in the accomplishment of its established goals.

Archives are used to preserve corporate memory; provide production information, policy direction, personnel information, and financial information; maintain public relations activities; provide legal advantage and research service; and to prepare commemorative histories.

### Preserve Corporate Memory

Historical records are used to document the activities of the organization and, in that way, preserve corporate memory. For example, it may be important to know issue dates of patents, initial distribution dates of products, and actions of the governing body, and to provide documentation of these facts.

### Provide Product Information

Documentation of product development, the success or failure of prior products, and marketing strategies used are all relevant to the creation, development, or introduction of a new product. For example, if a manufacturer is contemplating a change in product design, knowing the history of that product may be helpful.

## Provide Policy Direction

Historical records may provide direction for reviewing the effectiveness of existing policies or in considering new ones. For example, access to records regarding the effectiveness of past policies and procedures would give direction for maintaining or changing policies.

## Provide Personnel Information

Personnel departments may find organizational history helpful when conducting employee orientation and building company identification. Personnel information may also be useful when it is necessary to contact previous employees. For example, in 1969 the archives staff of Eli Lilly and Company was asked to assist in locating surviving members of the families of deceased Lilly employees. When new benefits for survivors were added to the company's survivor benefits program, these benefits were made retroactive for eligible survivors of every qualified employee who had died at any time since the company began its retirement program. As a result of obtaining this personnel information, over 300 eligible survivors began receiving benefits.

## Provide Financial Information

The use of early financial records may prove valuable in forecasting activities. Planning departments frequently use financial records in long-term strategic planning.

## Maintain Public Relations Activities

Having complete and accurate information available for use in public relations campaigns is essential. A proven record of accomplishment, operational continuity, and length of service to the public provides a wealth of promotional material. For example, Ford Motor Co. once constructed an entire television commercial around a letter of approval the company received from the gangster Clyde Barrow (of Bonnie and Clyde fame). The Coca-Cola Company also has offered trays and glasses that are facsimilies of those used many years ago to advertise Coca-Cola.

## Provide Legal Advantage

Legal departments often need historical records to document their positions. For example, Eli Lilly and Company found archives information to be essential in establishing their right to a trademark registration. Other organizations have used their archives to justify tax positions, product rights, and so forth.

## Provide Research Service

Researchers need a source for their information. Essential tools of the historian are original records. Without original records, the researcher must rely on hearsay, tradition, recollections, and summary documentation. Archives provide the researcher with accurate information which is accessible to users and preserved so that the information is still available. Often, knowing exactly when something happened allows for easier identification of the reason or causes for the event.

## Prepare Commemorative Histories

Businesses often wish to prepare a commemorative history for an anniversary. Historical records are essential to an accurate portrayal of the early years of a company. When there is no documentation, oral histories must be relied upon to provide the necessary information. Although these personal recollections provide color, they may be inaccurate or only partial recollections. Many companies prepare commemorative histories as they approach significant milestones in their lives; 25-, 50-, 75-, and 100-year anniversaries are typical commemorative years.

# APPROACHES TO ARCHIVES MANAGEMENT

Historically, there have been three different approaches to archives management—unstructured internal approach, structured internal approach, and external approach. Some organizations have made a progression through all three approaches, with changes made as the needs of the organization changed.

## Unstructured Internal Approach

In the unstructured internal approach to archives management, someone is assigned the task of sorting records to determine which records are valuable and should be preserved and which records have no lasting value and therefore should be destroyed. This is usually accomplished on an "as-needed" basis to clean out existing records in order to provide storage space for incoming records. Records tend to accumulate faster than they are destroyed, and the need for the process begins to occur more frequently as the need for storage accelerates. With the unstructured approach, the sorting is not usually a permanently assigned task. Several persons sorting and making decisions for retention or destruction may cause inconsistency and result in failure to preserve the most important records.

## Structured Internal Approach

Beginning in 1943 with the establishment of a business archives by Firestone Tire & Rubber Co., other organizations began to see the value of establishing a formal system to collect and maintain their own historical records. This approach has been adopted by a number of large organizations including Eli Lilly and Company, Walt Disney Productions, Ford Motor Co., Colonial Williamsburg Foundation, Coca-Cola Company, International Business Machines Corp., universities, and governmental agencies.

## External Approach

Some organizations have elected to preserve and maintain their historical records in university libraries, historical societies, and other collection agencies such as the National Archives. Although this approach provides a place for historical records, the disadvantages associated with the external approach have caused a number of organizations to withdraw their collections and begin their own archival programs. This approach separates important records by housing them in two places: active records within the organization, and selected inactive records outside the organization. Some of the records housed in the external depositories are bulky, little used, and expensive to maintain. The external approach seems to be more appropriate for organizations which are no longer in business rather than for active organizations.

## RECORD SELECTION

What records should be preserved and maintained in archival storage? Record selection is largely dependent upon the purpose for which each archival facility is established. Questions that should be asked prior to selection of records to be placed in archival storage include

- Will the archives function as a purely administrative tool?
- Will its collections be available only to insiders?
- Will the archives serve scholars and other interested individuals?
- Will only company records be collected or will materials documenting the organization's role in community and civic affairs be included?
- Will the personal records of company officials be collected?

The answers to these questions, in addition to affecting the selection of the records being considered for preservation and archival storage, will determine the scope of the program.

## Record Content

Record selection is a two-phase operation. The first phase is a determination of the administrative units most likely to produce records whose preservation may be important to the organization. The second phase is a determination of the record types to be preserved and maintained. The content of the record, rather than the age of the record, dominates the selection decision. Preserving records simply because they are old is difficult to justify when one considers the expense involved in the preservation and maintenance of the records in the archives program. Final selection is based on the organization's perceived value of the records for future reference and research.

## Record Types

Most of the records selected for preservation and for archival storage are paper documents. However, archival records are not limited to paper documents. Many forms of organizational history are chosen for inclusion in archives because the various types make a contribution to the preservation of corporate history.

Walt Disney Productions archivist David R. Smith identified for his unique type of archives three types of records—business, creative, and product. Included in the business category are all of the traditional records. Creative records include the many types of materials generated in planning and producing films and in planning and constructing Disneyland, Walt Disney World, and Epcot Center. The product records include films, books, comic books, phonograph records, press clippings, still photographs, insignia, character merchandise, employee publications, audioanimatronics, props, costumes, and Walt Disney memorabilia.

Another example of records other than paper that have been used to preserve corporate history are those items selected by Eli Lilly and Company. Its archives include samples of Lilly products, anniversary souvenirs, advertising promotions, bottles, and packaging material.

Photographs are an important part of an archives collection. Pictures of people, equipment, products, and buildings add color and dimension to the archival records maintained by an organization.

Oral histories—valuable assets of any company—are particularly valuable when based on the experiences of the organization's key executives. These histories may be preserved in the form of tapes and/or transcripts, and videotapes. Original company catalogs are also a source of information.

All of these types of records are appropriate for archival preservation and storage. Final selection should be based upon the needs of the individual organization.

## Reference Value

It is difficult to differentiate the reference value of archives from the research value. In general, the distinction lies with the user and the intent rather than with the record and its content. Archives provide information regarding the organization's policies, philosophies, performances, product, and people. When this information is used internally, its value is primarily reference. Company personnel requiring information for the performance of their daily activities would benefit from the reference value of the archives. These records may provide validation or reinforcement for their decisions.

## Research Value

The research value of archives most frequently lies with external users or with organizational personnel who are engaged in researching the development of the organization's policies, philosophy, performance, product, or people. The archives enable qualified historians to have the information required to write factual business histories.

# RESPONSIBILITY

Efficient archives management requires defining responsibility for the preservation of the organization's history and an understanding of the need for coordination of shared responsibilities among those involved in the management of the archives.

## Placement

The placement of responsibility for an archives management program is not clearly defined. There are three major schools of thought regarding who should have ultimate responsibility and authority for the establishment and maintenance of an archives program. One group believes that archives management is one element of a comprehensive records management system; therefore, the responsibility and authority should rest with the records manager. The second group believes that an archivist should have the responsibility and authority for administering the total system. The third group believes that a distinct delineation of functions exists between an archivist and a records manager; therefore, a delineation of responsibility and authority should exist. In this definition, the records manager assumes the responsibility for efficient generation of records, arrangement and use of records for business purposes, and eventual records disposal when the records no longer serve a business need. The archivist assumes the responsibility for collecting, preserving, and making available for research the records selected for long-term preservation on historical grounds. There is some overlap of interests in this arrangement. (See Figure 1.) Overlapping functions and divided responsibility and authority may create problems which may be resolved through coordination, cooperation, and communication.

## Coordination

Each of the three arrangements for sharing responsibility for records management requires a high degree of coordination, cooperation, and communication among the participants. When the records manager is responsible for managing a total program that includes archives management, coordination of activities must be maintained between those who process active records and those who preserve inactive records. When the archivist is responsible for managing a total program that includes both functions, the same requirement for coordination exists. When the functions are di-

Figure 1
Responsibilities of Records Managers/Archivists

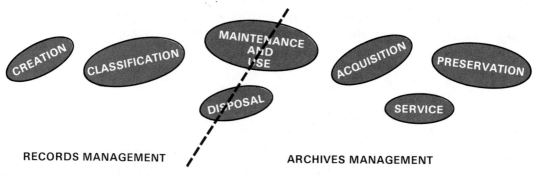

RECORDS MANAGEMENT                     ARCHIVES MANAGEMENT

*Source: Jay Atherton, "Archives and Records Management." Presentation at Association of Records Managers and Administrators, Inc.: Boston, 1980.*

vided and responsibility is shared, the degree to which coordination and cooperation exist determines the degree to which the program is effective.

## ARCHIVES STORAGE

Storage of records in an archives involves ensuring that the records are maintained in the proper arrangement according to the principles of provenance and original order, that the records are correctly prepared for storage, that the records are preserved so as to retain their value, and that appropriate housing for the records is secured.

### Arrangement

Archivists follow two generally accepted principles of records arrangement in handling records received for archival storage. These two principles are the principle of provenance and the principle of original order.

**Provenance**
The principle of provenance is that records of a given unit within the organization should be retained as a separate group rather than being interfiled with similar records of another unit. For example, under the provenance principle, the product division records regarding the manufacture of a specific product should not be merged with sales department records pertaining to that same product.

## Original Order

The principle of original order preserves records in the same order as they were filed in the office of origin. For example, records originally filed by subject classification should be filed by subject classification by the receiving unit; they should be retained in the subject order in which they were received.

The principles of provenance and original order preserve file integrity by maintaining the original records in the arrangement in which they were created and used.

## Preparation

The selection of proper methods for preparing and storing records is important to their future accessibility and use.

### Records Preparation

Records must be properly prepared for storage. All metal clips and staples should be removed unless they are rustproof. All rubber bands should be removed. Duplicate copies of records should be destroyed. Letters should be removed from their envelopes and unfolded. Records that are in poor condition should be noted for special treatment. Pressure-sensitive tape should never be used to repair valuable records.

### Equipment

Storing archival records in filing cabinets is an unacceptable practice. Folders in file cabinets often become jammed and searches create undue wear; documents have a tendency to curl. Additionally, file cabinets are expensive, inflexible, space consuming, and cause slow retrieval. Open steel shelving is preferred for storage of documents. Other types of archives may require special storage equipment. Certain kinds of "collectibles" may require a glass-enclosed cabinet for protection from dust or handling. Tapes, disks, photographs, and maps require special housing, as discussed in Chapter 6.

## Preservation

Various methods of preserving archival records, such as using acid-free containers, acid-free folders, lamination, encapsulation, and microforms, are available.

### Containers

Acidity in the storage containers destroys the records inside. The acidity is measured in pH; an acceptable range is 6.5 to 8.5, which is a neutral to basic pH rating. To combat possible destruction by acidity, records should be stored in acid-free boxes and/or folders. The preference, though expensive, is to use acid-free containers as well as acid-free folders. A gray fiberboard box called a "Hollinger" carton is acid-free, available in various sizes to accommodate different types of records, and widely accepted as a most suitable container for archival records. Hollinger cartons are more expensive than traditional records center cartons and, when cost is a major factor, some organizations use Hollinger cartons for only the most valuable records. Corrugated, fitted-lid records center cartons, together with acid-free folders, are used for all other records.

### Folders

Acid-free folders are available in both standard and legal sizes from most office supply firms. These folders, made from Perma-life paper, protect the contents from acidity damage.

### Lamination

Records may be preserved by lamination. This process requires technicians knowledgeable both in the preparation of the records for lamination and in the process itself. Lamination may make records in poor condition (torn, dirty, or ragged) usable. Records must be washed, deacidified, and dried before they can be laminated. Commercially available plastic film should not be used for this process, nor should the process be performed by anyone other than a skilled technician.

### Encapsulation

Encapsulation is the process of placing a document between sheets of polyester film and sealing the edges with double-faced tape. This process can be performed in-house by archives employees. Unlike lamination, encapsulation requires no outside professional assistance, no expensive equipment, and no chemicals.

### Microforms

Records may also be preserved by microfilming the originals. The original microfilm copies of long-term records should not be used for reference purposes. Negative or positive duplication of the original camera film is made available for use; the original records and film are protected from damage caused by use.

In 1947, the Dead Sea Scrolls were discovered. The original manuscripts are showing increasing deterioration from exposure to light and humidity; predictions are that by the year 2010 the manuscripts will have deteriorated. To preserve their value for researchers, the Dead Sea Scrolls have been filmed and are available in both microfilm and microfiche.

## Housing

Important factors to consider when planning archival records storage include building construction, safety controls, temperature and humidity controls, and space allocations.

### Building

The building housing the archives should comply with the requirements for three-hour fire resistant construction. Fire walls, smoke-handling systems, and fire/smoke alarms are among the safety components that should be a part of the plan for the building or for its conversion. Temperature and humidity controls, as discussed in Chapter 20, are important for the preservation and maintenance of the archives.

### Space

Space requirements for archival facilities are the same as the ones for records centers—a stack area, processing area, office area, and reference area. The amount of space required depends upon the volume of records in the facility, the projected accessions, and the reference activity within the facility.

Archives management is a broad field of endeavor and cannot be completely addressed in a chapter or an appendix within a book. Entire books have been written on the subject. The purpose of this appendix is to provide an overview of archives management and to look at areas that differ from records management. For readers whose interests have been aroused by this discussion, further information may be obtained from the Society of American Archivists. The Society has published basic manuals dealing with surveys, appraisal and accessioning, arrangement and description, reference and access, security, and business archives. These manuals are available from

The Society of American Archivists
330 South Wells, Suite 810
Chicago, IL 60606

# READINGS AND REFERENCES

Atherton, Jay. "Archives and Records Management." Presentation at Association of Records Managers and Administrators: Boston, 1980.

Bridges, Edwin C. "Can State Archives Meet the Challenges of the Eighties?" *Records Management Quarterly,* Vol. 20, No. 2 (April, 1986), p. 15.

Cushman, Helen. "Using Business History." *Records Management Quarterly,* Vol. 11, No. 3 (July, 1977).

"86: The Year of the Optical Disk," *Modern Office Technology,* Vol. 31, No. 1 (January, 1986), p. 118.

Hedlin, Edie. *Business Archives: An Introduction.* Society of American Archivists: Chicago, 1978.

Hives, Christopher L. "Records, Information, and Archives Management in Business," *Records Management Quarterly,* Vol. 20, No. 1 (January, 1986), p. 3.

Lowell, Howard P. "Preservation Microfilming: An Overview." *Records Management Quarterly,* Vol. 19, No. 1 (January, 1985), p. 22.

Lowell, Howard P. "Preserving Recorded Information — The Physical Deterioration of Paper." *Records Management Quarterly,* Vol. 13, No. 2 (April, 1979).

Minkler, Whitney S., and Robert W. Starbird. "Determination of Harmful Residual Chemicals on Archival Film — An Important Aspect of Micrographic File Management." *Records Management Quarterly,* Vol. 19, No. 1 (January, 1985), p. 30.

Riley, Thomas W., and John G. Adorjan. "Company History — A By-Product of Good Records Management." *Records Management Quarterly,* Vol. 15, No. 4 (October, 1981), p. 5.

Sanders, Robert L. "The Company Index: Information Retrieval Thesauri for Organizations and Institutions," *Records Management Quarterly,* Vol. 20, No. 2 (April, 1986), p. 3.

Schultz, Charles R. "Archives in Business and Industry: Identification, Preservation, and Use." *Records Management Quarterly,* Vol. 15 , No. 1 (January, 1981), p. 5.

White, Karen. "Establishing a Business Archives." *Records Management Quarterly,* Vol. 15, No. 4 (October, 1981), p. 10.

# APPENDIX B
## History of Records Management

### HISTORY PRIOR TO 1900

The need for evidence of previous transactions caused records to be created. The earliest need recorded was the need for records of taxes collected — what was collected, from whom, by whom, and when. Even thousands of years ago, governments were collecting and recording taxes!

### Recording Media

The earliest recordkeepers obviously had none of today's technology to assist them in their task. Early records were carved into stone or clay tablets or recorded in wax on wood or animal skins. This was quite time consuming and prohibited keeping any but the most important records. Papyrus was developed by the Egyptians and was in widespread use from about 400 B.C. to A.D. 400.

### Storage Procedures

Initially places for storing government records were called archives. (This term has evolved along with the need of other organizations to preserve records of historical or other lasting value.) There were some rather interesting methods of protecting records which were stored in the archives. Clay tablets were tagged and racked. Rolls of papyrus were often stored in hollow crocodile skins.

The first known retention schedule came into being about A.D. 1200. At that time, the city states of Northern Italy enacted statutes regulating the retention and disposal of files. Prior to that time, retention and disposition decisions had been made on a very individual basis by the person currently in charge of the records. When records were no longer deemed to be of value, they were often dumped in an area that resembled a modern landfill.

### Introduction of Paper Records

The fifteenth century brought the development of paper. Paper allowed a new ease of recording information, and the number of records made and preserved rapidly multiplied.

## HISTORY FROM 1900 TO 1960

By the early 1900s, the typewriter was coming into prominent use in business and government offices, and businesses and governments were generating even greater numbers of records, The paperwork explosion had begun; numerous steps were taken by local, state, and federal governments to control the creation, maintenance, storage, and disposition of records for government use. This section and the one which follows highlight some of the more important actions taken at the federal level. Table I, pages 608 and 609, summarizes some of the major actions affecting records management.

### National Archives

The National Archives was founded in 1934. Prior to that time, each government agency or department had been responsible for maintaining its own records and determining what their retention periods should be. Because there had been no central recordkeeping organization, one of the first actions taken by the National Archives staff was to conduct the first government-wide records survey. This survey, conducted from 1935–1937, revealed a complete lack of consistency in the manner in which records were created and retained within government agencies. The National Archives staff found it very difficult to determine which records were duplicative and which should be reported to the Congress for destruction.

### The 1940s

Two federal statutes of the early 1940s were direct outcomes of the first government-wide records survey. The first of these was the Federal Reports Act of 1942, This act was the federal government's first attempt to control the paperwork burden placed on citizens and businesses through government paperwork requirements. However, this act did not include the Internal Revenue Service. In 1943, the Congress passed the Records Disposal Act which authorized the use of the disposition schedule developed by the National Archives after its initial records survey.

A major stride toward records management consistency was taken in 1946 when President Truman issued Executive Order 9784, which required all agencies in the executive branch to implement continuing programs for records management and disposition. This executive order also increased the records management authority of the National Archives. Prior to that time, primary responsibility for records management had resided in the individual agencies; results of this were inconsistent procedures and unequal concern.

The Hoover Commission on the Organization of the Executive Branch of the Government, established by the Lodge-Brown Act of 1947, made its report in 1948. The three recommendations in this report were based on the findings of the Commission's Task Force on Paperwork Management led by Emmett J. Leahy, executive director of the National Records Management Council. The first recommendation was that the National Archives should be incorporated into a Records Management Bureau established in the Office of General Services. The Records Management Bureau would also be responsible for establishing and operating general records centers and developing and promoting government-wide improvements and economies in records management. The second recommendation was that provisions for more effective creation, preservation, management, storage, and disposal of records in the federal government should be legislated in a Federal Records Act. The final recommendation was that each department and agency of the federal government should be required to implement and conduct an adequate program of records management; these programs would include controls of creation, storage, and disposition of records.

One result of the work of the first Hoover Commission was the Federal Property and Administrative Services Act of 1949. This act created the General Services Administration (GSA) and authorized it to make surveys of government records and records management procedures and to promote more effective records management. This act also transferred the National Archives to the GSA.

## The 1950s

Another result of the work of the first Hoover Commission was the Federal Records Act of 1950. This act required each federal agency to establish an ongoing program for economic and efficient management of its records; to establish controls over creation, maintenance, and use; and to cooperate with the National Archives and Records Service (NARS) in promoting effective government-wide records management. This act provided the first definition of records management in a federal statute. In addition, the GSA was authorized to establish and operate records centers for government records. By June 30, 1952, NARS had established nine federal records centers throughout the country; by June 30, 1954, 95 percent of the records of federal agencies were covered by retention schedules.

A second Hoover Commission was provided for by the Brown-Ferguson Act. This commission established a Task Force on Paperwork Management which was again led by Emmett J. Leahy. In 1954, this Commission made two recommendations. The first recommendation contained three parts. First, a government-wide paperwork management program should be established by executive order of the President; second, general supervision of all phases of paperwork management throughout the executive branch of the government should be given to the GSA to simplify, improve, and reduce the costs; and third, staff functions of paperwork management which had existed in the NARS should be consolidated into the GSA to implement these recommendations. Each agency was to designate one individual to be responsible for cooperating with the GSA in reviewing, simplifying, and reducing the volume of forms, correspondence, and reports. The administrators of the GSA decided that NARS should retain its paperwork management function, but its importance should be emphasized by its assignment to the newly created Office of Records Management.

In 1955, the first *Guide to Record Retention Requirements* was published as an aid to the Task Force on Paperwork Management. This compilation of federal record retention requirements for businesses, private persons, and state and local governments is now published annually.

## HISTORY FROM 1960 TO THE PRESENT

From the 1960s to the present, a number of legislative changes have affected the availability of information and the extensive federal paperwork requirements. These changes have caused subsequent revisions in records management practices in many organizations.

### The 1960s

The 1960s brought one statute that has had widespread effects on records management programs in federal agencies. This statute was the Freedom of Information Act of 1966. This act made provision for individuals to obtain, upon request, information on the operation of federal agencies.

## The 1970s

Amendments to the Freedom of Information Act of 1966 were passed in 1974. These amendments were designed to improve the administration of the act and to expedite the handling of requests for information.

In 1974, the Privacy Act was passed to provide for the protection of information about individuals. The act established the right of individuals to access information about themselves, the right to exclude others from access to personal information without consent, and the right of individuals to know who has accessed their records.

The Federal Records Management Amendments of 1976 were passed to supplement and update the Federal Records Act of 1950. These amendments defined records management over the life cycle of a record and established a new statutory program objective of reducing paperwork while maintaining needed program documentation. These amendments charged the GSA with presenting an annual report to Congress on the records management activities of federal agencies.

In 1977, the Privacy Protection Study Commission, established under the Privacy Act of 1974, made 162 specific recommendations for the protection of the privacy of individuals and determined that the principles of the Privacy Act should be extended to the private sector.

The Commission on Federal Paperwork, created by Congress in 1975 in response to complaints about the burden of federal paperwork, made its report to the President in 1977. The Commission issued 37 reports. The summary report characterized the paperwork burden as a hidden tax. The full report included over 800 recommendations in two categories: 650 recommendations on specific forms or recordkeeping requirements in areas such as health, education, or energy; and 150 recommendations for government-wide reforms.

## The 1980s

The Paperwork Reduction Act of 1980 (effective April 1, 1981) was passed in response to the findings of the Commission on Federal Paperwork and addressed the need to manage information as a resource which should be planned, managed, and included in the budget. Specific provisions of this act addressed minimizing the federal paperwork burden; minimizing the cost to the federal government of collecting, maintaining, using, and disseminating information; maximizing the usefulness of information collected; coordinating, and where possible making uniform, federal information policies and practices; and ensuring that collection, maintenance, use, and dissemination of information by the federal government is consistent with the Privacy Act.

Table I
Major Actions Affecting Records Management
(1900 to Present)

| | |
|---|---|
| 1934 | National Archives was founded. |
| 1935–1937 | National Archives conducted the first government-wide records survey. |
| 1942 | Federal Reports Act provided a mechanism for controlling federal paper-work requirements (excluded IRS). |
| 1943 | Records Disposal Act authorized the use of the disposition schedule developed by the National Archives. |
| 1946 | Executive Order 9784 (issued by President Truman) required all agencies in the executive branch to implement continuing records management programs. |
| 1948 | Report of the first Hoover Commission recommended that the National Archives should be incorporated into the Office of General Services; that provisions for records creation, preservation, management, and disposal should be legislated in a Federal Records Act; and that each department and agency should be required to have an adequate records management program. |
| 1949 | Federal Property and Administrative Services Act created the General Services Administration (GSA) and authorized it to make surveys of government records. The act also transferred the National Archives to the GSA. |
| 1950 | Federal Records Act required each federal agency to establish an ongoing program for the economic and efficient administration of records and to cooperate with the National Archives and Records Service (NARS) in government-wide records surveys; provided the first definition of records management in a federal statute; and authorized the GSA to establish and operate records centers. |
| 1952 | By June 30, 1952, NARS had established nine federal records centers throughout the country. |
| 1954 | By June 30, 1954, 95 percent of the records of federal agencies were covered by retention schedules. Task Force on Paperwork Management established by the second Hoover Commission recommended that a government-wide paperwork management program be established under the supervision of the GSA. The administrators of the GSA decided that NARS should retain its |

paperwork management function, but its importance should be emphasized by its assignment to the newly created Office of Records Management.

1955    The first *Guide to Record Retention Requirements* was published as an aid to the Task Force on Paperwork Management.

1966    Freedom of Information Act made provision for individuals to obtain, upon request, information on the operation of federal agencies.

1974    Amendments to the Freedom of Information Act expedited the handling of requests for information.

Privacy Act provided for the protection of information about individuals. The act established the right of individuals to access information about themselves, the right to exclude others from access to personal information without consent, and the right of individuals to know who has accessed their records.

1976    Federal Records Management Amendments were passed to supplement and update the Federal Records Act of 1950. These amendments defined records management over the life cycle of a record and established a new statutory program objective of reducing paperwork.

1977    Privacy Protection Study Commission, established under the Privacy Act of 1974, made 162 specific recommendations for the protection of the privacy of individuals and determined that the principles.of the Privacy Act should be extended to the private sector.

The Commission on Federal Paperwork, created by Congress in 1975 in response to complaints about the burden of federal paperwork, made its report to the President. The summary report characterized the paperwork burden as a hidden tax. The full report included over 800 recommendations.

1980    Paperwork Reduction Act of 1980 (effective April 1, 1981) addressed the need to manage information as a resource which should be planned, managed, and included in the budget.

ARMA undertook nationwide campaign to eliminate use of legal-size files called Project ELF (Eliminate Legal-size Files).

1983    Judicial Conference of the United States implemented letter-size paper as the standard for use in all federal courts.

## ADMINISTRATION OF FEDERAL RECORDS PROGRAMS

Administration of federal records programs continues to be a function of the GSA. Within the GSA, records management responsibilities are divided between the Office of Records Management and the Office of Federal Records Centers.

The Office of Records Management is responsible for establishing and maintaining standards, evaluating automation plans, providing technical assistance to federal agencies in all phases of records management, and evaluating the effectiveness of records management programs. The Office of Federal Records Centers is responsible for developing and updating retention schedules, storing records, and referencing inactive records.

## ACTIVITIES OF PROFESSIONAL ORGANIZATIONS

Many of the activities of professional organizations have widespread effects on records management procedures. Educational programs are one example of this. Other examples are presentations made before Congressional committees and the publication of policy statements. The Association of Records Managers and Administrators, Inc. (ARMA), presented testimony at Congressional hearings in support of the Paperwork Reduction Act of 1980.

ARMA and records and information management professionals are now beginning to reap the benefits of ARMA's standards program begun in the early 1980's. The standards program seeks to document procedures and benchmarks for successful records management programs. Numerous professionals have donated time to developing standards in eight areas: records retention, records center operations, vital records, technology applications, job descriptions, disaster recovery, filing systems, and terminology. ARMA is also sponsoring a technical publications program and a seminar program.

## CURRENT STATUS OF RECORDS MANAGEMENT IN BUSINESS

Records management has expanded from the storage and retrieval of documents into a field which includes responsibility for personnel, equipment, and procedures for records creation, distribution, use, maintenance, storage, and disposition. Today, the records manager is responsible for the organization's most valuable resource—information. The efficient handling of that resource requires a thorough knowledge of all technologies which might be used in its management—word processing, data processing, micrographics, and telecommunications. The records manager must know how these technologies can best be used and integrated to meet the needs of an organization.

# APPENDIX C
## Filing Rules

### RULE 1: ORDER OF INDEXING UNITS

#### A. Personal Names

A personal name is indexed in this manner: (1) the surname (last name) is the key unit, (2) the given name (first name) or initial is the second unit, and (3) the middle name or initial is the third unit. Unusual or obscure (often foreign) names are indexed in the same manner. If it is not possible to determine the surname in a name, consider the last name as the surname.

Examples of Rule 1A

Index Order of Units in Names

| Names | Key Unit | Unit 2 | Unit 3 |
|---|---|---|---|
| George H. Colden | Colden | George | H |
| Missy D. Cullen | Cullen | Missy | D |
| Sylvia Marie Juarez | Juarez | Sylvia | Marie |
| C. M. Klein | Klein | C | M |
| Carroll Thomas | Thomas | Carroll | |

#### B. Business Names

Business names are filed *as written** using letterheads or trade-marks as guides. Business names containing personal names are indexed as written. Newspapers and periodicals are indexed as written. For newspapers and periodicals having identical names that do not include the city name, consider the city name as the last indexing unit. If necessary, the state name may follow the city name.

*As written* means the order of the words or names *as written or printed* on the person's, organization's, or publication's signature, letterhead, or title.

Examples of Rule 1B

### Index Order of Units in Names

| *Names* | *Key Unit* | *Unit 2* | *Unit 3* |
|---|---|---|---|
| Coleman Construction Company | Coleman | Construction | Company |
| First National Bank | First | National | Bank |
| Major Automobile Agency | Major | Automobile | Agency |
| Mary Coleman Nurseries | Mary | Coleman | Nurseries |
| Scott Manufacturing | Scott | Manufacturing | |

## RULE 2: MINOR WORDS IN BUSINESS NAMES

Each complete English word in a business name is considered a separate indexing unit. Prepositions, conjunctions, symbols, and articles are included; symbols (&, ¢, $, #, %) are considered as spelled in full (and, Cent, Dollar, Number, Percent). All spelled-out symbols except "and" begin with a capital letter.

When the word "The" appears as the first word of a business name, it is considered the last indexing unit.

Examples of Rule 2

### Index Order of Units in Names

| *Names* | *Key Unit* | *Unit 2* | *Unit 3* | *Unit 4* |
|---|---|---|---|---|
| Bank of Boston | Bank | of | Boston | |
| The Beef Place | Beef | Place | The | |
| Brinn Medicine and Sundries | Brinn | Medicine | and | Sundries |
| In Town Motel | In | Town | Motel | |
| Inn at the Woods | Inn | at | the | Woods |

## RULE 3: PUNCTUATION AND POSSESSIVES

All punctuation is disregarded when indexing personal and business names. Commas, periods, hyphens, and apostrophes are disregarded, and names are indexed as written. (For example, Smith's Playhouse would be filed after Smiths' Bakery.)

## Examples of Rule 3

### Index Order of Units in Names

| Names | Key Unit | Unit 2 | Unit 3 |
|---|---|---|---|
| Willie West | West | Willie | |
| The West-End Inn | WestEnd | Inn | The |
| West's Products Company | Wests | Products | Company |
| Williams' Bicycle Repair | Williams | Bicycle | Repair |
| William's Sub Shoppe | Williams | Sub | Shoppe |

# RULE 4: SINGLE LETTERS AND ABBREVIATIONS

## A. Personal Names

Initials in personal names are considered separate indexing units. Abbreviations of personal names (Wm., Jos., Thos.,) and brief personal names or nicknames (Liz, Bill) are indexed as they are written.

## B. Business Names

Single letters in business names are indexed as written. If there is a space between single letters, index each letter as a separate unit. An acronym (a word formed from the first, or first few, letters of several words) is indexed as one unit. Abbreviations are indexed as one unit regardless of punctuation or spacing (AAA, Y M C A, Y.W.C.A.). Radio and television station call letters are indexed as one word. Cross-reference spelled-out names to their acronyms if necessary. For example: American Automobile Association SEE AAA.

## Examples of Rule 4

### Index Order of Units in Names

| Names | Key Unit | Unit 2 | Unit 3 | Unit 4 |
|---|---|---|---|---|
| ARMA | ARMA | | | |
| Carolyn Hairworks, Inc. | Carolyn | Hairworks | Inc | |
| CBN Television Station | CBN | Television | Station | |
| R & G Associates | R | and | G | Associates |
| J. L. Randolph | Randolph | J | L | |
| Wm. N. Wilson | Wilson | Wm | N | |

# RULE 5: TITLES

## A. Personal Names

A personal title (Miss, Mr., Mrs., Ms.) is considered the last indexing unit when it appears. If a seniority title is required for identification, it is considered the last indexing unit in abbreviated form, with numeric titles (II, III) filed before alphabetic titles (Jr., Sr.). When professional titles (D.D.S., M.D., CRM, Dr., Mayor) are required for identification, they are considered the last units and filed alphabetically as written. Royal and religious titles followed by either a given name or a surname only (Father Leo) are indexed and filed as written. When all units of identical names, *including titles*, have been compared and there are no differences, filing order is determined by the addresses.

**Note:** Titles are indexed as written without punctuation. For example: Jr., Dr., Maj., Major are indexed as Jr, Dr, Maj, Major.

Examples of Rule 5A

| | Index Order of Units in Names | | | |
| --- | --- | --- | --- | --- |
| *Names* | *Key Unit* | *Unit 2* | *Unit 3* | *Unit 4* |
| Miss Pamela Lancowski | Lancowski | Pamela | Miss | |
| Sister Mary | Sister | Mary | | |
| Stan L. Thompkins II | Thompkins | Stan | L | II |
| Stanley W. Tompkins, D.D.S. | Tompkins | Stanley | W | DDS |
| Judge Suzanne J. Weatherby | Weatherby | Suzanne | J | Judge |

## B. Business Names

Titles in business names are filed as written. See Rules 1 and 2.

Examples of Rule 5B

| | Index Order of Units in Names | | |
| --- | --- | --- | --- |
| *Names* | *Key Unit* | *Unit 2* | *Unit 3* |
| Coca Cola Bottlers | Coca | Cola | Bottlers |
| Doctor Pet Shop | Doctor | Pet | Shop |
| Miss Sarah's Pancakes | Miss | Sarahs | Pancakes |
| Mrs. Smith's Pies | Mrs | Smiths | Pies |
| Ms. Magazine | Ms | Magazine | |

## RULE 6: MARRIED WOMEN

A married woman's name is filed as she writes it. It is indexed according to Rule 1. If more than one form of a name is known, the alternate name may be cross-referenced.

**Note:** A married woman's name in a business name is indexed as written and follows Rules 1B and 5B.

Examples of Rule 6

| | Index Order of Units in Names | | | |
|---|---|---|---|---|
| *Names* | *Key Unit* | *Unit 2* | *Unit 3* | *Unit 4* |
| Mrs. Ronald S. Dean | Dean | Ronald | S | Mrs |
| Ms. Bonnie N. Deaner | Deaner | Bonnie | N | Ms |
| x (Mrs. Bonnie Deaner Rollins) | | | | |
| x (Mrs. Jason C. Rollins) | | | | |
| Mrs. Katherine Z. Deene | Deene | Katherine | Z | Mrs |
| x (Ms. Katherine Zaneveld) | | | | |
| Mrs. Betty Jean Diener | Diener | Betty | Jean | Mrs |
| x (Mrs. Robert Bell Diener) | | | | |
| Ms. Susan N. Diner | Diner | Susan | N | Ms |

## RULE 7: ARTICLES AND PARTICLES

A foreign article or particle in a personal or business name is combined with the part of the name following it to form a single indexing unit. The indexing order is not affected by a space between a prefix and the rest of the name, and the space is disregarded when indexing. Examples of articles and particles are: a la, D', Da, De, Del, De la, Della, Den, Des, Di, Dos, Du, El, Fitz, Il, L', La, Las, Le, Les, Lo, Los, M', Mac, Mc, O', Per, Saint, San, Santa, Santo, St., Ste., Te, Ten, Ter, Van, Van de, Van der, Von, Von der.

Examples of Rule 7

| | Index Order of Units in Names | | |
|---|---|---|---|
| *Names* | *Key Unit* | *Unit 2* | *Unit 3* |
| Delores Del Rio | DelRio | Delores | |
| Arthur M. DuPuy | DuPuy | Arthur | M |
| L'Maisson Restaurant | LMaisson | Restaurant | |
| Johnnie Macintosh | Macintosh | Johnnie | |
| Mc Dougal Irish Linens | McDougal | Irish | Linens |

# RULE 8: IDENTICAL NAMES

When personal names and names of businesses, institutions, and organizations are identical, filing order is determined by the addresses. Cities are considered first, followed by states or provinces, street names, house numbers or building numbers in that order.

**Note 1:** When the first units of street names are written as figures, the names are considered in ascending numeric order and placed together before alphabetic street names.

**Note 2:** Street names with compass directions are considered as written. Numbers after compass directions are considered before alphabetic names (East 8th, East Main, Sandusky, SE Eighth, Southeast Eighth).

**Note 3:** House and building numbers written as figures are considered in ascending numeric order and placed together before spelled-out building names (The Charter House). If a street address and a building name are included in an address, disregard the building name. ZIP Codes are not considered in determining filing order.

**Note 4:** Seniority titles are indexed according to Rule 5 and are considered *before* addresses.

Examples of Rule 8

|  | Index Order of Units in Names | | | | |
|---|---|---|---|---|---|
| *Names* | *Key Unit* | *Unit 2* | *Unit 3* | *Unit 4* | *Address* |
| (Names of Cities Used to Determine Filing Order) | | | | | |
| John Adams School Lexington, KY | John | Adams | School | | <u>L</u>exington KY |
| John Adams School Richmond, KY | John | Adams | School | | <u>R</u>ichmond KY |
| (Names of States Used to Determine Filing Order) | | | | | |
| The Waffle Shop Miami, FL | Waffle | Shop | The | | Miami <u>FL</u> |
| The Waffle Shop Miami, OH | Waffle | Shop | The | | Miami <u>OH</u> |
| (Names of Streets and Building Numbers Used to Determine Filing Order) | | | | | |
| Center Shoe Store 714 Dana Ave. Portland, Oregon | Center | Shoe | Store | | 714 <u>D</u>ana Ave |

### Index Order of Units in Names

| Names | Key Unit | Unit 2 | Unit 3 | Unit 4 | Address |
|---|---|---|---|---|---|
| Center Shoe Store 271 E. Main Portland, Oregon | Center | Shoe | Store | | 271 <u>E</u> Main |
| Center Shoe Store 416 W. Main Portland, Oregon | Center | Shoe | Store | | 416 <u>W</u> Main |

(Seniority Titles Used to Determine Filing Order)

| Names | Key Unit | Unit 2 | Unit 3 | Unit 4 |
|---|---|---|---|---|
| Ray E. Adams, Jr. | Adams | Ray | E. | <u>Jr</u> |
| Ray E. Adams, Sr. | Adams | Ray | E | <u>Sr</u> |
| Marvin T. Jones | <u>Jones</u> | Marvin | T | |
| Marvin T. Jones II | Jones | Marvin | T | <u>II</u> |
| Marvin T. Jones III | Jones | Marvin | T | <u>III</u> |

## RULE 9: NUMBERS IN BUSINESS NAMES

Numbers spelled out in a business name are considered as written and filed alphabetically. Numbers written in digit form are considered one unit. Names with numbers written in digit form as the first unit are filed in ascending order before alphabetic names. Arabic numerals are filed before Roman numerals (2, 3; II, III). Names with inclusive numbers (33–37) are arranged by the first number only (33). Names with numbers appearing in other than the first position (Pier 36 Cafe) are filed alphabetically within the appropriate section and immediately before a similar name without a number (Pier and Port Cafe).

**Note:** In indexing numbers written in digit form which contain *st*, *d*, and *th* (1st, 2d, 3d, 4th), ignore the letter endings and consider the digits (1, 2, 3, 4).

Examples of Rule 9

### Index Order of Units in Names

| Names | Key Unit | Unit 2 | Unit 3 | Unit 4 |
|---|---|---|---|---|
| 6th Day Inn | <u>6</u> | Day | Inn | |
| 18th Street Dry Cleaners | <u>18</u> | Street | Dry | Cleaners |
| The 600 Book Store | <u>600</u> | Book | Store | The |
| 1608 Music Co. | <u>1608</u> | Music | Co | |
| Harley 5 Garden Shop | <u>Harley</u> | 5 | Garden | Shop |
| Sixth Street Bakery | <u>Sixth</u> | Street | Bakery | |

## RULE 10: ORGANIZATIONS AND INSTITUTIONS

Banks and other financial institutions, clubs, colleges, hospitals, hotels, lodges, motels, museums, religious institutions, schools, unions, universities, and other organizations and institutions are indexed and filed according to the names written on their letterheads. *The* used as the first word in these names is considered the last filing unit.

Examples of Rule 10

| | Index Order of Units in Names | | | |
|---|---|---|---|---|
| *Names* | *Key Unit* | *Unit 2* | *Unit 3* | *Unit 4* |
| Bank of Denver | Bank | of | Denver | |
| Church of Christ | Church | of | Christ | |
| Data Processing Mgmt. Assoc. | Data | Processing | Mgmt | Assoc |
| Denver Savings & Loan | Denver | Savings | and | Loan |
| Episcopal Church of Portsmouth | Episcopal | Church | of | Portsmouth |
| Galilee Episcopal Church | Galilee | Episcopal | Church | |

## RULE 11: SEPARATED SINGLE WORDS

When a single word is separated into two or more parts in a business name, the parts are considered separate indexing units. If a name contains two compass directions separated by a space (South East Car Rental), each compass direction is a separate indexing unit. *Southeast* and *south-east* are considered single indexing units. Cross-reference if necessary. For example: South East SEE ALSO Southeast, South-East.

Examples of Rule 11

| | Index Order of Units in Names | | | |
|---|---|---|---|---|
| *Names* | *Key Unit* | *Unit 2* | *Unit 3* | *Unit 4* |
| Air Port Hotel | Air | Port | Hotel | |
| Airport Sandwich Shoppe | Airport | Sandwich | Shoppe | |
| Mid-Lands Printing, Inc. | MidLands | Printing | Inc | |
| Midlands Resort Hotel | Midlands | Resort | Hotel | |
| North West Auto Sales | North | West | Auto | Sales |
| Northwest Record Corp. | Northwest | Record | Corp | |

# RULE 12: HYPHENATED NAMES

## A. Personal Names

Hyphenated personal names are considered one indexing unit and the hyphen is ignored. *Jones-Bennett* is a single indexing unit — *JonesBennett*.

## B. Business Names

Hyphenated business and place names and coined business names are considered one indexing unit and the hyphen is ignored. *La-Z-Boy* is a single indexing unit — *LaZBoy*.

Examples of Rule 12

| | Index Order of Units in Names | | | |
|---|---|---|---|---|
| *Names* | *Key Unit* | *Unit 2* | *Unit 3* | *Unit 4* |
| A-l Skating Rink | Al | Skating | Rink | |
| Dr. Ann R. Allen-Brown | AllenBrown | Ann | R | Dr |
| All-Star Athletic Apparel | AllStar | Athletic | Apparel | |
| Mario's North-West Pizza | Marios | NorthWest | Pizza | |
| Mid-Atlantic Services, Inc. | MidAtlantic | Services | Inc | |
| South-Side Ski Rentals | SouthSide | Ski | Rentals | |

# RULE 13: COMPOUND NAMES

## A. Personal Names

When separated by a space, compound personal names are considered separate indexing units. *Mary Lea Gerson* is three units.
**Note:** Although *St. John* is a compound name, *St.* (Saint) is a prefix and follows Rule 7 which considers it a single indexing unit.

## B. Business Names

Compound business or place names with spaces between the parts of the name follow Rule 11, and the parts are considered separate units. New Jersey and Mid America are considered two indexing units each.

Examples of Rule 13

Index Order of Units in Names

| Names | Key Unit | Unit 2 | Unit 3 | Unit 4 |
|---|---|---|---|---|
| All Star Athletic Apparel | All | Star | Athletic | Apparel |
| New Orleans Office Supplies | New | Orleans | Office | Supplies |
| Robert T. Saint John | SaintJohn | Robert | T | |
| San Jose Apartments | SanJose | Apartments | | |
| St. Louis Mfg. Co. | StLouis | Mfg | Co | |
| Trans-Allied Movers | TransAllied | Movers | | |

# RULE 14: GOVERNMENT NAMES

## Federal

The name of a federal government agency is indexed by the name of the government unit (United States Government) followed by the most distinctive name of the office, bureau, department, etc., as written (Internal Revenue Service). The words "Office of," "Department of," "Bureau of," etc., *if needed* for clarity and in the official name, are added and considered separate indexing units. **Note:** If "of" is not a part of the official name as written, it is not added.

## State and Local

The names of state, province, county, parish, city, town, township, and village governments/political divisions are indexed by their distinctive names. The words "State of," "County of," "City of," "Department of," etc., are added only *if needed* for clarity and in the official name, and are considered separate indexing units (Wisconsin/Transportation/Department/of).

## Foreign

The distinctive English name is the first indexing unit for foreign government names. This is followed, *if needed* and in the official name, by the balance of the formal name of the government. Branches, departments, and divisions follow in order by their distinctive names. States, colonies, provinces, cities, and other divisions of foreign governments are followed by their distinctive or official names as spelled in English (Canada; Poland; France, Paris). Cross-reference the written foreign name to the English name, if necessary.

**Note:** The *United States Government Manual* and the *Congressional Directory,* published annually, report a current list of United States government agencies and offices. *Countries, Dependencies, Areas of Special Sovereignty, and Their Principal Administrative Divisions,* published by the U. S. Department of Commerce, National Bureau of Standards, provides a list of geographic and political entities of the world and associated standard codes. The *State Information Book* by Susan Lukowski provides an up-to-date list of state departments and their addresses. The *World Almanac and Book of Facts,* updated annually, includes facts and statistics on many foreign nations, and is helpful as a source which gives the English spellings of many foreign names.

## Examples of Rule 14

| Names | Index Form of Names |
|---|---|
| Department of Transportation | Arkansas State of* |
| State of Arkansas | Transportation Department of* |
| | |
| Information Branch | Canada Government of* |
| Ministry of Agriculture and Food | Agriculture and Food Ministry of* |
| Government of Canada | Information Branch |
| Ottawa, Canada | Ottawa Canada |
| | |
| Department of Public Works | Charlotte City |
| Charlotte, North Carolina | Public Works Department of* |
| | Charlotte North Carolina |
| | |
| Office of Records Management | United States Government |
| National Archives and Records Service | General Services Administration |
| General Services Administration | National Archives and Records Service |
| United States Government | Records Management Office of* |
| | |
| Apprenticeship and Training Bureau | United States Government |
| U.S. Department of Labor | Labor Department of* |
| | Apprenticeship and Training Bureau |

*"of" can be omitted; it is not needed

# GLOSSARY

**Accession book**  A book containing a list of numbers previously assigned to correspondents/subjects and numbers available for assignment to new records.

**Accuracy ratio**  A measure of the effectiveness of the records system and its personnel which is determined by dividing the number of records found by the number of records requested.

**Active record**  A record that is referenced (used) on a regular basis.

**Active records staff**  Personnel responsible for controlling all records that are accessed at least once a month and for the determination of when records should be transferred to inactive status.

**Administrative audit**  A review of the effectiveness of the system in terms of the functional quality and quantity of the records available.

**Administrative manual**  Contains standard operating procedures that facilitate the completion of tasks requiring the work of more than one unit of the organization.

**Administrative value**  The value of a record series to the creating office in the performance of its assigned operations within the organization.

**Alphabetic classification system**  An arrangement of records that classifies records alphabetically by letter, word, or unit.

**Alphanumeric classification system**  An arrangement of records which uses a combination of words and numbers.

**Aperture card**  An 80-column keypunch card ($7\frac{3}{8}''$ by $3\frac{1}{4}''$) into which an opening(s) has been cut to accommodate the insertion of a frame(s) of microfilm.

**Association for Information and Image Management (AIIM)**  A professional organization for records and information management professionals.

**Association of Records Managers and Administrators, Inc. (ARMA)**  A professional organization for records and information management professionals.

**Audio teleconferencing**  Voice communication over telephone lines between two or more remote locations.

**Audit**  A regular examination and verification of a specific activity.

**Audit trail**  A procedure which provides documentation for regular examination and verification.

**Automated operation and retrieval**  Storing, retrieving, and controlling information using a computer or microprocessor.

**Bar coding**  A pattern of clear and opaque bars between images on roll film.

**Basic classification index**  A categorical grouping of subjects with appropriate subheadings.

**Biometric devices**  Scanners that measure and record fingerprints, voice, or retinal eye patterns.

**Blast freezing**  A process by which material is frozen very quickly.

**Blip coding**  A method of coding accomplished by placing a blip (an opaque, optical rectangle) below each image to identify it. Also called "image count marking."

**Block integrity**  All records related to one subject are filed together.

**Block sort**  Rough sorting records into groups of alphabetic letters (A, B, C, D, E, F) or in groups of numbers (1–10, 11–20), and so forth.

**Camera operator targets**  Frame of microfilm on which the date filmed and operator are identified.

**Central clearing point**  Unit whose function is to provide coordination for the directives program.

**Centralized records storage system**  A system for providing housing for all active records in one location within the organization.

**Certificate of authenticity/identification**  Frame on each roll of microfilm that identifies the date filmed and the operator, and verifies the accuracy and completeness of the reproductions.

**Certified Records Manager (CRM)**  The designation awarded to an individual who has met the experience and education requirements established by the Board of Regents of the ICRM and has satisfactorily passed a six-part examination.

**Charge-out**  Procedure for checking out records for use by requester.

**Chip**  A piece of film containing a microimage and optical or magnetic coding for automated retrieval.

**Chronologic classification system**  An arrangement in which records are stored in date order.

**Cine mode**  The positioning of microimages on film which takes its name from cinema film and is achieved by feeding documents into the camera with the headings or tops of each sheet entering the camera first.

**Class 1 records**  See **Vital records.**

**Class 2 records**  See **Important records.**

**Class 3 records**  See **Useful records.**

**Class 4 records**  See **Nonessential records.**

**Classification system**  A logical, systematic ordering of records using numbers, letters, or a combination of numbers and letters for record identification.

**Coding**  Indicating on a record where it is to be stored.

**COM recorder**  A microfilm unit which converts data from a computer into human-readable language and records it on microfilm.

**Combination manual**  Contains information on records policies, the structure and responsibilities of the records unit in relation to other units, administrative procedures, and operating procedures.

**Combination records storage system**  A system for housing active records in individual departments under centralized control.

**Comic mode**  The positioning of microimages on film which takes its name from the manner in which frames of a comic strip are presented and is achieved by feeding the document into the camera with the heading to the left or to the right.

**Communications subsystem**  The means of getting information to users in a timely manner.

**Computer input microfilm (CIM)**  Microfilm containing images which are converted to electronic signals for storage on magnetic tape to be used as input to a computer.

**Computer output microfilm (COM)**  An integration of computer and microform technology that converts information on computer tapes or from computer memory to a microform.

**Computer-assisted locator (CAL)**  A system that tracks records as they are circulated within the organization.

**Computer-assisted retrieval (CAR)**  Using the computer to aid in locating and retrieving records.

**Concurrent control**  A type of control that takes place as work is being performed.

**Contact printing**  Method of duplication achieved by placing the emulsion side of the original developed camera film in contact with the emulsion side of the copy film and directing a light beam through the original image to the copy. The copy film is then developed.

**Content security**  Providing for the protection of the content of records from destruction, disclosure, modification, or breach of confidentiality.

**Contracted microforms services**  Microforms produced through contract with a service bureau.

**Control**  The function that compares achieved results with planned goals.

**Control function**  The process of ordering, evaluating, and providing feedback to the records management system.

**Controlling**  The management function that compares achieved results with planned goals.

**Convenience copiers**  Self-service, unattended copiers that are located throughout the facility to provide for convenient copies.

**Copy**  A duplicate of the original record.

**Copy control device**  Mechanism attached to copy machines to limit access to authorized users.

**Copy distribution costs**  Costs associated with distributing the copies to the appropriate recipients.

**Copy maintenance costs**  Costs related to storing and retrieving copies.

**Copy management**  The management of copying practices, procedures, and devices to ensure the effective and economical creation of copies.

**Copy practices**  How the copying equipment is used.

**Copy procedures**  The requirements for making duplicate records.

**Copy processing costs** Costs involved in making necessary copies, including equipment and equipment maintenance, materials, supplies, and clerical time.

**Copy user costs** Costs that represent the time the user must take to interpret and use the information.

**Correction target** Frame of microfilm showing that the preceding document has been refilmed.

**Correspondence distribution costs** Costs associated with distributing correspondence to the appropriate recipients.

**Correspondence maintenance costs** Costs associated with storing and retrieving correspondence.

**Correspondence manual** Contains policies on the creation and distribution of correspondence, guidelines on efficient and effective document creation, form letters, formats for letters and other communications, guidelines for selecting the most effective type of communication, and guidelines on effective dictation techniques.

**Correspondence origination costs** Costs directly related to writing and research time necessary to draft correspondence.

**Correspondence processing costs** Costs involved in actual preparation of documents including equipment, materials, supplies, and administrative support.

**Correspondence user costs** Costs that represent user time to correctly interpret and use the information contained in the correspondence.

**Cost benefit analysis** A comparison of the benefits of a new procedure, system, or technology with its costs.

**Cross-reference** An additional notation that directs the user to another location where the record or information may be found.

**Cross-reference target** Frame of microfilm that provides information regarding the location of related records.

**Data** Symbols which represent people, objects, events, or concepts.

**Data processing** The use of a computer to manipulate data to achieve a desired result.

**Data set** Groups of data or information stored on magnetic tape.

**Decentralized records storage system** A system for housing records in individual departments or offices that create or receive the records.

**Decimal numbering arrangement** Arrangement used primarily in libraries (Dewey Decimal System) that uses numbers, decimals to classify records into ten major categories.

**Density** A numeric measurement of the amount of light which passes through a black background of negative microfilm.

**Direct access** A storage system which permits access to records without reference to an index.

**Directing** The management function of leading and motivating by providing a climate that stimulates employees to work toward achieving organizational goals and unit objectives.

**Directive** An instruction from management, usually addressing policy and/or procedure.

**Directive on directives**  A document describing the framework and philosophy of the directives control program.

**Directives control program**  Systematic method for establishing, implementing, maintaining, and evaluating an organization's directives.

**Directives manual**  Handbook containing all of the organizational directives and the directive on directives.

**Directives program appraisal**  A directives evaluation addressing the policies and procedures for establishing, implementing, maintaining, and evaluating the total directives control program.

**Directives system appraisal**  A directives evaluation addressing the operational aspects of the delivery system itself.

**Dispersal**  A method of providing a copy of an original document by having access to a copy distributed externally or internally.

**Document tracking system**  A computerized system which tracks the location of file folders as they move between departments or individuals.

**Documentary materials**  All forms of correspondence (letters, memos, directives, and reports); forms; drawings; specifications; maps; photographs; and creative materials.

**Duo mode**  A method of microfilming in which images are placed in consecutive order down one half of a strip of film and then back down the other half.

**Duplex mode**  A method of microfilming both sides of a document simultaneously with the images presented side by side.

**Duplex order**  A classification arrangement using numbers with two or more parts separated by a dash, space, or comma.

**Duplication**  A method of providing a copy of an original document by reproducing the original in paper, microfilm, microfiche, magnetic, or other media used by the organization.

**Electronic storage**  The depositing of information in an online computer database or in the memory of a word processor.

**Encyclopedic order**  Records arranged alphabetically by subject, as used in an encyclopedia.

**Executive summary**  A two- to three-page concise summary of a report made especially for top management.

**Facilitative area**  The section of a form, usually at the top, which provides printed information that, although necessary, is peripheral to the main purpose of the form, such as organization name, form number, and instructions.

**Facsimile transmission**  The electronic transmission of hard-copy data over telephone lines.

**Feasibility study**  An examination of the practicality of implementing new or modified procedures, methods, or technologies.

**Feedback control**  A type of control that concentrates on past performance as compared to current performance data.

**Fiber optics**  Transparent glass fibers which may transmit both analog (tonal) and digital signals by lasers.

**File**   A collection of records arranged according to a predetermined system.

**File group**   A collection of records with similar characteristics that should be separated from other record groups.

**File integrity**   Accuracy and completeness of the file.

**Filing**   The action of storing a record.

**Filing features**   Characteristics, such as name of originator or organization, date, or form number by which records are stored and retrieved.

**Filing manual**   Contains rules and regulations for filing which standardize procedures, assist in training personnel, and make storage/retrieval more efficient.

**Filing segment**   The entire name, subject, or number that is used for filing purposes.

**Fiscal value**   Value attributed to a record series which documents financial transactions.

**Flash targets**   Method used to divide a roll of film into batches of information.

**Floor load capacity**   The weight of records and equipment that a floor can safely accommodate.

**Folders**   Containers for documents within the storage system.

**Forms**   Carefully designed documents used to gather and transmit information necessary for operational functions and for historical records.

**Forms analysis**   The process of determining whether a form is necessary and, if so, how it should be designed to assure maximum efficiency.

**Forms control program**   A records management function designed to achieve the efficient collection and distribution of information through the use of forms.

**Forms staff**   Personnel responsible for establishing forms operating procedures, analysis procedures, and design and specification standards, and for controlling forms throughout the organization.

**Forms survey**   An inventory, by department, of the forms currently in use or in stock.

**Freedom of Information and Privacy Acts**   Two acts that combine to protect personal information collected by a government agency.

**Functional forms file**   A forms control file which groups forms according to their purpose.

**Functional reports file**   A reports control file which maintains information about reports with a like function.

**Geographic order**   An arrangement in which related records are grouped by place or location.

**Goals**   General statements of the philosophy and aspirations of management for the organization.

**Guide letters**   Letters that provide a suggested pattern of responses for routine letters.

**Guides**   Items used for separating records into sections to facilitate storage and retrieval and for supporting folders by keeping them upright in a cabinet or on a shelf.

**Historical reports file**   A reports control file which maintains a history of each report.

**Historical value**   Value attributed to a record which completes the picture of an organization's accomplishments and will aid future researchers with an interest in the organization, industry, or prominent individuals within the organization.

**Human resources development plan**   A comprehensive, systematic plan for the recruitment, selection, training, and evaluation of personnel.

**Image orientation**   The positioning of images on film.

**Important records**   Those records necessary to the continued life of a business; also called Class 2 records.

**Inactive record**   A record that is referenced fewer than ten times annually.

**Indexing**   The mental process of deciding where a record is to be stored.

**Indirect access**   A storage system which requires reference to an index before a record can be accessed.

**Information**   Data placed into a meaningful context for users.

**In-house copy facilities**   Copying facilities located within an organization as either centralized or decentralized operations.

**In-house training**   That training which is offered within the organization by its own personnel, as compared with that which might be developed and presented by special consultants or outside firms, or offered to the public by educational institutions.

**Institute of Certified Records Managers (ICRM)**   A group of CRMs who administer and evaluate the Certified Records Manager examination.

**Integrated information system**   A group of automated subsystems working together and communicating with each other to process information, distribute it in a timely manner to the appropriate persons, store information (records) for efficient retrieval, and dispose of stored information (records) when it is no longer needed.

**Jacket**   A transparent plastic carrier for strips of microfilm.

**Job analysis**   The systematic study of a job to determine its characteristics — its function, specific duties, and qualifications.

**Job description**   A written summary of the job which states (or lists) duties to be performed by the employee; the description will include areas of responsibility and specific duties.

**Labels**   Items used to identify the contents of folders, drawers, shelves, binders, trays, and boxes.

**Landlord/tenant agreement**   Describes a self-service type of commercial records center operating under a landlord/tenant agreement.

**Legal value**   Value attributed to a record series which documents business ownership, agreements, and transactions.

**Life cycle**   Creation, distribution, use, maintenance, and disposition of a record.

**Locator file**   A special card file or automated index which lists records contents and their locations.

**Long-term cross-reference**   An additional notation that is used to provide a trail or forwarding address for a record.

**Long-term record**   A record that has continuing value to the organization.

**Machine dictation**   Dictation of correspondence into a recording machine as opposed to face-to-face dictation to a secretary.

**Magnetic media**   Depository of information off-line from the computer data base or word processing memory which may take the form of computer tapes or disks, word processor disks, or optical disks.

**Magnetic storage and retrieval**   Depositing and retrieving information offline from the computer database or word processing memory.

**Manual operation and retrieval**   The process of storing and retrieving records without the aid of mechanical or automated devices.

**Mechanical operation and retrieval**   The use of mechanized equipment to store and retrieve records.

**Memory**   The capacity to retain data within the system to form a database.

**Microfiche**   A sheet of film containing multiple miniature images in a grid pattern.

**Microform**   Any medium which contains miniature images.

**Micrographics**   The procedures for creating, using, and storing microforms.

**Micrographics staff**   Personnel responsible for converting certain records or types of records to microforms.

**Microimage**   A reduced copy of the original document that may be stored on a film roll, fiche, aperture card, jacket, or opaque.

**Microimage storage and retrieval**   The process of storing and retrieving records that have been reduced in size and stored on roll film, fiche, aperture cards, jackets, and opaques.

**Micro-opaque**   A sheet of opaque paper stock containing multiple miniature images in a grid pattern similar to a microfiche.

**Microrecords**   Records stored on microforms.

**Middle digit order**   A type of duplex arrangement in which the middle two digits are primary digits, the first two digits are secondary digits, and the last two digits are tertiary digits.

**Missing document target**   Frame of microfilm documenting records that were missing when records were originally received.

**Mobile aisle systems**   Space-conserving cabinets of shelves or trays which move on track (either manually or electrically) to create aisles for accessing records.

**Name order**   An arrangement in which records are classified by name of organization or person.

**Negative polarity**   The light to dark relationship of a film image in which clear characters are produced on a black background.

**Nonessential records**   Those records having no present value to the organization; also called Class 4 records.

**Nonrecord copy**   A copy of a record maintained in addition to the record copy, such as materials not identified in the retention schedule; documents not required to be retained; materials available from public sources.

**Numeric classification system**   An arrangement in which records are classified by number rather than by name.

**Numeric forms file**   A forms control file which documents the history of each form and which contains such information as the original request for the form, a sample of the original form and each subsequent revision, a reorder record, and any correspondence related to that form.

**Objective**   A statement of how one step in reaching a goal is to be completed and measured.

**Odometer indexing**   Method of indexing which indicates the distance of each image from the beginning of the roll of film.

**Offsite records center**   A storage facility located away from the organization site.

**Onsite records center**   A storage facility located on the same site as the organization.

**Operational audit**   A review of the effectiveness of the system as a process to ensure that specific tasks are performed effectively and efficiently.

**Operational manual**   Contains detailed information on the structure, policies, and procedures of one department/division of an organization.

**Optical character recognition (OCR)**   An input device which bypasses the keyboard and feeds pretyped data directly into word or data processing equipment.

**Optical disks**   An information storage medium which resembles a phonograph record.

**Organization chart**   A formal representation of the firm's organizational structure—a diagram of who reports to whom within an organization.

**Organization of information target**   Frame of microfilm showing the order in which the records were received and filmed.

**Organizational manual**   Describes the structure, duties, and responsibilities of each department/division and explains the relationships between other departments/divisions and the records unit.

**Organizing**   The management function of putting plans into action through allocating available resources and providing a structure for the implementation of the plans.

**Originating subsystem**   The means of putting information into the integrated information system.

**Originating unit**  Department creating the directive or responsible for the function or subject described in the directive.

**Periodic transfer**  The transfer of inactive records to the records center or to another low-cost storage area at regularly scheduled intervals.

**Perpetual transfer**  The transfer of records to the records center or to another low-cost storage area as they become inactive.

**Personnel ratio**  A measure of the adequacy of the records staff to perform selected records functions.

**Phonetic order**  An alphanumeric arrangement of records by sound, regardless of the spelling of the name.

**Planetary camera**  A flatbed camera used primarily to film stationary engineering drawings and other large documents.

**Planning**  The management function of determining what the organization wishes to achieve and deciding the means for achieving the desired outcomes.

**Policy**  Guideline for decision making.

**Policy manual**  Contains written general guidelines used for consistent decision making.

**Positive polarity**  The light to dark relationship of a film image in which black characters are produced on a clear background.

**Power elevator lateral files**  Multiple-tier units which utilize a Ferris wheel approach to electrically bring the desired shelf to the user when needed.

**Precontrol**  A type of control that takes place before work is performed and concentrates on preventing problems before they occur.

**Procedure**  Statements of how to implement a policy.

**Processing subsystem**  The means of manipulating data within the information system to achieve desired results.

**Project ELF**  A project (Eliminate Legal-size Files) focused on eliminating legal-size files from offices and converting to standard-size paper files.

**Quick copy**  Centralized copying facility representing one of the forms of in-house copying.

**Record copy**  A record that serves the documentation needs of the organization.

**Record series**  A group of records filed together in a unified arrangement which results from, or relates to, the same function or activity.

**Records**  Recorded information (books, papers, photographs, maps, or other documentary materials) regardless of form or characteristics, made or received for legal or operational purposes in connection with the transaction of business.

**Records analyst**  A specialist in systems and procedures used in creating, processing, and disposing of records.

**Records analyst staff**  Personnel responsible for providing assistance in reviewing existing records systems and preparing revisions for improvement.

**Records and information administrator**   Manager responsible for translating organizational records and information plans for implementation by the individual records divisions and for controlling the records information system throughout the organization.

**Records appraisal**   An examination of the data gathered through the records inventory to determine the value of each record series to the organization.

**Records center staff**   Personnel responsible for controlling all inactive records of the organization.

**Records centers**   Storage facilities to house inactive records and to serve as reference service centers.

**Records destruction**   The disposal of records no longer needed by the organization.

**Records disposition**   The determination of whether a record should be placed in archival storage, destroyed, or discarded based on its continued usefulness and level of confidentiality.

**Records inventory**   A complete listing of the locations and contents of an organization's records.

**Records management**   The systematic control of records from creation to final disposition.

**Records management manual**   A guide to how the records management system works.

**Records retention manual**   Contains the records retention schedule, procedures for establishing retention periods, procedures for transferring inactive records to the records center, and procedures for the destruction of records.

**Records retention schedule**   An established timetable for maintaining the organization's records, transferring inactive records to storage, and destroying records which are no longer valuable to the organization.

**Records time/activity chart**   Provides information regarding the volume, types of records activity within each department or file station, and time spent in records activities.

**Reduction ratio**   The size of a microimage as compared to the size of the original document, usually expressed as 24x, 30x, or 24:1, 30:1, and so forth.

**Reference ratio**   The measure of file activity which is determined by dividing the number of retrieval requests by the number of pieces stored.

**Relative index**   A dictionary-type listing of all words and combinations of words by which records may be requested.

**Release mark**   A notation that the immediate need for the record has passed and the record may now be stored.

**Report**   A written presentation of information useful in the decision-making process.

**Reports staff**   Personnel responsible for the development, implementation, and control of reports throughout the organization.

**Resolution**   The sharpness of a microimage.

**Retrieval**   Finding a requested file or information contained within the file.

**Retrieval time**   The time required to locate a record is determined by dividing the time used to retrieve items (shown in hours but converted to minutes) by total number of requests received.

**Reversal processing**   A procedure which changes the polarity of film.

**Rotary camera**   A type of microfilm camera that photographs documents while the documents and film are being moved by transport mechanisms at the same speed.

**Scope of study**   Defines the boundaries of the study in terms of who will be included.

**Scroll**   A roll of extra-wide film (105mm) used in some automated retrieval systems.

**Semiactive record**   A record that is referenced once a month.

**Serial order**   An arrangement in which records are stored using consecutive numbers.

**Sorting**   Arranging records in filing order according to the classification system used.

**Space numbering system**   A method of designating the storage location of records.

**Specifications forms file**   A forms control file which groups forms according to the manner in which they are printed.

**Staffing**   Planning for the human resource needs of an organization, including determining types and number of personnel required, recruiting, selecting, training, promoting, appraising, and terminating employees.

**Step and repeat camera**   A flatbed camera designed to expose images in uniform rows and columns for the preparation of microfiche.

**Storage subsystem**   The means of storing, retrieving, and disposing of information according to the organization's needs.

**Strips**   Short lengths of film containing microimages which are containerized and coded for use in automated retrieval systems.

**Subject order**   An arrangement of records by the subjects of the records.

**Subject-numeric order**   An alphanumeric arrangement in which records are stored using an encyclopedia arrangement; related materials are stored together under major headings and subheadings.

**Substandard document target**   Frame showing that the original record was not completely legible and that the quality of the microimage is below standard.

**Supplies**   Consumable items which assist in storing and retrieving records.

**System**   A group of interrelated parts acting together to accomplish a goal.

**Tab**   A projection from the top or side of a guide or folder used to identify the contents.

**Telecommunications**   Those communications sent over telephone lines.

**Templates**   Blank forms stored electronically in a computerized information processing system.

**Temporary record**   A record that does not have continuing or lasting value to the oganization; sometimes called a transitory record.

**Terminal digit order**   A type of duplex numeric arrangement in which the last two digits are the primary digits, the middle two digits are the secondary digits, and the first two digits are the tertiary digits.

**Topical order**   An arrangement of records in alphabetic order by subject.

**Ultrafiche**   A microfiche produced at a reduction ratio of 90x or greater and containing microimages of 4,000 or more pages.

**Uniform Classification System (UCS)**   A standard classification system used throughout an organization.

**Unit box lateral files**   A shelf filing system which uses specially designed boxes which hang from rails to hold file folders.

**Updatable microfiche camera**   A step and repeat camera which allows additional images to be added to the microfiche at any time (if space for these additional images exists).

**Updatable microfilm/fiche**   Form of microrecord that allows all file information to accumulate on one record and for corrections to be made and the file to be updated.

**Useful records**   Those records useful to the uninterrupted operation of the business; also called Class 3 records.

**Vital record**   A record that is essential to the operation of the organization, the continuation and/or resumption of operations following a disaster, the recreation of legal or financial status of the organization, or to the fulfillment of its obligations to stockholders and employees in the event of a disaster; also called Class 1 record.

**Vital records protection manual**   A manual listing all vital records of an organization according to department; contains both the vital record code number and the retention date.

**Working area**   The section of a form which requests information necessary to achieve the purpose for which the form was designed.

# INDEX